The Supreme Court Compendium

The Supreme Court Compendium
Data, Decisions, and Developments

Lee Epstein
Washington University in St. Louis

Jeffrey A. Segal
State University of New York at Stony Brook

Harold J. Spaeth
Michigan State University

Thomas G. Walker
Emory University

Congressional Quarterly Inc.
Washington, D.C.

Printed in the United States of America

Cover design: Paula Anderson

Library of Congress Cataloging-in-Publication Data

Epstein, Lee, 1958-
    The Supreme Court compendium : data, decisions, and developments / Lee Epstein ... [et al.].
        p. cm.
    Includes bibliographical references and index.
    ISBN 0-87187-771-6 (c) : ISBN 0-87187-770-8 (p)
    1. United States. Supreme Court. 2. Judges--United States. 3. Judicial review--United States. 4. Law and politics. I. United States. Supreme Court. II. Title.
KF8742.E68 1993
347.73'26--dc20   93-23845
[347.30735]   CIP

In memory of my grandfather, Martin Buxbaum

L.E.

For Paul

J.A.S.

For my coauthors, who made the compilation of this book
a thoroughly enjoyable endeavor

H.J.S.

For Victoria Nowak and Ann Walker

T.G.W.

Contents

Tables and Figures

Tables

Figures

Preface

As professors who teach courses and conduct research on courts and the law, we became increasingly frustrated with the absence of a comprehensive collection of information on the U.S. Supreme Court. It seemed that each time we needed even the simplest datum, whether it be a Senate vote on a particular nominee or the number of cases argued during a given term, we had to consult three or four different books and articles to find the desired information. This sense of frustration led to the compilation of the present volume.

Our goal in *The Supreme Court Compendium: Data, Decisions, and Developments* is to provide a comprehensive collection of data and relevant information on the U.S. Supreme Court. We attempt to cover all bases, from characteristics of the Court and its members, to the environment in which it operates, to the public's views on its decisions and perceptions about the Court itself, as well as much more. In addition, we seek to provide readers with some insight into how we collected the data and why we consider them important. The reader should use the general introduction and the chapter introductions as guides to the information presented in the tables and figures that follow. We also urge readers to pay particular attention to table notes, where we identify data sources and, when relevant, caution readers about potential irregularities in data interpretation.

Putting together a volume of this nature required work with a great deal of data. While we took pains to check and recheck all the tables, it is entirely possible that we committed errors of omission and commission. Naturally, we take full responsibility for both. But we do ask readers who find errors in the text or the tables to please contact us so that we may remedy them for subsequent editions.

Many people assisted us in producing *The Supreme Court Compendium*. The folks at CQ Press were, as always, terrific. We initially pitched the project to Brenda Carter, who provided a great deal of encouragement. Our editor, Jeanne Ferris, could not have been more helpful or patient. She read the entire text and considered all the tables with an eye toward clarity and readability. The final product would have been far the worse had Jeanne not taken such a keen interest. Tracy W. Villano, our copy editor, not only performed the usual tasks with great skill but went far beyond the call, rearranging data and tables, calculating numerical information to make the chapter introductions more interesting, and catching inconsistencies and typographical errors missed by four other pairs of eyes. We also thank Gregory Caldeira of Ohio State University for his excellent suggestions upon review of the manuscript. His contributions strengthened considerably the final volume. We would also like to thank him and Jan Palmer of Ohio University for providing specific items of interest.

Students at our respective institutions performed various essential tasks throughout the undertaking. We thank Robert Oritz at SUNY Stony Brook, Paul Fabrizio at Emory University, and Marjorie George and Jim Spriggs at Washington University.

While a four-person collaboration was a great deal of fun for us, it was our home institutions that bore the costs of extended phone calls and faxes, as well as photocopying and mailing expenses. Epstein is especially grateful to John Sprague, chair of the Department of Political Science at Washington University, who complained not at all and encouraged always; Segal thanks Lee Koppelman and the staff at the Center for Regional Policy Studies, SUNY Stony Brook, for making their fax line available whenever needed; Spaeth thanks the Law and Social Science Program of the National Science Foundation for its continuing support of his Supreme Court database; and Walker acknowledges the staff and faculty in the political science department at Emory University for creating an atmosphere that makes academic research so enjoyable.

L. E.
St. Louis

J. A. S.
Stony Brook

H. J. S.
East Lansing

T. G. W.
Atlanta

Introduction

Until now, there has been no comprehensive collection of data on the U.S. Supreme Court. This is unfortunate, not only because of the importance of the Court in the American government, but also because the absence of reliable data makes it hard to understand the Court, the justices, and case decisions. *The Supreme Court Compendium* is an effort to rectify this deficiency.

We hope that readers will find useful the data and information presented in the following pages. Before continuing, though, we urge them to read this introduction and those opening each chapter so that they might better understand the choices we made in compiling this work. Here, we provide information on data sources, the scope of the data, data presentation, and the overall organization of the volume. In the introductions preceding each chapter, we provide more specific details on the tables they contain.

Data Sources and Scope of the Data

Our sources of information vary widely, depending on what dimension of the Court we are examining. The primary source is the reports of the Court's decisions. The official record is the *United States Reports.*[1] Three privately printed sources are also employed: *The Lawyers' Edition,*[2] *The Supreme Court Reporter,*[3] and *United States Law Week.*[4] In Table 1-4 we provide additional information about these various systems. Two major legal electronic information retrieval systems, LEXIS and WESTLAW, also contain the Court's decisions. We used these sources when gathering data requiring specific search delimiters. A third source of electronically transmitted information was initiated by the Supreme Court in 1990. The experimental Project Hermes provides electronic transmission of Court decisions. Researchers can access these files through Internet, Bitnet, or the National Public Telecomputing Network.[5]

We also obtained information from archived databases. Harold J. Spaeth's computer-dependent United States Supreme Court Judicial Database[6] provides a wealth of data beginning with the Warren Court through to the present. Among the many attributes of Court decisions coded by Spaeth are the names of the courts making the original decision, the identities of the parties to a case, the policy context of a case, and the votes of each justice. It and accompanying documentation are freely available to faculty, staff, and students of colleges and universities who are members of the Inter-University Consortium for Political and Social Research in Ann Arbor, Michigan. Along with the Gallup Poll, the Harris Survey, and unpublished press releases issued by the *New York Times,* we use data gathered by the National Opinion Research Center (and archived as the General Social Survey) as sources for information on public opinion. Because survey responses are extremely sensitive to question wording, we eschew one-time "snap-shots" of public opinion on questions relevant to the judiciary and focus instead on trends over time.

We compiled additional data from governmental reports. *Historical Statistics of the United States, Colonial Times to 1970*[7] and the *Statistical Abstract of the United States*[8] (published annually since 1878) are "the standard summar[ies] of statistics on the social, political, and economic organization of the United States."[9] For our purposes, they are particularly useful sources of court caseload statistics. Another very helpful source is *The Constitution of the United States of America: Analysis and Interpretation.*[10] Among other things, it lists all Court decisions overruled by subsequent decisions and all cases in which the Court held unconstitutional acts of federal, state, and local governments. We also rely on reports issued by various governmental actors and agencies. Examples include the *Register of the U.S. Department of Justice and the Federal Courts,*[11] which provides information on individuals who have served as attorneys and solicitors general; the Administrative Office of the United States Courts,[12] which issues annual reports on court caseloads; and the *Annual Report of the Attorney General of the United States,*[13] which contains various data on the processing of Court litigation.

Finally, we scoured historical accounts and secondary material to fill in blanks and verify other sources. This was particularly the case in collecting information about the lives of the justices. While there has been a great deal written about the most famous of the justices, little is known about many of the others. Much of the data on the justices come from well-established biographical sources, including Leon Friedman and Fred Israel's *The Justices of the United States Supreme Court,*[14] The

Judicial Conference of the United States' *Judges of the United States,*[15] *The National Cyclopaedia of American Biography,*[16] and *The Dictionary of American Biography.*[17] *The First One Hundred Justices*[18] by Albert P. Blaustein and Roy M. Mersky was especially helpful. Similarly, a great deal of information was gleaned from John Schmidhauser's classic study of the backgrounds of the justices.[19] Data from this important work are archived at the Inter-University Consortium for Political and Social Science Research.[20] Even with the wealth of information contained in these sources, significant gaps remained. We filled these holes by consulting scores of biographies on the justices, newspaper accounts, and studies of the various historical periods. At the end of this process, we were still plagued with missing information and instances where contradictory claims in the biographical literature could not be resolved to our complete satisfaction. Unfortunately, such difficulties are inevitable when dealing with incomplete historical records. Notes to the tables alert readers to these and other problems.

The scope of our information also varies considerably. Whenever possible we tried to present data dating back to the Court's inception in February 1790. Unfortunately, this was more the exception than the rule, as such longitudinal data have seldom been compiled and, when they have, are often riddled with inconsistency. We were especially handicapped in our ability to offer information on voting behavior prior to the Warren Court era, as our most reliable source, Spaeth's United States Supreme Court Judicial Database, does not antedate 1953.

For data other than voting behavior, though, we were often able to locate information going back to the early 1900s and occasionally even the 1800s. We do want to alert readers to the fact that, while we sought to verify historical data against other sources, we did not attempt to research the primary data sources. In some instances, therefore, we cannot vouch for accuracy. Once again, table notes alert readers to these potential problems.

Presentation of the Data

Two major concerns guided our presentation of the data. First, we sought to be as comprehensive as possible. Accordingly, we provide data well fitted to tabular presentation as well as data that are not. Examples of the latter are a chronology of events in the Court's history (Table 1-1) and catalogs of landmark decisions (Table 2-10). In order to organize and communicate the data in usable fashion, we exercised our judgment of how best to present them, as most of the data have either not been compiled at all or have not appeared in any systematic fashion. Where possible, we have conformed to customary and conventional categorization, such as chronological, alphabetical, or topical. But for the vast majority of the data, conventions simply do not exist. Hence, we proceeded on the bases of clarity and understanding.

We also sought to minimize the technical character of the data. This is not an easy task since the Court and its activities are complex matters typically characterized by a somewhat arcane vocabulary (notwithstanding the inroads made on legalese by the plain English movement of recent years). Although we eliminated technical terms to the extent possible, they are by no means absent. For this reason (and several others noted above), it is especially important that readers review the notes following the tables. Legal definitions typically lack even imprecise meaning. What rights, for example, are objectively within—or outside—"the very essence of a scheme of ordered liberty"?[21] What principles of justice are "so rooted in the traditions and conscience of our people as to be ranked as fundamental"?[22] Is a declaration of unconstitutionality or the overruling of a precedent beyond dispute? Moreover, many legal definitions create distinctions between things that arguably have no meaningful differences. A jurisdictional dissent, for example, includes dissents from the Court's refusal to decide a case, from the Court's affirmation of a lower court's decision without oral argument, and from the Court's assertion of jurisdiction over a case. None address the merits of the controversy. Should they be distinguished from one another or simply lumped together? Does it really matter? In short, we had to formulate our own operationally meaningful definitions, as the notes to the tables point out.

In addition, technical terms do not necessarily have conventional meanings. Jurisdictional dissents provide a good example, as do concurring opinions. Is a concurring opinion that fully agrees with the contents of the majority opinion to be treated the same as one that agrees only with the result reached by the majority? We do not think so; hence, we separate them into "regular" and "special" concurrences. In our view, the justices who join the former type are full-fledged members of the majority opinion coalition, while those joining the latter are not. And if enough justices specially concur, no opinion of the Court will result—only a judgment. In such a case, the decision provides little guidance either to the litigants or to others similarly situated. Consider also the basic question of how to count cases. Should each citation be treated separately, or should one count the number of docketed cases under a given citation? Further, should one limit analysis only to "formally" decided cases—that is, to those cases that have been orally argued? And if so, should orally argued cases with the prevailing opinion signed by a justice be included alone, or in tandem with those decided per curiam (in which no individual justice authors the prevailing opinion)? Because no convention dictates the answers to these and other matters, the explanatory notes following the tables are particularly important.

Finally, apart from convention, certain matters are sufficiently unusual that they must be treated in an ad hoc fashion. Although we sometimes report anomalies in separate tables (see Table 4-14, for example), such peculiarities will often affect the contents of related tables. This further points up the need to pay close attention to the notes that accompany the tables.

The fact that the Court operates in a technical fashion need not cloud comprehension and understanding. We have defined terms in a nontechnical fashion, and the tables themselves do not require advanced interpretive skills. The book is based on simple numerical data, not the results of complicated statistical analyses. It should be useful to the methodologically skilled and unskilled alike.

The Organization of the Book

Chapter organization progresses logically. We begin in Chapters 1 through 3 with an institutional overview of the Court's history, the constitutional and congressional provisions that govern the Court and its jurisdiction, the Court's caseload, and landmark decisions. We also identify various chronological and topical trends apparent in the Court's decisions and opinions.

Chapters 4, 5, and 6 shift the focus from cases to the individual justices. We identify family backgrounds, childhood environments, marital status, educational and employment histories, and political experiences; dates and circumstances of nomination and confirmation are supplied as well, as are dates of court service. The circumstances surrounding retirements, resignations, and deaths are reviewed. The justices' scholarly credentials are identified and quotations from classic opinions excerpted. The justices' voting behavior is viewed ideologically, and trends in voting agreement are presented. We also identify the justices' opinion-writing proclivities, and those who agreed between themselves.

Chapter 7 considers the political environment in which the Court operates. Accordingly, we identify congressional legislation most frequently the subject of Court litigation, amendments ratified to alter Court decisions, and key congressional members whose legislative activities affect the judicial system (for example, the chairs of the House and Senate Judiciary Committees). We map the organization of the Justice Department and the Office of the Solicitor General, and list the names and dates of service of persons heading these agencies. We also chart the success of the United States as a party before the Supreme Court, noting as well the rates of success of various administrative agencies. Finally, we enumerate the frequency with which states participate in Court litigation and the rates of success they achieve in so doing.

Chapter 8 summarizes the public's views of the Court, both overall and by subgroup. Questions reviewed include "How knowledgeable is the public about the Court?" and "To what extent does the public support the Court's resolution of specific controversial issues?" Chapter 9 addresses the impact of the Court on certain public policy questions. Abortion, capital punishment, school desegregation, voter registration, and reapportionment are examples of issues covered.

Chapter 10 focuses on other courts within the judicial system: federal district courts, circuit courts of appeal, specialized federal courts, and state courts. At the federal court level, we specify the number of judges in service, party affiliations, caseloads handled by the courts, and the extent to which the Supreme Court has reversed and affirmed lower court decisions. For the state courts, we detail organization, methods by which members are seated, caseloads, and Supreme Court review of state court decisions.

In compiling the data contained in the pages that follow, detailed and voluminous though they be, we have made no attempt to resolve the questions and controversies that presently surround the Court. Questions such as "Are the justices overworked, too old, too unrepresentative?" "Is the Court rendering too many liberal decisions, or too many conservative ones?" "Is the Court addressing pertinent issues of broad public concern?" "Does the solicitor general exercise too much influence over the justices?" are not answered here. The data we supply are simply that: information about the Court and its environment. We have compiled and reported these data as accurately and as objectively as possible. They do not cover the totality of the activity that occurs within the confines of the justices' "Marble Palace." For example, we know little of what has transpired within the justices' secret conferences where they choose cases to be heard and decided and cast initial votes on the merits of the cases.[23] Our data, rather, are an appropriate starting point for analysis. But by no means are they the last word on the subjects to which they pertain.

Notes

1. *United States Reports* (Washington, D.C.: Government Printing Office).
2. *The Lawyers' Edition* (Rochester, N.Y.: Lawyers Co-operative Publishing Co.).
3. *The Supreme Court Reporter* (Minneapolis, Minn.: West Publishing Co.).

4. *United States Law Week* (Washington, D.C.: Bureau of National Affairs).

5. See the *Newsletter of the Law and Courts Section of the American Political Science Association*, Summer 1992, 11.

6. Ann Arbor, Mich., Inter-University Consortium for Political and Social Research, published and updated annually as study #9422.

7. U.S. Bureau of the Census, *Historical Statistics of the United States, Colonial Times to 1970* (Washington, D.C.: Government Printing Office, 1975).

8. U.S. Bureau of the Census, *Statistical Abstract of the United States* (Washington, D.C.: Government Printing Office).

9. Ibid., v.

10. U.S. Library of Congress, Congressional Research Service, *The Constitution of the United States of America: Analysis and Interpretation: Annotations of Cases Decided by the Supreme Court of the United States* (Washington, D.C.: Government Printing Office).

11. U.S. Department of Justice, *Register of the U.S. Department of Justice and the Federal Courts* (Washington, D.C.: Government Printing Office).

12. Administrative Office of the United States Courts, *Annual Report of the Director of the Administrative Office of the United States Courts* (Washington, D.C.: Government Printing Office).

13. U.S. Department of Justice, *Annual Report of the Attorney General of the United States* (Washington, D.C.: Government Printing Office).

14. Leon Friedman and Fred L. Israel, eds., *The Justices of the United States Supreme Court: Their Lives and Major Opinions* (New York: R. R. Bowker, 1969-1978).

15. *Judges of the United States*, 2d ed. (Washington, D.C.: Judicial Conference of the United States, 1983).

16. *The National Cyclopaedia of American Biography* (New York: James T. White).

17. *The Dictionary of American Biography* (New York: Charles Scribner's Sons).

18. Albert P. Blaustein and Roy M. Mersky, *The First One Hundred Justices* (Hamden, Conn.: Shoe String Press, 1978).

19. John Schmidhauser, "The Justices of the Supreme Court: A Collective Portrait," *Midwest Journal of Political Science* 3 (February 1959): 1-57.

20. Ann Arbor, Mich., Inter-University Consortium for Political and Social Research, published as study #7240.

21. *Palko v. Connecticut*, 302 U.S. 319 (1937), at 325.

22. *Snyder v. Massachusetts*, 291 U.S. 95 (1934), at 105.

23. The exception is the Vinson Court (1946-1953). Jan Palmer's dataset draws on the private docket books of most of the justices who sat on that Court. See *The Vinson Court Era: The Supreme Court's Conference Votes* (New York: AMS Press, 1990). Having gained access to these docket books, Palmer systematically presents all the votes—preliminary and final—cast by each of the justices in every case in which the Vinson Court justices voted. See also H. W. Perry, Jr., *Deciding to Decide: Agenda Setting in the United States Supreme Court* (Cambridge: Harvard University Press, 1991).

1

The Supreme Court:
An Institutional Perspective

The material in this chapter provides an overview of the Court's activities. The perspective here is largely historical, starting with a chronology of the events in the Court's history in Table 1-1. We have attempted to be reasonably detailed in compiling the contents of this table. However, more recent events appear with greater frequency than those from earlier years. We provide at least one entry for each of the past thirteen years, and for thirty of the last thirty-one. By contrast, an entry appears for only eight of the fourteen years between the Constitutional Convention and the accession of John Marshall to the chief justiceship in 1801. This may reflect a recency bias but we believe it demonstrates the greater importance of the modern Supreme Court as a national policy maker. The events recounted in Table 1-1 are predominantly decisions of the Court, along with changes in the Court's personnel and various unusual and noteworthy events that affected the Court.

Tables 1-2 and 1-3 outline and specify the major legislation Congress has enacted to implement its constitutional powers concerning the federal judiciary in general and the Supreme Court in particular. As Table 1-2 indicates, this legislation addresses the number of justices and the scope of the Court's jurisdiction. Table 1-3 contains the pertinent provisions of the United States Code that specify the sorts of cases the Supreme Court may hear and decide. The writ of certiorari referred to here is the primary method by which those who have lost a case bring it to the Court's attention. Unlike the traditional writ of appeal, the Court can choose to grant or deny a petitioner's writ of certiorari.

The primary means of disseminating the decisions of a court are its published reports. Not all decisions of all courts are published. More so than most American courts, state and federal, the reports of the U.S. Supreme Court contain a relatively complete record of its decisions.

Prior to the twentieth century, however, records are less than complete. During the 1790s, fewer than half the Court's decisions were published, and many of those were compiled from the notes of the attorneys who argued the cases.[1] Incompleteness continued to afflict the Court's reports until well after the Civil War. Numerous cases can be found in the privately published *Lawyers' Edition* of the Court's reports that are absent from the official *United States Reports*.[2] For at least the last half-century, however, the official reports do not materially differ from the privately printed ones. The differences among them are largely limited to such unofficial matter as notes, summaries, and indices, as Table 1-4 indicates.

The remaining tables and figure provide information on the Court's budget, calendar, and personnel. Tables 1-5 through 1-8 provide a fairly complete set of the Court's budgetary, salary, and pension data. They show that the Court comprises but a tiny fraction of the federal government's expenditures. The Court's calendar and the processing of cases from the initial filing to the publication of its decisions are the subjects of Table 1-9 and Figure 1-1. The number of full-time positions is identified in Table 1-10, and the names and dates of service of the Court's administrative officials are presented in Table 1-11.

Notes

1. Susan W. Brenner, *Precedent Inflation* (New Brunswick, N.J.: Transaction, 1992), 84, 94-95.
2. For example, *Thatcher v. Kaucher*, 24 L. Ed. 511 (1877), *Keogh v. Orient Fire Insurance Co.*, 24 L. Ed. 650 (1878).

Table 1-1   Chronology of Important Events in the Supreme Court's
History, 1787-1993

1787 The Constitutional Convention meets.
1789 The Constitution is ratified.
President George Washington signs the Judiciary Act of 1789, which establishes a federal court structure.
1790 The Supreme Court holds its first session in New York City.
The Court issues its first formal rule, creating the Office of the Clerk of the Court.
1791 The Bill of Rights becomes part of the Constitution.
The Court moves from New York City to Philadelphia.
1793 The Court announces its first major decision, *Chisholm v. Georgia*, which authorizes citizens of one state to sue another state in the Supreme Court. Ironically, the Eleventh Amendment, ratified in 1795, nullifies this decision.
The Court refuses Secretary of State Thomas Jefferson's request to answer questions concerning the appropriate role America should play in the ongoing English-French war. In so doing, it sets an important precedent regarding advisory opinions: issuing them would violate the separation of powers principle.
1795 The first chief justice, John Jay, resigns to become governor of New York. Washington nominates John Rutledge of South Carolina as Jay's successor, but for the first time the Senate refuses to confirm a Supreme Court nominee. In January of 1796, William Cushing, the senior associate, is nominated. He declines because of age. Washington then offers the post to Oliver Ellsworth, whom the Senate confirms the next day.
The Eleventh Amendment, prohibiting a nonresident from suing a state in federal court, is ratified.
1796 John Marshall makes his only appearance as an attorney before the Supreme Court when he argues the case of *Ware v. Hylton*. In stark contrast to the nationalist position he espoused as chief justice, Marshall here alleges the supremacy of state laws that conflict with federal treaties. He loses the case.
1801 Marshall is appointed chief justice by lame-duck president John Adams shortly before Jefferson takes office.
The Court moves to Washington, D.C., and holds sessions in a room in the Capitol building.
Congress passes the Circuit Court Act of 1801, which eliminates circuit court duty for the justices, reduces the number of justices from six to five, and increases the number of circuits from three to six.
Chief Justice Marshall begins the practice of issuing opinions of the Court, rather than having the justices deliver individual opinions in each case.
1802 Congress repeals the Circuit Court Act of 1801; the number of justices is returned to six.
1803 *Marbury v. Madison*, which enunciates the doctrine of judicial review, is decided.
1804 For the only time in history, the House of Representatives votes to

(Table continues)

Table 1-1   *(Continued)*

---

impeach a Supreme Court justice, Samuel Chase. However, one year later the Senate fails to muster the two-thirds vote required to convict Chase on charges of partisan political behavior.

The Twelfth Amendment, governing the election of the president and vice-president, is ratified.

1805   Justice William Johnson delivers the Court's first opinion labeled as a dissent, in *Huidekoper's Lessee v. Douglass.*

1807   Congress creates a seventh circuit and, accordingly, increases the Court's membership to seven.

1810   The Court declares a state law unconstitutional for the first time in *Fletcher v. Peck.*

1811   On his fourth attempt to fill the vacancy created by the death of the last of the Court's original members, William Cushing, President James Madison nominates, and the Senate confirms, Joseph Story, at 32 years old the youngest person ever to sit on the Court.

1813   The U.S. Attorney General files the Court's first *amicus curiae* brief (*Beatty's Administrator v. Burnes's Administrators*).

1816   The Court rules in *Martin v. Hunter's Lessee* that it, rather than the state courts, has final authority to determine the meaning of constitutional provisions and acts of Congress.

Henry Wheaton becomes the first Court reporter formally appointed by the Court. His two predecessors, Alexander J. Dallas and William Cranch, held the position on an unofficial basis.

Congress authorizes the official publication of Supreme Court decisions.

1819   The doctrine of implied powers is formulated in *McCulloch v. Maryland.*
In *Dartmouth College v. Woodward,* the Court broadly construes the contract clause to prevent states from abridging corporate charters as well as public grants.

1823   The longest period in the Court's history without a change of personnel (twelve years) ends with the death of Justice Henry Livingston.

Henry Clay files the first nongovernmental *amicus curiae* brief in a Supreme Court case (*Green v. Biddle).*

1824   The Court decides *Gibbons v. Ogden* in an opinion by Chief Justice Marshall that broadly defines the scope of Congress's power to regulate interstate commerce.

1832   An attempt by Georgia to subject Cherokee Indians to its authority, notwithstanding a Court decision to the contrary (*Worcester v. Georgia),* ends when President Andrew Jackson reverses his pro-state position and supports expanded federal judicial power.

1833   *Barron v. Baltimore,* Chief Justice Marshall's last major constitutional opinion, holds that the Bill of Rights applies only to the federal government, not to the states.

1835   Chief Justice Marshall dies.
James M. Wayne of Georgia, the only incumbent member of the House of Representatives to be appointed to the Court, takes his seat.

1836   Because of Senate opposition to the nomination of Roger Taney as Marshall's successor, the Supreme Court, for the only term in its history,

Table 1-1   *(Continued)*

is without a chief justice.

Taney is finally confirmed by the Senate, notwithstanding the opposition of two giants of American constitutional law, Daniel Webster and Henry Clay.

1837   Three major decisions, *Charles River Bridge v. Warren Bridge, New York v. Miln,* and *Briscoe v. Bank of Kentucky,* portend an increase in the rights of the states vis-à-vis the national government by limiting the scope of the contract clause and upholding state regulations affecting interstate commerce.

Congress divides the United States into nine circuits and increases the Court's membership to nine.

1842   *Prigg v. Pennsylvania* holds that the federal government, not the states, has authority over fugitive slaves.

1844   The longest vacancy in Supreme Court history begins with the death of Justice Henry Baldwin. Because of partisan conflict between President John Tyler—the first nonelected president—and the Senate, Tyler is unsuccessful in filling the vacancy before he leaves office in 1845. Incoming president James Polk faces similar difficulties in naming a replacement for Baldwin. His first choice declines and his second choice is rejected by the Senate. Finally, twenty-seven months after Baldwin's death, the Senate confirms Robert Grier for the post.

1849   The Court places time limits on oral arguments: two hours per side.

1851   Benjamin Curtis, the only Whig to sit on the Court, takes his seat.

1857   The *Dred Scott* decision rules that slaves are property with which Congress may not interfere, and that neither they nor any of their descendants are citizens under the Constitution.

1861   Jeremiah Black, nominated by lame-duck president James Buchanan, is rejected by the closest vote in history, 25 to 26.

1863   The Emancipation Proclamation declares southern slaves free.

For the first time, a president clearly identified with one political party nominates a formally affiliated member of another political party to the Supreme Court when Abraham Lincoln selects Stephen J. Field.

Congress abolishes the Circuit Court of California, created in 1855, and replaces it with a tenth circuit. It also increases the size of the Court to ten. This gives Lincoln the opportunity to make his fourth appointment.

1864   Chief Justice Taney dies and is succeeded by Salmon P. Chase.

1865   General Robert E. Lee surrenders at Appomattox, ending the Civil War. Five days later John Wilkes Booth assassinates President Lincoln.

The Thirteenth Amendment, abolishing slavery, is ratified.

1866   Congress reduces the size of the Court from ten to seven to thwart President Andrew Johnson.

In *Ex parte Milligan,* the Supreme Court rules that military tribunals have no jurisdiction over civilians where civil courts are open and operating.

1867   Congress establishes the Office of the Marshal of the Supreme Court, which manages the Court's chamber.

1868   The Fourteenth Amendment, prohibiting the states from depriving

(Table continues)

Table 1-1 *(Continued)*

---

persons of due process or denying them equal protection of the laws, is ratified.

President Andrew Johnson is impeached.

After the Court hears arguments in *Ex parte McCardle*, Congress removes the Court's authority to hear appeals emanating under the 1867 Habeas Corpus Act. The justices then redocket the case, but decline to decide it. Their action indicates that Congress possesses the authority to remove the Court's appellate jurisdiction as it deems necessary.

1869   Congress increases the size of the Supreme Court to nine, where it has remained ever since.

1870   The last of the Civil War amendments, the Fifteenth, is ratified, prohibiting the states or the United States from denying anyone the right to vote because of race.

By a 4-to-3 vote, the Court rules in *Hepburn v. Griswold* that Congress has no power to authorize paper money as legal payment of debts, the method used to finance the Civil War. President Ulysses S. Grant fills the Court's two vacancies with individuals sympathetic to the use of paper money, and, fifteen months after the initial decision, the Court reverses itself and rules that the Legal Tender Acts were a proper exercise of congressional power.

Congress creates the Department of Justice and the post of solicitor general.

1873   By a 5-to-4 vote, the Court holds in the *Slaughterhouse Cases* that nothing in the Fourteenth Amendment expands the scope of individual rights against state action.

With only Chief Justice Chase dissenting, the Court rules in *Bradwell v. Illinois* that a state violates no constitutional provision in denying a woman a license to practice law because of her sex.

Chief Justice Chase dies.

1874   After two unsuccessful attempts to fill the chief justiceship—the most in history—Grant nominates Morrison Waite, a little-known Ohio attorney without judicial experience who had never argued a case before the Court.

1875   Court Reporter John W. Wallace retires. Because of a change in policy, he is the last to see his name on the cover of the reports of the Court. The official reports of the Court now are known as *United States Reports*.

1877   Five members of the Court serve on the electoral commission that resolves the disputed election of 1876. The justices split 3 to 2 along party lines, thereby making the Republican nominee, Rutherford B. Hayes, president.

In *Munn v. Illinois*, the Court reaffirms its 1873 decision in the *Granger Cases*, which asserted that the Fourteenth Amendment does not prevent states from regulating the use of private property.

1880   For the first time since the Civil War, President Hayes nominates a person from a Confederate state, William B. Woods, to sit on the Court. Woods, however, was not a native of the South, having migrated to Georgia after Appomattox.

Table 1-1   *(Continued)*

1881   Stanley Mathews, the only person besides John Jay ever to be nominated to the same seat by two different presidents, is confirmed by the closest vote in history, 24 to 23.

1882   Justice Horace Gray is the first Supreme Court justice to hire law school graduates as clerks.

1883   In the *Civil Rights Cases*, the Court narrowly defines what constitutes state action under the due process and equal protection clauses of the Fourteenth Amendment and, as a result, declares the Civil Rights Act of 1875 unconstitutional. Not until after World War II would the Court with any regularity support civil rights claims.

1886   In *Santa Clara County v. Southern Pacific R. Co.*, the Court claims that corporations are not citizens and thus not entitled to the protections afforded by the Fourteenth Amendment. They are nevertheless "persons" who cannot be deprived of liberty or property without due process of law. This decision heralds the Court's integration of the doctrines of laissez-faire economics into the Constitution.
Congress authorizes each justice to hire a stenographic clerk.

1887   The Interstate Commerce Act is passed, creating the first regulatory commission in United States history. Supreme Court decisions, however, sap the strength from its provisions, making the commission impotent to regulate the railroads, which are the focus of the Act.

1888   L.Q.C. Lamar of Mississippi is appointed to the Court. He is the first Democrat to be seated in a quarter century.
Chief Justice Waite dies. He is replaced by Melville Fuller, a Chicago railroad attorney.

1890   Congress enacts the Sherman Antitrust Act. Because of lax enforcement and hostile Court decisions, the law does little to curb the growth of concentrated economic power.

1891   Congress establishes federal appellate courts, allowing district court judges to sit in place of Supreme Court justices, virtually eliminating circuit-riding duty.

1894   Edward D. White, the first incumbent senator to be selected for the Court in 48 years, is nominated and confirmed on the same day. It will be another 43 years before a subsequent incumbent senator, Hugo Black, is chosen.

1895   In *United States v. E.C. Knight Co.*, the Court rules that the Sherman Antitrust Act, which is based on Congress's power to regulate interstate commerce, does not apply to manufacturing because manufacturing is not commerce.
Overruling a 100-year-old precedent, the Court declares the income tax unconstitutional in *Pollock v. Farmers' Loan & Trust Co.*, occasioning the adoption of the Sixteenth Amendment eighteen years later.
A unanimous Court in *In re Debs* approves the use of federal judicial power to stop strikes through the use of the labor injunction.

1896   The Court formulates the separate but equal doctrine in *Plessy v. Ferguson*, thereby legitimizing the segregated society created by Jim Crow laws.

(Table continues)

Table 1-1 *(Continued)*

1897   In *Allgeyer v. Louisiana,* the Court holds that the Fourteenth Amendment protects the freedom of contract, including the right of individuals to sell their labor without governmental regulation of hours, wages, or working conditions.

1898   In *Smyth v. Ames,* the Court further extends its probusiness judicial activism, holding that if states set the rates railroads may charge, those rates must provide a fair return on investment, and that the federal courts will determine what is and is not fair.

1902   Theodore Roosevelt appoints Massachusetts Supreme Court chief justice and legal scholar Oliver Wendell Holmes to the U.S. Supreme Court.

1905   *Lochner v. New York* is decided, precluding a state from restricting bakers to a ten-hour day and a sixty-hour week on the basis of freedom of contract.

1908   In *Adair v. United States,* freedom of contract also invalidates the act of Congress outlawing yellow-dog contracts, which employers utilize to fire employees if they join a labor union.
Although the Sherman Act does not particularly restrain labor activity, the Court construes it to ban secondary boycotts by labor unions in *Loewe v. Lawlor.*
As a result of the advocacy of Louis D. Brandeis, who would join the Supreme Court eight years later, the Court, in *Muller v. Oregon,* accepts limitations on freedom of contract in the case of women. Accordingly, a state may restrict women laundry workers to a ten-hour day.

1909   William Howard Taft takes the oath of office as president. During his tenure, six justices are seated, more than under any other single-term president. Only Washington's ten successful nominees and Franklin Roosevelt's nine exceed this number.
The first of Taft's nominees, Horace H. Lurton, at 65, is the oldest member to be seated as an associate justice in history. Harlan Fiske Stone and Charles Evans Hughes were 68 years, 8 months, and 67 years, 10 months, respectively, when promoted to the chief justiceship.

1910   Chief Justice Fuller dies. For the first time, an associate justice, Edward D. White, is promoted to the chief justiceship.

1911   In *Standard Oil Co. v. United States,* the Court states that the Sherman Act only outlaws unreasonable restraints of trade even though it contains no such qualification. The federal courts determine for themselves what is and is not reasonable.
Congress completely relieves justices of circuit-riding duty.

1913   The Sixteenth (income tax) and Seventeenth (popular election of senators) amendments are ratified.

1914   World War I begins.
The Clayton Antitrust Act, which supplements and strengthens the Sherman Act, is passed.

1916   President Woodrow Wilson nominates the first Jew, Louis Brandeis, to the Supreme Court. Over the opposition of former president—and soon-to-be chief justice—Taft and various bar and business leaders, Brandeis is confirmed after four months of acrimonious hearings. Although his

Table 1-1 *(Continued)*

opponents describe him as a trouble-making radical, anti-Semitism fuels much of the opposition.

1917 The United States declares war on Germany.

1918 By a 5-to-4 vote in *Hammer v. Dagenhart,* the Court declares unconstitutional Congress's effort to outlaw child labor.
The armistice ending World War I is signed.

1919 The "noble experiment," Prohibition, spearheaded by the Women's Christian Temperance Union and the Anti-Saloon League, is written into the Constitution as the Eighteenth Amendment.

1920 Women earn the right to vote with the ratification of the Nineteenth Amendment.

1921 Chief Justice White dies. President Warren Harding chooses former president Taft as his successor.

1922 Congress's second effort to ban child labor, based this time on the power to tax rather than the interstate commerce clause, is struck down as a result of the Court's decision in *Bailey v. Drexel Furniture Co.*
Congress allows Court law clerks to be hired at government expense.

1923 The Court rules in *Adkins v. Children's Hospital* that a federal minimum wage law for women violates freedom of contract.

1925 In the course of upholding the conviction of a left-wing radical for distributing a pamphlet urging the overthrow of the government, the Court, in *Gitlow v. New York,* notes that freedoms of speech and of the press are among the fundamental rights and liberties that the Fourteenth Amendment protects from state abridgment.
Congress enacts the Judiciary Act of 1925, reducing significantly the proportion of cases the Court must hear.
The Court develops the Rule of Four: at least four justices must agree before the Court will hear a case under its discretionary jurisdiction.

1928 The Court reduces oral argument from two hours to one hour per side.

1929 The stock market crashes; the Great Depression begins.
The Tenth Circuit Court of Appeals is created.

1930 President Herbert Hoover replaces Chief Justice Taft, who resigns, with Charles Evans Hughes, who had left the Supreme Court in 1916 to accept the Republican nomination for president.
John J. Parker is rejected by a vote of 39 to 41. Not since 1894 has a nominee failed to gain confirmation, and not until 1968 will another one do so.

1931 In *Stromberg v. California,* the Court strikes down a California law prohibiting the display of a red flag as a symbol of opposition to government as a violation of First Amendment rights. Two weeks later, in *Near v. Minnesota,* the Court rules that a state law prohibiting publication of a scandal sheet violates the First Amendment's guarantee of freedom of the press.

1932 The Norris-LaGuardia Act forbids the federal courts to issue injunctions in labor disputes to prevent strikes, boycotts, or picketing.
Two months shy of his 91st birthday, Oliver Wendell Holmes resigns, the

(Table continues)

Table 1-1   *(Continued)*

---

only nonagenarian ever to sit on the Supreme Court.

1933   Franklin D. Roosevelt takes office. The New Deal begins. Major regulatory legislation is enacted, including the Agricultural Adjustment Act and the National Industrial Recovery Act. Congress creates the Civilian Conservation Corps to provide outdoor work for unemployed males between the ages of eighteen and twenty-five, and establishes the Tennessee Valley Authority to construct dams and power plants in especially depressed parts of Appalachia.

The Twentieth Amendment, which ends the practice of congressional lame-duck sessions, is ratified.

The Twenty-first Amendment, repealing Prohibition is ratified.

1934   Major federal regulatory commissions are created, including the Securities and Exchange Commission, the Federal Communications Commission, and the Federal Housing Administration.

In *Nebbia v. New York*, the Court rules that the Fourteenth Amendment does not prevent a state from fixing the maximum and minimum prices of milk.

1935   Congress enacts the National Labor Relations Act, which gives labor the legal right to bargain collectively, and the Social Security Act, which provides unemployment compensation, old-age pension benefits, aid to blind and disabled persons, and aid to families with dependent children.

The Court declares unconstitutional the National Industrial Recovery Act and the Railroad Retirement Act, which established a comprehensive pension system for railroad workers.

May 27 goes down in history as Black Monday when the Court deals the Roosevelt administration three losses on a single day (*Schechter Poultry Corporation v. United States, Humphrey's Executor v. United States*, and *Louisville Joint Stock Land Bank v. Radford*).

Oliver Wendell Holmes dies. He leaves his estate to the United States, which uses the money to fund a study of the Court's history.

The Court meets in its new (and current) building, "the Marble Palace," in Washington, D.C.

1936   The Court continues to strike down major portions of the New Deal in *United States v. Butler* and *Carter v. Carter Coal Co.*, invalidating the Agricultural Adjustment Act and the Bituminous Coal Conservation Act, respectively.

The Court declares in *Morehead v. New York* and *ex rel. Tipaldo* that all state minimum wage laws, including those that apply to women and children, violate due process.

1937   The Court unanimously rules in *DeJonge v. Oregon* that the due process clause of the Fourteenth Amendment makes binding on the states the First Amendment's guarantee of freedom of assembly.

Following his landslide reelection in 1936, President Roosevelt submits to Congress a so-called Court-packing plan that will allow him to appoint additional justices to the Supreme Court for the unexpressed purpose of preventing further invalidation of New Deal legislation. But Justice Owen Roberts's switch in vote, immortalized as "the switch in time that saved nine," produces a pro-New Deal majority and makes Roosevelt's

Table 1-1   *(Continued)*

Court-packing scheme a moot issue.

West Coast Hotel Co. v. Parrish overrules the 1923 decision, *Adkins v. Children's Hospital,* and the 1936 decision, *Morehead v. New York ex rel. Tipaldo,* and upholds the state of Washington's minimum wage law. As the justices earlier read freedom of contract into the Constitution, they now read it out.

In *National Labor Relations Board v. Jones & Laughlin Steel Corp.,* the Court finally accepts that manufacturing is a part of commerce that Congress has power to regulate. As a result, the National Labor Relations Act is ruled to be constitutional.

Steward Machine Co. v. Davis upholds the unemployment compensation provisions of the Social Security Act. *Helvering v. Davis* upholds its old-age pension benefits.

Justice Willis Van Devanter retires. Roosevelt has his first opportunity to fill a seat on the Court and thereby increase judicial support for the New Deal. His selection, Senator Hugo Black, is confirmed five days after nomination.

1938   Justice George Sutherland becomes the second anti-New Deal member to resign. By the middle of 1941, Roosevelt has filled seven Court vacancies. The Fair Labor Standards Act prohibits child labor and establishes a nationwide minimum wage and maximum hour law. The Court upholds its constitutionality three years later in *United States v. Darby.*

1939   Felix Frankfurter, the last foreign-born justice, becomes an associate justice.

World War II begins with the Nazi invasion of Poland.

1940   In an opinion by Justice Frankfurter in *Minersville School District v. Gobitis,* the Court holds that children attending public school may be compelled to salute the flag, notwithstanding their religious objections.

With President Roosevelt's elevation of Frank Murphy, his appointees now comprise a majority of the Court.

1941   Chief Justice Hughes resigns. For the second time in history, a president crosses party lines to select a chief justice when Roosevelt nominates Harlan Fiske Stone.

James F. Byrnes, the last justice to sit without having attended law school, is appointed. He neither attended college nor graduated from high school.

Japan attacks Pearl Harbor.

The last of the anti-New Deal justices, James McReynolds, leaves the Court.

1942   In *Wickard v. Filburn,* the justices unanimously assert that Congress's power to regulate interstate commerce gives it control over activities that are neither commercial nor interstate.

1943   The Court overrules its compulsory flag salute decision of 1940 in *West Virginia State Board of Education v. Barnette.*

1944   In *Korematsu v. United States,* the Court asserts that unsubstantiated "military necessity" permits citizens to be summarily imprisoned solely

(Table continues)

Table 1-1 *(Continued)*

---

because of their race.

Justice William Douglas selects the first woman to serve as a law clerk.

1945   President Roosevelt dies; Harry Truman succeeds him. World War II ends and the Cold War begins.

President Truman crosses party lines to nominate Republican incumbent senator Harold H. Burton to the Supreme Court.

1946   Chief Justice Stone dies. Fred Vinson succeeds to the chief justiceship.

1947   In *Everson v. Board of Education,* the First Amendment's religious establishment clause is made binding on the states.

1948   In *Shelley v. Kraemer,* the Court rules that state courts may not constitutionally enforce racially restrictive housing covenants.

Justice Frankfurter selects the first African American to serve as a law clerk.

1949   In *Wolf v. Colorado,* the Fourth Amendment's ban on unreasonable searches and seizures is held to apply to the states.

1950–
1952   A series of decisions upholds federal and state legislation curbing alleged subversive activity.

1951   The Twenty-second Amendment, limiting presidential terms, is ratified.

1952   In *Burstyn v. Wilson,* the Court rules that motion pictures are a significant medium of expression protected by the First Amendment.

The Court curbs presidential power in *Youngstown Sheet and Tube Co. v. Sawyer* by ruling unconstitutional President Truman's seizure of the steel mills to avoid a strike that would disrupt U.S. military actions in Korea.

1953   Chief Justice Vinson dies. California governor Earl Warren becomes chief justice.

The Court meets in special session to decide the fate of Ethel and Julius Rosenberg. Its decision to lift the stay of their death sentences leads to their execution.

1954   The separate but equal doctrine of *Plessy v. Ferguson* is overruled in *Brown v. Board of Education,* paving the way for school desegregation.

1955   The Court begins taping oral arguments.

The Court announces that it will no longer hear oral arguments on Fridays, reserving that day for conference.

1956   The American Bar Association's Standing Committee on the Federal Judiciary begins screening and rating Court candidates.

1957   In *Yates v. United States,* the Court makes the conviction of alleged subversives more difficult by requiring prosecutors to show that the accused took some action to overthrow the U.S. government by force.

The Court declares obscenity to be without constitutional protection in *Roth v. United States* and *Alberts v. California.*

1961–
1969   The Warren Court begins to expand the rights of persons accused of crime by using various provisions in the Fourth to Eighth amendments to restrict state and local law enforcement activities.

1961   The Court holds in *Mapp v. Ohio* that the judicially created constitution-

Table 1-1   *(Continued)*

---

ally based exclusionary rule prohibits the use of illegally seized evidence in state, as well as federal, trials.

The Twenty-third Amendment is ratified, allowing the District of Columbia to participate in presidential elections.

1962   The Court rules in *Baker v. Carr* that redistricting malapportioned legislative bodies is a judicial, not a political, question. Within the next twenty-seven months, the Court formulates a "one person, one vote" rule and applies it to the House of Representatives and both houses of the states' legislatures. These decisions break the historical rural domination of legislative politics and shift power to cities and their suburbs.

In *Engle v. Vitale,* the Court rules that officially sanctioned prayer in the public schools violates the Constitution's establishment of religion clause.

1963   The Court rules in *Gideon v. Wainwright* that the Sixth Amendment requires that all persons accused of serious crimes be provided an attorney.

President John F. Kennedy is assassinated.

1964   The Twenty-fourth Amendment, prohibiting poll and other voting taxes, is ratified.

In *New York Times v. Sullivan,* the Court determines that the First Amendment prevents public officials from collecting damages for libelous media statements unless they prove the statement was made "with knowledge that it was false or with reckless disregard of whether it was false or not."

The Court holds in *Malloy v. Hogan* that the Fifth Amendment's protection against self-incrimination applies to state criminal defendants.

The Court unanimously upholds the constitutionality of the Civil Rights Act of 1964 and its ban on discrimination in places of public accommodations in *Heart of Atlanta Motel v. United States.*

1965   In *Pointer v. Texas,* the Court makes defendants' Sixth Amendment right to confront and crossexamine their accusers binding on the state, as well as the federal, governments.

The Court rules in *Griswold v. Connecticut* that "penumbras" in the First, Third, Fourth, Fifth, Ninth, and Fourteenth amendments guarantee a right to personal privacy, which prohibits a state from criminalizing the use of contraceptives.

Abe Fortas, the fifth Jewish justice, takes his seat.

1966   In *South Carolina v. Katzenbach,* the Court upholds the constitutionality of the Voting Rights Act of 1965. As a result, for the first time since Reconstruction southern blacks are able to vote with relative ease.

In *Miranda v. Arizona,* the Court decides that suspects must be read their rights before police questioning. The collapse of law enforcement is widely forecast, and efforts to impeach Chief Justice Warren gain additional force.

1967   The Twenty-fifth Amendment, governing the order of succession in cases of presidential incompetence, is ratified.

(Table continues)

Table 1-1   *(Continued)*

A unanimous Court in *Loving v. Virginia* rules that criminalizing interracial marriage violates due process as well as equal protection.

In *Washington v. Texas*, the Court rules that defendants in state courts have as much right to obtain favorable witnesses as does the prosecution.

Thurgood Marshall, the first African American nominated to the Supreme Court, takes his seat.

1968   The Court holds in *Duncan v. Louisiana* that the due process clause of the Fourteenth Amendment requires states to provide a trial by jury to persons accused of serious crimes.

A unanimous Court in *Green v. County School Board* terminates the "with all deliberate speed" formula for desegregating southern schools under the mandate of *Brown v. Board of Education* and orders desegregation "now."

The Court rules in *United States v. O'Brien* that the First Amendment does not protect draft card burning.

President Lyndon Johnson nominates Abe Fortas to succeed Earl Warren as chief justice and Homer Thornberry to occupy Fortas's seat as associate justice. Opposition from Republicans and conservative Democrats forces the lame-duck Johnson to withdraw Fortas's nomination, which also precludes action on Thornberry.

Richard Nixon defeats Hubert Humphrey in the presidential election.

1969   The Court rules in *Tinker v. Des Moines School District* that the First Amendment protects symbolic speech and applies to children as well as adults. Hence, students may wear armbands to protest the Vietnam War.

Under investigation for his dealings with a convicted felon, Justice Fortas resigns. He is the only justice to resign under threat of impeachment.

The Court rules in *Benton v. Maryland* that the due process clause prohibits the states from denying individuals protection from double jeopardy.

President Nixon nominates Warren Burger to succeed Chief Justice Warren, who has announced his intention to resign at the end of the Court's term.

1969-
1970   President Nixon's initial efforts to fill the Fortas vacancy are unsuccessful. The Senate rejects his first two nominees, Clement Haynsworth and Harrold Carswell. Not since 1894 have two successive nominees been rejected. The Senate, however, does confirm his third choice, Harry Blackmun, by a vote of 94 to 0.

1970   In *In re Winship* the Court determines that juvenile defendants are entitled to the same evidentiary standard as adults: beyond a reasonable doubt.

The Court in *Oregon v. Mitchell* rules that Congress has power to lower the voting age to eighteen only for federal, not state and local, elections. As a consequence, the Twenty-sixth Amendment is proposed and ratified one year later.

The Court reduces its dockets from three (original, appellate, miscellaneous) to two (original and all others).

The Court reduces the time allotted to oral arguments from one hour per side to one-half hour per side.

Table 1-1 *(Continued)*

1971   The Court holds that cross-district busing, racial quotas, and redrawn school district boundaries are permissible means of ending southern school segregation in *Swann v. Charlotte-Mecklenburg County Board of Education.*

       With each justice writing an opinion in *New York Times Co. v. United States,* the Court denies the government's request for an injunction prohibiting the publication of the "Pentagon Papers," classified documents pertaining to American involvement in Vietnam.

       In *Reed v. Reed,* the Court for the first time voids a law because it discriminates against women.

1972   White House aides break into Democratic headquarters in the Watergate office building in Washington, D.C.

       In *Argersinger v. Hamlin,* the Court rules that the right to counsel applies to all cases in which a jail sentence is possible.

       With each justice again writing an opinion, the Court voids all death penalty statutes in the United States in *Furman v. Georgia.*

1973   *Roe v. Wade* is decided. The due process clause entitles women to an abortion "without undue governmental interference."

       The Court decides in *San Antonio Independent School District v. Rodriguez* that because the Constitution nowhere mentions education, it is not a fundamental right insofar as the equal protection clause is concerned. Hence, states are free to finance their schools by local property taxes even though the dollars available vary widely from district to district.

1974   By an 8-to-0 vote, the Court in *United States v. Nixon* requires President Nixon to comply with a subpoena of certain White House tapes dealing with the Watergate affair. Seventeen days later Nixon resigns.

       The Court rules in *Milliken v. Bradley* that a multi-district remedy for school desegregation may involve only districts that have themselves discriminated. Hence, suburban Detroit districts cannot constitutionally be required to participate in the desegregation of the Detroit schools.

       The Supreme Court Historical Society is founded.

1975   The justices unanimously agree in *O'Connor v. Donaldson* that the guarantee of liberty in the due process clause prevents involuntary confinement in mental hospitals of persons dangerous to no one and capable of surviving in the outside world.

       Justice Douglas resigns after thirty-six years on the Court, longer than any justice in history.

       The Court limits oral arguments to Mondays, Tuesdays, and Wednesdays.

1976   In *Gregg v. Georgia,* the Court determines that carefully crafted statutes authorizing the death penalty for first degree murder do not necessarily violate the Eighth Amendment.

1977   In a series of three decisions, the Court rules that neither the Constitution nor the Social Security Act requires states to pay for nontherapeutic abortions. Furthermore, public hospitals may, as a matter of policy, refuse to perform abortions. Such actions do not constitute unreasonable governmental interference with a woman's right to an abortion.

(Table continues)

Table 1-1 *(Continued)*

1978   The Supreme Court decides the *Bakke* case, the first major decision involving affirmative action. Numerical quotas are illegal, but goals are not. Furthermore, race may not be the sole criterion for such programs, but may be one of several.

1980   Ronald Reagan is elected president.

1981   Sandra Day O'Connor becomes the first woman to sit on the Supreme Court. In anticipation of her arrival, the justices drop the traditional title of "Mr. Justice" to simply "Justice."

1982   In *Globe Newspaper Co. v. Superior Court*, the Court rules that a state may ban media coverage of the testimony of child molestation victims in criminal trials only on a case-by-case basis.

1983   The one-house legislative veto is ruled unconstitutional in *Immigration and Naturalization Service v. Chadha*.

        Michigan v. Long, posing a major threat to the autonomy of state courts, is decided. The Court overturns its traditional presumption that state court decisions containing a mixture of state and federal issues rest "on an adequate and independent state ground." Since *Long*, if the basis for the state court's decision is unclear, the Court assumes it to be based on federal grounds.

1984   The Court rules in *Lynch v. Donnelly* that the inclusion of a nativity scene in a city's secular Christmas display does not violate the Constitution's establishment clause.

1985   The Court determines in *New Hampshire Supreme Court v. Piper* that, although the privileges and immunities clause of Article IV of the Constitution allows states to discriminate against nonresidents for "substantial" reasons, New Hampshire's denial of a license to a Vermont lawyer does not qualify as such.

        In *Wallace v. Jaffree*, the Court holds that a legislatively mandated moment of silence for meditation or voluntary prayer in the public schools violates the establishment clause.

1986   The Court in *Bowers v. Hardwick* holds that the Constitution confers no right on consenting adult homosexuals to engage in oral or anal sex.

        The Court decides in *Wygant v. Jackson Board of Education* that affirmative action plans need not be "victim specific," but that racial preferences in hiring and promotion are constitutionally preferable to layoffs.

        President Reagan promotes Justice William Rehnquist to replace Chief Justice Burger. Antonin Scalia takes Rehnquist's seat.

1987   The Court unanimously rules in *St. Francis College v. Al-Khazraji* that members of white ethnic groups are also protected from employment, housing, and other forms of discrimination.

        The Court decides in *Edwards v. Aguillard* that a Louisiana law requiring schools that teach evolution to teach creation science too violates the establishment of religion clause.

        President Reagan's first two attempts to fill the seat vacated by Lewis Powell fail when the Senate rejects Robert Bork by a 42-to-58 vote, and Douglas Ginsberg withdraws because of allegations of marijuana use while a professor at Harvard Law School. In January 1988, the Democrati-

Table 1-1   *(Continued)*

---

cally controlled Senate approves Reagan's third choice, Anthony Kennedy, by a 97-to-0 vote.

1988   Congress enacts legislation virtually eliminating the Court's nondiscretionary appellate jurisdiction.

1989   The Court rules in *Perry v. Lynaugh* and *Stanford v. Kentucky* that mentally retarded persons and those as young as sixteen may constitutionally be sentenced to death.

1990   In *Cruzan v. Missouri Department of Health,* the Court decides that, for persons making their wishes clearly known, the Constitution recognizes a right to die.

Justice William Brennan resigns after more than thirty-three years, the seventh longest tenure. President George Bush nominates, and the Senate confirms, David Souter to replace him.

1991   Thurgood Marshall, the first African American justice, resigns. He is replaced by Clarence Thomas, the second African American justice, after acrimonious hearings involving alleged sexual harassment.

1992   In *Planned Parenthood of Southeastern Pennsylvania v. Casey,* the Court reaffirms the constitutional right to obtain an abortion.

In a unanimous ruling in *R.A.V. v. City of St. Paul,* the Court strikes down a "hate speech" ordinance as a violation of the First Amendment.

The Twenty-seventh Amendment, which provides that congressional pay raises shall not take effect until an intervening election has occurred, is ratified. The amendment was first proposed to the states in 1789.

1993   Thurgood Marshall dies of heart failure.

Justice Byron White announces his retirement from the Court. Accordingly, after eleven successive Republican appointments, President William J. Clinton is the first Democrat since Lyndon B. Johnson to appoint a Supreme Court justice. He nominates Ruth Bader Ginsburg, whom the Senate confirms by a 96-3 vote.

Note: This list reflects the judgment of the authors.

Table 1-2 Key Congressional Legislation Relating to the Supreme Court

Act	Description
Judiciary Act of 1789	Provided basic appellate jurisdiction Created a three-tier judiciary staffed by Supreme Court justices and district court judges Required Supreme Court justices to ride circuits Mandated that the Court consist of a chief justice and five associate justices, any four of whom shall be a quorum
Acts of 1793, 1801, 1802, and 1803	Provided rotation system for circuit riding, then eliminated the responsibilities, only to have the Jeffersonians reinstate circuit-riding duties
Act of 1807	Added seventh circuit and justice
Act of 1837	Divided country into nine circuits Brought number of justices to nine Expanded Court's jurisdiction to include appeals from new states and territories in 1825, 1828, and 1848.
Acts of 1855 and 1863	Added California as tenth circuit Added tenth justice
Acts of 1866, 1867, 1869, and 1871	Expanded federal jurisdiction over civil rights Reorganized the country into nine circuits Reduced number of justices to seven (1866), and later fixed the number at nine (1869) Expanded Court's jurisdiction over writs of habeas corpus and state court decisions
Act of 1875	Greatly expanded Court's jurisdiction over civil disputes Gave Court full review over writs of error Granted Court full federal question review of state court decisions
Act of 1887	Curbed access by raising jurisdictional amount in diversity cases Provided for writ of error in all capital cases
Circuit Court of Appeals Act of 1891	Established nine circuit courts and judgeships Broadened review over criminal cases Provided for limited discretionary review via writs of certiorari
Act of 1892	Provided for *in forma pauperis* filings

Table 1-2   *(Continued)*

Act	Description
Act of 1893	Created District of Columbia Circuit
Acts of 1903 and 1907	Provided direct appeal under antitrust and interstate commerce acts Granted government right of direct appeal in dismissals of criminal prosecutions
Acts of 1910, 1911, and 1913	Altered federal injunctive power; established three-judge district courts in response to single judges' enjoining state economic regulation; later extended the jurisdiction of three-judge district courts and direct appeals to the Court
Acts of 1914, 1915, and 1916	Made discretionary jurisdiction over some state cases Eliminated right to review in bankruptcy, trademark, and Federal Employers' Liability Act cases
Judiciary Act of 1925	Greatly extended Court's discretionary jurisdiction by replacing mandatory appeals with petitions for certiorari
Act of 1928	Made appeals the sole method of mandatory appellate review
Act of 1939	Expanded review of Court of Claims decisions to include both law and fact
Act of 1948	Revised, codified, and enacted into law judicial code
Act of 1950 (Hobbs Act)	Eliminated three-judge district court requirement in certain areas
Voting Rights Act of 1965	Provided direct appeal of decisions of three-judge district courts in area of voting rights
Acts of 1970, 1971, 1974, 1975, and 1976	Reorganized District of Columbia courts Expanded Court's discretionary review Repealed direct government appeals under 1907 Act Eliminated direct appeals in antitrust and Interstate Commerce Commission cases Further cut back jurisdiction and direct appeals from three-judge district courts, with the exception of voting rights and reapportionment
Federal Courts Improvement Act of 1982	Created Court of Appeals for the Federal Circuit by combining the Court of Claims and the Court of Customs and Patent Appeals

(Table continues)

Table 1-2 *(Continued)*

Act	Description
1988 Act to Improve the Administration of Justice	Eliminated virtually all Court's nondiscretionary jurisdiction, except for appeals in reapportionment cases and suits under the Civil Rights and Voting Rights Acts, antitrust laws, and Presidential Election Campaign Fund Act

Sources: David M. O'Brien, *Storm Center* (New York: W.W. Norton, 1990), 185-187, and U.S. Senate, "Creation of the Federal Judiciary," Sen. Doc. No. 91, 75th Cong., 1st Sess., July 22, 1937 (Washington, D.C.: Government Printing Office, 1938).

Table 1-3   Sections on the Jurisdiction of the Supreme Court in the United States Code Annotated, 1992

---

§ 1251. Original Jurisdiction

(a) The Supreme Court shall have original and exclusive jurisdiction of all controversies between two or more States.

(b) The Supreme Court shall have original but not exclusive jurisdiction of:

(1) All actions or proceedings to which ambassadors, other public ministers, consuls, or vice consuls of foreign states are parties;

(2) All controversies between the United States and a State;

(3) All actions or proceedings by a State against the citizens of another State or against aliens.

§ 1253. Direct appeals from decisions of three-judge courts

Except as otherwise provided by law, any party may appeal to the Supreme Court from an order granting or denying, after notice and hearing, an interlocutory or permanent injunction in any civil action, suit or proceeding required by any Act of Congress to be heard and determined by a district court of three judges.

§ 1254. Courts of appeals; certiorari; appeal; certified questions

Cases in the courts of appeals may be reviewed by the Supreme Court by the following methods:

(1) By writ of certiorari granted upon the petition of any party to any civil or criminal case, before or after rendition of judgment or decree;

(2) By certification at any time by a court of appeals of any question of law in any civil or criminal case as to which instructions are desired, and upon such certification the Supreme Court may give binding instructions or require the entire record to be sent up for decision of the entire matter in controversy.

§ 1257. State courts; appeal; certiorari

(a) Final judgments or decrees rendered by the highest court of a State in which a decision could be had, may be reviewed by the Supreme Court by writ of certiorari where the validity of a treaty or statute of the United States is drawn in question or where the validity of a statute of any State is drawn in question on the ground of its being repugnant to the Constitution, treaties, or laws of the United States, or where any title, right, privilege, or immunity is specially set up or claimed under the Constitution or the treaties or statutes of, or any commission held or authority exercised under, the United States.

(b) For the purposes of this section, the term "highest court of a State" includes the District of Columbia Court of Appeals.

§ 1258. Supreme Court of Puerto Rico; certiorari

Final judgments or decrees rendered by the Supreme Court of the Commonwealth of Puerto Rico may be reviewed by the Supreme Court by writ of

(Table continues)

Table 1-3   *(Continued)*

certiorari where the validity of a treaty or statute of the United States is drawn in question or where the validity of a statute of the Commonwealth of Puerto Rico is drawn in question on the ground of its being repugnant to the Constitution, treaties, or laws of the United States, or where any title, right, privilege, immunity is specially set up or claimed under the Constitution or the treaties or statutes of, or any commission held or authority exercised under, the United States.

§ 1259. Court of Military Appeals; certiorari

Decisions by the United States Court of Military Appeals may be reviewed by the Supreme Court by writ of certiorari in the following cases:

(1) Cases reviewed by the Court of Military Appeals under section 867(a)(1) of title 10 [10 USCS § 867(a)(1)].

(2) Cases certified to the Court of Military Appeals by the Judge Advocate General under section 867(a)(2) of title 10 [10 USCS § 867(a)(2)].

(3) Cases in which the Court of Military Appeals granted a petition for review under section 867(a)(3) of title 10 [10 USCS § 867(a)(3)].

(4) Cases, other than those described in paragraphs (1), (2), and (3) of this subsection in which the Court of Military Appeals granted relief.

Source: 28 U.S.C.A. § 1251, 1253-1254, 1257-1259.

Table 1-4 Reporting Systems

Reporter/publisher	Form of citation	Description
United States Reports Government Printing Office	U.S. Dall. 1-4 Cranch 1-15 Wheat. 1-12 Pet. 1-16 How. 1-24 Black 1-2 Wall. 1-23	Contain official text of opinions of the Court. Include tables of cases reported, cases and statutes cited, miscellaneous materials, and subject index. Include most of the Court's decisions.
United States Supreme Court Reports, Lawyers' Edition Lawyers Co-Operative Publishing Company	L.Ed. L.Ed.2d	Contain official reports of opinions of the Court. Additionally, provide per curiam and other decisions not found elsewhere. Summarize individual majority and dissenting opinions and counsel briefs.
Supreme Court Reporter West Publishing Company	S.Ct.	Contains official reports of opinions of the Court. Contains annotated reports and indexes of case names. Includes opinions of justices in chambers. Appears semi-monthly.
United States Law Week Bureau of National Affairs	U.S.L.W.	Weekly periodical service containing full text of Court decisions. Includes four indexes: topical, table of cases, docket number table, and proceedings section. Contains summary of cases filed recently, journal of proceedings, summary of orders, arguments before the Court, argued cases awaiting decisions, review of Court's work, and review of Court's docket.

Note: Citations can be read as follows: *Roe v. Wade* (1973) is 410 U.S. 113, where 410 is the volume number and 113 is the page on which the case begins. All reporters/reports listed above use the same volume/page system.

Sources: Elder Witt, *Congressional Quarterly's Guide to the U.S. Supreme Court* (Washington, D.C.: Congressional Quarterly, 1990), 767, and Fenton S. Martin and Robert U. Goehlert, *The U.S. Supreme Court* (Washington, D.C.: Congressional Quarterly, 1990), 12-13.

Table 1-5   Supreme Court Budget Appropriations, 1930-1993

Fiscal year	Salaries and expenses [a]	Building and grounds [b]	Other	Total
1930	$343,420	c		$343,420
1931	343,420	$1,000,000 [d]	$50,000 [e]	1,393,420
1932	343,420	3,750,000		4,093,420
1933	324,500	1,000,000		1,324,500
1934	315,173	3,490,000		3,805,173
1935	358,830	30,348		389,178
1936	486,000	49,080		535,080
1937	508,500	55,000		563,500
1938 [f]	470,900	60,000		530,900
1939	479,160	61,500		540,660
1940	504,000 [g]	62,500		566,500
1941	500,000	65,000		573,000
1942	601,460	70,017		671,477
1943	569,161	70,566		639,727
1944	642,214	76,600		718,814
1945	652,959	80,000		732,959
1946	668,500	104,100		772,600
1947	801,906	121,231		923,137
1948	852,920	122,800		975,720
1949	990,400	190,700		1,181,100
1950	944,100	152,000		1,096,100
1951	1,080,800	159,200		1,240,000
1952	1,152,050	172,500		1,324,550
1953	1,189,550	174,100		1,363,650
1954	1,193,236	174,100		1,367,336
1955	1,194,985	350,800		1,545,785
1956	1,294,285	367,400		1,661,685
1957	1,361,285	201,500		1,562,785
1958	1,423,835	218,200		1,642,035
1959	1,519,800	219,200		1,811,000
1960 [h]	1,536,000	347,000		1,883,000
1961	1,642,000	287,000		1,929,000
1962	1,712,000	284,000		1,996,000
1963	1,752,000	323,000		2,075,000
1964	1,853,000	355,000		2,208,000
1965	2,195,000	305,000		2,500,000
1966	2,270,000	319,000		2,589,000
1967	2,305,000	324,000		2,629,000
1968	2,356,000	334,000		2,690,000
1969	2,602,000	361,000		2,963,000
1970	3,138,000	410,000		3,548,000
1971	3,746,000	502,000		4,248,000
1972	4,180,000	561,000		4,741,000
1973 [f]	4,719,000	1,014,000	95,000 [i]	5,828,000
1974	5,353,000	1,493,000	75,000 [i]	6,921,000
1975	5,892,000	1,004,000	372,000 [i]	7,268,000
1976	6,582,000	1,454,000		8,036,000

Table 1-5   *(Continued)*

Fiscal year	Salaries and expenses[a]	Building and grounds[b]	Other	Total
1976[j]	1,576,000	196,000		1,772,000
1977	7,732,000	831,000		8,563,000
1978	8,691,000	1,588,000		10,279,000
1979	9,690,000	1,475,000		11,165,000
1980	10,363,000	2,182,000		12,545,000
1981	11,840,000	1,568,000	645,000[k]	14,053,000
1982	11,635,000	1,654,000		13,289,000
1983	12,675,000	2,000,000		14,675,000
1984	13,635,000	2,571,000		16,206,000
1985	14,143,000	2,242,000		16,385,000
1986	14,399,000	2,223,000		16,622,000
1987	15,513,000	2,336,000		17,849,000
1988	15,247,000	2,110,000		17,357,000
1989	15,901,000	2,131,000		18,032,000
1990	17,497,000	4,369,000		21,866,000
1991	19,083,000	3,453,000		22,536,000
1992 (est.)	20,787,000	3,801,000		24,588,000
1993 (est.)	22,286,000	3,611,000		25,897,000

Note: The figures shown are actual amounts appropriated for the designated fiscal years with the exception of the estimated figures for 1992 and 1993.

[a] Include salaries for Court employees, printing and binding of decisions, purchase of books and periodicals (after 1939), committees on the preparation of rules for criminal and civil procedure (1936-1938, 1942-1954), automobile and driver for the chief justice (after 1954), and miscellaneous expenses.
[b] Include improvements, maintenance, repairs, equipment, supplies, materials, special clothing for workers, snow removal, and miscellaneous expenses.
[c] Building rental costs were part of the Department of Justice appropriations at this time and consequently are not included.
[d] Construction of the Supreme Court building began in 1931 and continued through 1934, accounting for the large expenditures for buildings and grounds.
[e] Cost of purchase of printing plates for volumes 1-265 of the *Supreme Court Reports.*
[f] Beginning in 1938 all court appropriations were included in a separate Judiciary section of the federal budget. Previously appropriations for the federal courts had been part of the budget for the Justice Department.
[g] An appropriation for books and periodicals is included in the Court's budget for the first time. Prior to 1940 such library expenses were part of the Library of Congress budget.
[h] Beginning with fiscal year 1960 budgetary figures are stated in thousands of dollars rather than actual expenditures.
[i] Additional appropriation of funds for the care of the building and grounds.
[j] In 1976 the federal government moved the end of the fiscal year from June 30 to September 30. To accomplish this a special transition fiscal quarter was necessary.
[k] Acquisition of property as an addition to the grounds of the Supreme Court.

Sources: Office of Management and Budget, *Budget of the United States Government* (Washington, D.C.: Government Printing Office, 1932-1962) and *Appendix to the Budget* (Washington, D.C.: Government Printing Office, 1963-1993).

Table 1-6   Supreme Court Budget, Fiscal Year 1991

Budgetary categories	Appropriation
Salaries and expenses	
Personnel compensation	
Full-time permanent	$11,709,000
Other than full-time permanent	458,000
Total personnel compensation	12,167,000
Civilian personnel benefits	2,373,000
Benefits for former personnel	27,000
Travel and transportation of persons	76,000
Transportation of things	9,000
Communications, utilities, and miscellaneous charges	377,000
Printing and reproduction	690,000
Other services	960,000
Supplies and materials	629,000
Equipment	1,775,000
Total obligations	19,083,000
Budget appropriation	19,083,000
Care of building and grounds	
Personnel compensation	
Full-time permanent	$848,000
Other personnel compensation	153,000
Total personnel compensation	1,001,000
Civilian personnel benefits	160,000
Communications, utilities, and miscellaneous charges	592,000
Other services	2,082,000
Supplies and materials	26,000
Equipment	14,000
Land and structures	9,000
Total obligations	3,884,000
Unobligated balance available, start of year	−1,765,000
Unobligated balance available, end of year	911,000
Unobligated balance expiring	423,000
Budget appropriation	3,453,000
Total Court appropriation	22,536,000

Source: Office of Management and Budget, *The Budget of the United States Government, Fiscal Year 1993* (Washington, D.C.: Government Printing Office, 1992), Appendix One, p. 191.

Table 1-7 Salaries of the Justices, 1789-1992

Years	Chief justice	Associate justices
1789-1818	$4,000	$3,500
1819-1854	5,000	4,500
1855-1870	6,500	6,000
1871-1872	8,500	8,000
1873-1902	10,500	10,000
1903-1910	13,000	12,500
1911-1925	15,000	14,500
1926-1945	20,500	20,000
1946-1954	25,500	25,000
1955-1963	35,500	35,000
1964-1968	40,000	39,500
1969-1974	62,500	60,000
1975	65,625	63,000
1976	68,000	66,000
1977	75,000	72,000
1978	79,100	76,000
1979	84,700	81,300
1980	92,400	88,700
1981	96,800	93,000
1982-1983	100,700	96,700
1984	104,700	100,600
1985-1986	108,400	104,100
1987-1989	115,000	110,000
1990	124,000	118,000
1991	160,600	153,600
1992	166,200	159,000

Sources: Elder Witt, *Congressional Quarterly's Guide to the U.S. Supreme Court,* 2d ed. (Washington, D.C.: Congressional Quarterly, 1990) and *World Almanac and Book of Facts* (New York: Pharos Books, various years).

Table 1-8   Retirement and Pension Provisions

Year of enactment	Provisions
1869	The first judicial pension statute is passed. Justices having reached the age of seventy with at least ten years of service may resign their office and receive for life the same salary that was payable to them at the time of their resignation.
1909	Justices having reached the age of seventy with at least ten years of continuous service as a federal judge may resign their office and receive for life the salary that was payable at the time of their resignation for the office held ten years before the date of resignation.
1911	Justices having reached the age of seventy with at least ten years of continuous service as a federal judge may resign their office and receive for life the salary that was payable to them at the time of resignation for the office held at the time of resignation.
1929	Federal law is amended so that the ten years of judicial service required for pension eligibility need no longer be continuous.
1937	Justices having reached the age of seventy with at least ten years of service as a federal judge are allowed to retire in senior status rather than to resign. Senior justices retain the authority to perform judicial duties in any circuit when called upon by the Chief Justice. Senior justices receive the same pension benefits as resigned justices. (Lower court judges were given the "senior status" option in 1919.)
1939	The first judicial disability statute is enacted. Justices who become permanently disabled may retire regardless of age. Disabled justices who have less than ten years of service as a federal judge receive for life one-half of the annual salary being received on the date of retirement. Disabled justices with more than ten years of service as a federal judge receive for life the full annual salary being received on the date of retirement.
1948	Justices having reached the age of seventy with ten years of service as a federal judge who resign their office receive for life the full salary payable to them at the time of their resignations. Justices having reached the age of seventy with ten years of service as a federal judge who retire from office in senior status continue to receive the salary of their office for life. This includes any salary increases that might be granted to sitting justices. Disabled justices retiring receive the same benefits as other senior status justices, subject to the service provisions of the 1939 act.
1984	Federal law removes the term resignation from the pension regulations. Justices having reached the age of sixty-five may retire from

Table 1-8 *(Continued)*

Year of enactment	*Provisions*
	office provided that the sum of their age and years of judicial service equal at least eighty. Such retired justices receive for life the salary of their office at the time of their retirement. Justices having reached the age of sixty-five may retire in senior status provided that the sum of their age and years of judicial service equal at least eighty. Such senior justices will receive for life the salary of the office.
1989	Justices retiring in senior status are required to perform actual judicial duties in order to continue to receive the same salary increases as sitting members of the Court. Each year such justices must certify that during the previous twelve months they have been engaged in judicial work generally equivalent to what a regular sitting member of the judiciary would accomplish in three months.

Sources: U.S.C. and *Statutes at Large,* various years.

38

Figure 1-1 The Processing of Cases

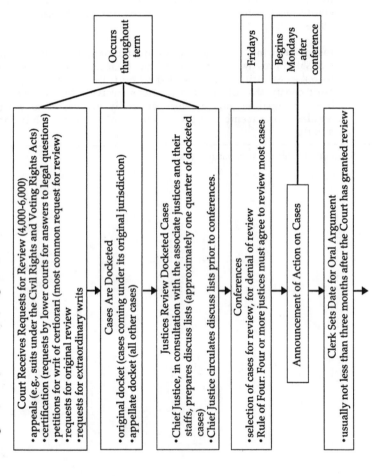

Court Receives Requests for Review (4,000-6,000)
- appeals (e.g., suits under the Civil Rights and Voting Rights Acts)
- certification (requests by lower courts for answers to legal questions)
- petitions for writ of certiorari (most common request for review)
- requests for original review
- requests for extraordinary writs

Cases Are Docketed
- original docket (cases coming under its original jurisdiction)
- appellate docket (all other cases)

Justices Review Docketed Cases
- Chief Justice, in consultation with the associate justices and their staffs, prepares discuss lists (approximately one quarter of docketed cases)
- Chief Justice circulates discuss lists prior to conferences.

Conferences
- selection of cases for review, for denial of review
- Rule of Four: Four or more justices must agree to review most cases

Announcement of Action on Cases

Clerk Sets Date for Oral Argument
- usually not less than three months after the Court has granted review

Occurs throughout term

Fridays

Begins Mondays after conference

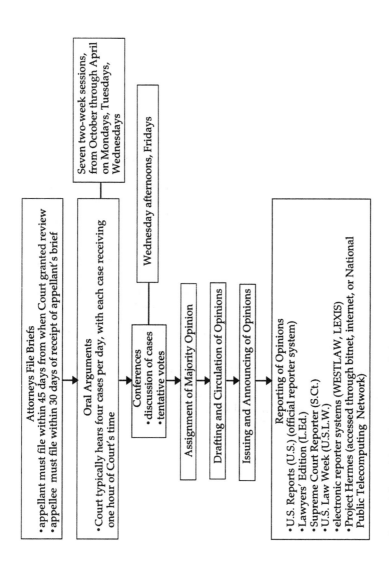

Attorneys File Briefs
•appellant must file within 45 days from when Court granted review
•appellee must file within 30 days of receipt of appellant's brief

Oral Arguments
•Court typically hears four cases per day, with each case receiving one hour of Court's time

Seven two-week sessions, from October through April on Mondays, Tuesdays, Wednesdays

Conferences
•discussion of cases
•tentative votes

Wednesday afternoons, Fridays

Assignment of Majority Opinion

Drafting and Circulation of Opinions

Issuing and Announcing of Opinions

Reporting of Opinions
•U.S. Reports (U.S.) (official reporter system)
•Lawyers' Edition (L.Ed.)
•Supreme Court Reporter (S.Ct.)
•U.S. Law Week (U.S.L.W.)
•electronic reporter systems (WESTLAW, LEXIS)
•Project Hermes (accessed through bitnet, internet, or National Public Telecomputing Network)

Source: Adapted from Lee Epstein and Thomas G. Walker, *Constitutional Law for a Changing America: Rights, Liberties, and Justice* (Washington, D.C. : CQ Press, 1992), 662-664.

Table 1-9   The Supreme Court's Calendar

Activity	Time
Start of term	First Monday in October
Oral argument cycle	October-April on Mondays, Tuesdays and, Wednesdays in seven two-week sessions
Recess cycle	October-April, two or more consecutive weeks after two weeks of oral arguments and at Christmas and Easter holidays
Conferences	Wednesday afternoon following Monday oral arguments (discussion of four Monday cases) Friday following Tuesday and Wednesday oral arguments (discussion of Tuesday-Wednesday cases; certiorari petitions) Friday before two-week oral argument period
Majority opinion assignment	Following oral arguments/conference
Opinion announcement	Throughout term, with bulk coming in spring/summer
Summer recess	Late June/early July until first Monday in October
Initial conference	Late September (resolve old business, consider certiorari petitions from the summer)

Source: Adapted from Lee Epstein and Thomas G. Walker, *Constitutional Law for a Changing America: Rights, Liberties, and Justice* (Washington, D.C.: CQ Press, 1992), 662-664.

Table 1-10   Supreme Court Employees: Full-time Permanent Positions, 1930-1993

Year	Court employees[a]	Building employees[b]	Other employees
1930	52.5		
1931	50.8		
1932	51.8		
1933	52.8		
1934	51.8		
1935	54.5	18.4	
1936	156.9[c]	29.0[c]	7.4[d]
1937	160.5	30.2	7.4[d]
1938	172.8	32.0	0.4[d]
1939	173.8	32.0	
1940	176.8	32.0	
1941	177.8	32.0	
1942	179.0	32.4	4.7[e]
1943	172.7	29.1	5.7[e, f]
1944	144.5	28.7	3.9[e, f]
1945	144.1	29.7	3.0[e, f]
1946	133.4	31.8	2.7[e, f]
1947	142.0	34.0	
1948	151.0	34.9	
1949	157.0	36.0	
1950	159.0	36.0	
1951	162.0	37.0	
1952	162.0	37.0	
1953	163.0	37.0	
1954	163.0	37.0	
1955	162.0	38.0	1.0[g]
1956	162.0	33.0	1.0
1957	163.0	33.0	1.0
1958	163.0	33.0	1.0
1959	164.0	33.0	1.0
1960	164.0	33.0	1.0
1961	166.0	33.0	1.0
1962	168.0	33.0	1.0
1963	168.0	33.0	1.0
1964	168.0	33.0	1.0
1965	189.0	33.0	1.0
1966	189.0	33.0	1.0
1967	190.0	33.0	1.0
1968	190.0	33.0	1.0
1969	191.0	33.0	1.0
1970	204.0	33.0	1.0
1971	220.0	33.0	1.0
1972	227.0	33.0	1.0
1973	238.0	33.0	1.0

(Table continues)

Table 1-10   *(Continued)*

Year	Court employees[a]	Building employees[b]	Other employees
1974	243.0	33.0	1.0
1975	254.0	33.0	
1976	274.0	33.0	
1977	297.0	33.0	
1978	304.0	33.0	
1979	325.0	33.0	
1980	325.0	33.0	
1981	325.0	33.0	
1982	316.0	30.0	
1983	320.0	33.0	
1984	322.0	33.0	
1985	317.0	33.0	
1986	318.0	33.0	
1987	319.0	33.0	
1988	319.0	33.0	
1989	319.0	33.0	
1990	329.0	26.0	
1991	338.0	28.0	
1992 (est.)[h]	340.0	33.0	
1993 (est.)	341.0	33.0	

Note: The personnel figures shown are for the actual full-time permanent positions appropriated for the fiscal years listed with the exceptions of 1992 and 1993 where the figures are estimates.

[a] Individuals providing administrative and other services under the authority of the Supreme Court.

[b] Individuals assigned to the care of the Supreme Court building and grounds under statutory authority granted to the Architect of the Capitol.

[c] The move to the new Supreme Court building required the hiring of many additional employees, including almost 30 positions for guards and 40 janitorial positions.

[d] Advisory committee on preparation of a unified system of general rules for cases in equity and actions of law. This commission ceased to exist in 1938.

[e] Advisory committee on the preparation of rules for criminal proceedings. It was funded for personnel through 1946.

[f] Advisory committee on the preparation of rules for civil proceedings. It was funded for personnel through 1946.

[g] Beginning in 1955, the newly created position of a driver for the chief justice was placed in the "other" category. After 1974, this position was not itemized separately.

[h] Beginning with the budget for fiscal 1992 (which contains the actual figures for 1990), the government eliminated the classification "full-time permanent positions." It was replaced with the classification "total compensable work years: full-time equivalent employment."

Sources: Office of Management and Budget, *Budget of the United States Government* (Washington, D.C.: Government Printing Office, 1932-1962) and *Appendix to the Budget* (Washington, D.C.: Government Printing Office, 1963-1993).

Table 1-11 Administrative Officers of the Court, 1790-1993

Position	Officer	Years of service
Clerk of the Court[a]	John Tucker	1790-1791
	Samuel Bayard	1791-1800
	Elias B. Caldwell	1800-1825
	William Griffith	1826-1827
	William T. Carroll	1827-1863
	D. W. Middleton	1863-1880
	J. H. McKenney	1880-1913
	James D. Maher	1913-1921
	William R. Stansbury	1921-1927
	C. Elmore Cropley	1927-1952
	Harold B. Willey	1952-1956
	John T. Fey	1956-1958
	James R. Browning	1958-1961
	John F. Davis	1961-1970
	E. Robert Seaver	1970-1972
	Michael Rodak, Jr.	1972-1981
	Alexander Stevas	1981-1985
	Joseph F. Spaniol, Jr.	1985-1991
	William K. Suter	1991-
Reporter of Decisions[b]	Alexander J. Dallas	1790-1800
	William Cranch	1801-1815
	Henry Wheaton	1816-1827
	Richard Peters, Jr.	1828-1842
	Benjamin C. Howard	1843-1860
	Jeremiah S. Black	1861-1863
	John W. Wallace	1863-1874
	William T. Otto	1875-1882
	J. C. Bancroft Davis	1883-1902
	Charles Henry Butler	1902-1915
	Ernest Knaebel	1916-1946
	Walter Wyatt	1946-1963
	Henry Putzel, Jr.	1964-1979
	Henry C. Lind	1979-1987
	Frank D. Wagner	1987-
Marshal of the Court[c]	Richard C. Parsons	1867-1872
	John C. Nicolay	1872-1887
	John Montgomery Wright	1888-1915
	Frank Key Green	1915-1938
	Thomas E. Waggaman	1938-1952
	T. Perry Lippitt	1952-1972
	Frank M. Hepler	1972-1976
	Alfred Wong	1976-
Librarian of the Court[d]	Henry Deforest Clarke	1887-1900

(Table continues)

Table 1-11   *(Continued)*

Position	Officer	Years of service
	Frank Kay Green	1900-1915
	Oscar Deforest Clarke	1915-1947
	Helen C. Newman	1947-1965
	Henry Charles Hallam, Jr.	1965-1972
	Edward G. Hudon	1972-1976
	Betty H. Clowers (acting)	1976-1978
	Roger F. Jacobs	1978-1985
	Stephen G. Margeton	1985-1988
	Shelley L. Dowling	1989-

[a] Responsible for administering and processing the Court's records and paperwork, including administration of the docket, receiving case filings, distributing papers to the justices, communicating with attorneys, and preparation of orders and judgments.
[b] Responsible for editing, printing, and publishing the decisions and opinions of the Court.
[c] Initially responsible for the Court's security, but over time also assumed responsibility for maintaining the Court's building and grounds and for administering the fiscal affairs of the institution.
[d] Responsible for the acquisition and maintenance of the Court's books, periodicals, and other resources for legal research.

Sources: Elder Witt, *Congressional Quarterly's Guide to the U.S. Supreme Court,* 2d ed. (Washington, D.C.: Congressional Quarterly, 1990); *United States Reports,* various years.

2

The Supreme Court's Review Process, Caseload, and Cases

The material in this chapter provides basic information on the Court's work. We begin with the review process and the Court's rules governing the process's operations and procedures. Those rules governing the steps litigants must take to secure Court review of their cases and the criteria the Court uses in acting on their petitions appear in Table 2-1. Note especially the detailed jurisdictional statement of Rule 15. This results because all of the federal courts are so-called courts of limited jurisdiction. This means that they may only resolve disputes within the compass of Article III of the Constitution (see pages 710-711). For them to exceed these limits would intrude upon the reserved powers of the states in violation of the federal character of the constitutional system. To ensure that this does not happen, the Supreme Court requires the party petitioning the Court to review his or her case to provide the information requested in Rule 15. The concern of the justices not to exceed jurisdictional limits is evidenced by the frequency with which the Court either resolves cases on jurisdictional bases without reaching the merits of the controversy, or addresses the merits but only after a sometimes lengthy discussion of the reasons why it is proper for the Supreme Court, or the lower federal courts, to exercise jurisdiction over the case. Although Rule 15 technically governs only writs of appeal, similar language governs litigants who petition the Court to review their cases by writ of certiorari. We do not include that rule in this table.

Note also the criteria in Rule 17 that the Court specifies for granting a writ of certiorari. This is the most common method whereby cases reach the Supreme Court. Although the list is vague, allowing the justices to use their own discretion in granting or denying petitions, four of the seven reasons listed in sections (a), (b), and (c) pertain to decisions in conflict with those of other courts. All things considered, a case in conflict with another appreciably enhances the likelihood that the justices will hear the matter.

The Court's caseload is considered from five different standpoints in Tables 2-2 through 2-6. The raw totals of Tables 2-5 and 2-6 show a five-fold increase in the total of docketed cases since 1880, with the number of new cases increasing tenfold. These increases suggest that the Court has difficulty remaining abreast of its docket. The data in Tables 2-3 and 2-4, however, indicate the opposite. Cases remaining on the Court's dockets at the end of the term have not appreciably increased since the mid 1960s. Tables 2-5 and 2-6 show why: the justices simply accept for review a number of cases independent of the number filed.

Use of the writ of certiorari by the Court began with an 1891 Act of Congress, which made some types of lower court decisions "reviewable only upon the issuance" of a writ. According to one account, though, between 1891 and 1893 the Court granted only two writs. Between the mid 1890s and the end of the 1920s that figure grew and stabilized at about 16 percent. Still, the vast majority of the cases fell under the Court's obligatory jurisdiction. Accordingly (and with a good deal of prodding by the justices), Congress enacted the Judiciary Act of 1925, which greatly increased the Court's discretionary jurisdiction by replacing mandatory appeals with petitions for certiorari.[1]

Thus, for example, in 1971 the Court accepted 11.5 percent of the 2,070 cases on its major (appellate) docket and 2.5 percent of the 2,445 *in forma pauperis* petitions. In 1989, the justices accepted only 4.3 percent of the cases on the appellate docket (103 of 2,416) and 0.5 percent of those filing *in forma pauperis* (19 of 3,316). It is important to add, however, that despite the limited number of cases accepted by the Court, no lay or professional sources allege that it is failing to decide many important cases.

Tables 2-7 through 2-13 present data about the cases that the Court has decided. Table 2-7 lists the number of formally decided cases: those that the Court decided after hearing oral argument. They comprise two forms: those in which the prevailing opinion is signed by an individual justice, and those in which no individual justice authors the prevailing opinion (per curiam). The Court initially decided its cases seriatim—that is, with the authoring justices identifying their individual opinions, but with no opinion constituting the opinion of the Court. Beginning in 1875 and continuing until 1925, the Court typically decided more than 200 cases per term. In 1925, Congress authorized the Court to decide for itself which cases it would hear. As a result, the Court now averages only about 125 signed opinions per term. The difference in the figures between the first two columns of Table 2-7, signed opinions and cases disposed of by signed opinion, results because of the Court's practice of deciding related cases together under a single signed opinion. Although this practice long antedates 1926, no compilation for preceding years exists. It appears as though orally argued per curiam decisions, the subject of the third column, do not antedate 1940. An equivalent device nevertheless did exist: the practice of an individual justice announcing the Court's decision in a brief opinion without any designation other than the name of the authoring justice. Such opinions, however, are not labeled "the opinion of the Court." [2] Per curiam opinions generally address relatively uncomplicated matters that do not require more than a brief opinion.

Table 2-8 lists the number of Court cases decided ·between 1933 and 1987 falling into fourteen major policy areas; Table 2-9 breaks down the Court's formally decided cases (signed opinions and orally argued per curiams) since the beginning of the Warren Court in 1953 into thirteen issue areas. Both tables show a slow decline in the number and proportion of economically based litigation and a corresponding increase in that pertaining to noneconomic rights and liberties. Thus, as Table 2-9 indicates, the proportion of economic activity cases has dropped from approximately one in three to one in five. Additionally, 68 federal income tax cases were decided during the first eight terms of the Warren Court, while only 74 were decided in the most recent nineteen terms. By contrast, the other sizable economic category, unions, has maintained a much more consistent number of decisions per term: 65 during the first eight terms displayed; 68 during the most recent twelve. In the noneconomic sector, all categories have increased in absolute number, with the possible exception of First Amendment freedoms. Criminal procedure (overall the largest category), civil rights, due process, and the small privacy and attorney sets produce markedly more decisions currently than they did during the 1950s and the early 1960s. Like unions, judicial power and federalism have maintained a relatively constant number of decisions, notwithstanding the current perception that the Rehnquist Court considers decentralization a matter of some priority.

The foregoing categorization of the Court's decisions is in gross numbers and treats all cases falling within a given grouping as equally important. To rectify these shortcomings, we have compiled Table 2-10, which orders the Court's most important decisions topically. Obviously, any list of the Court's landmark decisions is a subjective venture. Nonetheless, all such lists contain more overlap than they do cases unique to any one compilation. While not minimizing cases of purely historical significance, our list emphasizes topics and cases of current interest. Hence, we include many more cases from the Warren, Burger, and Rehnquist Courts than from earlier Courts. Moreover, where choice could appropriately be exercised, we erred on the side of inclusion. Hence, some 400 cases under 75 topics appear in these tables.

Among the cases that have shaped modern American constitutional law are those that have made various provisions of the Bill of Rights binding on state and local governments. According to the literal language of the Constitution, and the authoritative interpretation given that language by Chief Justice John Marshall,[3] the guarantees in the Bill of Rights limit only the federal government. Accordingly, any state could, for example, deny individuals freedom of speech, impose taxes on all to support a specific religious denomination, employ cruel and unusual punishments, or deny persons a trial by jury. Not until the 1920s did the justices alter this original interpretation by reading into the due process clause of the Fourteenth Amendment, which was binding on state and local governments, various provisions of the Bill of Rights. Table 2-11 identifies these cases and the provision incorporated into the due process clause. Note that approximately half of them resulted from decisions of the Warren Court handed down between 1961 and 1969.

Tables 2-12 and 2-13 concern the exercise of the most momentous of the Court's powers: judicial review. Judicial review is the capacity of the Court to declare unconstitutional the actions of Congress, as well as the legal provisions of state and local governments. While the power to void actions of state and local governments fairly derives from the language of the supremacy clause of Article VI of the Constitution (see page 713), no comparable provision authorizes the Court to declare unconstitutional actions of the other branches of the federal government. Marshall simply inferred the existence of such authority in his masterful opinion in *Marbury v. Madison* (1803).[4]

Whereas the decision of a court declaring legislation unconstitutional is upsetting to those who view the will of the people, as reflected by legislative majorities, to be the essence of democracy, the decision of a court to overrule itself is upsetting to those who view the law, and especially the Constitution, as fixed and stable. Nonetheless, as Tables 2-12 and 2-13, on the one hand, and Table 2-14 on the other, demonstrate, the Court has not been reluctant either to declare legislation unconstitutional or to overrule its own previous decisions. And though the frequency of the former is several times the frequency of the latter, by no means is the number of instances when the Court formally altered its own precedents trivial. Indeed, when one considers that in 1789 the Court had no precedents of its own at all, and very few until well after the Civil War, legal stability and fixity is at most a sometime thing.

Notes

1. Doris Marie Provine, *Case Selection in the United States Supreme Court* (Chicago: University of Chicago Press, 1980), chapter one.
2. See, for example, *Morse v. Anderson*, 150 U.S. 156 (1893).
3. In *Barron v. Baltimore*, 7 Pet. 243 (1833).
4. 1 Cranch 137.

Table 2-1   Rules Governing the Supreme Court's Review Process

---

PART III. ORIGINAL JURISDICTION

Rule 9
Procedure in Original Actions

.1. This Rule applies only to actions within the Court's original jurisdiction under Article III of the Constitution of the United States. Original applications for writs in aid of the Court's appellate jurisdiction are governed by Part VII of these Rules.

.2. The form of pleadings and motions in original actions shall be governed, so far as may be, by the Federal Rules of Civil Procedure, and in other respects those Rules, where their application is appropriate, may be taken as a guide to procedure in original actions in this Court.

.3. The initial pleading in any original action shall be prefaced by a motion for leave to file such pleading, and both shall be printed in conformity with Rule 33. A brief in support of the motion for leave to file, which shall comply with Rule 33, may be filed with the motion and pleading. Sixty copies of each document, with proof of service as prescribed by Rule 28, are required, except that, when an adverse party is a State, service shall be made on the Governor and Attorney General of such State. See Rule 28.1.

.4. The case will be placed upon the original docket when the motion for leave to file is filed with the Clerk. The docket fee must be paid at that time, and the appearance of counsel for the plaintiff entered.

.5. Within 60 days after receipt of the motion for leave to file and allied documents, any adverse party may file, with proof of service as prescribed by Rule 28, 60 printed copies of a brief in opposition to such motion. The brief shall conform to Rule 33. When such brief in opposition has been filed, or when the time within which it may be filed has expired, the motion, pleading, and briefs will be distributed to the Court by the Clerk. The Court may thereafter grant or deny the motion, set it down for argument, or take other appropriate action.

.6. Additional pleadings may be filed, and subsequent proceedings had, as the Court may direct. See Rule 28.1.

.7. A summons issuing out of this Court in any original action shall be served on the defendent 60 days before the return day set out therein; and if the defendant, on such service, shall not respond by the return day, the plaintiff shall be at liberty to proceed *ex parte*.

.8. Any process against a State issued from the Court in an original action shall be served on the Governor and Attorney General of such State.

PART IV. JURISDICTION ON APPEAL

Rule 10
Appeal—How Taken—Parties—Cross-Appeal

.1. An appeal to this Court permitted by law shall be taken by filing a notice of appeal in the form, within the time, and at the place prescribed by this rule, and shall be perfected by docketing the case in this Court as provided in Rule 12.

.2. The notice of appeal shall specify the parties taking the appeal, shall designate the judgment or part thereof appealed from, giving the date of its entry, and shall specify the statute or statutes under which the appeal to this

Table 2-1 *(Continued)*

Court is taken. A copy of the notice of appeal shall be served on all parties to the proceeding in the court where the judgment appealed from was issued, in the manner prescribed by Rule 28, and proof of service shall be filed with the notice of appeal.

.3. If the appeal is taken from a federal court, the notice of appeal shall be filed with the clerk of that court. If the appeal is taken from a state court, the notice of appeal shall be filed with the clerk of the court from whose judgment the appeal is taken, and a copy of the notice of appeal shall be filed with the court possessed of the record.

.4. All parties to the proceeding in the court from whose judgment the appeal is being taken shall be deemed parties in this Court, unless the appellant shall notify the Clerk of this Court in writing of the appellant's belief that one or more of the parties below has no interest in the outcome of the appeal. A copy of such notice shall be served on all parties to the proceeding below and a party noted as no longer interested may remain a party hereby notifying the Clerk, with service on the other parties, that he has an interest in the appeal. All parties other than appellants shall be appellees, but any appellee who supports the position of an appellant shall meet the time schedule for filing papers which is provided for that appellant, except that any response by such appellee to a jurisdictional statement shall be filed within 20 days after receipt of the statement.

.5. The Court may permit an appellee, without filing a cross-appeal, to defend a judgment on any ground that the law and record permit and that would not expand the relief he has been granted.

.6. Parties interested jointly, severally, or otherwise in a judgment may join in an appeal therefrom; or any one or more of them may appeal separately; or any two or more of them may join in an appeal. Where two or more cases that involve identical or closely related questions are appealed from the same court, it will suffice to file a single jurisdictional statement covering all the issues.

.7. An appellee may take a cross-appeal by perfecting an appeal in the normal manner or, without filing a notice of appeal, by docketing the cross-appeal within the time permitted by Rule 12.4

Rule 15
Jurisdictional Statement

.1. The jurisdictional statement required by Rule 12 shall contain, in the order here indicated:

(a) The questions presented by the appeal, expressed in the terms and circumstances of the case but without unnecessary detail. The statement of the questions should be short and concise and should not be argumentative or repetitious. The statement of a question presented will be deemed to comprise every subsidiary question fairly included therein. Only the questions set forth in the jurisdictional statement or fairly included therein will be considered by the Court.

(b) A list of all parties to the proceeding in the court whose judgment is sought to be reviewed, except where the caption of the case in this Court

(Table continues)

Table 2-1 *(Continued)*

contains the names of all such parties. This listing may be done in a footnote. See Rule 28.1.

(c) A table of contents and table of authorities, if required by Rule 33.5.

(d) A reference to the official and unofficial reports of any opinions delivered in the courts or administrative agency below.

(e) A concise statement of the grounds on which the jurisdiction of this Court is invoked, showing:

(i) The nature of the proceeding and, if the appeal is from a federal court, the statutory basis for federal jurisdiction.

(ii) The date of the entry of the judgment or decree sought to be reviewed, the date of any order respecting a rehearing, the date the notice of appeal was filed, and the court in which it was filed. In the case of a cross-appeal docketed under Rule 12.4, reliance upon that Rule shall be expressly noted, and the date of. receipt of the appellant's jurisdictional statement by the appellee-cross-appellant shall be stated.

(iii) The statutory provision believed to confer jurisdiction of the appeal on this Court, and, if deemed necessary, the cases believed to sustain jurisdiction.

(f) The constitutional provisions, treaties, statutes, ordinances, and regulations that the case involves, setting them out verbatim, and giving the appropriate citation therefor. If the provisions involved are lengthy, their citation alone will suffice at this point, and their pertinent text then shall be set forth in the appendix referred to in subparagraph 1 (j) of this Rule.

(g) A *concise* statement of the case containing the facts material to consideration of the questions presented. The statement of the case shall also specify the stage in the proceedings (both in the court of first instance and in the appellate court) at which the questions sought to be reviewed were raised; the method or manner of raising them; and the way in which they were passed upon by the court.

(h) A statement of the reasons why the questions presented are so substantial as to require plenary consideration, with briefs on the merits and oral argument, for their resolution.

(i) If the appeal is from a decree of a district court granting or denying a preliminary injunction, a showing of the matters in which it is contended that the court has abused its discretion by such action. See *United States v. Corrick*, 298 U.S. 435 (1936); *Mayo v. Lakeland Highlands Canning Co.*, 309 U.S. 310 (1940).

(j) An appendix containing, in the following order:

(i) Copies of any opinions, orders, findings of fact, and conclusions of law, whether written or oral (if recorded and transcribed), delivered upon the rendering of the judgment or decree by the court whose decision is sought to be reviewed.

(ii) Copies of any other such opinions, orders, findings of fact, and conclusions of law rendered by courts or administrative agencies in the case, and, if reference thereto is necessary to ascertain the grounds of the judgment or decree, of those in companion cases. Each of these documents shall include the caption showing the name of the issuing court or agency, the title and number of the case, and the date of its entry.

(iii) A copy of the judgment or decree appealed from and any order on rehearing, including in each the caption showing the name of the issuing court or agency, the title and number of the case, and the date of entry of the

Table 2-1   *(Continued)*

judgment, decree, or order on rehearing.

(iv) A copy of the notice of appeal showing the date it was filed and the name of the court where it was filed.

(v) Any other appended materials.

If what is required by this paragraph to be appended to the statement is voluminous, it may, if more convenient, be separately presented.

.2. The jurisdictional statement shall be produced in conformity with Rule 33. The Clerk shall not accept any jurisdictional statement that does not comply with this Rule and with Rule 33, except that a party proceeding *in forma pauperis* may proceed in the manner provided in Rule 46.

.3. The jurisdictional statement shall be as short as possible, but may not exceed 30 pages, excluding the subject index, table of authorities, any verbatim quotation required by subparagraph 1(f) of this Rule, and the appendices.

PART V. JURISDICTION ON WRIT OF CERTIORARI

Rule 17
Considerations Governing Review on Certiorari

.1. A review on writ of certiorari is not a matter of right, but of judicial discretion, and will be granted only when there are special and important reasons therefor. The following, while neither controlling nor fully measuring the Court's discretion, indicate the character of reasons that will be considered.

(a) When a federal court of appeals has rendered a decision in conflict with the decision of another federal court of appeals on the same matter; or has decided a federal question in a way in conflict with a state court of last resort; or has so far departed from the accepted and usual course of judicial proceedings, or so far sanctioned such a departure by a lower court, as to call for an exercise of this Court's power of supervision.

(b) When a state court of last resort has decided a federal question in a way in conflict with the decision of another state court of last resort or of a federal court of appeals.

(c) When a state court or a federal court of appeals has decided an important question of federal law which has not been, but should be, settled by this Court, or has decided a federal question in a way in conflict with applicable decisions of this Court.

.2. The same general considerations outlined above will control in respect of petitions for writs of certiorari to review judgments of . . . any other court whose judgments are reviewable by law on writ of certiorari.

Rule 19
Review on Certiorari—How Sought—Parties

.1. A party intending to file a petition for certiorari, prior to filing the case in this Court or at any time prior to action by this Court on the petition, may request the clerk of the court possessed of the record to certify it, or any part of it, and to provide for its transmission to this Court, but the filing of the record in this Court is not a requisite for docketing the petition. If the petitioner has not

(Table continues)

Table 2-1 *(Continued)*

done so, the respondent may request such clerk to certify and transmit the record or any part of it. Thereafter, the Clerk of this Court or any party to the case may request that additional parts of the record be certified and transmitted to this Court. Copies of all requests for certification and transmission shall be sent to all parties to the proceeding. Such requests to certify the record prior to action by the Court on the petition for certiorari, however, should not be made as a matter of course but only when the record is deemed essential to a proper understanding of the case by this Court.

.2. When requested to certify and transmit the record, or any part of it, the clerk of the court possessed of the record shall number the documents to be certified and shall transmit with the record a numbered list of the documents, identifying each with reasonable definiteness. If the record, or stipulated portions thereof, has been printed for the use of the court below, such printed record plus the proceedings in the court below may be certified as the record unless one of the parties or the Clerk of this Court otherwise requests. The provisions of Rule 13.3 with respect to original papers shall apply to all cases sought to be reviewed on writ of certiorari.

.3. Counsel for the petitioner shall enter an appearance, pay the docket fee, and file, with proof of service as provided by Rule 28, 40 copies of a petition which shall comply in all respects with Rule 21. The case will then be placed on the docket. It shall be the duty of counsel for the petitioner to notify all respondents, on a form supplied by the Clerk, of the date of filing and of the docket number of the case. Such notice shall be served as required by Rule 28.

.4. Parties interested jointly, severally, or otherwise in a judgment may join in a petition for a writ of certiorari therefrom; or any one or more of them may petition separately; or any two or more of them may join in a petition. When two or more cases are sought to be reviewed on certiorari to the same court and involve identical or closely related questions, it will suffice to file a single petition for writ of certiorari covering all the cases.

.5. Not more than 30 days after receipt of the petition for certiorari, counsel for a respondent wishing to file a cross-petition that would otherwise be untimely shall enter an appearance, pay the docket fee, and file, with proof of service as prescribed by Rule 28, 40 copies of a cross-petition for certiorari, which shall comply in all respects with Rule 21. The cross-petition will then be placed on the docket subject, however, to the provisions of Rule 20.5. It shall be the duty of counsel for the cross-petitioner to notify the cross-respondent on a form supplied by the Clerk of the date of docketing and of the docket number of the cross-petition. Such notice shall be served as required by Rule 28. A cross-petition for certiorari may not be joined with any other pleading. The Clerk shall not accept any pleadings so joined. The time for filing a cross-petition may not be extended.

.6. All parties to the proceeding in the court whose judgment is sought to be reviewed shall be deemed parties in this Court, unless the petitioner shall notify the Clerk of the Court in writing of petitoner's belief that one or more of the parties below has no interest in the outcome of the petition. A copy of such notice shall be served on all parties to the proceeding below and a party noted as no longer interested may remain a party here by notifying the Clerk, with service on the other parties, that he has an interest in the petition. All parties other than petitioners shall be respondents, but any respondent who supports the position of a petitioner shall meet the time schedule for filing papers which

Table 2-1   *(Continued)*

is provided for that petitioner, except that any response by such respondent to the petition shall be filed within 20 days after receipt of the petition. The time for filing such response may not be extended.

PART VII. JURISDICTION TO ISSUE EXTRAORDINARY WRITS

Rule 26
Considerations Governing Issuance of Extraordinary Writs

The issuance by the Court of any extraordinary writ authorized by 28 U.S.C. § 1651 (a) is not a matter of right, but of discretion sparingly exercised. To justify the granting of any writ under that provision, it must be shown that the writ will be in aid of the Court's appellate jurisdiction, that there are present exceptional circumstances warranting the exercise of the Court's discretionary powers, and that adequate relief cannot be had in any other form or from any other court.

Rule 27
Procedure in Seeking an Extraordinary Writ

.1. The petition in any proceeding seeking the issuance by this Court of a writ authorized by 28 U.S.C. §§ 1651 (a), 2241, or 2254 (a), shall comply in all respects with Rule 33, except that a party proceeding *in forma pauperis* may proceed in the manner provided in Rule 46. The petition shall be captioned "In re (name of petitioner)." All contentions in support of the petition shall be included in the petition. The case will be placed upon the docket when 40 copies, with proof of service as prescribed by Rule 28 (subject to paragraph .3 (b) of this Rule), are filed with the Clerk and the docket fee is paid. The appearance of counsel for the petitioner must be entered at this time. The petition shall be as short as possible, and in any event may not exceed 30 pages.

.2.(a) If the petition seeks issuance of a writ of prohibition, a writ of mandamus, or both in the alternative, it shall identify by names and office or function all persons against whom relief is sought and shall set forth with particularity why the relief sought is not available in any other court. There shall be appended to such petition a copy of the judgment or order in respect of which the writ is sought, including a copy of any opinion rendered in that connection, and such other papers as may be essential to an understanding of the petition.

(b) The petition shall follow, insofar as applicable, the form for the petition for writ of certiorari prescribed by Rule 21. The petition shall be served on the judge or judges to whom the writ is sought to be directed, and shall also be served on every other party to the proceeding in respect of which relief is desired. The judge or judges, and the other parties, within 30 days after receipt of the petition, may file 40 copies of a brief or briefs in opposition thereto, which shall comply fully with Rules 22.1 and 22.2, including the 30-page limit. If the judge or judges concerned do not desire to respond to the petition, they shall so advise the Clerk and all parties by letter. All persons served pursuant to this paragraph shall be deemed respondents for all purposes in the proceedings in

(Table continues)

Table 2-1   *(Continued)*

this Court.

.3. (a) If the petition seeks issuance of a writ of habeas corpus, it shall comply with the requirements of 28 U.S.C. § 2242, and in particular with the requirement in the last paragraph thereof that it state the reasons for not making application to the district court of the district in which the petitioner is held. If the relief sought is from the judgment of a state court, the petition shall set forth specifically how and wherein the petitioner has exhausted his remedies in the state courts or otherwise comes within the provisions of 28 U.S.C. § 2254 (b). To justify the granting of a writ of habeas corpus, it must be shown that there are present exceptional circumstances warranting the exercise of the Court's discretionary powers and that adequate relief cannot be had in any other form or from any other court. Such writs are rarely granted.

(b) Proceedings under this paragraph .3 will be *ex parte*, unless the Court requires the respondent to show cause why the petition for a writ of habeas corpus should not be granted. If a response is ordered, it shall comply fully with Rules 22.1 and 22.2, including the 30-page limit. Neither denial of the petition, without more, nor an order of transfer under authority of 28 U.S.C. § 2241 (b), is an adjudication on the merits, and the former action is to be taken as without prejudice to a further application to any other court for the relief sought.

.4. If the petition seeks issuance of a common- law writ of certiorari under 28 U.S.C. § 1651 (a), there may also be filed, at the time of docketing, a certified copy of the record, including all proceedings in the court to which the writ is sought to be directed. However, the filing of such record is not required. The petition shall follow, insofar as applicable, the form for a petition for certiorari prescribed by Rule 21, and shall set forth with particularity why the relief sought is not available in any other court, or cannot be had through other appellate process. The respondent, within 30 days after receipt of the petition, may file 40 copies of a brief in opposition, which shall comply fully with Rules 22.1 and 22.2, including the 30-page limit.

.5. When a brief in opposition under paragraphs .2 and .4 has been filed, or when a response under paragraph .3 has been ordered and filed, or when the time within which it may be filed has expired, or upon an express waiver of the right to file, the papers will be distributed to the Court by the Clerk.

.6. If the Court orders the cause set down for argument, the Clerk will notify the parties whether additional briefs are required, when they must be filed, and, if the case involves a petition for common-law certiorari, that the parties shall proceed to print a joint appendix pursuant to Rule 30.

Note: For the text of those rules mentioned, but not included, here, see 445 U.S. 987-1047.

Source: 445 U.S. 987-1047.

Table 2-2   The Supreme Court's Caseload, 1880-1992 Terms

Term	New cases filed (percentage change)	Total cases on docket [a] (percentage change)
1880	417	1,212
1881	411 (−1.4)	1,254 (+3.1)
1882	434 (+5.6)	1,275 (+1.7)
1883	439 (+1.2)	1,313 (+3.0)
1884	477 (+8.7)	1,325 (+0.9)
1885	493 (+3.4)	1,348 (+1.7)
1886	499 (+1.2)	1,403 (+4.1)
1887	489 (−2.0)	1,437 (+2.4)
1888	556 (+13.7)	1,571 (+9.3)
1889	500 (−10.1)	1,648 (+4.9)
1890	636 (+27.2)	1,816 (+10.2)
1891	383 (−39.8)	1,582 (−12.9)
1892	290 (−24.3)	1,369 (−13.5)
1893	280 (−3.4)	1,224 (−10.6)
1894	341 (+21.8)	1,062 (−13.2)
1895	386 (+13.2)	1,033 (−2.7)
1896	295 (−23.6)	834 (−19.3)
1897	307 (+4.1)	689 (−17.4)
1898	523 (+70.4)	839 (+21.8)
1899	384 (−26.6)	692 (−17.5)
1900	406 (+5.7)	723 (+4.5)
1901	386 (−4.9)	732 (+1.2)

(Table continues)

Table 2-2   *(Continued)*

Term	New cases filed (percentage change)	Total cases on docket [a] (percentage change)
1902	391 (+1.3)	746 (+1.9)
1903	430 (+9.9)	749 (+0.4)
1904	403 (−6.3)	698 (−6.8)
1905	502 (+24.6)	794 (+13.8)
1906	484 (−3.6)	801 (+0.9)
1907	480 (−0.9)	832 (+3.9)
1908	494 (+2.9)	923 (10.9)
1909	514 (+4.0)	1,000 (+8.3)
1910	516 (+0.4)	1,116 (+11.6)
1911	532 (+3.1)	1,182 (+5.9)
1912	521 (−2.1)	1,201 (+1.6)
1913	526 (+1.0)	1,142 (−4.9)
1914	530 (+0.8)	1,075 (−5.9)
1915	557 (+5.1)	1,093 (+1.7)
1916	658 (+18.1)	1,200 (+9.8)
1917	590 (−10.3)	1,145 (−4.6)
1918	593 (+0.5)	1,112 (−2.9)
1919	587 (−1.0)	1,019 (−8.4)
1920	565 (−3.7)	975 (−4.3)
1921	673 (+19.1)	1,040 (+6.7)
1922	720 (+7.0)	1,157 (+11.3)
1923	631 (−12.4)	1,123 (−2.9)
1924	909 (+44.1)	1,316 (+17.2)

Table 2-2   *(Continued)*

Term	New cases filed (percentage change)	Total cases on docket[a] (percentage change)
1925	790 (−13.1)	1,309 (−0.5)
1926	718 (−9.11)	1,183 (−9.6)
1927	751 (+4.6)	1,032 (−12.8)
1928	776 (+3.3)	962 (−6.8)
1929	838 (+8.0)	981 (+2.0)
1930	845 (+0.8)	1,034 (+5.4)
1931	877 (+3.8)	1,024 (−1.0)
1932	897 (+2.3)	1,041 (+1.7)
1933	1,005 (+12.0)	1,132 (+8.7)
1934	937 (−6.8)	1,040 (−8.1)
1935	983 (+4.9)	1,092 (+5.0)
1936	950 (−3.4)	1,052 (−3.7)
1937	981 (+3.3)	1,091 (+3.7)
1938	942 (−4.0)	1,020 (−6.5)
1939	981 (+4.1)	1,078 (+5.7)
1940	977 (−0.4)	1,109 (+2.9)
1941	1,178 (+20.6)	1,302 (+17.4)
1942	984 (−16.5)	1,118 (−14.1)
1943	997 (+1.3)	1,118 (0.0)
1944	1,237 (+24.8)	1,393 (+24.6)
1945	1,316 (+6.4)	1,460 (+4.8)
1946	1,510 (+14.7)	1,678 (+14.9)

(Table continues)

Table 2-2 *(Continued)*

Term	New cases filed (percentage change)	Total cases on docket [a] (percentage change)
1947	1,295 (−14.2)	1,453 (−13.4)
1948	1,465 (+13.1)	1,596 (+9.8)
1949	1,270 (−13.3)	1,441 (−9.7)
1950	1,181 (−7.0)	1,321 (−8.3)
1951	1,234 (+4.5)	1,353 (+2.4)
1952	1,283 (+4.0)	1,429 (+5.6)
1953	1,302 (+1.5)	1,453 (+1.7)
1954	1,397 (+7.3)	1,557 (+7.2)
1955	1,644 (+17.7)	1,849 (+18.8)
1956	1,802 (+9.6)	2,021 (+9.3)
1957	1,639 (−9.0)	1,990 (−1.5)
1958	1,819 (+11.0)	2,044 (+2.7)
1959	1,862 (+2.4)	2,143 (+4.8)
1960	1,940 (+4.2)	2,296 (+7.1)
1961	2,185 (+12.6)	2,570 (+11.9)
1962	2,373 (+8.6)	2,801 (+9.0)
1963	2,294 (−3.3)	2,768 (−1.2)
1964	2,288 (−0.3)	2,655 (−4.1)
1965	2,774 (+21.2)	3,256 (+22.6)
1966	2,752 (−0.8)	3,343 (+2.7)
1967	3,106 (+12.9)	3,559 (+6.5)
1968	3,271 (+5.3)	3,884 (+9.1)
1969	3,405 (+4.1)	4,172 (+7.4)

Table 2-2 *(Continued)*

Term	New cases filed (percentage change)	Total cases on docket [a] (percentage change)
1970	3,419 (+0.4)	4,212 (+1.0)
1971	3,643 (+6.6)	4,533 (+7.6)
1972	3,749 (+2.9)	4,640 (+2.4)
1973	3,943 (+5.2)	5,079 (+9.5)
1974	3,661 (−7.2)	4,668 (−8.1)
1975	3,939 (+7.6)	4,761 (+2.0)
1976	3,873 (−1.7)	4,731 (−0.6)
1977	3,839 (−0.9)	4,704 (−0.6)
1978	3,893 (+1.4)	4,731 (+0.6)
1979	4,067 (+4.5)	4,781 (+1.1)
1980	4,252 (+4.5)	5,144 (+7.6)
1981	4,363 (+2.6)	5,311 (+3.2)
1982	4,201 (−3.7)	5,079 (−4.4)
1983	4,222 (+0.5)	5,100 (+0.4)
1984	4,046 (−4.2)	5,006 (−1.8)
1985	4,413 (+9.1)	5,158 (+3.0)
1986	4,251 (−3.7)	5,123 (−0.7)
1987	4,494 (+5.7)	5,268 (+2.8)
1988	4,776 (+6.3)	5,657 (+7.4)
1989	4,919 (+3.0)	5,746 (+1.6)
1990	5,502 (+11.9)	6,316 (+9.9)
1991	5,866 (+6.6)	6,770 (+7.2)
1992	6,303 (+7.5)	7,245 (+7.0)

(Notes follow)

Table 2-2   *(Continued)*

Note: Consistent and reliable data not available prior to 1880.

[a] Includes all cases on all dockets in effect. The number of cases on the docket exceeds the number of cases filed because the Court carries over a certain number of cases each term.

Sources: New cases filed, 1880-1974: Gerhard Casper and Richard A. Posner, *The Workload of the Supreme Court* (Chicago: American Bar Foundation, 1976), 3; 1974-1989: Administrative Office of the United States Courts, *Annual Report of the Director of the Administrative Office of the United States Court* (Washington, D.C.: Government Printing Office, successive editions), Table A-1; 1990-1991: Clerk of the U.S. Supreme Court. Total cases on docket, 1880-1885 and 1900-1935: U.S. Department of Justice, *Annual Report of the Attorney General of the United States* (Washington, D.C.: Government Printing Office, successive editions); 1885-1900: U.S. Senate, "Creation of the Federal Judiciary," Sen. Doc. No. 91, 75th Cong., 1st Sess., July 22, 1937 (Washington, D.C.: Government Printing Office, 1938), 44; 1935-1969: Federal Judicial Center, *Report of the Study Group on the Case Load of the Supreme Court* (Washington, D.C.: Federal Judicial Center, 1972), Table A1; 1970-1989: U.S. Bureau of the Census, *Statistical Abstract of the United States* (Washington, D.C.: Government Printing Office, successive editions); 1990-1992: Clerk of the U.S. Supreme Court.

Table 2-3 Cases on the Dockets of the Supreme Court, 1935-1969 Terms

Term	Original docket			Appellate docket			Miscellaneous docket			
	Filed	Disposed [a]	Remaining [b]	Filed	Disposed [a]	Remaining [b]	Filed	Disposed [a]	Transferred	Remaining [b]
1935	3	4	12	980	986	90				
1936	1	1	12	949	941	98				
1937	10	9	13	971	1,004	65				
1938	—	1	12	942	922	85				
1939	3	4	11	978	942	121				
1940	4	6	9	973	979	115				
1941	3	2	10	1,175	1,166	124				
1942	5	5	10	979	992	111				
1943	1	2	9	996	960	147				
1944	2	—	11	1,235	1,249	133				
1945	1	—	12	1,184	1,161	156				
1946	—	—	12	1,356	1,366	146				
1947	—	—	12	733	772	107				
1948	2	1	13	773	747	142	690	677	9	16
1949	—	—	13	718	757	110	552	544	7	17
1950	—	5	8	659	687	96	522	510	14	15
1951	1	—	9	716	714	113	517	493	15	24
1952	2	—	11	742	742	121	539	536	8	19
1953	—	—	11	684	694	121	618	599	10	28
1954	—	—	11	713	721	122	684	631	9	72
1955	4	4	11	891	865	155	749	761	7	53
1956	3	3	11	974	900	260	825	767	31	80
1957	2	1	12	826	967	137	811	797	18	76
1958	3	3	12	886	886	155	930	874	18	114
1959	—	—	12	857	860	187	1,005	927	35	157

(Table continues)

Table 2-3 *(Continued)*

Term	Original docket Filed	Disposed [a]	Remaining [b]	Appellate docket Filed	Disposed [a]	Remaining [b]	Miscellaneous docket Filed	Disposed [a]	Transferred	Remaining [b]
1960	—	1	11	842	887	159	1,098	1,023	17	215
1961	2	—	13	888	860	202	1,295	1,282	15	213
1962	2	7	8	957	972	210	1,414	1,348	23	256
1963	1	2	7	1,017	1,036	202	1,276	1,363	11	158
1964	4	2	9	1,038	1,027	220	1,246	1,144	7	253
1965	8	9	8	1,188	1,182	254	1,578	1,474	28	329
1966	5	5	8	1,202	1,232	237	1,545	1,653	13	208
1967	2	2	8	1,276	1,338	202	1,828	1,606	27	403
1968	1	—	9	1,323	1,288	271	1,947	1,829	34	487
1969	6	5	10	1,457	1,433	325	1,942	1,941	30	458

Note: Consistent and reliable data not available prior to 1935. Appellate docket prior to 1947 includes appeals and petitions for certiorari. Beginning in 1947, all petitions for certiorari containing motions for leave to proceed *in forma pauperis* were placed on the miscellaneous docket. If the Court granted certiorari to such a case, it was then transferred to the appellate docket. No transfer was made if the motion was granted and the case was then disposed of "on the merits by the same order."

Beginning in 1954, all appeals containing motions to proceed *in forma pauperis* were placed on the miscellaneous docket, as were "all petitions seeking the issuance of special writs," including writs of habeas corpus, mandamus, and prohibition. Petitions for certiorari containing motions for leave to proceed *in forma pauperis* continued to to be placed on the miscellaneous docket.

Beginning in 1970, the Court utilized a different numbering system (see Table 2-4).

[a] Includes those cases that the Court denied, dismissed, withdrew, or decided summarily.
[b] Cases on which the Court took no action during the term.

Sources: Administrative Office of the United States Courts, *Annual Report of the Director of the Administrative Office of the United States Court* (Washington, D.C.: Government Printing Office, successive editions), Table A-1.

Table 2-4 Cases on the Dockets of the Supreme Court, 1970-1992 Terms

| | Original cases | | Appellate cases | | | | | |
| | | | Excluding in forma pauperis | | | In forma pauperis | | |
Term	On docket	Disposed [a]	On docket	Disposed [a]	Not acted on [b]	On docket	Disposed [a]	Not acted on [b]
1970	20	7	1,903	1,399	290	2,289	1,761	487
1971	18	8	2,070	1,514	318	2,445	1,962	422
1972	21	8	2,183	1,617	349	2,436	1,947	454
1973	14	4	2,480	1,719	532	2,585	1,983	572
1974	12	4	2,308	1,732	341	2,348	1,948	372
1975	14	7	2,352	1,656	452	2,395	1,969	398
1976	8	2	2,324	1,782	305	2,398	2,053	315
1977	14	3	2,341	1,755	362	2,349	1,936	389
1978	17	0	2,383	1,813	360	2,331	1,969	335
1979	23	1	2,509	1,851	459	2,249	1,806	411
1980	24	7	2,749	2,089	425	2,371	2,000	344
1981	22	6	2,935	2,214	422	2,354	2,026	315
1982	17	3	2,710	2,005	413	2,352	2,001	339
1983	18	7	2,688	1,973	468	2,394	1,978	402
1984	15	8	2,575	2,012	322	2,416	2,064	329
1985	10	2	2,571	1,941	386	2,577	2,160	388
1986	12	1	2,547	1,947	358	2,564	2,224	314
1987	16	5	2,577	1,985	353	2,675	2,231	412
1988	14	2	2,587	2,048	316	3,056	2,609	418
1989	14	2	2,416	1,925	320	3,316	2,859	425
1990	14	3	2,351	1,883	309	3,951	3,397	515
1991	12	1	2,451	1,966	326	4,307	3,738	539
1992	12	1	2,441	2,004	301	4,792	4,234	531

Note: Prior to 1970, the Court utilized a different numbering system (see Table 2-3).

[a] Includes those cases that the Court denied, dismissed, withdrew, or decided summarily.
[b] Cases on which the Court took no action during the term.

Source: 1970-1989: U.S. Bureau of the Census, *Statistical Abstract of the United States* (Washington, D.C.: Government Printing Office, successive editions); 1990-1992: Clerk of the U.S. Supreme Court.

Table 2-5 Number of Petitions Granted Review, 1926-1969 Terms

Term	Petitions for certiorari, excluding in forma pauperis		Petitions for certiorari, in forma pauperis	
	Number on docket	Number granted review (proportion granted)	Number on docket	Number granted review (proportion granted)
1926	586	117 (.20)		
1927	587	102 (.17)		
1928	649	99 (.15)		
1929	692	133 (.19)		
1930	726	159 (.22)		
1931	738	137 (.19)		
1932	797	148 (.19)		
1933	880	148 (.17)		
1934	835	165 (.20)		
1935	842	142 (.17)	59	8 (.14)
1936	809	149 (.18)	60	4 (.07)
1937	804	140 (.17)	97	15 (.16)

Year							
1938	760	125	(.16)	85	7	(.08)
1939	806	170	(.21)	117	18	(.15)
1940	814	174	(.21)	120	19	(.16)
1941	832	150	(.18)	178	16	(.09)
1942	786	158	(.20)	147	8	(.05)
1943	736	127	(.17)	214	12	(.06)
1944	865	176	(.20)	339	10	(.03)
1945	774	155	(.20)	393	15	(.04)
1946	785	148	(.19)	528	8	(.02)
1947	698	97	(.14)	426	17	(.04)
1948	733	144	(.20)	456	18	(.04)
1949	699	85	(.12)	454	7	(.02)
1950	640	89	(.14)	415	17	(.04)
1951	668	94	(.14)	425	19	(.05)
1952	711	104	(.15)	454	11	(.02)

(Table continues)

68

Table 2-5 *(Continued)*

Term	Petitions for certiorari, excluding in forma pauperis		Petitions for certiorari, in forma pauperis	
	Number on docket	Number granted review (proportion granted)	Number on docket	Number granted review (proportion granted)
1953	669	78 (.12)	542	10 (.02)
1954	695	108 (.16)	568	12 (.02)
1955	842	123 (.15)	645	16 (.03)
1956	927	139 (.15)	689	38 (.06)
1957	840	110 (.13)	747	34 (.05)
1958	820	108 (.13)	837	24 (.03)
1959	838	122 (.15)	933	55 (.06)
1960	789	87 (.11)	1,085	22 (.02)
1961	852	103 (.12)	1,330	38 (.03)
1962	907	115 (.13)	1,412	88 (.06)
1963	972	118 (.12)	1,307	69 (.05)
1964	1,041	116 (.11)	1,170	21 (.02)

1965	1,164	124	(.12)	1,610	43	(.03)
1966	1,198	121	(.10)	1,615	56	(.04)
1967	1,269	166	(.13)	1,798	84	(.05)
1968	1,255	101	(.08)	2,121	62	(.03)
1969	1,425	108	(.08)	2,228	38	(.02)

Note: Prior to the early 1920s, petitions *in forma pauperis* were few in number. Figures for them prior to 1935 are not available. The figures listed for the 1925-1934 terms probably include all petitions.

Sources: 1926-1934: "The Supreme Court at October Term, 1930," 45 (1931): 284, and "The Supreme Court at October Term, 1934," 49 (1935): 78; 1935-1969: Administrative Office of the United States Courts, *Annual Report of the Director of the Administrative Office of the United States Courts* (Washington, D.C.: Government Printing Office, successive editions).

Table 2-6 Number of Petitions Granted Review, 1970-1992 Terms

Term	Petitions for certiorari, excluding in forma pauperis		Petitions for certiorari, in forma pauperis	
	Number on docket	Number granted review (proportion granted)	Number on docket	Number granted review (proportion granted)
1970	1,903	214 (.11)	2,289	41 (.02)
1971	2,070	238 (.12)	2,445	61 (.03)
1972	2,183	217 (.10)	2,436	35 (.01)
1973	2,480	229 (.09)	2,585	30 (.02)
1974	2,308	235 (.10)	2,348	28 (.01)
1975	2,352	244 (.10)	2,395	28 (.01)
1976	2,324	237 (.10)	2,398	30 (.01)
1977	2,341	224 (.10)	2,349	24 (.01)
1978	2,383	210 (.09)	2,331	27 (.01)
1979	2,509	199 (.08)	2,249	32 (.01)
1980	2,749	167 (.06)	2,371	17 (.01)
1981	2,935	203 (.07)	2,354	7 (.003)

Year						
1982	2,710	169	(.06)	2,352	10	(.004)
1983	2,688	140	(.05)	2,394	9	(.004)
1984	2,575	167	(.07)	2,416	18	(.01)
1985	2,571	166	(.07)	2,577	20	(.01)
1986	2,547	152	(.06)	2,564	15	(.02)
1987	2,577	157	(.06)	2,675	23	(.02)
1988	2,587	130	(.05)	3,056	17	(.02)
1989	2,416	103	(.04)	3,316	19	(.01)
1990	2,351	114	(.05)	3,951	27	(.007)
1991	2,451	103	(.04)	4,307	17	(.004)
1992	2,441	83	(.03)	4,792	14	(.003)

Sources: 1970–1989: U.S. Bureau of the Census, *Statistical Abstract of the United States* (Washington, D.C.: Government Printing Office, successive editions); 1990–1992: Clerk of the U.S. Supreme Court.

Table 2-7   Number of Signed Opinions and Number of Cases Disposed of by Signed Opinion and by Per Curiam Opinion, 1926-1992 Terms

Term	Number of signed opinions of the Court	Number of cases disposed of by signed opinion [a]	Number of cases disposed of by per curiam opinion after oral argument [b]
1926	199	223	
1927	175	214	
1928	129	141	
1929	134	156	
1930	166	235	
1931	150	175	
1932	168	187	
1933	158	179	
1934	156	185	
1935	145	187	
1936	149	180	
1937	152	180	
1938	139	174	
1939	137	151	
1940	165	195	20
1941	151	175	14
1942	147	196	14
1943	130	154	6
1944	156	199	7
1945	134	170	4
1946	142	190	8
1947	110	143	14
1948	114	147	18
1949	87	108	14
1950	91	114	15
1951	83	96	25
1952	104	122	10
1953	65	84	23
1954	78	86	16
1955	82	103	18
1956	100	112	23
1957	104	125	27
1958	99	116	23
1959	97	110	20
1960	110	125	22
1961	85	100	21
1962	110	129	19
1963	111	123	20
1964	91	103	17
1965	97	120	8
1966	100	132	15
1967	110	156	17
1968	99	116	14

Table 2-7   *(Continued)*

Term	Number of signed opinions of the Court	Number of cases disposed of by signed opinion[a]	Number of cases disposed of by per curiam opinion after oral argument[b]
1969	88	105	21
1970	109	137	22
1971	129	140	24
1972	140	159	18
1973	141	161	8
1974	123	144	20
1975	138	160	16
1976	126	154	22
1977	129	153	8
1978	130	153	8
1979	130	143	12
1980	123	144	8
1981	141	170	10
1982	151	174	6
1983	151	174	6
1984	139	159	11
1985	146	161	10
1986	145	164	10
1987	139	151	9
1988	133	156	12
1989	129	143	3
1990	112	121	4
1991	107	120	3
1992	107	111	4

[a] Data not available prior to 1926. Includes number of cases decided by a single opinion of the Court, not just the opinion itself.

[b] Data not available prior to 1940.

Sources: Number of signed opinions of the Court, 1926: Albert P. Blaustein and Roy M. Mersky, *The First One Hundred Justices* (Hamden, Conn.: Shoe String Press, 1978), 140; 1927-1974: Gerhard Casper and Richard A. Posner, *The Workload of the Supreme Court* (Chicago: American Bar Foundation, 1976), 76; 1975-1989: U.S. Bureau of the Census, *Statistical Abstract of the United States* (Washington, D.C.: Government Printing Office, successive editions); 1990-1991: Clerk of the U.S. Supreme Court. Number of cases disposed of by signed opinion, 1926-1934: "The Business of the Supreme Court," *Harvard Law Review* 49 (1935): 70; 1935-1971: Federal Judicial Center, *Report of the Study Group on the Case Load of the Supreme Court* (Washington, D.C.: Federal Judicial Center, 1972), A7; 1972-1989: U.S. Bureau of the Census, *Statistical Abstract of the United States* (Washington, D.C.: Government Printing Office, successive editions); 1990-1991: Clerk of the U.S. Supreme Court. Cases disposed of by per curiam opinion after argument, 1940-1969: Administrative Office of the United States Courts, *Annual Report of the Director of the Administrative Office of the United States Court* (Washington, D.C.: Government Printing Office, successive editions); 1970-1989: U.S. Bureau of the Census, *Statistical Abstract of the United States* (Washington, D.C.: Government Printing Office, successive editions); 1990-1992: Clerk of the U.S. Supreme Court.

Table 2-8 Supreme Court Cases by Major Policy Area, 1933-1987

Policy area	1933-1937	1938-1942	1943-1947	1948-1952	1953-1957	1958-1962	1963-1967	1968-1972	1973-1977	1978-1982	1983-1987	Total (n)
Due process	41 (5.2)	54 (7.1)	66 (10.0)	73 (14.4)	84 (17.1)	124 (20.9)	165 (25.0)	222 (31.0)	233 (27.8)	213 (26.8)	222 (29.6)	1,497
Substantive rights	9 (1.2)	32 (4.2)	31 (4.7)	43 (8.5)	38 (7.7)	62 (10.5)	63 (9.5)	116 (16.2)	120 (14.3)	80 (10.1)	80 (10.7)	674
Equality	11 (1.4)	8 (1.0)	18 (2.7)	25 (4.9)	25 (5.1)	31 (5.2)	82 (12.4)	86 (12.0)	105 (12.5)	102 (12.8)	124 (16.6)	617
Criminal law	12 (1.5)	20 (2.6)	17 (2.6)	20 (3.9)	24 (4.9)	19 (3.2)	16 (2.4)	22 (3.1)	17 (2.0)	14 (1.8)	13 (1.7)	194
Government as provider	3 (0.4)	4 (0.5)	0 (0.0)	0 (0.0)	2 (0.4)	4 (0.7)	2 (0.3)	6 (0.8)	12 (1.4)	8 (1.0)	13 (1.7)	54
Foreign affairs	12 (1.5)	15 (2.0)	41 (6.2)	21 (4.1)	12 (2.4)	2 (0.3)	5 (0.8)	1 (0.1)	5 (0.6)	4 (0.5)	2 (0.3)	120
Separation of powers	6 (0.4)	2 (0.3)	2 (0.3)	4 (0.8)	5 (1.0)	3 (0.5)	2 (0.3)	8 (1.1)	11 (1.3)	14 (1.8)	9 (1.2)	66
Federalism	109 (14.0)	108 (14.1)	90 (13.6)	59 (11.6)	49 (10.0)	45 (7.6)	47 (7.1)	39 (5.4)	78 (9.3)	89 (11.2)	75 (10.0)	788
U.S. regulation	220 (27.8)	258 (33.8)	232 (35.7)	166 (33.9)	162 (33.0)	202 (34.1)	202 (30.6)	139 (19.4)	165 (19.7)	168 (21.2)	133 (17.8)	2,047

												Total
Internal revenue	139 (17.8)	123 (16.1)	73 (11.1)	33 (6.5)	41 (8.4)	43 (7.3)	29 (4.4)	26 (3.6)	27 (3.2)	20 (2.5)	24 (3.2)	578
State regulation	79 (10.1)	46 (6.0)	19 (2.9)	16 (3.2)	10 (2.0)	17 (2.9)	8 (1.2)	16 (2.2)	24 (2.9)	29 (3.6)	8 (1.1)	272
State as litigant	14 (1.8)	4 (0.5)	7 (1.1)	2 (0.4)	6 (1.2)	3 (0.5)	8 (1.2)	11 (1.5)	11 (1.3)	19 (2.4)	5 (0.7)	90
United States as litigant	11 (1.4)	29 (3.8)	24 (3.6)	15 (3.0)	6 (1.2)	14 (2.4)	6 (0.9)	5 (0.7)	6 (0.7)	11 (1.4)	19 (2.5)	146
Ordinary economic	126 (16.1)	61 (8.0)	39 (5.9)	30 (5.9)	26 (5.3)	24 (4.0)	24. (3.6)	20 (2.8)	22 (2.6)	22 (2.8)	22 (2.9)	416
Total	792	764	659	507	490	593	659	717	836	793	749	7,559

Note: Data include all cases that received an opinion of one page or more in the *United States Reports*. Figures listed are the number of cases in each issue area. Figures in parentheses are the percent of cases falling into that area for the time interval.

The policy areas are defined as follows: Due process: criminal procedure cases and due process considerations of administrative proceedings; Substantive rights: primarily First Amendment and privacy cases, including abortion; Equality: civil rights cases involving discrimination on the basis of race, gender, age, disability, or similar factors; Criminal law: cases that turn on a substantive interpretation of a criminal statute; Government as provider: post-New Deal cases dealing with the expansion of government power; Foreign affairs: governmental power in international affairs; Separation of powers: cases involving the Court's attempts to regulate the boundaries between the judiciary and other branches of government or between the legislative and executive branches; Federalism: cases involving the boundaries between federal and subnational authority; U.S. regulation: economic regulation of private industries by the federal government, including labor relations, securities regulation, commerce, environmental concerns, patents and copyrights, bank regulation, food and drug regulation, and antitrust questions; Internal revenue: interpretation of the tax codes and Internal Revenue Service policies; State regulation: economic regulation of private industries by states, including labor relations, energy regulation, and state taxation; State as litigant: boundary disputes between two states, navigable water cases, and state liability for certain actions; United States as litigant: disputes concerning government contracts and United States liability for, or immunity from, certain actions; Ordinary economic: miscellaneous cases with a common economic denominator, such as the allocation of a good or service between competing litigants.

Source: Richard L. Pacelle, *The Transformation of the Supreme Court's Agenda* (Boulder, Colo.: Westview, 1991), 56-57.

Table 2-9 Formally Decided Cases by Issue Area, 1953-1991

Term	Crim	Civ	1st	DP	Priv	Atty	Un'n	Econ	JudP	Fed	IR	FTax	Misc	Total
1953	15 (.18)	8 (.10)	4 (.05)	1 (.01)	0 (.00)	0 (.00)	6 (.07)	33 (.39)	8 (.10)	6 (.07)	0 (.00)	3 (.04)	0 (.00)	84
1954	18 (.19)	10 (.11)	5 (.05)	3 (.03)	0 (.00)	1 (.01)	4 (.04)	23 (.25)	13 (.14)	4 (.04)	0 (.00)	11 (.12)	1 (.01)	93
1955	12 (.12)	11 (.11)	5 (.05)	2 (.02)	0 (.00)	0 (.00)	10 (.10)	29 (.30)	13 (.13)	3 (.03)	3 (.03)	7 (.07)	3 (.03)	98
1956	20 (.17)	12 (.10)	9 (.07)	4 (.03)	0 (.00)	3 (.02)	11 (.09)	32 (.26)	17 (.14)	5 (.04)	0 (.00)	8 (.07)	0 (.00)	121
1957	32 (.25)	14 (.11)	9 (.07)	6 (.05)	1 (.01)	1 (.01)	4 (.03)	30 (.24)	16 (.13)	5 (.04)	0 (.00)	9 (.07)	0 (.00)	127
1958	26 (.22)	6 (.05)	11 (.09)	0 (.00)	0 (.00)	0 (.00)	5 (.04)	44 (.37)	13 (.11)	5 (.04)	2 (.02)	6 (.05)	0 (.00)	118
1959	16 (.14)	10 (.09)	7 (.06)	3 (.03)	0 (.00)	0 (.00)	14 (.12)	28 (.24)	16 (.14)	7 (.06)	0 (.00)	14 (.12)	0 (.00)	115
1960	30 (.23)	14 (.11)	22 (.17)	1 (.01)	0 (.00)	0 (.00)	11 (.09)	27 (.21)	11 (.09)	2 (.02)	0 (.00)	10 (.08)	0 (.00)	128
1961	17 (.17)	9 (.09)	8 (.08)	5 (.05)	0 (.00)	0 (.00)	9 (.09)	29 (.29)	11 (.11)	5 (.05)	0 (.00)	7 (.07)	1 (.01)	101

Year																											Total
1962	21	(.17)	17	(.14)	8	(.06)	3	(.02)	0	(.00)	1	(.01)	10	(.08)	35	(.28)	12	(.10)	10	(.08)	0	(.00)	8	(.06)	0	(.00)	125
1963	22	(.17)	27	(.21)	9	(.07)	0	(.00)	0	(.00)	0	(.00)	9	(.07)	30	(.23)	16	(.12)	9	(.07)	2	(.02)	6	(.05)	0	(.00)	130
1964	16	(.15)	14	(.13)	11	(.10)	2	(.02)	1	(.01)	0	(.00)	11	(.10)	18	(.17)	19	(.18)	3	(.03)	2	(.02)	9	(.08)	0	(.00)	106
1965	16	(.16)	14	(.14)	13	(.13)	3	(.03)	0	(.00)	0	(.00)	3	(.03)	25	(.25)	16	(.16)	4	(.04)	0	(.00)	8	(.08)	0	(.00)	102
1966	28	(.25)	19	(.17)	11	(.10)	0	(.00)	0	(.00)	1	(.01)	7	(.06)	23	(.21)	18	(.16)	3	(.03)	0	(.00)	2	(.02)	0	(.00)	112
1967	36	(.30)	16	(.13)	13	(.11)	1	(.01)	0	(.00)	3	(.02)	9	(.07)	25	(.20)	10	(.08)	6	(.05)	0	(.00)	3	(.02)	0	(.00)	122
1968	27	(.24)	23	(.21)	10	(.09)	3	(.03)	0	(.00)	0	(.00)	4	(.04)	17	(.15)	19	(.17)	4	(.04)	0	(.00)	4	(.04)	0	(.00)	111
1969	27	(.25)	26	(.24)	10	(.09)	1	(.01)	0	(.00)	1	(.01)	6	(.06)	10	(.09)	14	(.13)	4	(.04)	1	(.01)	7	(.07)	0	(.00)	107
1970	24	(.19)	28	(.22)	22	(.18)	4	(.03)	1	(.01)	1	(.01)	9	(.07)	16	(.13)	15	(.12)	1	(.01)	0	(.00)	4	(.03)	0	(.00)	125
1971	34	(.23)	28	(.19)	16	(.11)	11	(.07)	1	(.01)	0	(.00)	7	(.05)	32	(.22)	11	(.07)	1	(.01)	2	(.01)	4	(.03)	0	(.00)	147

(Table continues)

Table 2-9 (Continued)

Term	Crim	Civ	1st	DP	Priv	Atty	Un'n	Econ	JudP	Fed	IR	FTax	Misc	Total
1972	35 (.23)	33 (.22)	18 (.12)	5 (.03)	3 (.02)	1 (.01)	6 (.04)	29 (.19)	15 (.10)	3 (.02)	2 (.01)	3 (.02)	0 (.00)	153
1973	30 (.20)	36 (.24)	14 (.09)	6 (.04)	1 (.01)	2 (.01)	8 (.05)	21 (.14)	19 (.13)	4 (.03)	1 (.01)	6 (.04)	0 (.00)	148
1974	24 (.17)	29 (.21)	8 (.06)	7 (.05)	3 (.02)	1 (.01)	6 (.04)	28 (.20)	21 (.15)	8 (.06)	0 (.00)	4 (.03)	0 (.00)	139
1975	33 (.22)	28 (.19)	13 (.09)	13 (.09)	2 (.01)	0 (.00)	5 (.03)	28 (.19)	23 (.15)	3 (.02)	2 (.01)	1 (.01)	0 (.00)	151
1976	30 (.21)	35 (.24)	12 (.08)	7 (.05)	1 (.01)	1 (.01)	7 (.05)	19 (.13)	15 (.10)	7 (.05)	1 (.01)	4 (.03)	0 (.00)	143
1977	29 (.21)	26 (.19)	8 (.06)	5 (.04)	4 (.03)	4 (.03)	5 (.04)	30 (.22)	14 (.10)	5 (.04)	0 (.00)	7 (.05)	1 (.01)	135
1978	29 (.22)	34 (.25)	8 (.06)	8 (.06)	4 (.03)	0 (.00)	5 (.04)	27 (.20)	12 (.09)	3 (.02)	0 (.00)	4 (.03)	0 (.00)	134
1979	32 (.23)	22 (.16)	10 (.07)	11 (.08)	6 (.04)	4 (.03)	6 (.04)	31 (.22)	13 (.09)	2 (.01)	4 (.03)	0 (.00)	0 (.00)	141
1980	25 (.20)	27 (.21)	9 (.07)	6 (.05)	1 (.01)	0 (.00)	8 (.06)	25 (.20)	17 (.13)	5 (.04)	0 (.00)	4 (.03)	1 (.01)	128

Year														Total
1981	19 (.13)	34 (.23)	12 (.08)	9 (.06)	4 (.03)	3 (.02)	9 (.06)	25 (.17)	23 (.16)	5 (.03)	0 (.00)	3 (.02)	2 (.01)	148
1982	30 (.19)	27 (.17)	11 (.07)	7 (.05)	4 (.03)	2 (.01)	7 (.05)	33 (.21)	16 (.10)	10 (.06)	2 (.01)	4 (.03)	2 (.01)	155
1983	40 (.26)	29 (.19)	12 (.08)	10 (.06)	2 (.01)	2 (.01)	6 (.04)	27 (.17)	13 (.08)	8 (.05)	2 (.01)	4 (.03)	0 (.00)	155
1984	33 (.23)	25 (.18)	11 (.08)	11 (.08)	1 (.01)	6 (.04)	5 (.04)	30 (.21)	8 (.06)	8 (.06)	0 (.00)	4 (.03)	0 (.00)	142
1985	43 (.28)	29 (.19)	14 (.09)	7 (.05)	1 (.01)	4 (.03)	3 (.02)	16 (.10)	20 (.13)	10 (.07)	0 (.00)	5 (.03)	1 (.01)	153
1986	41 (.27)	24 (.16)	12 (.08)	12 (.08)	1 (.01)	3 (.02)	5 (.03)	23 (.15)	15 (.10)	11 (.07)	1 (.01)	4 (.03)	1 (.01)	153
1987	31 (.22)	21 (.15)	12 (.08)	9 (.06)	1 (.01)	3 (.02)	7 (.05)	26 (.18)	20 (.14)	9 (.06)	0 (.00)	3 (.02)	2 (.01)	144
1988	30 (.21)	26 (.19)	15 (.11)	5 (.04)	4 (.03)	5 (.04)	5 (.04)	17 (.12)	18 (.13)	0 (.00)	9 (.06)	4 (.03)	2 (.01)	140
1989	35 (.27)	9 (.07)	14 (.11)	5 (.04)	3 (.02)	4 (.03)	4 (.03)	22 (.17)	18 (.14)	9 (.07)	1 (.01)	7 (.05)	0 (.00)	131
1990	29 (.25)	16 (.14)	5 (.04)	3 (.03)	1 (.01)	2 (.02)	8 (.07)	24 (.21)	16 (.14)	4 (.04)	2 (.02)	2 (.02)	2 (.02)	114

(Table continues)

Table 2-9 (*Continued*)

Term	Crim	Civ	1st	DP	Priv	Atty	Un'n	Econ	JudP	Fed	IR	FTax	Misc	Total
1991	21 (.19)	18 (.17)	8 (.07)	5 (.05)	2 (.02)	2 (.02)	1 (.01)	27 (.25)	16 (.15)	5 (.05)	0 (.00)	4 (.04)	0 (.00)	109
Total	1,056	834	429	204	54	61	265	1,014	600	215	30	207	19	4,988

Note: Formally decided cases include those with signed opinions and orally argued per curiams. Figures listed are the number of cases in each issue area. Figures in parentheses are the proportion of cases falling into that area each term.

The issue areas are defined as follows: Criminal procedure (Crim): the rights of persons accused of crime except for the due process rights of prisoners; Civil rights (Civ): non-First Amendment freedom cases that pertain to classifications based on race (including Native Americans), age, indigence, voting, residence, military or handicapped status, sex, or alienage; First Amendment (1st): guarantees contained therein; Due process (DP): noncriminal procedural guarantees, plus court jurisdiction over nonresident litigants and the takings clause of the Fifth Amendment; Privacy (Priv): abortion, contraception, the Freedom of Information Act and related federal statutes; Attorneys (Atty): attorneys' fees, commercial speech, admission to and removal from the bar, and disciplinary matters; Unions (Un'n): labor union activity; Economics (Econ): commercial business activity, plus litigation involving injured persons or things, employee actions vis-à-vis employers, zoning regulations, and governmental regulation of corruption other than that involving campaign spending; Judicial power (JudP): the exercise of the judiciary's own power and authority; Federalism (Fed): conflicts between the federal and state governments, excluding those between state and federal courts, and those involving the priority of federal fiscal claims; Interstate relations (IR): conflicts between states, boundary disputes, and nonproperty disputes commonly arising under the full faith and credit clause of the Constitution; Federal taxation (FTax): the Internal Revenue Code and related statutes; Miscellaneous (Misc): legislative veto, separation of powers, and matters not included in any other issue area.

Source: U.S. Supreme Court Judicial Detabase, with orally argued citation as unit of analysis.

Table 2-10   Landmark Decisions, Topically Ordered

Abortion

Roe v. Wade, 410 U.S. 113 (1973)
Doe v. Bolton, 410 U.S. 179 (1973)
Planned Parenthood of Central Missouri v. Danforth, 428 U.S. 52 (1976)
Beal v. Doe, 432 U.S. 438 (1977)
Harris v. McRae, 448 U.S. 297 (1980)
Akron v. Akron Center for Reproductive Health, 462 U.S. 416 (1983)
Thornburgh v. American College of Obstetricians and Gynecologists, 476 U.S.
 747 (1986)
Webster v. Reproductive Health Services, 106 L. Ed. 2d 410 (1989)
Hodgson v. Minnesota, 111 L. Ed. 2d 344 (1990)
Planned Parenthood of Southeastern Pennsylvania v. Casey, 120 L. Ed. 2d 674
 (1992)

Affirmative Action

Regents of the University of California v. Bakke, 438 U.S. 265 (1978)
United Steelworkers of America v. Weber, 444 U.S. 193 (1979)
Fullilove v. Klutznick, 448 U.S. 448 (1980)
Firefighters Local Union v. Stotts, 467 U.S. 561 (1984)
Wygant v. Jackson Board of Education, 476 U.S. 267 (1986)
Firefighters v. Cleveland, 478 U.S. 501 (1986)
Johnson v. Transportation Agency, 480 U.S. 616 (1987)
Richmond v. Croson Company, 102 L. Ed. 2d 854 (1989)
Metro Broadcasting Co. v. FCC, 111 L. Ed. 2d 445 (1990)

Aliens

Truax v. Raich, 239 U.S. 33 (1915)
Graham v. Richardson, 403 U.S. 365 (1971)
Ambach v. Norwick, 441 U.S. 68 (1979)
Plyler v. Doe, 457 U.S. 202 (1982)

Assembly and Association, Freedom of

DeJonge v. Oregon, 299 U.S. 353 (1937)
Hague v. C.I.O., 307 U.S. 496 (1939)
NAACP v. Alabama, 357 U.S. 449 (1958)
Shelton v. Tucker, 364 U.S. 479 (1960)
Edwards v. South Carolina, 372 U.S. 229 (1963)
Cox v. Louisiana, 379 U.S. 536 (1965)
Communist Party of Indiana v. Whitcomb, 414 U.S. 441 (1974)
Rutan v. Illinois Republican Party, 111 L. Ed. 2d 52 (1990)

Bail, ·Right to

United States v. Salerno, 481 U.S. 739 (1987)

(Table continues)

Table 2-10   *(Continued)*

Bill of Rights, Applicability to the States

Barron v. Baltimore, 7 Pet. 243 (1833)
Twining v. New Jersey, 211, U.S. 78 (1908)
Gitlow v. New York, 268 U.S. 652 (1925)
Palko v. Connecticut, 302 U.S. 319 (1937)
United States v. Carolene Products Co., 304 U.S. 144 (1938)

Business, Federal Regulation of

United States v. E. C. Knight Co., 156 U.S. 1 (1895)
Northern Securities Co. v. United States, 193 U.S. 197 (1904)
Swift & Co. v. United States, 196 U.S. 375 (1905)
Standard Oil Co. v. United States, 221 U.S. 1 (1911)
Schechter Poultry Co. v. United States, 295 U.S. 495 (1935)
National Labor Relations Board v. Jones and Laughlin Steel Corp., 301 U.S. 1
  (1937)

Citizenship

Scott v. Sandford, 19 How. 393 (1857)
United States v. Wong Kim Ark, 169 U.S. 649 (1898)
Perez v. Brownell, 356 U.S. 44 (1958)
Schneider v. Rusk, 377 U.S. 163 (1964)
Afroyim v. Rusk, 387 U.S. 253 (1967)

Comity and the Abstention Doctrine

Railroad Commission of Texas v. Pullman Co., 312 U.S. 496 (1941)
Younger v. Harris, 401 U.S. 37 (1971)
Michigan v. Long, 463 U.S. 1032 (1983)

Congressional Membership and Prerogatives

McGrain v. Daugherty, 273 U.S. 135 (1927)
Bond v. Floyd, 385 U.S. 116 (1966)
Powell v. McCormack, 395 U.S. 486 (1969)
Gravel v. United States, 408 U.S. 606 (1972)
Doe v. McMillan, 412 U.S. 306 (1973)
Hutchinson v. Proxmire, 443 U.S. 111 (1979)

Confrontation and Cross-Examination of Witnesses

Pointer v. Texas, 380 U.S. 400 (1965)
Davis v. Alaska, 415 U.S. 308 (1974)
Ohio v. Roberts, 448 U.S. 56 (1980)
Maryland v. Craig, 111 L. Ed. 2d 666 (1990)

Table 2-10   *(Continued)*

Contract Clause

Fletcher v. Peck, 6 Cranch 87 (1810)
Dartmouth College v. Woodward, 4 Wheat. 518 (1819)
Charles River Bridge v. Warren Bridge, 11 Pet. 420 (1837)
Home Building and Loan Association v. Blaisdell, 290 U.S. 398 (1934)

Counsel, Right to

Powell v. Alabama (First Scottsboro Case), 287 U.S. 45 (1932)
Johnson v. Zerbst, 304 U.S. 458 (1938)
Gideon v. Wainwright, 372 U.S. 335 (1963)
Escobedo v. Illinois, 378 U.S. 478 (1964)
Argersinger v. Hamlin, 407 U.S. 25 (1972)
Nix v. Whiteside, 475 U.S. 157 (1986)

Cruel and Unusual Punishment

Louisiana ex rel. Francis v. Resweber, 329 U.S. 459 (1947)
Trop v. Dulles, 356 U.S. 86 (1958)
Furman v. Georgia, 408 U.S. 238 (1972)
Gregg v. Georgia, 428 U.S. 153 (1976)
Ingraham v. Wright, 430 U.S. 651 (1977)
Coker v. Georgia, 433 U.S. 584 (1977)
Ford v. Wainwright, 477 U.S. 399 (1986)
McCleskey v. Kemp, 481 U.S. 279 (1987)
Penry v. Lynaugh, 106 L. Ed. 2d 256 (1989)
Stanford v. Kentucky, 106 L. Ed. 2d 306 (1989)
Payne v. Tennessee, 115 L. Ed. 2d 720 (1991)
Harmelin v. Michigan, 115 L. Ed. 2d 836 (1991)

Die, Right to

Cruzan v. Director, Missouri Department of Health, 111 L. Ed. 2d 224 (1990)

Diversity Of Citizenship

Swift v. Tyson, 16 Pet. 1 (1842)
Erie Railroad Co. v. Tompkins, 304 U.S. 64 (1938)

Double Jeopardy

Palko v. Connecticut, 302 U.S. 319 (1937)
Louisiana ex rel. Francis v. Resweber, 329 U.S. 459 (1947)
Bartkus v. Illinois, 359 U.S. 121 (1959)
Benton v. Maryland, 395 U.S. 784 (1969)
Waller v. Florida, 397 U.S. 387 (1970)

(Table continues)

Table 2-10   *(Continued)*

Ashe v. Swenson, 397 U.S. 436 (1970)
Crist v. Bretz, 437 U.S. 28 (1978)

Education

Missouri ex rel. Gaines v. Canada, 305 U.S. 337 (1938)
McLaurin v. Oklahoma State Regents, 339 U.S. 637 (1950)
Sweatt v. Painter, 339 U.S. 629 (1950)
Brown v. Board of Education, 347 U.S. 483, 349 U.S. 294 (1954, 1955)
Bolling v. Sharpe, 347 U.S. 497 (1954)
Green v. County School Board, 391 U.S. 430 (1968)
Swann v. Charlotte-Mecklenburg County Board of Education, 402 U.S. 1 (1971)
San Antonio Independent School District v. Rodriguez, 411 U.S. 1 (1973)
Milliken v. Bradley, 418 U.S. 717 (1974)
Missouri v. Jenkins, 109 L. Ed. 2d 31 (1990)

Employment Discrimination

Griggs v. Duke Power Co., 401 U.S. 424 (1971)
St. Francis College v. Al-Khazraji, 481 U.S. 604 (1987)

Establishment of Religion

Everson v. Board of Education, 330 U.S. 1 (1947)
McCollum v. Board of Education, 333 U.S. 203 (1948)
Zorach v. Clauson, 343 U.S. 306 (1952)
Engel v. Vitale, 370 U.S. 421 (1962)
School District of Abington Township v. Schempp, 374 U.S. 203 (1963)
Walz v. Tax Commission of the City of New York, 397 U.S. 664 (1970)
Lemon v. Kurtzman, 403 U.S. 602 (1971)
Tilton v. Richardson, 403 U.S. 672 (1971)
Mueller v. Allen, 463 U.S. 388 (1983)
Lynch v. Donnelly, 465 U.S. 668 (1984)
Wallace v. Jaffree, 472 U.S. 38 (1985)
Grand Rapids School District v. Ball, 473 U.S. 373 (1985)
Edwards v. Aguillard, 482 U.S. 578 (1987)
Lee v. Weisman (1992)

Extradition

Kentucky v. Dennison, 24 How. 66 (1861)
Puerto Rico v. Branstad, 483 U.S. 219 (1987)

Fair Procedure

Pennoyer v. Neff, 95 U.S. 714 (1878)
International Shoe Co. v. Washington, 326 U.S. 310 (1945)
Mullane v. Central Hanover Bank & Trust Co., 339 U.S. 306 (1950)
Sheppard v. Maxwell, 384 U.S. 333 (1966)
Goldberg v. Kelly, 397 U.S. 254 (1970)

Table 2-10   *(Continued)*

Jackson v. Metropolitan Edison Co., 419 U.S. 345 (1975)
Goss v. Lopez, 419 U.S. 565 (1975)
Mathews v. Eldridge, 424 U.S. 319 (1976)
Bishop v. Wood, 426 U.S. 341 (1976)
Shaffer v. Heitner, 433 U.S. 186 (1977)
Board of Curators of the University of Missouri v. Horowitz, 435 U.S. 78 (1978)
Memphis Light, Gas and Water Division v. Craft, 436 U.S. 1 (1978)
World-Wide Volkswagen Corp. v. Woodson, 444 U.S. 286 (1980)
Rush v. Savchuk, 444 U.S. 320 (1980)
Pacific Mutual Life Insurance Company v. Haslip, 113 L. Ed. 2d 1 (1991)

Family Rights

Meyer v. Nebraska, 262 U.S. 390 (1923)
Loving v. Virginia, 388 U.S. 1 (1967)
Mathews v. Lucas, 427 U.S. 495 (1976)
Lassiter v. Department of Social Services, 452 U.S. 18 (1981)
Santosky v. Kramer, 455 U.S. 745 (1982)
Palmore v. Sidoti, 466 U.S. 429 (1984)

Federal Supremacy

United States v. Peters, 5 Cranch 115 (1809)
Ableman v. Booth, 21 How. 506 (1859)
Pennsylvania v. Nelson, 350 U.S. 497 (1956)

Foreign Affairs

Foster v. Neilson, 2 Pet. 253 (1829)
United States v. Curtiss-Wright Export Corp., 299 U.S. 304 (1936)

Fourteenth Amendment as a Limitation on State Economic Regulation

The Slaughterhouse Cases, 16 Wall. 36 (1873)
Munn v. Illinois, 94 U.S. 113 (1877)
Euclid v. Ambler Realty Co., 272 U.S. 365 (1926)
Tyson & Brother v. Banton, 273 U.S. 418 (1927)
Nebbia v. New York, 291 U.S. 502 (1934)
West Coast Hotel Co. v. Parrish, 300 U.S. 379 (1937)

Free Exercise of Religion

Pierce v. Society of Sisters, 268 U.S. 510 (1925)
Cantwell v. Connecticut, 310 U.S. 296 (1940)
Minersville School District v. Gobitis, 310 U.S. 586 (1940)
West Virginia State Board of Education v. Barnette, 319 U.S. 628 (1943)
Wisconsin v. Yoder, 406 U.S. 205 (1972)
Wooley v. Maynard, 430 U.S. 705 (1977)

(Table continues)

Table 2-10   *(Continued)*

Thomas v. Review Board of the Indiana Employment Security Division, 450 U.S. 707 (1981)
Employment Division, Oregon Department of Human Resources v. Smith, 108 L. Ed. 2d 876 (1990)

Full Faith and Credit

Atherton v. Atherton, 181 U.S. 155 (1901)
Haddock v. Haddock, 201 U.S. 562 (1906)
Williams v. North Carolina, 317 U.S. 287 (1942)
Williams v. North Carolina, 325 U.S. 226 (1945)
Estin v. Estin, 334 U.S. 541 (1948)

Handicapped Persons

Buck v. Bell, 274 U.S. 200 (1927)
O'Connor v. Donaldson, 422 U.S. 563 (1975)
Youngberg v. Romeo, 457 U.S. 307 (1982)
Cleburne v. Cleburne Living Center, 473 U.S. 432 (1985)

Implied Powers

McCulloch v. Maryland, 4 Wheat. 316 (1819)

Indians, Status and Regulation of

Cherokee Nation v. Georgia, 5 Pet. 1 (1831)
Worcester v. Georgia, 6 Pet. 515 (1832)
United States v. Winans, 198 U.S. 371 (1905)
Williams v. Lee, 358 U.S. 217 (1959)
White Mountain Apache Tribe v. Bracker, 448 U.S. 136 (1980)

Interstate Commerce, State Regulation of

Cooley v. Board of Wardens, 12 How. 299 (1851)
Shreveport Rate Cases, 234 U.S. 342 (1914)
South Carolina Highway Dept. v. Barnwell Bros., 303 U.S. 177 (1938)
Southern Pacific Co. v. Arizona, 325 U.S. 761 (1945)
Huron Portland Cement Co. v. Detroit, 362 U.S. 440 (1960)
Kassel v. Consolidated Freightways Corp., 450 U.S. 662 (1981)

Interstate Commerce Power, Scope of

Gibbons v. Ogden, 9 Wheat. 1 (1824)
Wickard v. Filburn, 317 U.S. 111 (1942)
Katzenbach v. McClung, 379 U.S. 294 (1964)

Judicial Organization

Ex parte Bakelite Corporation, 279 U.S. 438 (1929)

Table 2-10   *(Continued)*

Glidden Co. v. Zdanok, 370 U.S. 530 (1962)
Northern Pipeline Construction Co. v. Marathon Pipe Line Co., 458 U.S. 50
  (1982)

Judicial Review

Marbury v. Madison, 1 Cranch 137 (1803)
Martin v. Hunter's Lessee, 1 Wheat. 304 (1816)
United States v. Nixon, 418 U.S. 683 (1974)

Jurisdiction of the Federal Courts

Chisholm v. Georgia, 2 Dall. 419 (1793)
Martin v. Hunter's Lessee, 1 Wheat. 304 (1816)
Cohens v. Virginia, 6 Wheat. 264 (1821)
Ex parte McCardle, 7 Wall. 506 (1869)
Nashville, Chattanooga, and St. Louis R. Co. v. Wallace, 288 U.S. 249 (1933)
Pennhurst State School & Hospital v. Halderman, 465 U.S. 89 (1984)

Jury Trial

Strauder v. West Virginia, 100 U.S. 303 (1880)
Hurtado v. California, 110 U.S. 516 (1884)
Maxwell v. Dow, 176 U.S. 581 (1900)
Patton v. United States, 281 U.S. 276 (1930)
Norris v. Alabama (Second Scottsboro Case), 294 U.S. 537 (1935)
Duncan v. Louisiana, 391 U.S. 145 (1968)
United States v. Jackson, 390 U.S. 570 (1968)
Witherspoon v. Illinois, 391 U.S. 510 (1968)
Taylor v. Louisiana, 419 U.S. 522 (1975)
Ballew v. Georgia, 435 U.S. 223 (1978)
Burch v. Louisiana, 441 U.S. 130 (1979)
Batson v. Kentucky, 476 U.S. 79 (1986)
Lockhart v. McCree, 476 U.S. 162 (1986)

Juveniles

Kent v. United States, 383 U.S. 541 (1966)
In re Gault, 387 U.S. 1 (1967).
Tinker v. Des Moines Independent Community School District, 393 U.S. 503
  (1969)
In re Winship, 397 U.S. 358 (1970)
McKeiver v. Pennsylvania, 403 U.S. 528 (1971)
Goss v. Lopez, 419 U.S. 565 (1975)
Parham v. J.R., 442 U.S. 584 (1979)
Santosky v. Kramer, 455 U.S. 745 (1982)
Schall v. Martin, 467 U.S. 253 (1984)

(Table continues)

Table 2-10 *(Continued)*

DeShaney v. Winnebago County Department of Social Services, 103 L. Ed. 2d 249 (1989)
Maryland v. Craig, 111 L. Ed. 2d 666 (1990)

Labor, Federal Regulation of

Adair v. United States, 208 U.S. 161 (1908)
Loewe v. Lawlor, 208 U.S. 274 (1908)
Wilson v. New, 243 U.S. 332 (1917)
Hammer v. Dagenhart, 247 U.S. 251 (1918)
Adkins v. Children's Hospital, 261 U.S. 525 (1923)
United States v. Darby, 312 U.S. 100 (1941)

Labor, State Regulation of

Holden v. Hardy, 169 U.S. 366 (1898)
Lochner v. New York, 198 U.S. 45 (1905)
Muller v. Oregon, 208 U.S. 412 (1908)
West Coast Hotel Co. v. Parrish, 300 U.S. 379 (1937)

Legislative Apportionment and Districting

Colegrove v. Green, 328 U.S. 549 (1946)
Baker v. Carr, 369 U.S. 186 (1962)
Wesberry v. Sanders, 376 U.S. 1 (1964)
Reynolds v. Sims, 377 U.S. 533 (1964)
Kirkpatrick v. Preisler, 394 U.S. 526 (1969)
Hadley v. Junior College District, 397 U.S. 50 (1970)
Mahan v. Howell, 410 U.S. 315 (1973)
Salyer Land Co. v. Tulare Water Storage District, 410 U.S. 719 (1973)

Legislative Investigations

Kilbourn v. Thompson, 103 U.S. 168 (1881)
Watkins v. United States, 354 U.S. 178 (1957)
Barenblatt v. United States, 360 U.S. 109 (1959)

Miranda Warnings

Miranda v. Arizona, 377 U.S. 201 (1966)
Harris v. New York, 401 U.S. 222 (1971)
Doyle v. Ohio, 427 U.S. 610 (1976)
Rhode Island v. Innis, 446 U.S. 291 (1980)
New York v. Quarles, 467 U.S. 649 (1984)

Obscenity

Roth v. United States, 354 U.S. 476 (1957)
Jacobellis v. Ohio, 378 U.S. 184 (1964)
Memoirs v. Massachusetts, 383 U.S. 413 (1966)

Table 2-10 *(Continued)*

Redrup v. New York, 386 U.S. 767 (1967)
Stanley v. Georgia, 394 U.S. 557 (1969)
Miller v. California, 413 U.S. 15 (1973)
Jenkins v. Georgia, 418 U.S. 153 (1974)
New York v. Ferber, 458 U.S. 747 (1982)
Osborne v. Ohio, 109 L. Ed. 2d 98 (1990)
Barnes v. Glen Theatre, Inc., 115 L. Ed. 2d 504 (1991)

Pardoning Power

Ex parte Garland, 4 Wall. 333 (1867)
Ex parte Grossman, 267 U.S. 87 (1925)
Schick v. Reed, 419 U.S. 256 (1974)

Poverty Law

Goldberg v. Kelly, 397 U.S. 254 (1970)
Dandridge v. Williams, 397 U.S. 471 (1970)
Fuentes v. Shevin, 407 U.S. 67 (1972)
Mathews v. Eldridge, 424 U.S. 319 (1976)

President as Commander in Chief

The Prize Cases, 2 Black 635 (1863)
Ex parte Milligan, 4 Wall. 2 (1866)
Ex parte Quirin, 317 U.S. 1 (1942)
Korematsu v. United States, 323 U.S. 214 (1944)
Toth v. Quarles, 350 U.S. 11 (1955)

Presidential Prerogatives

Kendall v. United States, 12 Pet. 524 (1838)
Mississippi v. Johnson, 4 Wall. 475 (1867)
In re Neagle, 135 U.S. 1 (1890)
In re Debs, 158 U.S. 564 (1895)
Panama Refining Co. v. Ryan, 293 U.S. 388 (1935)
U.S. v. Curtiss-Wright Export Corp., 299 U.S. 304 (1936)
Nixon v. Administrator of General Services, 433 U.S. 425 (1977)
Butz v. Economou, 438 U.S. 478 (1978)
Nixon v. Fitzgerald, 457 U.S. 731 (1982)

Press, Freedom of

Near v. Minnesota, 283 U.S. 697 (1931)
Grosjean v. American Press Co., 297 U.S. 233 (1936)
New York Times v. Sullivan, 376 U.S. 254 (1964)
Branzburg v. Hayes, 408 U.S. 665 (1972)
Miami Herald Publishing Co. v. Tornillo, 418 U.S. 241 (1974)

(Table continues)

Table 2-10 *(Continued)*

Time, Inc. v. Firestone, 424 U.S. 448 (1976)

Press, Freedom of Versus the Right to a Fair Trial

Nebraska Press Association v. Stuart, 427 U.S. 539 (1976)
Zurcher v. The Stanford Daily, 436 U.S. 547 (1978)
Richmond Newspapers, Inc. v. Virginia, 448 U.S. 555 (1980)
Globe Newspaper Co. v. Superior Court, 457 U.S. 596 (1982)

Privacy

Griswold v. Connecticut, 381 U.S. 479 (1965)
Eisenstadt v. Baird, 405 U.S. 438 (1972)
Whalen v. Roe, 429 U.S. 589 (1977)
Bowers v. Hardwick, 478 U.S. 186 (1986)

Privileges and Immunities

Baldwin v. Fish and Game Commission of Montana, 436 U.S. 371 (1978)
Hicklin v. Orbeck, 437 U.S. 518 (1978)
Supreme Court of New Hampshire v. Piper, 470 U.S. 274 (1985)

Race Discrimination

Scott v. Sandford, 19 How. 393 (1857)
Civil Rights Cases, 109 U.S. 3 (1883)
Yick Wo v. Hopkins, 118 U.S. 356 (1886)
Plessy v. Ferguson, 163 U.S. 537 (1896)
Buchanan v. Warley, 245 U.S. 60 (1917)
Morgan v. Virginia, 328 U.S. 373 (1946)
Shelley v. Kraemer, 334 U.S. 1 (1948)
Brown v. Board of Education, 347 U.S. 483, 349 U.S. 394 (1954, 1955)
Heart of Atlanta Motel v. United States, 379 U.S. 241 (1964)
Washington v. Davis, 426 U.S. 229 (1976)
Village of Arlington Heights v. Metropolitan Housing Development Corp., 429
   U.S. 25 (1977)
Bob Jones University v. United States, 461 U.S. 574 (1983)
Batson v. Kentucky, 476 U.S. 79 (1986)
St. Francis College v. Al-Khazraji, 481 U.S. 604 (1987)

Removal Power

Myers v. United States, 272 U.S. 52 (1926)
Humphrey's Executor (Rathbun) v. United States, 295 U.S. 602 (1935)
Wiener v. United States, 357 U.S. 349 (1958)

Republican Form of Government

Luther v. Borden, 7 How. 1 (1849)
Pacific States Telephone and Telegraph Co. v. Oregon, 223 U.S.118 (1912)

Table 2-10   *(Continued)*

Search and Seizure

Rochin v. California, 342 U.S. 165 (1952)
Mapp v. Ohio, 367 U.S. 643 (1961)
Terry v. Ohio, 392 U.S. 1 (1968)
United States v. Matlock, 415 U.S. 164 (1974)
Zurcher v. The Stanford Daily, 436 U.S. 547 (1978)
Mincey v. Arizona, 437 U.S. 385 (1978)
United States v. Ross, 456 U.S. 798 (1982)
Illinois v. Gates, 462 U.S. 213 (1983)
United States v. Leon, 468 U.S. 897 (1984)
Michigan Dept. of State Police v. Sitz, 110 L. Ed. 2d 412 (1990)
California v. Acevedo, 114 L. Ed. 2d 619 (1991)

Separation of Powers

Youngstown Sheet & Tube Co. v. Sawyer, 343 U.S. 579 (1952)
Train v. New York City, 420 U.S. 35 (1975)
Nixon v. Administrator of General Services, 433 U.S. 425 (1977)
Immigration and Naturalization Service v. Chadha, 462 U.S. 919 (1983)
Bowsher v. Synar, 478 U.S. 714 (1986)
Morrison v. Olson, 108 S.Ct. 2597 (1988)
Mistretta v. United States, 109 S.Ct. 647 (1989)

Second Amendment

United States v. Miller, 307 U.S. 174 (1939)

Self-Incrimination

Twining v. New Jersey, 211 U.S. 78 (1908)
Chambers v. Florida, 309 U.S. 227 (1940)
Adamson v. California, 322 U.S. 46 (1947)
Ullman v. United States, 350 U.S. 422 (1956)
Slochower v. Board of Higher Education of New York City, 350 U.S. 551 (1956)
Mallory v. United States, 354 U.S. 449 (1957)
Malloy v. Hogan, 378 U.S. 1 (1964)
Albertson v. Subversive Activities Control Board, 382 U.S. 70 (1965)
Zicarelli v. New Jersey State Commission of Investigation, 406 U.S. 472 (1972)

Sex Discrimination

Bradwell v. Illinois, 16 Wall. 130 (1873)
Hoyt v. Florida, 368 U.S. 57 (1961)
Reed v. Reed, 404 U.S. 71 (1971)
Cleveland Board of Education v. LaFleur, 414 U.S. 632 (1974)
Taylor v. Louisiana, 419 U.S. 522 (1975)
Craig v. Boren, 429 U.S. 190 (1976)

(Table continues)

Table 2-10 *(Continued)*

Califano v. Goldfarb, 430 U.S. 199 (1977)
Rostker v. Goldberg, 453 U.S. 57 (1979)
Mississippi University for Women v. Hogan, 458 U.S. 718 (1982)
Arizona Governing Committee v. Norris, 463 U.S. 1073 (1983)
Hishon v. King & Spalding, 467 U.S. 69 (1984)
Meritor Savings Bank, FSB v. Vinson, 477 U.S. 57 (1986)
Johnson v. Transportation Agency, 480 U.S. 616 (1987)
United Automobile Workers v. Johnson Controls, 113 L. Ed. 2d 158 (1991)

Speech, Commercial

Bigelow v. Virginia, 421 U.S. 809 (1975)
Virginia State Pharmacy Board v. Virginia Citizens Consumer Council, Inc., 425
  U.S. 748 (1976)
Bates v. State Bar of Arizona, 433 U.S. 350 (1977)
Bolger v. Youngs Drug Products Corp., 463 U.S. 60 (1983)

Speech, Freedom of

Schenck v. United States, 249 U.S. 47 (1919)
Whitney v. California, 274 U.S. 357 (1927)
Chaplinsky v. New Hampshire, 315 U.S. 568 (1942)
American Communications Association v. Douds, 339 U.S. 94 (1950)
Dennis v. United States, 341 U.S. 494 (1951)
Adler v. Board of Education, 342 U.S. 485 (1952)
Burstyn v. Wilson, 343 U.S. 195 (1952)
Yates v. United States, 355 U.S. 66 (1957)
Barenblatt v. United States, 360 U.S. 109 (1959)
Scales v. United States, 367 U.S. 203 (1961)
Communist Party v. Subversive Activities Control Board, 367 U.S. 1 (1961)
Keyishian v. Board of Regents, 385 U.S. 589 (1967)
Brandenburg v. Ohio, 395 U.S. 444 (1969)
R.A.V. v. City of St. Paul, 120 L. Ed. 2d 305 (1992)

Speech, Symbolic

Stromberg v. California, 283 U.S. 359 (1931)
Thornhill v. Alabama, 310 U.S. 88 (1940)
United States v. O'Brien, 391 U.S. 367 (1968)
Tinker v. Des Moines Independent Community School District, 393 U.S. 503
  (1969)
Cohen v. California, 403 U.S. 15 (1971)
Texas v. Johnson, 105 L. Ed. 2d 342 (1989)
United States v. Eichman, 110 L. Ed. 2d 287 (1990)

Standing to Sue

Frothingham v. Mellon, 262 U.S. 447 (1923)
Flast v. Cohen, 392 U.S. 83 (1968)
Warth v. Seldin, 422 U.S. 490 (1975)

Table 2-10   *(Continued)*

State Autonomy

Texas v. White, 7 Wall. 700 (1869)
Stearns v. Minnesota, 179 U.S. 223 (1900)
Coyle v. Smith, 221 U.S. 559 (1911)

Takings Clause

Berman v. Parker, 348 U.S. 26 (1954)
Penn Central Transportation Co. v. New York City, 438 U.S. 104 (1978)
Pruneyard Shopping Center v. Robins, 447 U.S. 74 (1980)
Hawaii Housing Authority v. Midkiff, 467 U.S. 229 (1984)

Taxing and Spending Power

Pollock v. Farmers' Loan and Trust Co., 157 U.S. 429, 158 U.S. 601 (1895)
McCray v. United States, 195 U.S. 27 (1904)
Bailey v. Drexel Furniture Co., 259 U.S. 20 (1922)
United States v. Butler, 297 U.S. 1 (1936)
Steward Machine Co. v. Davis, 301 U.S. 548 (1937)
Helvering v. Davis, 301 U.S. 619 (1937)
Mulford v. Smith, 307 U.S. 38 (1939)

Tenth Amendment

Maryland v. Wirtz, 392 U.S. 183 (1968)
National League of Cities v. Usery, 426 U.S. 833 (1976)
United Transportation Union v. Long Island Rail Road Co., 455 U.S. 678 (1982)
Garcia v. San Antonio Metropolitan Transit Authority, 469 U.S. 528 (1985)

Thirteenth Amendment: Servitude

Pollock v. Williams, 322 U.S. 4 (1944)
Jones v. Alfred H. Meyer Co., 392 U.S. 409 (1968)

Travel, Right to

Kent v. Dulles, 357 U.S. 116 (1958)
Aptheker v. Secretary of State, 378 U.S. 500 (1964)
Zemel v. Rusk, 381 U.S. 1 (1965)

Treaties and Executive Agreements

Head Money Cases, 112 U.S. 580 (1884)
Missouri v. Holland, 252 U.S. 416 (1920)
United States v. Belmont, 301 U.S. 324 (1937)
Reid v. Covert, 351 U.S. 487, 354 U.S. 1 (1956, 1957)

(Table continues)

Table 2-10 *(Continued)*

Voting

Ex parte Siebold, 100 U.S. 371 (1880)
Guinn v. United States, 238 U.S. 437 (1915)
Harper v. Virginia State Board of Elections, 383 U.S. 667 (1966)
South Carolina v. Katzenbach, 383 U.S. 301 (1966)
Oregon v. Mitchell, 400 U.S. 112 (1970)
Dunn v. Blumstein, 405 U.S. 330 (1972)
Rosario v. Rockefeller, 410 U.S. 752 (1973)
Buckley v. Valeo, 424 U.S. 1 (1976)
Mobile v. Bolden, 446 U.S. 55 (1980)

War Powers

Selective Draft Law Cases, 245 U.S. 366 (1918)
Block v. Hirsh, 256 U.S. 135 (1921)
Ashwander v. Tennessee Valley Authority, 297 U.S. 288 (1936)
Woods v. Miller Co., 333 U.S. 138 (1948)
Feres v. United States, 340 U.S. 135 (1950)
United States v. Stanley, 483 U.S. 669 (1987)

Wiretapping

Olmstead v. United States, 277 U.S. 438 (1928)
Katz v. United States, 389 U.S. 347 (1967)
United States v. United States District Court, 407 U.S. 297 (1972)
United States v. Kahn, 415 U.S. 143 (1974)

Note: This list reflects the judgment of the authors.

Table 2-11   Cases Incorporating Provisions of the Bill of Rights into the Due Process Clause of the Fourteenth Amendment

Provision	Case
First Amendment	
Freedom of speech and press	*Gitlow v. New York*, 268 U.S. 652 (1925)
Freedom of assembly	*DeJonge v. Oregon*, 299 U.S. 353 (1937)
Free exercise of religion	*Cantwell v. Connecticut*, 310 U.S. 296 (1940)
Establishment of religion	*Everson v. Board of Education*, 330 U.S. 1 (1947)
Fourth Amendment	
Unreasonable search and seizure	*Wolf v. Colorado*, 338 U.S. 25 (1949)
Exclusionary rule	*Mapp v. Ohio*, 367 U.S. 643 (1961)
Fifth Amendment	
Payment of compensation for the taking of private property	*Chicago, Burlington and Quincy R. Co. v. Chicago*, 166 U.S. 226 (1897)
Self-incrimination	*Malloy v. Hogan*, 378 U.S. 1 (1964)
Double jeopardy	*Benton v. Maryland*, 395 U.S. 784 (1969)
When jeopardy attaches	*Crist v. Bretz*, 437 U.S. 28 (1978)
Sixth Amendment	
Public trial	*In re Oliver*, 333 U.S. 257 (1948)
Right to counsel	*Gideon v. Wainwright*, 372 U.S. 335 (1963)
Confrontation and cross-examination of adverse witnesses	*Pointer v. Texas*, 380 U.S. 400 (1965)
Speedy trial	*Klopfer v. North Carolina*, 386 U.S. 213 (1967)
Compulsory process to obtain witnesses	*Washington v. Texas*, 388 U.S. 14 (1967)
Jury trial	*Duncan v. Louisiana*, 391 U.S. 145 (1968)
Eighth Amendment	
Cruel and unusual punishment	*Louisiana ex rel. Francis v. Resweber*, 329 U.S. 459 (1947)

Source: United States Reports.

Table 2-12   Supreme Court Decisions Holding Acts of Congress
Unconstitutional in Whole or in Part, 1789-1990

Marshall Court (January 27, 1801-March 14, 1836)

Marbury v. Madison, 1 Cranch (5 U.S.) 137 (1803)

Taney Court (March 15, 1836-December 5, 1864)

Scott v. Sandford, 19 How. (60 U.S.) 393 (1857)

Chase Court (December 6, 1864-January 20, 1874)

Gordon v. United States, 2 Wall. (69 U.S.) 561 (1865)
Ex parte Garland, 4 Wall. (71 U.S.) 333 (1867)
Reichart v. Felps, 6 Wall. (73 U.S.) 160 (1868)
The Alicia, 7 Wall. (74 U.S.) 571 (1869)
Hepburn v. Griswold, 8 Wall. (75 U.S.) 603 (1870)
The Justices v. Murray, 9 Wall. (76 U.S.) 274 (1870)
United States v. Dewitt, 9 Wall. (76 U.S.) 41 (1870)
United States v. Klein, 13 Wall. (80 U.S.) 128 (1872)

Waite Court (January 21, 1874-July 19, 1888)

United States v. Reese, 92 U.S. 214 (1876)
United States v. Fox, 95 U.S. 670 (1878)
Trade-Mark Cases, 100 U.S. 82 (1879)
United States v. Harris, 106 U.S. 629 (1883)
Civil Rights Cases, 109 U.S. 3 (1883)
Boyd v. United States, 116 U.S. 616 (1886)
Baldwin v. Franks, 120 U.S. 678 (1887)
Callan v. Wilson, 127 U.S. 540 (1888)

Fuller Court (July 20, 1888-December 11, 1910)

Monongahela Navigation Co. v. United States, 148 U.S. 312 (1893)
Pollock v. Farmers' Loan & Trust Co., 157 U.S. 429 (1895)
Wong Wing v. United States, 163 U.S. 228 (1896)
Kirby v. United States, 174 U.S. 47 (1899)
Jones v. Meehan, 175 U.S. 1 (1899)
Fairbank v. United States, 181 U.S. 283 (1901)
James v. Bowman, 190 U.S. 127 (1903)
Matter of Heff, 197 U.S. 488 (1905)
Rassmussen v. United States, 197 U.S. 516 (1905)
Hodges v. United States, 203 U.S. 1 (1906)
The Employers' Liability Cases, 207 U.S. 463 (1908)
Adair v. United States, 208 U.S. 161 (1908)
Keller v. United States, 213 U.S. 138 (1909)
United States v. Evans, 213 U.S. 297 (1909)

White Court (December 12, 1910-June 29, 1921)

Coyle v. Smith, 221 U.S. 559 (1911)

Table 2-12 *(Continued)*

Muskrat v. United States, 219 U.S. 346 (1911)
Choate v. Trapp, 224 U.S. 665 (1912)
United States v. Hvoslef, 237 U.S. 1 (1915)
Thames & Mersey Marine Ins. Co. v. United States, 237 U.S. 19 (1915)
Hammer v. Dagenhart, 247 U.S. 251 (1918)
Eisner v. Macomber, 252 U.S. 189 (1920)
Knickerbocker Ice Co. v. Stewart, 253 U.S. 149 (1920)
Evans v. Gore, 253 U.S. 245 (1920)
United States v. L. Cohen Grocery Co., 255 U.S. 81 (1921)
Weeds, Inc. v. United States, 255 U.S. 109 (1921)
Newberry v. United States, 256 U.S. 232 (1921)

Taft Court (June 30, 1921-February 12, 1930)

United States v. Moreland, 258 U.S. 433 (1922)
Bailey v. Drexel Furniture Co. (Child Labor Tax Case), 259 U.S. 20 (1922)
Hill v. Wallace, 259 U.S. 44 (1922)
Keller v. Potomac Electric Co., 261 U.S. 428 (1923)
Adkins v. Children's Hospital, 261 U.S. 525 (1923)
Washington v. Dawson & Co., 264 U.S. 219 (1924)
Miles v. Graham, 268 U.S. 501 (1925)
Trusler v. Crooks, 269 U.S. 475 (1926)
Myers v. United States, 272 U.S. 52 (1926)
Nicholds v. Coolidge, 274 U.S. 531 (1927)
Untermeyer v. Anderson, 276 U.S. 440 (1928)
National Life Ins. v. United States, 277 U.S. 508 (1928)

Hughes Court (February 13, 1930-June 11, 1941)

Heiner v. Donnan, 285 U.S. 312 (1932)
Booth v. United States, 291 U.S. 339 (1934)
Lynch v. United States, 292 U.S. 571 (1934)
Perry v. United States, 294 U.S. 330 (1935)
Panama Refining Co. v. Ryan, 293 U.S. 388 (1935)
Railroad Retirement Board v. Alton Railroad Co., 295 U.S. 330 (1935)
Schechter Poultry Corp. v. United States, 295 U.S. 495 (1935)
Louisville Bank v. Radford, 295 U.S. 555 (1935)
United States v. Constantine, 296 U.S. 287 (1935)
Hopkins Savings Association v. Cleary, 296 U.S. 315 (1935)
United States v. Butler, 297 U.S. 1 (1936)
Rickert Rice Mills v. Fontenot, 297 U.S. 110 (1936)
Ashton v. Cameron County District, 298 U.S. 513 (1936)
Carter v. Carter Coal Co., 298 U.S. 238 (1936)

Stone Court (June 12, 1941-June 19, 1946)

Tot v. United States, 319 U.S. 463 (1943)

(Table continues)

Table 2-12   *(Continued)*

United States v. Lovett, 328 U.S. 303 (1946)

Vinson Court (June 20, 1946-September 29, 1953)

United States v. Cardiff, 344 U.S. 174 (1952)

Warren Court (September 30, 1953-June 8, 1969)

Bolling v. Sharpe, 347 U.S. 497 (1954)
Toth v. Quarles, 350 U.S. 11 (1955)
Reid v. Covert, 354 U.S. 1 (1957)
Trop v. Dulles, 356 U.S. 86 (1958)
Kinsella v. United States, 361 U.S. 234 (1960)
Grisham v. Hagan, 361 U.S. 278 (1960)
McElroy v. United States, 361 U.S. 281 (1960)
Kennedy v. Mendoza-Martinez, 372 U.S. 144 (1963)
Schneider v. Rusk, 377 U.S. 163 (1964)
Aptheker v. Secretary of State, 378 U.S. 500 (1964)
Lamont v. Postmaster General, 381 U.S. 301 (1965)
United States v. Brown, 381 U.S. 437 (1965)
Albertson v. Subversive Activities Control Board, 382 U.S. 70 (1965)
United States v. Romano, 382 U.S. 136 (1965)
Afroyim v. Rusk, 387 U.S. 253 (1967)
United States v. Robel, 389 U.S. 258 (1967)
Marchetti v. United States, 390 U.S. 39 (1968)
Grosso v. United States, 390 U.S. 62 (1968)
Haynes v. United States, 390 U.S. 85 (1968)
United States v. Jackson, 390 U.S. 570 (1968)
Shapiro v. Thompson, 394 U.S. 618 (1969)
Leary v. United States, 395 U.S. 6 (1969)
O'Callahan v. Parker, 395 U.S. 258 (1969)

Burger Court (June 9, 1969-September 16, 1986)

Turner v. United States, 396 U.S. 398 (1970)
Schacht v. United States, 398 U.S. 58 (1970)
Oregon v. Mitchell, 400 U.S. 112 (1970)
Blount v. Rizzi, 400 U.S. 410 (1971)
United States v. United States Coin & Currency, 401 U.S. 715 (1971)
Tilton v. Richardson, 403 U.S. 672 (1971)
Chief of Capitol Police v. Jeannette Rankin Brigade, 409 U.S. 972 (1972)
Richardson v. Davis, 409 U.S. 1069 (1972)
Frontiero v. Richardson, 411 U.S. 677 (1973)
U.S. Dept. of Agriculture v. Murry, 413 U.S. 508 (1973)
U.S. Dept. of Agriculture v. Moreno, 413 U.S. 528 (1973)
Jimenez v. Weinberger, 417 U.S. 628 (1974)
Weinberger v. Wiesenfeld, 420 U.S. 636 (1975)
Buckley v. Valeo, 424 U.S. 1 (1976)
National League of Cities v. Usery, 426 U.S. 833 (1976)

Table 2-12   *(Continued)*

Califano v. Goldfarb, 430 U.S. 199 (1977)
Califano v. Silbowitz, 430 U.S. 934 (1977)
Railroad Retirement Bd. v. Kalina, 431 U.S. 909 (1977)
Marshall v. Barlow's, Inc., 436 U.S. 307 (1978)
Califano v. Westcott, 443 U.S. 76 (1979)
United States v. Will, 449 U.S. 200 (1980)
Railroad Labor Executives' Assn. v. Gibbons, 455 U.S. 457 (1982)
Northern Pipeline Construction Co. v. Marathon Pipe Line Co., 458 U.S. 50 (1982)
United States v. Grace, 461 U.S. 171 (1983)
Immigration and Naturalization Service v. Chadha, 462 U.S. 919 (1983)
Bolger v. Youngs Drug Products Corp., 463 U.S. 60 (1983)
Process Gas Consumers Group v. Consumer Energy Council, 463 U.S. 1216 (1983)
U.S. Senate v. Federal Trade Commission, 463 U.S. 1216 (1983)
Federal Communications Commission v. League of Women Voters of California, 468 U.S. 364 (1984)
Regan v. Time, Inc., 468 U.S. 641 (1984)
Federal Election Commission v. National Conservative Political Action Committee, 470 U.S. 480 (1985)
Bowsher v. Synar, 478 U.S. 714 (1986)

Rehnquist Court (September 17, 1986-)

Federal Election Commission v. Massachusetts Citizens for Life, Inc., 479 U.S. 238 (1986)
Hodel v. Irving, 481 U.S. 704 (1987)
Boos v. Barry, 485 U.S. 312 (1988)
Sable Communications of California, Inc. v. Federal Communications Commission, 106 L. Ed. 2d 93 (1989)
United States v. Eichman, 110 L. Ed. 2d 287 (1990)

Note: Determination of which decisions have voided acts of Congress is not a clear-cut matter. For example, the source used here invokes criteria different from those of the Supreme Court database, which lists these decisions since the onset of the Warren Court in 1953. For purposes of longitudinal consistency, we report only those cases listed in the Library of Congress source.

Source: U.S. Library of Congress, Congressional Research Service, *The Constitution of the United States of America, Analysis and Interpretation: Annotations of Cases Decided by the Supreme Court of the United States* (Washington, D.C.: Government Printing Office, 1973), 1597-1619 and supplements.

Table 2-13 Supreme Court Decisions Holding State Constitutional and
Statutory Provisions and Municipal Ordinances
Unconstitutional on Their Face or as Administered,
1789-1990

Marshall Court (January 27, 1801-March 14, 1836)

United States v. Peters, 5 Cranch (9 U.S.) 115 (1809)
Fletcher v. Peck, 6 Cranch (10 U.S.) 87 (1810)
New Jersey v. Wilson, 7 Cranch (11 U.S.) 164 (1812)
Terrett v. Taylor, 9 Cranch (13 U.S.) 43 (1815)
Sturges v. Crowninshield, 4 Wheat. (17 U.S.) 122 (1819)
McMillan v. McNeil, 4 Wheat. (17 U.S.) 209 (1819)
McCulloch v. Maryland, 4 Wheat. (17 U.S.) 316 (1819)
Dartmouth College v. Woodward, 4 Wheat. (17 U.S.) 518 (1819)
Farmers' & Mechanics' Bank v. Smith, 6 Wheat. (19 U.S.) 131 (1812)
Green v. Biddle, 8 Wheat. (21 U.S.) 1 (1823)
Society for the Propagation of the Gospel v. New Haven, 8 Wheat. (21 U.S.) 464
  (1823)
Gibbons v. Ogden, 9 Wheat. (22 U.S.) 1 (1824)
Osborn v. Bank of the United States, 9 Wheat. (22 U.S.) 738 (1824)
Ogden v. Saunders, 12 Wheat. (25 U.S.) 213 (1827)
Brown v. Maryland, 12 Wheat. (25 U.S.) 419 (1827)
Weston v. City Council of Charleston, 2 Pet. (27 U.S.) 449 (1829)
Craig v. Missouri, 4 Pet. (29 U.S.) 410 (1830)
Worcester v. Georgia, 6 Pet. (31 U.S.) 515 (1832)
Boyle v. Zacharie & Turner, 6 Pet. (31 U.S.) 635 (1832)

Taney Court (March 15, 1836-December 5, 1864)

Dobbins v. The Commissioners of Erie County, 16 Pet. (41 U.S.) 435 (1842)
Prigg v. Pennsylvania, 16 Pet. (41 U.S.) 539 (1842)
Bronson v. Kinzie, 1 How. (42 U.S.) 311 (1843)
McCracken v. Hayward, 2 How. (43 U.S.) 608 (1844)
Gordon v. Appeal Tax Court, 3 How. (44 U.S.) 133 (1845)
Searight v. Stokes, 3 How. (44 U.S.) 151 (1845)
Neil, Moore & Co. v. Ohio, 3 How. (44 U.S.) 720 (1845)
Planters' Bank v. Sharp, 6 How. (47 U.S.) 301 (1848)
Passenger Cases, 7 How. (48 U.S.) 283 (1849)
Woodruff v. Trapnall, 10 How. (51 U.S.) 190 (1851)
Achison v. Huddleson, 12 How. (53 U.S.) 293 (1852)
Trustees for Vincennes University v. Indiana, 14 How. (55 U.S.) 269 (1853)
Curran v. Arkansas, 15 How. (56 U.S.) 304 (1854)
State Bank of Ohio v. Knoop, 16 How. (57 U.S.) 369 (1854)
Hays v. The Pacific Mail Steamship Co., 17 How. (58 U.S.) 596 (1855)
Dodge v. Woolsey, 18 How. (59 U.S.) 331 (1856)
Sinnot v. Davenport, 22 How. (63 U.S.) 227 (1860)
   accord: Foster v. Davenport, 22 How. (63 U.S.) 244 (1860)
Almy v. California, 24 How. (65 U.S.) 169 (1861)
Howard v. Bugbee, 24 How. (65 U.S.) 461 (1861)

Table 2-13   *(Continued)*

Bank of Commerce v. New York City, 2 Black (67 U.S.) 620 (1863)
    accord: Bank Tax Case, 2 Wall. (69 U.S.) 244 (1865)

Chase Court (December 6, 1864-January 20, 1874)

Hawthorne v. Calef, 2 Wall. (69 U.S.) 10 (1865)
The Binghamton Bridge, 3 Wall. (70 U.S.) 51 (1866)
Van Allen v. The Assessors, 3 Wall. (70 U.S.) 573 (1866)
Bradley v. Illinois, 4 Wall. (71 U.S.) 459 (1867)
McGee v. Mathis, 4 Wall. (71 U.S.) 143 (1867)
Cummings v. Missouri, 4 Wall. (71 U.S.) 277 (1867)
The Moses Taylor, 4 Wall. (71 U.S.) 411 (1867)
Von Hoffman v. Quincy, 4 Wall. (71 U.S.) 535 (1867)
The Hine v. Trevor, 4 Wall (71 U.S.) 555 (1867)
Christmas v. Russell, 5 Wall. (72 U.S.) 290 (1867)
The Kansas Indians, 5 Wall. (72 U.S.) 737 (1867)
The New York Indians, 5 Wall. (72 U.S.) 761 (1867)
Steamship Company v. Portwardens, 6 Wall. (73 U.S.) 31 (1867)
Crandall v. Nevada, 6 Wall. (73 U.S.) 35 (1868)
Bank v. Supervisors, 7 Wall. (74 U.S.) 26 (1868)
Northern Central Ry. Co. v. Jackson, 7 Wall. (74 U.S.) 262 (1869)
The Belfast, 7 Wall. (74 U.S.) 624 (1869)
Furman v. Nichol, 8 Wall. (75 U.S.) 44 (1869)
Home of the Friendless v. Rouse, 8 Wall. (75 U.S.) 430 (1869)
The Washington University v. Rouse, 8 Wall. (75 U.S.) 439 (1869)
State Tonnage Tax Cases, 12 Wall. (79 U.S.) 204 (1871)
Ward v. Maryland, 12 Wall. (79 U.S.) 418 (1871)
Gibson v. Chouteau, 13 Wall. (80 U.S.) 92 (1872)
Wilmington Railroad v. Reid, 13 Wall. (80 U.S.) 264 (1872)
White v. Hart, 13 Wall. (80 U.S.) 646 (1872)
Osborne v. Nicholson, 13 Wall. (80 U.S.) 654 (1872)
Delmas v. Insurance Company, 14 Wall. (81 U.S.) 661 (1872)
Case of the State Freight Tax, 15 Wall. (82 U.S.) 232 (1873)
State Tax on Foreign-Held Bonds, 15 Wall. (82 U.S.) 300 (1873)
Gunn v. Barry, 15 Wall. (82 U.S.) 610 (1873)
Pierce v. Carskadon, 16 Wall. (83 U.S.) 234 (1873)
Humphrey v. Pegues, 16 Wall. (83 U.S.) 244 (1873)
Walker v. Whitehead, 16 Wall. (83 U.S.) 314 (1873)
Barings v. Dabney, 19 Wall. (86 U.S.) 1 (1873)

Waite Court (January 21, 1874-July 19, 1888)

Cannon v. New Orleans, 20 Wall. (87 U.S.) 577 (1874)
Murray v. Charleston, 96 U.S. 432 (1874)
Peete v. Morgan, 19 Wall. (86 U.S.) 581 (1874)

(Table continues)

Table 2-13 *(Continued)*

Pacific Railroad Company v. Maguire, 20 Wall. (87 U.S.) 36 (1874)
Insurance Company v. Morse, 20 Wall. (87 U.S.) 445 (1874)
Loan Association v. Topeka, 20 Wall. (87 U.S.) 655 (1875)
Wilmington & Weldon R. Co. v. King, 91 U.S. 3 (1875)
Welton v. Missouri, 91 U.S. 275 (1876)
Morrill v. Wisconsin, 154 U.S. 626 (1877)
Henderson v. Mayor of New York, 92 U.S. 259 (1876)
Chy Lung v. Freeman, 92 U.S. 275 (1876)
Inman Steamship Co. v. Tinker, 94 U.S. 238 (1877)
Foster v. Masters of New Orleans, 94 U.S. 246 (1877)
New Jersey v. Yard, 95 U.S. 104 (1877)
Hannibal & St. Joseph R. Co. v. Husen, 95 U.S. 465 (1878)
Hall v. DeCuir, 95 U.S. 485 (1878)
Farrington v. Tennessee, 95 U.S. 679 (1878)
Pensacola Tel. Co. v. Western Union Tel Co., 96 U.S. 1 (1878)
Edwards v. Kearzey, 96 U.S. 595 (1878)
Keith v. Clark, 97 U.S. 454 (1878)
Cook v. Pennsylvania, 97 U.S. 566 (1878)
Northwestern University v. Illinois ex rel. Miller, 99 U.S. 309 (1878)
Strauder v. West Virginia, 100 U.S. 303 (1880)
Guy v. Baltimore, 100 U.S. 434 (1880)
Tiernan v. Rinker, 102 U.S. 123 (1880)
Hartman v. Greenhow, 102 U.S. 672 (1880)
Hall v. Wisconsin, 103 U.S. 5 (1880)
Webber v. Virginia, 103 U.S. 344 (1881)
United States ex rel. Wolff v. New Orleans, 103 U.S. 358 (1881)
   accord: Louisiana v. Pilsbury, 105 U.S. 278 (1881)
Asylum v. New Orleans, 105 U.S. 362 (1881)
Western Union Telegraph Co. v. Texas, 105 U.S. 460 (1881)
Ralls County Court v. United States, 105 U.S. 733 (1881)
Parkersburg v. Brown, 106 U.S. 487 (1882)
New York v. Compagnie Gén. Transatlantique, 107 U.S. 59 (1882)
Kring v. Missouri, 107 U.S. 221 (1883)
Nelson v. St. Martin's Parish, 111 U.S. 716 (1884)
Moran v. New Orleans, 112 U.S. 69 (1884)
Cole v. La Grange, 113 U.S. 1 (1885)
Gloucester Ferry Co. v. Pennsylvania, 114 U.S. 196 (1885)
Virginia Coupon Cases, 114 U.S. 269 (1885)
New Orleans Gas Co. v. Louisiana Light Co., 115 U.S. 650 (1885)
New Orleans Water-Works Co. v. Rivers, 115 U.S. 674 (1885)
Effinger v. Kenney, 115 U.S. 566 (1885)
Louisville Gas Co. v. Citizens' Gas Co., 115 U.S. 683 (1885)
Fiske v. Jefferson Police Jury, 116 U.S. 131 (1885)
Mobile v. Watson, 116 U.S. 289 (1886)
Walling v. Michigan, 116 U.S. 446 (1886)
Royall v. Virginia, 116 U.S. 572 (1886)

Table 2-13   *(Continued)*

Pickard v. Pullman Southern Car Co., 117 U.S. 34 (1886)
Van Brocklin v. Tennessee, 117 U.S. 151 (1886)
Sprague v. Thompson, 118 U.S 90 (1886)
Wabash, St. Louis & P. Ry. Co. v. Illinois, 118 U.S. 557 (1886)
Yick Wo v. Hopkins, 118 U.S. 356 (1886)
Robbins v. Shelby Taxing District, 120 U.S. 489 (1887)
Corson v. Maryland, 120 U.S. 502 (1887)
Barron v. Burnside, 121 U.S. 186 (1887)
Fargo v. Michigan, 121 U.S. 230 (1887)
Seibert v. Lewis, 122 U.S. 284 (1887)
Philadelphia Steamship Co. v. Pennsylvania, 122 U.S. 326 (1887)
Western Union Telegraph Co. v. Pendleton, 122 U.S. 347 (1887)
Bowman v. Chicago & Nw. Ry. Co., 125 U.S. 465 (1888)
Western Union Telegraph Co. v. Massachusetts, 125 U.S. 530 (1888)
California v. Pacific Railroad Co., 127 U.S. 1 (1888)
Ratterman v. Western Union Tel. Co., 127 U.S. 411 (1888)
Leloup v. Port of Mobile, 127 U.S. 640 (1888)

Fuller Court (July 20, 1888-December 11, 1910)

Asher v. Texas, 128 U.S. 129 (1888)
Stoutenburgh v. Hennick, 129 U.S. 141 (1889)
Western Union Telegraph Co. v. Alabama, 132 U.S. 472 (1889)
Medley, Petitioner, 134 U.S. 160 (1890)
Chicago, Minneapolis & St. Paul Ry. Co. v. Minnesota, 134 U.S. 418 (1890)
Leisy v. Hardin, 135 U.S. 100 (1890)
Lyng v. Michigan, 135 U.S. 161 (1890)
McGahey v. Virginia, 135 U.S. 662 (1890)
Norfolk & Western R. Co. v. Pennsylvania, 136 U.S. 114 (1890)
Minnesota v. Barber, 136 U.S. 313 (1890)
McCall v. California, 136 U.S. 104 (1890)
Brimmer v. Rebman, 138 U.S. 78 (1891)
Pennoyer v. McConnaughy, 140 U.S. 1 (1891)
Crutcher v. Kentucky, 141 U.S. 47 (1891)
Voight v. Wright, 141 U.S. 62 (1891)
Harman v. Chicago, 147 U.S. 396 (1893)
Brennan v. Titusville, 153 U.S. 289 (1894)
Mobile & Ohio Railroad v. Tennessee, 153 U.S. 486 (1894)
New York, L.E. & W.R. Co. v. Pennsylvania, 153 U.S. 628 (1894)
Covington & Cincinnati Bridge Co. v. Kentucky, 154 U.S. 204 (1894)
Gulf, C. & S.F. Ry. Co. v. Hefley, 158 U.S. 98 (1896)
Bank of Commerce v. Tennessee, 161 U.S. 134 (1896)
Barnitz v. Beverly, 163 U.S. 118 (1896)
Illinois Central Ry. v. Illinois, 163 U.S. 142 (1896)
Missouri Pacific Railway v. Nebraska, 164 U.S. 403 (1896)

(Table continues)

Table 2-13 *(Continued)*

Scott v. Donald, 165 U.S. 58 (1897)
Gulf, C. & S.F. Ry. Co. v. Ellis, 165 U.S. 150 (1897)
Allgeyer v. Louisiana, 165 U.S. 578 (1897)
Smyth v. Ames, 169 U.S. 466 (1898)
Houston & Texas Central Ry. v. Texas, 170 U.S. 243 (1898)
Thompson v. Utah, 170 U.S. 343 (1898)
Walla Walla v. Walla Walla Water Co., 172 U.S. 1 (1898)
Schollenberger v. Pennsylvania, 171 U.S. 1 (1898)
Collins v. New Hampshire, 171 U.S. 30 (1898)
Blake v. McClung, 172 U.S. 239 (1898)
Norwood v. Baker, 172 U.S. 269 (1898)
Dewey v. Des Moines, 173 U.S. 193 (1899)
Ohio v. Thomas, 173 U.S. 276 (1899)
Lake Shore & Mich. S. Ry. Co. v. Smith, 173 U.S. 684 (1899)
Houston & Texas Central R. Co. v. Texas, 177 U.S. 66 (1900)
Cleveland, C.C. & St. Louis Ry. Co. v. Illinois, 177 U.S. 514 (1900)
Stearns v. Minnesota, 179 U.S. 223 (1900)
Duluth & I.R.R. Co. v. Kentucky, 179 U.S. 302 (1900)
Los Angeles v. Los Angeles Water Co., 177 U.S. 558 (1900)
Cotting v. Kansas City Stock Yards Co., 183 U.S. 79 (1901)
Louisville & Nashville R. Co. v. Eubank, 184 U.S. 27 (1902)
Connolly v. Union Sewer Pipe Co., 184 U.S. 540 (1902)
Detroit v. Detroit Citizens' St. Ry. Co., 184 U.S. 368 (1902)
Stockard v. Morgan, 185 U.S. 27 (1902)
Louisville & J. Ferry Co. v. Kentucky, 188 U.S. 385 (1903)
The Roanoke, 189 U.S. 185 (1903)
The Robert W. Parsons, 191 U.S. 17 (1903)
Allen v. Pullman Company, 191 U.S. 171 (1903)
Caldwell v. North Carolina, 187 U.S. 622 (1903)
Postal Telegraph-Cable Co. v. Taylor, 192 U.S. 64 (1904)
Cleveland v. Cleveland City Ry. Co., 194 U.S. 517 (1904)
Bradley v. Lightcap, 195 U.S. 1 (1904)
Dobbins v. Los Angeles, 195 U.S. 223 (1904)
Central of Georgia Ry. Co. v. Murphey, 196 U.S. 194 (1905)
Lochner v. New York, 198 U.S. 45 (1905)
Union Transit Co. v. Kentucky, 199 U.S. 194 (1905)
Houston & Texas Central Railroad v. Mayes, 201 U.S. 321 (1906)
Powers v. Detroit & Grand Haven Ry., 201 U.S. 543 (1906)
Vicksburg v. Waterworks Co., 202 U.S. 453 (1906)
Cleveland v. Cleveland Electric Ry., 201 U.S. 529 (1906)
Rearick v. Pennsylvania, 203 U.S. 507 (1906)
American Smelting Co. v. Colorado, 204 U.S. 103 (1907)
Home Savings Bank v. Des Moines, 205 U.S. 503 (1907)
Adams Express Co. v. Kentucky, 206 U.S. 129 (1907)
   accord: American Express Co. v. Kentucky, 206 U.S. 139 (1907)
Vicksburg v. Vicksburg Waterworks Co., 206 U.S. 496 (1907)

Table 2-13   *(Continued)*

Central of Georgia Ry. v. Wright, 207 U.S. 127 (1907)
Darnell & Son v. Memphis, 208 U.S. 113 (1908)
Ex parte Young, 209 U.S. 123 (1908)
Londoner v. Denver, 210 U.S. 373 (1908)
Galveston, Houston & San Antonio Ry. Co. v. Texas, 210 U.S. 217 (1908)
Willcox v. Consolidated Gas Co., 212 U.S. 19 (1909)
Louisville & Nashville R. Co. v. Stock Yards Co., 212 U.S. 132 (1909)
Nielson v. Oregon, 212 U.S. 315 (1909)
Adams Express Co. v. Kentucky, 214 U.S. 218 (1909)
Louisiana ex rel. Hubert v. New Orleans, 215 U.S. 170 (1909)
Minneapolis v. Street Railway Co., 215 U.S. 417 (1910)
North Dakota ex rel. Flaherty v. Hanson, 215 U.S. 515 (1910)
Western Union Tel. Co. v. Kansas, 216 U.S. 1 (1910)
Ludwig v. Western Union Tel. Co., 216 U.S. 146 (1910)
Southern Railway Co. v. Greene, 216 U.S. 400 (1910)
International Textbook Co. v. Pigg, 217 U.S. 91 (1910)
St. Louis S.W. Ry. v. Arkansas, 217 U.S. 136 (1910)
Missouri Pacific Ry. v. Nebraska, 217 U.S. 196 (1910)
Dozier v. Alabama, 218 U.S. 124 (1910)
Herndon v. Chicago, R.I. & P. R. Co., 218 U.S. 135 (1910)

White Court (December 12, 1910–June 29, 1921)

Bailey v. Alabama, 219 U.S. 219 (1911)
Oklahoma v. Kansas Nat. Gas Co., 221 U.S. 229 (1911)
Berryman v. Whitman College, 222 U.S. 334 (1912)
Northern Pacific Ry. Co. v. Washington, 222 U.S. 370 (1912)
Southern Ry. Co. v. Reid, 222 U.S. 424 (1912)
    accord: Southern Ry. Co. v. Reil & Beam, 222 U.S. 444 (1912)
    accord: Southern Ry. Co. v. Burlington Lumber Co., 225 U.S. 99 (1912)
Louisville & Nashville R. v. Cook Brewing Co., 223 U.S. 70 (1912)
Atchison Topeka & Santa Fe Ry. Co. v. O'Connor, 223 U.S. 280 (1912)
Oklahoma v. Wells, Fargo & Co., 223 U.S. 298 (1912)
Haskell v. Kansas Natural Gas Co., 224 U.S. 217 (1912)
St. Louis, I.M. & S. Ry. Co. v. Wynne, 224 U.S. 354 (1912)
Bucks Stove Co. v. Vickers, 226 U.S. 205 (1912)
Eubank v. Richmond, 226 U.S. 137 (1912)
Williams v. Talladega, 226 U.S. 404 (1912)
Chicago R.I. & P. Ry. Co. v. Hardwick Elevator Co., 226 U.S. 426 (1913)
    accord: St. Louis, Iron Mt. & S. Ry. v. Edwards, 227 U.S. 265 (1913)
Adams Express Co. v. Croninger, 226 U.S. 491 (1913)
    accord: Chicago, B. & Q. Ry. v. Miller, 226 U.S. 513 (1913)
    accord: Chicago, St. Paul, Minneapolis, & Omaha Ry. Co. v. Latta, 226 U.S. 519
    (1913)
New York Central Railroad Co. v. Hudson County, 227 U.S. 248 (1913)

(Table continues)

Table 2-13 *(Continued)*

Grand Trunk Western Ry. v. South Bend, 227 U.S. 544 (1913)
Crenshaw v. Arkansas, 227 U.S. 389 (1913)
  accord: Rogers v. Arkansas, 227 U.S. 401 (1913)
  accord: Stewart v. Michigan, 232 U.S. 665 (1914)
McDermott v. Wisconsin, 228 U.S. 115 (1913)
Missouri, K. & T. Ry. v. Harriman Bros., 227 U.S. 657 (1914)
Ettor v. Tacoma, 228 U.S. 148 (1913)
St. Louis, S.F. & T. Ry. Co. v. Seale, U.S. 156 (1913)
Chicago, B. & Q. R. v. Hall, 229 U.S. 511 (1913)
Owensboro v. Cumberland Telephone Co., 230 U.S. 58 (1913)
Boise Water Co. v. Boise City, 230 U.S. 84 (1913)
Old Colony Trust Co. v. Omaha, 230 U.S. 100 (1913)
Missouri Pacific Ry. Co. v. Tucker, 230 U.S. 340 (1913)
Chicago, Minneapolis & St. Paul Ry. Co. v. Polt, 232 U.S. 165 (1914)
  accord: Chicago, M. & St. P. Ry. Co. v. Kennedy, 232 U.S. 626 (1914)
Harrison v. St. Louis, S.F. & T.R. Co., 232 U.S. 318 (1914)
Foote v. Maryland, 232 U.S. 495 (1914)
Farmers Bank v. Minnesota, 232 U.S. 516 (1914)
Russell v. Sebastian, 233 U.S. 195 (1914)
Singer Sewing Machine Co. v. Brickell, 233 U.S. 304 (1914)
Tennessee Coal Co. v. George, 233 U.S. 354 (1914)
Carondelet Canal Co. v. Louisiana, 233 U.S. 362 (1914)
Smith v. Texas, 233 U.S. 630 (1914)
Erie R.R. Co. v. New York, 233 U.S. 671 (1914)
International Harvester Co. v. Kentucky, 234 U.S. 216 (1914)
  accord: International Harvester v. Kentucky, 234 U.S. 579 (1914)
  accord: Collins v. Kentucky, 234 U.S. 634 (1914)
  accord: American Machine Co. v. Kentucky, 236 U.S. 660 (1915)
Missouri Pacific Ry. Co. v. Larabee, 234 U.S. 459 (1914)
Western Union Telegraph Co. v. Brown, 234 U.S. 542 (1914)
United States v. Reynolds, 235 U.S. 133 (1914)
McCabe v. Atchison, Topeka & Santa Fe Ry. Co., 235 U.S. 151 (1914)
Sioux Remedy Co. v. Cope, 235 U.S. 197 (1914)
Choctaw & Gulf R.R. v. Harrison, 235 U.S. 292 (1914)
Adams Express Co. v. New York, 232 U.S. 12 (1914)
U.S. Express Co. v. New York, 232 U.S. 35 (1914)
Sault Ste. Marie v. International Transit Co., 234 U.S. 333 (1914)
South Covington Ry. v. Covington, 235 U.S. 537 (1915)
Coppage v. Kansas, 236 U.S. 1 (1915)
Heyman v. Hays, 236 U.S. 178 (1915)
  accord: Southern Operating Co. v. Hayes, 236 U.S. 188 (1915)
Globe Bank v. Martin, 236 U.S. 288 (1915)
Southern Ry. Co. v. R.R. Comm., 236 U.S. 439 (1915)
Kirmeyer v. Kansas, 236 U.S. 568 (1915)
Northern Pac. Ry. v. North Dakota ex rel. McCue, 236 U.S. 585 (1915)
Norfolk & West Ry. v. Conley, 236 U.S. 605 (1915)

Table 2-13 *(Continued)*

Wright v. Central of Georgia Ry., 236 U.S. 674 (1915)
  accord: Wright v. Louisville & Nashville R., 236 U.S. 687 (1915)
Davis v. Virginia, 236 U.S. 697 (1915)
Chicago B. & Q. Ry. v. Wisconsin R.R. Com., 237 U.S. 220 (1915)
Coe v. Armour Fertilizer Works, 237 U.S. 413 (1915)
Charleston & W.C. Ry. Co. v. Varnville Co., 237 U.S. 597 (1915)
Atchison, Topeka & Santa Fe Ry. Co. v. Vosburg, 238 U.S. 56 (1915)
Rossi v. Pennsylvania, 238 U.S. 62 (1915)
Guinn v. United States, 238 U.S. 347 (1915)
  accord: Mayers v. Anderson, 238 U.S. 368 (1915)
Southwestern Tel. Co. v. Danaher, 238 U.S. 482 (1915)
Chicago, Minneapolis & St. Paul R. v. Wisconsin, 238 U.S. 491 (1915)
Traux v. Raich, 239 U.S. 33 (1915)
Provident Savings Assn. v. Kentucky, 239 U.S. 103 (1915)
Gast Realty Co. v. Schneider Granite Co., 240 U.S. 55 (1916)
Indian Oil Co. v. Oklahoma, 240 U.S. 522 (1916)
Rosenberger v. Pacific Express Co., 241 U.S. 48 (1916)
McFarland v. American Sugar Co., 241 U.S. 79 (1916)
Wisconsin v. Philadelphia & Reading Coal Co., 241 U.S. 329 (1916)
Detroit United Ry. v. Michigan, 242 U.S. 238 (1916)
Buchanan v. Warley, 245 U.S. 60 (1917)
  accord: Harmon v. Tyler, 273 U.S. 668 (1927)
  accord: City of Richmond v. Deans, 281 U.S. 704 (1930)
Rowland v. Boyle, 244 U.S. 106 (1917)
New York Central R. Co. v. Winfield, 244 U.S. 147 (1917)
  accord: Erie R.R. Co. v. Winfield, 244 U.S. 170 (1917)
Southern Pacific Co. v. Jensen, 244 U.S. 205 (1917)
  accord: Clyde S.S. Co. v. Walker, 244 U.S. 255 (1917)
  accord: Steamship Bowdoin Co. v. Indust. Accident Comm. of California, 246
  U.S. 648 (1918)
Seaboard Air Line Ry. v. Blackwell, 244 U.S. 310 (1917)
Western Oil Refg. Co. v. Lipscomb, 244 U.S. 346 (1917)
Adams v. Tanner, 244 U.S. 590 (1917)
American Express Company v. Caldwell, 244 U.S. 617 (1917)
Hendrickson v. Apperson, 245 U.S. 105 (1917)
  accord: Hendrickson v. Creager, 245 U.S. 115 (1917)
Looney v. Crane Co., 245 U.S. 178 (1917)
Crew Levick v. Pennsylvania, 245 U.S. 292 (1917)
International Paper Co. v. Massachusetts, 246 U.S. 135 (1918)
  accord: Locomobile Co. v. Massachusetts, 246 U.S. 146 (1918)
Cheney Brothers Co. v. Massachusetts, 246 U.S. 147 (1918)
New York Life Ins. Co. v. Dodge, 246 U.S. 357 (1918)
Georgia v. Cincinnati So. Ry., 248 U.S. 26 (1918)
Union Pac. R. Co. v. Pub. Service Comm., 248 U.S. 67 (1918)
Northern Ohio Traction & Light Co. v. Ohio ex rel. Pontius, 245 U.S. 574 (1918)

(Table continues)

Table 2-13   *(Continued)*

Denver v. Denver Union Water Co., 246 U.S. 178 (1918)
Covington v. South Covington St. Ry. Co., 246 U.S. 413 (1918)
Detroit United Railway v. Detroit, 248 U.S. 429 (1919)
Los Angeles v. Los Angeles Gas Corp., 251 U.S. 32 (1919)
Flexner v. Farson, 248 U.S. 289 (1919)
Central of Georgia Ry. Co. v. Wright, 248 U.S. 525 (1919)
Union Tank Line Co. v. Wright, 249 U.S. 275 (1919)
Standard Oil Co. v. Graves, 249 U.S. 389 (1919)
Chalker v. Birmingham & N.W. Ry. Co., 249 U.S. 522 (1919)
New Orleans & N.E.R.R. Co. v. Scarlet, 249 U.S. 528 (1919)
   accord: Yazoo & M.V.R.R. Co. v. Mullins, 249 U.S. 531 (1919)
Pennsylvania R. Co. v. Public Service Comm., 250 U.S. 566 (1919)
Postal Tel.-Cable Co. v. Warren-Godwin Co., 251 U.S. 27 (1919)
Western Union Telegraph Co. v. Boegli, 251 U.S. 315 (1920)
Travis v. Yale & Towne Mfg. Co., 252 U.S. 60 (1920)
Oklahoma Operating Co. v. Love, 252 U.S. 331 (1920)
   accord: Oklahoma Gin Co. v. Oklahoma, 252 U.S. 339 (1920)
Askren v. Continental Oil Co., 252 U.S. 444 (1920)
Wallace v. Hines, 253 U.S. 66 (1920)
Hawke v. Smith (No. 1), 253 U.S. 221 (1920)
   accord: Hawke v. Smith (No. 2), 253 U.S. 221 (1920)
Ohio Valley Co. v. Ben Avon Borough, 253 U.S. 287 (1920)
Royster Guano Co. v. Virginia, 253 U.S. 412 (1920)
Johnson v. Maryland, 254 U.S. 51 (1920)
Turner v. Wade, 254 U.S. 64 (1920)
Bank of Minden v. Clement, 256 U.S. 126 (1921)
Bethlehem Motors Co. v. Flynt, 256 U.S. 421 (1921)
Merchant's National Bank v. Richmond, 256 U.S. 635 (1921)
Bowman v. Continental Oil Co., 256 U.S. 642 (1921)
Kansas City So. Ry. v. Road Imp. Dist. No. 6, 256 U.S. 658 (1921)

Taft Court (June 30, 1921-February 12, 1930)

Eureka Pipe Line Co. v. Hallanan, 257 U.S. 265 (1921)
United Fuel Gas Co. v. Hallanan, 257 U.S. 277 (1921)
Dahnke-Walker Co. v. Bondurant, 257 U.S. 282 (1921)
Truax v. Corrigan, 257 U.S. 312 (1921)
Gillespie v. Oklahoma, 257 U.S. 501 (1922)
Terral v. Burke Constr. Co., 257 U.S. 529 (1922)
Lemke v. Farmers Grain Co., 258 U.S. 50 (1922)
   accord: Lemke v. Homer Farmers Elevator Co., 258 U.S. 65 (1922)
Newton v. Consolidated Gas Co., 258 U.S. 165 (1922)
   accord: Newton v. New York Gas Co., 258 U.S. 178 (1922)
   accord: Newton v. Kings County Lighting Co., 258 U.S. 180 (1922)
   accord: Newton v. Brooklyn Union Gas Co., 258 U.S. 604 (1922)
   accord: Newton v. Consolidated Gas Co., 259 U.S. 101 (1922)

Table 2-13   *(Continued)*

Forbes Pioneer Boat Line v. Everglades Drainage Dist., 258 U.S. 338 (1922)
Texas Co. v. Brown, 258 U.S. 466 (1922)
Chicago & N.W. Ry. v. Nye Schneider Fowler Co., 260 U.S. 35 (1922)
St. Louis Compress Co. v. Arkansas, 260 U.S. 346 (1922)
Champlain Co. v. Brattleboro, 260 U.S. 366 (1922)
Pennsylvania Coal Co. v. Mahon, 260 U.S. 393 (1922)
Houston v. Southwestern Tel. Co., 259 U.S. 318 (1922)
Paducah v. Paducah Ry., 261 U.S. 267 (1923)
Columbia R., Gas & Electric Co. v. South Carolina, 261 U.S. 236 (1923)
Federal Land Bank v. Crosland, 261 U.S. 374 (1923)
Phipps v. Cleveland Refg. Co., 261 U.S. 449 (1923)
Thomas v. Kansas City So. Ry., 261 U.S. 481 (1923)
Davis v. Farmers Co-operative Co., 262 U.S. 313 (1923)
First National Bank v. California, 262 U.S. 366 (1923)
Meyer v. Nebraska, 262 U.S. 390 (1923)
Bartels v. Iowa, 262 U.S. 404 (1923)
Bohning v. Ohio, 262 U.S. 404 (1923)
Georgia Ry. Co. v. Decatur, 262 U.S. 432 (1923)
    accord: Georgia Ry. Co. v. College Park, 262 U.S. 441 (1923)
Wolff Packing Co. v. Industrial Court, 262 U.S. 522 (1923)
    accord: Dorchy v. Kansas, 264 U.S. 286 (1924)
    accord: Wolff Packing Co. v. Industrial Court, 267 U.S. 552 (1925)
Kentucky Co. v. Paramount Exch., 262 U.S. 544 (1923)
Pennsylvania v. West Virginia, 262 U.S. 553 (1923)
Bunch v. Cole, 263 U.S. 250 (1923)
Clallam County v. United States, 263 U.S. 341 (1923)
Texas Transp. Co. v. New Orleans, 264 U.S. 150 (1924)
Asakura v. Seattle, 265 U.S. 332 (1924)
Sperry Oil Co. v. Chisholm, 264 U.S. 488 (1924)
Burns Baking Co. v. Bryan, 264 U.S. 504 (1924)
Missouri ex rel. Burnes National Bank v. Duncan, 265 U.S. 17 (1924)
Atchison, Topeka & Santa Fe Ry. Co. v. Wells, 265 U.S. 101 (1924)
Air-Way Corp. v. Day, 266 U.S. 71 (1924)
Aetna Life Ins. Co. v. Dunken, 266 U.S. 389 (1924)
Real Silk Mills v. Portland, 268 U.S. 325 (1925)
Tampa Interocean Steamship Co. v. Louisiana, 266 U.S. 594 (1925)
Ozark Pipe Line v. Monier, 266 U.S. 555 (1925)
Michigan Commission v. Duke, 266 U.S. 570 (1925)
Flanagan v. Federal Coal Co., 267 U.S. 222 (1925)
Buck v. Kuykendall, 267 U.S. 307 (1925)
    accord: Bush Co. v. Maloy, 267 U.S. 317 (1925)
    accord: Allen v. Galveston Truck Line Corp., 289 U.S. 708 (1933)
Missouri Pacific R. Co. v. Stroud, 267 U.S. 404 (1925)
Lancaster v. McCarty, 267 U.S. 427 (1925)
Shafer v. Farmers Grain Co., 268 U.S. 189 (1925)

(Table continues)

Table 2-13 *(Continued)*

Alpha Cement Co. v. Massachusetts, 268 U.S. 203 (1925)
Frick v. Pennsylvania, 268 U.S. 473 (1925)
Pierce v. Society of Sisters, 268 U.S. 510 (1925)
Davis v. Cohen, 268 U.S. 638 (1925)
Lee v. Osceola Imp. Dist., 268 U.S. 643 (1925)
First National Bank v. Anderson, 269 U.S. 341 (1926)
Connally v. General Const. Co., 269 U.S. 385 (1926)
Browning v. Hooper, 269 U.S. 396 (1926)
Rhode Island Trust Co. v. Doughton, 270 U.S. 69 (1926)
Oregon-Washington Co. v. Washington, 270 U.S. 87 (1926)
Schlesinger v. Wisconsin, 270 U.S. 230 (1926)
    accord: Uihlein v. Wisconsin, 273 U.S. 642 (1926)
Weaver v. Palmer Bros. Co., 270 U.S. 402 (1926)
Fidelity & Deposit Co. v. Tafoya, 270 U.S. 426 (1926)
Childers v. Beaver, 270 U.S. 555 (1926)
Appleby v. City of New York, 271 U.S. 365 (1926)
Appleby v. Delaney, 271 U.S. 403 (1926)
Frost Trucking Co. v. Railroad Comm., 271 U.S. 583 (1926)
Jaybird Mining Co. v. Wier, 271 U.S. 609 (1926)
Hughes Bros. Co. v. Minnesota, 272 U.S. 469 (1926)
Hanover Ins. Co. v. Harding, 272 U.S. 494 (1926)
Wachovia Trust Co. v. Doughton, 272 U.S. 567 (1926)
Ottinger v. Consolidated Gas Co., 272 U.S. 576 (1926)
    accord: Ottinger v. Brooklyn Union Co., 272 U.S. 579 (1926)
Napier v. Atlantic Coast Line, 272 U.S. 605 (1926)
Miller v. Milwaukee, 272 U.S. 713 (1927)
DiSanto v. Pennsylvania, 273 U.S. 34 (1927)
Missouri Pacific v. Porter, 273 U.S. 341 (1927)
Tyson & Brother v. Banton, 273 U.S. 418 (1927)
Tumey v. Ohio, 273 U.S. 510 (1927)
Nixon v. Herndon, 273 U.S. 536 (1927)
First National Bank v. Hartford, 273 U.S. 548 (1927)
    accord: Minnesota v. First National Bank, 273 U.S. 561 (1927)
    accord: Commercial National Bank v. Custer County, 275 U.S. 502 (1927)
    accord: Keating v. Public National Bank, 284 U.S. 587 (1932)
Fairmont Co. v. Minnesota, 274 U.S. 1 (1927)
Ohio Pub. Serv. Co. v. Ohio ex rel. Fritz, 274 U.S. 12 (1927)
Southern Ry. Co. v. Kentucky, 274 U.S. 76 (1927)
Road Improvement Dist. v. Missouri Pacific R. Co., 274 U.S. 188 (1927)
Fiske v. Kansas, 274 U.S. 380 (1927)
Cline v. Frink Dairy Co., 274 U.S. 445 (1927)
Power Mfg. Co. v. Saunders, 274 U.S. 490 (1927)
Northwestern Ins. Co. v. Wisconsin, 275 U.S. 136 (1927)
Mayor of Vidalia v. McNeely, 274 U.S. 676 (1927)
Delaware L. & W. R.R. v. Morristown, 276 U.S. 182 (1928)
Sprout v. South Bend, 277 U.S. 163 (1928)

Table 2-13 *(Continued)*

Nectow v. Cambridge, 277 U.S. 183 (1928)
Washington ex rel. Seattle Trust Co. v. Roberge, 278 U.S. 116 (1928)
Wuchter v. Pizzutti, 276 U.S. 13 (1928)
  accord: Consolidated Flour Mills Co. v. Muegge, 278 U.S. 559 (1928)
Missouri ex rel. Robertson v. Miller, 276 U.S. 174 (1928)
Montana National Bank v. Yellowstone County, 276 U.S. 479 (1928)
New Brunswick v. United States, 276 U.S. 547 (1928)
Brooke v. Norfolk, 277 U.S. 27 (1928)
Louisville Gas Co. v. Coleman, 277 U.S. 32 (1928)
Long v. Rockwood, 277 U.S. 142 (1928)
Standard Pipe Line v. Highway Dist., 277 U.S. 160 (1928)
Panhandle Oil Co. v. Missouri ex rel. Knox, 277 U.S. 218 (1928)
  accord: Graysburg Oil Co. v. Texas, 278 U.S. 582 (1929)
Ribnik v. McBride, 277 U.S. 350 (1928)
Quaker City Cab Co. v. Pennsylvania, 277 U.S. 389 (1928)
Foster-Fountain Packing Co. v. Haydel, 278 U.S. 1 (1928)
  accord: Johnson v. Haydel, 278 U.S. 16 (1928)
Hunt v. United States, 278 U.S. 96 (1928)
Louis K. Liggett Co. v. Baldridge, 278 U.S. 105 (1928)
Williams v. Standard Oil Co., 278 U.S. 235 (1929)
International Shoe Co. v. Pinkus, 278 U.S. 261 (1929)
Cudahy Co. v. Hinkle, 278 U.S. 460 (1929)
Frost v. Corporation Commission, 278 U.S. 515 (1929)
Manley v. Georgia, 279 U.S. 1 (1929)
Nielsen v. Johnson, 279 U.S. 47 (1929)
Carson Petroleum Co. v. Vial, 279 U.S. 95 (1929)
London Guarantee & Accident Co. v. Industrial Comm., 279 U.S. 109 (1929)
Helson v. Kentucky, 279 U.S. 245 (1929)
Macallen Co. v. Massachusetts, 279 U.S. 620 (1929)
Western & Atlantic Ry. Co. v. Henderson, 279 U.S. 639 (1929)
Safe Deposit & T. Co. v. Virginia, 280 U.S. 83 (1929)
Farmers Loan Co. v. Minnesota, 280 U.S. 204 (1930)
New Jersey Tel. Co. v. Tax Board, 280 U.S. 338 (1930)
Carpenter v. Shaw, 280 U.S. 363 (1930)

Hughes Court (February 13, 1930-June 11, 1941)

Moore v. Mitchell, 281 U.S. 18 (1930)
Lindgren v. United States, 281 U.S. 38 (1930)
Baizley Iron Works v. Span, 281 U.S. 222 (1930)
  accord: Employers' Liability Assurance Co. v. Cook, 281 U.S. 233 (1930)
Missouri ex rel. Missouri Ins. Co. v. Gehner, 281 U.S. 313 (1930)
Home Ins. Co. v. Dick, 281 U.S. 397 (1930)
Baldwin v. Missouri, 281 U.S. 586 (1930)
Surplus Trading Co. v. Cook, 281 U.S. 647 (1930)

(Table continues)

Table 2-13   *(Continued)*

Beidler v. South Carolina Tax Comm., 282 U.S. 1 (1930)
Chicago, St. Paul, Minneapolis & P. Ry. v. Holmberg, 282 U.S. 162 (1930)
Furst v. Brewster, 282 U.S. 493 (1931)
Coolidge v. Long, 282 U.S. 582 (1931)
Hans Rees' Sons v. North Carolina ex rel. Maxwell, 283 U.S. 123 (1931)
Interstate Transit, Inc. v. Lindsey, 283 U.S. 183 (1931)
Stromberg v. California, 283 U.S. 359 (1931)
Smith v. Cahoon, 283 U.S. 553 (1931)
Near v. Minnesota ex rel. Olsen, 283 U.S. 697 (1931)
Santovincenzo v. Egan, 284 U.S. 30 (1931)
State Tax Comm. v. Interstate Natural Gas Co., 284 U.S. 41 (1931)
Hoeper v. Tax Commission, 284 U.S. 206 (1931)
Van Huffel v. Harkelrode, 284 U.S. 225 (1931)
First National Bank v. Maine, 284 U.S. 312 (1932)
Henkel v. Chicago, St. Paul, Minneapolis & O. Ry. Co., 284 U.S. 444 (1932)
New State Ice Co. v. Liebmann, 285 U.S. 262 (1932)
Coombes v. Getz, 285 U.S. 434 (1932)
Nixon v. Condon, 286 U.S. 73 (1932)
Champlin Rfg. Co. v. Corporation Comm., 286 U.S. 210 (1932)
Anglo-Chilean Corp. v. Alabama, 288 U.S. 218 (1933)
Louis K. Liggett Co. v. Lee, 288 U.S. 517 (1933)
Consolidated Textile Co. v. Gregory, 289 U.S. 85 (1933)
Johnson Oil Co. v. Oklahoma ex rel. Mitchell, 290 U.S. 158 (1933)
Southern Ry. Co. v. Virginia, 290 U.S. 190 (1933)
Morrison v. California, 291 U.S. 82 (1934)
Standard Oil Co. v. California, 291 U.S. 242 (1934)
Murray v. Gerrick & Co., 291 U.S. 315 (1934)
Hartford Accident & Insurance Co. v. Delta Pine Land Co., 292 U.S. 143 (1934)
McKnett v. St. Louis & S. F. Ry. Co., 292 U.S. 230 (1934)
W.B. Worthen Co. v. Thomas, 292 U.S. 426 (1934)
Concordia Ins. Co. v. Illinois, 292 U.S. 535 (1934)
Jennings v. United States Fidelity & Guaranty Co., 294 U.S. 216 (1935)
   accord: Old Company's Lehigh v. Meeker, 294 U.S. 227 (1935)
Cooney v. Mountain States Tel. Co., 294 U.S. 384 (1935)
Baldwin v. G.A.F. Seelig, 294 U.S. 511 (1935)
Stewart Dry Goods Co. v. Lewis, 294 U.S. 550 (1935)
   accord: Valentine v. A. & P. Tea Co., 299 U.S. 32 (1936)
Panhandle Co. v. Highway Comm., 294 U.S. 613 (1935)
Broderick v. Rosner, 294 U.S. 629 (1935)
Worthen Co. v. Kavanaugh, 295 U.S. 56 (1935)
Georgia Ry. & Electric Co. v. Decatur, 295 U.S. 165 (1935)
Senior v. Braden, 295 U.S. 422 (1935)
Schuylkill Trust Co. v. Pennsylvania, 296 U.S. 113 (1935)
Colgate v. Harvey, 296 U.S. 404 (1935)
Oklahoma v. Barnsdall Corp., 296 U.S. 521 (1936)
Treigle v. Acme Homestead Assn., 297 U.S. 189 (1936)

Table 2-13 *(Continued)*

Grosjean v. American Press Co., 297 U.S. 233 (1936)
    accord: Arizona Publishing Co. v. O'Neil, 304 U.S. 543 (1938)
Mayflower Farms v. Ten Eyck, 297 U.S. 266 (1936)
Bingaman v. Golden Eagle Lines, 297 U.S. 626 (1936)
Fisher's Blend Station v. State Tax Comm., 297 U.S. 650 (1936)
International Steel & I. Co. v. National Surety Co., 297 U.S. 657 (1936)
Graves v. Texas Company, 298 U.S. 393 (1936)
Morehead v. New York ex rel. Tipaldo, 298 U.S. 587 (1936)
Binney v. Long, 299 U.S. 280 (1936)
De Jonge v. Oregon, 299 U.S. 353 (1937)
New York ex rel. Rogers v. Graves, 299 U.S. 401 (1937)
Lawrence v. Shaw, 300 U.S. 245 (1937)
Ingles v. Morf, 300 U.S. 290 (1937)
Herndon v. Lowry, 301 U.S. 242 (1937)
Lindsey v. Washington, 301 U.S. 397 (1937)
Hartford Ins. Co. v. Harrison, 301 U.S. 459 (1937)
Puget Sound Co. v. Tax Commission, 302 U.S. 90 (1937)
James v. Dravo Contracting Co., 302 U.S. 134 (1937)
Connecticut General Life Ins. Co. v. Johnson, 303 U.S. 77 (1938)
Indiana ex rel. Anderson v. Brand, 303 U.S. 95 (1938)
Indiana ex rel. Valentine v. Marker, 303 U.S. 628 (1938)
Adams Mfg. Co. v. Storen, 304 U.S. 307 (1938)
Collins v. Yosemite Park Co., 304 U.S. 518 (1938)
Missouri ex rel. Gaines v. Canada, 305 U.S. 337 (1938)
Lovell v. Griffin, 303 U.S. 444 (1938)
Hague v. C.I.O., 307 U.S. 496 (1939)
Schneider v. City of Irvington, 308 U.S. 147 (1939)
Gwin, White & Prince, Inc. v. Henneford, 305 U.S. 434 (1939)
Hale v. Bimco Trading Co., 306 U.S. 375 (1939)
Lanzetta v. New Jersey, 306 U.S. 451 (1939)
Lane v. Wilson, 307 U.S. 268 (1939)
Thornhill v. Alabama, 310 U.S. 88 (1940)
Cantwell v. Connecticut, 310 U.S. 296 (1940)
McCarroll v. Dixie Lines, 309 U.S. 176 (1940)
Best v. Maxwell, 311 U.S. 454 (1940)
McGoldrick v. Gulf Oil Corp., 309 U.S. 414 (1940)
Carlson v. California, 310 U.S. 106 (1940)
Hines v. Davidowitz, 312 U.S. 52 (1941)
Wood v. Lovett, 313 U.S. 362 (1941)

Stone Court (June 12, 1941-June 19, 1946)

Federal Land Bank v. Bismarck Co., 314 U.S. 95 (1941)
Edwards v. California, 314 U.S. 160 (1941)
Taylor v. Georgia, 315 U.S. 25 (1942)

(Table continues)

Table 2-13   *(Continued)*

Cloverleaf Butter Co. v. Patterson, 315 U.S. 148 (1942)
Tulee v. Washington, 315 U.S. 681 (1942)
Skinner v. Oklahoma ex rel. Wilwinson, 316 U.S. 535 (1942)
Pacific Coast Dairy v. Dept. of Agriculture, 318 U.S. 285 (1943)
Jones v. Opelika, 319 U.S. 103 (1943)
Mayo v. United States, 319 U.S. 441 (1943)
Taylor v. Mississippi, 319 U.S. 583 (1943)
Jamison v. Texas, 318 U.S. 413 (1943)
Largent v. Texas, 318 U.S. 418 (1943)
Murdock v. Pennsylvania, 319 U.S. 105 (1943)
Martin v. Struthers, 319 U.S. 141 (1943)
Follett v. McCormick, 321 U.S. 573 (1944)
Pollack v. Williams, 322 U.S. 4 (1944)
United States v. Allegheny County, 322 U.S. 174 (1944)
McLeod v. Dilworth Co., 322 U.S. 327 (1944)
Thomas v. Collins, 323 U.S. 516 (1945)
Hoover & Allison Co. v. Evatt, 324 U.S. 652 (1945)
Hill v. Florida ex rel. Watson, 325 U.S. 538 (1945)
Southern Pacific Co. v. Arizona, 325 U.S. 761 (1945)
Marsh v. Alabama, 326 U.S. 501 (1946)
Tucker v. Texas, 326 U.S. 517 (1946)
Republic Pictures Corp. v. Kappler, 327 U.S. 757 (1946)
First Iowa Hydro-Electric Coop. v. FPC, 328 U.S. 152 (1946)
Morgan v. Virginia, 328 U.S. 373 (1946)

Vinson Court (June 20, 1946-September 29, 1953)

Richfield Oil Corp. v. State Board, 329 U.S. 69 (1946)
Freeman v. Hewit, 329 U.S. 239 (1946)
Nippert v. Richmond, 327 U.S. 416 (1946)
Joseph v. Carter & Weekes Co., 330 U.S. 422 (1947)
Bethlehem Steel Co. v. New York Employment Relations Board, 330 U.S. 767
    (1947)
    accord: Plankington Packing Co. v. WERB, 338 U.S. 953 (1950)
Rice v. Sante Fe Elevator Corp., 331 U.S. 218 (1947)
Order of Travelers v. Wolfe, 331 U.S. 586 (1947)
United States v. California, 332 U.S. 19 (1947)
Sipuel v. Board of Regents, 332 U.S. 631 (1948)
Oyama v. California, 332 U.S. 633 (1948)
Seaboard R. Co. v. Daniel, 333 U.S. 118 (1948)
Winters v. New York, 333 U.S. 507 (1948)
Toomer v. Witsell, 334 U.S. 385 (1948)
Takahaski v. Fish Comm., 334 U.S. 410 (1948)
Greyhound Lines v. Mealey, 334 U.S. 653 (1948)
Saia v. New York, 334 U.S. 558 (1948)
Terminiello v. Chicago, 337 U.S. 1 (1949)

Table 2-13   *(Continued)*

La Crosse Tel. Corp. v. WERB, 336 U.S. 18 (1949)
Hood & Sons v. Du Mond, 336 U.S. 525 (1949)
Schnell v. Davis, 336 U.S. 933 (1949)
Union National Bank v. Lamb, 337 U.S. 38 (1949)
Wheeling Steel Corp. v. Glander, 337 U.S. 562 (1949)
Treichler v. Wisconsin, 338 U.S. 251 (1949)
Wissner v. Wissner, 338 U.S. 655 (1950)
New Jersey Insurance Co. v. Div. of Tax Appeals, 338 U.S. 665 (1950)
Mullane v. Central Hanover Bank & Trust Co., 339 U.S. 306 (1950)
United Automobile Workers v. O'Brien, 339 U.S. 454 (1950)
Sweatt v. Painter, 339 U.S. 629 (1950)
United States v. Louisiana, 339 U.S. 699 (1950)
United States v. Texas, 339 U.S. 707 (1950)
McLaurin v. Oklahoma State Regents, 339 U.S. 637 (1950)
Bus Employees v. WERB, 340 U.S. 383 (1951)
Norton Co. v. Dept. of Revenue, 340 U.S. 534 (1951)
Spector Motor Service v. O'Connor, 340 U.S. 602 (1951)
Hughes v. Fetter, 341 U.S. 609 (1951)
Kunz v. New York, 340 U.S. 290 (1951)
Dean Milk Co. v. Madison, 340 U.S. 349 (1951)
Gelling v. Texas, 343 U.S. 960 (1952)
Carson v. Roane-Anderson Co., 342 U.S. 232 (1952)
    accord: General Electric Co. v. Washington, 347 U.S. 909 (1954)
Standard Oil Co. v. Peck, 342 U.S. 382 (1952)
Memphis Steam Laundry v. Stone, 342 U.S. 389 (1952)
First National Bank v. United Air Lines, 342 U.S. 396 (1952)
Joseph Burstyn, Inc. v. Wilson, 343 U.S. 495 (1952)
Kedroff v. St. Nicholas Cathedral, 344 U.S. 94 (1952)
Wieman v. Updegraff, 344 U.S. 183 (1952)
Fowler v. Rhode Island, 345 U.S. 67 (1953)
Dameron v. Brodhead, 345 U.S. 322 (1953)

Warren Court (September 30, 1953-June 8, 1969)

Kern-Limerick, Inc. v Scurlock, 347 U.S. 110 (1954)
Michigan-Wisconsin Pipe Line Co. v. Calvert, 347 U.S. 157 (1954)
Miller Bros. Co. v. Maryland, 347 U.S. 340 (1954)
Railway Express Agency v. Virginia, 347 U.S. 359 (1954)
Franklin National Bank v. New York, 347 U.S. 373 (1954)
Brown v. Board of Education, 347 U.S. 483 (1954)
Castle v. Hayes Freight Lines, 348 U.S. 61 (1954)
Society for Savings v. Bowers, 349 U.S. 143 (1955)
Pennsylvania v. Nelson, 350 U.S. 497 (1956)
Holmes v. City of Atlanta, 350 U.S. 879 (1955)
Indiana Dept. of Revenue v. Nebeker, 348 U.S. 933 (1955)

(Table continues)

Table 2-13 *(Continued)*

Slochower v. Board of Higher Education, 350 U.S. 551 (1956)
Griffin v. Illinois, 351 U.S. 12 (1956)
Covey v. Town of Somers, 351 U.S. 141 (1956)
Railway Employees' Dept. v. Hansen, 351 U.S. 225 (1956)
Walker v. Hutchinson City, 352 U.S. 112 (1956)
Leslie Miller, Inc. v. Arkansas, 352 U.S. 187 (1956)
Butler v. Michigan, 352 U.S. 380 (1957)
Gayle v. Browder, 352 U.S. 903 (1956)
Guss v. Utah Labor Board, 353 U.S. 1 (1957)
West Point Wholesale Grocery Co. v. Opelika, 354 U.S. 390 (1957)
Morey v. Doud, 354 U.S. 457 (1957)
Lambert v. California, 355 U.S. 225 (1957)
Staub v. Baxley, 355 U.S. 313 (1958)
Public Utility Commission v. United States, 355 U.S. 534 (1958)
Eskridge v. Washington Prison Bd., 357 U.S. 214 (1958)
Chicago v. Atchison, Topeka & Santa Fe R. Co., 357 U.S. 77 (1958)
Speiser v. Randall, 357 U.S. 513 (1958)
First Unitarian Church v. Los Angeles, 357 U.S. 545 (1958)
Teamsters Union v. Oliver, 358 U.S. 283 (1959)
Bibb v. Navajo Freight Lines, Inc., 359 U.S. 520 (1959)
San Diego Unions v. Garmon, 359 U.S. 236 (1959)
    accord: Devries v. Baumgartner's Electric Co., 359 U.S. 498 (1959)
    accord: Superior Court v. Washington ex rel. Yellow Cab, 361 U.S. 373 (1960)
    accord: Bogle v. Jakes Foundry Co., 362 U.S. 401 (1960)
    accord: McMahon v. Milam Manufacturing Company, 368 U.S. 7 (1961)
    accord: Marine Engineers v. Interlake Co., 370 U.S 173 (1962)
    accord: Waxman v. Virginia, 371 U.S. 4 (1962)
    accord: Construction Laborers v. Curry, 371 U.S. 542 (1963)
    accord: Journeymen & Plumbers' Union v. Borden, 373 U.S. 690 (1962)
    accord: Iron Workers v. Perko, 373 U.S. 701 (1963)
State Athletic Comm. v. Dorsey, 359 U.S. 533 (1959)
Kingsley Pictures Corp. v. Regents, 360 U.S. 684 (1959)
Smith v. California, 361 U.S. 147 (1959)
Faubus v. Aaron, 361 U.S. 197 (1959)
Phillips Chemical Co. v. Dumas Independent School District, 361 U.S. 376 (1960)
Rohr Corp. v. San Diego County, 362 U.S. 628 (1960)
Bates v. Little Rock, 361 U.S. 516 (1960)
Talley v. California, 362 U.S. 60 (1960)
Gomillion v. Lightfoot, 364 U.S. 339 (1960)
Boynton v. Virginia, 364 U.S. 454 (1960)
Shelton v. Tucker, 364 U.S. 479 (1960)
Bush v. Orleans School Board, 364 U.S. 500 (1961)
Orleans Parish School Board v. Bush, 365 U.S. 569 (1961)
Ferguson v. Georgia, 365 U.S. 570 (1961)
Louisiana v. N.A.A.C.P. ex rel. Gremillion, 366 U.S. 293 (1961)
United States v. Oregon, 366 U.S. 643 (1961)

Table 2-13   *(Continued)*

United States v. Shimer, 367 U.S. 374 (1961)
Torcaso v. Watkins, 367 U.S. 488 (1961)
Marcus v. Search Warrant, 367 U.S. 717 (1961)
Tugwell v. Bush, 367 U.S. 907 (1961)
Legislature of Louisiana v. United States, 367 U.S. 908 (1961)
Federal Land Bank v. Kiowa County, 368 U.S. 146 (1961)
Cramp v. Board of Public Instruction, 368 U.S. 278 (1961)
United States v. Union Central Life Ins. Co., 368 U.S. 291 (1961)
Campbell v. Hussey, 368 U.S. 297 (1961)
St. Helena Parish School Board v. Hall, 368 U.S. 515 (1962)
Bailey v. Patterson, 369 U.S. 31 (1962)
Turner v. Memphis, 369 U.S. 350 (1962)
Free v. Bland, 369 U.S. 663 (1962)
State Board of Ins. v. Todd Shipyards, 370 U.S. 451 (1962)
Central R. Co. v. Pennsylvania, 370 U.S. 607 (1962)
Robinson v. California, 370 U.S. 660 (1962)
Lassiter v. United States, 371 U.S. 10 (1962)
United States v. Buffalo Savings Bank, 371 U.S. 228 (1963)
Paul v. United States, 371 U.S. 245 (1963)
Schroeder v. New York City, 371 U.S. 208 (1962)
N.A.A.C.P. v. Button, 371 U.S. 415 (1963)
Gideon v. Wainwright, 372 U.S. 335 (1963)
Gray v. Sanders, 372 U.S. 368 (1963)
Lane v. Brown, 372 U.S. 477 (1963)
Michigan National Bank v. Robertson, 372 U.S. 591 (1963)
    accord: Mercantile Nat. Bank v. Langdeau, 371 U.S. 555 (1963)
Halliburton Oil Well Cementing Co. v. Reily, 373 U.S. 64 (1963)
Willner v. Committee on Character & Fitness, 373 U.S. 96 (1963)
Peterson v. Greenville, 373 U.S. 244 (1963)
    accord: Gober v. Birmingham, 373 U.S. 374 (1963)
Lombard v. Louisiana, 373 U.S. 267 (1963)
Wright v. Georgia, 373 U.S. 284 (1963)
Sperry v. Florida ex rel. Florida Bar, 373 U.S. 379 (1963)
Bus Employees v. Missouri, 374 U.S. 74 (1963)
Abington Township School District v. Schempp, 374 U.S. 203 (1963)
Sherbert v. Verner, 374 U.S. 398 (1963)
Polar Ice Cream & Creamery Co. v. Andrews, 375 U.S. 361 (1964)
Anderson v. Martin, 375 U.S. 399 (1964)
Wesberry v. Sanders, 376 U.S. 1 (1964)
    accord: Martin v. Bush, 376 U.S. 222 (1964)
City of New Orleans v. Barthe, 376 U.S. 189 (1964)
Sears, Roebuck & Co. v. Stiffel Co., 376 U.S. 225 (1964)
Hostetter v. Idlewild Bon Voyage Liquor Corp., 377 U.S. 324 (1964)
    accord: Dept. of Alcoholic Beverage Control of Cal. v. Ammex Warehouse Co.,
378 U.S. 124 (1964)

(Table continues)

Table 2-13 *(Continued)*

Dept. of Revenue v. James B. Beam Distilling Co., 377 U.S. 341 (1964)
Baggett v. Bullitt, 377 U.S. 360 (1964)
Chamberlin v. Dade County Board of Public Instruction, 377 U.S. 402 (1964)
Reynolds v. Sims, 377 U.S. 533 (1964)
   accord: WMCA, Inc. v. Lomenzo, 377 U.S. 633 (1964)
   accord: Maryland Committee for Fair Representation v. Tawes, 377 U.S. 656 (1964)
   accord: Davis v. Mann, 377 U.S. 678 (1964)
   accord: Roman v. Sincock, 377 U.S. 695 (1964)
   accord: Lucas v. Forty-Fourth General Assembly of Colorado, 377 U.S. 713 (1964)
   accord: Meyers v. Thigpen, 378 U.S. 554 (1964)
   accord: Williams v. Moss, 378 U.S. 558 (1964)
   accord: Pinney v. Butterworth, 378 U.S. 564 (1964)
   accord: Hill v. Davis, 378 U.S. 565 (1964)
A Quantity of Copies of Books v. Kansas, 378 U.S. 205 (1964)
Tancil v. Woolls; Virginia Board of Elections v. Hamm, 379 U.S. 19 (1964)
Garrison v. Louisiana, 379 U.S. 64 (1964)
McLauglin v. Florida, 379 U.S. 184 (1964)
Stanford v. Texas, 379 U.S. 476 (1965)
Cox v. Louisiana, 379 U.S. 536 (1965)
Freedman v. Maryland, 380 U.S. 51 (1965)
Carrington v. Rash, 380 U.S. 89 (1965)
Louisiana v. United States, 380 U.S. 145 (1965)
Reserve Life Insurance Co. v. Bowers, 380 U.S. 258 (1965)
American Oil Co. v. Neill, 380 U.S. 451 (1965)
Dombrowski v. Pfister, 380 U.S. 479 (1965)
Harman v. Forssenius, 380 U.S. 528 (1965)
Corbett v. Stergios, 381 U.S. 124 (1965)
Jordan v. Silver, 381 U.S. 415 (1965)
Griswold v. Connecticut, 381 U.S. 479 (1965)
Giaccio v. Pennsylvania, 382 U.S. 399 (1966)
Baxstrom v. Herold, 383 U.S. 107 (1966)
Harper v. Virginia Board of Elections, 383 U.S. 663 (1966)
   accord: Texas v. United States, 384 U.S. 155 (1966)
Elfbrandt v. Russell, 384 U.S. 11 (1966)
Mills v. Alabama, 384 U.S. 214 (1966)
Rinaldi v. Yeager, 384 U.S. 305 (1966)
Alton v. Tawes, 384 U.S. 315 (1966)
Carr v. City of Altus, 385 U.S. 35 (1966)
Swann v. Adams, 385 U.S. 440 (1967)
   accord: Kirkpatrick v. Preisler, 385 U.S. 450 (1967)
Short v. Ness Produce Co., 385 U.S. 537 (1967)
Keyishian v. Board of Regents, 385 U.S. 589 (1967)
National Bellas Hess, Inc. v. Dept. of Revenue of Illinois, 386 U.S. 753 (1967)
Holding v. Blankenship, 387 U.S. 94 (1967)

Table 2-13   *(Continued)*

Reitman v. Mulkey, 387 U.S. 369 (1967)
Camara v. Municipal Court, 387 U.S. 523 (1967)
See v. Seattle, 387 U.S. 541 (1967)
Loving v. Virginia, 388 U.S. 1 (1967)
Washington v. Texas, 388 U.S. 14 (1967)
Berger v. New York, 388 U.S. 41 (1967)
Whitehill v. Elkins, 389 U.S. 54 (1967)
Lucas v. Rhodes, 389 U.S. 212 (1967)
Nash v. Florida Industrial Commission, 389 U.S. 235 (1967)
Rockefeller v. Wells, 389 U.S. 421 (1967)
Zschernig v. Miller, 389 U.S. 429 (1968)
Dinis v. Volpe, 389 U.S. 570 (1968)
Louisiana Financial Assistance Comm. v. Poindexter, 389 U.S. 571 (1968)
Kirk v. Gong, 389 U.S. 572 (1968)
James v. Gilmore, 389 U.S. 572 (1968)
Tietel Film Corp. v. Cusack, 390 U.S. 139 (1968)
Lee v. Washington, 390 U.S. 333 (1968)
Avery v. Midland County, 390 U.S. 474 (1968)
Interstate Circuit, Inc. v. Dallas, 390 U.S. 676 (1968)
Scafati v. Greenfield, 390 U.S. 713 (1968)
Levy v. Louisiana, 391 U.S. 68 (1968)
   accord: Glona v. American Guarantee Liability Insurance Co., 391 U.S. 73
   (1968)
Rabeck v. New York, 391 U.S. 462 (1968)
Witherspoon v. Illinois, 391 U.S. 510 (1968)
Louisiana Education Comm. for Needy Children v. Poindexter, 393 U.S. 17
   (1968)
Williams v. Rhodes, 393 U.S. 23 (1968)
Epperson v. Arkansas, 393 U.S. 97 (1968)
WHYY, Inc. v. Glassboro, 393 U.S. 117 (1968)
South Carolina State Board of Education v. Brown, 393 U.S. 222 (1968)
Hunter v. Erickson, 393 U.S. 385 (1969)
Kirkpatrick v. Preisler, 394 U.S. 526 (1969)
   accord: Wells v. Rockefeller, 394 U.S. 542 (1969)
Stanley v. Georgia, 394 U.S. 557 (1969)
Street v. New York, 394 U.S. 576 (1969)
Shapiro v. Thompson, 394 U.S. 618 (1969)
Moore v. Ogilvie, 394 U.S. 814 (1969)
Sniadach v. Family Finance Corp. 395 U.S. 337 (1969)
Brandenburg v. Ohio, 395 U.S. 444 (1969)
Kramer v. Union Free School District, 395 U.S. 621 (1969)
Cipriano v. City of Houma, 395 U.S. 701 (1969)

Burger Court (June 9, 1969-September 16, 1986)

Turner v. Fouche, 396 U.S. 346 (1970)

(Table continues)

Table 2-13 *(Continued)*

Wyman v. Bowens, 397 U.S. 49 (1970)
Hadley v. Junior College District, 397 U.S. 50 (1970)
In re Winship, 397 U.S. 358 (1970)
Rosado v. Wyman, 397 U.S. 397 (1970)
Lewis v. Martin, 397 U.S. 552 (1970)
Baldwin v. New York, 399 U.S. 66 (1970)
Phoenix v. Kolodziejski, 399 U.S. 204 (1970)
Williams v. Illinois, 399 U.S. 235 (1970)
Wisconsin v. Constantineau, 400 U.S. 433 (1971)
Groppi v. Wisconsin, 400 U.S. 505 (1971)
Rockefeller v. Socialist Workers Party, 400 U.S. 806 (1970)
Parish School Board v. Stewart, 400 U.S. 884 (1970)
Bower v. Vaughan, 400 U.S. 884 (1970)
Rafferty v. MacKay, 400 U.S. 954 (1970)
Boddie v. Connecticut, 401 U.S. 371 (1971)
Tate v. Short, 401 U.S. 395 (1971)
North Carolina State Board of Education v. Swann, 402 U.S. 43 (1971)
California Dept. of Human Resources Development v. Java, 402 U.S. 121 (1971)
Bell v. Burson, 402 U.S. 535 (1971)
Coates v. Cincinnati, 402 U.S. 611 (1971)
Perez v. Campbell, 402 U.S. 637 (1971)
Nyquist v. Lee, 402 U.S. 935 (1971)
Whitcomb v. Chavis, 403 U.S. 124 (1971)
Connell v. Higginbotham, 403 U.S. 207 (1971)
Graham v. Richardson, 403 U.S. 365 (1971)
Sailer v. Leger, 403 U.S. 365 (1971)
Lemon v. Kurtzman, 403 U.S. 602 (1971)
  accord: Sanders v. Johnson, 403 U.S. 955 (1971)
Pease v. Hansen, 404 U.S. 70 (1971)
Reed v. Reed, 404 U.S. 71 (1971)
Townsend v. Swank, 404 U.S. 282 (1971)
Dunn v. Rivera, 404 U.S. 1054 (1972)
Wyman v. Lopez, 404 U.S. 1055 (1972)
Lindsey v. Normet, 405 U.S. 56 (1972)
Bullock v. Carter, 405 U.S. 134 (1972)
Papachristou v. Jacksonville, 405 U.S. 156 (1972)
Dunn v. Blumstein, 405 U.S. 330 (1972)
  accord: Caniffe v. Burg, 405 U.S. 1034 (1972)
  accord: Davis v. Kohn, 405 U.S. 1034 (1972)
  accord: Cody v. Andrews, 405 U.S. 1034 (1972)
  accord: Donovan v. Keppel, 405 U.S. 1034 (1972)
  accord: Whitcomb v. Affeldt, 405 U.S. 1034 (1972)
  accord: Amos v. Hadnott, 405 U.S. 1035 (1972)
  accord: Virginia State Board of Elections v. Bufford, 405 U.S. 1035 (1972)
Eisenstadt v. Baird, 405 U.S. 438 (1972)
Gooding v. Wilson, 405 U.S. 518 (1972)

Table 2-13   *(Continued)*

Stanley v. Illinois, 405 U.S. 645 (1972)
Weber v. Aetna Casualty & Surety Co. 406 U.S. 164 (1972)
Wisconsin v. Yoder, 406 U.S. 205 (1972)
Brooks v. Tennessee, 406 U.S. 605 (1972)
Jackson v. Indiana, 406 U.S. 715 (1972)
Fuentes v. Shevin, 406 U.S. 67 (1972)
James v. Strange, 406 U.S. 128 (1972)
United States v. Scotland Neck City Board of Education, 406 U.S. 484 (1972)
State Dept. of Health & Rehab. Services v. Zarate, 407 U.S. 918 (1972)
Police Dept. of Chicago v. Mosley, 408 U.S. 92 (1972)
Furman v. Georgia, 408 U.S. 238 (1972)
Ward v. Village of Monroeville, 409 U.S. 57 (1972)
Evco v. Jones, 409 U.S. 91 (1972)
Philpott v. Essex County Welfare Board, 409 U.S. 413 (1973)
Gomez v. Perez, 409 U.S. 535 (1973)
Georges v. McCellan, 409 U.S. 535 (1973)
Texas Board of Barber Examiners v. Bolton, 409 U.S. 807 (1972)
Essex v. Wolman, 409 U.S. 808 (1972)
Sterrett v. Mothers' and Children's Rights Organization, 409 U.S. 809 (1972)
Cason v. City of Columbia, 409 U.S. 1053 (1972)
Robinson v. Hanrahan, 409 U.S. 38 (1972)
Amos v. Sims, 409 U.S. 942 (1972)
Fugate v. Potomac Electric Power Co., 409 U.S. 942 (1972)
Roe v. Wade, 410 U.S. 113 (1973)
Doe v. Bolton, 410 U.S. 179 (1973)
Mahan v. Howell, 410 U.S. 315 (1973)
Whitcomb v. Communist Party of Indiana, 410 U.S. 976 (1973)
Mescalero Apache Tribe v. Jones, 411 U.S. 145 (1973)
McClanahan v. Arizona State Tax Commission, 411 U.S. 164 (1973)
New Jersey Welfare Rights Organization v. Cahill, 411 U.S. 619 (1973)
City of Burbank v. Lockheed Air Terminal, Inc., 411 U.S. 624 (1973)
Parker v. Levy, 411 U.S. 978 (1973)
Gagnon v. Scarpelli, 411 U.S. 778 (1973)
Vlandis v. Kline, 412 U.S. 441 (1973)
Wardius v. Oregon, 412 U.S. 470 (1973)
White v. Regester, 412 U.S. 755 (1973)
White v. Weiser, 412 U.S. 783 (1973)
Miller v. Gomez, 412 U.S. 914 (1973)
Levitt v. Committee for Public Education & Religious Liberty, 413 U.S. 472 (1973)
Sugarman v. Dougall, 413 U.S. 634 (1973)
Committee for Public Education & Religious Liberty v. Nyquist, 413 U.S. 756 (1973)
Sloan v. Lemon, 413 U.S. 825 (1973)
   accord: Grit v. Wolman, 413 U.S. 902 (1973)
Stevenson v. West, 413 U.S. 902 (1973)

(Table continues)

Table 2-13   *(Continued)*

Nelson v. Miranda, 413 U.S. 902 (1973)
Department of Game v. Puyallup Tribe, 414 U.S. 44 (1973)
Kusper v. Pontikes, 414 U.S. 51 (1973)
Lefkowitz v. Turley, 414 U.S. 70 (1973)
Communist Party of Indiana v. Whitcomb, 414 U.S. 441 (1974)
O'Brien v. Skinner, 414 U.S. 524 (1974)
Texas v. Pruett, 414 U.S. 802 (1973)
Danforth v. Rodgers, 414 U.S. 1035 (1973)
Lewis v. New Orleans, 415 U.S. 130 (1974)
Memorial Hospital v. Maricopa County, 415 U.S. 250 (1974)
Davis v. Alaska, 415 U.S. 308 (1974)
Smith v. Goguen, 415 U.S. 566 (1974)
Lubin v. Panish, 415 U.S. 709 (1974)
Wallace v. Sims, 415 U.S. 902 (1974)
Beasley v. Food Fair, 416 U.S. 653 (1974)
Schwegmann Bros. Giant Super Markets v. Louisiana Milk Comm., 416 U.S. 922
   (1974)
Indiana Real Estate Comm. v. Satoskar, 417 U.S. 938 (1974)
Marburger v. Public Funds for Public Schools, 417 U.S. 961 (1974)
Miami Herald Publishing Co. v. Tornillo, 418 U.S. 241 (1974)
Letter Carriers v. Austin, 418 U.S. 264 (1974)
Spence v. Washington, 418 U.S. 405 (1974)
   accord: Cahn v. Long Island Vietnam Moratorium Committee, 418 U.S. 906
   (1974)
Taylor v. Louisiana, 419 U.S. 522 (1975)
Goss v. Lopez, 419 U.S. 565 (1975)
North Georgia Finishing, Inc. v. Di-Chem, Inc., 419 U.S. 601 (1975)
Franchise Tax Board v. United Americans, 419 U.S. 890 (1974)
Cox Broadcasting Corp. v. Cohn, 420 U.S. 469 (1975)
Austin v. New Hampshire, 420 U.S. 656 (1975)
Stanton v. Stanton, 421 U.S. 7 (1975)
Hill v. Stone, 421 U.S. 289 (1975)
Meek v. Pittenger, 421 U.S. 349 (1975)
Bigelow v. Virginia, 421 U.S. 809 (1975)
Erznoznik v. Jacksonville, 422 U.S. 205 (1975)
Herring v. New York, 422 U.S. 853 (1975)
Turner v. Department of Employment Security, 423 U.S. 44 (1975)
Schwartz v. Vanasco, 423 U.S. 1041 (1976)
Tucker v. Salera, 424 U.S. 959 (1976)
Moe v. Salish & Kootenai Tribes, 425 U.S. 463 (1976)
Hynes v. Mayor & Council of Oradell, 425 U.S. 610 (1976)
Virginia State Board of Pharmacy v. Virginia Citizens Consumer Council, Inc.,
   425 U.S. 748 (1976)
   accord: California State Board of Pharmacy v. Terry, 426 U.S. 913 (1976)
Kleppe v. New Mexico, 425 U.S. 529 (1976)
Bryan v. Itasca County, 426 U.S. 373 (1976)

Table 2-13   *(Continued)*

Planned Parenthood of Central Missouri v. Danforth, 427 U.S. 52 (1976)
    accord: Gerstein v. Coe, 428 U.S. 901 (1976)
Machinists & Aerospace Workers v. WERC, 427 U.S. 132 (1976)
Woodson v. North Carolina, 427 U.S. 280 (1976)
    accord: Roberts v. Louisiana, 427 U.S. 325 (1976)
    accord: Williams v. Oklahoma, 428 U.S. 907 (1976)
Craig v. Boren, 429 U.S. 190 (1976)
Boston Stock Exchange v. State Tax Commission, 429 U.S. 318 (1977)
Sendak v. Arnold, 429 U.S. 968 (1976)
Exon v. McCarthy, 429 U.S. 972 (1976)
Lefkowitz v. C.D.R. Enterprises, 429 U.S. 1031 (1977)
Guste v. Weeks, 429 U.S. 1056 (1977)
Bowen v. Women's Services, 429 U.S. 1067 (1977)
Jones v. Rath Packing Co., 430 U.S. 519 (1977)
Wooley v. Maynard, 430 U.S. 705 (1977)
Trimble v. Gordon, 430 U.S. 762 (1977)
United States Trust Co. v. New Jersey, 431 U.S. 1 (1977)
Linmark Associates v. Willingboro, 431 U.S. 85 (1977)
Chapelle v. Greater Baton Rouge Airport Dist., 431 U.S. 159 (1977)
Douglas v. Seacoast Products, 431 U.S. 265 (1977)
Moore v. East Cleveland, 431 U.S. 494 (1977)
Roberts v. Louisiana, 431 U.S. 633 (1977)
Carey v. Population Services International, 431 U.S. 678 (1977)
Lefkowitz v. Cunningham, 431 U.S. 801 (1977)
Nyquist v. Mauclet, 432 U.S. 1 (1977)
Hunt v. Washington State Apple Advertising Commission, 432 U.S. 333 (1977)
Shaffer v. Heitner, 433 U.S. 186 (1977)
Wolman v. Walter, 433 U.S. 229 (1977)
Dothard v. Rawlinson, 433 U.S. 321 (1977)
Coker v. Georgia, 433 U.S. 584 (1977)
Jernigan v. Lendall, 433 U.S. 901 (1977)
New York v. Cathedral Academy, 434 U.S. 125 (1977)
Carter v. Miller, 434 U.S. 356 (1978)
Zablocki v. Redhail, 434 U.S. 374 (1978)
Maher v. Buckner, 434 U.S. 898 (1977)
Ray v. Atlantic Richfield Co., 435 U.S. 151 (1978)
Ballew v. Georgia, 435 U.S. 223 (1978)
McDaniel v. Paty, 435 U.S. 618 (1978)
First National Bank of Boston v. Bellotti, 435 U.S. 765 (1978)
Landmark Communications v. Virginia, 435 U.S. 839 (1978)
Hicklin v. Orbeck, 437 U.S. 518 (1978)
City of Philadelphia v. New Jersey, 437 U.S. 617 (1978)
Allied Structural Steel Co. v. Spannaus, 438 U.S. 234 (1978)
Lockett v. Ohio, 438 U.S. 586 (1978)
Duren v. Missouri, 439 U.S. 357 (1979)

(Table continues)

Table 2-13 *(Continued)*

Colautti v. Franklin, 439 U.S. 379 (1979)
Hisquierdo v. Hisquierdo, 439 U.S. 572 (1979)
Miller v. Youakim, 440 U.S. 125 (1979)
Illinois State Board of Elections v. Socialist Workers Party, 440 U.S. 173 (1979)
Orr v. Orr, 440 U.S. 268 (1979)
Ashcroft v. Freiman, 440 U.S. 941 (1979)
Quern v. Hernandez, 440 U.S. 951 (1979)
Burch v. Louisiana, 441 U.S. 130 (1979)
Arizona Public Service Co. v. Snead, 441 U.S. 141 (1979)
Hughes v. Oklahoma, 441 U.S. 322 (1979)
Caban v. Mohammed, 441 U.S. 380 (1979)
Japan Line, Ltd. v. Los Angeles County, 441 U.S. 434 (1979)
Torres v. Puerto Rico, 442 U.S. 465 (1979)
Beggans v. Public Funds for Public Schools, 442 U.S. 907 (1979)
Smith v. Daily Mail Publishing Co., 443 U.S. 97 (1979)
Bellotti v. Baird, 443 U.S. 622 (1979)
Village of Schaumberg v. Citizens for a Better Environment, 444 U.S. 620 (1980)
California Retail Liquor Dealers Assn. v. Midcal Aluminum, Inc., 445 U.S. 97
  (1980)
Vance v. Universal Amusement Co., Inc., 445 U.S. 308 (1980)
Vitek v. Jones, 445 U.S. 480 (1980)
Payton v. New York, 445 U.S. 573 (1980)
Ventura County v. Gulf Oil Corp., 445 U.S. 947 (1980)
Wengler v. Druggists Mutual Insurance Co., 446 U.S. 142 (1980)
Lewis v. BT Investment Managers, Inc., 447 U.S. 27 (1980)
Washington v. Confederated Tribes, 447 U.S. 134 (1980)
Carey v. Brown, 447 U.S. 455 (1980)
Beck v. Alabama, 447 U.S. 625 (1980)
White Mountain Apache Tribe v. Bracker, 448 U.S. 136 (1980)
Central Machinery Co. v. Arizona State Tax Comm., 448 U.S. 160 (1980)
Minnesota v. Planned Parenthood, 448 U.S. 901 (1980)
Stone v. Graham, 449 U.S. 39 (1980)
Democratic Party of United States v. Wisconsin, 449 U.S. 107 (1981)
Webb's Fabulous Pharmacies, Inc. v. Beckwith, 449 U.S. 155 (1980)
Kirchberg v. Feenstra, 449 U.S. 455 (1981)
Kassel v. Consolidated Freightways Corp., 449 U.S. 662 (1981)
Edwards v. Service Machine & Shipbuilding Corp., 449 U.S. 913 (1980)
Town of Southampton v. Troyer, 449 U.S. 988 (1980)
Weaver v. Graham, 450 U.S. 24 (1981)
Chicago & North Western Transp. Co. v. Kalo Brick & Tile Co., 450 U.S. 311
  (1981)
Jefferson County v. United States, 450 U.S. 901 (1981)
Alessi v. Raybestos-Manhattan, Inc., 451 U.S. 504 (1981)
Maryland v. Louisiana, 451 U.S. 725 (1981)
Little v. Streater, 452 U.S. 1 (1981)
Schad v. Borough of Mount Ephraim, 452 U.S. 61 (1981)

Table 2-13 *(Continued)*

McCarty v. McCarty, 453 U.S. 210 (1981)
Metromedia, Inc. v. San Diego, 453 U.S. 490 (1981)
Campbell v. John Donnelly & Sons, 453 U.S. 916 (1981)
Citizens Against Rent Control v. Berkeley, 454 U.S. 290 (1981)
Agsalud v. Standard Oil Co., 454 U.S. 801 (1981)
Louisiana Dairy Stabilization Bd. v. Dairy Fresh Corp., 454 U.S. 884 (1981)
Brockett v. Spokane Arcades, 454 U.S. 1022 (1981)
Firestone v. Let's Help Florida, 454 U.S. 1130 (1981)
Santosky v. Kramer, 455 U.S. 745 (1982)
Treen v. Karen B., 455 U.S. 912 (1982)
Brown v. Hartlage, 456 U.S. 45 (1982)
Mills v. Habluetzel, 456 U.S. 91 (1982)
California State Bd. of Equalization v. United States, 456 U.S. 141 (1982)
Larson v. Valente, 456 U.S. 228 (1982)
Greene v. Lindsay, 456 U.S. 444 (1982)
Rusk v. Espinosa, 456 U.S. 951 (1982)
Zobel v. Williams, 457 U.S. 55 (1982)
Blum v. Bacon, 457 U.S. 132 (1982)
Plyler v. Doe, 457 U.S. 202 (1982)
Globe Newspaper Co. v. Superior Court, 457 U.S. 596 (1982)
Edgar v. Mite Corp., 457 U.S. 624 (1982)
Fidelity Federal Savings & Loan Assn. v. De la Cuesta, 458 U.S. 141 (1982)
Loretto v. Teleprompter Manhattan CATV Corp., 458 U.S. 419 (1982)
Washington v. Seattle School Disrict No. 1, 458 U.S. 457 (1982)
Enmund v. Florida, 458 U.S. 782 (1982)
Ramah Navajo School Bd. v. Bureau of Revenue, 458 U.S. 832 (1982)
Sporhase v. Nebraska ex rel. Douglas, 458 U.S. 941 (1982)
Brown v. Socialist Workers '74 Campaign Committee, 459 U.S. 87 (1982)
Larkin v. Grendel's Den, Inc., 459 U.S. 116 (1982)
Memphis Bank & Trust Co. v. Garner, 459 U.S. 392 (1983)
King v. Sanchez, 459 U.S. 801 (1982)
Giacabbe v. Andrews, 459 U.S. 801 (1982)
Busbee v. Georgia, 459 U.S. 1166 (1983)
Minneapolis Star & Tribune Co. v. Minnesota Commissioner of Revenue, 460 U.S. 575 (1983)
Anderson v. Celebrezze, 460 U.S. 780 (1983)
Kolender v. Lawson, 461 U.S. 352 (1983)
Pennsylvania Public Utility Comm'n v. CONRAIL, 461 U.S. 912 (1983)
Pickett v. Brown, 462 U.S. 1 (1983)
Exxon Corp. v. Eagerton, 462 U.S. 176 (1983)
Philco Aviation v. Shacket, 462 U.S. 406 (1983)
Akron v. Akron Center for Reproductive Health, Inc., 462 U.S. 416 (1983)
Planned Parenthood Association v. Ashcroft, 462 U.S. 476 (1983)
Karcher v. Daggett, 462 U.S. 725 (1983)
Mennonite Board of Missions v. Adams, 462 U.S. 791 (1983)

(Table continues)

Table 2-13   *(Continued)*

Shaw v. Delta Airlines, 463 U.S. 85 (1983)
American Bank & Trust Co. v. Dallas County, 463 U.S. 855 (1983)
Arcudi v. Stone & Webster Engineering, 463 U.S. 1220 (1983)
Aloha Airlines v. Director of Taxation, 464 U.S. 7 (1983)
Healy v. United States Brewers Ass'n, 464 U.S. 909 (1983)
Southland Corp. v. Keating, 465 U.S. 1 (1984)
Texas v. KVUE-TV, 465 U.S. 1092 (1984)
Westinghouse Electric Corp. v. Tully, 466 U.S. 388 (1984)
Wallace v. Jaffree, 466 U.S. 924 (1984)
Bernal v. Fainter, 467 U.S. 216 (1984)
Michigan Canners & Freezers Ass'n v. Agricultural Marketing and Bargaining
  Bd., 467 U.S. 461 (1984)
Armco Inc. v. Hardesty, 467 U.S. 638 (1984)
Capital Cities Cable v. Crisp, 467 U.S. 691 (1984)
Brown v. Brandon, 467 U.S. 1223 (1984)
Secretary of State of Maryland v. Joseph H. Munson Co., 467 U.S. 947 (1984)
Bacchus Imports, Ltd. v. Dias, 468 U.S. 263 (1984)
Lawrence County v. Lead-Deadwood School District, 469 U.S. 256 (1985)
Deukmejian v. National Meat Ass'n, 469 U.S. 1100 (1985)
Westhafer v. Worrell Newspapers, 469 U.S. 1200 (1985)
Metropolitan Life Insurance Co. v. Ward, 470 U.S. 869 (1985)
Oklahoma City Board of Education v. National Gay Task Force, 470 U.S. 903
  (1985)
Hunter v. Underwood, 471 U.S. 222 (1985)
Williams v. Vermont, 472 U.S. 14 (1985)
Wallace v. Jaffree, 472 U.S. 38 (1985)
Jensen v. Quaring, 472 U.S. 478 (1985)
Brockett v. Spokane Arcades, 472 U.S. 491 (1985)
Hooper v. Bernalillo County Assessor, 472 U.S. 612 (1985)
Estate of Thornton v. Caldor, Inc., 472 U.S. 703 (1985)
City of Cleburne v. Cleburne Living Center, Inc., 473 U.S. 432 (1985)
Gerace v. Grocery Mfrs. of America, 474 U.S. 801 (1985)
Wisconsin Dep't of Industry v. Gould, Inc., 475 U.S. 282 (1986)
Exxon Corp. v. Hunt, 475 U.S. 355 (1986)
Philadelphia Newspapers, Inc. v. Hepps, 475 U.S. 767 (1986)
Hudnut v. American Booksellers Ass'n, 475 U.S. 1001 (1986)
Brown-Foreman Distillers Corp. v. New York State Liquor Authority, 476 U.S.
  573 (1986)
Thornburgh v. American College of Obstetricians & Gynecologists, 476 U.S. 747
  (1986)
Three Affiliated Tribes v. World Engineering, 476 U.S. 877 (1986)
Attorney General of New York v. Soto-Lopez, 476 U.S. 898 (1986)
Offshore Logistics v. Tallentire, 477 U.S. 207 (1986)
Roberts v. Burlington Industries, 477 U.S. 901 (1986)
Brooks v. Burlington Industries, 477 U.S. 901 (1986)
Thornburg v. Gingles, 478 U.S. 30 (1986)

Table 2-13   *(Continued)*

Rehnquist Court (September 17, 1986-)

Rose v. Arkansas State Police, 479 U.S. 1 (1986)
Tashjian v. Republican Party of Connecticut, 479 U.S. 208 (1986)
324 Liquor Corp. v. Duffy, 479 U.S. 335 (1987)
Babbitt v. Planned Parenthood, 479 U.S. 925 (1986)
California v. Cabazon Band of Mission Indians, 480 U.S. 202 (1987)
Wilkinson v. Jones, 480 U.S. 926 (1987)
Arkansas Writers' Project, Inc. v. Ragland, 481 U.S. 221 (1987)
Miller v. Florida, 482 U.S. 423 (1987)
City of Houston v. Hill, 482 U.S. 451 (1987)
Perry v. Thomas, 482 U.S. 483 (1987)
Booth v. Maryland, 482 U.S. 496 (1987)
Board of Airport Commissioners for the City of Los Angeles v. Jews for Jesus,
  Inc., 482 U.S. 569 (1987)
Edwards v. Aguillard, 482 U.S. 578 (1987)
Sumner v. Shuman, 483 U.S. 66 (1987)
Tyler Pipe Industries, Inc. v. Washington Dept. of Revenue, 483 U.S. 232 (1987)
American Trucking Associations, Inc. v. Scheiner, 483 U.S. 266 (1987)
Hartigan v. Zbaraz, 484 U.S. 171 (1987)
Montana v. Crow Tribe of Indians, 484 U.S. 997 (1988)
Schneidewind v. ANR Pipeline Co., 485 U.S. 293 (1988)
Bennett v. Arkansas, 485 U.S. 395 (1988)
City of Manassas v. United States, 485 U.S. 1017 (1988)
New Energy Company of Indiana v. Limbach, 100 L. Ed. 2d 302 (1988)
Maynard v. Cartwright, 100 L. Ed. 2d 372 (1988)
Meyer v. Grant, 100 L. Ed. 2d 425 (1988)
Clark v. Jeter, 100 L. Ed. 2d 465 (1988)
Shapero v. Kentucky Bar Assn., 100 L. Ed. 2d 475 (1988)
Lakewood v. Plain Dealer Publishing Co., 100 L. Ed. 2d 771 (1988)
Bendix Autolite Corp. v. Midwesco Enterprises, Inc., 100 L. Ed. 2d 896 (1988)
Riley v. National Federation of the Blind, 101 L. Ed. 2d 669 (1988)
Mackey v. Lanier Collection Agency and Service, Inc., 486 U.S. 888 (1988)
Supreme Court of Virginia v. Friedman, 487 U.S. 59 (1988)
Felder v. Casey, 487 U.S. 131 (1988)
Boyle v. United Technologies Corp., 487 U.S. 500 (1988)
Thompson v. Oklahoma, 487 U.S. 815 (1988)
Coy v. Iowa, 487 U.S. 1012 (1988)
Richmond v. J. A. Croson Co., 102 L. Ed. 2d 854 (1989)
Texas Monthly, Inc. v. Bullock, 103 L. Ed. 2d 1 (1989)
Bonito Boats, Inc. v. Thunder Craft Boats, Inc., 103 L. Ed. 2d 118 (1989)
Eu v. San Francisco County Democratic Central Committee, 103 L. Ed. 2d 271
  (1989)
Board of Estimate of New York City v. Morris, 103 L. Ed. 2d 717 (1989)
Davis v. Michigan Dept. of Treasury, 103 L. Ed. 2d 891 (1989)

(Table continues)

Table 2-13   *(Continued)*

Quinn v. Millsap, 105 L. Ed. 2d 74 (1989)
Healy v. Beer Institute, Inc., 105 L. Ed. 2d 275 (1989)
Texas v. Johnson, 105 L. Ed. 2d 342 (1989)
Allegheny Pittsburgh Coal Co. v. Webster County Comm'n., 488 U.S. 336 (1989)
Barnard v. Thorstenn, 109 S. Ct. 1294 (1989)
The Florida Star v. B.J.F., 109 S. Ct. 2603 (1989)
FW/PBS, Inc. v. Dallas, 107 L. Ed. 2d 603 (1990)
McKoy v. North Carolina, 108 L. Ed. 2d 369 (1990)
Butterworth v. Smith, 108 L. Ed. 2d 572 (1990)
Peel v. Attorney Registration & Disciplinary Commission, 110 L. Ed. 2d 83 (1990)
Hodgson v. Minnesota, 111 L. Ed. 2d 344 (1990)

Note: Determination of which decisions have declared state and local legislation unconstitutional is not a clear-cut matter. For example, the source we have used to identify these
cases invokes criteria different from those of the Supreme Court database, which lists these
decisions since the onset of the Warren Court in 1953. For cases appearing here, the
Library of Congress source includes "decisions in which provisions of state constitutions,
statutes, and municipal ordinances were found to be unconstitutional either in substance
or as enforced, including provisions which conflicted with federal legislative acts and
were therefore void because of the supremacy clause" (p. 1623). The database, by contrast,
lists only decisions in which the Court clearly indicates that it has voided a legislative
enactment of some level of government. For purposes of longitudinal consistency, we
report only those cases listed in the Library of Congress source.

Source: U.S. Library of Congress, Congressional Research Service, *The Constitution of the
United States of America, Analysis and Interpretation: Annotations of Cases Decided by the Supreme
Court of the United States* (Washington, D.C.: Government Printing Office, 1973), 1623-1785
and supplements.

Table 2-14 Supreme Court Decisions Overruled by Subsequent Decisions, 1789-1990

Court	Overruling case	Overruled case
Marshall Court (January 27, 1801-March 14, 1836)	Hudson v. Guestier, 6 Cranch 281 (1810)	Rose v. Himley, 4 Cranch 241 (1808)
Taney Court (March 15, 1836-December 5, 1864)	The Genesse Chief, 12 How. 443 (1851)	The Thomas Jefferson, 10 Wheat. 428 (1825) The Orieans v. Phoebus, 11 Pet. 175 (1837)
	Gazzam v. Phillip's Lessee, 20 How. 372 (1858)	Brown's Lessee v. Clements, 3 How. 650 (1845)
Chase Court (December 6, 1864-January 20, 1874)	Mason v. Eldred, 6 Wall. 231 (1868)	Sheehy v. Mandeville, 6 Cranch 253 (1810)
Waite Court (January 21, 1874-July 19, 1888)	Hornbuckle v. Toombs, 18 Wall. 648 (1874)	Noonan v. Lee, 2 Black 499 (1863) Orchard v. Hughes, 1 Wall. 73 (1864) Dunphy v. Kleinsmith, 11 Wall. 610 (1871)
	Union Pac. R. Co. v. McShane, 22 Wall. 444 (1874)	Kansas Pac. R. Co. v. Prescott, 16 Wall. 803 (1873) (in part)
	County of Cass v. Johnston, 95 U.S. 360 (1877)	Harshman v. Bates County, 92 U.S. 569 (1875)
	Fairfield v. County of Gallatin, 100 U.S. 47 (1879)	Town of Concord v. Savings-Bank, 92 U.S. 625 (1875)

(Table continues)

Table 2-14 *(Continued)*

Court	Overruling case	Overruled case
	Tilghman v. Proctor, 102 U.S. 707 (1880)	Mitchell v. Tilghman, 19 Wall. 287 (1873)
	United States v. Phelps, 107 U.S. 320 (1883)	Shelton v. The Collector, 5 Wall. 113 (1867)
	Kountze v. Omaha Hotel Co., 107 U.S. 378 (1883)	Stafford v. The Union Bank of Louisiana, 16 How. 135 (1853)
	Morgan v. United States, 113 U.S. 476 (1885)	Texas v. White, 7 Wall. 700 (1869)
	Leloup v. Port of Mobile, 127 U.S. 640 (1888)	Osbourne v. Mobile, 16 Wall. 479 (1873)
Fuller Court (July 20, 1888–December 11, 1910)	Leisy v. Hardin, 135 U.S. 100, 118 (1890)	Peirce v. New Hampshire, 5 How. 504 (1847)
	Brenham v. German-American Bank, 144 U.S. 173 (1892)	Rogers v. Burlington, 3 Wall. 654 (1866) Mitchell v. Burlington, 4 Wall. 270 (1867)
	Roberts v. Lewis, 153 U.S. 367 (1894)	Giles v. Little, 104 U.S. 291 (1881)
White Court (December 12, 1910–June 29, 1921)	Garland v. Washington, 232 U.S. 642 (1914)	Crain v. United States, 162 U.S. 625 (1896)
	United States v. Nice, 241 U.S. 591 (1916)	Matter of Heff, 197 U.S. 488 (1905)
	Rosen v. United States, 245 U.S. 467 (1918)	United States v. Reid, 12 How. 361 (1851)

130

Taft Court (June 30, 1921- February 12, 1930)	Boston Store v. American Graphophone Co., 246 U.S. 8 (1918) and Motion Picture Co. v. Universal Film Co., 243 U.S. 502 (1917)	Henry v. Dick Co., 224 U.S. 1 (1912)
	Terrel v. Burke Constr. Co., 257 U.S. 529 (1922)	Doyle v. Continental Ins. Co., 94 U.S. 535 (1877) Security Mutual Life Ins. Co. v. Prewitt, 202 U.S. 246 (1906)
	Lee v. Chesapeake & Ohio Ry., 260 U.S. 653 (1923)	Ex Parte Wisner, 203 U.S. 449 (1906) In re Moore, 209 U.S. 490 (1908) (qualifying)
	Alpha Cement Co. v. Massachusetts, 268 U.S. 203 (1925)	Baltic Mining Co. v. Massachusetts, 231 U.S. 68 (1913)
	Gleason v. Seaboard Ry., 278 U.S. 349 (1929)	Friedlander v. Texas & Railway Co., 130 U.S. 416 (1889)
Hughes Court (February 13, 1930- June 11, 1941)	Farmers Loan Co. v. Minnesota, 280 U.S. 204 (1930)	Blackstone v. Miller, 188 U.S. 189 (1903)
	East Ohio Gas Co. v. Tax Comm., 283 U.S. 465 (1931)	Penna. Gas Co. v. Pub. Service Comm., 292 U.S. 23 (1920)
	Chicago & E.I.R. Co. v. Commission, 284 U.S. 296 (1932)	Erie R.R. Co. v. Collins, 253 U.S. 77 (1920) Erie R.R. Co. v. Szary, 253 U.S. 86 (1920)
	Funk v. United States, 290 U.S. 371 (1933); see also Hawkins v. United States, 358 U.S. 74 (1958)	Stein v. Bowman, 13 Pet. 209 (1839) (in part) Hendrix v. United States, 219 U.S. 79 (1911) Jin Fuey Moy v. United States, 254 U.S. 189 (1920)

(Table continues)

Table 2-14 *(Continued)*

Court	Overruling case	Overruled case
	West Coast Hotel Co. v. Parrish, 300 U.S. 379 (1937)	Adkins v. Children's Hospital, 261 U.S. 525 (1923)
	Helvering v. Producers Corp., 303 U.S. 376 (1938)	Gillespie v. Oklahoma, 257 U.S. 501 (1922) Burnet v. Coronado Oil & Gas Co., 285 U.S. 393 (1932)
	Erie R. Co. v. Tompkins, 304 U.S. 64 (1938).	Swift v. Tyson, 16 Pet. 1 (1842)
	Graves v. N.Y. ex rel. O'Keefe, 306 U.S. 466 (1939)	Collector v. Day, 11 Wall. 113 (1871) N.Y. ex rel. Rogers v. Graves, 299 U.S. 401 (1937)
	O'Malley v. Woodrough, 307 U.S. 277 (1939)	Miles v. Graham, 268 U.S. 501 (1925)
	Madden v. Kentucky, 309 U.S. 83 (1940)	Colgate v. Harvey, 296 U.S. 404 (1935)
	Helvering v. Hallock, 309 U.S. 106 (1940)	Helvering v. St. Louis Trust Co., 296 U.S. 48 (1935) Becker v. St. Louis Trust Co., 296 U.S. 48 (1935)
	United States v. Darby, 312 U.S. 100 (1941)	Hammer v. Dagenhart, 247 U.S. 251 (1918) Carter v. Carter Coal Co., 298 U.S. 238 (1936) (limited)
	United States v. Chicago, M. St. P. & P.R. Co., 312 U.S. 592 (1941)	United States v. Lynah, 188 U.S. 445 (1903) (in part)
	Nye v. United States, 313 U.S. 33 (1941)	Toledo Newspaper v. Heyward, 250 U.S. 633 (1918)
	California v. Thompson, 313 U.S. 109 (1941)	Di Santo v. Pennsylvania, 273 U.S. 34 (1927)
	Olson v. Nebraska, 313 U.S. 236 (1941)	Ribnik v. McBride, 277 U.S. 350 (1928)

Court	Case (overruling)	Case(s) overruled
Stone Court (June 12, 1941–June 19, 1946)	Alabama v. King & Boozer, 314 U.S. 1 (1941)	Panhandle Oil Co. v. Knox, 277 U.S. 218 (1928) Graves v. Texas Co., 298 U.S. 393 (1936)
	State Tax Comm. v. Aldrich, 316 U.S. 174 (1942)	First National Bank v. Maine, 284 U.S. 312 (1932)
	Williams v. North Carolina, 317 U.S. 287 (1942)	Haddock v. Haddock, 201 U.S. 562 (1906)
	Brady v. Roosevelt S.S. Co., 317 U.S. 575 (1943)	Johnson v. Fleet Corp., 280 U.S. 320 (1930)
	Jones v. Opelika, 319 U.S. 103 (1943) (reargument)	Jones v. Opelika, 316 U.S. 584 (1942)
	Board of Education v. Barnette, 319 U.S. 624 (1943)	Minersville District v. Gobitis, 310 U.S. 586 (1940)
	Smith v. Allwright, 321 U.S. 649 (1944)	Grovey v. Townsend, 295 U.S. 45 (1935)
	Girouard v. United States, 328 U.S. 61 (1946)	United States v. MacIntosh, 283 U.S. 605 (1931) United States v. Bland, 283 U.S. 636 (1931)
Vinson Court (June 20, 1946–September 29, 1953)	Angel v. Buelington, 330 U.S. 183 (1947)	David Lupton's Sons v. Auto Club of Am., 225 U.S. 489 (1912) (rendered obsolete by previous law)
	Comr. v. Estate of Church, 335 U.S. 632 (1949)	May v. Heiner, 281 U.S. 238 (1930)
	Oklahoma Tax Comm. v. Texas Co., 336 U.S. 342 (1949)	Choctaw & Gulf R.R. v. Harrison, 235 U.S. 292 (1914) Indian Oil Co. v. Oklahoma, 240 U.S. 522 (1916) Howard v. Gipsy Oil Co., 247 U.S. 503 (1918) Large Oil Co. v. Howard, 248 U.S. 549 (1919) Oklahoma v. Barnsdall Corp., 296 U.S. 521 (1936)

(Table continues)

Table 2-14 *(Continued)*

Court	Overruling case	Overruled case
	Cosmopolitan Co. v. McAllister, 337 U.S. 783 (1949)	Hust v. Moore-McCormack Lines, 328 U.S. 707 (1946)
	United States v. Rabinowitz, 339 U.S. 56 (1950)	Trupiano v. United States, 334 U.S. 699 (1948) McDonald v. United States, 335 U.S. 451 (1948)
	Joseph Burstyn, Inc. v. Wilson, 343 U.S. 495 (1952)	Mutual Film Corp. v. Ohio Indus'l Comm., 236 U.S. 230 (1915)
Warren Court (September 30, 1953-June 8, 1969)	Brown v. Board of Education, 347 U.S. 483 (1954)	Cumming v. Board of Education, 175 U.S. 528 (1899) Gong Lum v. Rice, 275 U.S. 78 (1927)
	Reid v. Covert, 354 U.S. 1 (1957)	Kinsella v. Krueger, 351 U.S. 470 (1956) Reid v. Covert, 351 U.S. 487 (1956)
	Vanderbilt v. Vanderbilt, 354 U.S. 416 (1957); see also Armstrong v. Armstrong, 350 U.S. 568 (1956)	Thompson v. Thompson, 226 U.S. 551 (1913)
	Ladner v. United States, 358 U.S. 169 (1958) (on rehearing)	Ladner v. United States, 355 U.S. 282 (1958)
	United States v. Raines, 362 U.S. 17 (1960)	United States v. Reese, 92 U.S. 214 (1876)
	Elkins v. United States, 364 U.S. 206 (1960) Rios v. United States, 364 U.S. 253 (1960)	Weeks v. United States, 232 U.S. 383 (1914) (in part) Center v. United States, 267 U.S. 575 (1925) Byars v. United States, 273 U.S. 28 (1927) (in part) Feldman v. United States, 322 U.S. 487 (1944) (in part)

James v. United States, 366 U.S. 213 (1961)	CIR v. Wilcox, 327 U.S. 404 (1946)
Mapp v. Ohio, 367 U.S. 643 (1961); see also Ker v. California, 374 U.S. 23 (1963)	Wolf v. Colorado, 338 U.S. 25 (1949) (in part) Irvine v. California, 347 U.S. 128 (1954)
Baker v. Carr, 369 U.S. 186 (1962)	Colegrove v. Green, 328 U.S. 549 (1946) (in part)
Wesberry v. Sanders, 376 U.S. 1 (1964)	Colegrove v. Green, 328 U.S. 549 (1946)
Smith v. Evening News Association, 371 U.S. 195 (1962); see also Truck Drivers Union v. Riss & Co., 372 U.S. 517 (1923)	Westinghouse Employees v. Westinghouse Corp., 348 U.S. 437 (1955) (in part)
Construction & General Laborers' Union v. Curry, 371 U.S. 542 (1962)	Building Union v. Ledbetter Co., 344 U.S. 178 (1952) (in part)
Gideon v. Wainwright, 372 U.S. 335 (1963)	Betts v. Brady, 316 U.S. 455 (1942)
Gray v. Sanders, 372 U.S. 368 (1963)	Cook v. Fortson, 329 U.S. 675 (1946) South v. Peters, 339 U.S. 276 (1950) Cox v. Peters, 342 U.S. 936 (1952) Hartsfield v. Sloan, 357 U.S. 916 (1958)
Fay v. Noia, 372 U.S. 391 (1963)	Darr v. Burford, 339 U.S. 200 (1950) (in part)
Ferguson v. Skrupa, 372 U.S. 726 (1963)	Adams v. Tanner, 244 U.S. 590 (1917)
Malloy v. Hogan, 378 U.S. 1 (1964)	Twining v. New Jersey, 211 U.S. 78 (1908) Adamson v. California, 332 U.S. 46 (1947)

(Table continues)

Table 2-14 (Continued)

Court	Overruling case	Overruled case
	Murphy v. Waterfront Commission, 378 U.S. 52 (1964)	Jack v. Kansas, 199 U.S. 372 (190)
		United States v. Murdock, 284 U.S. 141 (1931)
		Feldman v. United States, 332 U.S. 487 (1944)
		Knapp v. Schweitzer, 357 U.S. 371 (1958)
		Mills v. Louisiana, 360 U.S. 230 (1959)
	Jackson v. Denno, 378 U.S. 368 (1964)	Stein v. New York, 346 U.S. 156 (1953)
	Pointer v. Texas, 380 U.S. 400 (1965)	West v. Louisiana, 194 U.S. 258 (1904)
	Swift & Co. v. Wickham, 382 U.S. 111 (1965)	Kesler v. Dep't of Public Safety, 369 U.S. 153 (1962)
	Harris v. United States, 382 U.S. 162 (1965)	Brown v. United States, 359 U.S. 41 (1959)
	Harper v. Virginia Board of Elections, 383 U.S. 663 (1966)	Breedlove v. Suttles, 302 U.S. 277 (1937)
		Butler v. Thompson, 341 U.S. 937 (1937)
	Spevack v. Klein, 385 U.S. 511 (1967)	Cohen v. Hurley, 366 U.S. 177 (1961)
	Afroyim v. Rusk, 387 U.S. 253 (1967)	Perez v. Brownell, 356 U.S. 44 (1958)
	Warden v. Hayden, 387 U.S. 294 (1967)	Gouled v. United States, 255 U.S. 298 (1921)
	Camara v. Municipal Court, 387 U.S. 523 (1967)	Frank v. Maryland, 359 U.S. 360 (1959)
	Katz v. United States, 389 U.S. 347 (1967)	Olmstead v. United States, 277 U.S. 438 (1928)

Peyton v. Rowe, 391 U.S. 54 (1968)

Bruton v. United States, 391 U.S. 123 (1968)

Carafas v. LaVallee, 391 U.S. 234 (1968)

Lee v. Florida, 392 U.S. 378 (1968)

Jones v. Alfred H. Mayer Co., 392 U.S. 409 (1968)

Moore v. Ogilvie, 394 U.S. 814 (1969)

Brandenburg v. Ohio, 395 U.S. 444 (1969)

Chimel v. California, 395 U.S. 752 (1969)

Benton v. Maryland, 395 U.S. 784 (1969)

Ashe v. Swenson, 397 U.S. 436 (1970)

Burger Court
(June 9, 1969-
September 16, 1986)

Boys Markets v. Retail Clerks, 398 U.S. 235 (1970)

Prince v. Georgia, 398 U.S. 323, (1970)

McNally v. Hill, 293 U.S. 131 (1934)

Delli Paoli v. United States, 352 U.S. 232 (1957)

Parker v. Ellis, 362 U.S. 574 (1960)

Schwartz v. Texas, 344 U.S. 199 (1952)

Hodges v. United States, 203 U.S. 1 (1906)

MacDougall v. Green, 335 U.S. 281 (1958)

Whitney v. California, 274 U.S. 357 (1927)

Harris v. United States, 331 U.S. 145 (1947)
United States v. Rabinowitz, 339 U.S. 56 (1950)

Palko v. Connecticut, 302 U.S. 319 (1937)

Hoag v. New Jersey, 356 U.S. 464 (1958)

Sinclair v. Refining Co. v. Atkinson, 370 U.S. 195 (1962)

Brantley v. Georgia, 217 U.S. 284 (1910)

(Table continues)

Table 2-14 (*Continued*)

Court	Overruling case	Overruled case
	Moragne v. States Marine Lines, Inc., 398 U.S. 375 (1970)	The Harrisburg, 119 U.S. 199 (1886)
	Williams v. Florida, 399 U.S. 78 (1970)	Thompson v. Utah, 170 U.S. 343 (1898) (in part) Rassmussen v. United States, 197 U.S. 516 (1905) (in part)
	Blonder-Tongue Laboratories, Inc. v. University of Illinois Foundation, 402 U.S. 313 (1971)	Triplett v. Lowell, 297 U.S. 638 (1936)
	Perez v. Campbell, 402 U.S. 637 (1971)	Kesler v. Dep't of Public Safety, 369 U.S. 153 (1962)
	Griffin v. Breckenridge, 403 U.S. 88 (1971)	Collins v. Hardyman, 341 U.S. 651 (1951) (in part)
	Dunn v. Blumstein, 405 U.S. 330 (1972)	Pope v. Williams, 193 U.S. 621 (1904)
	Andrews v. Louisville & Nashville R. Co., 406 U.S. 320 (1972)	Moore v. Ill. Cent. R. Co., 312 U.S. 630 (1941)
	Lehnhausen v. Lake Shore Auto Parts Co., 410 U.S. 356 (1973)	Quaker City Cab v. Pennsylvania, 277 U.S. 389 (1928)
	Braden v. 30th Judicial Circuit Court, 410 U.S. 484 (1973)	Ahrens v. Clark, 335 U.S. 188 (1948)
	Miller v. California, 413 U.S. 15 (1973)	A Book Named "John Cleland's Memoirs of a Woman of Pleasure" v. Attorney General, 383 U.S. 413 (1966)

North Dakota Pharmacy Board v. Snyder's Drug Stores, 414 U.S. 156 (1973)	Liggett Co. v. Baldridge, 278 U.S. 105 (1929)
Edelman v. Jordan, 415 U.S. 651 (1974)	Shapiro v. Thompson, 394 U.S. 618 (1969) (in part) State Dep't of Health & Rehabilitation Services v. Zarate, 407 U.S. 918 (1972) Sterett v. Mothers' & Children's Rights Organization, 409 U.S. 67 (1972)
Mitchell v. W.T. Grant Co., 416 U.S. 600 (1974)	Fuentes v. Shevin, 407 U.S. 67 (1972)
Taylor v. Louisiana, 419 U.S. 522 (1975)	Hoyt v. Florida, 368 U.S. 57 (1971) (in effect)
United States v. Reliable Transfer Co., 421 U.S. 397 (1975)	Schooner Catherine v. Dickinson, 17 How. 170 (1854)
Michelin Tire Co. v. Wages, 423 U.S. 276 (1976)	Low v. Austin, 13 Wall. 29 (1871)
Dove v. United States, 423 U.S. 325 (1976)	Durham v. United States, 401 U.S. 481 (1971)
Hudgens v. National Labor Relations Board, 424 U.S. 507 (1976)	Amalgamated Food Employees Union v. Logan Valley Plaza, 391 U.S. 308 (1968)
Virginia Board of Pharmacy v. Virginia Citizens Consumer Council, 425 U.S. 748 (1976)	Valentine v. Chrestensen, 316 U.S. 52 (1942)
National League of Cities v. Usery, 426 U.S. 833 (1976)	Maryland v. Wirtz, 392 U.S. 183 (1968)
Machinists & Aerospace Workers v. Wisconsin Employment Relations Commission, 427 U.S. 132 (1976)	UAW v. WERB, 336 U.S. 245 (1957)

(Table continues)

Table 2-14 (Continued)

Court	Overruling case	Overruled case
	New Orleans v. Dukes, 427 U.S. 297 (1976)	Morey v. Doud, 354 U.S. 457 (1957)
	Gregg v. Georgia, 428 U.S. 153 (1976)	McGautha v. California, 402 U.S. 183 (1971)
	Craig v. Boren, 429 U.S. 190 (1976)	Goesaert v. Cleary, 335 U.S. 464 (1948)
	Oregon ex rel. State Land Board v. Corvallis Sand Gravel Co., 429 U.S. 363 (1976)	Bonelli Cattle Co. v. Arizona, 414 U.S. 313 (1973)
	Complete Auto Transit, Inc. v. Brady, 430 U.S. 274 (1977)	Spector Motor Service v. O'Connor, 340 U.S. 602 (1951)
	Continental T. V., Inc. v. GTE Sylvania Inc., 433 U.S. 36 (1977)	United States v. Arnold, Schwinn & Co., 388 U.S. 365 (1967)
	Shaffer v. Heitner, 433 U.S. 186 (1977)	Pennoyer v. Neff, 95 U.S. 714 (1878)
	Revenue Dept. v. Washington Stevedoring Cos., 435 U.S. 734 (1978)	Puget Sound Stevedoring Co. v. State Tax Comm'n, 302 U.S. 90 (1937) Joseph v. Carter & Weeks Stevedoring Co., 330 U.S. 422 (1947)
	Monell v. Dept. of Social Services, 436 U.S. 658 (1978)	Monroe v. Pape, 365 U.S. 167 (1961) (in part) City of Kenosha v. Bruno, 412 U.S. 507 (1973) (in part) Morr v. County of Almeda, 411 U.S. 693 (1973)

Burks v. United States, 437 U.S. 1 (1978)	Bryan v. United States, 338 U.S. 552 (1950) (in part) Sapir v. United States, 348 U.S. 373 (1955) (in part) Yates v. United States, 354 U.S. 298 (1957) (in part) Forman v. United States, 361 U.S. 416 (1960) (in part)
United States v. Scott, 437 U.S. 82 (1978)	United States v. Jenkins, 420 U.S. 358 (1975)
Duren v. Missouri, 439 U.S. 357 (1978)	Hoyt v. Florida, 368 U.S. 57 (1961)
Hughes v. Oklahoma, 441 U.S. 322 (1979)	Geer v. Connecticut, 161 U.S. 519 (1896)
Trammel v. United States, 445 U.S. 40 (1980)	Hawkins v. United States, 358 U.S. 74 (1958)
United States v. Salvucci, 448 U.S. 83 (1981)	Jones v. United States, 362 U.S. 257 (1964)
Commonwealth Edison Co. v. Montana (1981)	Heisler v. Thomas Colliery Co., 260 U.S. 245 (1922)
United States v. Ross, 456 U.S. 798 (1982)	Robbins v. California, 453 U.S. 420 (1981)
Sporhase v. Nebraska ex rel. Douglas, 458 U.S. 941 (1982)	Hudson County Water Co. v. McCarter, 209 U.S. 349 (1908)
Illinois v. Gates, 462 U.S. 213 (1983)	Aquilar v. Texas, 378 U.S. 108 (1964) Spinelli v. United States, 393 U.S. 410 (1969)
Pennhurst State School & Hosp. v. Halderman	Rolston v. Missouri Fund Comm'rs, 120 U.S. 390 (1887) (in part)

(Table continues)

Table 2-14 (Continued)

Court	
Overruling case	Overruling case
	Siler v. Louisville & Nashville R.R. Co., 213 U.S. 175 (1909) (in part)
	Atchison, T. & S.F. Ry. Co. v. O'Connor, 223 U.S. 280 (1912) (in part)
	Greene v. Louisville & Interurban R.R. Co., 244 U.S. 499 (1917) (in part)
	Johnson v. Lankford, 245 U.S. 541 (1918) (in part)
	Numerous other cases fall more or less under the Pennhurst doctrine. See 465 U.S. 109-111 nn.17-21, 117-121 (maj. op.) and id., 130-37, 159-163, 165-166 nn.50 & 52 (dissent) (listing 28 cases)
United States v. One Assortment of 89 Firearms, 465 U.S. 354 (1984)	Coffey v. United States, 116 U.S. 436 (1886)
Limbach v. Hooven & Allison Co., 466 U.S. 353 (1984)	Hooven & Allison Co. v. Evatt, 324 U.S. 652 (1945)
Copperweld Corp. v. Independence Tube Corp., 467 U.S. 752 (1984)	United States v. Yellow Cab Co., 332 U.S. 218 (1947) Kiefer-Stewart Co. v. Jos. E. Seagram & Sons, 340 U.S. 211 (1951)
Garcia v. San Antonio Metropolitan Transit Authority, 469 U.S. 528 (1985)	National League of Cities v. Usery, 426 U.S. 833 (1976)
United States v. Miller, 471 U.S. 130 (1985)	Ex parte Bain, 121 U.S. 1 (1887) (in part)
Daniels v. Williams, 474 U.S. 327 (1986)	Parratt v. Taylor, 451 U.S. 527 (1981) (in part)

	United States v. Lane, 474 U.S. 438 (1986)	McElroy v. United States, 164 U.S. 76 (1896)
	Batson v. Kentucky, 476 U.S. 79 (1986)	Swain v. Alabama, 380 U.S. 202 (1965) (in part)
Rehnquist Court (September 17, 1986-)	Puerto Rico v. Branstad, 483 U.S. 219 (1987)	Kentucky v. Dennison, 24 How. 66 (1861)
	Solorio v. United States, 483 U.S. 435 (1987)	O'Callahan v. Parker, 395 U.S. 258 (1969)
	Welch v. Texas Dept. of Highways and Public Transportation, 483 U.S. 468 (1987)	Parden v. Terminal Ry., 377 U.S. 84 (1964) (in part)
	Gulfstream Aerospace Corp. v. Mayacamas Corp., 99 L. Ed. 2d 296 (1988)	Enelow v. New York Life Ins. Co., 293 U.S. 379 (1935) Ettelson v. Metropolitan Life Ins. Co., 317 U.S. 188 (1942)
	South Carolina v. Baker, 99 L. Ed. 2d 592 (1988)	Pollock v. Farmers' Loan & Trust Co., 157 U.S. 429 (1895)
	Thornburgh v. Abbott, 104 L. Ed. 2d 459 (1989)	Procunier v. Martinez, 416 U.S. 396 (1974) (in part)
	Rodriguez de Quijas v. Shearson/American Express, Inc. 104 L. Ed. 2d 526 (1989)	Wilko v. Swann, 346 U.S. 427 (1953)
	Alabama v. Smith, 104 L. Ed. 2d 865 (1989)	Simpson v. Rice, 395 U.S. 711 (1969)
	Healy v. Beer Institute, 105 L. Ed. 2d 205 (1989)	Joseph E. Seagram & Sons v. Hostetter, 384 U.S. 35 (1966)

(Table continues)

Table 2-14 (Continued)

Court	Overruling case	Overruled case
	W. S. Kirkpatrick & Co. v. Environmental Tectronics Corp., 110 S.Ct. 701 (1990)	American Banana Co. v. United Fruit Co., 213 U.S. 347 (1909)
	Collins v. Youngblood, 111 L. Ed. 2d 30 (1990)	Kring v. Missouri, 107 U.S. 221 (1883) Thompson v. Utah, 170 U.S. 343 (1898)

Note: Determination of whether or not the Court has formally altered one of its own precedents is a subjective judgment, as acknowledged by the Library of Congress source used here, which includes only "reversals stated in express terms by the Supreme Court." The Supreme Court Judicial Database, in contrast, defines such wording as "formal alteration of precedent," "disapproved," "no longer good law," "can no longer be considered controlling," or "modify and narrow" as evidence of overruling. For purposes of consistency, however, the Library of Congress source is used here exclusively.

Source: U.S. Library of Congress, Congressional Research Service, *The Constitution of the United States of America, Analysis and Interpretation: Annotations of Cases Decided by the Supreme Court of the United States* (Washington, D.C.: Government Printing Office, 1973) and supplements.

3

The Supreme Court's Opinion, Decision, and Outcome Trends

This chapter provides longitudinal data on several aspects of the Court's opinions, decisions, and outcomes. The information contained in the tables that follow deals exclusively with the *institutional output of the Court as a whole,* not with that of particular justices. Readers interested in the voting behavior of the Court's members will find such data in Chapter 5.

Chapter 3 begins with information on the Court's opinion trends. Tables 3-1 through 3-4 provide the number and proportion of cases that were decided unanimously, with dissenting opinions, with concurring opinions, and by 4-to-3 or 5-to-4 votes. As noted in the introduction to the book, the accuracy of the data that antedate 1953 cannot be confirmed as the sources do not report reliability. It is also important to note that, given the varied data sources used to compile these tables, some inconsistency may arise as the result of differing definitions of unanimity and dissent. Results are simply reported, with no attempt to impose consistency on the data.

These data show that unanimity remained high throughout the nineteenth century, notwithstanding the small number of cases decided in many terms. Not until the 1940s does substantial dissent appear. Since then, the trend has been essentially flat, with approximately two-fifths of the cases decided unanimously, and the other three-fifths with dissent. Prior to 1940, the proportion of one-vote decisions never exceeded 10 percent. Since then, they have ranged between 2 and 28 percent. A higher proportion results when the justices are relatively evenly divided ideologically and confront many cases that trigger their ideological divisions.

Although numerous closely divided decisions may belie judicial objectivity, most of them have produced an authoritative result: a decision backed by an opinion with which a majority of the participating justices agree. Markedly more embarrassing are cases in which a majority is unable to agree on the reasons for its decision. These are termed judgments of the Court, and are the subject of Table 3-5. Although they have reached double digits in only four terms since 1953, they most often occur in highly salient issue areas, such as civil rights and civil liberties. They result because one or more of the justices in the majority decision coalition specially concurs—that is, agrees with the result the majority has reached, but refuses to agree with the reasoning sustaining that outcome.

Unlike other federal and most state courts, the justices are free to determine which of the cases brought to their attention by losing litigants they will decide. Table 3-6 shows that, overall, the justices accept cases from lower courts that they wish to overturn. In only three terms since 1953 have the justices affirmed more cases than they have reversed. Reversal rates have exceeded 60 percent in 27 of the past 38 terms, including all but one term between 1961 and 1984.

The final two tables (Tables 3-7 and 3-8) divide the cases the Court has chosen to decide into broad issue areas and specify the proportion that were decided in a liberal direction. Although these data indicate increases in the conservative proportion across the issue areas since the heyday of the Warren Court, marked variation in the conservative proportion exists from one issue to another. These results may reflect the changes in the Court's membership and the attitudes of the more recently appointed justices. Note too that Table 3-8 only includes those issues where there are a sufficient number of cases for annual analysis. It also merges union and economic activity into a single economics category.

Table 3-1   Unanimous Decisions, 1900-1991 Terms

Term	Number of unanimous decisions	Total number of cases[a]	Proportion of cases that were unanimous
1900	151	197	.766
1910	150	168	.893
1920	178	217	.820
1930	148	166	.892
1931	124	150	.827
1932	141	168	.839
1933	132	158	.835
1934	134	156	.859
1935	119	145	.821
1936	118	149	.792
1937	106	152	.697
1938	89	139	.640
1939	95	137	.693
1940	118	165	.715
1941	92	151	.609
1942	72	147	.490
1943	50	130	.385
1944	62	156	.397
1945	57	134	.425
1946	54	142	.380
1947	28	110	.255
1948	23	114	.202
1949	22	87	.253
1950	29	91	.319
1951	16	83	.193
1952	17	104	.163
1953	30	84	.357
1954	41	93	.441
1955	42	98	.429
1956	35	121	.289
1957	37	127	.291
1958	49	118	.415
1959	30	115	.261
1960	41	128	.320
1961	37	101	.366
1962	48	125	.384
1963	57	130	.438
1964	44	106	.415
1965	42	102	.412
1966	37	112	.330
1967	47	122	.385

(Table continues)

Table 3-1   *(Continued)*

Term	Number of unanimous decisions	Total number of cases[a]	Proportion of cases that were unanimous
1968	41	111	.369
1969	40	107	.374
1970	43	125	.344
1971	54	147	.367
1972	43	153	.281
1973	47	148	.318
1974	53	139	.381
1975	59	151	.391
1976	49	143	.343
1977	46	135	.341
1978	51	134	.381
1979	39	141	.277
1980	45	128	.352
1981	54	148	.365
1982	62	155	.400
1983	71	155	.458
1984	63	142	.444
1985	51	153	.333
1986	48	153	.314
1987	64	144	.444
1988	59	140	.421
1989	44	131	.336
1990	45	114	.395
1991	43	109	.394

[a] For 1953-1991, the total number of cases includes those with signed opinions and orally argued per curiams; for earlier terms, includes signed opinions of the Court only.

Sources: Number of unanimous decisions, 1900, 1910, 1920, 1930, 1935-1944: C. Herman Pritchett, "The Divided Supreme Court," *Michigan Law Review* 44 (1945): 428; 1931-1934: Karl M. ZoBell, "Dissenting Opinions," *Cornell Law Quarterly* 44 (1959): 205; 1945-1952: C. Herman Pritchett, *Civil Liberties and the Vinson Court* (Chicago: University of Chicago Press, 1954), 21; 1953-1991: U.S. Supreme Court Judicial Database, with orally argued citation as unit of analysis. Total number of cases and proportions therefrom, 1900-1926: Albert P. Blaustein and Roy M. Mersky, *The First One Hundred Justices* (Hamden, Conn.: Shoe String Press, 1978), 137-140; 1927-1952: Gerhard Casper and Richard A. Posner, *The Workload of the Supreme Court* (Chicago: American Bar Foundation, 1976), 76; 1953-1991: U.S. Supreme Court Judicial Database, with citation as unit of analysis.

Table 3-2   Dissenting Opinions, 1800-1991 Terms

Term[a]	Number of cases with dissenting opinions	Total number of cases[b]	Proportion of cases with at least one dissenting opinion[c]
1800	0	0	.000
1801	0	4	.000
1803	0	11	.000
1804	0	15	.000
1805	1	10	.100
1806	0	17	.000
1807	0	10	.000
1808	4	21	.190
1809	4	37	.108
1810	1	27	.037
1812	1	31	.032
1813	3	39	.077
1814	5	46	.109
1815	2	39	.051
1816	3	40	.075
1817	1	40	.025
1818	2	36	.056
1819	0	32	.000
1820	3	26	.115
1821	1	33	.030
1822	1	29	.034
1823	2	27	.074
1824	4	39	.103
1825	0	27	.000
1826	0	29	.000
1827	1	45	.022
1828	3	53	.057
1829	2	42	.048
1830	7	51	.137
1831	7	40	.175
1832	5	50	.100
1833	2	38	.053
1834	2	59	.034
1835	3	38	.079
1836	1	48	.021
1837	5	19	.263
1838	5	40	.125
1839	5	51	.098
1840	3	41	.073
1841	0	31	.000
1842	2	42	.048
1843	4	26	.154
1844	3	39	.077

(Table continues)

Table 3-2 *(Continued)*

Term[a]	Number of cases with dissenting opinions	Total number of cases[b]	Proportion of cases with at least one dissenting opinion[c]
1845	13	49	.265
1846	2	46	.043
1847	5	35	.143
1848	3	35	.086
1849	8	40	.200
1850	25	156	.160
1851	10	94	.106
1852	12	53	.226
1853	16	80	.200
1854	15	71	.211
1855	14	90	.156
1856	8	63	.127
1857	9	70	.129
1858	6	69	.087
1859	4	115	.035
1860	3	64	.047
1861	2	74	.027
1862	7	41	.171
1863	4	75	.053
1864	5	55	.091
1865	7	70	.100
1866	6	128	.047
1867	7	96	.073
1868	13	114	.114
1869	14	169	.083
1870	15	151	.099
1871	21	148	.142
1872	23	157	.146
1873	21	193	.109
1874	17	186	.091
1875	23	200	.115
1876	16	219	.073
1877	21	248	.085
1878	23	198	.116
1879	18	205	.088
1880	9	221	.041
1881	11	232	.047
1882	17	267	.064
1883	14	277	.051
1884	11	271	.041
1885	18	280	.064
1886	12	298	.040
1887	13	287	.045
1888	6	242	.025
1889	16	282	.057

Table 3-2 *(Continued)*

Term[a]	Number of cases with dissenting opinions	Total number of cases[b]	Proportion of cases with at least one dissenting opinion[c]
1890	14	297	.047
1891	20	252	.115
1892	22	231	.095
1893	23	280	.082
1894	23	225	.102
1895	25	257	.097
1896	12	228	.053
1897	16	184	.087
1898	14	173	.081
1899	15	214	.070
1900	22	197	.112
1901	12	179	.067
1902	18	213	.085
1903	20	208	.096
1904	17	194	.088
1905	22	168	.131
1906	12	205	.059
1907	15	176	.085
1908	14	181	.077
1909	9	175	.051
1910	13	168	.077
1911	9	230	.039
1912	10	271	.037
1913	5	285	.018
1914	16	257	.062
1915	5	235	.021
1916	16	207	.077
1917	13	208	.062
1918	14	213	.066
1919	23	168	.137
1920	16	217	.074
1921	24	171	.140
1922	15	223	.067
1923	12	212	.057
1924	10	232	.043
1925	12	210	.057
1926	24	199	.121
1927	32	175	.183
1928	14	129	.109
1929	14	134	.104
1930	13	166	.078
1931	16	150	.107
1932	17	168	.101

(Table continues)

Table 3-2 *(Continued)*

Term [a]	Number of cases with dissenting opinions	Total number of cases [b]	Proportion of cases with at least one dissenting opinion [c]
1933	18	158	.114
1934	11	156	.071
1935	20	145	.138
1936	17	149	.114
1937	26	152	.171
1938	35	139	.252
1939	20	137	.146
1940	27	165	.164
1941	44	151	.291
1942	63	147	.429
1943	68	130	.523
1944	79	156	.506
1945	67	134	.500
1946	80	142	.563
1947	70	110	.636
1948	86	114	.754
1949	56	87	.644
1950	56	91	.615
1951	69	83	.831
1952	90	104	.865
1953	47	84	.560
1954	43	93	.462
1955	49	98	.500
1956	82	121	.678
1957	84	127	.661
1958	63	118	.534
1959	83	115	.722
1960	84	128	.656
1961	60	101	.594
1962	71	125	.568
1963	70	130	.538
1964	58	106	.547
1965	57	102	.559
1966	75	112	.670
1967	74	122	.607
1968	69	111	.622
1969	64	107	.598
1970	81	125	.648
1971	92	147	.626
1972	107	153	.699
1973	101	148	.682
1974	81	139	.583
1975	91	151	.603
1976	94	143	.657
1977	89	135	.659

Table 3-2   *(Continued)*

Term[a]	Number of cases with dissenting opinions	Total number of cases[b]	Proportion of cases with at least one dissenting opinion[c]
1978	83	134	.619
1979	105	141	.745
1980	83	128	.648
1981	94	148	.635
1982	94	155	.606
1983	85	155	.548
1984	79	142	.556
1985	101	153	.660
1986	106	153	.693
1987	80	144	.556
1988	84	140	.600
1989	84	131	.641
1990	70	114	.614
1991	65	109	.596

[a] Court did not meet during 1802 or 1811.

[b] For 1953-1991, total number of cases includes those with signed opinions and orally argued per curiams; for earlier terms, includes signed opinions of the Court only.

[c] Due to ambiguity in the description of data prior to the 1953 term, we cannot determine whether data represent the number of dissenting opinions or the number of cases with dissenting opinions. Hence, the proportion may not be comparable across all terms.

Sources: Number of dissenting opinions, 1800-1952: Albert P. Blaustein and Roy M. Mersky, *The First One Hundred Justices* (Hamden, Conn.: Shoe String Press, 1978), 137-140; 1953-1992: U.S. Supreme Court Judicial Database, with orally argued citation as unit of analysis. Total number of cases and proportions therefrom, 1800-1926: Albert P. Blaustein and Roy M. Mersky, *The First One Hundred Justices* (Hamden, Conn.: Shoe String Press, 1978), 137-140; 1927-1952: Gerhard Casper and Richard A. Posner, *The Workload of the Supreme Court* (Chicago: American Bar Foundation, 1976), 76; 1953-1991: U.S. Supreme Court Judicial Database, with citation as unit of analysis.

Table 3-3 Concurring Opinions, 1800-1991 Terms

Term[a]	Number of cases with concurring opinions	Total number of cases[b]	Proportion of cases with at least one concurring opinion[c]
1800	0	0	.000
1801	0	4	.000
1803	0	11	.000
1804	1	15	.067
1805	1	10	.100
1806	0	17	.000
1807	0	10	.000
1808	2	21	.095
1809	0	37	.000
1810	1	27	.037
1812	1	31	.032
1813	3	39	.077
1814	0	46	.000
1815	2	39	.051
1816	1	40	.025
1817	0	40	.000
1818	0	36	.000
1819	0	32	.000
1820	0	26	.000
1821	0	33	.000
1822	0	29	.000
1823	0	27	.000
1824	1	39	.026
1825	1	27	.037
1826	0	29	.000
1827	1	45	.022
1828	1	53	.019
1829	1	42	.024
1830	1	51	.020
1831	2	40	.050
1832	1	50	.020
1833	0	38	.000
1834	0	59	.000
1835	1	38	.026
1836	0	48	.000
1837	2	19	.105
1838	3	40	.075
1839	2	51	.039
1840	4	41	.098
1841	0	31	.000
1842	6	42	.143
1843	0	26	.000
1844	1	39	.026
1845	0	49	.000
1846	2	46	.043

Table 3-3 *(Continued)*

Term[a]	Number of cases with concurring opinions	Total number of cases[b]	Proportion of cases with at least one concurring opinion[c]
1847	4	35	.114
1848	1	35	.029
1849	0	40	.000
1850	0	156	.000
1851	3	94	.032
1852	0	53	.000
1853	7	80	.087
1854	5	71	.070
1855	7	90	.078
1856	7	63	.111
1857	2	70	.029
1858	1	69	.014
1859	0	115	.000
1860	0	64	.000
1861	2	74	.027
1862	0	41	.000
1863	4	75	.053
1864	1	55	.018
1865	1	70	.014
1866	2	128	.016
1867	0	96	.000
1868	3	114	.026
1869	0	169	.000
1870	3	151	.020
1871	0	148	.000
1872	7	157	.045
1873	9	193	.047
1874	2	186	.011
1875	1	200	.005
1876	3	219	.014
1877	4	248	.016
1878	5	198	.025
1879	1	205	.005
1880	2	221	.009
1881	0	232	.000
1882	3	267	.011
1883	4	277	.014
1884	2	271	.007
1885	4	280	.014
1886	1	298	.003
1887	4	287	.014
1888	1	242	.004
1889	3	282	.011

(Table continues)

Table 3-3 *(Continued)*

Term[a]	Number of cases with concurring opinions	Total number of cases[b]	Proportion of cases with at least one concurring opinion[c]
1890	2	297	.007
1891	3	252	.012
1892	0	231	.000
1893	1	280	.004
1894	1	225	.004
1895	1	257	.004
1896	0	228	.000
1897	3	184	.016
1898	1	173	.006
1899	4	214	.019
1900	5	197	.025
1901	3	179	.017
1902	4	213	.019
1903	3	208	.014
1904	7	194	.036
1905	5	168	.030
1906	4	205	.020
1907	5	176	.028
1908	3	181	.017
1909	7	175	.040
1910	1	168	.006
1911	0	230	.000
1912	1	271	.004
1913	3	285	.011
1914	1	257	.004
1915	1	235	.004
1916	1	207	.005
1917	1	208	.005
1918	0	213	.000
1919	3	168	.018
1920	7	217	.032
1921	1	171	.006
1922	1	223	.004
1923	3	212	.014
1924	0	232	.000
1925	0	210	.000
1926	8	199	.040
1927	2	175	.011
1928	2	129	.016
1929	2	134	.015
1930	2	166	.012
1931	1	150	.007
1932	1	168	.006
1933	4	158	.025
1934	7	156	.045

Table 3-3   *(Continued)*

Term[a]	Number of cases with concurring opinions	Total number of cases[b]	Proportion of cases with at least one concurring opinion[c]
1935	4	145	.028
1936	2	149	.013
1937	11	152	.072
1938	11	139	.079
1939	5	137	.036
1940	5	165	.030
1941	17	151	.113
1942	24	147	.163
1943	16	130	.123
1944	31	156	.199
1945	36	134	.269
1946	31	142	.218
1947	31	110	.282
1948	32	114	.281
1949	10	87	.115
1950	22	91	.242
1951	17	83	.205
1952	24	104	.231
1953	14	84	.167
1954	15	93	.161
1955	17	98	.173
1956	21	121	.174
1957	24	127	.189
1958	29	118	.246
1959	32	115	.278
1960	34	128	.266
1961	33	101	.327
1962	36	125	.288
1963	39	130	.300
1964	40	106	.377
1965	32	102	.314
1966	32	112	.286
1967	59	122	.484
1968	52	111	.468
1969	44	107	.411
1970	62	125	.496
1971	56	147	.381
1972	49	153	.320
1973	51	148	.345
1974	43	139	.309
1975	70	151	.464
1976	67	143	.469
1977	56	135	.415

(Table continues)

Table 3-3 *(Continued)*

Term[a]	Number of cases with concurring opinions	Total number of cases[b]	Proportion of cases with at least one concurring opinion[c]
1978	63	134	.470
1979	58	141	.411
1980	66	128	.516
1981	70	148	.473
1982	58	155	.374
1983	55	155	.355
1984	53	142	.373
1985	64	153	.418
1986	61	153	.399
1987	53	144	.368
1988	68	140	.486
1989	58	131	.443
1990	40	114	.351
1991	47	109	.431

[a] Court did not meet during 1802 or 1811.

[b] For 1953-1991, total number of cases includes those with signed opinions and orally argued per curiams; for earlier terms, includes signed opinions of the Court only.

[c] Due to ambiguity in the description of data prior to the 1953 term, we cannot determine whether data represent the number of concurring opinions or the number of cases with concurring opinions. Hence, the proportion may not be comparable across all terms.

Sources: Number of concurring opinions, 1800-1952: Albert P. Blaustein and Roy M. Mersky, *The First One Hundred Justices* (Hamden, Conn.: Shoe String Press, 1978), 137-140; 1953-1992: U.S. Supreme Court Judicial Database, with orally argued citation as unit of analysis. Total number of cases and proportions therefrom, 1800-1926: Albert P. Blaustein and Roy M. Mersky, *The First One Hundred Justices* (Hamden, Conn.: Shoe String Press, 1978), 137-140; 1927-1952: Gerhard Casper and Richard A. Posner, *The Workload of the Supreme Court* (Chicago: American Bar Foundation, 1976), 76; 1953-1991: U.S. Supreme Court Judicial Database, with citation as unit of analysis.

Table 3-4 Cases Decided by a 5-to-4 or 4-to-3 Vote, 1800-1991 Terms

Term[a]	Number of cases decided by a one-vote margin	Total number of cases[b]	Proportion of cases decided by a one-vote margin
1800	0	0	.000
1801	0	4	.000
1803	0	11	.000
1804	0	15	.000
1805	0	10	.000
1806	0	17	.000
1807	1	10	.100
1808	2	21	.095
1809	0	37	.000
1810	3	27	.111
1812	0	31	.000
1813	0	39	.000
1814	1	46	.022
1815	0	39	.000
1816	0	40	.000
1817	0	40	.000
1818	1	36	.028
1819	0	32	.000
1820	0	26	.000
1821	1	33	.030
1822	1	29	.034
1823	0	27	.000
1824	0	39	.000
1825	0	27	.000
1826	1	29	.034
1827	1	45	.022
1828	1	53	.019
1829	0	42	.071
1830	0	51	.000
1831	3	40	.075
1832	0	50	.000
1833	0	38	.000
1834	0	59	.000
1835	0	38	.000
1836	0	48	.000
1837	1	19	.053
1838	3	40	.075
1839	0	51	.000
1840	1	41	.024
1841	0	31	.000
1842	1	42	.024
1843	0	26	.000
1844	0	39	.000
1845	0	49	.000

(Table continues)

Table 3-4   *(Continued)*

Term[a]	Number of cases decided by a one-vote margin	Total number of cases[b]	Proportion of cases decided by a one-vote margin
1846	0	46	.000
1847	0	35	.000
1848	0	35	.000
1849	2	40	.050
1850	7	156	.045
1851	0	94	.000
1852	1	53	.019
1853	3	80	.037
1854	1	71	.014
1855	1	90	.011
1856	0	63	.000
1857	2	70	.029
1858	0	69	.000
1859	0	115	.000
1860	0	64	.000
1861	0	74	.000
1862	1	41	.024
1863	0	75	.000
1864	2	55	.036
1865	1	70	.014
1866	3	128	.023
1867	0	96	.000
1868	0	114	.000
1869	1	169	.006
1870	0	151	.000
1871	1	148	.007
1872	6	157	.038
1873	3	193	.016
1874	3	186	.016
1875	2	200	.010
1876	3	219	.014
1877	2	248	.008
1878	1	198	.005
1879	0	205	.000
1880	0	221	.000
1881	0	232	.000
1882	3	267	.007
1883	0	277	.004
1884	3	271	.011
1885	7	280	.020
1886	2	298	.007
1887	2	287	.007
1888	0	242	.000
1889	0	282	.000
1890	1	297	.003
1891	2	252	.008

Table 3-4   *(Continued)*

Term[a]	Number of cases decided by a one-vote margin	Total number of cases[b]	Proportion of cases decided by a one-vote margin
1892	1	231	.004
1893	2	280	.007
1894	3	225	.013
1895	2	257	.008
1896	6	228	.026
1897	3	184	.016
1898	6	173	.035
1899	7	214	.033
1900	15	197	.076
1901	7	179	.039
1902	3	213	.014
1903	10	208	.048
1904	7	194	.036
1905	9	168	.054
1906	2	205	.010
1907	3	176	.017
1908	1	181	.006
1909	6	175	.034
1910	2	168	.012
1911	3	230	.013
1912	5	271	.018
1913	1	285	.004
1914	6	257	.023
1915	0	235	.000
1916	8	207	.039
1917	4	208	.019
1918	9	213	.042
1919	10	168	.060
1920	6	217	.028
1921	2	171	.012
1922	0	223	.000
1923	0	212	.000
1924	2	232	.009
1925	1	210	.005
1926	4	199	.020
1927	6	175	.034
1928	1	129	.008
1929	0	134	.000
1930	6	166	.036
1931	2	150	.013
1932	3	168	.018
1933	6	158	.038
1934	8	156	.051
1935	7	145	.048

(Table continues)

Table 3-4   *(Continued)*

Term[a]	Number of cases decided by a one-vote margin	Total number of cases[b]	Proportion of cases decided by a one-vote margin
1936	13	149	.087
1937	3	152	.020
1938	6	139	.043
1939	4	137	.029
1940	5	165	.030
1941	15	151	.099
1942	10	147	.068
1943	17	130	.131
1944	30	156	.192
1945	6	134	.045
1946	25	142	.176
1947	25	110	.227
1948	31	114	.272
1949	5	87	.057
1950	12	91	.132
1951	11	83	.133
1952	8	104	.077
1953	11	84	.131
1954	2	93	.022
1955	13	98	.133
1956	13	121	.107
1957	29	127	.228
1958	24	118	.203
1959	25	115	.217
1960	27	128	.211
1961	9	101	.089
1962	13	125	.104
1963	12	130	.092
1964	6	106	.057
1965	12	102	.118
1966	20	112	.179
1967	2	122	.016
1968	5	111	.045
1969	2	107	.019
1970	29	125	.232
1971	31	147	.211
1972	30	153	.196
1973	30	148	.203
1974	16	139	.115
1975	14	151	.093
1976	23	143	.161
1977	20	135	.148
1978	25	134	.187
1979	27	141	.191
1980	17	128	.133
1981	34	148	.230

Table 3-4   *(Continued)*

Term[a]	Number of cases decided by a one-vote margin	Total number of cases[b]	Proportion of cases decided by a one-vote margin
1982	31	155	.200
1983	27	155	.174
1984	20	142	.141
1985	35	153	.229
1986	42	153	.275
1987	16	144	.111
1988	33	140	.236
1989	37	131	.282
1990	21	114	.184
1991	13	109	.119

[a] Court did not meet during 1802 or 1811.

[b] For 1953-1991, total number of cases includes those with signed opinions and orally argued per curiams; for earlier terms, includes signed opinions of the Court only.

Sources: Number of cases decided by a one-vote margin, 1800-1923: U.S. Senate, "Creation of the Federal Judiciary," Sen. Doc. No. 91, 75th Cong., 1st Sess., July 22, 1937 (Washington, D.C.: Government Printing Office, 1938), 260-272; 1923-1952: "Five-Four Decisions of the United States Supreme Court—Resurrection of the Extraordinary Majority," Suffolk University Law Review 7 (1973): 916; 1953-1990: U.S. Supreme Court Judicial Database, with orally argued citation as unit of analysis. Total number of cases and proportions therefrom, 1800-1926: Albert P. Blaustein and Roy M. Mersky, *The First One Hundred Justices* (Hamden, Conn.: Shoe String Press, 1978), 137-140; 1927-1952: Gerhard Casper and Richard A. Posner, *The Workload of the Supreme Court* (Chicago: American Bar Foundation, 1976), 76; 1953-1990: U.S. Supreme Court Judicial Database, with citation as unit of analysis.

Table 3-5 Cases Decided by a Judgment of the Court, 1953-1991 Terms

Term	Number of cases decided by a judgment	Total number of cases	Proportion of cases decided by a judgment
1953	5	90	.060
1954	1	86	.012
1955	1	104	.010
1956	4	112	.036
1957	1	125	.008
1958	2	116	.017
1959	2	111	.018
1960	9	123	.073
1961	4	102	.039
1962	1	130	.008
1963	2	123	.016
1964	1	105	.010
1965	3	122	.025
1966	4	132	.030
1967	1	159	.006
1968	2	116	.017
1969	3	105	.029
1970	16	126	.127
1971	7	143	.049
1972	6	160	.038
1973	3	161	.019
1974	0	142	.000
1975	10	160	.063
1976	7	157	.045
1977	8	154	.052
1978	6	153	.039
1979	12	145	.083
1980	6	145	.041
1981	4	170	.024
1982	8	183	.044
1983	1	174	.006
1984	2	159	.013
1985	5	161	.031
1986	6	164	.037
1987	3	154	.019
1988	12	156	.077
1989	5	143	.035
1990	3	121	.025
1991	3	119	.025

Note: A judgment is a decision of the Court, the opinion in support of which is joined by less than a majority of the participating justices. Only those decisions that the Court clearly labels as a judgment are counted as such. If reference is made to a judgment and an opinion of the Court, it is counted as an opinion. Only signed opinion cases may produce a judgment of the Court. Count is by docket number. Included are *Ker v. California,* 374 U.S. 23 (1963), wherein a majority agreed on the standard whereby state searches and seizures are to be evaluated, but only a plurality agreed on the application of that standard, and two of the three docket numbers of *County of Allegheny v. American Civil Liberties Union,* 106 L. Ed. 2d 472 (1989) that were decided by a judgment of the Court.

Source: U.S. Supreme Court Judicial Database.

Table 3-6   Disposition of Cases, 1953-1991 Terms

Term	Total number of cases[a]	Reversals[b]
1953	112	48.2%
1954	105	64.8
1955	118	54.2
1956	135	63.7
1957	154	55.2
1958	139	57.6
1959	129	58.9
1960	145	52.4
1961	122	68.9
1962	146	74.0
1963	144	75.2
1964	119	71.4
1965	128	71.1
1966	146	69.9
1967	177	65.2
1968	128	71.1
1969	125	64.0
1970	142	56.3
1971	161	60.9
1972	174	67.2
1973	168	67.3
1974	158	67.7
1975	172	66.3
1976	177	63.3
1977	160	68.1
1978	159	65.4
1979	150	60.7
1980	152	65.1
1981	179	64.2
1982	185	63.2
1983	177	71.8
1984	168	61.3
1985	168	57.7
1986	173	60.7
1987	160	49.4
1988	167	49.1
1989	145	55.2
1990	123	61.8
1991	120	64.2

[a] Includes all orally argued docket numbers excluding cases arising under original jurisdiction.
[b] Any decision in which the petitioning party prevailed.

Source: U.S. Supreme Court Judicial Database.

Table 3-7 Direction of Court Decisions by Issue Area and Chief Justice, 1953–1991 Terms

Issue area	Warren (1953–1968) % liberal	Warren N cases	Burger (1969–1985) % liberal	Burger N cases	Rehnquist (1986–1991) % liberal	Rehnquist N cases	Total % liberal	Total N cases
Civil liberties	67.7	780	43.6	1,421	42.8	437	50.6	2,638
Criminal procedure	59.4	352	34.2	517	33.2	187	42.4	1,056
Civil rights	76.3	224	51.8	496	55.3	114	58.9	834
First Amendment	69.0	155	48.6	208	48.5	66	55.9	429
Due process	83.8	37	44.5	128	43.6	39	51.5	204
Privacy	50.0	2	27.5	40	33.3	12	29.6	54
Attorneys	90.0	10	53.1	32	47.4	19	57.4	61
Unions	70.1	127	57.4	108	40.0	30	61.5	265
Economic activity	72.5	448	51.8	427	49.6	139	60.7	1,014
Judicial power	40.8	228	27.9	269	44.7	103	35.7	600
Federalism	66.7	81	64.4	87	59.6	47	64.2	215
Federal taxation	77.4	115	72.1	68	70.8	24	74.9	207

Note: The issue areas are defined as follows: Civil liberties: combines criminal procedure, civil rights, First Amendment, due process, privacy, and attorneys issue areas; Criminal procedure: the rights of persons accused of crime except for the due process rights of prisoners; Civil rights: non-First Amendment freedom cases that pertain to classifications based on race (including native Americans), age, indigence, voting, residence, military or handicapped status, sex, or alienage; First Amendment: guarantees contained therein; Due process: non-criminal procedural guarantees, plus court jurisdiction over non-resident litigants and the takings clause of the Fifth Amendment; Privacy: abortion, contraception, the Freedom of Information Act and related federal statutes; Attorneys: attorneys' fees, commercial speech, admission to and removal from the bar, and disciplinary matters; Unions: labor union activity; Economic activity: commercial business activity, plus litigation involving injured persons or things, employee actions vis-à-vis employers, zoning regulations, and governmental regulation of corruption other than that involving campaign spending; Judicial power: the exercise of the judiciary's own power and authority; Federalism: conflicts between the federal and state governments, excluding those between state and federal courts, and those involving the priority of federal fiscal claims; Federal taxation: the Internal Revenue Code and related statutes.

The term *liberal* represents the voting direction of the justices across the various issue areas. It is most appropriate in the areas of civil liberties, criminal procedure, civil rights, First Amendment, due process, privacy, and attorneys where it signifies pro-defendant votes in criminal procedure cases, pro-women or -minorities in civil rights cases, pro-individual against the government in First Amendment, due process, and privacy cases, and pro-attorney in attorneys' fees and bar membership cases. In takings clause cases, however, a pro-government/anti-owner vote is considered liberal. The use of the term is perhaps less appropriate in union cases, where it represents pro-union votes against both individuals and the government, and in economic cases, where it represents pro-government votes against challenges to federal regulatory authority and pro-competition, anti-business, pro-liability, pro-injured person, and pro-bankruptcy votes. In federalism and federal taxation, liberal indicates pro-national government positions; in judicial power cases, the term represents pro-judiciary positions.

Source: U.S. Supreme Court Judicial Database, with orally argued citation as unit of analysis.

Table 3-8   Outcome Trends by Issue Area, 1953-1991 Terms
(percent liberal)

Term	Civil liberties	Criminal procedure	Civil rights	First Amendment	Economics
1953	50.0	40.0	62.5	50.0	51.3
1954	64.9	50.0	70.0	80.0	81.5
1955	56.7	41.7	63.6	80.0	82.1
1956	60.4	65.0	33.3	55.6	83.7
1957	60.3	43.8	71.4	77.8	70.6
1958	58.1	46.2	66.7	81.8	65.3
1959	50.0	43.8	70.0	42.9	73.8
1960	55.2	66.7	57.1	36.4	63.2
1961	76.9	70.6	88.9	87.5	71.1
1962	84.0	71.4	94.1	100.0	77.8
1963	84.5	72.7	92.6	88.9	76.9
1964	72.7	56.3	85.7	72.7	65.5
1965	71.7	56.3	85.7	69.2	75.0
1966	62.7	64.3	68.4	54.5	76.7
1967	76.8	75.0	81.3	69.2	64.7
1968	79.4	63.0	87.0	100.0	76.2
1969	56.9	44.4	69.2	60.0	56.3
1970	47.5	29.2	50.0	54.5	60.0
1971	52.2	41.2	64.3	43.8	48.7
1972	40.0	31.4	54.5	22.2	65.7
1973	43.8	33.3	47.2	64.3	48.3
1974	55.6	54.2	58.6	62.5	52.9
1975	37.1	18.2	53.6	53.8	42.4
1976	37.8	36.7	42.9	33.3	46.2
1977	50.7	58.6	38.5	62.5	65.7
1978	41.0	37.9	44.1	25.0	46.9
1979	49.4	37.5	59.1	70.0	51.4
1980	35.3	40.0	33.3	44.4	60.6
1981	46.9	26.3	55.9	75.0	64.7
1982	39.5	26.7	55.6	45.5	55.0
1983	35.8	20.0	58.6	33.3	42.4
1984	41.4	30.3	60.0	45.5	45.7
1985	37.8	27.9	41.4	42.9	42.1
1986	44.1	34.1	58.3	50.0	46.4
1987	49.4	45.2	47.6	50.0	51.5
1988	38.8	23.3	50.0	46.7	40.9
1989	35.7	25.7	55.6	35.7	53.8
1990	41.1	31.0	68.8	40.0	46.9
1991	48.2	42.9	55.6	75.0	46.4

Note: The issue areas are defined as follows: Civil liberties: combines criminal procedure, civil rights, First Amendment, due process, privacy, and attorneys issue areas; Criminal procedure: the rights of persons accused of crime except for the due process rights of prisoners; Civil rights: non-First Amendment freedom cases that pertain to classifications based on race (including native Americans), age, indigence, voting, residence, military or handicapped status, sex, or alienage; First Amendment: guarantees contained therein;

(Notes continue)

Table 3-8   *(Continued)*

Economics: labor union activity, commercial business activity, plus litigation involving injured persons or things, employee actions vis-à-vis employers, zoning regulations, and governmental regulation of corruption other than that involving campaign spending.

The term *liberal* represents the voting direction of the justices across the various issue areas. It is most appropriate in the areas of civil liberties, criminal procedure, civil rights, First Amendment, due process, privacy, and attorneys where it signifies pro-defendant votes in criminal procedure cases, pro-women or -minorities in civil rights cases, pro-individual against the government in First Amendment, due process, and privacy cases and pro-attorney in attorneys' fees and bar membership cases. In takings clause cases, however, a pro-government/anti-owner vote is considered liberal. The use of the term is perhaps less appropriate in union cases, where it represents pro-union votes against both individuals and the government, and in economic cases, where it represents pro-government votes against challenges to federal regulatory authority and pro-competition, anti-business, pro-liability, pro-injured person, and pro-bankruptcy votes. In federalism and federal taxation, liberal indicates pro-national government positions; in judicial federal power cases, the term represents pro-judiciary positions.

Source: U.S. Supreme Court Judicial Database, with orally argued citation as unit of analysis.

4

The Justices: Backgrounds, Nominations, and Confirmations

From its inception through the 1992 term, 107 individuals have served on the United States Supreme Court. Their names and dates of service are listed in Table 4-1. These individuals have participated in crucial legal and political decisions that have shaped the powers of our government and determined our personal rights. Yet little is known about those who have sat on the highest bench of the land. The purpose of this chapter is to provide information about those justices.

The first question is what kinds of individuals have been tapped for Supreme Court service. Tables 4-2 through 4-9 deal with the backgrounds and personal characteristics of the justices. It does not take a great deal of study to conclude that the justices have tended to be drawn from the ranks of the nation's political and social elites. Table 4-2 shows that the justices tended to come from economically secure families. With the exception of the Jacksonian era, members of elite families dominated the Court from its beginning until the aftermath of the Great Depression. Relatively few of the justices prior to the mid-twentieth century emerged from humble family origins. In the more recent period, however, individuals chosen for Court service appear from the middle and lower socioeconomic classes. Yet the tilt in favor of elite backgrounds remains. Most were reared in childhood environments that reflected the lifestyle of the economic elite. In the early periods, this frequently meant being raised on plantations or large farms. Later, it meant spending childhood years in comfortable surroundings in large metropolitan areas.

Similarly, the justices have tended to come from the ethnic and religious traditions of mainstream America. During the earlier periods of Court history, religious and ethnic factors were quite important in the appointment process, reflecting their significance in American politics generally. In the modern era, however, ethnic and religious distinctions have become less important. Tables 4-2 and 4-3 illustrate that most of the justices trace their family roots to northern European countries, most frequently the British Isles. After the initial years, only three individuals were appointed to the Court who were born in foreign lands: David Brewer, born in Asia Minor; George Sutherland, born in England; and Felix Frankfurter, born in Austria. No person of African descent had ever been selected until Thurgood Marshall broke that pattern in 1967; no person of Italian background had been appointed before Antonin Scalia in 1986; no woman until Sandra Day O'Connor in 1981. A justice of Latin American origins has yet to be selected. In matters of religious preference, Episcopalians and Presbyterians have dominated the Court throughout its history. This is not surprising given that these denominations historically have attracted the nation's social and economic elite. The first Catholic did not reach the High Court until Roger Taney was appointed in 1836, and it took more than a half century for the second member of that church (Edward White) to be nominated. Louis Brandeis became the first Jewish justice in 1916, and only five others (Cardozo, Frankfurter, Goldberg, Fortas, and Ginsburg) have followed. The Court remains overwhelmingly Protestant.

One of the reasons the elite have dominated the Court is that a sound education is a prerequisite for judicial service. Over a good portion of our history, education, especially education that included legal training, was available only to the upper classes, who could afford to send their children to the appropriate schools or tutors. Individuals from the lower socioeconomic groups rarely had the opportunity to obtain the proper training and experience to qualify for the Court. Table 4-4 summarizes the educational records of the justices. As a group, the justices represent the highest in educational attainment, most having attended highly prestigious educational institutions or studied under renowned private tutors. Similarly exceptional has been the justices' legal training. During the colonial period and the first century after independence, it was customary for legal aspirants to study law privately under the direction of established attorneys. Those who reached the Supreme Court frequently were privileged to have had some of the nation's most prestigious private practitioners as their mentors. Later, when law school became the customary route to acquiring a legal education, Supreme Court justices frequently had attended the elite Ivy League law schools.

As the future justices reached adulthood, most married and had families, often with large numbers of children (Table 4-5). Only Benjamin Cardozo, John Clarke, James McReynolds, William Moody, Frank Murphy, and David Souter remained single. The early careers of the justices normally included a period of private practice, and sometimes a law professorship (Table 4-6). One-third served in the armed forces when the nation was drawn into war (Table 4-7). Almost all of the justices were involved in some form of political activity prior to their appointment. Table 4-8 shows that many were state or federal legislators, governors, or cabinet officials. One, William Howard Taft, had even been president. A majority of the justices also served as judges in the lower state or federal courts. A surprising one-third of the members, however, had had absolutely no judicial experience before putting on the robe of a Supreme Court justice (Table 4-9).

The remaining tables deal with the nomination process. Table 4-10 lists all Supreme Court nominees, along with information on their ages, home states, and occupational positions when nominated. Table 4-11 supplies comparative data concerning justices whom nominees were set to replace. A number of factors tending to influence the president's selection of a nominee have remained important over the years. First, the president prefers to nominate an individual from the ranks of his own political party. This allows the chief executive to reward political supporters as well as to select individuals who have an acceptable political ideology. This partisan tradition was started by George Washington, who appointed exclusively Federalists to the High Court. When presidents select from outside their own political party, they tend to do so only when the nominee has a similar ideological stance. Second, the president considers the qualifications of the nominee. These extend both to questions of personal character as well as to legal competence. No president wants to be known for having selected unqualified justices, or wishes to nominate those whose qualifications may make confirmation difficult. Third, representational concerns often come into play. In the period prior to the Civil War, regional representation was a major factor in the nomination process. As time went on, regional considerations declined in importance to be replaced by ethnic and religious factors. Today, representation of racial minorities and women is a significant issue.

After being nominated to a seat on the Court, a successful candidate must obtain Senate confirmation. As Table 4-12 illustrates, approximately 20 percent of all Supreme Court nominees have failed to be confirmed by the Senate. Although this means that most candidates are successful, Supreme Court nominations have a higher rejection rate than those of any other federal office. Most of the rejections have been clustered at certain points in history. President John Tyler suffered the most rebuffs from the Senate. During his short tenure in office, Tyler submitted six Supreme Court nominations. Only one (Samuel Nelson) achieved favorable Senate action. The twentieth century has witnessed five rejections—John Parker in 1930, Abe Fortas in 1968, Clement Haynsworth in 1969, Harrold Carswell in 1970, and Robert Bork in 1987. Often nominees' ideological orientations and interest group reactions affect these nomination outcomes. Table 4-13 provides data on these subjects. Finally, Table 4-14 describes some nomination anomalies, such as individuals who have been nominated for the Court more than once or those who have been nominated and confirmed, but never served.

Table 4-1   The Justices of the Supreme Court

Appointment number/justice [a]	Position	Appointing president	Years of service [b]
1. John Jay	Chief justice	Washington	1789-1795
2. John Rutledge[c]	Associate justice	Washington	1789-1791
3. William Cushing	Associate justice	Washington	1789-1810
4. James Wilson	Associate justice	Washington	1789-1798
5. John Blair, Jr.	Associate justice	Washington	1789-1796
6. James Iredell	Associate justice	Washington	1790-1799
7. Thomas Johnson	Associate justice	Washington	1791-1793
8. William Paterson	Associate justice	Washington	1793-1806
9. John Rutledge[d]	Chief justice	Washington	1795
10. Samuel Chase	Associate justice	Washington	1796-1811
11. Oliver Ellsworth	Chief justice	Washington	1796-1800
12. Bushrod Washington	Associate Justice	J. Adams	1798-1829
13. Alfred Moore	Associate justice	J. Adams	1799-1804
14. John Marshall	Chief justice	J. Adams	1801-1835
15. William Johnson	Associate justice	Jefferson	1804-1834
16. Henry Brockholst Livingston	Associate justice	Jefferson	1806-1823
17. Thomas Todd	Associate justice	Jefferson	1807-1826
18. Gabriel Duvall	Associate justice	Madison	1811-1835
19. Joseph Story	Associate justice	Madison	1811-1845
20. Smith Thompson	Associate justice	Monroe	1823-1843
21. Robert Trimble	Associate justice	J. Q. Adams	1826-1828
22. John McLean	Associate justice	Jackson	1829-1861
23. Henry Baldwin	Associate justice	Jackson	1830-1844

(Table continues)

Table 4-1   *(Continued)*

Appointment number/justice [a]	Position	Appointing president	Years of service [b]
24. James Moore Wayne	Associate justice	Jackson	1835-1867
25. Roger Brooke Taney	Chief justice	Jackson	1836-1864
26. Philip Pendleton Barbour	Associate justice	Jackson	1836-1841
27. John Catron	Associate justice	Jackson	1837-1865
28. John McKinley	Associate justice	Van Buren	1837-1852
29. Peter Vivian Daniel	Associate justice	Van Buren	1841-1860
30. Samuel Nelson	Associate justice	Tyler	1845-1872
31. Levi Woodbury	Associate justice	Polk	1846-1851
32. Robert Cooper Grier	Associate justice	Polk	1846-1870
33. Benjamin Robbins Curtis	Associate justice	Fillmore	1851-1857
34. John Archibald Campbell	Associate justice	Pierce	1853-1861
35. Nathan Clifford	Associate justice	Buchanan	1858-1881
36. Noah Haynes Swayne	Associate justice	Lincoln	1862-1881
37. Samuel Freeman Miller	Associate justice	Lincoln	1862-1890
38. David Davis	Associate justice	Lincoln	1862-1877
39. Stephen Johnson Field	Associate justice	Lincoln	1863-1897
40. Salmon Portland Chase	Chief justice	Lincoln	1864-1873
41. William Strong	Associate justice	Grant	1870-1880
42. Joseph P. Bradley	Associate justice	Grant	1870-1892
43. Ward Hunt	Associate justice	Grant	1872-1882
44. Morrison Remick Waite	Chief justice	Grant	1874-1888
45. John Marshall Harlan	Associate justice	Hayes	1877-1911
46. William Burnham Woods	Associate justice	Hayes	1880-1887
47. Stanley Matthews	Associate justice	Garfield	1881-1889

Table 4-1   *(Continued)*

Appointment number/justice[a]	Position	Appointing president	Years of service[b]
48. Horace Gray	Associate justice	Arthur	1881-1902
49. Samuel Blatchford	Associate justice	Arthur	1882-1893
50. Lucius Quintus Cincinnatus Lamar	Associate justice	Cleveland	1888-1893
51. Melville Weston Fuller	Chief justice	Cleveland	1888-1910
52. David Josiah Brewer	Associate justice	Harrison	1889-1910
53. Henry Billings Brown	Associate justice	Harrison	1890-1906
54. George Shiras, Jr.	Associate justice	Harrison	1892-1903
55. Howell Edmunds Jackson	Associate justice	Harrison	1893-1895
56. Edward Douglass White[c]	Associate justice	Cleveland	1894-1910
57. Rufus Wheeler Peckham	Associate justice	Cleveland	1895-1909
58. Joseph McKenna	Associate justice	McKinley	1898-1925
59. Oliver Wendell Holmes, Jr.	Associate justice	T. Roosevelt	1902-1932
60. William Rufus Day	Associate justice	T. Roosevelt	1903-1922
61. William Henry Moody	Associate justice	T. Roosevelt	1906-1910
62. Horace Harmon Lurton	Associate justice	Taft	1909-1914
63. Charles Evans Hughes[c]	Associate justice	Taft	1910-1916
64. Edward Douglass White[d]	Chief justice	Taft	1910-1921
65. Willis Van Devanter	Associate justice	Taft	1910-1937
66. Joseph Rucker Lamar	Associate justice	Taft	1910-1916
67. Mahlon Pitney	Associate justice	Taft	1912-1922
68. James Clark McReynolds	Associate justice	Wilson	1914-1941
69. Louis Dembitz Brandeis	Associate justice	Wilson	1916-1939
70. John Hessin Clarke	Associate justice	Wilson	1916-1922

(Table continues)

Table 4-1 *(Continued)*

Appointment number/justice [a]	Position	Appointing president	Years of service [b]
71. William Howard Taft	Chief justice	Harding	1921-1930
72. George Sutherland	Associate justice	Harding	1922-1938
73. Pierce Butler	Associate justice	Harding	1922-1939
74. Edward Terry Sanford	Associate justice	Harding	1923-1930
75. Harlan Fiske Stone [c]	Associate justice	Coolidge	1925-1941
76. Charles Evans Hughes [d]	Chief justice	Hoover	1930-1941
77. Owen Josephus Roberts	Associate justice	Hoover	1930-1945
78. Benjamin Nathan Cardozo	Associate justice	Hoover	1932-1938
79. Hugo Lafayette Black	Associate justice	F. Roosevelt	1937-1971
80. Stanley Forman Reed	Associate justice	F. Roosevelt	1938-1957
81. Felix Frankfurter	Associate justice	F. Roosevelt	1939-1962
82. William Orville Douglas	Associate justice	F. Roosevelt	1939-1975
83. Francis William (Frank) Murphy	Associate justice	F. Roosevelt	1940-1949
84. Harlan Fiske Stone [d]	Chief justice	F. Roosevelt	1941-1946
85. James Francis Byrnes	Associate justice	F. Roosevelt	1941-1942
86. Robert Houghwout Jackson	Associate justice	F. Roosevelt	1941-1954
87. Wiley Blount Rutledge	Associate justice	F. Roosevelt	1943-1949
88. Harold Hitz Burton	Associate justice	Truman	1945-1958
89. Fred Moore Vinson	Chief justice	Truman	1946-1953
90. Tom Campbell Clark	Associate justice	Truman	1949-1967
91. Sherman Minton	Associate justice	Truman	1949-1956
92. Earl Warren	Chief justice	Eisenhower	1953-1969
93. John Marshall Harlan	Associate justice	Eisenhower	1955-1971

Table 4-1   *(Continued)*

Appointment number/justice[a]	Position	Appointing president	Years of service[b]
94. William Joseph Brennan, Jr.	Associate justice	Eisenhower	1956-1990
95. Charles Evans Whittaker	Associate justice	Eisenhower	1957-1962
96. Potter Stewart	Associate justice	Eisenhower	1958-1981
97. Byron Raymond White	Associate justice	Kennedy	1962-1993
98. Arthur Joseph Goldberg	Associate justice	Kennedy	1962-1965
99. Abe Fortas	Associate justice	Johnson	1965-1969
100. Thurgood Marshall	Associate justice	Johnson	1967-1991
101. Warren Earl Burger	Chief justice	Nixon	1969-1986
102. Harry Andrew Blackmun	Associate justice	Nixon	1970-
103. Lewis Franklin Powell, Jr.	Associate justice	Nixon	1971-1987
104. William Hubbs Rehnquist[c]	Associate justice	Nixon	1971-1986
105. John Paul Stevens	Associate justice	Ford	1975-
106. Sandra Day O'Connor	Associate justice	Reagan	1981-
107. William Hubbs Rehnquist[d]	Chief justice	Reagan	1986-
108. Antonin Scalia	Associate justice	Reagan	1986-
109. Anthony McLeod Kennedy	Associate justice	Reagan	1988-
110. David H. Souter	Associate justice	Bush	1990-
111. Clarence Thomas	Associate justice	Bush	1991-
112. Ruth Bader Ginsburg	Associate justice	Clinton	1993-

[a] Ordered according to date of appointment.
[b] Begin with date of Senate confirmation or date of recess appointment (whichever occurred first); end with date of service termination.
[c] Served subsequently as chief justice.
[d] Served previously as associate justice.

Source: Elder Witt, *Congressional Quarterly's Guide to the U.S. Supreme Court,* 2d ed. (Washington, D.C.: Congressional Quarterly, 1990).

Table 4-2 Births and Childhoods

Justice (appointment number)	Date/place of birth	Childhood location[a]	Childhood surroundings[b]	Family status[c]	Judicial family[d]
Baldwin, Henry (23)	January 14, 1780; New Haven, Connecticut	Same	Family farm	Lower-middle	No
Barbour, Philip P. (26)	May 25, 1783; Orange County, Virginia	Same	Family farm	Upper	Yes
Black, Hugo L. (79)	February 27, 1886; Harlan, Alabama	Ashland, Alabama	Small town	Lower-middle	No
Blackmun, Harry A. (102)	November 12, 1908; Nashville, Illinois	Minneapolis, Minnesota	Urban	Middle	No
Blair, John, Jr. (5)	1732; Williamsburg, Virginia	Same	Family plantation	Upper	No
Blatchford, Samuel (49)	March 9, 1820; New York City, New York	Same	Urban	Upper	No
Bradley, Joseph P. (42)	March 14, 1813; Berne, New York	Same	Family farm	Lower-middle	No
Brandeis, Louis D. (69)	November 13, 1856; Louisville, Kentucky	Same	Urban	Upper	No

Name	Birth date; place		Setting	Class	
Brennan, William J., Jr. (94)	April 25, 1906; Newark, New Jersey	Same	Urban	Middle	No
Brewer, David J. (52)	June 20, 1837; Smyrna, Asia Minor (Turkey)	Wethersfield, Connecticut	Small town	Upper-middle	Yes
Brown, Henry B. (53)	March 2, 1836; South Lee, Massachusetts	Same	Small town	Upper-middle	No
Burger, Warren E. (101)	September 17, 1907; St. Paul, Minnesota	Same	Urban	Lower-middle	No
Burton, Harold H. (88)	June 22, 1888; Jamaica Plain, Massachusetts	Same	Urban	Middle	No
Butler, Pierce (73)	March 17, 1866; Northfield, Minnesota	Pine Bend, Minnesota	Family farm	Lower-middle	No
Byrnes, James F. (85)	May 2, 1879; Charleston, South Carolina	Same	Urban	Lower	No
Campbell, John A. (34)	June 24, 1811; Washington, Georgia	Same	Small town	Upper-middle	Yes
Cardozo, Benjamin (78)	May 24, 1870; New York City, New York	Same	Urban	Upper-middle	Yes

(Table continues)

Table 4-2 (Continued)

Justice (appointment number)	Date/place of birth	Childhood location [a]	Childhood surroundings [b]	Family status [c]	Judicial family [d]
Catron, John (27)	1786; Pennsylvania [e]	Virginia and Kentucky	Rural	Lower	No
Chase, Salmon P. (40)	January 13, 1808; Cornish, New Hampshire	Keene, New Hampshire	Small town	Middle	No
Chase, Samuel (10)	April 17, 1741; Somerset County, Maryland	Baltimore, Maryland	Urban	Upper-middle	No
Clark, Tom C. (90)	September 23, 1899; Dallas, Texas	Same	Urban	Upper-middle	No
Clarke, John H. (70)	September 18, 1857; Lisbon, Ohio	Same	Small town	Upper-middle	Yes
Clifford, Nathan (35)	August 18, 1803; Rumney, New Hampshire	Western New Hampshire	Rural	Lower	No
Curtis, Benjamin R. (33)	November 4, 1809; Watertown, Massachusetts	Same	Small town	Middle	Yes
Cushing, William (3)	March 1, 1732; Scituate, Massachusetts	Same	Small town	Upper	Yes
Daniel, Peter V. (29)	April 24, 1784; Stafford County, Virginia	Same	Family plantation	Upper	No

Davis, David (38)	March 9, 1815; Cecil County, Maryland	Same	Rural	Middle	No
Day, William R. (60)	April 17, 1849; Ravenna, Ohio	Same	Small town	Upper	Yes
Douglas, William O. (82)	October 16, 1898; Maine, Minnesota	Yakima, Washington	Small town	Lower	No
Duvall, Gabriel (18)	December 6, 1752; Prince George's County, Maryland	Buena Vista, Maryland	Family plantation	Upper	No
Ellsworth, Oliver (11)	April 29, 1745; Windsor, Connecticut	Same	Family farm	Upper	No
Field, Stephen J. (39)	November 4, 1816; Haddam, Connecticut	Stockbridge, Massachusetts	Small town	Upper-middle	No
Fortas, Abe (99)	June 19, 1910; Memphis, Tennessee	Same	Urban	Lower-middle	No
Frankfurter, Felix (81)	November 15, 1882; Vienna, Austria	Vienna, Austria; New York City	Urban	Lower-middle	No
Fuller, Melville W. (51)	February 11, 1833; Augusta, Maine	Same	Small city	Upper	Yes
Ginsburg, Ruth Bader (112)	March 15, 1933; Brooklyn, New York	Same	Urban	Middle	No

(Table continues)

Table 4-2 (Continued)

Justice (appointment number)	Date/place of birth	Childhood location [a]	Childhood surroundings [b]	Family status [c]	Judicial family [d]
Goldberg, Arthur J. (98)	August 8, 1908; Chicago, Illinois	Same	Urban	Lower	No
Gray, Horace (48)	March 24, 1828; Boston, Massachusetts	Same	Urban	Upper	Yes
Grier, Robert C. (32)	March 5, 1794; Cumberland County, Pennsylvania	Lycoming County, Pennsylvania	Rural	Middle	No
Harlan, John Marshall I (45)	June 1, 1833; Boyle County, Kentucky	Same	Rural	Upper	No
Harlan, John Marshall II (93)	May 20, 1899; Chicago, Illinois	Same	Urban	Upper	Yes
Holmes, Oliver W., Jr. (59)	March 8, 1841; Boston, Massachusetts	Same	Urban	Upper	Yes
Hughes, Charles Evans (63, 76)	April 11, 1862; Glens Falls, New York	Same	Small town	Middle	No
Hunt, Ward (43)	June 14, 1810; Utica, New York	Same	Small city	Upper-middle	No

Name	Birth date and place	Location	Setting	Class	
Iredell, James (6)	October 5, 1751; Lewes, England	Bristol, England	Urban	Upper-middle	No
Jackson, Howell E. (55)	April 8, 1832; Paris, Tennessee	Jackson, Tennessee	Small town	Middle	No
Jackson, Robert H. (86)	February 13, 1892; Spring Creek, Pennsylvania	Frewsburg, New York	Small town	Middle	No
Jay, John (1)	December 12, 1745; New York, New York	Rye, New York	Family farm	Upper	No
Johnson, Thomas (7)	November 4, 1732; Calvert County, Maryland	Same	Family plantation	Upper	No
Johnson, William (15)	December 27, 1771; Charleston, South Carolina	Same	Urban	Upper-middle	No
Kennedy, Anthony (109)	July 23, 1936; Sacramento, California	Same	Urban	Upper-middle	No
Lamar, Joseph R. (66)	October 14, 1857; Elbert County, Georgia	Ruckersville, Georgia	Family plantation	Upper-middle	Yes
Lamar, Lucius Q.C. (50)	September 17, 1825; Eatonton, Georgia	Same	Family plantation	Upper	Yes
Livingston, Henry Brockholst (16)	November 25, 1757; New York, New York	New York, New York; Elizabethtown, New Jersey	Urban	Upper	Yes

(Table continues)

Table 4-2 (*Continued*)

Justice (appointment number)	Date/place of birth	Childhood location [a]	Childhood surroundings [b]	Family status [c]	Judicial family [d]
Lurton, Horace (62)	February 26, 1844; Newport, Kentucky	Clarksville, Tennessee	Small town	Upper-middle	No
Marshall, John (14)	September 24, 1755; Germantown, Virginia	Same	Rural	Upper-middle	No
Marshall, Thurgood (100)	July 2, 1908; Baltimore, Maryland	Same	Urban	Lower-middle	No
Matthews, Stanley (47)	July 21, 1824; Cincinnati, Ohio	Same	Urban	Middle	No
McKenna, Joseph (58)	August 10, 1843; Philadelphia, Pennsylvania	Same	Urban	Lower-middle	No
McKinley, John (28)	May 1, 1780; Culpepper County, Virginia	Lincoln County, Kentucky	Rural	Upper-middle	No
McLean, John (22)	March 11, 1785; Morris County, New Jersey	Virginia, Kentucky, Ohio	Rural	Lower-middle	No
McReynolds, James C. (68)	February 3, 1862; Elkton, Kentucky	Same	Family farm	Upper-middle	No
Miller, Samuel (37)	April 5, 1816; Richmond, Kentucky	Madison County, Kentucky	Family farm	Lower-middle	No

Minton, Sherman (91)	October 20, 1890; Georgetown, Indiana	New Albany, Indiana	Family farm	Lower-middle	No
Moody, William H. (61)	December 23, 1853; Newbury, Massachusetts	Same	Family farm	Upper	Yes
Moore, Alfred (13)	May 21, 1755; Brunswick County, North Carolina	Same	Rural	Upper	Yes
Murphy, Frank (83)	April 13, 1890; Harbor Beach, Michigan	Same	Small town	Middle	No
Nelson, Samuel (30)	November 10, 1792; Hebron, New York	Washington County, New York	Family farm	Upper-middle	No
O'Connor, Sandra Day (106)	March 26, 1930; El Paso, Texas	El Paso; Southeastern Arizona	Urban; family ranch	Upper-middle	No
Paterson, William (8)	December 24, 1745; County Antrim, Ireland	Princeton, New Jersey	Small town	Upper-middle	No
Peckham, Rufus W. (57)	November 8, 1838; Albany, New York	Same	Urban	Upper	Yes

(Table continues)

188

Table 4-2 (*Continued*)

Justice (appointment number)	Date/place of birth	Childhood location[a]	Childhood surroundings[b]	Family status[c]	Judicial family[d]
Pitney, Mahlon (67)	February 5, 1858; Morristown, New Jersey	Same	Family farm	Upper	Yes
Powell, Lewis F., Jr. (103)	September 19, 1907; Suffolk, Virginia	Norfolk, Virginia	Urban	Upper	No
Reed, Stanley F. (80)	December 31, 1884; Minerva, Kentucky	Same	Small town	Upper-middle	No
Rehnquist, William (104, 107)	October 1, 1924; Milwaukee, Wisconsin	Same	Urban	Upper-middle	No
Roberts, Owen J. (77)	May 2, 1875; Germantown, Pennsylvania	Philadelphia, Pennsylvania	Urban	Middle	No
Rutledge, John (2, 9)	September, 1739; Charleston, South Carolina	Same	Urban	Upper	No
Rutledge, Wiley B. (87)	July 20, 1894; Cloverport, Kentucky	Same	Small town	Middle	No
Sanford, Edward T. (74)	July 23, 1865; Knoxville, Tennessee	Same	Small city	Upper	No
Scalia, Antonin (108)	March 11, 1936; Trenton, New Jersey	Queens, New York	Urban	Middle	No

Shiras, George, Jr. (54)	January 26, 1832; Pittsburgh, Pennsylvania	Western Pennsylvania	Family farm	Upper	Yes
Souter, David H. (110)	September 17, 1939; Melrose, Massachusetts	Weare, New Hampshire	Small town	Middle	No
Stevens, John Paul (105)	April 20, 1920; Chicago, Illinois	Same	Urban	Upper	No
Stewart, Potter (96)	January 23, 1915; Jackson, Michigan	Cincinnati, Ohio	Urban	Upper	Yes
Stone, Harlan Fiske (75, 84)	October 11, 1872; Chesterfield, New Hampshire	Same	Family farm	Middle	No
Story, Joseph (19)	September 18, 1779; Marblehead, Massachusetts	Same	Small town	Upper	Yes
Strong, William (41)	May 6, 1808; Somers, Connecticut	Same	Small town	Upper-middle	No
Sutherland, George (72)	March 25, 1862; Buckinghamshire, England	Provo, Utah	Small town	Lower-middle	No
Swayne, Noah H. (36)	December 7, 1804; Frederick County, Virginia	Same	Rural	Middle	No

(Table continues)

189

Table 4-2 (*Continued*)

Justice (appointment number)	Date/place of birth	Childhood location [a]	Childhood surroundings [b]	Family status [c]	Judicial family [d]
Taft, William H. (71)	September 15, 1857; Cincinnati, Ohio	Same	Urban	Upper	Yes
Taney, Roger B. (25)	March 17, 1777; Calvert County, Maryland	Same	Family plantation	Upper	No
Thomas, Clarence (111)	June 23, 1948; Savannah, Georgia	Pin Point, Georgia	Small town	Lower	No
Thompson, Smith (20)	January 17, 1768; Dutchess County, New York	Same	Rural	Upper-middle	No
Todd, Thomas (17)	January 23, 1765; King and Queen County, Virginia	Same	Rural	Lower-middle	No
Trimble, Robert (21)	November 17, 1776; Augusta County, Virginia	Jefferson County, Kentucky	Rural	Lower-middle	No
Van Devanter, Willis (65)	April 17, 1859; Marion, Indiana	Same	Small town	Upper-middle	No
Vinson, Fred M. (89)	January 22, 1890; Louisa, Kentucky	Same	Small town	Lower-middle	No

Name	Birth date; place	Location	Setting	Class	Column
Waite, Morrison (44)	November 29, 1816; Lyme, Connecticut	Same	Small town	Upper	Yes
Warren, Earl (92)	March 19, 1891; Los Angeles, California	Bakersfield, California	Small town	Lower-middle	No
Washington, Bushrod (12)	June 5, 1762; Westmoreland County, Virginia	Same	Family plantation	Upper	Yes
Wayne, James M. (24)	1790; Savannah, Georgia	Same	Family plantation	Upper	No
White, Byron R. (97)	June 8, 1917; Fort Collins, Colorado	Wellington, Colorado	Small town	Middle	No
White, Edward D. (56, 64)	November 3, 1845; Lafourche Parish, Louisiana	Same	Family plantation	Upper	Yes
Whittaker, Charles E. (95)	February 22, 1901; Troy, Kansas	Same	Family farm	Lower-middle	No
Wilson, James (4)	September 14, 1742; Caskardy, Scotland	Same	Rural	Lower	No
Woodbury, Levi (31)	December 22, 1789; Francestown, New Hampshire	Same	Family farm	Upper-middle	No

(Table continues)

191

Table 4-2 (Continued)

Justice (appointment number)	Date/place of birth	Childhood location[a]	Childhood surroundings[b]	Family status[c]	Judicial family[d]
Woods, William B. (46)	August 3, 1824; Newark, Ohio	Same	Small town	Upper-middle	No

[a] "Same" indicates that the location of the justice's childhood was the same as his or her place of birth.

[b] Refers to the general environment in which the justice spent his or her formative years. In several cases a justice's family moved one or more times during the justice's childhood. In such cases, the more prominent childhood experience is listed.

[c] Indicates general socioeconomic status of the justice's family during his or her childhood. The families of some of the justices, especially in the earlier years of the nation, experienced major upward or downward shifts in their economic status. In such cases, the justices are categorized according to the status that best describes the largest segment of their childhood.

[d] Indicates whether or not the justice grew up in a family with a tradition of judicial service.

[e] Both the date and place of John Catron's birth are unclear. Some scholars estimate it to have been as early as 1778, and there is some evidence that it may have occurred in Virginia.

Sources: Elder Witt, *Congressional Quarterly's Guide to the U.S. Supreme Court,* 2d ed. (Washington, D.C.: Congressional Quarterly, 1990); Leon Friedman and Fred L. Israel, eds., *The Justices of the United States Supreme Court: Their Lives and Major Opinions* (New York: R.R. Bowker, 1969-1978); Harold W. Chase et al., *Biographical Dictionary of the American Judiciary* (Detroit: Gale Research, 1976); *Judges of the United States,* 2d ed. (Washington, D.C.: Judicial Conference of the United States, 1983); *The National Cyclopaedia of American Biography* (New York: James T. White, various years); *Dictionary of American Biography* (New York: Charles Scribner's Sons, various editions); John R. Schmidhauser, *Supreme Court Justices Biographical Data 1958* (Ann Arbor, Mich.: Inter-University Consortium for Political Research, 1972).

Table 4-3 Family Backgrounds

Justice (appointment number)	Religion	Ethnic background	Father/ mother	Father's occupation	Political offices held by father
Baldwin, Henry (23)	Episcopalian	English	Michael Baldwin / Theodora Wolcott	Small farmer; skilled craftsman	None
Barbour, Philip P. (26)	Episcopalian	Scotch	Thomas Barbour / Mary P. Thomas	Plantation owner	Virginia legislator
Black, Hugo L. (79)	Baptist	Scotch/Irish	William L. Black / Martha A. Toland	Storekeeper; farmer	None
Blackmun, Harry A. (102)	Methodist	English/German	Corwin Blackmun / Theo Reuter	Businessman	None
Blair, John, Jr. (5)	Episcopalian [a]	Scotch/Irish	John Blair / Mary Monro	Plantation owner	Virginia legislator, governor's council acting governor
Blatchford, Samuel (49)	Episcopalian [a]	English	Richard Blatchford / Julia Ann Mumford	Lawyer; banker	New York legislator
Bradley, Joseph P. (42)	Dutch Reform [b]	English	Philo Bradley / Mercy Gardiner	Small farmer; teacher	None
Brandeis, Louis D. (69)	Jewish	German	Adolph Brandeis / Fredericka Dembitz	Grain merchant	None

(Table continues)

194

Table 4-3 (*Continued*)

Justice (appointment number)	Religion	Ethnic background	Father/ mother	Father's occupation	Political offices held by father
Brennan, William J., Jr. (94)	Roman Catholic	Irish	William J. Brennan / Agnes McDermott	Labor organizer; brewery worker	New Jersey local official
Brewer, David J. (52)	Congregational	English	Josiah Brewer / Emilia Field	Congregational minister	None
Brown, Henry B. (53)	Congregational	English	Billings Brown / Mary Tyler	Merchant; manufacturer	None
Burger, Warren E. (101)	Presbyterian	Swiss/German	Charles J. Burger / Katharine Schnittger	Railroad cargo inspector; small farmer; salesman	None
Burton, Harold H. (88)	Unitarian	English/Swiss	Alfred E. Burton / Gertrude Hitz	Professor	None
Butler, Pierce (73)	Roman Catholic	Irish	Patrick Butler / Mary Gaffney	Small farmer	None
Byrnes, James F. (85)[c]	Episcopalian[d]	Irish	James Byrnes / Elizabeth McSweeney	Municipal clerk	None
Campbell, John A. (34)	Episcopalian[a]	Scotch/Irish	Duncan Campbell / Mary Williamson	Lawyer; teacher	Georgia legislator

Cardozo, Benjamin (78)	Jewish	Spanish	Albert Cardozo / Rebecca Washington	Lawyer	New York judge
Catron, John (27)	Presbyterian	German	Peter Catron / Unknown	Small farmer	None
Chase, Salmon P. (40)[e]	Episcopalian	English/Scotch	Ithamar Chase / Janette Ralston	Tavern owner	New Hampshire local official
Chase, Samuel (10)	Episcopalian	English	Thomas Chase / Martha Walker	Episcopal clergy	None
Clark, Tom C. (90)	Presbyterian	Scotch	William H. Clark / Jennie Falls	Lawyer	Texas local official
Clarke, John H. (70)	Protestant	Scotch/Irish	John Clarke / Melissa Hessin	Lawyer	Ohio judge
Clifford, Nathan (35)	Unitarian[f]	English	Nathaniel Clifford / Lydia Simpson	Small farmer	None
Curtis, Benjamin R. (33)[g]	Episcopalian[h]	English	Benjamin Curtis / Lois Robbins	Ship captain	None
Cushing, William (3)	Congregational[i]	English	John Cushing / Mary Cotton	Lawyer	Massachusetts judge
Daniel, Peter V. (29)	Episcopalian	English	Travers Daniel / Frances Moncure	Plantation owner	Virginia legislator

(Table continues)

Table 4-3 (Continued)

Justice (appointment number)	Religion	Ethnic background	Father/ mother	Father's occupation	Political offices held by father
Davis, David (38)[j]	Presbyterian[a]	English/Welsh	David Davis / Ann Mercer	Physician	None
Day, William R. (60)	Lutheran	English	Luther Day / Emily Spalding	Lawyer	Ohio chief justice
Douglas, William O. (82)[k]	Presbyterian	Scotch	William Douglas / Julia F. Bickford	Presbyterian minister	None
Duvall, Gabriel (18)	Episcopalian	French	Benjamin Duvall / Susanna Tyler	Plantation owner	Unknown
Ellsworth, Oliver (11)	Congregational	English	David Ellsworth / Jemima Leavitt	Farm owner; captain, Connecticut militia	Connecticut local official
Field, Stephen J. (39)	Episcopalian	English	David Dudley Field / Submit Dickinson	Congregational minister	None
Fortas, Abe (99)	Jewish	English	William Fortas / Ray Berson	Cabinetmaker	None
Frankfurter, Felix (81)	Jewish[l]	Austrian	Leopold Frankfurter / Emma Winter	Merchant	None

197

Fuller, Melville W. (51) [m]	Episcopalian	English	Frederick A. Fuller / Catherine Weston	Lawyer	Maine local official
Ginsburg, Ruth Bader (112)	Jewish	German	Nathan Bader / Celia Amster	Merchant	None
Goldberg, Arthur J. (98)	Jewish	Russian	Joseph Goldberg / Rebecca Perlstein	Carter, peddler	None
Gray, Horace (48)	Unitarian	English	Horace Gray / Harriet Upham	Businessman	None
Grier, Robert C. (32)	Presbyterian	Scotch	Issac Grier / Elizabeth Cooper	Presbyterian minister; farmer; teacher	None
Harlan, John Marshall I (45)	Presbyterian	English	James Harlan / Eliza S. Davenport	Lawyer	Kentucky attorney general, secretary of state; U.S. representative
Harlan, John Marshall II (93)	Presbyterian	English	John M. Harlan / Elizabeth Flagg	Lawyer	Illinois local official
Holmes, Oliver W., Jr. (59)	Unitarian	English	Oliver W. Holmes / Amelia Lee Jackson	Professor; poet; physician	None
Hughes, Charles E. (63, 76)	Baptist	English	David C. Hughes / Mary C. Connelly	Baptist minister	None

(Table continues)

Table 4-3 (*Continued*)

Justice (appointment number)	Religion	Ethnic background	Father/ mother	Father's occupation	Political offices held by father
Hunt, Ward (43)	Episcopalian	English	Montgomery Hunt Elizabeth Stringham	Banker	None
Iredell, James (6)	Episcopalian	English/Irish	Francis Iredell Margaret McCulloch	Merchant	None
Jackson, Howell E. (55)	Baptist	Scotch	Alexander Jackson Mary Hurt	Physician	None
Jackson, Robert H. (86)	Episcopalian	Scotch	William E. Jackson Angelina Houghwout	Farm owner; livery stable owner	None
Jay, John (1)	Episcopalian[n]	French/Dutch	Peter Jay Mary Van Cortlandt	Merchant	None
Johnson, Thomas (7)	Episcopalian	English	Thomas Johnson Dorcas Sedgwick	Plantation owner	Maryland legislator
Johnson, William (15)	Presbyterian[a]	English/Dutch	William Johnson Sarah Nightingale	Blacksmith; landowner	South Carolina legislator
Kennedy, Anthony (109)	Roman Catholic	Irish	Anthony Kennedy Gladys McLeod	Lawyer; lobbyist	None
Lamar, Joseph R. (66)[o]	Disciples of Christ	French	James S. Lamar Mary Rucker	Lawyer; Disciples of Christ minister	None

Name	Religion	Ethnicity	Parents	Father's occupation	Father's political position
Lamar, Lucius Q.C. (50) [p]	Methodist	French	Lucius Q. C. Lamar / Sarah Bird	Plantation owner; lawyer	Georgia judge
Livingston, H. Brockholst (16)	Presbyterian	Scotch/Dutch	William Livingston / Susanna French	Landowner	New Jersey governor
Lurton, Horace (62)	Episcopalian	English	Lycurgus Lurton / Sarah Ann Harmon	Physician; Episcopal minister	None
Marshall, John (14)	Episcopalian	English/Welsh	Thomas Marshall / Mary Randolph Keith	Farmer; surveyor; land speculator	Virginia revenue collector, legislator
Marshall, Thurgood (100)	Episcopalian	African	William Marshall / Norma Williams	Club steward	None
Matthews, Stanley (47)	Presbyterian	English	Thomas J. Matthews / Isabella Brown	Professor	None
McKenna, Joseph (58) [q]	Roman Catholic	Irish	John McKenna / May Ann Johnson	Baker	None
McKinley, John (28)	Protestant	Scotch	Andrew McKinley / Mary Logan	Physician	None
McLean, John (22)	Methodist [r]	Scotch/Irish	Fergus McLean / Sophia Blackford	Weaver; small farmer	None

(Table continues)

Table 4-3 (Continued)

Justice (appointment number)	Religion	Ethnic background	Father/ mother	Father's occupation	Political offices held by father
McReynolds, James C. (68)	Disciples of Christ	Scotch/Irish	John McReynolds Ellen Reeves	Physician; farmer	None
Miller, Samuel (37)	Unitarian	German	Frederick Miller Patsy Freeman	Small farmer	None
Minton, Sherman (91)	Protestant	English	John E. Minton Emma Lyvers	Small farmer	None
Moody, William H. (61)	Episcopalian	English	Henry Moody Melissa Emerson	Businessman; farmer	None
Moore, Alfred (13)	Episcopalian	English/Irish	Maurice Moore Anne Grange	Lawyer	North Carolina judge
Murphy, Frank (83)	Roman Catholic	Irish	John Murphy Mary Brennan	Lawyer	None
Nelson, Samuel (30)	Episcopalian	Scotch/Irish	John Rogers Nelson Jane McCarter[s]	Farm owner	None
O'Connor, Sandra Day (106)	Episcopalian	English	Harry A. Day Ada Mae Wilkey	Rancher	None

Paterson, William (8)	Presbyterian	Scotch/Irish	Richard Paterson Mary	Manufacturer of tin plate; merchant; real estate investor	None
Peckham, Rufus W. (57)	Episcopalian	English	Rufus W. Peckham Isabella Lacey	Lawyer	New York judge, district attorney; U.S. representative
Pitney, Mahlon (67)	Presbyterian	English	Henry C. Pitney Sarah L. Halsted	Lawyer	New Jersey judge
Powell, Lewis F., Jr. (103)	Presbyterian	English/Welsh	Lewis F. Powell Mary Gwathmey	Businessman	None
Reed, Stanley F. (80)	Protestant	English	John A. Reed Frances Forman	Physician	None
Rehnquist, William (104, 107)	Lutheran	Scandinavian	William B. Rehnquist Margery Peck	Sales	None
Roberts, Owen J. (77)	Episcopalian	Welsh/Dutch/Scotch/Irish	Josephus Roberts Emma Laferty	Businessman	Pennsylvania local official
Rutledge, John (2, 9)	Episcopalian	Scotch/English	John Rutledge Sarah Hext	Physician	None
Rutledge, Wiley B. (87)	Unitarian	English	Wiley Rutledge Mary Lou Wigginton	Baptist minister	None

(Table continues)

Table 4-3 *(Continued)*

Justice (appointment number)	Religion	Ethnic background	Father/ mother	Father's occupation	Political offices held by father
Sanford, Edward T. (74)	Episcopalian	English/Swiss	Edward J. Sanford Emma Chavannes	Lumber and construction business	None
Scalia, Antonin (108)	Roman Catholic	Italian	Eugene Scalia Catherine Panaro	Professor	None
Shiras, George, Jr. (54)	Presbyterian [t]	Scotch	George Shiras Eliza Herron	Brewer; peach farmer	None
Souter, David H. (110)	Episcopalian	English	Joseph A. Souter Helen A. Hackett	Banker	None
Stevens, John Paul (105)	Protestant	English	Ernest J. Stevens Elizabeth Street	Businessman	None
Stewart, Potter (96)	Episcopalian	English	James G. Stewart Harriet L. Potter	Lawyer	Cincinnati mayor; Ohio supreme court
Stone, Harlan Fiske (75, 84)	Episcopalian	English	Frederick L. Stone Ann Sophia Butler	Farm owner	New Hampshire local official
Story, Joseph (19)	Unitarian [u]	English	Elisha Story Mehitable Pedrick	Physician	None

Strong, William (41)	Presbyterian	English	William L. Strong Harriet Deming	Presbyterian minister	None
Sutherland, George (72)	Episcopalian	Scotch/English	Alexander Sutherland Frances Slater	Lawyer; postman; prospector	None
Swayne, Noah H. (36)[v]	Quaker	English	Joshua Swayne Rebecca Smith	Farm owner	None
Taft, William H. (71)	Unitarian	Scotch/English	Alphonso Taft Louisa M. Torrey	Lawyer	Ohio judge; U.S. secretary of war; U.S. attorney general
Taney, Roger B. (25)	Roman Catholic	English	Michael Taney Monica Brooke	Tobacco planter; plantation owner	Virginia legislator
Thomas, Clarence (111)[w]	Roman Catholic[x]	African	M. C. Thomas Leola Anderson	Farm worker	None
Thompson, Smith (20)	Presbyterian	English	Ezra Thompson Rachel Smith	Farm owner	New York local official
Todd, Thomas (17)[y]	Presbyterian[a]	English	Richard Todd Elizabeth Richards	Plantation owner	Local official
Trimble, Robert (21)	Presbyterian	Scotch	William Trimble Mary McMillan	Pioneer settler; farmer	Kentucky local official

(Table continues)

Table 4-3 *(Continued)*

Justice (appointment number)	Religion	Ethnic background	Father/ mother	Father's occupation	Political offices held by father
Van Devanter, Willis (65)	Episcopalian	Dutch	Isaac Van Devanter Violetta Spencer	Lawyer	None
Vinson, Fred M. (89)	Methodist	English	James Vinson Virginia Ferguson	County jailer	Kentucky local official
Waite, Morrison (44)	Episcopalian	English	Henry Matson Waite Maria Selden	Lawyer; farmer	Connecticut chief justice
Warren, Earl (92)	Protestant	Scandinavian	Methias Warren Chrystal Hernlund	Railroad car mechanic	None
Washington, Bushrod (12)	Episcopalian	English	John A. Washington Hannah Bushrod	Plantation owner	Virginia legislator; county judge
Wayne, James M. (24)	Episcopalian	English	Richard Wayne Elizabeth Clifford	Plantation owner	Georgia local official
White, Byron R. (97)	Episcopalian	English	Alpha A. White Maude Burger	Lumber company manager	Mayor of Wellington, Colorado
White, Edward D. (56, 64)[z]	Roman Catholic	Irish	Edward White Catherine Ringgold	Plantation owner; lawyer	Louisiana judge, governor; U.S. representative

Whittaker, Charles E. (95)	Methodist	English	Charles Whittaker Ida Miller	Farm owner	None
Wilson, James (4)	Episcopalian	Scotch	William Wilson Alison Lansdale	Small farmer	None
Woodbury, Levi (31)	Presbyterian [a]	English	Peter Woodbury Mary Woodbury	Merchant; farmer	New Hampshire legislator
Woods, William B. (46)	Protestant	Scotch/English	Ezekiel Woods Sarah J. Burnham	Farm owner; merchant	None

Note: During the historical period in which all but the most recent justices were reared, families tended to depend upon the father for financial support and mothers generally remained at home to administer the household and care for the children. Similarly, politics was a sphere of activity almost exclusively reserved for men. Consequently, listed here are the occupations of the fathers as an indicator of the economic and social status of the family. Also listed are the political offices held by the fathers as an indicator of the political atmosphere in the home. Specific notes (see below) indicate family situations in which these traditional roles were not in place.

[a] For a number of justices there is some confusion as to whether they belonged to the Presbyterian Church or the Episcopal Church. Both strains of Protestantism traditionally have attracted individuals from the upper socio-economic groups. Here we list the affiliation most commonly cited in the literature, but some sources identify the justice with membership in the other church.

[b] Some sources claim that as an adult Bradley affiliated with either the Lutheran or Presbyterian churches.

[c] Byrnes's father died several weeks before he was born. His mother supported the family as a dressmaker.

[d] Byrnes converted from Roman Catholicism.

[e] Chase's father died when he was nine. He spent the rest of his childhood with an uncle in Ohio.

[f] Clifford converted from the Congregational Church.

[g] When Curtis was five years old his father died at sea while on a voyage to Chile. He was raised by his mother, who supported the family by running a boarding house and library.

[h] Curtis converted from Unitarianism.

[i] Some sources claim that Cushing became affiliated with the Unitarian faith.

[j] Davis's father died before his birth. He was raised by his mother, who remarried when Davis was five years old. Davis's stepfather was a bookseller and stationer.

(Notes continue)

Table 4-3 (*Continued*)

k Douglas's father died when he was six. He was raised by his mother.

l Frankfurter's religious faith was largely agnostic.

m When Fuller was still an infant, his mother won divorce from his father on grounds of adultery. His mother moved in with her father and supported herself and two children as a piano teacher. When she remarried, the eleven-year-old Fuller decided to remain with his grandfather.

n Jay was raised in the French Huguenot religious tradition.

o When Lamar was eight his mother died. His father remarried two years later and moved the family to Augusta, Georgia.

p Lamar's father committed suicide when he was nine. He was raised by his mother with the help of other family members.

q McKenna's father died when he was fifteen. The eldest of six children, McKenna aided his mother in raising the family.

r McLean converted from Presbyterianism.

s Listed as Jean McArthur by some sources.

t Shiras became an agnostic in his advanced years.

u Some scholars claim Story to have been a member of the Congregational Church.

v Swayne's father died when he was four. He was raised by his mother.

w When Thomas was a young child his father deserted the family. His mother worked as a crab picker. Shortly thereafter he went to live with his grandparents who played a major role in his upbringing.

x Thomas was born into a Baptist family, but was raised by his grandparents as a Roman Catholic and studied for the Catholic priesthood. In his later adult years he regularly attended a charismatic Episcopal church.

y Todd's father died when he was an infant. His mother ran a boardinghouse and raised him until she died several years later. Todd was entrusted to guardians until he reached maturity.

z White was two when his father died. His mother remarried not long thereafter. White spent much of his childhood in boarding schools.

Sources: Elder Witt, *Congressional Quarterly's Guide to the U.S. Supreme Court,* 2d ed. (Washington, D.C.: Congressional Quarterly, 1990); Leon Friedman and Fred L. Israel, eds., *The Justices of the United States Supreme Court: Their Lives and Major Opinions* (New York: R.R. Bowker, 1969-1978); Harold W. Chase et al., *Biographical Dictionary of the American Judiciary* (Detroit: Gale Research, 1976); *Judges of the United States,* 2d ed. (Washington, D.C.: Judicial Conference of the United States, 1983); John R. Schmidhauser, *Supreme Court Justices Biographical Data 1958* (Ann Arbor, Mich.: Inter-University Consortium for Political Research, 1972); *The National Cyclopaedia of American Biography* (New York: James T. White, various years); *Dictionary of American Biography* (New York: Charles Scribner's Sons, various editions).

207

Table 4-4 Education and Legal Training

Justice (appointment number)	Undergraduate education		Graduate education		Law school		Read the law[a]	
	School	Status/dates	School	Status/dates	School	Status/dates	Mentor/state	Dates studied
Baldwin, Henry (23)	Yale	Graduated 1797					Alexander Dallas (Pennsylvania)	1798
Barbour, Philip P. (26)	William and Mary	Attended 1801					Self taught (Virginia)	1800
Black, Hugo L. (79)	Birmingham Medical	Attended 1903-04			Alabama	Graduated 1906		
Blackmun, Harry A. (102)	Harvard	B.A. 1929			Harvard	Graduated 1932		
Blair, John, Jr. (5)	William and Mary	Graduated 1754			Middle Temple (England)	Attended 1755-56		
Blatchford, Samuel (49)	Columbia	B.A. 1837					William H. Seward (New York)	1837-41
Bradley, Joseph P. (42)	Rutgers	Graduated 1836					Archer Gifford (New Jersey)	1836-39

(Table continues)

Table 4-4 (Continued)

Justice (appointment number)	Undergraduate education		Graduate education		Law school		Read the law[a]	
	School	Status/dates	School	Status/dates	School	Status/dates	Mentor/state	Dates studied
Brandeis, Louis D. (69)	Annen Real Schule (Germany)	Attended 1873-75			Harvard	Graduated 1877		
Brennan, William J., Jr. (94)	Pennsylvania	B.S. 1928			Harvard	Graduated 1931		
Brewer, David J. (52)	Wesleyan Yale	Attended 1852-53 B.A. 1856			Albany	Graduated 1858	David Dudley Field (New York)	1856-57
Brown, Henry B. (53)	Yale	B.A. 1856			Yale Harvard	Attended 1858-59 Attended 1859	Local attorneys (Michigan)	1859-60
Burger, Warren E. (101)	Minnesota	Attended 1925-27			St. Paul	Graduated 1931		
Burton, Harold H. (88)	Bowdoin	B.A. 1909			Harvard	Graduated 1912		
Butler, Pierce (73)	Carleton	B.A., B.S. 1887					J. W. Pinch and John Twohy (Minnesota)	1887-88

Name	College	College degree	Graduate school	Graduate degree	Law study	Dates
Byrnes, James F. (85)	None				Self taught (South Carolina)	1896-1903
Campbell, John A. (34)	Georgia West Point	Graduated 1825 Attended 1825-28			Self taught (Georgia)	1829
Cardozo, Benjamin (78)	Columbia	B.A. 1889	Columbia	M.A. 1890	Columbia Attended 1890-91	
Catron, John (27)	None				Self taught (Tennessee)	1813-14
Chase, Salmon P. (40)	Dartmouth	Graduated 1826			William Wirt (Washington, D.C.)	1827-30
Chase, Samuel (10)	None				John Hammond and John Hall (Maryland)	1759-61
Clark, Tom C. (90)	Virginia Military Texas	Attended 1917-18 B.A. 1921	Texas	Graduated 1922		
Clarke, John H. (70)	Western Reserve	B.A. 1877	Western Reserve	M.A. 1880	John Clarke (Ohio)	1877-78

(Table continues)

Table 4-4 (Continued)

Justice (appointment number)	Undergraduate education		Graduate education		Law school		Read the law[a]	
	School	Status/dates	School	Status/dates	School	Status/dates	Mentor/state	Dates studied
Clifford, Nathan (35)	None						Josiah Quincy (New Hampshire)	1826-27
Curtis, Benjamin R. (33)	Harvard	Graduated 1829			Harvard	Graduated 1832		
Cushing, William (3)	Harvard	Graduated 1751					Jeremiah Gridley (Massachusetts)	1753-55
Daniel, Peter V. (29)	Princeton	Attended 1802-03					Edmund Randolph (Virginia)	1805-08
Davis, David (38)	Kenyon	Graduated 1832			Yale	Attended 1835	Henry W. Bishop (Massachusetts)	1833-34
Day, William R. (60)	Michigan	B.S. 1870			Michigan	Attended 1871-72	George Robinson (Ohio)	1871
Douglas, William O. (82)	Whitman	B.A. 1920			Columbia	Graduated 1925		
Duvall, Gabriel (18)	None						Local lawyers (Maryland)	1775-78

	College		Law study	
Ellsworth, Oliver (11)	Yale Princeton	Attended 1762-64 Graduated 1766	Self taught (Connecticut)	1767-71
Field, Stephen J. (39)	Williams	Graduated 1837	David Dudley Field and John Van Buren (New York)	1838-40
Fortas, Abe (99)	Southwestern	B.A. 1930	Yale	Graduated 1933
Frankfurter, Felix (81)	College of the City of New York	B.A. 1902	Harvard	Graduated 1906
Fuller, Melville W. (51)	Bowdoin	B.A. 1853	Harvard	Attended 1854-55
Ginsburg, Ruth Bader (112)	Cornell	B.A. 1954	Harvard Columbia	Attended 1956-58 Graduated 1959
Goldberg, Arthur J. (98)	Crane Jr. College DePaul Northwestern	Attended 1924-26 Attended 1924-26 B.S.L. 1929	North-western	Graduated 1930

(Table continues)

Table 4-4 (*Continued*)

Justice (appointment number)	Undergraduate education		Graduate education		Law school		Read the law[a]	
	School	Status/dates	School	Status/dates	School	Status/dates	Mentor/state	Dates studied
Gray, Horace (48)	Harvard	B.A. 1845			Harvard	Graduated 1849	John Lowell (Massachusetts)	1849-51
Grier, Robert C. (32)	Dickinson	Graduated 1812					Self taught (Pennsylvania)	1815-17
Harlan, John Marshall I (45)	Centre	Graduated 1850			Transylvania	Attended 1851-53	James Harlan, Thomas Marshal, and George Robertson (Kentucky)	1853
Harlan, John Marshall II (93)	Princeton	B.A. 1920	Oxford	Rhodes Scholar 1920-23	New York	Graduated 1925		
Holmes, Oliver W., Jr. (59)	Harvard	B.A. 1861			Harvard	Graduated 1866		
Hughes, Charles E. (63, 76)	Colgate Brown	Attended 1876-78 B.A. 1881	Brown	M.A. 1884	Columbia	Graduated 1884	William Gleason (New York)	1881-82
Hunt, Ward (43)	Union	Graduated 1828			Litchfield	Attended 1831	Hiram Denio (New York)	1829-31

Name	College	Law School	Legal Apprenticeship
Iredell, James (6)	None		Samuel Johnston 1768-70 (North Carolina)
Jackson, Howell E. (55)	West Tennessee B.A. 1849 Virgina Attended 1851-52	Cumberland Graduated 1856	A. W. O. Totten and Milton Brown (Tennessee) 1851-54
Jackson, Robert H. (86)	None	Albany Attended 1912	
Jay, John (1)	Columbia Graduated 1764		Benjamin Kissam 1765-68 (New York)
Johnson, Thomas (7)	None		Stephen Bordley 1759-60 (Maryland)
Johnson, William (15)	Princeton Graduated 1790		Charles Pinckney 1790-93 (South Carolina)
Kennedy, Anthony (109)	Stanford B.A. 1958 London School of Economics Attended 1957-58	Harvard Graduated 1961	
Lamar, Joseph R. (66)	Georgia Attended 1874-75 Bethany B.A. 1877	Washington and Lee Attended 1877	Henry Clay Foster (Georgia) 1878

(Table continues)

Table 4-4 *(Continued)*

Justice (appointment number)	Undergraduate education		Graduate education		Law school		Read the law[a]	
	School	Status/dates	School	Status/dates	School	Status/dates	Mentor/state	Dates studied
Lamar, Lucius Q. C. (50)	Emory	B.A. 1845					Absalom Chappell (Georgia)	1845-47
Livingston, H. Brockholst (16)	Princeton	Graduated 1774					Peter Yates (New York)	1782-83
Lurton, Horace (62)	Chicago	Attended 1859-60			Cumberland	Graduated 1867		
Marshall, John (14)	None				William and Mary	Attended 1780	Self taught (Virginia)	1780
Marshall, Thurgood (100)	Lincoln	B.A. 1930			Howard	Graduated 1933		
Matthews, Stanley (47)	Kenyon	B.A. 1840					Self taught (Ohio)	1840-42
McKenna, Joseph (58)	Benicia Institute	Graduated 1865			Columbia	Attended 1897	Self taught (California)	1864-65
McKinley, John (28)	None						Self taught (Kentucky)	1798-1800

Name				
McLean, John (22)	None		John Gano and Arthur St. Clair, Jr. (Ohio)	1804-06
McReynolds, James C. (68)	Vanderbilt	B.S. 1882	Virginia	Graduated 1884
Miller, Samuel (37)	Transylvania	M.D. 1838	Self taught (Kentucky)	1846-47
Minton, Sherman (91)	None		Indiana	Graduated 1915
			Yale	LL.M. 1917
Moody, William H. (61)	Harvard	B.A. 1876	Harvard	Attended 1876-77
			Richard H. Dana (Massachusetts)	1877-78
Moore, Alfred (13)	None		Maurice Moore (North Carolina)	1754-55
Murphy, Frank (83)	Michigan	B.A. 1912	Michigan	Graduated 1914
			Lincoln's Inn (England)	Attended 1919
			Trinity College (Ireland)	Attended 1919

(Table continues)

Table 4-4 (*Continued*)

Justice (appointment number)	Undergraduate education		Graduate education		Law school		Read the law[a]	
	School	Status/dates	School	Status/dates	School	Status/dates	Mentor/state	Dates studied
Nelson, Samuel (30)	Middlebury	Graduated 1813					Law offices of Savage and Woods (New York)	1814-17
O'Connor, Sandra Day (106)	Stanford	B.A. 1950			Stanford	Graduated 1952		
Paterson, William (8)	Princeton	Graduated 1763	Princeton	M.A. 1766			Richard Stockton (New Jersey)	1766-69
Peckham, Rufus W. (57)	None						Rufus Peckham (New York)	1857-59
Pitney, Mahlon (67)	Princeton	B.A. 1879	Princeton	M.A. 1882			Henry C. Pitney (New Jersey)	1879-82
Powell, Lewis F., Jr. (103)	Washington and Lee	B.S. 1929			Washington and Lee Harvard	Graduated 1931 LL.M 1932		
Reed, Stanley F. (80)	Kentucky Wesleyan	B.A. 1902			Virginia	Attended 1906-07		

	Yale	B.A. 1906			Columbia University of Paris	Attended 1908-09 Attended 1909-10	
Rehnquist, William (104, 107)	Stanford	B.A. 1948	Stanford Harvard	M.A. 1948 M.A. 1950	Stanford	Graduated 1952	
Roberts, Owen J. (77)	Pennsylvania	B.A. 1895			Pennsylvania	Graduated 1898	
Rutledge, John (2, 9)	None				Middle Temple (England)	Attended 1758-60	Andrew Rutledge 1753-55 (South Carolina) James Parsons 1755-57 (South Carolina)
Rutledge, Wiley B. (87)	Maryville	Attended 1910-12	Wisconsin	B.A. 1914	Indiana Colorado	Attended 1914-15 Graduated 1922	
Sanford, Edward T. (74)	Tennessee Harvard	B.A., Ph.B. 1883 B.A. 1884	Harvard	M.A. 1889	Harvard	Graduated 1889	
Scalia, Antonin (108)	Georgetown	B.A. 1957	Fribourg (Switzerland)	Attended 1957	Harvard	Graduated 1960	

(Table continues)

Table 4-4 (Continued)

Justice (appointment number)	Undergraduate education		Graduate education		Law school		Read the law[a]	
	School	Status/dates	School	Status/dates	School	Status/dates	Mentor/state	Dates studied
Shiras, George, Jr. (54)	Ohio Yale	Attended 1849-51 B.A. 1853			Yale	Attended 1853-54	Hopewell Hepburn (Pennsylvania)	1854-55
Souter, David H. (110)	Harvard	B.A. 1961	Oxford	Rhodes Scholar 1961-63	Harvard	Graduated 1966		
Stevens, John Paul (105)	Chicago	B.A. 1941			Northwestern	Graduated 1947		
Stewart, Potter (96)	Yale	B.A. 1937	Cambridge	Fellow 1937-38	Yale	Graduated 1941		
Stone, Harlan Fiske (75, 84)	Amherst	B.A. 1894	Amherst	M.A. 1897	Columbia	Graduated 1898		
Story, Joseph (19)	Harvard	Graduated 1798					Samuel Sewall and Samuel Putnam (Massachusetts)	1798-1801
Strong, William (41)	Yale	B.A. 1828	Yale	M.A. 1831	Yale	Attended 1832	Local lawyers (New Jersey)	1829-32

Name	College		Law School		Legal Study	
Sutherland, George (72)	Brigham Young	Attended 1878-1881	Michigan	Attended 1883		
Swayne, Noah H. (36)	None				John Scott and Francis Brooks (Virginia)	1821-23
Taft, William H. (71)	Yale	B.A. 1878	Cincinnati	Graduated 1880		
Taney, Roger B. (25)	Dickinson	Graduated 1795			Jeremiah Chase (Maryland)	1796-98
Thomas, Clarence (111)	Immaculate Conception Holy Cross	Attended 1967-68 B.A. 1971	Yale	Graduated 1974		
Thompson, Smith (20)	Princeton	Graduated 1788			Gilbert Livingston and James Kent (New York)	1789-92
Todd, Thomas (17)	Washington and Lee	Graduated 1783			Harry Innes (Virginia)	1784-88
Trimble, Robert (21)	Transylvania	Attended 1796-97			George Nicholas and James Brown (Kentucky)	1801-03

(Table continues)

Table 4-4 (Continued)

Justice (appointment number)	Undergraduate education		Graduate education		Law school		Read the law[a]	
	School	Status/dates	School	Status/dates	School	Status/dates	Mentor/state	Dates studied
Van Devanter, Willis (65)	DePauw	B.A. 1878			Cincinnati	Graduated 1881		
Vinson, Fred M. (89)	Centre	B.A. 1909			Centre	Graduated 1911		
Waite, Morrison (44)	Yale	Graduated 1837					Samuel Young (Ohio)	1838-39
Warren, Earl (92)	California	B.A. 1912			California	Graduated 1914		
Washington, Bushrod (12)	William and Mary	Graduated 1778					James Wilson (Pennsylvania)	1782-84
Wayne, James M. (24)	Princeton	Graduated 1808					John Noel (Georgia) Charles Chauncey (Connecticut)	1808-09 1809-1810
White, Byron R. (97)	Colorado	B.A. 1938	Oxford	Rhodes Scholar 1939	Yale	Graduated 1946		

Justice					
White, Edward D. (56, 64)	Mount St. Mary's	Attended 1856	Louisiana	Attended 1866-68	Edward Bermudez (Louisiana) 1866-68
	Georgetown	Attended 1857-61			
Whittaker, Charles E. (95)	None		Kansas City	Graduated 1924	
Wilson, James (4)	St. Andrews (Scotland)	Attended 1756-60			John Dickinson (Pennsylvania) 1766-67
Woodbury, Levi (31)	Dartmouth	Graduated 1809	Tapping-Reeve	Attended 1810	Samuel Dana and Jeremiah Smith (Massachusetts) 1810-12
Woods, William B. (46)	Western Reserve	Attended 1841-44			S. D. King (Ohio) 1845-47
	Yale	Graduated 1845			

Note: Colleges and universities listed by names used today. During earlier periods, some institutions had different names. For example, Columbia University was known as King's College and Princeton as the College of New Jersey. In the earlier historical periods, colleges and universities often "graduated" students without conferring degrees. In later periods, graduates were given degrees (e.g., bachelor of arts, bachelor of science) indicating the course of study taken. Also, in the earlier historical periods an undergraduate education frequently took less time than the standard four-year curriculum of today.

[a] During the early years of the nation's history it was common for lawyers to be trained by "reading the law" rather than attending law school. This was accomplished through self study or by serving as an apprentice under an experienced lawyer. Only in the more modern period have justices trained in a formal law school setting.

Sources: Elder Witt, *Congressional Quarterly's Guide to the U.S. Supreme Court,* 2d ed. (Washington, D.C.: Congressional Quarterly, 1990); Leon Friedman and Fred L. Israel, eds., *The Justices of the United States Supreme Court: Their Lives and Major Opinions* (New York: R.R. Bowker, 1969-1978); Harold W. Chase et al., *Biographical Dictionary of the American Judiciary* (Detroit: Gale Research, 1976); *Judges of the United States,* 2d ed. (Washington, D.C.: Judicial Conference of the United States, 1983); *The National Cyclopaedia of American Biography* (New York: James T. White, various years); *Dictionary of American Biography* (New York: Charles Scribner's Sons, various editions).

Table 4-5 Marriages and Children

Justice (appointment number)	Spouse (date of marriage)	Children[a]
Baldwin, Henry (23)	Marianna Norton (1802, d. 1803); Sally Ellicott (1805)	1
Barbour, Philip P. (26)	Frances Todd Johnson (1804)	7
Black, Hugo L. (79)	Josephine Foster (1921, d. 1951); Elizabeth Seay DeMeritte (1957)	3
Blackmun, Harry A. (102)	Dorothy E. Clark (1941)	3
Blair, John, Jr. (5)	Jean Balfour (1756)	Unknown
Blatchford, Samuel (49)	Caroline Appleton (1844)	2
Bradley, Joseph P. (42)	Mary Hornblower (1844)	7
Brandeis, Louis D. (69)	Alice Goldmark (1891)	2
Brennan, William J., Jr. (94)	Marjorie Leonard (1928, d. 1982); Mary Fowler (1983)	3
Brewer, David J. (52)	Louisa R. Landon (1861, d. 1898); Emma Miner Mott (1901)	4
Brown, Henry B. (53)	Caroline Pitts (1864, d. 1901); Josephine Tyler (1904)	Unknown
Burger, Warren E. (101)	Elvera Stromberg (1933)	2
Burton, Harold H. (88)	Selma Florence Smith (1912)	4
Butler, Pierce (73)	Annie M. Cronin (1891)	8
Byrnes, James F. (85)	Maude Busch (1906)	0
Campbell, John A. (34)	Anna Esther Goldthwaite (1830s)	5
Cardozo, Benjamin (78)	Unmarried	
Catron, John (27)	Mary Childress (1807)	0
Chase, Salmon P. (40)	Katharine Jane Garniss (1834, d. 1835); Eliza Ann Smith (1839, d. 1845); Sarah Belle Dunlop Ludlow (1846)	6

Table 4-5   *(Continued)*

Justice (appointment number)	*Spouse (date of marriage)*	*Children*[a]
Chase, Samuel (10)	Anne Baldwin (1762, d.); Hannah Kitty Giles (1784)	7
Clark, Tom C. (90)	Mary Jane Ramsey (1924)	3
Clarke, John H. (70)	Unmarried	
Clifford, Nathan (35)	Hannah Ayer (1828)	6
Curtis, Benjamin R. (33)	Eliza Maria Woodward (1833, d. 1844); Anna Wroe Curtis (1846, d. 1860); Maria Malleville Allen (1861)	12
Cushing, William (3)	Hannah Phillips (1774)	0
Daniel, Peter V. (29)	Lucy Randolph (1809, d. 1847); Elizabeth Harris (1853)	5
Davis, David (38)	Sarah Walker Woodruff (1838, d. 1879); Adeline Burr (1883)	2
Day, William R. (60)	Mary Elizabeth Schaefer (1875)	4
Douglas, William O. (82)	Mildred Riddle (1923, divorced 1954); Mercedes Hester (1954, divorced 1963); Joan Martin (1963, divorced 1966); Cathleen Heffernan (1966)	2
Duvall, Gabriel (18)	Mary Bryce (1787, d. 1790); Jane Gibbon (1795)	1
Ellsworth, Oliver (11)	Abigale Wolcott (1772)	7
Field, Stephen J. (39)	Virginia Swearingen (1859)	0
Fortas, Abe (99)	Carolyn Eugenia Agger (1935)	0
Frankfurter, Felix (81)	Marion A. Denman (1919)	0
Fuller, Melville W. (51)	Calista Ophelia Reynolds (1858, d. 1864); Mary E. Coolbaugh (1866)	8

(Table continues)

Table 4-5   *(Continued)*

Justice (appointment number)	*Spouse (date of marriage)*	*Children*[a]
Ginsburg, Ruth Bader (112)	Martin D. Ginsburg (1954)	2
Goldberg, Arthur J. (98)	Dorothy Kurgans (1931)	2
Gray, Horace (48)	Jane Matthews (1889)	0
Grier, Robert C. (32)	Isabella Rose (1829)	2
Harlan, John Marshall I (45)	Malvina F. Shanklin (1856)	6
Harlan, John Marshall II (93)	Ethel Andrews (1928)	1
Holmes, Oliver W., Jr. (59)	Fanny Bowdich Dixwell (1872)	0
Hughes, Charles E. (63, 76)	Antoinette Carter (1888)	4
Hunt, Ward (43)	Mary Ann Savage (1837, d. 1845); Marie Taylor (1853)	3
Iredell, James (6)	Hannah Johnston (1773)	3
Jackson, Howell E. (55)	Sophia Malloy (1859, d. 1873); Mary E. Harding (1874)	7
Jackson, Robert H. (86)	Irene Gerhardt (1916)	2
Jay, John (1)	Sarah Van Brugh Livingston (1774)	7
Johnson, Thomas (7)	Ann Jennings (1766)	8
Johnson, William (15)	Sarah Bennett (1794)	10
Kennedy, Anthony (109)	Mary Davis (1963)	3
Lamar, Joseph R. (66)	Clarinda Huntington Pendleton (1879)	3
Lamar, Lucius Q. C. (50)	Virginia Longstreet (1847, d. 1884); Henrietta Dean Holt (1887)	4
Livingston, H. Brockholst (16)	Catharine Keteltas; Ann Ludlow; Catharine Kortright (marriage dates unknown)	11

Table 4-5   *(Continued)*

Justice (appointment number)	Spouse (date of marriage)	Children[a]
Lurton, Horace (62)	Mary Francis Owen (1867)	4
Marshall, John (14)	Mary Willis Ambler (1783)	10
Marshall, Thurgood (100)	Vivian Burey (1929, d. 1955); Cecilia Suyat (1955)	2
Matthews, Stanley (47)	Mary Ann Black (1843, d. 1885); Mary Theaker (1887)	8
McKenna, Joseph (58)	Amanda F. Bornemann (1869)	4
McKinley, John (28)	Juliana Bryan; Elizabeth Armistead (marriage dates unknown)	Unknown
McLean, John (22)	Rebecca Edwards (1807, d. 1840); Sarah Bellow Ludlow Garrard (1843)	8
McReynolds, James C. (68)	Unmarried	
Miller, Samuel (37)	Lucy Ballinger (1839, d. 1854); Elizabeth Winter Reeves (1857)	5
Minton, Sherman (91)	Gertrude Gurtz (1917)	3
Moody, William H. (61)	Unmarried	
Moore, Alfred (13)	Susanna Eagles (1775)	4
Murphy, Frank (83)	Unmarried	
Nelson, Samuel (30)	Pamela Woods (1819, d. 1822); Catherine Ann Russell (1825)	4
O'Connor, Sandra Day (106)	John O'Connor (1952)	3
Paterson, William (8)	Cornelia Bell (1779, d. 1783); Euphemia White (1785)	3
Peckham, Rufus W. (57)	Harriette M. Arnold (1866)	2
Pitney, Mahlon (67)	Florence T. Shelton (1891)	3

(Table continues)

Table 4-5 *(Continued)*

Justice (appointment number)	*Spouse (date of marriage)*	*Children*[a]
Powell, Lewis F., Jr. (103)	Josephine M. Rucker (1936)	4
Reed, Stanley F. (80)	Winifred Elgin (1908)	2
Rehnquist, William (104, 107)	Natalie Cornell (1953)	3
Roberts, Owen J. (77)	Elizabeth Caldwell Rogers (1904)	1
Rutledge, John (2, 9)	Elizabeth Grimke (1763)	10
Rutledge, Wiley B. (87)	Annabel Person (1917)	3
Sanford, Edward T. (74)	Lutie Mallory Woodruff (1891)	2
Scalia, Antonin (108)	Maureen McCarthy (1960)	9
Shiras, George, Jr. (54)	Lillie E. Kennedy (1857)	2
Souter, David H. (110)	Unmarried	
Stevens, John Paul (105)	Elizabeth Jane Sheeren (1942, divorced 1979); Maryan Mulholland Simon (1980)	4
Stewart, Potter (96)	Mary Ann Bertles (1943)	3
Stone, Harlan F. (75, 84)	Agnes Harvey (1899)	2
Story, Joseph (19)	Mary Lynde Oliver (1804, d. 1805); Sarah Waldo Wetmore (1808)	7
Strong, William (41)	Priscilla Lee Mallery (1836, d. 1844); Rachel Davies Bull (1849)	7
Sutherland, George (72)	Rosamund Lee (1883)	3
Swayne, Noah H. (36)	Sarah Ann Wager (1832)	5
Taft, William H. (71)	Helen Herron (1886)	3
Taney, Roger B. (25)	Anne P. C. Key (1806)	7
Thomas, Clarence (111)	Kate Ambush (1971, divorced, 1984); Virginia Lamp (1987)	1

Table 4-5 *(Continued)*

Justice (appointment number)	Spouse (date of marriage)	Children[a]
Thompson, Smith (20)	Sarah Livingston (1794, d. 1833); Eliza Livingston (1836)	7
Todd, Thomas (17)	Elizabeth Harris (1788, d. 1811); Lucy Payne (1812)	8
Trimble, Robert (21)	Nancy Timberlake (1803)	10
Van Devanter, Willis (65)	Dellice Burhans (1883)	2
Vinson, Fred M. (89)	Roberta Dixson (1923)	2
Waite, Morrison (44)	Amelia C. Warner (1840)	5
Warren, Earl (92)	Nina P. Meyers (1925)	6
Washington, Bushrod (12)	Julia Ann Blackburn (1785)	0
Wayne, James M. (24)	Mary Johnson Campbell (1813)	3
White, Byron R. (97)	Marion Stearns (1946)	2
White, Edward D. (56, 64)	Virginia Montgomery Kent (1894)	0
Whittaker, Charles E. (95)	Winifred R. Pugh (1928)	3
Wilson, James (4)	Rachel Bird (1771, d. 1786); Hanna Gray (1793)	7
Woodbury, Levi (31)	Elizabeth Williams Clapp (1819)	5
Woods, William B. (46)	Anne E. Warner (1855)	2

[a] Because infant mortality rates were high in the early periods of American history, sources often vary as to number of children credited to each justice. Some sources count all live births, while others count only those children who survived infancy. Here, the most commonly cited figures in the biographical literature are used.

Sources: Elder Witt, *Congressional Quarterly's Guide to the U.S. Supreme Court,* 2d ed. (Washington, D.C.: Congressional Quarterly, 1990); Leon Friedman and Fred L. Israel, eds., *The Justices of the United States Supreme Court: Their Lives and Major Opinions* (New York: R.R.

(Notes continue)

Table 4-5   *(Continued)*

Bowker, 1969-1978); Harold W. Chase et al., *Biographical Dictionary of the American Judiciary* (Detroit: Gale Research, 1976); *Judges of the United States*, 2d ed. (Washington, D.C.: Judicial Conference of the United States, 1983); *The National Cyclopaedia of American Biography* (New York: James T. White, various years); *Dictionary of American Biography* (New York: Charles Scribner's Sons, various editions).

Table 4-6 Private Practice and Law Professorships

Justice (appointment number)	Bar admission, state/year	Private law practice, location/years[a]	Law school	Rank	Years of service
Baldwin, Henry (23)	Pennsylvania, 1798	Pennsylvania, 1798-1816, 1822-29			
Barbour, Philip P. (26)	Virginia, 1800	Kentucky, 1800; Virginia, 1802-13			
Black, Hugo L. (79)	Alabama, 1906	Alabama, 1906-15, 1918-26			
Blackmun, Harry A. (102)	Minnesota, 1932	Minnesota, 1933-59	Mitchell College of Law University of Minnesota	Instructor Instructor	1935-41 1945-47
Blair, John, Jr. (5)	Virginia, 1756	Virginia, 1756-77			
Blatchford, Samuel (49)	New York, 1842	New York, 1842-67			
Bradley, Joseph P. (42)	New Jersey, 1839	New Jersey, 1839-70			
Brandeis, Louis D. (69)	Massachusetts, 1878	Missouri, 1878-79; Massachusetts, 1879-1916			
Brennan, William J., Jr. (94)	New Jersey, 1931	New Jersey, 1931-42, 1946-49			

(Table continues)

Table 4-6 *(Continued)*

Justice (appointment number)	Bar admission, state/year	Private law practice, location/years[a]	Law school	Rank	Years of service
Brewer, David J. (52)	New York, 1858; Kansas, 1859	Kansas, 1859-61	George Washington University	Lecturer	1890s
Brown, Henry B. (53)	Michigan, 1860	Michigan, 1860-61, 1868-75	University of Michigan Detroit Medical College	Lecturer Lecturer	1860s 1868-71
Burger, Warren E. (101)	Minnesota, 1931	Minnesota, 1931-53	Mitchell College of Law	Lecturer	1931-48
Burton, Harold H. (88)	Ohio, 1912; Utah, 1914	Ohio, 1912-14, 1918-35; Utah, 1914-16; Idaho, 1916-17	Western Reserve University	Instructor	1923-25
Butler, Pierce (73)	Minnesota, 1888	Minnesota, 1888-91, 1897-1922			
Byrnes, James F. (85)	South Carolina, 1903	South Carolina, 1925-30, 1947-50			
Campbell, John A. (34)	Georgia, 1829	Alabama, 1830-52; Louisiana, 1865-89			
Cardozo, Benjamin (78)	New York, 1891	New York, 1891-1914			
Catron, John (27)	Tennessee, 1815	Tennessee, 1815-24, 1834-37			
Chase, Salmon P. (40)	Ohio, 1830	Ohio, 1830-49			

Chase, Samuel (10)	Maryland, 1761	Maryland, 1761-87		
Clark, Tom C. (90)	Texas, 1922	Texas, 1922-27, 1932-37		
Clarke, John H. (70)	Ohio, 1878	Ohio, 1878-1914		
Clifford, Nathan (35)	New Hampshire, 1827	Maine, 1827-34, 1843-46, 1849-57		
Curtis, Benjamin R. (33)	Massachusetts, 1832	Massachusetts, 1832-51, 1857-74		
Cushing, William (3)	Massachusetts, 1755	Massachusetts, 1755-72		
Daniel, Peter V. (29)	Virginia, 1808	Virginia, 1808-18		
Davis, David (38)	Illinois, 1835	Illinois, 1835-48		
Day, William R. (60)	Ohio, 1872	Ohio, 1872-86, 1890-97		
Douglas, William O. (82)	New York, 1925	New York, 1925-26; Washington, 1927-28	Columbia University Yale University	Assistant Professor 1928 1929-36
Duvall, Gabriel (18)	Maryland, 1778	Maryland, 1778-94		
Ellsworth, Oliver (11)	Connecticut, 1771	Connecticut, 1771-84		
Field, Stephen J. (39)	New York, 1841	New York, 1841-48; California, 1849-57		

(Table continues)

Table 4-6 (*Continued*)

Justice (appointment number)	Bar admission, state/year	Private law practice, location/years[a]	Law school	Rank	Years of service
Fortas, Abe (99)	Connecticut, 1934; District of Columbia, 1945	District of Columbia, 1947-65	Yale University	Associate Professor	1933-37 1946-47
Frankfurter, Felix (81)	New York, 1905	New York, 1905-06	Harvard University	Professor	1914-41
Fuller, Melville W. (51)	Maine, 1855; Illinois, 1856	Maine, 1855-56; Illinois, 1856-88			
Ginsburg, Ruth Bader (112)	New York, 1959; District of Columbia, 1975		Rutgers University Rutgers University Rutgers University Columbia University	Assistant Associate Professor Professor	1963-66 1966-69 1969-72 1972-80
Goldberg, Arthur J. (98)	Illinois, 1929	Illinois, 1929-42, 1945-61	John Marshall Law School	Professor	1945-48
Gray, Horace (48)	Massachusetts, 1851	Massachusetts, 1851-64			
Grier, Robert C. (32)	Pennsylvania, 1817	Pennsylvania, 1817-33			
Harlan, John Marshall I (45)	Kentucky, 1853	Kentucky, 1853-61, 1867-77	George Washington University	Lecturer	1889-1910
Harlan, John Marshall II (93)	New York, 1925	New York, 1925, 1927, 1931-42, 1946-51			

Name					
Holmes, Oliver W., Jr. (59)	Massachusetts, 1867	Massachusetts, 1867-82	Harvard University Lowell Institute Harvard University	Instructor Lecturer Professor	1870-71 1880 1882
Hughes, Charles Evans (63, 76)	New York, 1884	New York, 1884-91, 1893-1906, 1917-21, 1925-30	Cornell University New York University	Professor Lecturer Lecturer	1891-93 1893-95 1893-1900
Hunt, Ward (43)	New York, 1831	New York, 1831-66			
Iredell, James (6)	North Carolina, 1770	North Carolina, 1770-77; 1782-90			
Jackson, Howell E. (55)	Tennessee, 1856	Tennessee, 1856-61, 1865-80	Southwest Baptist University	Professor	1875-80
Jackson, Robert H. (86)	New York, 1913	New York, 1913-34			
Jay, John (1)	New York, 1768	New York, 1768-74			
Johnson, Thomas (7)	Maryland, 1760	Maryland, 1760-76			
Johnson, William (15)	South Carolina, 1793	South Carolina, 1793-99			
Kennedy, Anthony (109)	California, 1961	California, 1961-76	University of the Pacific	Lecturer	1965-88

(Table continues)

Table 4-6 *(Continued)*

Justice (appointment number)	Bar admission, state/year	Private law practice, location/years[a]	Law school	Rank	Years of service
Lamar, Joseph R. (66)	Georgia, 1878	Georgia, 1880-1903, 1906-10			
Lamar, Lucius Q.C. (50)	Georgia, 1847	Georgia, 1847-48, 1852-55; Mississippi, 1849-52, 1855-56, 1866-72	University of Mississippi	Professor	1867-70
Livingston, H. Brockholst (16)	New York, 1783	New York, 1783-1802			
Lurton, Horace (62)	Tennessee, 1867	Tennessee, 1867-75, 1878-86	Vanderbilt University	Professor Dean	1898-1905 1905-09
Marshall, John (14)	Virginia, 1780	Virginia, 1780-97			
Marshall, Thurgood (100)	Maryland, 1933	Maryland, 1933-36			
Matthews, Stanley (47)	Tennessee, 1842 Ohio, 1844	Tennessee, 1842-44; Ohio, 1844-51, 1854-58, 1865-77, 1879-81			
McKenna, Joseph (58)	California, 1865	California, 1865-66, 1870-85			
McKinley, John (28)	Kentucky, 1800	Kentucky, 1800-18; Alabama, 1818-26			
McLean, John (22)	Ohio, 1807	Ohio, 1807-11			

McReynolds, James C. (68)	Tennessee, 1884	Tennessee, 1884-1903, 1907-12	Vanderbilt University	Lecturer	1900-03
Miller, Samuel (37)	Kentucky, 1847	Kentucky, 1847-50; Iowa, 1850-62			
Minton, Sherman (91)	Indiana, 1915	Indiana, 1915-16, 1919-25, 1928-33; Florida, 1925-28			
Moody, William H. (61)	Massachusetts, 1878	Massachusetts, 1878-88			
Moore, Alfred (13)	North Carolina, 1775	North Carolina, 1775-76, 1777-82, 1791-99			
Murphy, Frank (83)	Michigan, 1914	Michigan, 1914-17, 1920-23	University of Detroit	Lecturer	1914-17, 1922-27
Nelson, Samuel (30)	New York, 1817	New York, 1817-20			
O'Connor, Sandra Day (106)	California, 1952; Arizona, 1957	Arizona, 1959-65, 1969-75			
Paterson, William (8)	New Jersey, 1769	New Jersey, 1769-76, 1783-88			
Peckham, Rufus W. (57)	New York, 1859	New York, 1859-69, 1872-81			

(Table continues)

Table 4-6 *(Continued)*

Justice (appointment number)	Bar admission, state/year	Private law practice, location/years[a]	Law school	Rank	Years of service
Pitney, Mahlon (67)	New Jersey, 1882	New Jersey, 1882-94, 1899-1901			
Powell, Lewis F., Jr. (103)	Virginia, 1933	Virginia, 1933-71			
Reed, Stanley F. (80)	Kentucky, 1910	Kentucky, 1910-29			
Rehnquist, William (104, 107)	Arizona, 1953	Arizona, 1953-69			
Roberts, Owen J. (77)	Pennsylvania, 1898	Pennsylvania, 1898-1901, 1905-24	University of Pennsylvania	Lecturer Dean	1898-1919 1948-51
Rutledge, John (2, 9)	England, 1760	South Carolina, 1761-74			
Rutledge, Wiley B. (87)	Colorado, 1922	Colorado, 1922-24	University of Colorado Washington University University of Iowa	Professor Professor Dean Professor and dean	1924-26 1926-35 1930-35 1935-39
Sanford, Edward T. (74)	Tennessee, 1888	Tennessee, 1890-1906	University of Tennessee	Lecturer	1898-1906
Scalia, Antonin (108)	Ohio, 1962; Virginia, 1970	Ohio, 1961-67	University of Virginia University of Chicago	Professor Professor	1967-74 1977-82
Shiras, George, Jr. (54)	Pennsylvania, 1855	Iowa, 1855-58; Pennsylvania, 1858-92			

Name			University	Position	Years
Souter, David H. (110)	New Hampshire, 1966	New Hampshire, 1966-68			
Stevens, John Paul (105)	Illinois, 1949	Illinois, 1948-51; 1952-70	Northwestern University University of Chicago	Lecturer Lecturer	1950-54 1977-82
Stewart, Potter (96)	Ohio, 1942; New York, 1942	New York, 1941-42, 1945-47; Ohio, 1947-54			
Stone, Harlan Fiske (75, 84)	New York, 1898	New York, 1899-1924	Columbia University	Professor Dean	1899-1905 1910-23
Story, Joseph (19)	Massachusetts, 1801	Massachusetts, 1801-08, 1810-11	Harvard University	Professor	1829-45
Strong, William (41)	Pennsylvania, 1832	Pennsylvania, 1832-46, 1868-70			
Sutherland, George (72)	Michigan, 1883; Utah, 1883	Utah, 1883-1900, 1903-05; District of Columbia, 1917-22			
Swayne, Noah H. (36)	Virginia, 1823	Ohio, 1825-30, 1841-61			
Taft, William H. (71)	Ohio, 1880	Ohio, 1880-81, 1883-85	University of Cincinnati Yale University	Professor and dean Professor	1896-1900 1913-21
Taney, Roger B. (25)	Maryland, 1799	Maryland, 1799-1826			
Thomas, Clarence (111)	Missouri, 1974	Missouri, 1977-79			

(Table continues)

Table 4-6 *(Continued)*

Justice (appointment number)	Bar admission, state/year	Private law practice, location/years[a]	Law school	Rank	Years of service
Thompson, Smith (20)	New York, 1792	New York, 1793-1802			
Todd, Thomas (17)	Virginia, 1788	Kentucky, 1788-1801			
Trimble, Robert (21)	Kentucky, 1803	Kentucky, 1803-06, 1809-13			
Van Devanter, Willis (65)	Indiana, 1881	Indiana, 1881-83; Wyoming, 1884-88, 1890-97	George Washington University	Lecturer	1898-1903
Vinson, Fred M. (89)	Kentucky, 1911	Kentucky, 1911-21, 1929-30			
Waite, Morrison (44)	Ohio, 1839	Ohio, 1839-74			
Warren, Earl (92)	California, 1914	California, 1914-17			
Washington, Bushrod (12)	Virginia, 1784	Virginia, 1784-98			
Wayne, James M. (24)	Georgia, 1810	Georgia, 1810-19			
White, Byron R. (97)	Colorado, 1947	Colorado, 1947-61			
White, Edward D. (56, 64)	Louisiana, 1868	Louisiana, 1868-78, 1880-90			

Whittaker, Charles E. (95)	Missouri, 1923	Missouri, 1923-54	
Wilson, James (4)	Pennsylvania, 1767	Pennsylvania, 1768-89	University of Pennsylvania	Professor 1789-90
Woodbury, Levi (31)	New Hampshire, 1812	New Hampshire, 1812-16	
Woods, William B. (46)	Ohio, 1847	Ohio, 1847-62; Alabama, 1866-67	

a Legal practice may have been combined with such activities as farming, business ventures, teaching, or part-time political positions. Includes work as a solo practitioner, in a law firm, or with a corporation. Does not include full-time employment with the government or interest groups, or those years the justices may have practiced law on an irregular or part-time basis while holding a major public office. The years of private practice for justices during the early periods of American history are difficult to identify accurately because law was often practiced on a less formal basis than in later years.

Sources: Elder Witt, *Congressional Quarterly's Guide to the U.S. Supreme Court,* 2d ed. (Washington, D.C.: Congressional Quarterly, 1990); Leon Friedman and Fred L. Israel, eds., *The Justices of the United States Supreme Court: Their Lives and Major Opinions* (New York: R.R. Bowker, 1969-1978); Harold W. Chase et al., *Biographical Dictionary of the American Judiciary* (Detroit: Gale Research, 1976); *Judges of the United States,* 2d ed. (Washington, D.C.: Judicial Conference of the United States, 1983); *The National Cyclopaedia of American Biography* (New York: James T. White, various years); *Dictionary of American Biography* (New York: Charles Scribner's Sons, various editions).

Table 4-7 Military Experience

Justice (appointment number)	Service	Dates	Rank	Wars
Black, Hugo L. (79)	Army	1917-18	Captain	World War I
Brennan, William J., Jr. (94)	Army	1942-46	Colonel	World War II
Burton, Harold H. (88)	Army	1917-18	Captain	World War I
Catron, John (27)	Army	1812	Enlisted soldier	War of 1812
Clark, Tom C. (90)	Army	1918	Infantryman	World War I
Douglas, William O. (82)	Army	1918	Private	World War I
Duvall, Gabriel (18)	Continental Army	1776-81	Private, mustermaster	Revolution
Goldberg, Arthur J. (98)	Army	1942-44	Captain, major	World War II
Harlan, John Marshall I (45)	Union Army	1861-63	Colonel	Civil War
Harlan, John Marshall II (93)	Army Air Force	1943-45	Colonel	World War II
Holmes, Oliver W., Jr. (59)	Union Army	1861-64	Lieutenant, captain	Civil War
Jay, John (1)	New York Militia	1776-78	Colonel	Revolution
Johnson, Thomas (7)	Maryland Militia	1776-77	Brigadier general	Revolution
Kennedy, Anthony (109)	National Guard	1961	Private first class	
Lamar, Lucius Q. C. (50)	Confederate Army	1861-65	Colonel, judge advocate	Civil War
Livingston, H. Brockholst (16)	Continental Army	1776-79	Lt. colonel	Revolution
Lurton, Horace (62)	Confederate Army	1861-65	Sgt. major	Civil War
Marshall, John (14)	Continental Army	1776-81	Captain	Revolution
Matthews, Stanley (47)	Union Army	1861-63	Colonel	Civil War
Minton, Sherman (91)	Army	1917-18	Captain	World War I
Moore, Alfred (13)	Continental Army	1776-77	Captain	Revolution
Murphy, Frank (83)	Army	1917-18	Lieutenant, captain	World War I
	Army	1942	Lt. colonel	World War II
Paterson, William (8)	Minutemen[a]	1776-78	Officer	Revolution
Powell, Lewis F., Jr. (103)	Army Air Force	1942-46	Colonel	World War II
Reed, Stanley F. (80)	Army	1917-18	Lieutenant	World War I
Rehnquist, William (104, 107)	Army Air Force	1943-46	Sergeant	World War II
Stevens, John Paul (105)	Navy	1942-45	Lt. commander	World War II

Stewart, Potter (96)	Navy	1942-45	Lieutenant	World War II
Todd, Thomas (17)	Continental Army	1781	Private	Revolution
Warren, Earl (92)	Army	1917-18	Lieutenant	World War I
Washington, Bushrod (12)	Continental Army	1780-81	Private	Revolution
Wayne, James M. (24)	Georgia Militia	1812	Captain	War of 1812
White, Byron R. (97)	Navy	1942-46	Lieutenant	World War II
White, Edward D. (56, 64)	Confederate Army	1861-65	Private, lieutenant	Civil War
Woods, William B. (46)	Union Army	1862-66	Brigadier general	Civil War

[a] American citizen army at the time of the Revolution whose members volunteered to be ready for military service at a minute's notice.

Sources: Elder Witt, Congressional Quarterly's Guide to the U.S. Supreme Court, 2d ed. (Washington, D.C.: Congressional Quarterly, 1990); Leon Friedman and Fred L. Israel, eds., The Justices of the United States Supreme Court: Their Lives and Major Opinions (New York: R.R. Bowker, 1969-1978); Harold W. Chase et al., Biographical Dictionary of the American Judiciary (Detroit: Gale Research, 1976); Judges of the United States, 2d ed. (Washington, D.C.: Judicial Conference of the United States, 1983); The National Cyclopaedia of American Biography (New York: James T. White, various years); Dictionary of American Biography (New York: Charles Scribner's Sons, various editions).

Table 4-8 Political Experience

Justice (appointment number)	Political experience[a] State	Federal
Baldwin, Henry (23)		House of Representatives (Pennsylvania), 1817-22
Barbour, Philip P. (26)	Virginia House of Delegates, 1812-14; president, Virginia Constitutional Convention, 1829-30	House of Representatives (Virginia), 1814-25, 1827-30; Speaker of the House, 1821-23
Black, Hugo L. (79)	Solicitor, Jefferson County, Alabama, 1915-17	Senate (Alabama), 1927-37
Blair, John, Jr. (5)	Virginia House of Burgesses, 1766-70; clerk, Virginia Governor's Council, 1770-75; member, Virginia Governor's Council, 1776; delegate, Virginia constitutional convention, 1776	Delegate, Constitutional Convention, 1787
Brewer, David J. (52)	County attorney, Leavenworth, Kansas, 1869-70	
Brown, Henry B. (53)		Deputy marshal, eastern district of Michigan, 1861; assistant U.S. attorney, eastern district of Michigan, 1863-68
Burger, Warren E. (101)		Assistant attorney general, 1953-56
Burton, Harold H. (88)	Ohio House of Representatives, 1929; director of law, Cleveland, Ohio, 1929-32; acting mayor, Cleveland, Ohio, 1931-32; mayor, Cleveland, Ohio, 1935-40	Senate (Ohio), 1941-45

Butler, Pierce (73)	Assistant county attorney, Ramsey County, Minnesota, 1891-93; county attorney, Ramsey County, Minnesota, 1893-97; Board of Regents, University of Minnesota, 1907-24
Byrnes, James F. (85)	House of Representatives (South Carolina), 1911-25; Senate (South Carolina), 1931-41
Campbell, John A. (34)	Circuit court solicitor, South Carolina, 1908-10
Chase, Salmon P. (40)	Alabama House of Representatives, 1837, 1843
Chase, Samuel (10)	Senate (Ohio), 1849-55; secretary of the Treasury, 1861-64
	Governor, Ohio, 1856-60
	Maryland General Assembly, 1764-84; member, Maryland Committee of Correspondence, 1774; member, Maryland Convention and Council of Safety, 1775; delegate, Maryland convention to ratify the U.S. Constitution, 1788
	Continental Congress (Maryland), 1774-78; signed Declaration of Independence, 1776; Congress (Maryland), 1784-85
Clark, Tom C. (90)	Civil district attorney, Dallas, Texas, 1927-32
	Special assistant, Justice Department, 1937-43; assistant attorney general, 1943-45; attorney general, 1945-49
Clifford, Nathan (35)	Maine House of Representatives, 1830-34; speaker, Maine House of Representatives, 1832-34; attorney general, Maine, 1834-38
	House of Representatives (Maine), 1839-43; attorney general, 1846-48; minister to Mexico, 1848-49
Curtis, Benjamin R. (33)	Massachusetts House of Representatives, 1849-51

(Table continues)

Table 4-8 (*Continued*)

Justice (*appointment number*)	Political experience[a]	
	State	Federal
Cushing, William (3)	Member, Massachusetts convention to ratify the U.S. Constitution, 1788; member, Massachusetts constitutional convention, 1779	Presidential elector, 1788
Daniel, Peter V. (29)	Virginia House of Delegates, 1809-12; Privy Council, Virginia, 1812-35; lieutenant governor, Virginia, 1818-35	
Davis, David (38)	Illinois House of Representatives, 1845-47; member, Illinois constitutional convention, 1847	
Day, William R. (60)		Assistant secretary of state, 1897-98; secretary of state, 1898; delegate, Paris Peace Conference, 1898-99
Douglas, William O. (82)		Member, Securities and Exchange Commission, 1936-39; chairman, Securities and Exchange Commission, 1937-39
Duvall, Gabriel (18)	Clerk, Maryland Convention, 1775-77; clerk, Maryland House of Delegates, 1777-1787; member, Maryland State Council, 1782-85; Maryland House of Delegates, 1787-94	House of Representatives (Maryland), 1794-96; presidential elector, 1796, 1800; comptroller of the Treasury, 1802-11

Ellsworth, Oliver (11)	Continental Congress (Connecticut), 1777-82; Congress (Connecticut), 1782-84; delegate, Constitutional Convention, 1787; Senate (Connecticut), 1789-96
Field, Stephen J. (39)	Alcalde, Marysville, California, 1850; California House of Representatives, 1850-51
Fortas, Abe (99)	Assistant director, Securities and Exchange Commission, 1937-39; general counsel, Public Works Administration, 1939-40; director, division of power, Interior Department, 1941-42; under secretary, Interior Department, 1942-46
Frankfurter, Felix (81)	Assistant U.S. attorney, southern district of New York, 1906-09; law officer, War Department, 1910-14; secretary and counsel, President's Mediation Commission, 1917; assistant to secretary of labor, 1917-18
Fuller, Melville W. (51)	City council, Augusta, Maine, 1856; member, Illinois constitutional convention, 1861; Illinois House of Representatives, 1863-64
Goldberg, Arthur J. (98)	Secretary of labor, 1961-62
Harlan, John Marshall I (45)	Adjutant general, Kentucky, 1851; attorney general, Kentucky, 1863-67

(Table continues)

Table 4-8 (Continued)

Justice (appointment number)	Political experience[a]	
	State	Federal
Harlan, John Marshall II (93)	Special assistant attorney general, New York, 1928-30; chief counsel, New York State Crime Commission, 1951-53	Assistant U.S. attorney, southern district of New York, 1925-27
Hughes, Charles Evans (63, 76)	Special counsel, New York House of Representatives, 1905-06; governor, New York, 1907-10	Secretary of state, 1921-25
Hunt, Ward (43)	New York General Assembly, 1839; mayor, Utica, New York, 1844	
Iredell, James (6)	Attorney general, North Carolina, 1779-81; member, North Carolina Council of State, 1787; delegate, North Carolina convention to ratify the U.S. Constitution, 1788	Comptroller of customs, Edenton, North Carolina, 1768-74[b]; collector of customs, North Carolina, 1774-76[b]
Jackson, Howell E. (55)	Tennessee House of Representatives, 1880	Receiver of alien property, 1861-64[c]; Senate (Tennessee), 1881-86
Jackson, Robert H. (86)		General counsel, Internal Revenue Bureau, 1934-36; special counsel, Securities and Exchange Commission, 1935; assistant attorney general, 1936-38; solicitor general, 1938-39; attorney general, 1940-41

Jay, John (1)	New York provincial Congress, 1776-77	Continental Congress (New York), 1774-79; minister to Spain, 1779; secretary of foreign affairs, 1784-89
Johnson, Thomas (7)	Maryland Provincial Assembly, 1762; delegate, Maryland constitutional convention, 1776; governor, Maryland, 1777-79; Maryland House of Delegates, 1780, 1786, 1787; member, Maryland convention to ratify the U.S. Constitution, 1788	Delegate, Annapolis Convention, 1774; Continental Congress (Maryland), 1774-77
Johnson, William (15)	South Carolina House of Representatives, 1794-98; South Carolina Speaker of the House, 1798; founder and trustee, University of South Carolina.	
Lamar, Joseph R. (66)	Georgia House of Representatives, 1886-89; member, commission to codify Georgia laws, 1893	
Lamar, Lucius Q. C. (50)	Georgia House of Representatives, 1853	Delegate, Mississippi secession convention, 1861[c]; special envoy to Russia, 1862[c]; House of Representatives (Mississippi), 1857-60, 1873-77; Senate (Mississippi), 1877-85; secretary of interior, 1885-88
Livingston, H. Brockholst (16)	New York General Assembly, 1786, 1800-02	

(Table continues)

Table 4-8 *(Continued)*

Justice *(appointment number)*	Political experience[a]	
	State	Federal
Marshall, John (14)	Executive Council of State, Virginia, 1782-84; Virginia House of Delegates, 1782-85, 1787-90, 1795-96; delegate, Virginia convention to ratify the U.S. Constitution, 1788	Minister to France, 1797-98; House of Representatives (Virginia), 1799-1800; secretary of state, 1800-01
Marshall, Thurgood (100)		Solicitor general, 1965-67
Matthews, Stanley (47)	Assistant prosecutor, Hamilton County, Ohio, 1845; clerk, Ohio House of Representatives, 1848-49; Ohio Senate, 1855-58	U.S. attorney, southern district of Ohio, 1858-61; presidential elector, 1864, 1868; counsel, Hayes-Tilton electoral commission, 1877; Senate (Ohio), 1877-79
McKenna, Joseph (58)	District attorney, Solano County, California, 1866-70; California House of Representatives, 1875-76	House of Representatives (California), 1885-92; attorney general, 1897
McKinley, John (28)	Alabama House of Representatives, 1820, 1831, 1836	Senate (Alabama), 1826-31, 1837; House of Representatives (Alabama), 1833-35
McLean, John (22)		Examiner, U.S. Land Office, 1811-12; House of Representatives (Ohio), 1813-16; commissioner, General Land Office, 1822-23; postmaster general, 1823-29
McReynolds, James C. (68)		Assistant attorney general, 1903-07; attorney general, 1913-14

Minton, Sherman (91)	Counselor, Indiana Public Service Commission, 1933-34	Senate (Indiana), 1935-41; administrative assistant to the president, 1941
Moody, William H. (61)	City solicitor, Haverhill, Massachusetts, 1888-90; district attorney, Eastern district of Massachusetts, 1890-95	House of Representatives (Massachusetts), 1895-1902; secretary of the navy, 1902-04; attorney general, 1904-06
Moore, Alfred (13)	North Carolina Senate, 1782; attorney general, North Carolina, 1782-91; North Carolina House of Commons, 1792	
Murphy, Frank (83)	Mayor, Detroit, Michigan, 1930-33; governor, Michigan, 1937-39	Assistant U.S. attorney, eastern district of Michigan, 1919-20; governor of the Philippines, 1933-35; high commission to the Philippines, 1935-36; attorney general, 1939-40
Nelson, Samuel (30)	Delegate, New York state constitutional convention, 1821	Presidential elector, 1820; postmaster, Cortland, New York, 1820-23
O'Connor, Sandra Day (106)	Deputy county attorney, San Mateo, California, 1952-53; assistant attorney general, Arizona, 1965-69; Arizona Senate, 1969-75; majority leader, Arizona Senate, 1973-74	
Paterson, William (8)	New Jersey Provincial Congress, 1775-76; delegate, New Jersey state constitutional convention, 1776; attorney general, New Jersey, 1776-83; governor, New Jersey, 1790-93	Delegate, Constitutional Convention, 1787; Senate (New Jersey), 1789-90

(Table continues)

250

Table 4-8 *(Continued)*

Justice (appointment number)	Political experience [a]	
	State	Federal
Peckham, Rufus W. (57)	District attorney, Albany County, New York, 1869-72; city attorney, Albany, New York, 1881-83	
Pitney, Mahlon (67)	New Jersey Senate, 1899-1901; president, New Jersey Senate, 1901	House of Representatives (New Jersey), 1895-99
Powell, Lewis F., Jr. (103)	President, Richmond, Virginia, school board, 1952-61; member, Virginia state school board, 1961-69; president, Virginia state school board, 1968-69	
Reed, Stanley F. (80)	Kentucky House of Representatives, 1912-16	General counsel, Federal Farm Board, 1929-32; general counsel, Reconstruction Finance Corporation, 1932-35; special assistant to the attorney general, 1935; solicitor general, 1935-38
Rehnquist, William (104, 107)		Assistant attorney general, 1969-71
Roberts, Owen J. (77)	Assistant district attorney, Philadelphia, Pennsylvania, 1901-04	Special deputy attorney general, 1918; special U.S. attorney, 1924-30

Rutledge, John (2, 9)	South Carolina Assembly, 1761-76; attorney general pro tem, South Carolina, 1764-65; president, Republic of South Carolina, 1776-78; governor, South Carolina, 1779-82; member, South Carolina convention to ratify the U.S. Constitution, 1788	Continental Congress (South Carolina), 1774-76; Congress (South Carolina), 1782-83; delegate, Constitutional Convention, 1787
Sanford, Edward T. (74)	Trustee, University of Tennessee, 1897-1923	Special assistant to attorney general, 1906-07; assistant attorney general, 1907-08
Scalia, Antonin (108)		General counsel, White House Office of Telecommunications Policy, 1971-72; chairman, Administrative Conference of the United States, 1972-74; assistant attorney general, 1974-77
Shiras, George, Jr. (54)		Presidential elector, 1888
Souter, David H. (110)	Assistant attorney general, New Hampshire, 1968-71; deputy attorney general, New Hampshire, 1971-76; attorney general, New Hampshire, 1976-78	
Stevens, John Paul (105)		Associate counsel, House Judiciary Committee, 1951; attorney general's committee to study anti-trust laws, 1953-55
Stewart, Potter (96)	City council, Cincinnati, Ohio, 1950-53; vice mayor, Cincinnati, Ohio, 1952-53	
Stone, Harlan Fiske (75, 84)		Attorney general, 1924-25

(Table continues)

Table 4-8 (Continued)

Justice (appointment number)	Political experience[a]	
	State	Federal
Story, Joseph (19)	Massachusetts House of Representatives, 1805-08, 1811; Massachusetts Speaker of the House, 1811	House of Representatives (Massachusetts), 1808-09
Strong, William (41)		House of Representatives (Pennsylvania), 1847-51
Sutherland, George (72)	Utah Senate, 1896-1900	House of Representatives (Utah), 1901-03; Senate (Utah), 1905-17; counsel, Norway-United States arbitration, 1921-22
Swayne, Noah H. (36)	Prosecuting attorney, Coshocton County, Ohio, 1826-29; Ohio House of Representatives, 1830, 1836; city council, Columbus, Ohio, 1834	U.S. attorney for the district of Ohio, 1830-41
Taft, William H. (71)	Assistant prosecutor, Hamilton County, Ohio, 1881-83; assistant solicitor, Hamilton County, Ohio, 1885-87	Solicitor general, 1890-92; chairman, the Philippine Commission, 1900-01; governor, Philippine Islands, 1901-04; secretary of war, 1904-08; president, 1909-13; joint chairman, National War Labor Board, 1918-19
Taney, Roger B. (25)	Maryland House of Delegates, 1799-1800; Maryland Senate, 1816-21; attorney general, Maryland, 1827-31	Attorney general, 1831-33; acting secretary of war, 1831; secretary of the Treasury (confirmation rejected), 1833-34

Thomas, Clarence (111)	Assistant attorney general, Missouri, 1974-77	Legislative assistant, Senate, 1979-81; assistant secretary for civil rights, Department of Education, 1981-82; chairman, Equal Employment Opportunity Commission, 1982-90
Thompson, Smith (20)	New York House of Representatives, 1800; member, New York constitutional convention, 1801; member, New York State Board of Regents, 1813	Secretary of the Navy, 1819-23
Todd, Thomas (17)	Clerk, Kentucky House of Representatives, 1792-1801	
Trimble, Robert (21)	Kentucky House of Representatives, 1802	U.S. attorney for the district of Kentucky, 1813-17
Van Devanter, Willis (65)	City attorney, Cheyenne, Wyoming, 1887-88; Wyoming territorial legislature, 1888	Assistant attorney general, 1897-03
Vinson, Fred M. (89)	City attorney, Louisa, Kentucky, 1913; commonwealth attorney, Kentucky, 1921-24	House of Representatives (Kentucky), 1923-29, 1931-38; director, Office of Economic Stabilization, 1943-45; administrator, Federal Loan Agency, 1945; director, Office of War Mobilization and Reconversion, 1945; secretary of the Treasury, 1945-46
Waite, Morrison (44)	Ohio House of Representatives, 1850-52; president, Ohio constitutional convention, 1873-74	Member, U.S. delegation to Geneva Arbitration Convention, 1871

(Table continues)

Table 4-8 *(Continued)*

| | Political experience[a] | |
Justice *(appointment number)*	State	Federal
Warren, Earl (92)	Deputy city attorney, Oakland, California, 1919-20; deputy assistant district attorney, Alameda County, California, 1920-23; chief deputy district attorney, Alameda County, California, 1923-25; district attorney, Alameda County, California, 1925-39; attorney general, California, 1939-43; governor, California, 1943-53	Republican vice-presidential nominee, 1948
Washington, Bushrod (12)	Virginia House of Delegates, 1787-88; member, Virginia convention to ratify the U.S. Constitution, 1788	
Wayne, James M. (24)	Georgia House of Representatives, 1815-16; mayor, Savannah, Georgia, 1817-19	House of Representatives (Georgia), 1829-35
White, Byron R. (97)		Deputy attorney general, 1961-62
White, Edward D. (56, 64)	Louisiana Senate, 1874	Senate (Louisiana), 1891-94
Wilson, James (4)	Member, Pennsylvania convention to ratify the U.S. Constitution, 1787	Continental Congress (Pennsylvania), 1775-77; signed Declaration of Independence, 1776; delegate, Constitutional Convention, 1787; Congress (Pennsylvania), 1783, 1785-87
Woodbury, Levi (31)	Clerk, New Hampshire Senate, 1816; governor, New Hampshire, 1823-24; speaker, New Hampshire House of Representatives, 1825	Senate (New Hampshire), 1825-31, 1841-45; secretary of the Navy, 1831-34; secretary of the Treasury, 1834-41

Woods, William B. (46) Mayor, Newark, Ohio, 1856; Ohio House of
Representatives, 1858-62; speaker, Ohio House of
Representatives, 1858-60

Note: The names of justices who held no state or federal offices prior to taking seat on the Supreme Court have been omitted.

[a] Includes nonjudicial governmental positions held by justice prior to taking seat on the Supreme Court.
[b] Office held under colonial English government.
[c] Office held under Confederate States of America.

Sources: Elder Witt, *Congressional Quarterly's Guide to the U.S. Supreme Court* 2d ed. (Washington, D.C.: Congressional Quarterly, 1990); Leon Friedman and Fred L. Israel, eds., *The Justices of the United States Supreme Court: Their Lives and Major Opinions* (New York: R.R. Bowker, 1969-1978); Harold W. Chase et al., *Biographical Dictionary of the American Judiciary* (Detroit: Gale Research, 1976); *Judges of the United States,* 2d ed. (Washington, D.C.: Judicial Conference of the United States, 1983); *The National Cyclopaedia of American Biography* (New York: James T. White, various years); *Dictionary of American Biography* (New York: Charles Scribner's Sons, various editions).

Table 4-9 Prior Judicial Experience

Justice (appointment number)	Judicial branch experience[a]	
	State	Federal
Barbour, Philip P. (26)	Judge, General Court, Virginia, 1825-27	Judge, Eastern District of Virginia, 1830-36
Black, Hugo L. (79)	Judge, Police Court, Birmingham, Alabama, 1910-11	
Blackmun, Harry A. (102)		Law clerk, Court of Appeals for the Eighth Circuit, 1932-33; Judge, Court of Appeals for the Eighth Circuit, 1959-70
Blair, John, Jr. (5)	Judge, General Court, Virginia, 1777-78; Chief judge, General Court, Virginia, 1779; Judge, Court of Appeals, Virginia, 1780-89; Judge, Supreme Court of Appeals, Virginia, 1789	
Blatchford, Samuel (49)		Judge, Southern District of New York, 1867-72; Judge, Second Judicial Circuit, 1872-82
Brennan, William J., Jr. (94)	Judge, Superior Court, New Jersey, 1949-50; Judge, Superior Court, Appellate Division, New Jersey, 1950-52; Judge, Supreme Court, New Jersey, 1952-56	
Brewer, David J. (52)	Judge, County Probate and Criminal Courts, Kansas, 1863-64; Judge, District Court, Kansas, 1865-69; Justice, Supreme Court, Kansas, 1870-84; Commissioner, Circuit Court, Kansas Division, 1861-62	Judge, Eighth Judicial Circuit, 1884-89

Brown, Henry B. (53)	Judge, Circuit Court, Michigan, 1868	Judge, Eastern District of Michigan, 1875-90
Burger, Warren E. (101)		Judge, Court of Appeals for the District of Columbia Circuit, 1956-69
Byrnes, James F. (85)	Reporter, Circuit Court, South Carolina, 1900-08	
Cardozo, Benjamin (78)	Justice, Supreme Court, New York, 1914; Judge, Court of Appeals, New York, 1914-26; Chief Judge, Court of Appeals, New York, 1926-32	
Catron, John (27)	Judge, Supreme Court, Tennessee, 1824-31; Chief Justice, Supreme Court, Tennessee, 1831-34	
Chase, Samuel (10)	Judge, Criminal Court, Baltimore, Maryland, 1788-96; Chief Judge, General Court, Maryland, 1791-96	
Clarke, John H. (70)		Judge, Northern District of Ohio, 1914-16
Cushing, William (3)	Judge, Probate Court, Massachusetts, 1760-61; Judge, Superior Court, Massachusetts, 1772-77; Chief Justice, Superior Court, Massachusetts, 1777-80; Judge, Supreme Court, Massachusetts, 1780-89	
Daniel, Peter V. (29)		Judge, Eastern District of Virginia, 1836-41
Davis, David (38)	Judge, Circuit Court, Illinois, 1848-62	

(Table continues)

Table 4-9 (*Continued*)

Justice (appointment number)	Judicial branch experience[a]	
	State	Federal
Day, William R. (60)	Judge, Court of Common Pleas, Ohio, 1886-90	Judge, Court of Appeals for the Sixth Circuit, 1899-1903
Duvall, Gabriel (18)	Chief Justice, General Court, Maryland, 1796-1802	
Ellsworth, Oliver (11)	Judge, Superior Court, Connecticut, 1785-89	
Field, Stephen J. (39)	Justice, Supreme Court, California, 1857-59; Chief Justice, Supreme Court, California, 1859-63	
Ginsburg, Ruth Bader (112)		Law clerk, Judge Edmund Palmieri, Southern District of New York, 1959-61; Judge, Court of Appeals for the District of Columbia, 1980-93
Gray, Horace (48)	Reporter, Supreme Court, Massachusetts, 1854-64; Associate Justice, Supreme Court, Massachusetts, 1864-73; Chief Justice, Supreme Court, Massachusetts, 1873-81	
Grier, Robert C. (32)	Presiding Judge, District Court, Pennsylvania, 1833-46	
Harlan, John Marshall I (45)	Judge, Franklin County Court, Kentucky, 1858-59	
Harlan, John Marshall II (93)		Judge, Court of Appeals for the Second Circuit, 1954-55

Holmes, Oliver W., Jr. (59)	Associate Justice, Supreme Court, Massachusetts, 1882-99; Chief Justice, Supreme Court, Massachusetts, 1899-1902
Hughes, Charles Evans (63, 76)	Judge, Permanent Court of Arbitration and International Court of Justice, 1926-30[b]
Hunt, Ward (43)	Judge, Court of Appeals, New York, 1866-68; Chief Judge, Court of Appeals, New York, 1868-69; Commissioner of Appeals, New York, 1869-73
Iredell, James (6)	Judge, Superior Court, North Carolina, 1778
Jackson, Howell E. (55)	Judge, Court of Arbitration, Tennessee, 1875-79 Judge, Sixth Judicial Circuit, 1886-91; Judge, Court of Appeals for the Sixth Circuit, 1891-93
Jay, John (1)	Chief Justice, Supreme Court, New York, 1777-78
Johnson, Thomas (7)	Chief Judge, General Court, Maryland, 1790-91
Johnson, William (15)	Judge, Court of Common Pleas, South Carolina, 1799-1804
Kennedy, Anthony (109)	Judge, Court of Appeals for the Ninth Circuit, 1976-88
Lamar, Joseph R. (66)	Associate Justice, Supreme Court, Georgia, 1903-05
Livingston, H. Brockholst (16)	Judge, Supreme Court, New York, 1802-07

(Table continues)

Table 4-9 (*Continued*)

Justice (*appointment number*)	Judicial branch experience[a]	
	State	Federal
Lurton, Horace (62)	Chancellor in Equity, Tennessee, 1875-78; Judge, Supreme Court, Tennessee, 1886-93	Judge, Court of Appeals for the Sixth Circuit, 1893-1909
Marshall, Thurgood (100)		Judge, Court of Appeals for the Second Circuit, 1961-65
Matthews, Stanley (47)	Judge, Court of Common Pleas, Ohio, 1851-53; Judge, Superior Court, Ohio, 1863-65	
McKenna, Joseph (58)		Judge, Court of Appeals for the Ninth Circuit, 1892-97
McLean, John (22)	Judge, Supreme Court, Ohio, 1816-22	
Miller, Samuel (37)	Justice of the Peace, Kentucky, 1844	
Minton, Sherman (91)		Judge, Court of Appeals for the Seventh Circuit, 1941-49
Moore, Alfred (13)	Judge, Superior Court, North Carolina, 1799	
Murphy, Frank (83)	Judge, Recorder's Court, Detroit, Michigan, 1923-30	

Nelson, Samuel (30)	Judge, Circuit Court, New York, 1823-31; Associate Justice, Supreme Court, New York, 1831-37; Chief Justice, Supreme Court, New York, 1837-45
O'Connor, Sandra Day (106)	Judge, Superior Court, Arizona, 1975-79; Judge, Court of Appeals, Arizona, 1979-81
Peckham, Rufus W. (57)	Judge, Supreme Court, New York, 1883-86; Judge, Court of Appeals, New York, 1886-95
Pitney, Mahlon (67)	Associate Justice, Supreme Court, New Jersey, 1901-08; Chancellor, New Jersey, 1908-12
Rehnquist, William (104, 107)	Law Clerk, Justice Robert Jackson, 1952-53
Rutledge, John (2, 9)	Chief Judge, Chancery Court, South Carolina, 1784-91
Rutledge, Wiley B. (87)	Judge, Court of Appeals for the District of Columbia Circuit, 1939-43
Sanford, Edward T. (74)	Judge, Middle and Eastern Districts of Tennessee, 1908-23
Scalia, Antonin (108)	Judge, Court of Appeals for the District of Columbia Circuit, 1982-86
Souter, David H. (110)	Judge, Superior Court, New Hampshire, 1978-83; Judge, Supreme Court, New Hampshire, 1983-90; Judge, Court of Appeals for the First Circuit, 1990

(Table continues)

Table 4-9 (*Continued*)

Justice (appointment number)	Judicial branch experience[a]	
	State	Federal
Stevens, John Paul (105)		Law Clerk, Justice Wiley Rutledge, 1947-48; Judge, Court of Appeals for the Seventh Circuit, 1970-75
Stewart, Potter (96)		Judge, Court of Appeals for the Sixth Circuit, 1954-58
Strong, William (41)	Justice, Supreme Court, Pennsylvania, 1857-68	
Taft, William H. (71)	Judge, Superior Court, Ohio, 1887-90	Judge, Court of Appeals for the Sixth Circuit, 1892-1900
Thomas, Clarence (111)		Judge, Court of Appeals for the District of Columbia Circuit, 1990-91
Thompson, Smith (20)	Associate Justice, Supreme Court, New York, 1802-14; Chief Justice, Supreme Court, New York, 1814-18	
Todd, Thomas (17)	Clerk, Court of Appeals, Kentucky, 1799-1801; Judge, Court of Appeals, Kentucky, 1801-06; Chief Justice, Court of Appeals, Kentucky, 1806-07	Clerk, District of Kentucky, 1792-1801
Trimble, Robert (21)	Judge, Court of Appeals, Kentucky, 1807-09	Judge, District of Kentucky, 1817-26

Van Devanter, Willis (65)	Chief Justice, Supreme Court, Wyoming Territory, 1889-90	Judge, Court of Appeals for the Eighth Circuit, 1903-10
Vinson, Fred M. (89)		Judge, Court of Appeals for the District of Columbia Circuit, 1938-43
Wayne, James M. (24)	Judge, Court of Common Pleas, Savannah, Georgia, 1820-22; Judge, Superior Court, Georgia, 1822-28	
White, Byron R. (97)		Law Clerk, Chief Justice Fred M. Vinson, 1946-47
White, Edward D. (56, 64)	Associate Justice, Supreme Court, Louisiana, 1878-80	
Whittaker, Charles E. (95)		Judge, Western District of Missouri, 1954-56; Judge, Court of Appeals for the Eighth Circuit, 1956-57
Woodbury, Levi (31)	Associate Justice, Superior Court, New Hampshire, 1817-23	
Woods, William B. (46)	Chancellor, Chancery Court, Alabama, 1868-69	Judge, Fifth Judicial Circuit, 1869-80

Note: The names of justices who held no local, state, or federal judicial branch position prior to taking seat on the Supreme Court have been omitted.

[a] Includes local, state, and federal judicial branch positions held by justice prior to taking seat on the Supreme Court.

[b] International jurisdiction; Hughes served in this capacity after his tenure on the Court as an associate justice, but prior to his second term on the Court as chief justice.

(Notes continue)

Table 4-9 *(Continued)*

Sources: Elder Witt, *Congressional Quarterly's Guide to the U.S. Supreme Court*, 2d ed. (Washington, D.C.: Congressional Quarterly, 1990); Leon Friedman and Fred L. Israel, eds., *The Justices of the United States Supreme Court: Their Lives and Major Opinions* (New York: R.R. Bowker, 1969-1978); Harold W. Chase et al., *Biographical Dictionary of the American Judiciary* (Detroit: Gale Research, 1976); *Judges of the United States*, 2d ed. (Washington, D.C.: Judicial Conference of the United States, 1983); *The National Cyclopaedia of American Biography* (New York: James T. White, various years); *Dictionary of American Biography* (New York: Charles Scribner's Sons, various editions).

Table 4-10 Supreme Court Nominees

President/nominee	Year	Position at time of nomination	Age	Home state
George Washington:				
John Jay[a]	1789	U.S. secretary of foreign affairs	43	New York
John Rutledge	1789	South Carolina Chancery Court judge	50	South Carolina
William Cushing	1789	Massachusetts Supreme Court judge	57	Massachusetts
Robert H. Harrison[b]	1789	Maryland General Court judge	44	Maryland
James Wilson	1789	Lawyer, business speculator	47	Pennsylvania
John Blair, Jr.	1789	Virginia Supreme Court judge	57	Virginia
James Iredell	1790	Lawyer	38	North Carolina
Thomas Johnson	1791	Maryland General Court judge	58	Maryland
William Paterson[b]	1793	New Jersey governor	47	New Jersey
William Paterson	1793	New Jersey governor	47	New Jersey
John Rutledge[a, b]	1795	South Carolina chief justice	55	South Carolina
William Cushing[a, b]	1796	Sitting associate justice	63	Massachusetts
Samuel Chase	1796	Maryland General Court judge	54	Maryland
Oliver Ellsworth[a]	1796	U.S. senator	50	Connecticut
John Adams:				
Bushrod Washington	1798	Lawyer	36	Virginia
Alfred Moore	1799	North Carolina Superior Court judge	44	North Carolina
John Jay[a, b]	1800	New York governor	55	New York
John Marshall[a]	1801	U.S. secretary of state	45	Virginia
Thomas Jefferson:				
William Johnson	1804	South Carolina Common Pleas judge	33	South Carolina

(Table continues)

Table 4-10 (Continued)

President/nominee	Year	Position at time of nomination	Age	Home state
H. Brockholst Livingston	1806	New York Supreme Court judge	49	New York
Thomas Todd	1807	Kentucky chief justice	42	Kentucky
James Madison:				
Levi Lincoln [b]	1811	Massachusetts Governor's Council	61	Massachusetts
Alexander Wolcott [b]	1811	U.S. revenue collector	52	Connecticut
John Quincy Adams [b]	1811	U.S. minister to Russia	43	Massachusetts
Gabriel Duvall	1811	U.S. controller of the Treasury	58	Maryland
Joseph Story	1811	Speaker of the Massachusetts House	32	Massachusetts
James Monroe:				
Smith Thompson	1823	U.S. secretary of the Navy	55	New York
John Quincy Adams:				
Robert Trimble	1826	U.S. District Court judge	49	Kentucky
John Crittenden [b]	1828	U.S. attorney	41	Kentucky
Andrew Jackson:				
John McLean	1829	U.S. postmaster general	43	Ohio
Henry Baldwin	1830	Lawyer, businessman	49	Pennsylvania
James M. Wayne	1835	U.S. House Of Representatives	45	Georgia
Roger Brooke Taney [b]	1835	Lawyer	57	Maryland
Roger Brooke Taney [a]	1835	Lawyer	58	Maryland
Philip P. Barbour	1835	U.S. District Court judge	51	Virginia
William Smith [b]	1837	Alabama House Of Representatives	75	Alabama
John Catron	1837	Lawyer	51	Tennessee

Name	Year	Position	Age	State
Martin Van Buren:				
John McKinley	1837	U.S. senator	57	Alabama
Peter V. Daniel	1841	U.S. District Court judge	56	Virginia
John Tyler:				
John C. Spencer [b]	1844	U.S. secretary of the Treasury	56	New York
Reuben H. Walworth [b]	1844	New York chancellor	55	New York
Edward King [b]	1844	Pennsylvania Common Pleas judge	50	Pennsylvania
Edward King [b]	1844	Pennsylvania Common Pleas judge	50	Pennsylvania
Samuel Nelson	1845	New York Supreme Court judge	52	New York
John M. Read [b]	1845	Lawyer	47	Pennsylvania
James K. Polk:				
George W. Woodward [b]	1845	Pennsylvania District Court judge	36	Pennsylvania
Levi Woodbury	1845	U.S. senator	56	New Hampshire
Robert C. Grier	1846	U.S. District Court judge	52	Pennsylvania
Millard Fillmore:				
Benjamin R. Curtis	1851	Massachusetts state representative	42	Massachusetts
Edward A. Bradford [b]	1852	Lawyer	38	Louisiana
George E. Badger [b]	1853	U.S. senator	57	North Carolina
William C. Micou [b]	1853	Lawyer	47	Louisiana
Franklin Pierce:				
John A. Campbell	1853	Lawyer	41	Alabama
James Buchanan:				
Nathan Clifford	1857	Lawyer	54	Maine
Jeremiah S. Black [b]	1861	U.S. secretary of state	51	Pennsylvania

(Table continues)

Table 4-10 (Continued)

President/nominee	Year	Position at time of nomination	Age	Home state
Abraham Lincoln:				
Noah H. Swayne	1862	Lawyer	56	Ohio
Samuel F. Miller	1862	Lawyer	46	Iowa
David Davis	1862	Illinois Circuit Court judge	47	Illinois
Stephen J. Field	1863	California Supreme Court judge	46	California
Salmon P. Chase [a]	1864	U.S. secretary of the Treasury	56	Ohio
Andrew Johnson:				
Henry Stanbery [b]	1866	Lawyer	63	Ohio
Ulysses S. Grant:				
Ebenezer R. Hoar [b]	1869	U.S. attorney general	53	Massachusetts
Edwin M. Stanton [b]	1869	Lawyer	54	Ohio
William Strong	1870	Lawyer	61	Pennsylvania
Joseph P. Bradley	1870	Lawyer	57	New Jersey
Ward Hunt	1872	New York commissioner of appeals	62	New York
George H. Williams [a, b]	1873	U.S. attorney general	50	Oregon
Caleb Cushing [a, b]	1874	U.S. minister to Spain	73	Massachusetts
Morrison R. Waite [a]	1874	Ohio Constitutional Convention, lawyer	57	Ohio
Rutherford B. Hayes:				
John Marshall Harlan I	1877	Louisiana Reconstruction Commission	44	Kentucky
William B. Woods	1880	U.S. Circuit Court judge	56	Georgia
Stanley Matthews [b]	1881	Lawyer	56	Ohio
James Garfield:				
Stanley Matthews	1881	Lawyer	56	Ohio

Chester Arthur:			
Horace Gray	1881	Massachusetts chief justice	Massachusetts
Roscoe Conkling [b]	1882	Lawyer	New York
Samuel Blatchford	1882	U.S. Circuit Court judge	New York
Grover Cleveland:			
Lucius Q. C. Lamar	1887	U.S. secretary of the Interior	Mississippi
Melville W. Fuller [a]	1888	Lawyer	Illinois
Benjamin Harrison:			
David J. Brewer	1889	U.S. Circuit Court judge	Kansas
Henry B. Brown	1890	U.S. District Court judge	Michigan
George Shiras, Jr.	1892	Lawyer	Pennsylvania
Howell E. Jackson	1893	U.S. Court of Appeals judge	Tennessee
Grover Cleveland:			
William B. Hornblower [b]	1893	Lawyer	New York
Wheeler H. Peckham [b]	1894	Lawyer	New York
Edward D. White	1894	U.S. senator	Louisiana
Rufus W. Peckham	1895	New York Court of Appeals judge	New York
William McKinley:			
Joseph McKenna	1897	U.S. attorney general	California
Theodore Roosevelt:			
Oliver W. Holmes, Jr.	1902	Massachusetts chief justice	Massachusetts
William Rufus Day	1903	U.S. Court of Appeals judge	Ohio
William H. Moody	1906	U.S. attorney general	Massachusetts

(Table continues)

Table 4-10 (Continued)

President/nominee	Year	Position at time of nomination	Age	Home state
William Howard Taft:				
Horace H. Lurton	1909	U.S. Court of Appeals judge	65	Tennessee
Charles E. Hughes	1910	New York governor	48	New York
Edward D. White [a]	1910	Sitting associate justice	65	Louisiana
Willis Van Devanter	1910	U.S. Court of Appeals judge	51	Wyoming
Joseph Rucker Lamar	1910	Lawyer	53	Georgia
Mahlon Pitney	1912	New Jersey chancellor	54	New Jersey
Woodrow Wilson:				
James C. McReynolds	1914	U.S. attorney general	52	Tennessee
Louis D. Brandeis	1916	Lawyer	59	Massachusetts
John H. Clarke	1916	U.S. District Court judge	58	Ohio
Warren Harding:				
William H. Taft [a]	1921	Law school professor	63	Ohio
George Sutherland	1922	Lawyer	60	Utah
Pierce Butler	1922	Lawyer	56	Minnesota
Edward T. Sanford	1923	U.S. District Court judge	57	Tennessee
Calvin Coolidge:				
Harlan Fiske Stone	1925	Law school dean	52	New York
Herbert Hoover:				
Charles E. Hughes [a]	1930	International Court of Justice judge	67	New York
John J. Parker [b]	1930	U.S. Court of Appeals judge	44	North Carolina
Owen J. Roberts	1930	U.S. special prosecutor	55	Pennsylvania
Benjamin N. Cardozo	1932	New York Court of Appeals judge	61	New York

Name	Year	Position	Age	State
Franklin Roosevelt:				
Hugo L. Black	1937	U.S. senator	51	Alabama
Stanley F. Reed	1938	U.S. solicitor general	53	Kentucky
Felix Frankfurter	1939	Law school professor	56	Massachusetts
William O. Douglas	1939	Securities and Exchange Commission	40	Connecticut
Frank Murphy	1940	U.S. attorney general	49	Michigan
Harlan Fiske Stone [a]	1941	Sitting associate justice	68	New York
James Francis Byrnes	1941	U.S. senator	62	South Carolina
Robert H. Jackson	1941	U.S. attorney general	49	New York
Wiley B. Rutledge	1943	U.S. Court of Appeals judge	48	Iowa
Harry S. Truman:				
Harold H. Burton	1945	U.S. senator	57	Ohio
Fred M. Vinson [a]	1946	U.S. secretary of the Treasury	56	Kentucky
Tom C. Clark	1949	U.S. attorney general	49	Texas
Sherman Minton	1949	U.S. Court of Appeals judge	58	Indiana
Dwight Eisenhower:				
Earl Warren [a]	1953	California governor	62	California
John Marshall Harlan II	1954	U.S. Court of Appeals judge	55	New York
William J. Brennan, Jr.	1956	New Jersey Supreme Court judge	50	New Jersey
Charles E. Whittaker	1957	U.S. Court of Appeals judge	56	Missouri
Potter Stewart	1959	U.S. Court of Appeals judge	43	Ohio
John Kennedy:				
Byron R. White	1962	U.S. deputy attorney general	44	Colorado
Arthur J. Goldberg	1962	U.S. secretary of Labor	54	Illinois

(Table continues)

Table 4-10 *(Continued)*

President/nominee	Year	Position at time of nomination	Age	Home state
Lyndon Johnson:				
Abe Fortas	1965	Lawyer	55	Tennessee
Thurgood Marshall	1967	U.S. solicitor general	58	New York
Abe Fortas [a,b]	1968	Sitting associate justice	58	Tennessee
Homer Thornberry [b]	1968	U.S. Court of Appeals judge	59	Texas
Richard Nixon:				
Warren E. Burger [a]	1969	U.S. Court of Appeals judge	61	Minnesota
Clement Haynsworth, Jr. [b]	1969	U.S. Court of Appeals judge	56	South Carolina
G. Harrold Carswell [b]	1970	U.S. Court of Appeals judge	50	Florida
Harry A. Blackmun	1970	U.S. Court of Appeals judge	61	Minnesota
Lewis F. Powell, Jr.	1971	Lawyer	64	Virginia
William H. Rehnquist	1971	U.S. assistant attorney general	47	Arizona
Gerald Ford:				
John Paul Stevens	1975	U.S. Court of Appeals judge	55	Illinois
Ronald Reagan:				
Sandra Day O'Connor	1981	Arizona Appeals Court judge	51	Arizona
William H. Rehnquist [a]	1986	Sitting associate justice	61	Arizona
Antonin Scalia	1986	U.S. Court of Appeals judge	50	Virginia
Robert H. Bork [b]	1987	U.S. Court of Appeals judge	60	D.C.
Anthony M. Kennedy	1987	U.S. Court of Appeals judge	51	California
George Bush:				
David H. Souter	1990	U.S. Court of Appeals judge	50	New Hampshire
Clarence Thomas	1991	U.S. Court of Appeals judge	43	Georgia

Bill Clinton:				
Ruth Bader Ginsburg	1993	U.S. Court of Appeals judge	60	New York

Note: Nominees are ordered chronologically according to the dates of their nominations or recess appointments, whichever came first. Only names of those officially nominated and sent to the Senate for confirmation are included. For example, Daniel Ginsburg, nominated by Ronald Reagan in 1987, is not included because his nomination was withdrawn before official submission to the Senate.

[a] Nomination for chief justice.
[b] Unsuccessful nomination. The nominee either failed to obtain Senate confirmation or did not serve after being confirmed.

Sources: Elder Witt, *Congressional Quarterly's Guide to the U.S. Supreme Court,* 2d ed. (Washington, D.C.: Congressional Quarterly, 1990); Leon Friedman and Fred L. Israel, eds., *The Justices of the United States Supreme Court: Their Lives and Major Opinions* (New York: R.R. Bowker, 1969-1978); Harold W. Chase et al., *Biographical Dictionary of the American Judiciary* (Detroit: Gale Research, 1976); *Judges of the United States,* 2d ed. (Washington, D.C.: Judicial Conference of the United States, 1983); *The National Cyclopaedia of American Biography* (New York: James T. White, various years); *Dictionary of American Biography* (New York: Charles Scribner's Sons, various editions).

Table 4-11 Supreme Court Nominees and the Vacancies To Be Filled

President/nominee	State	Party at time of appointment[a]	Previous party affiliations[a]	Justice to be replaced Name	State	Party[a]
George Washington (Fed):						
John Jay[b]	NY	Fed		[c]	—	—
John Rutledge	SC	Fed		[c]	—	—
William Cushing	MA	Fed		[c]	—	—
Robert H. Harrison[d]	MD	Fed		[c]	—	—
James Wilson	PA	Fed		[c]	—	—
John Blair, Jr.	VA	Fed		[c]	—	—
James Iredell	NC	Fed		[c]	—	—
Thomas Johnson	MD	Fed		John Rutledge	SC	Fed
William Paterson[d]	NJ	Fed		Thomas Johnson	MD	Fed
William Paterson	NJ	Fed		Thomas Johnson	MD	Fed
John Rutledge[b,d]	SC	Fed		John Jay	NY	Fed
William Cushing[b,d]	MA	Fed		John Jay	NY	Fed
Samuel Chase	MD	Fed		John Blair	VA	Fed
Oliver Ellsworth[b]	CT	Fed		John Jay	NY	Fed
John Adams (Fed):						
Bushrod Washington	VA	Fed		James Wilson	PA	Fed
Alfred Moore	NC	Fed		James Iredell	NC	Fed
John Jay[b,d]	NY	Fed		Oliver Ellsworth	CT	Fed
John Marshall[b]	VA	Fed		Oliver Ellsworth	CT	Fed
Thomas Jefferson (Dem-Rep):						
William Johnson	SC	Dem-Rep		Alfred Moore	NC	Fed

H. Brockholst Livingston	NY	Dem-Rep	Fed	William Paterson	NJ	Fed
Thomas Todd	KY	Dem-Rep		e	—	—
James Madison (Dem-Rep):						
Levi Lincoln[d]	MA	Dem-Rep		William Cushing	MA	Fed
Alexander Wolcott[d]	CT	Dem-Rep		William Cushing	MA	Fed
John Quincy Adams[d]	MA	Dem-Rep		William Cushing	MA	Fed
Gabriel Duvall	MD	Dem-Rep		Samuel Chase	MD	Fed
Joseph Story	MA	Dem-Rep		William Cushing	MA	Fed
James Monroe (Dem-Rep):						
Smith Thompson	NY	Dem-Rep		H. Brockholst Livingston	NY	Dem-Rep
John Quincy Adams (Dem-Rep):						
Robert Trimble	KY	Dem-Rep		Thomas Todd	KY	Dem-Rep
John Crittenden[d]	KY	Dem-Rep		Robert Trimble	KY	Dem-Rep
Andrew Jackson (Dem):						
John McLean	OH	Dem	Dem-Rep	Robert Trimble	KY	Dem-Rep
Henry Baldwin	PA	Dem	Fed	Bushrod Washington	VA	Fed
James M. Wayne	GA	Dem		William Johnson	SC	Dem-Rep
Roger Brooke Taney[d]	MD	Dem	Fed	Gabriel Duvall	MD	Dem-Rep
Roger Brooke Taney[b]	MD	Dem	Fed	John Marshall	VA	Fed
Philip P. Barbour	VA	Dem	Dem-Rep	Gabriel Duvall	MD	Dem-Rep
William Smith[d]	AL	Dem		e	—	—
John Catron	TN	Dem		e	—	—
Martin Van Buren (Dem):						
John McKinley	AL	Dem		e	—	—
Peter V. Daniel	VA	Dem	Dem-Rep	Philip Barbour	VA	Dem

Table 4-11 (Continued)

| President/nominee | State | Party at time of appointment[a] | Previous party affiliations[a] | Justice to be replaced | | Party[a] |
				Name	State	
John Tyler (Dem):						
John C. Spencer[d]	NY	Whig		Smith Thompson	NY	Dem-Rep
Reuben H. Walworth[d]	NY	Dem		Smith Thompson	NY	Dem-Rep
Edward King[d]	PA	Dem		Henry Baldwin	PA	Dem
Edward King[d]	PA	Dem		Henry Baldwin	PA	Dem
Samuel Nelson	NY	Dem	Dem-Rep	Smith Thompson	NY	Dem-Rep
John M. Read[d]	PA	Dem		Henry Baldwin	PA	Dem
James K. Polk (Dem):						
George W. Woodward[d]	PA	Dem		Henry Baldwin	PA	Dem
Levi Woodbury	NH	Dem	Dem-Rep	Joseph Story	MA	Dem-Rep
Robert C. Grier	PA	Dem		Henry Baldwin	PA	Dem
Millard Fillmore (Whig):						
Benjamin R. Curtis	MA	Whig		Levi Woodbury	NH	Dem
Edward A. Bradford[d]	LA	Whig		John McKinley	AL	Dem
George E. Badger[d]	NC	Whig		John McKinley	AL	Dem
William C. Micou[d]	LA	Whig		John McKinley	AL	Dem
Franklin Pierce (Dem):						
John A. Campbell	AL	Dem		John McKinley	AL	Dem
James Buchanan (Dem):						
Nathan Clifford	ME	Dem		Benjamin Curtis	MA	Whig
Jeremiah S. Black[d]	PA	Dem		Peter Daniel	VA	Dem

Nominee	State	Party	Prior affiliation	Justice replaced	State	Party
Abraham Lincoln (Rep):						
Noah H. Swayne	OH	Rep	Dem	John McLean	OH	Dem
Samuel F. Miller	IA	Rep	Whig	Peter Daniel	VA	Dem
David Davis	IL	Rep	Whig	John Campbell[e]	AL	Dem
Stephen J. Field	CA	Dem		—	—	—
Salmon P. Chase	OH	Rep	Whig, Anti-Slavery, Liberty, Free Soil	Roger Taney	MD	Dem
Andrew Johnson (Dem):						
Henry Stanbery[d]	OH	Rep		John Catron	TN	Dem
Ulysses S. Grant (Rep):						
Ebenezer R. Hoar[d]	MA	Rep		[f]	—	—
Edwin M. Stanton[d]	OH	Rep	Dem	Robert Grier	PA	Dem
William Strong	PA	Rep	Whig	Robert Grier	PA	Dem
Joseph P. Bradley	NJ	Rep	Dem, Free Soil	[f]	—	—
Ward Hunt	NY	Rep		Samuel Nelson	NY	Dem
George H. Williams[b,d]	OR	Rep		Salmon Chase	OH	Rep
Caleb Cushing[b,d]	MA	Rep	Whig	Salmon Chase	OH	Rep
Morrison R. Waite[c]	OH	Rep		Salmon Chase	OH	Rep
Rutherford B. Hayes (Rep):						
John Marshall Harlan I	KY	Rep	Whig, Know-Nothing, Union	David Davis	IL	Rep

(Table continues)

Table 4-11 (*Continued*)

President/nominee	State	Party at time of appointment[a]	Previous party affiliations[a]	Justice to be replaced		
				Name	State	Party[a]
William B. Woods[d]	GA	Rep	Dem	William Strong	PA	Rep
Stanley Matthews[d]	OH	Rep	Dem	Noah Swayne	OH	Rep
James Garfield (Rep):						
Stanley Matthews	OH	Rep		Noah Swayne	OH	Rep
Chester Arthur (Rep):						
Horace Gray	MA	Rep	Free Soil	Nathan Clifford	ME	Dem
Roscoe Conkling[d]	NY	Rep		Ward Hunt	NY	Rep
Samuel Blatchford	NY	Rep		Ward Hunt	NY	Rep
Grover Cleveland (Dem):						
Lucius Q. C. Lamar	MS	Dem		William Woods	GA	Rep
Melville W. Fuller[b]	IL	Dem		Morrison Waite	OH	Rep
Benjamin Harrison (Rep):						
David J. Brewer	KS	Rep		Stanley Matthews	OH	Rep
Henry B. Brown	MI	Rep		Samuel Miller	IA	Rep
George Shiras, Jr.	PA	Rep		Joseph Bradley	NJ	Rep
Howell E. Jackson	TN	Dem	Whig	Lucius Q. C. Lamar	MS	Dem
Grover Cleveland (Dem):						
William B. Hornblower[d]	NY	Dem		Samuel Blatchford	NY	Rep
Wheeler H. Peckham[d]	NY	Dem		Samuel Blatchford	NY	Rep
Edward D. White	LA	Dem		Samuel Blatchford	NY	Rep
Rufus W. Peckham	NY	Dem		Howell Jackson	TN	Dem

Appointee	State	Party		Sitting Justice	State	Party
William McKinley (Rep):				Stephen Field	CA	Dem
Joseph McKenna	CA	Rep				
Theodore Roosevelt (Rep):				Horace Gray	MA	Rep
Oliver W. Holmes, Jr.	MA	Rep		George Shiras	PA	Rep
William Rufus Day	OH	Rep		Henry B. Brown	MI	Rep
William H. Moody	MA	Rep				
William Howard Taft (Rep):				Rufus Peckham	NY	Dem
Horace H. Lurton	TN	Dem		David Brewer	KS	Rep
Charles E. Hughes	NY	Rep		Melville Fuller	IL	Dem
Edward D. White [c]	LA	Dem	Dem	Edward White	LA	Dem
Willis Van Devanter	WY	Rep		William Moody	MA	Rep
Joseph Rucker Lamar	GA	Dem		John M. Harlan I	KY	Rep
Mahlon Pitney	NJ	Rep				
Woodrow Wilson (Dem):				Horace Lurton	TN	Dem
James C. McReynolds	TN	Dem		Joseph Rucker Lamar	GA	Dem
Louis D. Brandeis	MA	Rep [g]		Charles E. Hughes	NY	Rep
John H. Clarke	OH	Dem				
Warren Harding (Rep):				Edward White	LA	Dem
William H. Taft [b]	OH	Rep		John H. Clarke	OH	Dem
George Sutherland	UT	Rep		William Rufus Day	OH	Rep
Pierce Butler	MN	Dem		Mahlon Pitney	NJ	Rep
Edward T. Sanford	TN	Rep				
Calvin Coolidge (Rep)				Joseph McKenna	CA	Rep
Harlan Fiske Stone	NY	Rep				

(Table continues)

Table 4-11 (Continued)

President / nominee	State	Party at time of appointment[a]	Previous party affiliations[a]	Justice to be replaced		
				Name	State	Party[a]
Herbert Hoover (Rep):						
Charles E. Hughes[b]	NY	Rep		William H. Taft	OH	Rep
John J. Parker[d]	NC	Rep		Edward T. Sanford	TN	Rep
Owen J. Roberts	PA	Rep		Edward T. Sanford	TN	Rep
Benjamin N. Cardozo	NY	Dem		Oliver W. Holmes	MA	Rep
Franklin Roosevelt (Dem):						
Hugo L. Black	AL	Dem		Willis Van Devanter	WY	Rep
Stanley F. Reed	KY	Dem		George Sutherland	UT	Rep
Felix Frankfurter	MA	Ind		Benjamin Cardozo	NY	Dem
William O. Douglas	CT	Dem		Louis D. Brandeis	MA	Rep[c]
Frank Murphy	MI	Dem		Pierce Butler	MN	Dem
Harlan Fiske Stone[b]	NY	Rep		Charles E. Hughes	NY	Rep
James Francis Byrnes	SC	Dem		James McReynolds	TN	Dem
Robert H. Jackson	NY	Dem		Harlan Fiske Stone	NY	Rep
Wiley B. Rutledge	IA	Dem		James F. Byrnes	SC	Dem
Harry S Truman (Dem):						
Harold H. Burton	OH	Rep		Owen Roberts	PA	Rep
Fred M. Vinson[b]	KY	Dem		Harlan Fiske Stone	NY	Rep
Tom C. Clark	TX	Dem		Frank Murphy	MI	Dem
Sherman Minton	IN	Dem		Wiley B. Rutledge	IA	Dem
Dwight Eisenhower (Rep):						
Earl Warren[c]	CA	Rep		Fred Vinson	KY	Dem

Nominee	State	Party	Justice replaced	State	Party
John Marshall Harlan II	NY	Rep	Robert Jackson	NY	Dem
William J. Brennan, Jr.	NJ	Dem	Sherman Minton	IN	Dem
Charles E. Whittaker	MO	Rep	Stanley Reed	KY	Dem
Potter Stewart	OH	Rep	Harold Burton	OH	Rep
John Kennedy (Dem):					
Byron R. White	CO	Dem	Charles Whittaker	MO	Rep
Arthur J. Goldberg	IL	Dem	Felix Frankfurter	MA	Ind
Lyndon Johnson (Dem):					
Abe Fortas	TN	Dem	Arthur Goldberg	IL	Dem
Thurgood Marshall	NY	Dem	Tom C. Clark	TX	Dem
Abe Fortas [b, d]	TN	Dem	Earl Warren	CA	Rep
Homer Thornberry [d]	TX	Dem	Abe Fortas	TN	Dem
Richard Nixon (Rep):					
Warren E. Burger	MN	Rep	Earl Warren	CA	Rep
Clement Haynsworth, Jr. [d]	SC	Dem	Abe Fortas	TN	Dem
G. Harrold Carswell [d]	FL	Rep	Abe Fortas	TN	Dem
Harry A. Blackmun	MN	Rep	Abe Fortas	TN	Dem
Lewis F. Powell, Jr.	VA	Dem	Hugo Black	AL	Dem
William H. Rehnquist	AZ	Rep	John M. Harlan II	NY	Rep
Gerald Ford (Rep):					
John Paul Stevens	IL	Rep	William O. Douglas	CT	Dem
Ronald Reagan (Rep):					
Sandra Day O'Connor	AZ	Rep	Potter Stewart	OH	Rep
William H. Rehnquist [b]	AZ	Rep	Warren E. Burger	MN	Rep

(Table continues)

Table 4-11 (*Continued*)

President/nominee	State	Party at time of appointment[a]	Previous party affiliations[a]	Justice to be replaced Name	State	Party[a]
Antonin Scalia	VA	Rep		William Rehnquist	AZ	Rep
Robert H. Bork[d]	DC	Rep		Lewis Powell	VA	Dem
Anthony M. Kennedy	CA	Rep		Lewis Powell	VA	Dem
George Bush (Rep):						
David H. Souter	NH	Rep		William J. Brennan	NJ	Dem
Clarence Thomas	GA	Rep		Thurgood Marshall	NY	Dem
Bill Clinton (Dem):						
Ruth Bader Ginsburg	NY	Dem		Byron White	CO	Dem

Note: Nominees are ordered chronologically according to the dates of their nominations or recess appointments, whichever came first. Only names of those officially nominated and sent to the Senate for confirmation are included.

[a] "Fed" indicates Federalist, "Dem-Rep" indicates Democratic Republican, "Dem" indicates Democrat, "Rep" indicates Republican, "Ind" indicates independent.

[b] Nomination for chief justice.

[c] Indicates original appointment.

[d] Unsuccessful nomination. The nominee either failed to obtain Senate confirmation or did not serve after being confirmed.

[e] Newly created seat.

[f] This seat was temporarily abolished upon the death of Justice James Wayne in 1867 as part of a congressional strategy to remove any opportunity for President Andrew Johnson to appoint a justice to the Court. Shortly after Ulysses Grant captured the presidency, the Republican Congress reestablished the seat. As part of the same strategy, Congress also abolished the seat held by James Catron. The Catron seat was not reestablished.

[g] Early in his career, Louis Brandeis registered as a Republican and officially remained so at the time of his nomination. Many scholars, however, classify him as a Democrat because he underwent a significant change in political identification in his later adult years and openly supported some Democratic candidates.

Sources: Elder Witt, *Congressional Quarterly's Guide to the U.S. Supreme Court,* 2d ed. (Washington, D.C.: Congressional Quarterly, 1990); Leon Friedman and Fred L. Israel, eds., *The Justices of the United States Supreme Court: Their Lives and Major Opinions* (New York: R.R. Bowker, 1969-1978); Harold W. Chase et al., *Biographical Dictionary of the American Judiciary* (Detroit: Gale Research, 1976); *Judges of the United States,* 2d ed. (Washington, D.C.: Judicial Conference of the United States, 1983); John R. Schmidhauser, *Supreme Court Justices Biographical Data 1958* (Ann Arbor, Mich.: Inter-University Consortium for Political Research, 1972); *The National Cyclopaedia of American Biography* (New York: James T. White, various years); *Dictionary of American Biography* (New York: Charles Scribner's Sons, various editions). We depart from CQ and follow the coding of Robert Scigliano, *The Supreme Court and the Presidency* (New York: Free Press, 1971), for John Tyler's and Andrew Johnson's political party.

Table 4-12 Senate Action on Supreme Court Nominees

President	Party	Nominee	Date of appointment	Confirmation or other action	Vote
Washington	Fed	John Jay[a]	Sept. 24, 1789	Sept. 26, 1789	Voice
		John Rutledge	Sept. 24, 1789	Sept. 26, 1789	Voice
		William Cushing	Sept. 24, 1789	Sept. 26, 1789	Voice
		Robert H. Harrison	Sept. 24, 1789	Sept. 26, 1789	Declined
		James Wilson	Sept. 24, 1789	Sept. 26, 1789	Voice
		John Blair	Sept. 24, 1789	Sept. 26, 1789	Voice
		James Iredell	Feb. 8, 1790	Feb. 10, 1790	Voice
		Thomas Johnson	Nov. 1, 1791	Nov. 7, 1791	Voice
		William Paterson	Feb. 27, 1793	Feb. 28, 1793	Withdrawn
		William Paterson	March 4, 1793	March 4, 1793	Voice
		John Rutledge[a]	July 1, 1795	Dec. 15, 1795	Rejected, 10-14
		William Cushing[a]	Jan. 26, 1796	Jan. 27, 1796	Declined
		Samuel Chase	Jan. 26, 1796	Jan. 27, 1796	Voice
		Oliver Ellsworth[a]	March 3, 1796	March 4, 1796	21-1
J. Adams	Fed	Bushrod Washington	Dec. 19, 1798	Dec. 20, 1798	Voice
		Alfred Moore	Dec. 6, 1799	Dec. 10, 1799	Voice
		John Jay[a]	Dec. 18, 1800	Dec. 19, 1800	Declined
		John Marshall[a]	Jan. 20, 1801	Jan. 27, 1801	Voice
Jefferson	D-R	William Johnson	March 22, 1804	March 24, 1804	Voice
		H. Brockholst Livingston	Dec. 13, 1806	Dec. 17, 1806	Voice
		Thomas Todd	Feb. 28, 1807	March 3, 1807	Voice
Madison	D-R	Levi Lincoln	Jan. 2, 1811	Jan. 3, 1811	Declined
		Alexander Walcott	Feb. 4, 1811	Feb. 13, 1811	Rejected, 9-24
		John Quincy Adams	Feb. 21, 1811	Feb. 22, 1811	Declined

President	Party	Nominee			
Monroe		Joseph Story	Nov. 15, 1811	Nov. 18, 1811	Voice
		Gabriel Duvall	Nov. 15, 1811	Nov. 18, 1811	Voice
J.Q. Adams	D-R	Smith Thompson	Dec. 8, 1823	Dec. 19, 1823	Voice
	D-R	Robert Trimble	April 11, 1826	May 9, 1826	27-5
		John J. Crittendon	Dec. 17, 1828	Feb. 12, 1829	Postponed
Jackson	Dem	John McLean	March 6, 1829	March 7, 1829	Voice
		Henry Baldwin	Jan. 4, 1830	Jan. 6, 1830	41-2
		James Wayne	Jan. 7, 1835	Jan. 9, 1835	Voice
		Roger B. Taney	Jan. 15, 1835	March 3, 1835	Postponed
		Roger B. Taney[a]	Dec. 28, 1835	March 15, 1836	29-15
		Philip P. Barbour	Dec. 28, 1835	March 15, 1836	30-11
		William Smith	March 3, 1837	March 8, 1837	23-16, declined
		John Catron	March 3, 1837	March 8, 1837	28-15
Van Buren	Dem	John McKinley	Sept. 18, 1837	Sept. 25, 1837	Voice
		Peter V. Daniel	Feb. 26, 1841	March 2, 1841	22-5
Tyler	Dem	John Spencer	Jan. 9, 1844	Jan. 31, 1844	Rejected, 21-26
		Reuben H. Walworth	March 13, 1844	June 17, 1844	Withdrawn
		Edward King	June 5, 1844	June 15, 1844	Postponed
		Edward King	Dec. 4, 1844	Feb. 7, 1845	Withdrawn
		Samuel Nelson	Feb. 4, 1845	Feb. 14, 1845	Voice
		John M. Read	Feb. 7, 1845	No action	
Polk	Dem	George G. Woodward	Dec. 23, 1845	Jan. 22, 1846	Rejected, 20-29
		Levi Woodbury	Dec. 23, 1845	Jan. 3, 1846	Voice
		Robert C. Grier	Aug. 3, 1846	Aug. 4, 1846	Voice

(Table continues)

Table 4-12 *(Continued)*

President	Party	Nominee	Date of appointment	Confirmation or other action	Vote
Fillmore	Whig	Benjamin Curtis	Dec. 11, 1851	Dec. 29, 1851	Voice
		Edward A. Bradford	Aug. 16, 1852	No action	Postponed
		George E. Badger	Jan. 10, 1853	Feb. 11, 1853	
		William Micou	Feb. 24, 1853	No action	
Pierce	Dem	John A. Campbell	March 22, 1853	March 25, 1853	Voice
Buchanan	Dem	Nathan Clifford	Dec. 9, 1857	Jan. 12, 1858	26-23
		Jeremiah S. Black	Feb. 5, 1861	Feb. 21, 1861	Rejected, 25-26
Lincoln	Rep	Noah H. Swayne	Jan. 21, 1862	Jan. 24, 1862	38-1
		Samuel F. Miller	July 16, 1862	July 16, 1862	Voice
		David Davis	Dec. 1, 1862	Dec. 8, 1862	Voice
		Stephen J. Field	March 6, 1863	March 10, 1863	Voice
		Salmon P. Chase	Dec. 6, 1864	Dec. 6, 1864	Voice
A. Johnson	Dem	Henry Stanbery	April 16, 1866	No action	
Grant	Rep	Ebenezer R. Hoar	Dec. 15, 1869	Feb. 3, 1870	Rejected, 24-33
		Edwin M. Stanton	Dec. 20, 1869	Dec. 20, 1869	46-11
		William Strong	Feb. 7, 1870	Feb. 18, 1870	46-11
		Joseph P. Bradley	Feb. 7, 1870	March 21, 1870	46-9
		Ward Hunt	Dec. 3, 1872	Dec. 11, 1872	Voice
		George H. Williams [a]	Dec. 1, 1873	Jan. 8, 1874	Withdrawn
		Caleb Cushing [a]	Jan. 9, 1874	Jan. 13, 1874	Withdrawn
		Morrison R. Waite [a]	Jan. 19, 1874	Jan. 21, 1874	63-0

President	Nominee	Party	Date of appointment	Date confirmed or other action	Vote
Hayes	John M. Harlan	Rep	Oct. 17, 1877	Nov. 29, 1877	Voice
	William B. Woods		Dec. 15, 1880	Dec. 21, 1880	39-8
	Stanley Matthews		Jan. 26, 1881	No action	
Garfield	Stanley Matthews	Rep	March 14, 1881	May 12, 1881	24-23
Arthur	Horace Gray	Rep	Dec. 19, 1881	Dec. 20, 1881	51-5
	Roscoe Conkling		Feb. 24, 1882	March 2, 1882	39-12, declined
	Samuel Blatchford		March 13, 1882	March 27, 1882	Voice
Cleveland	Lucius Q. C. Lamar	Dem	Dec. 6, 1887	Jan. 16, 1888	32-28
	Melvile W. Fuller[a]		April 30, 1888	July 20, 1888	41-20
B. Harrison	David J. Brewer	Rep	Dec. 4, 1889	Dec. 18, 1889	53-11
	Henry B. Brown		Dec. 23, 1890	Dec. 29, 1890	Voice
	George Shiras, Jr.		July 19, 1892	July 26, 1892	Voice
	Howell E. Jackson		Feb. 2, 1893	Feb. 18, 1893	Voice
Cleveland	William B. Hornblower	Dem	Sept. 19, 1893	Jan. 15, 1894	Rejected, 24-30
	Wheeler H. Peckham		Jan. 22, 1894	Feb. 16, 1894	Rejected, 32-41
	Edward D. White		Feb. 19, 1894	Feb. 19, 1894	Voice
	Rufus W. Peckham		Dec. 3, 1895	Dec. 9, 1895	Voice
McKinley	Joseph McKenna	Rep	Dec. 16, 1897	Jan. 21, 1898	Voice
T. Roosevelt	Oliver W. Holmes	Rep	Dec. 2, 1902	Dec. 4, 1902	Voice
	William R. Day		Feb. 19, 1903	Feb. 23, 1903	Voice
	William H. Moody		Dec. 3, 1906	Dec. 12, 1906	Voice

(Table continues)

Table 4-12 (Continued)

President	Party	Nominee	Date of appointment	Confirmation or other action	Vote
Taft	Rep	Horace H. Lurton	Dec. 13, 1909	Dec. 20, 1909	Voice
		Charles E. Hughes	April 25, 1910	May 2, 1910	Voice
		Edward D. White[a]	Dec. 12, 1910	Dec. 12, 1910	Voice
		Willis Van Devanter	Dec. 12, 1910	Dec. 15, 1910	Voice
		Jospeh R. Lamar	Dec. 12, 1910	Dec. 15, 1910	Voice
		Mahlon Pitney	Feb. 19, 1910	March 13, 1912	50-26
Wilson	Dem	James C. McReynolds	Aug. 19, 1914	Aug. 29, 1914	44-6
		Louis D. Brandeis	Jan. 28, 1916	June 1, 1916	47-22
		John H. Clarke	July 14, 1916	July 24, 1916	Voice
Harding	Rep	William H. Taft[a]	June 30, 1921	June 30, 1921	Voice
		George Sutherland	Sept. 5, 1922	Sept. 5, 1922	Voice
		Pierce Butler	Nov. 23, 1922	Dec. 21, 1922	61-8
		Edward T. Sanford	Jan. 24, 1923	Jan. 29, 1923	Voice
Coolidge	Rep	Harlan F. Stone	Jan. 25, 1925	Feb. 5, 1925	71-6
Hoover	Rep	Charles E. Hughes[a]	Feb. 3, 1930	Feb. 13, 1930	52-26
		John J. Parker	March 21, 1930	May 7, 1930	Rejected, 39-41
		Owen J. Roberts	May 9, 1930	May 20, 1930	Voice
		Benjamin N. Cardozo	Feb. 15, 1932	Feb. 24, 1932	Voice
F. Roosevelt	Dem	Hugo L. Black	Aug. 12, 1937	Aug. 17, 1937	63-16
		Stanley F. Reed	Jan. 15, 1938	Jan. 25, 1938	Voice
		Felix Frankfurter	Jan. 5, 1939	Jan. 17, 1939	Voice

President	Party	Nominee	Nomination date	Action date	Vote
		William O. Douglas	March 20, 1939	April 4, 1939	62-4
		Frank Murphy	Jan. 4, 1940	Jan. 15, 1940	Voice
		Harlan F. Stone [a]	June 12, 1941	June 27, 1941	Voice
		James F. Byrnes	June 12, 1941	June 12, 1941	Voice
		Robert H. Jackson	June 12, 1941	July 7, 1941	Voice
		Wiley B. Rutledge	Jan. 11, 1943	Feb. 8, 1943	Voice
Truman	Dem	Harold H. Burton	Sept 19, 1945	Sept. 19, 1945	Voice
		Fred M. Vinson [a]	June 6, 1946	June 20, 1946	Voice
		Tom C. Clark	Aug. 2, 1949	Aug. 18, 1949	73-8
		Sherman Minton	Sept. 15, 1949	Oct. 4, 1949	48-16
Eisenhower	Rep	Earl Warren [a]	Sept. 30, 1953	March 1, 1954	Voice
		John M. Harlan	Jan. 10, 1955	March 16, 1955	71-11
		William J. Brennan, Jr.	Jan. 14, 1957	March 19, 1957	Voice
		Charles E. Whittaker	March 2, 1957	March 19, 1957	Voice
		Potter Stewart	Jan. 17, 1959	May 5, 1959	70-17
Kennedy	Dem	Byron White	March 3, 1962	April 11, 1962	Voice
		Arthur J. Goldberg	Aug. 29, 1962	Sept. 25, 1962	Voice
L. Johnson	Dem	Abe Fortas	July 28, 1965	Aug. 11, 1965	Voice
		Thurgood Marshall	June 13, 1967	Aug. 30, 1967	69-11
		Abe Fortas [a]	June 26, 1968	Oct. 4, 1968	Withdrawn
		Homer Thornberry	June 26, 1968	No action	
Nixon	Rep	Warren E. Burger [a]	May 21, 1969	June 9, 1969	74-3
		Clement Haynsworth, Jr.	Aug. 18, 1969	Nov. 21, 1969	Rejected, 45-55
		G. Harrold Carswell	Jan. 19, 1970	April 8, 1970	Rejected, 45-51
		Harry A. Blackmun	April 14, 1970	May 12, 1970	94-0

(Table continues)

Table 4-12 (Continued)

President	Party	Nominee	Date of appointment	Confirmation or other action	Vote
		Lewis F. Powell, Jr.	Oct. 21, 1971	Dec. 6, 1971	89-1
		William H. Rehnquist	Oct. 21, 1971	Dec. 10, 1971	68-26
Ford	Rep	John Paul Stevens	Nov. 28, 1975	Dec. 17, 1975	98-0
Reagan	Rep	Sandra Day O'Connor	Aug 19, 1981	Sept. 21, 1981	99-0
		William H. Rehnquist[a]	June 20, 1986	Sept. 17, 1986	65-33
		Antonin Scalia	June 24, 1986	Sept. 17, 1986	98-0
		Robert H. Bork	July 1, 1987	Oct. 23, 1987	Rejected, 42-58
		Anthony Kennedy	Nov. 30, 1987	Feb. 3, 1988	97-0
Bush	Rep	David Souter	July 25, 1990	Oct. 2, 1990	90-9
		Clarence Thomas	July 1, 1991	Oct. 15, 1991	52-48
Clinton	Dem	Ruth Bader Ginsburg	June 14, 1993	Aug. 3, 1993	96-3

Note: "Fed" indicates Federalist, "D-R" indicates Democratic Republican, "Dem" indicates Democrat, "Rep" indicates Republican.

[a] Nominated for chief justice.

Sources: Updated from Elder Witt, *Congressional Quarterly's Guide to the U.S. Supreme Court,* 2d ed. (Washington, D.C: Congressional Quarterly, 1990), and Congressional Quarterly, *Presidential Elections Since 1789,* 4th ed. (Washington, D.C.: Congressional Quarterly, 1987). We depart from CQ and follow the coding of Robert Scigliano, *The Supreme Court and the Presidency* (New York: Free Press, 1971), for John Tyler's and Andrew Johnson's political party.

Table 4-13 Confirmation Factors, 1953-1991

Nominee	Perceived ideology	Perceived qualifications	Interest group support	Interest group opposition
Warren	.75	.74	0	2
Harlan	.88	.86	4	4
Brennan	1.00	1.00	0	0
Whittaker	.50	1.00	0	0
Stewart	.75	1.00	0	0
White	.50	.50	2	0
Goldberg	.75	.92	1	0
Fortas (1)	1.00	1.00	0	0
Marshall	1.00	.84	0	1
Fortas (2)	.85	.64	·7	4
Burger	.12	.96	3	0
Haynsworth	.16	.34	5	16
Carswell	.04	.11	1	3
Blackmun	.12	.97	5	0
Powell	.17	1.00	0	1
Rehnquist (1)	.05	.89	1	9
Stevens	.25	.96	11	3
O'Connor	.48	1.00	7	4
Scalia	.00	1.00	10	14
Rehnquist (2)	.05	.40	20	8
Bork	.10	.79	21	17
Kennedy	.37	.89	10	14
Souter	.33	.77	20	17
Thomas	.16	.41	21	32

Note: Nominee ideology: 1=most liberal, 0=most conservative; nominee qualifications: 1=most qualified, 0=least qualified. Interest group support and interest group opposition represent the number of groups presenting oral or written testimony for or against each nominee.

Sources: Nominee ideology and nominee qualifications are derived from a content analysis of editorial judgments in the *New York Times, Washington Post, Chicago Tribune,* and *Los Angeles Times.* Interest group support and opposition are derived from the Senate Judiciary Committee hearings for each nominee. See Jeffrey A. Segal, Charles M. Cameron, and Albert D. Cover, "A Spatial Model of Roll Call Voting: Senators, Constituents, Presidents and Interest Groups in Supreme Court Confirmations," *American Journal of Political Science* 36 (1992): 96.

Table 4-14 Appointment Anomalies

Justices Who Served Without Being Confirmed

Article II, section 2, of the Constitution authorizes the president to fill vacancies when the Senate is in recess. The individual nominated may serve in office until the Senate returns to session and acts on the nomination. A number of justices, especially in the Court's early history, received recess appointments but did not take their seats until after the Senate had confirmed their nominations. Five justices, however, received recess appointments and served a period of time without the benefit of Senate confirmation:

John Rutledge served as chief justice for four months in 1795.

Benjamin Curtis served as associate justice for two months in 1851.

Earl Warren served as chief justice for five months in 1953-54.

William Brennan served as associate justice for five months in 1956-57.

Potter Stewart served as associate justice for seven months in 1958-59.

Of these justices, all were later confirmed except Rutledge, whom the Senate rejected by a 10-14 vote in December of 1795.

Individuals Who Did Not Serve After Receiving Senate Confirmation

Eight individuals were nominated by the president and confirmed by the Senate and yet did not serve:

Robert H. Harrison was nominated to be associate justice by President George Washington and confirmed by the Senate in 1789. Because of health considerations and his selection to be Chancellor of Maryland, he declined the Supreme Court post to serve at the state level.

William Cushing, a sitting associate justice, was nominated to be chief justice by President Washington and confirmed by the Senate in 1796. Cushing declined the post because of age and health considerations, but he continued to serve as an associate justice.

John Jay, who had resigned the chief justiceship in 1795, was nominated again to be chief justice by President John Adams and was confirmed by the Senate in 1800. Jay declined to return to the federal bench.

Levi Lincoln, a former attorney general, was nominated to be associate justice by President James Madison and was confirmed by the Senate in 1811. Lincoln declined, citing poor health and age.

Table 4-14 *(Continued)*

John Quincy Adams, then minister to Russia, was nominated to be associate justice by President Madison and was confirmed by the Senate in 1811. Adams declined the post, preferring to pursue his political ambitions that ultimately led to the White House.

William Smith was nominated to be associate justice by President Andrew Jackson and confirmed by the Senate in 1837. He declined, preferring to engage in activities that offered higher remuneration.

Edwin Stanton, former secretary of war, received President Ulysses S. Grant's nomination to be associate justice and was confirmed by the Senate in 1869. Four days later, before he could take his seat, Stanton died.

Roscoe Conkling, a former senator from New York, received President Chester Arthur's nomination to be associate justice and was confirmed in 1882. He decided not to accept the position.

Justices Confirmed by the Senate Following a Previous Rejection

Three individuals attained a position on the Court after an unsuccessful first nomination:

William Paterson of New Jersey was nominated associate justice by President Washington on February 27, 1793. The nomination was withdrawn the next day because of a constitutional technicality. Paterson had been a member of the United States Senate and had participated in the development of the Supreme Court in the Judiciary Act of 1789. Article I, section 6, of the Constitution stipulates that no member of Congress "during the time for which he was elected" can be appointed to any office created during his term. Although Paterson was no longer a senator (he resigned in 1790 to become governor of New Jersey), the Senate term to which he was originally elected would not expire until March 4, 1793. Washington waited four more days and resubmitted the nomination. Paterson was confirmed the same day.

Roger Taney received President Jackson's nomination to be associate justice in 1835, but confirmation was indefinitely postponed by the Senate. Later that year, with a new Congress having been seated, Jackson nominated Taney to replace John Marshall as chief justice. In March of 1836 the Senate confirmed Taney by a 29-15 margin.

Stanley Matthews was nominated to be associate justice by Rutherford Hayes in January of 1881. Because of Matthews's close ties to unpopular railroad interests, the Senate killed the nomination by

(Table continues)

Table 4-14   *(Continued)*

inaction. The newly inaugurated James Garfield then renominated Matthews, and he was confirmed by a 24-23 vote in May of 1881.

Justices Who Served Under Two Successful Nominations and Confirmations

Six individuals who had already served on the Court received a second nomination and were confirmed. Two, William Cushing and John Jay, as described above, declined to serve. The remaining four, however, accepted service under the second appointment:

Edward White was confirmed as associate justice in 1894, and in 1910 was successfully promoted to chief justice, a position he held until his death in 1921.

Charles Evans Hughes served as associate justice from 1910 to 1916, when he resigned to seek the presidency. In 1930 he was confirmed as chief justice and served in that capacity until his retirement in 1941.

Harlan Fiske Stone was appointed associate justice in 1925 and after 16 years of service was promoted by Franklin Roosevelt to chief justice where he served until his death in 1946.

William Rehnquist became associate justice in 1971 and was later confirmed as chief justice in 1986.

Justices Whose Second Nominations Were Rejected by the Senate

Two individuals were successfully confirmed as associate justices, but later were rejected when nominated to become chief justice:

John Rutledge served as associate justice for eighteen months during Washington's first administration. He resigned to become chief justice of South Carolina. Four years later, in 1795, Washington gave Rutledge a recess appointment to be chief justice. He served for four months before the Senate returned to session and rejected the nomination.

Abe Fortas was successfully appointed associate justice by Lyndon Johnson in 1965. Three years later Johnson attempted to elevate Fortas to replace Earl Warren as chief justice. Because of charges of ethical impropriety, the Senate refused to confirm and the nomination was withdrawn.

Rejected Twice

In the history of the Court, only one person has been nominated twice and rejected both times:

Edward King, a distinguished Philadelphia legal scholar and judge,

Table 4-14   *(Continued)*

was nominated by President John Tyler to be associate justice in 1844. Tyler, who had assumed the presidency upon William Henry Harrison's death, was extremely unpopular in the Senate. The Senate killed the King nomination by voting to postpone action on it. Six months later Tyler once again submitted King's name, and once again the Senate refused to confirm. Before Tyler's term ended the Senate rejected a total of five of his nominations to the Supreme Court.

Sources: Elder Witt, *Congressional Quarterly's Guide to the U.S. Supreme Court,* 2d ed. (Washington, D.C.: Congressional Quarterly, 1990); Henry J. Abraham, *Justices and Presidents,* 2d ed. (New York: Oxford University Press, 1985); Albert P. Blaustein and Roy M. Mersky, *The First One Hundred Justices* (Hamden, Connecticut: Archon Books, 1978).

5

The Justices: Post-Confirmation Activities and Departures from the Court

Tables in the preceding chapter depict aspects of the justices' lives prior to their confirmation proceedings. In this chapter, we focus on the careers of the justices after their ascent to the bench. These data begin in Table 5-1 with the justices' lengths of service. Justice William O. Douglas served the longest, with a tenure in excess of 36 years. At the opposite extreme, Thomas Johnson sat on the Court for little more than a year. Table 5-2 then divides the Supreme Court's history into its component natural courts, a term used to identify periods of time in which the same set of justices served continuously. Such periods could vary greatly in length, from as long as 12 years to as short as one month. The average span, however, ran to just 24 months. A few natural court periods were too brief to allow much judicial activity. For example, the Court comprising Vinson 2 decided only one minor matter, *Telefilm v. Superior Court*, 338 U.S. 801 (1949).

Career data next extend to the justices' service on the various circuit courts (Tables 5-3 and 5-4). At the creation of the federal judicial system, Supreme Court justices were required to serve also as circuit court judges. During the first years of the operation of the federal judiciary no official assignments of individual judges to specific circuits occurred. There appears to have been a disagreement over who should make such assignments, Congress or the Court itself. The Judiciary Act of 1801, passed as the Federalists were leaving power, created six circuits, but did not require the justices to sit on the circuit courts. Consequently, the Act did not provide for circuit court assignments by the justices. The Act was repealed by the Jeffersonians in 1802, who subsequently assigned the justices to specific circuits (Table 5-3).

Much time was spent riding circuit, traveling throughout a multistate jurisdiction, often on horseback, hearing cases. In the earliest years, riding circuit demanded more time and effort from the justices than did their Supreme Court duties. The justices disliked this obligation and frequently petitioned Congress to eliminate it. Each justice was assigned a circuit for which he was responsible. The assigning was done at various times, either by Congress or by the Court. Usually a justice was assigned a circuit that included his home state. Congress periodically altered the number and composition of the circuits. This was prompted by westward expansion, political maneuvering, and the Civil War. The most significant of those circuit alterations are reflected in Table 5-3. After Congress revamped the structure of the circuits following the Civil War (Table 5-4), no major geographical changes in the configuration of the circuits occurred. The division of the Eighth Circuit in 1929 and the division of the Fifth in 1981 were the only significant alterations, and they were accomplished with no changes elsewhere. When new states were admitted or territories acquired, they were simply assigned as necessary to existing circuits. In 1891, Congress created the federal courts of appeals. This reform eliminated the justices' circuit riding responsibilities. Today the justices retain jurisdiction over one or more circuits assigned them by the Court. They are empowered to issue injunctions and stays of execution as well as handle emergency matters that arise out of their respective circuits. This is especially important when the Supreme Court is not in session and an urgent matter must be decided. The justices also perform an important, but largely informal, function of acting as a liaison between the Supreme Court and the lower federal court judges in the circuits.

Table 5-5 examines the nonjudicial activities of the justices while sitting on the Court. Participation in extra-judicial activities, commonplace and generally accepted during most of the Court's history, is unusual today. Since 1969, when Justice Abe Fortas was forced to resign under fire for ethical violations stemming from extra-judicial activities, members of the judiciary have been much more sensitive to the problems associated with becoming involved in pursuits not directly connected to their federal court duties. Failure to heed ethical considerations can lead to impeachment proceedings as in the case of Justice Fortas. Table 5-6 describes the occasions on which serious attempts to remove a justice by impeachment occurred. Two of these centered on the justiceship of William O. Douglas. It is notable that all were unsuccessful.

We next explore the justices' departures from the Court and their lives after judicial service. Table 5-7 outlines the circumstances surrounding each justice's termination of service. Slightly less than half died in office, while another large proportion retired after suffering debilitating health problems. After justices leave the Court (or sometimes while they are still on the bench), scholars and legal analysts rate their performances. The primary objective of such efforts has been to identify the truly great justices. A sample of these studies and their findings appear in Table 5-8. We include this because some readers might be interested in how observers of the Court have viewed the contributions of its members over time. Readers should be aware, however, that these rankings are, for the most part, quite subjective.

Many justices continued to be active in public affairs even after their time on the Court. Table 5-9 reviews the post-judicial activities of those members surviving their Court tenures. Finally, Table 5-10 lists the date and place of death of the justices, as well as the location of interment.

We conclude this chapter with four tables that will provide the reader with further resources by which to investigate more fully the work and lives of the justices. Table 5-11 is a listing of the libraries or other public depositories for scholarly study where the personal papers of the justices are located. Table 5-12 lists prominent books and articles written by the members of the Court, and Table 5-13 provides a sample of classic statements that can be found in the written opinions of the justices. Finally, for those who wish to read more about the lives of those individuals who have held the highest judicial post in the nation, Table 5-14 lists published biographical material on each of the justices.

Table 5-1   Length of Service (Ranked)

Justice (appointment number)[a]	Length of tenure[b]
1. Douglas, William O. (82)	36 years, 7 months
2. Field, Stephen J. (39)	34 years, 8 months
3. Marshall, John (14)	34 years, 5 months
4. Black, Hugo L. (79)	34 years, 1 month
5. Harlan, John Marshall I (45)	33 years, 10 months
6. Story, Joseph (19)	33 years, 9 months
7. Brennan, William J., Jr. (94)	33 years, 9 months
8. Wayne, James M. (24)	32 years, 5 months
9. McLean, John (22)	32 years, 2 months
10. White, Byron R. (97)	31 years, 2 months
11. Washington, Bushrod (12)	30 years, 11 months
12. Johnson, William (15)	30 years, 4 months
13. Holmes, Oliver W., Jr. (59)	29 years, 1 month
14. Taney, Roger B. (25)	28 years, 6 months
15. Miller, Samuel (37)	28 years, 2 months
16. Catron, John (27)	28 years, 2 months
17. Nelson, Samuel (30)	27 years, 9 months
18. White, Edward D. (56, 64)	27 years, 3 months
19. McKenna, Joseph (58)	26 years, 11 months
20. Van Devanter, Willis (65)	26 years, 5 months
21. McReynolds, James C. (68)	26 years, 5 months
22. Marshall, Thurgood (100)	24 years, 1 month
23. Frankfurter, Felix (81)	23 years, 7 months
24. Grier, Robert C. (32)	23 years, 6 months
25. Clifford, Nathan (35)	23 years, 6 months
26. Duvall, Gabriel (18)	23 years, 1 month
27. Stewart, Potter (96)	22 years, 8 months
28. Brandeis, Louis D. (69)	22 years, 8 months
29. Fuller, Melville W. (51)	21 years, 11 months
30. Bradley, Joseph P. (42)	21 years, 10 months
31. Stone, Harlan Fiske (75, 84)	21 years, 2 months
32. Cushing, William (3)	20 years, 11 months
33. Gray, Horace (48)	20 years, 8 months
34. Brewer, David J. (52)	20 years, 3 months
35. Thompson, Smith (20)	19 years, 11 months
36. Day, William R. (60)	19 years, 8 months
37. Daniel, Peter V. (29)	19 years, 2 months
38. Reed, Stanley F. (80)	19 years, 1 month
39. Swayne, Noah H. (36)	19 years
40. Todd, Thomas (17)	18 years, 11 months
41. Clark, Tom C. (90)	17 years, 9 months
42. Hughes, Charles Evans (63, 76)	17 years, 5 months
43. Burger, Warren E. (101)	17 years, 3 months
44. Butler, Pierce (73)	16 years, 10 months
45. Harlan, John Marshall II (93)	16 years, 6 months
46. Livingston, H. Brockholst (16)	16 years, 3 months
47. Warren, Earl (92)	15 years, 8 months
48. Powell, Lewis F., Jr. (103)	15 years, 6 months

Table 5-1   *(Continued)*

Justice (appointment number) [a]	Length of tenure [b]
49. Brown, Henry B. (53)	15 years, 4 months
50. Chase, Samuel (10)	15 years, 4 months
51. Sutherland, George (72)	15 years, 4 months
52. Roberts, Owen J. (77)	15 years, 2 months
53. McKinley, John (28)	14 years, 9 months
54. Baldwin, Henry (23)	14 years, 3 months
55. Davis, David (38)	14 years, 2 months
56. Waite, Morrison (44)	14 years, 2 months
57. Peckham, Rufus W. (57)	13 years, 10 months
58. Paterson, William (8)	13 years, 6 months
59. Jackson, Robert H. (86)	13 years, 3 months
60. Burton, Harold H. (88)	13 years
61. Blatchford, Samuel (49)	11 years, 3 months
62. Strong, William (41)	10 years, 9 months
63. Pitney, Mahlon (67)	10 years, 9 months
64. Shiras, George, Jr. (54)	10 years, 6 months
65. Iredell, James (6)	9 years, 8 months
66. Murphy, Frank (83)	9 years, 6 months
67. Hunt, Ward (43)	9 years, 1 month
68. Wilson, James (4)	8 years, 10 months
69. Taft, William H. (71)	8 years, 7 months
70. Chase, Salmon P. (40)	8 years, 5 months
71. Campbell, John A. (34)	8 years, 1 month
72. Matthews, Stanley (47)	7 years, 10 months
73. Vinson, Fred M. (89)	7 years, 2 months
74. Sanford, Edward T. (74)	7 years, 1 month
75. Minton, Sherman (91)	7 years
76. Rutledge, Wiley B. (87)	6 years, 7 months
77. Woods, William B. (46)	6 years, 4 months
78. Cardozo, Benjamin (78)	6 years, 4 months
79. Blair, John, Jr. (5)	6 years, 4 months
80. Clarke, John H. (70)	6 years, 1 month
81. Curtis, Benjamin R. (33)	5 years, 11 months
82. Jay, John (1)	5 years, 9 months
83. Woodbury, Levi (31)	5 years, 8 months
84. Lamar, Joseph R. (66)	5 years
85. Whittaker, Charles E. (95)	5 years
86. Lamar, Lucius Q. C. (50)	5 years
87. Barbour, Philip P. (26)	4 years, 11 months
88. Ellsworth, Oliver (11)	4 years, 6 months
89. Lurton, Horace (62)	4 years, 9 months
90. Moore, Alfred (13)	4 years, 1 month
91. Moody, William H. (61)	3 years, 11 months
92. Fortas, Abe (99)	3 years, 9 months
93. Goldberg, Arthur J. (98)	2 years, 10 months
94. Jackson, Howell E. (55)	2 years, 5 months

(Table continues)

Table 5-1   *(Continued)*

Justice (appointment number)[a]	*Length of tenure*[b]
95. Trimble, Robert (21)	2 years, 3 months
96. Rutledge, John (2, 9)	1 year, 10 months
97. Byrnes, James F. (85)	1 year, 3 months
98. Johnson, Thomas (7)	1 year, 2 months

[a] Only those justices who had departed the Court by the end of the 1992-93 term are included.

[b] Length of tenure measured from the date of confirmation to the date of departure, plus any time served under a recess appointment. Data are presented to the nearest completed month. Ties are broken by the number of days served beyond the last completed month.

Source: Elder Witt, *Congressional Quarterly's Guide to the U.S. Supreme Court,* 2d ed. (Washington, D.C.: Congressional Quarterly, 1990).

Table 5-2 Natural Courts

Natural court[a]	Justices[b]	Dates	U.S. Reports[c]
Jay 1	Jay (o October 19, 1789), J. Rutledge (o February 15, 1790), Cushing (o February 2, 1790), Wilson (o October 5, 1789), Blair (o February 2, 1790)	October 5, 1789-May 12, 1790	2
Jay 2	Jay, Rutledge (r March 5, 1791), Cushing, Wilson, Blair, Iredell (o May 12, 1790)	May 12, 1790-August 6, 1792	2
Jay 3	Jay, Cushing, Wilson, Blair, Iredell, T. Johnson (o August 6, 1792; r January 16, 1793)	August 6, 1792-March 11, 1793	2
Jay 4	Jay (r June 29, 1795), Cushing, Wilson, Blair, Iredell, Paterson (o March 11, 1793)	March 11, 1793-August 12, 1795	2-3
Rutledge 1	J. Rutledge (o August 12, 1795; rj December 15, 1795), Cushing, Wilson, Blair (r January 27, 1796), Iredell, Paterson	August 12, 1795-February 4, 1796	3
No chief justice	Cushing, Wilson, Iredell, Paterson, S. Chase (o February 4, 1796)	February 4, 1796-March 8, 1796	3
Ellsworth 1	Ellsworth (o March 8, 1796), Cushing, Wilson (d August 21, 1798), Iredell, Paterson, S. Chase	March 8, 1796-February 4, 1799	3
Ellsworth 2	Ellsworth, Cushing, Iredell (d October 20, 1799), Paterson, S. Chase, Washington (o February 4, 1799)	February 4, 1799-April 21, 1800	3-4
Ellsworth 3	Ellsworth (r December 15, 1800), Cushing, Paterson, S. Chase, Washington, Moore (o April 21, 1800)	April 21, 1800-February 4, 1801	4

(Table continues)

Table 5-2 (Continued)

Natural court[a]	Justices[b]	Dates	U.S. Reports[c]
Marshall 1	Marshall (o February 4, 1801), Cushing, Paterson, S. Chase, Washington, Moore (r January 26, 1804)	February 4, 1801-May 7, 1804	5-6
Marshall 2	Marshall, Cushing, Paterson (d September 9, 1806), S. Chase, Washington, W. Johnson (o May 7, 1804)	May 7, 1804-January 20, 1807	6-7
Marshall 3	Marshall, Cushing, S. Chase, Washington, W. Johnson, Livingston (o January 20, 1807)	January 20, 1807-May 4, 1807	8
Marshall 4	Marshall, Cushing (d September 13, 1810), Chase (d June 19, 1811), Washington, W. Johnson, Livingston, Todd (o May 4, 1807)	May 4, 1807-November 23, 1811	8-10
Marshall 5	Marshall, Washington, W. Johnson, Livingston, Todd, Duvall (o November 23, 1811)	November 23, 1811-February 3, 1812	11
Marshall 6	Marshall, Washington, W. Johnson, Livingston (d March 18, 1823), Todd, Duvall, Story (o February 3, 1812)	February 3, 1812-February 10, 1824	11-21
Marshall 7	Marshall, Washington, W. Johnson, Todd (d February 7, 1826), Duvall, Story, Thompson (o February 10, 1824)	February 10, 1824-June 16, 1826	22-24
Marshall 8	Marshall, Washington, W. Johnson, Duvall, Story, Thompson, Trimble (o June 16, 1826; d August 25, 1828)	June 16, 1826-January 11, 1830	25-27
Marshall 9	Marshall, W. Johnson (d August 4, 1834), Duvall (r January 14, 1835), Story, Thompson, McLean (o January 11, 1830), Baldwin (o January 18, 1830)	January 11, 1830-January 14, 1835	28-33

Marshall 10	Marshall (*d* July 6, 1835), Story, Thompson, McLean, Baldwin, Wayne (*o* January 14, 1835)	January 14, 1835-March 28, 1836	34-35
Taney 1	Taney (*o* March 28, 1836), Story, Thompson, McLean, Baldwin, Wayne	March 28, 1836-May 12, 1836	35
Taney 2	Taney, Story, Thompson, McLean, Baldwin, Wayne, Barbour (*o* May 12, 1836)	May 12, 1836-May 1, 1837	35-36
Taney 3	Taney, Story, Thompson, McLean, Baldwin, Wayne, Barbour, Catron (*o* May 1, 1837)	May 1, 1837-January 9, 1838	36
Taney 4	Taney, Story, Thompson, McLean, Baldwin, Wayne, Barbour (*d* February 25, 1841), Catron, McKinley (*o* January 9, 1838)	January 9, 1838-January 10, 1842	37-40
Taney 5	Taney, Story, Thompson (*d* December 18, 1843), McLean, Baldwin (*d* April 21, 1844), Wayne, Catron, McKinley, Daniel (*o* January 10, 1842)	January 10, 1842-February 27, 1845	40-44
Taney 6	Taney, Story (*d* September 10, 1845), McLean, Wayne, Catron, McKinley, Daniel, Nelson (*o* February 27, 1845)	February 27, 1845-September 23, 1845	44
Taney 7	Taney, McLean, Wayne, Catron, McKinley, Daniel, Nelson, Woodbury (*o* September 23, 1845)	September 23, 1845-August 10, 1846	44-45
Taney 8	Taney, McLean, Wayne, Catron, McKinley, Daniel, Nelson, Woodbury (*d* September 4, 1851), Grier (*o* August 10, 1846)	August 10, 1846-October 10, 1851	46-52
Taney 9	Taney, McLean, Wayne, Catron, McKinley (*d* July 19, 1852), Daniel, Nelson, Grier, Curtis (*o* October 10, 1851)	October 10, 1851-April 11, 1853	53-55

(Table continues)

Table 5-2 (Continued)

Natural court[a]	Justices[b]	Dates	U.S. Reports[c]
Taney 10	Taney, McLean, Wayne, Catron, Daniel, Nelson, Grier, Curtis (r September 30, 1857), Campbell (o April 11, 1853)	April 11, 1853-January 21, 1858	56-61
Taney 11	Taney, McLean (d April 4, 1861), Wayne, Catron, Daniel (d May 31, 1860), Nelson, Grier, Campbell (r April 30, 1861), Clifford (o January 21, 1858)	January 21, 1858-January 27, 1862	61-66
Taney 12	Taney, Wayne, Catron, Nelson, Grier, Clifford, Swayne (o January 27, 1862)	January 27, 1862-July 21, 1862	66
Taney 13	Taney, Wayne, Catron, Nelson, Grier, Clifford, Swayne, Miller (o July 21, 1862)	July 21, 1862-December 10, 1862	67
Taney 14	Taney, Wayne, Catron, Nelson, Grier, Clifford, Swayne, Miller, Davis (o December 10, 1862)	December 10, 1862-May 20, 1863	67
Taney 15	Taney (d October 12, 1864), Wayne, Catron, Nelson, Grier, Clifford, Swayne, Miller, Davis, Field (o May 20, 1863)	May 20, 1863-December 15, 1864	67-68
Chase 1	S. P. Chase (o December 15, 1864), Wayne (d July 5, 1867), Catron (d May 30, 1865), Nelson, Grier (r January 31, 1870), Clifford, Swayne, Miller, Davis, Field	December 15, 1864-March 14, 1870	69-76
Chase 2	S. P. Chase, Nelson (r November 28, 1872), Clifford, Swayne, Miller, Davis, Field, Strong (o March 14, 1870), Bradley (o March 23, 1870)	March 14, 1870-January 9, 1873	76-82
Chase 3	S. P. Chase (d May 7, 1873), Clifford, Swayne, Miller, Davis, Field, Strong, Bradley, Hunt (o January 9, 1873)	January 9, 1873-March 4, 1874	82-86

Waite 1	Waite (o March 4, 1874), Clifford, Swayne, Miller, Davis (r March 4, 1877), Field, Strong, Bradley, Hunt	March 4, 1874-December 10, 1877	86-95
Waite 2	Waite, Clifford, Swayne, Miller, Field, Strong (r December 14, 1880), Bradley, Hunt, Harlan I (o December 10, 1877)	December 10, 1877-January 5, 1881	95-103
Waite 3	Waite, Clifford, Swayne (r January 24, 1881), Miller, Field, Bradley, Hunt, Harlan I, Woods (o January 5, 1881)	January 5, 1881-May 17, 1881	103
Waite 4	Waite, Clifford (d July 25, 1881), Miller, Field, Bradley, Hunt, Harlan I, Woods, Matthews (o May 5, 1881)	May 17, 1881-January 9, 1882	103-104
Waite 5	Waite, Miller, Field, Bradley, Hunt (r January 27, 1882), Harlan I, Woods, Matthews, Gray (o January 9, 1882)	January 9, 1882-April 3, 1882	104-105
Waite 6	Waite, Miller, Field, Bradley, Harlan I, Woods (d May 14, 1887), Matthews, Gray, Blatchford (o April 3, 1882)	April 3, 1882-January 18, 1888	105-124
Waite 7	Waite (d March 23, 1888), Miller, Field, Bradley, Harlan I, Matthews, Gray, Blatchford, L. Lamar (o January 18, 1888)	January 18, 1888-October 8, 1888	124-127
Fuller 1	Fuller (o October 8, 1888), Miller, Field, Bradley, Harlan I, Matthews (d March 22, 1889), Gray, Blatchford, L. Lamar	October 8, 1888-January 6, 1890	128-132
Fuller 2	Fuller, Miller (d October 13, 1890), Field, Bradley, Harlan I, Gray, Blatchford, L. Lamar, Brewer (o January 6, 1890)	January 6, 1890-January 5, 1891	132-137
Fuller 3	Fuller, Field, Bradley (d January 22, 1892), Harlan I, Gray, Blatchford, L. Lamar, Brewer, Brown (o January 5, 1891)	January 5, 1891-October 10, 1892	137-145

(Table continues)

Table 5-2 *(Continued)*

Natural court[a]	Justices[b]	Dates	U.S. Reports[c]
Fuller 4	Fuller, Field, Harlan I, Gray, Blatchford, L. Lamar (*d* January 23, 1893), Brewer, Brown, Shiras (*o* October 10, 1892)	October 10, 1892-March 4, 1893	146-148
Fuller 5	Fuller, Field, Harlan I, Gray, Blatchford (*d* July 7, 1893), Brewer, Brown, Shiras, H. Jackson (*o* March 4, 1893)	March 4, 1893-March 12, 1894	148-151
Fuller 6	Fuller, Field, Harlan I, Gray, Brewer, Brown, Shiras, H. Jackson (*d* August 8, 1895), E. White (*o* March 12, 1894)	March 12, 1894-January 6, 1896	152-160
Fuller 7	Fuller, Field (*r* December 1, 1897), Harlan I, Gray, Brewer, Brown, Shiras, E. White, Peckham (*o* January 6, 1896)	January 6, 1896-January 26, 1898	160-169
Fuller 8	Fuller, Harlan I, Gray (*d* September 15, 1902), Brewer, Brown, Shiras, E. White, Peckham, McKenna (*o* January 26, 1898)	January 26, 1898-December 8, 1902	169-187
Fuller 9	Fuller, Harlan I, Brewer, Brown, Shiras (*r* February 23, 1903), E. White, Peckham, McKenna, Holmes (*o* December 8, 1902)	December 8, 1902-March 2, 1903	187-188
Fuller 10	Fuller, Harlan I, Brewer, Brown (*r* May 28, 1906), E. White, Peckham, McKenna, Holmes, Day (*o* March 2, 1903)	March 2, 1903-December 17, 1906	188-203
Fuller 11	Fuller, Harlan I, Brewer, E. White, Peckham (*d* October 24, 1909), McKenna, Holmes, Day, Moody (*o* December 17, 1906)	December 17, 1906-January 3, 1910	203-215
Fuller 12	Fuller (*d* July 4, 1910), Harlan I, Brewer (*d* March 28, 1910), E. White, McKenna, Holmes, Day, Moody, Lurton (*o* January 3, 1910)	January 3, 1910-October 10, 1910	215-217

No chief justice	Harlan I, E. White (p December 18, 1910), McKenna, Holmes, Day, Moody (r November 20, 1910), Lurton, Hughes (o October 10, 1910)	October 10, 1910-December 19, 1910	218
White 1	E. White (o December 19, 1910), Harlan I (d October 14, 1911), McKenna, Holmes, Day, Lurton, Hughes, Van Devanter (o January 3, 1911), J. Lamar (o January 3, 1911)	December 19, 1910-March 18, 1912	218-223
White 2	E. White, McKenna, Holmes, Day, Lurton (d July 12, 1914), Hughes, Van Devanter, J. Lamar, Pitney (o March 18, 1912)	March 18, 1912-October 12, 1914	223-234
White 3	E. White, McKenna, Holmes, Day, Hughes, Van Devanter, J. Lamar (d January 2, 1916), Pitney, McReynolds (o October 12, 1914)	October 12, 1914-June 5, 1916	235-241
White 4	E. White, McKenna, Holmes, Day, Hughes (r June 10, 1916), Van Devanter, Pitney, McReynolds, Brandeis (o June 5, 1916)	June 5, 1916-October 9, 1916	241
White 5	E. White (d May 19, 1921), McKenna, Holmes, Day, Van Devanter, Pitney, McReynolds, Brandeis, Clarke (o October 9, 1916)	October 9, 1916-July 11, 1921	242-256
Taft 1	Taft (o July 11, 1921), McKenna, Holmes, Day, Van Devanter, Pitney, McReynolds, Brandeis, Clarke (r September 18, 1922)	July 11, 1921-October 2, 1922	257-259
Taft 2	Taft, McKenna, Holmes, Day (r November 13, 1922), Van Devanter, Pitney (r December 31, 1922), McReynolds, Brandeis, Sutherland (o October 2, 1922)	October 2, 1922-January 2, 1923	260
Taft 3	Taft, McKenna, Holmes, Van Devanter, McReynolds, Brandeis, Sutherland, Butler (o January 2, 1923)	January 2, 1923-February 19, 1923	260
Taft 4	Taft, McKenna (r January 5, 1925), Holmes, Van Devanter, McReynolds, Brandeis, Sutherland, Butler, Sanford (o February 19, 1923)	February 19, 1923-March 2, 1925	260-267

(Table continues)

Table 5-2 (Continued)

Natural court[a]	Justices[b]	Dates	U.S. Reports[c]
Taft 5	Taft (r February 3, 1930), Holmes, Van Devanter, McReynolds, Brandeis, Sutherland, Butler, Sanford, Stone (o March 2, 1925)	March 2, 1925-February 24, 1930	267-280
Hughes 1	Hughes (o February 24, 1930), Holmes, Van Devanter, McReynolds, Brandeis, Sutherland, Butler, Sanford (d March 8, 1930), Stone	February 24, 1930-June 2, 1930	280-281
Hughes 2	Hughes, Holmes (r January 12, 1932), Van Devanter, McReynolds, Brandeis, Sutherland, Butler, Stone, Roberts (o June 2, 1930)	June 2, 1930-March 14, 1932	281-285
Hughes 3	Hughes, Van Devanter (r June 2, 1937), McReynolds, Brandeis, Sutherland, Butler, Stone, Roberts, Cardozo (o March 14, 1932)	March 14, 1932-August 19, 1937	285-301
Hughes 4	Hughes, McReynolds, Brandeis, Sutherland (r January 17, 1938), Butler, Stone, Roberts, Cardozo, Black (o August 19, 1937)	August 19, 1937-January 31, 1938	302-303
Hughes 5	Hughes, McReynolds, Brandeis, Butler, Stone, Roberts, Cardozo (d July 9, 1938), Black, Reed (o January 31, 1938)	January 31, 1938-January 30, 1939	303-305
Hughes 6	Hughes, McReynolds, Brandeis (r February 13, 1939), Butler, Stone, Roberts, Black, Reed, Frankfurter (o January 30, 1939)	January 30, 1939-April 17, 1939	306
Hughes 7	Hughes, McReynolds, Butler (d November 16, 1939), Stone, Roberts, Black, Reed, Frankfurter, Douglas (o April 17, 1939)	April 17, 1939-February 5, 1940	306-308
Hughes 8	Hughes (r July 1, 1941), McReynolds (r January 31, 1941), Stone (p July 2, 1941), Roberts, Black, Reed, Frankfurter, Douglas, Murphy (o February 5, 1940)	February 5, 1940-July 3, 1941	308-313

Stone 1	Stone (o July 3, 1941), Roberts, Black, Reed, Frankfurter, Douglas, Murphy, Byrnes (o July 8, 1941; r October 3, 1942), R. Jackson (o July 11, 1941)	July 3, 1941-February 15, 1943	314-318
Stone 2	Stone, Roberts (r July 31, 1945), Black, Reed, Frankfurter, Douglas, Murphy, R. Jackson, W. Rutledge (o February 15, 1943)	February 15, 1943-October 1, 1943	318-326
Stone 3	Stone (d April 22, 1946), Black, Reed, Frankfurter, Douglas, Murphy, R. Jackson, W. Rutledge, Burton (o October 1, 1945)	October 1, 1945-June 24, 1946	326-328
Vinson 1	Vinson (o June 24, 1946), Black, Reed, Frankfurter, Douglas, Murphy (d July 19, 1949), R. Jackson, W. Rutledge, Burton	June 24, 1946-August 24, 1949	329-338
Vinson 2	Vinson, Black, Reed, Frankfurter, Douglas, R. Jackson, W. Rutledge (d September 10, 1949), Burton, Clark (o August 24, 1949)	August 24, 1949-October 12, 1949	338
Vinson 3	Vinson (d September 8, 1953), Black, Reed, Frankfurter, Douglas, R. Jackson, Burton, Clark, Minton (o October 12, 1949)	October 12, 1949-October 5, 1953	338-346
Warren 1	Warren (o October 5, 1953), Black, Reed, Frankfurter, Douglas, R. Jackson (d October 9, 1954), Burton, Clark, Minton	October 5, 1953-March 28, 1955	346-348
Warren 2	Warren, Black, Reed, Frankfurter, Douglas, Burton, Clark, Minton (r October 15, 1956), Harlan II (o March 28, 1955)	March 28, 1955-October 16, 1956	348-352
Warren 3	Warren, Black, Reed (r February 25, 1957), Frankfurter, Douglas, Burton, Clark, Harlan II, Brennan (o October 16, 1956)	October 16, 1956-March 25, 1957	352
Warren 4	Warren, Black, Frankfurter, Douglas, Burton (r October 13, 1958), Clark, Harlan II, Brennan, Whittaker (o March 25, 1957)	March 25, 1957-October 14, 1958	352-358

(Table continues)

Table 5-2 (Continued)

Natural court[a]	Justices[b]	Dates	U.S. Reports[c]
Warren 5	Warren, Black, Frankfurter, Douglas, Clark, Harlan II, Brennan, Whittaker (r March 31, 1962), Stewart (o October 14, 1958)	October 14, 1958-April 16, 1962	358-369
Warren 6	Warren, Black, Frankfurter (r August 28, 1962), Douglas, Clark, Harlan II, Brennan, Stewart, B. White (o April 16, 1962)	April 16, 1962-October 1, 1962	369-370
Warren 7	Warren, Black, Douglas, Clark, Harlan II, Brennan, Stewart, B. White, Goldberg (o October 1, 1962; r July 25, 1965)	October 1, 1962-October 4, 1965	371-381
Warren 8	Warren, Black, Douglas, Clark (r June 12, 1967), Harlan II, Brennan, Stewart, B. White, Fortas (o October 4, 1965)	October 4, 1965-October 2, 1967	382-388
Warren 9	Warren (r June 23, 1969), Black, Douglas, Harlan II, Brennan, Stewart, B. White, Fortas (r May 14, 1969), T. Marshall (o October 2, 1967)	October 2, 1967-June 23, 1969	389-395
Burger 1	Burger (o June 23, 1969), Black, Douglas, Harlan II, Brennan, Stewart, B. White, T. Marshall	June 23, 1969-June 9, 1970	395-397
Burger 2	Burger, Black (r September 17, 1971), Douglas, Harlan II (r September 23, 1971), Brennan, Stewart, B. White, T. Marshall, Blackmun (o June 9, 1970)	June 9, 1970-January 7, 1972	397-404
Burger 3	Burger, Douglas (r November 12, 1975), Brennan, Stewart, B. White, T. Marshall, Blackmun, Powell (o January 7, 1972), Rehnquist (o January 7, 1972)	January 7, 1972-December 19, 1975	404-423
Burger 4	Burger, Brennan, Stewart (r July 3, 1981), B. White, T. Marshall, Blackmun, Powell, Rehnquist, Stevens (o December 19, 1975)	December 19, 1975-September 25, 1981	423-453

Burger 5	Burger (r September 26, 1986), Brennan, B. White, T. Marshall, Blackmun, Powell, Rehnquist (p September 26, 1986), Stevens, O'Connor (o September 25, 1981)	September 25, 1981-September 26, 1986	453-478
Rehnquist 1	Rehnquist (o September 26, 1986), Brennan, B. White, T. Marshall, Blackmun, Powell (r June 26, 1987), Stevens, O'Connor, Scalia (o September 26, 1986)	September 26, 1986-February 18, 1988	478-484
Rehnquist 2	Rehnquist, Brennan (r July 20, 1990), B. White, T. Marshall, Blackmun, Stevens, O'Connor, Scalia, Kennedy (o February 18, 1988)	February 18, 1988-October 9, 1990	484-
Rehnquist 3	Rehnquist, B. White, T. Marshall (r October 1, 1991), Blackmun, Stevens, O'Connor, Scalia, Kennedy, Souter (o October 9, 1990)	October 9, 1990-October 23, 1991	
Rehnquist 4	Rehnquist, B. White (r July 1, 1993), Blackmun, Stevens, O'Connor, Scalia, Kennedy, Souter, Thomas (o October 23, 1991)	October 23, 1991-August 10, 1993	
Rehnquist 5	Rehnquist, Blackmun, Stevens, O'Connor, Scalia, Kennedy, Souter, Thomas, Ginsburg (o August 10, 1993)	August 10, 1993-	

Note: The term *natural court* refers to a period of time during which the membership of the Court remains stable. There are a number of ways to determine the beginning and ending of a natural court. Here a natural court begins when a new justice takes the oath of office and continues until the next new justice takes the oath. When two or more justices join the Court within a period of fifteen or fewer days we treat it as the beginning of a single natural court (for example, Marshall 9, Chase 2, White 1, Stone 1).

a Numbered sequentially within the tenure of each chief justice.

b The name of the chief justice appears first, with associate justices following in order of descending seniority. In addition, the date a justice left the Court, creating a vacancy for the next justice to be appointed, is given, as well as the date the new justice took the oath of office. *o*=oath of office taken, *d*=died, *r*=resigned or retired, *rj*=recess appointment rejected by Senate, *p*= promoted from associate justice to chief justice.

c Volumes of *United States Reports* in which the actions of each natural court generally may be found. Because of the manner in which decisions were published prior to the twentieth century, these volume numbers may not contain all of the decisions of a given natural court. They do, however, provide a general guide to the location of each natural court's published decisions. Natural courts of short duration may have little business published in the reports.

Sources: Clare Cushman (ed.), *The Supreme Court Justices: Illustrated Biographies 1789-1993* (Washington, D.C.: The Supreme Court Historical Society and Congressional Quarterly, 1993); Kermit Hall (ed.), *The Oxford Companion to the Supreme Court* (New York: Oxford University Press, 1992); Commission on the Bicentennial of the United States Constitution, *The Supreme Court of the United States: Its Beginnings and Its Justices, 1790-1991* (Washington, D.C.: Supreme Court Historical Society, 1992); Administrative Office of the United States Courts, various reports.

Table 5-3   Circuit Justice Assignments, 1802-1867

Circuit	Justice assigned	Dates of service
First Circuit		
1802-1820: Massachusetts, New	William Cushing	1802-1810
Hampshire, Rhode Island; 1820-	Joseph Story	1811-1845
1867: Maine, Massachusetts, New	Levi Woodbury	1845-1851
Hampshire, Rhode Island	Benjamin Curtis	1851-1857
	Nathan Clifford	1858-1867
Second Circuit		
1802-1867: Connecticut, New York,	William Paterson	1802-1806
Vermont	Brockholst Livingston	1806-1823
	Smith Thompson	1823-1843
	Vacant	1844
	Samuel Nelson	1845-1867
Third Circuit		
1802-1867: New Jersey,	Bushrod Washington	1802-1829
Pennsylvania	Henry Baldwin	1830-1844
	Robert Grier	1846-1867
Fourth Circuit		
1802-1842: Delaware, Maryland;	Samuel Chase	1802-1811
1842-1863: Delaware, Maryland,	Gabriel Duvall	1811-1835
Virginia; 1863-1867: Delaware,	Roger Brooke Taney	1836-1864
Maryland, North Carolina, South	Salmon Chase	1864-1867
Carolina, Virginia, West Virginia		
Fifth Circuit		
1802-1842: North Carolina, Virginia;	John Marshall	1802-1835
1842-1863: Alabama, Louisiana;	Philip Barbour	1836-1841
1863-1867: Alabama, Florida,	Peter Daniel	1841-1845
Georgia, Mississippi	John McKinley	1845-1852
	John Campbell	1853-1861
	Vacant	1862
	James Wayne	1863-1867
Sixth Circuit		
1802-1842: Georgia, South Carolina;	Alfred Moore	1802-1804
1842-1862: Georgia, North Carolina,	William Johnson	1804-1834
South Carolina; 1862-1867:	James Wayne	1835-1863
Arkansas, Kentucky, Louisiana,	John Catron	1863-1865
Tennessee, Texas	Vacant	1866-1867
Seventh Circuit		
1807-1837: Kentucky, Ohio,	Thomas Todd	1807-1826
Tennessee; 1837-1862: Illinois,	Robert Trimble	1826-1828
Indiana, Michigan, Ohio; 1862-1867:	Vacant	1829

Table 5-3 *(Continued)*

Circuit	Justice assigned	Dates of service
Indiana, Ohio	John McLean	1830-1861
	Noah Swayne	1862-1867
Eighth Circuit		
1837-1862: Kentucky, Missouri,	John Catron	1837-1863
Tennessee; 1862-1867: Illinois,	David Davis	1863-1867
Michigan, Wisconsin		
Ninth Circuit		
1837-1842: Alabama, Arkansas,	John McKinley	1837-1845
Louisiana, Mississippi; 1842-1862:	Peter Daniel	1845-1860
Arkansas, Mississippi; 1862-1867:	Samuel Miller	1862-1867
Iowa, Kansas, Minnesota, Missouri		
Tenth Circuit		
1863-1865: California, Oregon; 1865-	Stephen Field	1863-1867
1867: California, Nevada, Oregon		
California Circuit		
1855-1863	No assignment	

Source: The Federal Cases Comprising Cases Argued and Determined in the Circuit and District Courts of the United States, Vol. I (St. Paul, Minn.: West Publishing, 1894), x-xvii.

Table 5-4 Circuit Justice Assignments, 1867-1992

Circuit	Justice assigned	Dates of service
First Circuit		
Maine, Massachusetts, New	Nathan Clifford	1867-1881
Hampshire, Rhode Island,	John Marshall Harlan I	1881
Puerto Rico [a]	Horace Gray	1882-1902
	Rufus Peckham	1902
	Oliver Wendell Holmes	1902-1932
	Louis Brandeis	1932-1939
	Felix Frankfurter	1939-1962
	Arthur Goldberg	1962-1965
	William Brennan	1969-1990
	David Souter	1990-
Second Circuit		
Connecticut, New York,	Samuel Nelson	1867-1872
Vermont	Ward Hunt	1873-1882
	Stephen Field	1882
	Samuel Blatchford	1882-1893
	Horace Gray	1893-1894
	Henry Brown	1894-1896
	Rufus Peckham	1896-1909
	Horace Lurton	1910-1911
	Charles Evans Hughes	1911-1916
	Louis Brandeis	1916-1925
	Harlan Fiske Stone	1925-1941
	Robert Jackson	1941-1945
	Stanley Reed	1945-1946
	Robert Jackson	1946-1954
	Felix Frankfurter	1954-1955
	John Marshall Harlan II	1955-1971
	Thurgood Marshall	1972-1991
	Clarence Thomas	1991-
Third Circuit		
Delaware, New Jersey,	Robert Grier	1867-1870
Pennsylvania, Virgin Islands [b]	William Strong	1870-1880
	Joseph Bradley	1881-1892
	John Marshall Harlan I	1892
	George Shiras	1892-1903
	Henry Brown	1903-1906
	Edward D. White	1906
	William Moody	1906-1910
	Horace Lurton	1911
	Mahlon Pitney	1911-1922
	Pierce Butler	1923-1925
	Louis Brandeis	1925-1930
	Owen Roberts	1930-1945
	Harold Burton	1945-1956

Table 5-4   *(Continued)*

Circuit	Justice assigned	Dates of service
	William Brennan	1956-1990
	David Souter	1990-
Fourth Circuit[c]		
Maryland, North Carolina,	Salmon Chase	1867-1873
South Carolina, Virginia, West	Morrison Waite	1874-1888
Virginia	Melville Fuller	1888-1910
	Edward D. White	1911-1921
	William Howard Taft	1921-1930
	Charles Evans Hughes	1930-1941
	Harlan Fiske Stone	1941-1946
	Fred Vinson	1946-1953
	Earl Warren	1953-1969
	Warren Burger	1969-1986
	William Rehnquist	1986-
Fifth Circuit		
Alabama,[d] Florida,[d] Georgia,[d]	James Wayne	1867
Louisiana, Mississippi, Texas,	Vacant	1868
Canal Zone[e]	Noah Swayne	1869
	Joseph Bradley	1870-1880
	William Woods	1881-1887
	John Marshall Harlan I	1887
	Lucius Lamar	1888-1893
	Howell Jackson	1893-1894
	Edward D. White	1894-1911
	Joseph Lamar	1911-1916
	Edward D. White	1916
	James McReynolds	1916-1923
	Edward Sanford	1923-1930
	Louis Brandeis	1930-1932
	Benjamin Cardozo	1932-1937
	Hugo Black	1937-1971
	Lewis Powell	1972-1981
	Byron White	1981-1987
	William Rehnquist	1987
	Byron White	1987-1990
	Antonin Scalia	1990-
Sixth Circuit		
Kentucky, Michigan, Ohio,	Noah Swayne	1867-1881
Tennessee	Stanley Matthews	1881-1889
	John Marshall Harlan I	1889-1890
	David Brewer	1890-1891
	Henry Brown	1892-1894
	Howell Jackson	1894-1896

(Table continues)

Table 5-4   *(Continued)*

Circuit	Justice assigned	Dates of service
	John Marshall Harlan I	1896-1911
	William Day	1911-1922
	James McReynolds	1922-1941
	Frank Murphy	1941
	Stanley Reed	1941-1957
	Harold Burton	1957-1958
	Potter Stewart	1958-1981
	Byron White	1981
	Sandra Day O'Connor	1981-1986
	Antonin Scalia	1986-1990
	John Paul Stevens	1990-
Seventh Circuit Illinois, Indiana, Wisconsin	David Davis	1867-1877
	John Marshall Harlan I	1878-1892
	Melville Fuller	1892-1894
	John Marshal Harlan I	1894-1896
	Henry Brown	1896-1903
	William Day	1903-1911
	Horace Lurton	1911-1914
	James McReynolds	1914-1916
	John Clarke	1916-1922
	George Sutherland	1922-1925
	Pierce Butler	1925-1929
	Willis Van Devanter	1929-1937
	Benjamin Cardozo	1937-1938
	Felix Frankfurter	1939
	William O. Douglas	1939-1940
	Frank Murphy	1940-1941
	James Byrnes	1941-1942
	Frank Murphy	1943-1949
	Sherman Minton	1949-1956
	Harold Burton	1956-1957
	Tom Clark	1957-1967
	Thurgood Marshall	1967-1972
	William Rehnquist	1972-1975
	John Paul Stevens	1975-
Eighth Circuit[f] Arkansas, Colorado, Iowa, Kansas, Minnesota, Missouri, Nebraska, New Mexico, North Dakota, Oklahoma, South Dakota, Utah, Wyoming	Samuel Miller	1867-1890
	David Brewer	1890-1910
	Willis Van Devanter	1911-1929
	Pierce Butler	1929-1939
	Stanley Reed	1940-1941
	Frank Murphy	1941-1943
	Wiley Rutledge	1943-1949
	Tom Clark	1949-1957
	Charles Whittaker	1957-1962

Table 5-4 *(Continued)*

Circuit	Justice assigned	Dates of service
	Tom Clark	1962
	Byron White	1962-1970
	Harry Blackmun	1970-
Ninth Circuit[g]		
Alaska, Arizona, California,	Stephen Field	1867-1897
Guam, Hawaii, Idaho, Montana,	David Brewer	1897-1898
Nevada, Northern Mariana	Joseph McKenna	1898-1925
Islands, Oregon, Washington	George Sutherland	1925-1938
	Stanley Reed	1938-1940
	William Douglas	1940-1975
	William Rehnquist	1975-1986
	Sandra Day O'Connor	1986-
Tenth Circuit		
Colorado, Kansas, New Mexico,	Willis Van Devanter	1929-1937
Oklahoma, Utah, Wyoming	Pierce Butler	1937-1939
	Stanley Reed	1940-1941
	Frank Murphy	1941-1943
	Wiley Rutledge	1943-1949
	Tom Clark	1949-1957
	Charles Whittaker	1957-1962
	William Douglas	1962
	Byron White	1962-
Eleventh Circuit		
Alabama, Georgia, Florida	Lewis Powell	1981-1987
	Sandra Day O'Connor	1987
	John Paul Stevens	1987-1988
	Anthony Kennedy	1988-
District of Columbia Circuit[h]	Charles Evans Hughes	1938-1941
	Harlan Fiske Stone	1941-1946
	Fred Vinson	1946-1953
	Earl Warren	1953-1969
	Warren Burger	1969-1986
	William Rehnquist	1986-
Federal Circuit[i]	Warren Burger	1982-1986
	William Rehnquist	1986-

[a] Added in 1915.
[b] Added in 1938.
[c] Traditionally, the chief justice has served as circuit justice for the Fourth Circuit.
[d] Moved to the newly created Eleventh Circuit in 1981.

(Notes continue)

Table 5-4   *(Continued)*

---

[e] Added in 1922, but removed from the circuit in 1979 with the implementation of the Panama Canal treaty that transferred the Canal Zone back to Panama.

[f] In 1867 the Eighth Circuit included only Arkansas, Iowa, Kansas, Minnesota, and Missouri. The states of Colorado, Nebraska, New Mexico, North Dakota, Oklahoma, South Dakota, Utah, and Wyoming were added as they achieved statehood. Colorado, Kansas, New Mexico, Oklahoma, Utah, and Wyoming were split off from the Eighth Circuit and combined to make a new Tenth Circuit in 1929.

[g] The Ninth Circuit contained only California, Nevada, and Oregon in 1867. As they attained statehood, Arizona, Idaho, Montana, and Washington were added. Alaska and Hawaii were added while still territories. Guam was included in 1966, and the Northern Mariana Islands in 1978.

[h] Became a full circuit in 1938. The chief justice traditionally serves as its circuit justice.

[i] Created in 1981. This court has no geographical jurisdiction but hears appeals concerning customs, patents, and special claims against the federal government. The chief justice has served as its circuit justice.

Sources: 1867-1891: *The Federal Courts Comprising Cases Argued and Determined in the Circuit and District Courts of the United States,* Vol. I (St. Paul, Minn.: West Publishing, 1894), x-xvii; 1891-1992: *The Supreme Court Reporter* (St. Paul, Minn.: West Publishing, annual volumes).

Table 5-5 Extra-Judicial Activities While Sitting on the Court

Justice (appointment number)[a]	Activity[b]
Blatchford, Samuel (49)	Trustee, Columbia University, 1882-93
Bradley, Joseph P. (42)	Member, commission to decide disputed Tilden-Hayes presidential election, 1877
Brandeis, Louis D. (69)	Advisor to President Woodrow Wilson; aided the development of the University of Louisville; active in Zionist causes
Brennan, William J., Jr. (94)	Participant, annual appellate judges seminar, New York University
Brewer, David J. (52)	President, Venezuela-British Guiana Border Commission, 1899; lecturer at Yale University and George Washington University; president, Associated Charities of Washington
Burger, Warren E. (101)	Participant, annual appellate judges seminar, New York University; lobbied for judicial reform
Butler, Pierce (73)	Trustee, Catholic University; member, Board of Regents, University of Minnesota
Byrnes, James F. (85)	Active in Franklin Roosevelt's administration, including drafting legislation, advising on appointments, and mediating disagreements among administrative agencies
Campbell, John A. (34)	Served as a mediator between Southern states and the incoming Lincoln administration, 1860-61
Catron, John (27)	Openly supported James Buchanan for president in 1856
Chase, Salmon P. (40)	Presided over impeachment trial of President Andrew Johnson, 1868; considered a possible presidential candidate, 1868 and 1872
Chase, Samuel (10)	Remained active in Federalist Party politics, including openly campaigning for the election of John Adams in 1800; campaigned for passage of Alien and Sedition acts

(Table continues)

Table 5-5   *(Continued)*

Justice (appointment number)[a]	*Activity*[b]
Clarke, John H. (70)	Active in promoting world peace and U.S. entry into the League of Nations
Clifford, Nathan (35)	Chair, commission to decide disputed Tilden-Hayes presidential election, 1877
Cushing, William (3)	Ran for governor of Massachusetts, 1794
Davis, David (38)	Nominee of Labor Reform Party for president, 1872
Douglas, William O. (82)	Advisor to Franklin Roosevelt; considered for Democratic vice-presidential nomination, 1944 and 1948; director, Parvin Foundation; executive, Center for the Study of Democratic Institutions; active in political, legal, and environmental writing
Ellsworth, Oliver (11)	Commissioner to France, 1799-1800
Field, Stephen J. (39)	Member, commission to decide disputed Tilden-Hayes presidential election, 1877; considered a possible Democratic presidential candidate, 1880 and 1884
Fortas, Abe (99)	Advisor to President Lyndon Johnson; instructor, American University Law School; consultant, Wolfson Foundation
Frankfurter, Felix (81)	Advisor to Franklin Roosevelt; active in scholarly writing
Fuller, Melville W. (51)	Member, Venezuela-British Guiana Border Commission, 1899; member, Permanent Court of Arbitration at the Hague, 1900-1910
Grier, Robert C. (32)	Advised President James Buchanan of decision in *Dred Scott* case before it was announced
Harlan, John Marshall I (45)	Member, Bering Sea Tribunal of Arbitration, 1893
Hughes, Charles E. (63, 76)	Member, federal postal rate commission; president, tribunal to arbitrate Guatemala-Honduras border dispute, 1930; extensive writing activities

Table 5-5 *(Continued)*

Justice (appointment number) [a]	*Activity* [b]
Jackson, Robert H. (86)	Chief prosecutor, Nuremberg war crimes trial, 1945-46; active in legal and political writing
Jay, John (1)	Secretary of foreign affairs, 1789; envoy to Great Britain, 1794-95; advisor to President George Washington and Treasury Secretary Alexander Hamilton throughout term of office
Johnson, Thomas (7)	Board of Commissioners of the Federal City, 1791-93
Johnson, William (15)	Advisor to President James Monroe; political writings
Lamar, Joseph R. (66)	Member, mediation conference on United States-Mexico relations, Niagara Falls, Canada, 1914
Livingston, H. Brockholst (16)	Trustee, Columbia University, 1806-23
Marshall, John (14)	Secretary of state, 1801; delegate, Virginia constitutional convention, 1829; member, Washington Historical Monument Society
McLean, John (22)	Honorary president, American Sunday School Union, 1849; several informal attempts to become a candidate for president
Miller, Samuel (37)	Member, commission to decide disputed Tilden-Hayes presidential election, 1877; considered a possible presidential candidate, 1880 and 1884; active in scholarly writing
Moody, William H. (61)	Advisor to Theodore Roosevelt
Moore, Alfred (13)	Trustee, University of North Carolina, 1799-1804
Murphy, Frank (83)	Lieutenant colonel, U.S. army, 1942
Nelson, Samuel (30)	Received support for 1860 Democratic presidential nomination; member, Alabama Claims Commission, 1871

(Table continues)

Table 5-5   *(Continued)*

Justice (appointment number)[a]	Activity[b]
Reed, Stanley F. (80)	Chair, President's Commission on Civil Service Improvement, 1939-41
Roberts, Owen J. (77)	Trustee, University of Pennsylvania; chair, Pearl Harbor Inquiry Board, 1941-42; member, Commission for the Protection and Salvage of Artistic and Historic Monuments in Europe, 1943-45
Rutledge, John (2, 9)	Chancery judge, South Carolina, 1789-91
Sanford, Edward T. (74)	Trustee, George Peabody College for Teachers, 1923-30
Stewart, Potter (96)	Active in American Bar Association committees
Stone, Harlan Fiske (75, 84)	Advisor to Herbert Hoover and Franklin Roosevelt; trustee, Amherst College; member of the boards of directors of several literary, artistic, and educational organizations
Story, Joseph (19)	Harvard University Board of Overseers, 1819-29; delegate, Massachusetts constitutional convention, 1820; fellow of the Harvard Corporation; professor of law, Harvard University, 1829-45; drafted federal statutes; member, Massachusetts Codification Commission, 1836-37; active in legal writing and publication
Strong, William (41)	Member, commission to decide disputed Tilden-Hayes presidential election, 1877
Swayne, Noah H. (36)	Campaigned for ratification of the Fifteenth Amendment
Taft, William H. (71)	Presidential and congressional advisor; active in the American Bar Association; diplomatic mission to Great Britain; trustee, Hampton Institute; lobbied bar and government groups for judicial reform
Taney, Roger B. (25)	Advisor to Presidents Andrew Jackson and Martin Van Buren; informally involved in Maryland politics

Table 5-5 *(Continued)*

Justice (appointment number)[a]	Activity[b]
Thompson, Smith (20)	Unsuccessful campaign for governor of New York, 1828
Todd, Thomas (17)	Stockholder in companies attempting to develop public roads in Kentucky; real estate investments in Kentucky
Van Devanter, Willis (65)	Arbitrated Great Britain-United States dispute over a ship seizure
Vinson, Fred M. (89)	Advisor to President Harry Truman
Waite, Morrison (44)	Trustee, Peabody Education Fund, 1874-88; member, Yale Corporation, 1882-88
Warren, Earl (92)	Chair, commission to investigate the assassination of President John F. Kennedy
Washington, Bushrod (12)	Executor of President Washington's estate; president, American Colonization Society, 1816
Wayne, James M. (24)	Active in developing transportation systems in Georgia; chair, Georgia State Railroad Convention, 1836; officer in various historical societies
White, Edward D. (56, 64)	Arbitrator of Panama-Costa Rica border dispute
Wilson, James (4)	Trustee, College of Philadelphia; unsuccessful business activities; jailed briefly for unsatisfied debts
Woodbury, Levi (31)	Contended for 1848 Democratic presidential nomination

[a] Justices without significant extra-judicial activities are not included.

[b] Refers to service beyond those activities normally expected. The years listed for each activity are only those concurrent with Supreme Court service.

Sources: Robert B. McKay, "The Judiciary and Nonjudicial Activities," *Law and Contemporary Problems* 35 (Winter 1970): 9-36; Elder Witt, *Congressional Quarterly's Guide to the U.S. Supreme Court,* 2d ed. (Washington, D.C.: Congressional Quarterly, 1990); Leon Friedman and Fred L. Israel, eds., *The Justices of the United States Supreme Court: Their Lives and Major Opinions* (New York: R.R. Bowker, 1969-1978); Harold W. Chase et al., *Biographical Dictionary of the American Judiciary* (Detroit: Gale Research, 1976); *Judges of the United States,* 2d ed. (Washington, D.C.: Judicial Conference of the United States, 1983); *The National Cyclopaedia of American Biography* (New York: James T. White, various years); *Dictionary of American Biography* (New York: Charles Scribner's Sons, various editions).

Table 5-6 Impeachment Actions Against Supreme Court Justices

Justice	Attempt	Outcome
Samuel Chase	On March 12, 1804, the House voted eight articles of impeachment by a 72-to-32 vote. Six of these called into question his actions "while presiding on circuit at treason and sedition trials." The other two centered on "addresses delivered to grand juries."	The Senate acquitted Chase of all charges on March 1, 1805.
William O. Douglas	On June 18, 1953, Rep. W. M. Wheeler (D-Ga.) introduced a resolution of impeachment against Douglas. The resolution came the day after Douglas had temporarily stayed the execution of Julius and Ethel Rosenberg. The Judiciary Committee created a subcommittee of "inquiry."	On June 19, the Supreme Court overruled Douglas. The Judiciary Committee tabled the resolution of impeachment on July 7.
	On April 15, 1970, Rep. Gerald Ford (R-Mich.), in a speech on the House floor, raised five charges against Douglas, centering on ethical violations (e.g., providing legal advice, failing to recuse). Ford called for the creation of a special committee, but the matter went to the House Judiciary Committee, which, on April 21, established a subcommittee to look into Ford's charges.	On April 21, the House subcommittee voted (3-1-1) that no grounds existed for impeachment.
Abe Fortas	On May 11, 1969, Rep. H. R. Gross (R-Iowa) stated that he had prepared articles of impeachment against Fortas, charging him with various ethical violations. Gross's announcement came a week after *Life* magazine had reported on Fortas's involvement with the Wolfson Foundation. On May 13, Rep. Clark MacGregor (R-Minn.) proposed that the House Judiciary Committee begin preliminary investigations.	Fortas resigned from the Court on May 14.

Source: Elder Witt, *Congressional Quarterly's Guide to the Supreme Court* (Washington, D.C.: Congressional Quarterly, 1991), 654-657.

Table 5-7 Departure from the Court

Justice (appointment number)	Year	Reason [a]	Age	Replacement
Baldwin, Henry (23)	1844	Died in office	64	Robert Grier
Barbour, Philip P. (26)	1841	Died in office	57	Peter Daniel
Black, Hugo L. (79)	1971	Declining health; stroke	85	Lewis Powell
Blair, John, Jr. (5)	1796	General decline in health; chronic headaches, weakness, decreased mental abilities; difficulties riding circuit	64	Samuel Chase
Blatchford, Samuel (49)	1893	Died in office	73	Edward White
Bradley, Joseph P. (42)	1892	Died in office	78	George Shiras
Brandeis, Louis D. (69)	1939	Advanced age	82	William O. Douglas
Brennan, William J., Jr. (94)	1990	Advanced age	84	David Souter
Brewer, David J. (52)	1910	Died in office	72	Charles E. Hughes
Brown, Henry B. (53)	1906	Declining health; blindness	70	William Moody
Burger, Warren E. (101) [b]	1986	Advanced age; desire to spend time chairing the Commission for the Bicentennial of the Constitution	79	William Rehnquist
Burton, Harold H. (88)	1958	Declining physical abilities due to Parkinson's disease	70	Potter Stewart
Butler, Pierce (73)	1939	Died in office	73	Frank Murphy

(Table continues)

Table 5-7 *(Continued)*

Justice (appointment number)	Year	Reason[a]	Age	Replacement
Byrnes, James F. (85)	1942	Resigned to assist war effort as director of the Office of Economic Stabilization	63	Wiley Rutledge
Campbell, John A. (34)	1861	Resigned to join the Confederacy	49	David Davis
Cardozo, Benjamin (78)	1938	Died in office	68	Felix Frankfurter
Catron, John (27)	1865	Died in office	79	Seat abolished
Chase, Salmon P. (40)[b]	1873	Died in office	65	Morrison Waite
Chase, Samuel (10)	1811	Died in office	70	Gabriel Duvall
Clark, Tom C. (90)	1967	Retired to remove possible conflicts of interest that might arise with his son's appointment as attorney general	67	Thurgood Marshall
Clarke, John H. (70)	1922	Resigned to campaign for U.S. participation in the League of Nations and other peace efforts	65	George Sutherland
Clifford, Nathan (35)	1881	Died in office	77	Horace Gray
Curtis, Benjamin R. (33)	1857	Resigned due to dissatisfaction with judicial salaries, circuit riding responsibilities, and strained relations on the Court	47	Nathan Clifford
Cushing, William (3)	1810	Died in office	78	Joseph Story
Daniel, Peter V. (29)	1860	Died in office	76	Samuel Miller
Davis, David (38)	1877	Resigned to take seat in U.S. Senate	61	John M. Harlan I

Justice	Reason	Year	Age	Successor
Day, William R. (60)	Advanced age; declining health	1922	73	Pierce Butler
Douglas, William O. (82)	Effects of a stroke	1975	77	John Paul Stevens
Duvall, Gabriel (18)	Advanced age; declining health; deafness	1835	82	Philip Barbour
Ellsworth, Oliver (11)[b]	Health problems aggravated by rigors of a lengthy diplomatic mission to Europe	1800	55	John Marshall
Field, Stephen J. (39)	Declining mental abilities	1897	81	Joseph McKenna
Fortas, Abe (99)	Resigned under criticism for unethical behavior	1969	58	Harry Blackmun
Frankfurter, Felix (81)	Effects of a stroke	1962	79	Arthur Goldberg
Fuller, Melville W. (51)[b]	Died in office	1910	77	Edward White
Goldberg, Arthur J. (98)	Resigned to accept position as U.S. ambassador to the United Nations	1965	56	Abe Fortas
Gray, Horace (48)	Died in office	1902	74	Oliver W. Holmes
Grier, Robert C. (32)	Severe decline in mental and physical abilities	1870	75	William Strong
Harlan, John Marshall I (45)	Died in office	1911	78	Mahlon Pitney
Harlan, John Marshall II (93)	Declining health	1971	72	William Rehnquist
Holmes, Oliver W., Jr. (59)	Advanced age	1932	90	Benjamin Cardozo

(Table continues)

Table 5-7 (*Continued*)

Justice (appointment number)	Year	Reason [a]	Age	Replacement
Hughes, Charles E. (63)	1916	Resigned to run for president	54	John H. Clarke
Hughes, Charles E. (76) [b]	1941	Advanced age; declining health	79	Harlan F. Stone
Hunt, Ward (43)	1882	Decline in ability due to a stroke; special retirement bill passed by Congress made him eligible for pension	71	Samuel Blatchford
Iredell, James (6)	1799	Died in office	48	Alfred Moore
Jackson, Howell E. (55)	1895	Died in office	63	Rufus Peckham
Jackson, Robert H. (86)	1954	Died in office	62	John M. Harlan II
Jay, John (1) [b]	1795	Resigned to become governor of New York	49	Oliver Ellsworth [c]
Johnson, Thomas (7)	1793	Health considerations; difficulties of riding circuit	60	William Paterson
Johnson, William (15)	1834	Died in office	63	James M. Wayne
Lamar, Joseph R. (66)	1916	Died in office	58	Louis Brandeis
Lamar, Lucius Q. C. (50)	1893	Died in office	67	Howell Jackson
Livingston, H. Brockholst (16)	1823	Died in office	65	Smith Thompson
Lurton, Horace (62)	1914	Died in office	70	James McReynolds
Marshall, John (14) [b]	1835	Died in office	79	Roger B. Taney

Marshall, Thurgood (100)	1991	Advanced age; declining health	83	Clarence Thomas
Matthews, Stanley (47)	1889	Died in office	64	David Brewer
McKenna, Joseph (58)	1925	Advanced age; declining mental abilities	81	Harlan F. Stone
McKinley, John (28)	1852	Died in office	72	John Campbell
McLean, John (22)	1861	Died in office	76	Noah Swayne
McReynolds, James C. (68)	1941	Advanced age; realization that further opposition to New Deal would be unsuccessful	78	James Byrnes
Miller, Samuel (37)	1890	Died in office	74	Henry Brown
Minton, Sherman (91)	1956	Debilitating effects of pernicious anemia	65	William J. Brennan
Moody, William H. (61)	1910	Severe arthritis	56	Joseph Lamar
Moore, Alfred (13)	1804	Declining health	48	William Johnson
Murphy, Frank (83)	1949	Died in office	59	Tom C. Clark
Nelson, Samuel (30)	1872	Advanced age; declining health aggravated by demands of serving on the Alabama Claims Commission	80	Ward Hunt
Paterson, William (8)	1806	Died in office	60	H. B. Livingston
Peckham, Rufus W. (57)	1909	Died in office	70	Horace Lurton

(Table continues)

Table 5-7 (Continued)

Justice (appointment number)	Year	Reason[a]	Age	Replacement
Pitney, Mahlon (67)	1922	Decreased ability due to stroke	64	Edward Sanford
Powell, Lewis F., Jr. (103)	1987	Advanced age	79	Anthony Kennedy
Reed, Stanley F. (80)	1957	Health considerations required reduced workload	72	Charles Whittaker
Rehnquist, William (104)	1986	Promoted to chief justice	61	Antonin Scalia
Roberts, Owen J. (77)	1945	Retired to pursue other activities, including the deanship of the University of Pennsylvania law school	70	Harold Burton
Rutledge, John (2)	1791	Resigned to become chief justice of South Carolina	51	Thomas Johnson
Rutledge, John (9)[b]	1795	Recess appointment rejected by Senate	56	Oliver Ellsworth
Rutledge, Wiley B. (87)	1949	Died in office	55	Sherman Minton
Sanford, Edward T. (74)	1930	Died in office	64	Owen Roberts
Shiras, George, Jr. (54)	1903	Retired in good health in order to enjoy retirement with family	71	William R. Day
Stewart, Potter (96)	1981	Retired in good health in order to enjoy retirement years and spend time with family	66	Sandra D. O'Connor
Stone, Harlan Fiske (75)	1941	Promoted to chief justice	68	Robert Jackson
Stone, Harlan Fiske (84)[b]	1946	Died in office	73	Fred Vinson

Name (age)	Year	Reason	Age	Successor
Story, Joseph (19)	1845	Died in office	65	Levi Woodbury
Strong, William (41)	1880	Retired to set an example for others to step down before suffering a decline in physical and mental abilities	72	William Woods
Sutherland, George (72)	1938	Advanced age; improved judicial retirement provisions; realization that further opposition to New Deal would be unsuccessful	75	Stanley Reed
Swayne, Noah H. (36)	1881	Declining mental abilities; a promise from President Rutherford B. Hayes to appoint his friend Stanley Matthews as his replacement	76	Stanley Matthews
Taft, William H. (71)[b]	1930	Declining health	72	Charles E. Hughes
Taney, Roger B. (25)[b]	1864	Died in office	87	Salmon Chase
Thompson, Smith (20)	1843	Died in office	75	Samuel Nelson
Todd, Thomas (17)	1826	Died in office	61	Robert Trimble
Trimble, Robert (21)	1828	Died in office	51	John McLean
Van Devanter, Willis (65)	1937	Advanced age; enactment of improved judicial retirement statute; realization that further opposition to New Deal would be unsuccessful	78	Hugo Black
Vinson, Fred M. (89)[b]	1953	Died in office	63	Earl Warren

Table 5-7 (Continued)

Justice (appointment number)	Year	Reason [a]	Age	Replacement
Waite, Morrison (44) [b]	1888	Died in office	71	Melville Fuller
Warren, Earl (92) [b]	1969	Advanced age	78	Warren Burger
Washington, Bushrod (12)	1829	Died in office	67	Henry Baldwin
Wayne, James M. (24)	1867	Died in office	77	Joseph Bradley [d]
White, Byron R. (97)	1993	Retired in good health to spend time with family and allow the appointment of a younger justice	76	Ruth Bader Ginsburg
White, Edward D. (56)	1910	Promoted to chief justice	65	Willis Van Devanter
White, Edward D. (64) [b]	1921	Died in office	75	William H. Taft
Whittaker, Charles E. (95)	1962	Health problems aggravated by Court's workload	61	Byron White
Wilson, James (4)	1798	Died in office	55	Bushrod Washington
Woodbury, Levi (31)	1851	Died in office	61	Benjamin Curtis
Woods, William B. (46)	1887	Died in office	62	Lucius Q. C. Lamar

[a] Lists factors cited at the time of departure. Other motives may also be involved. One of the more important is political timing. For example, a justice of advanced age enjoying relatively good health may be more prone to retire if the incumbent president is likely to appoint an acceptable replacement. Conversely, a justice of advanced age suffering health problems may attempt to postpone retirement if the incumbent president is likely to appoint a replacement whose political or legal views are at odds with his own.
[b] Chief justice.

(Notes continue)

[c] Jay was first replaced by John Rutledge, who received a recess appointment from George Washington. Rutledge served as chief justice only four months before the Senate reconvened and rejected the nomination.

[d] Bradley replaced Wayne after a three-year period during which the seat was temporarily abolished by Congress.

Sources: Elder Witt, *Congressional Quarterly's Guide to the U.S. Supreme Court*, 2d ed. (Washington, D.C.: Congressional Quarterly, 1990); Leon Friedman and Fred L. Israel, eds., *The Justices of the United States Supreme Court: Their Lives and Major Opinions* (New York: R.R. Bowker, 1969-1978); Harold W. Chase et al., *Biographical Dictionary of the American Judiciary* (Detroit: Gale Research, 1976); *Judges of the United States*, 2d ed. (Washington, D.C.: Judicial Conference of the United States, 1983); *The National Cyclopaedia of American Biography* (New York: James T. White, various years); *Dictionary of American Biography* (New York: Charles Scribner's Sons, various editions).

Table 5-8 Justices Rated "Great," Selected Studies

Hughes (1928)	Pound (1938)[a]	Frankfurter (1957)	Frank (1958)	Currie (1964)	Nagel (1970)	Asch (1971)	Blaustein and Mersky (1972)[b]	Schwartz (1979)[c]	Hambleton (1983)	Bradley (1991)[d]
J. Marshall	J. Marshall	J. Marshall	J. Marshall	J. Marshall	J. Marshall	Jay	J. Marshall	J. Marshall	J. Marshall	J. Marshall
Story	Story	W. Johnson	W. Johnson	W. Johnson	W. Johnson	J. Marshall	Story	Story	Story	Holmes
Curtis	Holmes	Story	Story	Story	Story	Taney	Taney	Holmes	Taney	Warren
Miller	Cardozo	Taney	McLean	Taney	Taney	Miller	Harlan I	Cardozo	Holmes	Brandeis
Field		Curtis	Taney	Miller	Curtis	Harlan I	Holmes	Black	Cardozo	Black
Bradley		Campbell	Curtis	Bradley	Campbell	Holmes	Hughes	Warren	Brandeis	Brennan
Gray		Miller	Campbell	Holmes	Miller	Brandeis	Brandeis		Hughes	Cardozo
Brewer		Field	Miller	Brandeis	Field	Hughes	Stone		Black	Frankfurter
		Bradley	Davis	Hughes	Bradley	Stone	Cardozo		Warren	Douglas
		Matthews	Field		Harlan I	Cardozo	Black			Rehnquist
		E. White	Bradley		Brewer	Frankfurter	Frankfurter			
		Holmes	Waite		Holmes	R. Jackson	Warren			
		Moody	Harlan I		Moody	Black				
		Hughes	Brewer		Hughes	Douglas				
		Brandeis	Holmes		Brandeis	Warren				
		Cardozo	Moody		Cardozo					
			Hughes		Black					
			Brandeis		Frankfurter					
			Taft		Douglas					
			Sutherland		R. Jackson					
			Butler		Warren					
			Stone							
			Cardozo							

Note: All studies list justices chronologically, with the exception of Bradley's, which lists in order of perceived greatness. Readers should be aware that these rankings are, for the most part, quite subjective. With the exceptions of the Blaustein and Mersky and Bradley studies, authors used their own judgments in devising their rankings.

[a] Pound's study also listed jurists who did not serve on the Supreme Court, including James Kent, John Bannister Gibson, Lemuel Shaw, Thomas Ruffin, Thomas McIntyre Cooley, and Charles Doe.

[b] Blaustein and Mersky asked 65 scholars to "grade" the justices in a continuum from A to E, where A is great, B is near great, C is average, D is below average, and E is failure. Included here are those rated A. (See source listed below for listings rated B through E.)

[c] Schwartz' study also listed jurists who did not serve on the Supreme Court, including James Kent, Lemuel Shaw, Arthur T. Vanderbilt, and Roger John Traynor.

[d] Bradley sent surveys to 493 lawyers, judges, and scholars. His response rates ranged from 37 percent (scholars) to 12 percent (judges).

Sources: Lists of great judges were compiled by Robert C. Bradley, "The Supreme Court: Who are the Great Justices and What Criteria did they Meet?," unpublished paper on record with the author, 1991, Appendix A. We supplemented those lists from the original sources: Sidney H. Asch, *The Supreme Court and its Great Justices* (New York: Arco, 1971); Albert P. Blaustein and Roy M. Mersky, *The First One Hundred Justices* (Hamden, Conn.: Archon Books, 1978); George R. Currie, "A Judicial All-star Nine," *Wisconsin Law Review* (1964): 3-31; John P. Frank, *Marble Palace* (New York: Alfred A. Knopf, 1958); Felix Frankfurter, "The Supreme Court in the Mirror of Justices," *University of Pennsylvania Law Review* 105 (1957): 781-796; James E. Hambleton, "The All-Time All-Star All-Era Supreme Court," *American Bar Association Journal* 69 (1983): 463-464; Charles Evans Hughes, *The Supreme Court of the United States* (New York: Columbia University Press, 1928); Stuart S. Nagel, "Characteristics of Supreme Court Greatness," *Journal of the American Bar Association* 56 (1970): 957-959; Roscoe Pound, *The Formative Era of American Law* (Boston: Little, Brown, 1938); Bernard Schwartz, "The Judicial Ten: America's Greatest Judges," *Southern Illinois University Law Review* (1979): 405-447.

Table 5-9 Post-Court Activities

Justice (appointment number)[a]	Post-Court Years	Post-Court activities
Black, Hugo L. (79)	1 week	Retired in poor health
Blair, John, Jr. (5)	4	Retired in declining health at his home in Williamsburg, Virginia
Brandeis, Louis D. (69)	2	Devoted his retirement years to the support of Zionist causes
Brennan, William J., Jr. (94)	—	Retired in poor health in Washington, D.C.
Brown, Henry B. (53)	7	Retired in declining health in New York; active in promoting legal reform
Burger, Warren E. (101)	—	Retired in Washington, D.C.; chaired Commission for the Bicentennial of the Constitution
Burton, Harold H. (88)	6	Retired in poor health in Washington, D.C.
Byrnes, James F. (85)	29	Director, Office of Economic Stabilization, 1942-43; director, Office of War Mobilization and Reconversion, 1943-45; secretary of state, 1945-47; private practice, Washington, D.C. and South Carolina, 1947-51; governor, South Carolina, 1951-55; retirement in South Carolina
Campbell, John A. (34)	27	Assistant secretary of war, Confederate States of America, 1862-65; built prosperous law practice, New Orleans, 1866-89; argued several appeals before the Supreme Court, including the *Slaughterhouse Cases* (1873)
Clark, Tom C. (90)	10	Chair, Board of Directors, American Judicature Society, 1967-69; judge, United States court of appeals, by designation, 1967-77; director, Federal Judicial Center, 1968-70

Clarke, John H. (70)	22	Retired in San Diego; worked for the cause of peace: president, League of Nations' Non-Partisan Association of the United States, 1922-30; trustee, World Peace Foundation, 1923-31
Curtis, Benjamin R. (33)	17	Operated successful law practice in Boston, 1857-74; Andrew Johnson's lead attorney in his 1868 impeachment proceedings; declined Johnson nomination to be attorney general
Davis, David (38)	9	United States senator from Illinois, 1877-83; president pro tem of the Senate, 1881-83; administrator of the Lincoln family estate; retirement in Bloomington, Illinois
Day, William R. (60)	7 months	Umpire, commission to settle World War I claims, 1922-23
Douglas, William O. (82)	4	Retired in poor health in Washington, D.C.
Duvall, Gabriel (18)	9	Retired in declining health to Marietta, his estate in Maryland; wrote a family history
Ellsworth, Oliver (11)	7	Governor's council of Connecticut, 1801-07; promoted agricultural development; retired at Elmwood, his estate in Windsor, Connecticut
Field, Stephen J. (39)	1	Retired in ill health
Fortas, Abe (99)	13	Private practice, Washington, D.C., 1969-82
Frankfurter, Felix (81)	2	Retired in poor health in Washington, D.C.
Goldberg, Arthur J. (98)	24	Ambassador to the United Nations, 1965-68; Democratic nominee for governor of New York, 1970; private practice
Grier, Robert C. (32)	7 months	Retired in ill health in Philadelphia

(Table continues)

Table 5-9 (Continued)

Justice (appointment number)[a]	Post-Court Years	Post-Court activities
Harlan, John Marshall II (93)	3 months	Retired in poor health in Washington, D.C.
Holmes, Oliver W., Jr. (59)	3	Divided his retirement years between Washington, D.C., and Massachusetts
Hughes, Charles Evans (63, 76)	13; 7	Following initial resignation as associate justice in 1916: Republican presidential nominee, 1916; secretary of state, 1921-25; president of the American Bar Association, 1924-25; judge, Permanent Court of International Justice, 1928-30; chair, New York State Reorganization Commission; lawyer in private practice. Following retirement as chief justice in 1941: retirement in declining health
Hunt, Ward (43)	4	Retired in poor health
Jay, John (1)	33	Governor of New York, 1795-1801; nominated and confirmed to be chief justice in 1800, but declined to serve; president of American Bible Society, 1821; retirement on his 800-acre estate in Westchester County, New York; conducted agricultural experiments; active in peace groups
Johnson, Thomas (7)	26	Board of commissioners to plan the development of nation's capitol in Washington, D.C., 1791-94; declined offer to serve as secretary of state, 1795; retirement in Frederick, Maryland
Marshall, Thurgood (100)	1	Retired in poor health in Washington, D.C.
McKenna, Joseph (58)	2	Retired in poor health in Washington, D.C.

McReynolds, James C. (68)	5	Retired in Washington, D.C.
Minton, Sherman (91)	8	Retired in poor health in New Albany, Indiana
Moody, William H. (61)	6	Retired in poor health due to crippling arthritis in Haverhill, Massachusetts
Moore, Alfred (13)	6	Retired to North Carolina; devoted his efforts to establishing the University of North Carolina, which he served as a trustee from 1789-1807
Nelson, Samuel (30)	1	Retired in declining health to his home in Cooperstown, New York
Pitney, Mahlon (67)	2	Retired in Washington, D.C., in poor health
Powell, Lewis F., Jr. (103)	—	Retired in Virginia
Reed, Stanley F. (80)	23	Chair, U.S. Civil Rights Commission, 1957; served by designation as a judge on the courts of appeals and the court of claims
Roberts, Owen J. (77)	10	Member, Amnesty Board, 1945-47; president, Pennsylvania Bar Association, 1947; dean, University of Pennsylvania Law School, 1948-51; trustee, University of Pennsylvania, 1943-55; president, American Philosophical Society, 1952; chair, Fund for the Advancement of Education, 1953; active in world federalist movement
Rutledge, John (2, 9)	9	Chief justice of South Carolina, 1791-95; nominated to be chief justice, served four months as recess appointment, confirmation rejected by Senate, 1795; South Carolina Assembly, 1798-99; unsuccessful suicide attempt
Shiras, George, Jr. (54)	21	Retired in good health spending time with family in Florida, Michigan, and Pennsylvania

(Table continues)

Table 5-9 (Continued)

Justice (appointment number)[a]	Post-Court Years	Post-Court activities
Stewart, Potter (96)	4	Retired in good health
Strong, William (41)	14	Retired in good health in Washington, D.C.; vice president, American Bible Society, 1871-95; president, American Tract Society, 1873-95; president, American Sunday School Union, 1883-95
Sutherland, George (72)	4	Retired in declining health
Swayne, Noah H. (36)	3	Retired in poor health
Taft, William H. (71)	1 month	Retired in poor health
Van Devanter, Willis (65)	3	Retired to New York; served by designation as a United States district judge
Warren, Earl (92)	5	Retired in Washington, D.C.; wrote memoirs
White, Byron R. (97)	—	Retired in good health in Washington, D.C.; sat by designation as a court of appeals judge
Whittaker, Charles E. (95)	11	Legal staff, General Motors Corporation, 1965; special counsel, Senate Committee on Standards and Conduct, to develop ethics code, 1966; law practice, Kansas City

[a] Justices who died in office and those sitting in 1993 are not included.

Sources: Elder Witt, *Congressional Quarterly's Guide to the U.S. Supreme Court,* 2d ed. (Washington, D.C.: Congressional Quarterly, 1990); Leon Friedman and Fred L. Israel, eds., *The Justices of the United States Supreme Court: Their Lives and Major Opinions* (New York: R.R. Bowker, 1969-1978); Harold W. Chase et al., *Biographical Dictionary of the American Judiciary* (Detroit: Gale Research, 1976); *Judges of the United States,* 2d ed. (Washington, D.C.: Judicial Conference of the United States, 1983); *The National Cyclopaedia of American Biography* (New York: James T. White, various years); *Dictionary of American Biography* (New York: Charles Scribner's Sons, various editions).

Table 5-10 The Deaths of the Justices

Justice (appointment number)	Date/place of death	Age	Interment
Baldwin, Henry (23)	April 21, 1844 Philadelphia, Penn.	64	Oak Hill Cemetery Washington, D.C.[a]
Barbour, Philip P. (26)	February 25, 1841 Washington, D.C.	57	Congressional Cemetery Washington, D.C.
Black, Hugo L. (79)	September 25, 1971 Washington, D.C.	85	Arlington National Cemetery Arlington, Va.
Blair, John, Jr. (5)	August 31, 1800 Williamsburg, Va.	68	Bruton Parish Church Williamsburg, Va.
Blatchford, Samuel (49)	July 7, 1893 Newport, R.I.	73	Green Wood Cemetery Brooklyn, N.Y.
Bradley, Joseph P. (42)	January 22, 1892 Washington, D.C.	78	Mount Pleasant Cemetery Newark, N.J.
Brandeis, Louis D. (69)	October 5, 1941 Washington, D.C.	84	University of Louisville Law School Louisville, Ky.
Brewer, David J. (52)	March 28, 1910 Washington, D.C.	72	Mount Muncie Cemetery Leavenworth, Kan.
Brown, Henry B. (53)	September 4, 1913 Bronxville, N.Y.	77	Elmwood Cemetery Detroit, Mich.

(Table continues)

Table 5-10 (*Continued*)

Justice (*appointment number*)	Date/place of death	Age	Interment
Burton, Harold H. (88)	October 28, 1964 Washington, D.C.	76	Highland Park Cemetery Cleveland, Ohio
Butler, Pierce (73)	November 16, 1939 Washington, D.C.	73	Calvary Cemetery St. Paul, Minn.
Byrnes, James F. (85)	April 9, 1972 Columbia, S.C.	92	Trinity Cathedral Graveyard Columbia, S.C.
Campbell, John A. (34)	March 12, 1889 Baltimore, Md.	77	Green Mount Cemetery Baltimore, Md.
Cardozo, Benjamin (78)	July 9, 1938 Port Chester, N.Y.	68	Cypress Hills Cemetery Brooklyn, N.Y.
Catron, John (27)	May 30, 1865 Nashville, Tenn.	79	Mount Olivet Cemetery Nashville, Tenn.
Chase, Salmon P. (40)	May 7, 1873 New York, N.Y.	65	Spring Grove Cemetery Cincinnati, Ohio
Chase, Samuel (10)	June 19, 1811 Baltimore, Md.	70	St. Paul's Cemetery Baltimore, Md.
Clark, Tom C. (90)	June 13, 1977 New York, N.Y.	77	Restland Memorial Park Dallas, Texas

Clarke, John H. (70)	March 22, 1945 San Diego, Calif.	87	Lisbon Cemetery Lisbon, Ohio
Clifford, Nathan (35)	July 25, 1881 Cornish, Maine	77	Evergreen Cemetery Portland, Maine
Curtis, Benjamin R. (33)	September 15, 1874 Newport, R.I.	64	Mount Auburn Cemetery Cambridge, Mass.
Cushing, William (3)	September 13, 1810 Scituate, Mass.	78	Family Cemetery Scituate, Mass.
Daniel, Peter V. (29)	May 31, 1860 Richmond, Va.	76	Hollywood Cemetery Richmond, Va.
Davis, David (38)	June 26, 1886 Bloomington, Ill.	71	Evergreen Memorial Cemetery Bloomington, Ill.
Day, William R. (60)	July 9, 1923 Mackinac Island, Mich.	74	West Lawn Cemetery Canton, Ohio
Douglas, William O. (82)	January 19, 1980 Washington, D.C.	81	Arlington National Cemetery Arlington, Va.
Duvall, Gabriel (18)	March 6, 1844 Prince George's Co., Md.	91	Family estate Prince George's Co., Md.
Ellsworth, Oliver (11)	November 26, 1807 Windsor, Conn.	62	Palisado Cemetery Windsor, Conn.

(Table continues)

Table 5-10 (Continued)

Justice (appointment number)	Date/place of death	Age	Interment
Field, Stephen J. (39)	April 9, 1899 Washington, D.C.	82	Rock Creek Cemetery Washington, D.C.
Fortas, Abe (99)	April 5, 1982 Washington, D.C.	71	Cremated, no interment
Frankfurter, Felix (81)	February 22, 1965 Washington, D.C.	82	Mount Auburn Cemetery Cambridge, Mass.
Fuller, Melville W. (51)	July 4, 1910 Sorrento, Maine	77	Graceland Cemetery Chicago, Ill.
Goldberg, Arthur J. (98)	January 19, 1990 Washington, D.C.	81	Arlington National Cemetery Washington D.C.
Gray, Horace (48)	September 15, 1902 Nahant, Mass.	74	Mount Auburn Cemetery Cambridge, Mass.
Grier, Robert C. (32)	September 25, 1870 Philadelphia, Penn.	76	West Laurel Hill Cemetery Bala-Cynwyd, Penn.
Harlan, John Marshall I (45)	October 14, 1911 Washington, D.C.	78	Rock Creek Cemetery Washington, D.C.
Harlan, John Marshall II (93)	December 29, 1971 Washington, D.C.	72	Emmanuel Church Cemetery Weston, Conn.

Name	Date and place of death	Age	Place of burial
Holmes, Oliver W., Jr. (59)	March 6, 1935 Washington, D.C.	93	Arlington National Cemetery Arlington, Va.
Hughes, Charles E. (63, 76)	August 27, 1948 Osterville, Mass.	86	The Woodlawn Cemetery Bronx, N.Y.
Hunt, Ward (43)	March 24, 1886 Washington, D.C.	75	Forest Hill Cemetery Utica, N.Y.
Iredell, James (6)	October 20, 1799 Edenton, N.C.	48	Hayes Plantation Edenton, N.C.
Jackson, Howell E. (55)	August 8, 1895 West Meade, Tenn.	63	Mount Olivet Cemetery Nashville, Tenn.
Jackson, Robert H. (86)	October 9, 1954 Washington, D.C.	62	Mapel Grove Cemetery Frewsburg, N.Y.
Jay, John (1)	May 17, 1829 Bedford, N.Y.	83	Family Cemetery Rye, N.Y.
Johnson, Thomas (7)	October 26, 1819 Frederick, Md.	86	Mount Olivet Cemetery Frederick, Md.
Johnson, William (15)	August 4, 1834 Brooklyn, N.Y.	62	Unknown[b]
Lamar, Joseph R. (66)	January 2, 1916 Washington, D.C.	58	Summerville Cemetery Augusta, Ga.

(Table continues)

Table 5-10 *(Continued)*

Justice (appointment number)	Date/place of death	Age	Interment
Lamar, Lucius Q. C. (50)	January 23, 1893 Vineville, Ga.	67	Riverside Cemetery[c] Macon, Ga.
Livingston, H. Brockholst (16)	March 18, 1823 Washington, D.C.	65	Trinity Church Churchyard New York, N.Y.
Lurton, Horace (62)	July 12, 1914 Atlantic City, N.J.	70	Greenwood Cemetery Clarksville, Tenn.
Marshall, John (14)	July 6, 1835 Philadelphia, Penn.	79	Shockoe Hill Cemetery Richmond, Va.
Marshall, Thurgood (100)	January 24, 1993 Washington, D.C.	84	Arlington National Cemetery Arlington, Va.
Matthews, Stanley (47)	March 22, 1889 Washington, D.C.	64	Spring Grove Cemetery Cincinnati, Ohio
McKenna, Joseph (58)	November 21, 1926 Washington, D.C.	83	Mount Olivet Cemetery Washington, D.C.
McKinley, John (28)	July 19, 1852 Louisville, Ky.	72	Cave Hill Cemetery Louisville, Ky.
McLean, John (22)	April 4, 1861 Cincinnati, Ohio	76	Spring Grove Cemetery Cincinnati, Ohio

McReynolds, James C. (68)	August 24, 1946 Washington, D.C.	84	Glenwood Cemetery Elkton, Ky.
Miller, Samuel (37)	October 13, 1890 Washington, D.C.	74	Oakland Cemetery Keokuk, Iowa
Minton, Sherman (91)	April 9, 1965 New Albany, Ind.	74	Holy Trinity Catholic Cemetery New Albany, Ind.
Moody, William H. (61)	July 2, 1917 Haverhill, Mass.	63	Byfield Parish Churchyard Georgetown, Mass.
Moore, Alfred (13)	October 15, 1810 Bladen County, N.C.	55	St. Philip's Churchyard Southport, N.C.
Murphy, Frank (83)	July 19, 1949 Detroit, Mich.	59	Our Lady of Lake Huron Cemetery Harbor Beach, Mich.
Nelson, Samuel (30)	December 13, 1873 Cooperstown, N.Y.	81	Lakewood Cemetery Cooperstown, N.Y.
Paterson, William (8)	September 9, 1806 Albany, N.Y.	60	Albany Rural Cemetery Menands, N.Y.
Peckham, Rufus W. (57)	October 24, 1909 Altamont, N.Y.	70	Albany Rural Cemetery Menands, N.Y.
Pitney, Mahlon (67)	December 9, 1924 Washington, D.C.	66	Evergreen Cemetery Morristown, N.J.

(Table continues)

Table 5-10 *(Continued)*

Justice (appointment number)	*Date/place of death*	*Age*	*Interment*
Reed, Stanley F. (80)	April 2, 1980 Huntington, N.Y.	95	Maysville Cemetery Maysville, Ky.
Roberts, Owen J. (77)	May 17, 1955 West Vincent, Penn.	80	St. Andrew's Cemetery West Vincent, Penn.
Rutledge, John (2, 9)	July 18, 1800 Charleston, S.C.	60	St. Michael's Cemetery Charleston, S.C.
Rutledge, Wiley B. (87)	September 10, 1949 York, Maine	55	Green Mountain Cemetery Boulder, Colo.
Sanford, Edward T. (74)	March 8, 1930 Washington, D.C.	64	Greenwood Cemetery Knoxville, Tenn.
Shiras, George, Jr. (54)	August 2, 1924 Pittsburgh, Penn.	92	Allegheny Cemetery Pittsburgh, Penn.
Stewart, Potter (96)	December 7, 1985 Hanover, N.H.	70	Arlington National Cemetery Arlington, Va.
Stone, Harlan Fiske (75, 84)	April 22, 1946 Washington, D.C.	73	Rock Creek Cemetery Washington, D.C.
Story, Joseph (19)	September 10, 1845 Cambridge, Mass.	65	Mount Auburn Cemetery Cambridge, Mass.

Strong, William (41)	August 19, 1895 Lake Minnewassa, N.Y.	87	Charles Evans Cemetery Reading, Penn.
Sutherland, George (72)	July 18, 1942 Stockbridge, Mass.	80	Cedar Hill Cemetery Suitland, Md.
Swayne, Noah H. (36)	June 8, 1884 New York, N.Y.	79	Oak Hill Cemetery Washington, D.C.
Taft, William H. (71)	March 8, 1930 Washington, D.C.	72	Arlington National Cemetery Arlington, Va.
Taney, Roger B. (25)	October 12, 1864 Washington, D.C.	87	St. John the Evangelist Cemetery Frederick, Md.
Thompson, Smith (20)	December 18, 1843 Poughkeepsie, N.Y.	75	Poughkeepsie Cemetery Poughkeepsie, N.Y.
Todd, Thomas (17)	February 7, 1826 Frankfort, Ky.	61	Frankfort Cemetery Frankfort, Ky.
Trimble, Robert (21)	August 25, 1828 Paris, Ky.	51	Paris Cemetery Paris, Ky.
Van Devanter, Willis (65)	February 8, 1941 Washington, D.C.	81	Rock Creek Cemetery Washington, D.C.
Vinson, Fred M. (89)	September 8, 1953 Washington, D.C.	63	Pinehill Cemetery Louisa, Ky.

(Table continues)

Table 5-10 (Continued)

Justice (appointment number)	Date/place of death	Age	Interment
Waite, Morrison (44)	March 23, 1888 Washington, D.C.	71	Woodlawn Cemetery Toledo, Ohio
Warren, Earl (92)	July 9, 1974 Washington, D.C.	83	Arlington National Cemetery Arlington, Va.
Washington, Bushrod (12)	November 26, 1829 Philadelphia, Penn.	67	Family vault Mount Vernon, Va.
Wayne, James M. (24)	July 5, 1867 Washington, D.C.	77	Laurel Grove Cemetery Savannah, GA
White, Edward D. (56, 64)	May 19, 1921 Washington, D.C.	75	Oak Hill Cemetery Washington, D.C.
Whittaker, Charles E. (95)	November 26, 1973 Kansas City, Mo.	72	Calvary Cemetery Kansas City, Mo.
Wilson, James (4)	August 21, 1798 Edenton, N.C.	55	Christ Churchyard Philadelphia, Penn.
Woodbury, Levi (31)	September 4, 1851 Portsmouth, N.H.	61	Harmony Grove Cemetery Portsmouth, N.H.
Woods, William B. (46)	May 14, 1887 Washington, D.C.	62	Cedar Hill Cemetery Newark, Ohio

[a] There is some evidence that Justice Baldwin's body was transferred to Glendale Cemetery in Meadville, Penn.

[b] Justice William Johnson died from complications of surgery in New York where he had gone for medical care. His body was to be shipped for burial in St. Philip's churchyard in Charleston, S.C. However, there is evidence that, although a monument to Johnson was erected at St. Philip's, the body never arrived. What happened to Johnson's body remains a mystery. See the Christensen source for a full account.

[c] An alternative claim is made that Justice Lamar is interred in St. Peter's Cemetery in Oxford, Miss.

Sources: George A. Christensen, "Here Lies the Supreme Court: Gravesites of the Justices," *1983 Supreme Court Historical Society Yearbook* (1983), 17-30; Elder Witt, *Congressional Quarterly's Guide to the U.S. Supreme Court,* 2d ed. (Washington, D.C.: Congressional Quarterly, 1990); Leon Friedman and Fred L. Israel, eds., *The Justices of the United States Supreme Court: Their Lives and Major Opinions* (N.Y.: R.R. Bowker, 1969-1978); Harold W. Chase et al., *Biographical Dictionary of the American Judiciary* (Detroit: Gale Research, 1976); *Judges of the United States,* 2d ed. (Washington, D.C.: Judicial Conference of the United States, 1983); *The National Cyclopaedia of American Biography* (New York: James T. White, various years); *Dictionary of American Biography* (New York: Charles Scribner's Sons, various editions).

Table 5-11 Locations of Justices' Personal Papers

Justice (appointment number)[a]	Size of collection[b]	Location of collection[c]
Baldwin, Henry (23)	Medium	National Archives Washington, D.C.
		Crawford County Historical Society Meadville, Penn.
Barbour, Philip P. (26)	Medium	Virginia Historical Society Richmond, Va.
		University of Virginia Charlottesville, Va.
Black, Hugo L. (79)	Large	Library of Congress, Manuscript Division Washington, D.C.
Blair, John, Jr. (5)	Very small	College of William and Mary Library Williamsburg, Va.
Blatchford, Samuel (49)	None	
Bradley, Joseph P. (42)	Medium	New Jersey Historical Society Newark, N.J.
Brandeis, Louis D. (69)	Large	University of Louisville Law School Louisville, Ky.

Name	Size	Repository
Brennan, William J., Jr. (94)	Large	Brandeis University Library, Waltham, Mass.
		Harvard Law School Library, Cambridge, Mass.
		American Jewish Archives, Cincinnati, Ohio
		Library of Congress, Manuscript Division, Washington, D.C.
Brewer, David J. (52)	Medium	Yale University Library, New Haven, Conn.
		Library of Congress, Manuscript Division, Washington, D.C.
Brown, Henry B. (53)	Small	Detroit Public Library, Detroit, Mich.
Burton, Harold H. (88)	Large	Yale University, New Haven, Conn.
		Library of Congress, Manuscript Division, Washington, D.C.
Butler, Pierce (73)	Very small	Minnesota Historical Society, St. Paul, Minn.

(Table continues)

Table 5-11 (*Continued*)

Justice (*appointment number*) [a]	Size of collection [b]	Location of collection [c]
Byrnes, James F. (85)	Large	Robert Muldrow Cooper Library Clemson University, S.C.
Campbell, John A. (34)	Small	Southern Historical Collection University of North Carolina Chapel Hill, N.C.
Cardozo, Benjamin (78)	Small	Columbia University Libraries New York, N.Y.
		American Jewish Archives Cincinnati, Ohio
		American Jewish Historical Society Waltham, Mass.
Catron, John (27)	None	
Chase, Salmon P. (40)	Large	Historical Society of Pennsylvania Philadelphia, Penn.
		Library of Congress, Manuscript Division Washington, D.C.
		Ohio Historical Society Columbus, Ohio

Name	Size	Location
Chase, Samuel (10)	Small	Maryland Historical Society Library, Baltimore, Md.
Clark, Tom C. (90)	Large	University of Texas Law Library, Austin, Texas
Clarke, John H. (70)	Small	Case Western Reserve University, Cleveland, Ohio
Clifford, Nathan (35)	Small	Maine Historical Society, Portland, Maine
Curtis, Benjamin R. (33)	Small	Library of Congress, Manuscript Division, Washington, D.C.
Cushing, William (3)	Small	Massachusetts Historical Society, Boston, Mass.
		Scituate Historical Society, Scituate, Mass.
		Library of Congress, Manuscript Division, Washington, D.C.
Daniel, Peter V. (29)	Small	Virginia Historical Society, Richmond, Va.
		University of Virginia Library, Charlottesville, Va.

(Table continues)

Table 5-11 (*Continued*)

Justice (appointment number)[a]	Size of collection[b]	Location of collection[c]
Davis, David (38)	Large	Illinois State Historical Society Library Springfield, Ill.
		Chicago Historical Society Chicago, Ill.
		Illinois Historical Survey Collection University of Illinois Urbana, Ill.
Day, William R. (60)	Large	Library of Congress, Manuscript Division Washington, D.C.
Douglas, William O. (82)	Large	Library of Congress, Manuscript Division Washington, D.C.
Duvall, Gabriel (18)	Small	Library of Congress, Manuscript Division Washington, D.C.
Ellsworth, Oliver (11)	Small	New York Public Library New York, N.Y.
		Connecticut Historical Society Hartford, Connecticut
		Connecticut State Library Hartford, Connecticut

Field, Stephen J. (39)	Small	Bancroft Library, Manuscript Division University of California, Berkeley, Calif.
		Oregon Historical Society Portland, Ore.
Fortas, Abe (99)	Large	Sterling Memorial Library Yale University New Haven, Conn.
Frankfurter, Felix (81)	Large	Harvard Law School Library Cambridge, Mass.
		Library of Congress, Manuscript Division Washington, D.C.
Fuller, Melville W. (51)	Large	Library of Congress, Manuscript Division Washington, D.C.
		Chicago Historical Society Library Chicago, Ill.
Gray, Horace (48)	Small	Library of Congress, Manuscript Division Washington, D.C.
Grier, Robert C. (32)	Very small	Historical Society of Pennsylvania Philadelphia, Penn.

(Table continues)

Table 5-11 (*Continued*)

Justice (appointment number)[a]	Size of collection[b]	Location of collection[c]
Harlan, John Marshall I (45)	Large	Library of Congress, Manuscript Division Washington, D.C.
		University of Louisville Law Library Louisville, Ky.
Harlan, John Marshall II (93)	Large	Seeley G. Mudd Manuscript Library Princeton University Princeton, N.J.
Holmes, Oliver W., Jr. (59)	Large	Harvard Law School Library Cambridge, Mass.
		Library of Congress, Manuscript Division Washington, D.C.
Hughes, Charles Evans (63, 76)	Large	Library of Congress, Manuscript Division Washington, D.C.
Hunt, Ward (43)	None	
Iredell, James (6)	Medium	North Carolina State Office of Archives and History Raleigh, N.C.

Name	Size	Location
Jackson, Howell E. (55)	Small	Southern Historical Collection University of North Carolina Chapel Hill, N.C. Duke University Durham, N.C. Tennessee State Library and Archives Memphis, Tenn.
Jackson, Robert H. (86)	Large	Southern Historical Collection University of North Carolina Chapel Hill, N.C. Library of Congress, Manuscript Division Washington, D.C.
Jay, John (1)	Medium	Columbia University Libraries New York, N.Y. New York Historical Society New York, N.Y.
Johnson, Thomas (7)	Small	C. Burr Artz Library Frederick, Md.
Johnson, William (15)	None	

(Table continues)

Table 5-11 *(Continued)*

Justice (appointment number)[a]	Size of collection[b]	Location of collection[c]
Lamar, Joseph R. (66)	Medium	University of Georgia Library Athens, Ga.
Lamar, Lucius Q. C. (50)	Small	Mississippi Department of Archives and History Jackson, Miss.
		Southern Historical Collection University of North Carolina Chapel Hill, N.C.
Livingston, H. Brockholst (16)	None	
Lurton, Horace (62)	Small	Library of Congress, Manuscript Division Washington, D.C.
Marshall, John (14)	Very small	Library of Congress, Manuscript Division Washington, D.C.
		National Archives Washington, D.C.
Marshall, Thurgood (100)	Large	Library of Congress, Manuscript Division Washington, D.C.
Matthews, Stanley (47)	Small	Cincinnati Historical Society Cincinnati, Ohio

McKenna, Joseph (58)	None	Wisconsin State Historical Society Madison, Wis.
McKinley, John (28)	None	Rutherford B. Hayes Library Fremont, Ohio
McLean, John (22)	Medium	Library of Congress, Manuscript Division Washington, D.C.
		Ohio Historical Society Columbus, Ohio
McReynolds, James C. (68)	Small	University of Virginia Library Charlottesville, Va.
Miller, Samuel (37)	None	
Minton, Sherman (91)	Small	Truman Library Independence, Mo.
Moody, William H. (61)	Large	Library of Congress, Manuscript Division Washington, D.C.
		Haverhill Historical Society Haverhill, Mass.

(Table continues)

Table 5-11 *(Continued)*

Justice *(appointment number)* [a]	Size of collection [b]	Location of collection [c]
		Essex Institute Salem, Mass.
Moore, Alfred (13)	Very small	North Carolina State Office of Archives and History Raleigh, N.C.
Murphy, Frank (83)	Large	Michigan Historical Collection University of Michigan Ann Arbor, Mich. Detroit Public Library Burton Historical Collection Detroit, Mich.
Nelson, Samuel (30)	None	
Paterson, William (8)	Medium	Princeton University Library Princeton, N.J. New York Public Library New York, N.Y. Library of Congress, Manuscript Division Washington, D.C.

Name	Size	Location
Peckham, Rufus W. (57)	Small	Rutgers University Library New Brunswick, N.J.
Pitney, Mahlon (67)	None	Library of Congress, Manuscript Division Washington, D.C.
Reed, Stanley F. (80)	Large	University of Kentucky Library Lexington, Ky.
Roberts, Owen J. (77)	None	
Rutledge, John (2, 9)	Small	Charleston Library Society Charleston, S.C.
Rutledge, Wiley B. (87)	Large	Library of Congress, Manuscript Division Washington, D.C.
Sanford, Edward T. (74)	Small	University of Tennessee Library Knoxville, Tenn.
Shiras, George, Jr. (54)	None	
Stewart, Potter (96)	Large	Sterling Memorial Library Yale University New Haven, Conn.
Stone, Harlan Fiske (75, 84)	Large	Library of Congress, Manuscript Division Washington, D.C.

(Table continues)

Table 5-11 (*Continued*)

Justice (appointment number)[a]	Size of collection[b]	Location of collection[c]
		Columbia University Libraries New York, N.Y.
Story, Joseph (19)	Medium	Library of Congress, Manuscript Division Washington, D.C.
		William Clements Library University of Michigan Ann Arbor, Mich.
		New York Historical Society New York, N.Y.
		Massachusetts Historical Society Boston, Mass.
		Humanities Research Center University of Texas Austin, Texas
Strong, William (41)	Very small	Historical Society of Pennsylvania Philadelphia, Penn.
Sutherland, George (72)	Medium	Library of Congress, Manuscript Division Washington, D.C.

Name	Size	Repository
Swayne, Noah H. (36)	Small	Ohio Historical Society Columbus, Ohio
Taft, William H. (71)	Large	Library of Congress, Manuscript Division Washington, D.C. Cincinnati Historical Society Cincinnati, Ohio Ohio Historical Society Columbus, Ohio
Taney, Roger B. (25)	Small	Library of Congress, Manuscript Division Washington, D.C. Maryland Historical Society Baltimore, Md. Dickinson College Library Carlisle, Penn.
Thompson, Smith (20)	Small	Library of Congress, Manuscript Division Washington, D.C. New York Historical Society New York, N.Y.
Todd, Thomas (17)	None	
Trimble, Robert (21)	None	

(Table continues)

Table 5-11 (Continued)

Justice (appointment number)[a]	Size of collection[b]	Location of collection[c]
Van Devanter, Willis (65)	Large	Library of Congress, Manuscript Division Washington, D.C.
		Case Western Reserve University Library Cleveland, Ohio
Vinson, Fred M. (89)	Large	University of Kentucky Library Lexington, Ky.
Waite, Morrison (44)	Large	Library of Congress, Manuscript Division Washington, D.C.
Warren, Earl (92)	Large	Library of Congress, Manuscript Division Washington, D.C.
		California State Archives Sacramento, Calif.
Washington, Bushrod (12)	Small	Library of Congress, Manuscript Division Washington, D.C.
		University of Virginia Charlottesville, Va.
		Historical Society of Pennsylvania Philadelphia, Penn.

Justice	Size	Location
Wayne, James M. (24)	Very small	Chicago Historical Society, Chicago, Ill. Georgia Historical Society, Savannah, Ga.
White, Edward D. (56, 64)	None	
Wilson, James (4)	Small	Historical Society of Pennsylvania, Philadelphia, Penn. Dickinson College Library, Carlisle, Penn.
Woodbury, Levi (31)	Large	Library of Congress, Manuscript Division, Washington, D.C. New Hampshire Historical Society, Concord, N.H.
Woods, William B. (46)	None	

Note: Lists collections of private papers deposited in libraries and other public institutions. Many of these collections have restrictions on use, and a number have limited numbers of items dealing with the justices' Supreme Court years.

[a] Recent Supreme Court justices not included as their personal papers are not yet available for public or scholarly use.
[b] Refers to combined holdings in all locations. Large = over 5,000 items; Medium = up to 5,000 items; Small = up to 1,000 items; Very small = scattered items; None = no known collections.
[c] Where more than one location listed, appear in descending order of collection size.

Source: Alexandra K. Wigdor, *The Personal Papers of Supreme Court Justices: A Descriptive Guide* (New York: Garland Publishing, 1986).

Table 5-12 Selected Books and Articles Written by the Justices

Justice (appointment number) [a]	Books and articles [b]
Baldwin, Henry (23)	*A General View of the Origin and Nature of the Constitution and Government of the United States.* Philadelphia: American Constitutional and Legal History Service, 1837.
Black, Hugo L. (79)	"The Lawyer and Individual Freedom." *Tennessee Law Review* 21 (December 1950): 461-471.
	"The Bill of Rights." *New York University Law Review* 35 (April 1960): 865-881.
	A Constitutional Faith. New York: Knopf, 1968.
Blackmun, Harry A. (102)	"Marital Deduction and Its Use in Minnesota." *Minnesota Law Review* 36 (December 1951): 50-64.
	"Thoughts about Ethics." *Emory Law Journal* 24 (Winter 1975): 3-20.
	"Section 1983 and Federal Protection of Individual Rights: Will the Statute Remain Alive or Fade Away?" *New York University Law Review* 60 (April 1985): 1-29.
Blatchford, Samuel (49)	*Blatchford's Circuit Court Reports*, 1852.
	Blatchford's and Howland's Reports, 1855.
Bradley, Joseph P. (42)	*Family Notes Respecting the Bradley Family of Fairfield.* Newark, N.J.: A. Pierson, 1894.
	Miscellaneous Writings of the Late Honorable Joseph P. Bradley and a Review of His Judicial Record. Edited by Charles Bradley. Newark, N.J.: L.J. Hardham, 1902.
Brandeis, Louis D. (69)	"The Right to Privacy" (with Samuel D. Warren). *Harvard Law Review* 4 (December 15, 1890): 193-220.
	Business: A Profession. Boston: Small, Maynard, 1914.
	Other People's Money: And How the Bankers Use It. New York: Stokes, 1914.

Table 5-12   *(Continued)*

Justice (appointment number) [a]	*Books and articles* [b]
	"The Living Law." *Illinois Law Review* 10 (February 1916): 461-471.
Brennan, William J., Jr. (94)	"The Bill of Rights and the States." *New York University Law Review* 36 (April 1961): 761-778.
	"Constitutional Adjudication." *Notre Dame Lawyer* 40 (August 1965): 559-569.
	An Affair with Freedom. New York: Atheneum, 1967.
	"Constitutional Adjudication and the Death Penalty: A View from the Court." *Harvard Law Review* 100 (December 1986): 313-331.
Brewer, David J. (52)	*The Income Tax Cases and Some Comments Thereon.* Iowa City: University of Iowa Press, 1895.
	The United States as a Christian Nation. Philadelphia: J.C. Winston Co., 1905.
	American Citizenship. New Haven, Conn.: Yale University Press, 1911.
Brown, Henry B. (53)	"The Dissenting Opinions of Mr. Justice Daniel." *American Law Review* 21 (November/December 1887): 869-900.
	"Judicial Independence." *American Bar Association Reports* 12 (1889): 265-288.
	"The Distribution of Property." *American Bar Association Reports* 16 (1893): 213-242.
Burger, Warren E. (101)	"New Chief Justice's Philosophy of Law in America." *New York State Bar Journal* 41 (October 1969): 454-479.
	"Thinking the Unthinkable." *Loyola Law Review* 31 (Spring 1985): 205-220.
	"The Time is Now for the Intercircuit Panel." *American Bar Association Journal* 71 (April 1985): 86-91.

(Table continues)

Table 5-12 *(Continued)*

Justice (appointment number)[a]	*Books and articles*[b]
Burton, Harold H. (88)	*The Story of the Place Where First and A Streets Formerly Met at What is Now the Site of the Supreme Court Building.* Washington, D.C.: Library of Congress, 1952.
	"Unsung Services of the Supreme Court of the United States." *Fordham Law Review* 24 (Summer 1955): 169-77.
	"Judging Is Also Administration: An Appreciation of Constructive Leadership." *Temple Law Quarterly* 21 (October 1947): 77-90.
Butler, Pierce (73)	"Some Opportunities and Duties of Lawyers." *American Bar Association Journal* 9 (September 1923): 583-587.
Byrnes, James F. (85)	*Speaking Frankly.* New York: Harper, 1947.
	All in One Lifetime. New York: Harper, 1958.
	"The Supreme Court and States Rights." *Alabama Lawyer* 20 (October 1959): 396-403.
Cardozo, Benjamin (78)	*The Nature of the Judicial Process.* New Haven, Conn.: Yale University Press, 1921.
	The Growth of the Law. New Haven, Conn.: Yale University Press, 1924.
	The Paradoxes of Legal Science. New York: Columbia University Press, 1928.
Chase, Salmon P. (40)	*Inside Lincoln's Cabinet: The Civil War Diaries of Salmon P. Chase.* Edited by David Donald. New York: Longman's Green, 1954.
Clark, Tom C. (90)	"Administrative Law." *Journal of the Bar Association of the District of Columbia* 18 (July 1951): 254-261.
	"Constitutional Adjudication and the Supreme Court." *Drake Law Review* 9 (May 1960): 59-65.
	"American Bar Association Standards for Criminal Justice: Prescription for an Ailing System." *Notre Dame Lawyer* 47 (February 1972): 429-441.

Table 5-12 *(Continued)*

Justice (appointment number)[a]	*Books and articles*[b]
Clarke, John H. (70)	"Practice Before the Supreme Court." *Virginia Law Register* 8 (August 1922): 241-252.
	"Reminiscences of the Courts and Law." *Proceedings of the California State Bar Association* 5 (1932): 20-31.
Curtis, Benjamin R. (33)	*Executive Power*. Cambridge, Mass.: Houghton, 1862.
	A Memoir of Benjamin Robbins Curtis. Boston: Little, Brown, 1879
Douglas, William O. (82)	*An Almanac of Liberty*. Garden City, N.Y.: Doubleday, 1954.
	Freedom of the Mind. Garden City, N.Y.: Doubleday, 1962.
	The Bible and the Schools. Boston: Little, Brown, 1966.
	Points of Rebellion. New York: Random House, 1970.
	Go East Young Man. New York: Random House, 1974.
	The Court Years, 1939-1975: The Autobiography of William O. Douglas. New York: Random House, 1980.
Ellsworth, Oliver (11)	*Essays on the Constitution of the United States, Published During Its Discussion by the People, 1787-1788*. Brooklyn, N.Y.: Historical Printing Club, 1892.
Field, Stephen J. (39)	"The Centenary of the Supreme Court of the United States." *American Law Review* 24 (May/June 1890): 351-368.
	Personal Reminiscences of Early Days in California with other Sketches. Washington, D.C., 1893. Reprint. New York: Da Capo Press, 1968.

(Table continues)

Table 5-12   *(Continued)*

Justice (appointment number)[a]	*Books and articles*[b]
Fortas, Abe (99)	*Concerning Dissent and Civil Disobedience.* New York: New American Library, 1968.
	"Criminal Justice 'Without Pity'." *Trial Lawyers Quarterly* 9 (Summer 1973): 9-14.
Frankfurter, Felix (81)	*The Case of Sacco and Vanzetti: A Critical Analysis for Lawyers and Laymen.* Boston: Little, Brown, 1927.
	The Business of the Supreme Court: A Study in the Federal Judicial System (with James M. Landis). New York: Macmillan, 1928.
	The Commerce Clause Under Marshall, Taney and Waite. Chapel Hill: University of North Carolina Press, 1937.
	Mr. Justice Holmes and the Constitution. Cambridge, Mass.: Harvard University Press, 1938.
	The Public and Its Government. Boston: Beacon Press, 1964.
Ginsburg, Ruth Bader (112)	*Civil Procedure in Sweden* (with Anders Bruzelius). The Hague: M. Nijhoff, 1965.
	Text, Cases and Materials on Sex-based Discrimination (with Kenneth M. Davidson and Herma Hill Kay). St. Paul, Minn.: West Publishing Co., 1974.
	"Some Thoughts on Autonomy and Equality in Relation to *Roe v. Wade.*" *North Carolina Law Review* 63 (January 1985): 375-386.
Goldberg, Arthur J. (98)	*AFL/CIO: Labor United.* New York: McGraw-Hill, 1956.
	"Declaring the Death Penalty Unconstitutional" (with Alan Dershowitz). *Harvard Law Review* 83 (June 1970): 1773-1819.
	Equal Justice: The Warren Era of the Supreme Court. Evanston, Ill.: Northwestern University Press, 1971.
Harlan, John Marshall I (45)	"The Supreme Court of the United States and Its Work." *American Law Review* 30 (November/December 1896): 900-902.

Table 5-12 *(Continued)*

Justice (appointment number)[a]	Books and articles[b]
	"James Wilson and the Formation of the Constitution." *American Law Review* 34 (July/August 1900): 481-504.
Harlan, John Marshall II (93)	"Some Aspects of the Judicial Process in the Supreme Court of the United States." *Australian Law Journal* 33 (August 1959): 108-125.
	"The Bill of Rights and the Constitution." *American Bar Association Journal* 50 (October 1964): 918-920.
Holmes, Oliver W., Jr. (59)	*The Common Law.* Boston: Little, Brown, 1881.
	The Holmes-Pollock Letters. Edited by Mark D. Howe. Cambridge, Mass.: Harvard University Press, 1941.
	The Holmes-Laski Letters. Edited by Mark D. Howe. Cambridge, Mass.: Harvard University Press, 1953.
	The Holmes-Einstein Letters. Edited by James B. Peabody. New York: St. Martin's Press, 1964.
Hughes, Charles E. (63, 76)	*Conditions of Progress in Democratic Government.* New Haven, Conn.: Yale University Press, 1910.
	Pathways of Peace. New York: Harper, 1925.
	The Supreme Court of the United States. New York: Columbia University Press, 1928.
	Pan American Peace Plans. New Haven, Conn.: Yale University Press, 1929.
Iredell, James (6)	"Letter of James Iredell to Johnson." *Massachusetts Historical Society Proceedings* 53 (1920): 27-28.
Jackson, Robert H. (86)	*The Struggle for Judicial Supremacy.* New York: Knopf, 1941.
	Full Faith and Credit: The Lawyer's Clause of the Constitution. New York: Columbia University Press, 1945.

(Table continues)

Table 5-12 *(Continued)*

Justice (appointment number)[a]	Books and articles[b]
	The Case Against the Nazi War Criminals. New York: Knopf, 1946.
	The Supreme Court in the American System of Government. Cambridge, Mass.: Harvard University Press, 1955.
Jay, John (1)	*An Address to the People of the State of New York on the Subject of the Constitution, Agreed upon at Philadelphia, September 17, 1787.* New York: Loudon, 1788.
	The Federalist Papers (with James Madison and Alexander Hamilton), ed. Garry Wills (New York: Bantam, 1982).
Johnson, William (15)	*Sketches of the Life and Correspondence of Nathanael Greene.* Charleston, S.C.: A.E. Miller, 1822.
Lamar, Joseph R. (66)	*A Century's Progress in Law.* Augusta, Ga.: Richards and Shaver, 1900.
	"History of the Establishment of the Supreme Court of Georgia." *Report of the Georgia Bar Association* 24 (1907): 85-103.
Lurton, Horace (62)	"Evolution of the Right of Trial." *Ohio Law Bulletin* 52 (1907): 442.
Marshall, John (14)	*The Life of George Washington,* 5 vols. Philadelphia: C. P. Wayne, 1804-1807.
	A History of the Colonies Planted by the English on the Continent of North America, from Their Settlement, to the Commencement of That War Which Terminated in Their Independence. Philadelphia: A. Small, 1824.
	The Writing of John Marshall upon the Federal Constitution. Boston: J. Munroe, 1839.
Marshall, Thurgood (100)	"The Supreme Court as Protector of Civil Rights: Equal Protection of the Laws." *Annals of the American Academy of Political and Social Sciences* 275 (May 1951): 101-110.

Table 5-12   *(Continued)*

Justice (appointment number) [a]	*Books and articles* [b]
	"The Continuing Challenge of the Fourteenth Amendment." *Georgia Law Review* 3 (Fall 1968): 1-10.
	"Financing Public Interest Law Practice: The Role of the Organized Bar." *American Bar Association Journal* 61 (December 1975): 1487-1491.
Matthews, Stanley (47)	*The Function of the Legal Profession in the Progress of Civilization.* Cincinnati: R. Clarke, 1881.
McLean, John (22)	*The Letters of John McLean to John Teesdale.* Edited by William Salter. Oberlin, Ohio: Bibliotheca Sacra, 1899.
Miller, Samuel (37)	*The Supreme Court of the United States.* Washington, D.C.: W.H. Barnes, 1877.
	The Constitution and the Supreme Court of the United States of America. New York: D. Appleton, 1889.
O'Connor, Sandra Day (106)	"The Changing of the Circuit Justice." *University of Toledo Law Review* 17 (Spring 1986): 521-526.
	"Swinford Lecture." *Kentucky Bench and Bar* 49 (Summer 1985): 20-22, 51-53.
Powell, Lewis F., Jr. (103)	"Myths and Misconceptions about the Supreme Court." *American Bar Association Journal* 61 (November 1975): 1344-1347.
	"Of Politics and the Court." *Supreme Court Historical Society Yearbook,* 1982 (1982): 23-26.
	"The Burger Court." *Washington and Lee Law Review* 44 (Winter 1987): 1-10.
Reed, Stanley F. (80)	"Our Constitutional Philosophy: Concerning the Significance of Judicial Review in the Evolution of American Democracy." *Kentucky State Bar Journal* 2 (June 1961): 136-146.

(Table continues)

Table 5-12 *(Continued)*

Justice (appointment number)[a]	*Books and articles*[b]
Rehnquist, William (104, 107)	"Political Battles for Judicial Independence." *Washington Law Review* 50 (August 1975): 835-851.
	"Sunshine in the Third Branch." *Washburn Law Journal* 16 (Spring 1977): 559-570.
	"Constitutional Law and Public Opinion." *Suffolk University Law Review* 20 (Winter 1986): 751-769.
	The Supreme Court: The Way It Was—the Way It Is. New York: Morrow, 1987.
	Grand Inquests: The Historic Impeachments of Justice Samuel Chase and President Andrew Johnson. New York: Morrow, 1992.
Roberts, Owen J. (77)	*The Court and the Constitution.* Cambridge, Mass.: Harvard University Press, 1951.
Rutledge, Wiley B. (87)	*A Declaration of Legal Faith.* Lawrence: University of Kansas Press, 1947.
Sanford, Edward T. (74)	*Blount College and the University of Tennessee.* Knoxville: University of Tennessee Press, 1894.
Scalia, Antonin (108)	"Vermont Yankee: The APA, the D.C. Circuit, and the Supreme Court." *Supreme Court Review,* 1978 (1978): 345-409.
	"Historical Anomalies in Administrative Law." *Supreme Court Historical Society Yearbook,* 1985 (1985): 101-111.
Stevens, John Paul (105)	*Mr. Justice Rutledge.* Chicago: University of Chicago Press, 1956.
	"Some Thoughts on Judicial Restraint." *Judicature* 66 (November 1983): 177-183.
	"Legal Questions in Perspective." *Florida State University Law Review* 13 (Spring 1985): 1-7.
	"The Third Branch of Liberty." *University of Miami Law Review* 41 (December 1986): 277-293.

Table 5-12   *(Continued)*

Justice (appointment number)[a]	*Books and articles*[b]
Stewart, Potter (96)	"The Nine of Us: 'Guardians of the Constitution'." *Florida Bar Journal* 41 (October 1967): 1090-1097.
	"A View From Inside the Court." *Cleveland Bar Association Journal* 39 (January 1968): 69-92.
	"Or of the Press." *Hastings Law Journal* 26 (January 1975): 631-637.
Stone, Harlan Fiske (75, 84)	*Law and Its Administration.* New York: Columbia University Press, 1915.
	"The Public Influence of the Bar." *Harvard Law Review,* 48 (November 1934): 1-14.
	"The Common Law in the United States." *Harvard Law Review* 50 (November 1936): 4-26.
	"Dissenting Opinions Are Not without Value." *Journal of the American Judicature Society* 26 (October 1942): 78.
Story, Joseph (19)	*Commentaries on the Constitution of the United States.* Boston: Hilliard, Gray, 1833.
	Commentaries on the Law, 9 vols., published between 1832-1845.
	Discourse upon the Life, Character and Services of the Honorable John Marshall. Boston: J. Munroe, 1835.
Strong, William (41)	*Two Lectures upon the Relations of Civil Law to Church Polity, Discipline, and Property.* New York: Dodd, Mead, 1875.
	"The Needs of the Supreme Court." *North American Review* 132 (May 1881): 437-450.
	"Relief for the Supreme Court." *North American Review* 151 (November 1890): 567-575.
Sutherland, George (72)	*Private Rights and Government Control.* Washington, D.C.: Government Printing Office, 1917.

(Table continues)

Table 5-12   *(Continued)*

Justice (appointment number)[a]	*Books and articles*[b]
	Constitutional Power and World Affairs. New York: Columbia University Press, 1919.
Taft, William H. (71)	*Four Aspects of Civic Duty.* New York: Charles Scribner's Sons, 1906.
	Popular Government: Its Essence, Its Permanence, and Its Perils. New Haven, Conn.: Yale University Press, 1913.
	The Anti-Trust Act and the Supreme Court. New York: Harper and Row, 1914.
	The President and His Powers. New York: Columbia University Press, 1916.
	Liberty Under Law: An Interpretation of the Principles of Our Constitutional Government. New Haven, Conn.: Yale University Press, 1922.
Taney, Roger B. (25)	*The Decision in the* Merryman *Case, upon the Writ of Habeas Corpus.* Philadelphia: John Campbell, 1862.
Thomas, Clarence (111)	"Commencement Address: Syracuse University College of Law," *Syracuse University Law Review* 42 (1991): 815-822.
Van Devanter, Willis (65)	"The Supreme Court of the United States." *Indiana Law Journal* 5 (May 1930): 553-562.
Vinson, Fred M. (89)	"Our Enduring Constitution." *Washington and Lee Law Review* 6 (1949): 1-11.
	"Supreme Court Work: Opinion on Dissents." *Oklahoma Bar Association Journal* 20 (September 1949): 1269-1275.
Waite, Morrison (44)	"The Supreme Court of the United States." *Albany Law Journal* 36 (October 15, 1887): 315-318.
Warren, Earl (92)	*Hughes and the Court.* Hamilton, N.Y.: Colgate University, 1962.
	"The Bill of Rights and the Military." *New York University Law Review* 37 (April 1962): 181-203.

Table 5-12   *(Continued)*

Justice (appointment number)[a]	*Books and articles*[b]
	"All Men Are Created Equal." *Record of the Association of the Bar of the City of New York* 25 (June 1970): 351-364.
	A Republic, if You Can Keep It. New York: Quadrangle Books, 1972.
	Memoirs. New York: Doubleday, 1977.
White, Byron R. (97)	"Supreme Court Review of Agency Decisions." *Administrative Law Review* 26 (Winter 1974): 107-112.
	"Challenges for the U. S. Supreme Court and the Bar: Contemporary Reflections." *Antitrust Law Journal* 51 (August 1982): 275-282.
	"Work of the Supreme Court: A Nuts and Bolts Description." *New York State Bar Journal* 54 (October 1982): 346-349.
White, Edward D. (56, 64)	"Supreme Court of the United States." *American Bar Association Journal* 7 (July 1921): 341-343.
Whittaker, Charles E. (95)	"Role of the Supreme Court." *Arizona Law Review* 17 (Fall 1963): 292-301.
Wilson, James (4)	*Commentaries on the Constitution of the United States* (with Thomas Mikean). Philadelphia: T. Lloyd, 1792.
	Works. Philadelphia: Lorenzo Press, 1804.
	Selected Political Essays. Edited by Randolph Adams. New York: Knopf, 1930.
Woodbury, Levi (31)	*Writings of Levi Woodbury, LL.D., Political, Judicial, and Literary.* Boston: Little, Brown, 1852.

[a] Justices with no significant books or articles credited to them not listed.

[b] Books and articles included should not be considered exhaustive. Several members of the Court were quite prolific authors. Where a justice published numerous books or articles, the more significant of those works are listed.

Sources: Fenton S. Martin and Robert U. Goehlert, *The United States Supreme Court: A Bibliography* (Washington, D.C.: Congressional Quarterly, 1990); Leon Friedman and Fred L. Israel, eds., *The Justices of the United States Supreme Court: Their Lives and Major Opinions,* 5 vols. (New York: Chelsea House, 1969-1978).

Table 5-13   Classic Statements from the Bench

---

abortion

This right of privacy, whether it be founded in the Fourteenth Amendment's concept of personal liberty and restrictions upon state action, as we feel it is, or, as the District Court determined, in the Ninth Amendment's reservation of rights to the people, is broad enough to encompass a woman's decision whether or not to terminate her pregnancy.

Harry Blackmun, for the Court, *Roe v. Wade*, 410 U.S. 113 (1973), at 152

Just as improvements in medical technology will move *forward* at the point at which the State may regulate for reasons of maternal health, different technological improvements will move *backward* the point of viability at which the State may proscribe abortions.... [T]he Roe framework ... is clearly on a collision course with itself.

Sandra Day O'Connor, dissenting, *Akron* v. *Akron Center for Reproductive Health*, 462 U.S. 416 (1983), at 456-458

Today, *Roe v. Wade* (1973) and the fundamental constitutional right of women to decide whether to terminate a pregnancy survive but are not secure....

I fear for the future. I fear for the liberty and equality of the millions of women who have lived and come of age in the 16 years since *Roe* was decided. I fear for the integrity of, and public esteem for, this Court.

I dissent.

Harry Blackmun, concurring in part and dissenting in part, *Webster v. Reproductive Health Services*, 492 U.S. 490 (1989), at 537-538

avoidance of constitutional questions

When the validity of an act of the Congress is drawn in question, and even if a serious doubt of constitutionality is raised, it is a cardinal principle that this Court will first ascertain whether a construction of the statute is fairly possible by which the question may be avoided.

Louis D. Brandeis, dissenting, *Ashwander v. Tennessee Valley Authority*, 297 U.S. 288 (1936), at 348

balancing of freedoms

...I do not agree that laws directly abridging First Amendment freedoms can be justified by a congressional or judicial balancing process....

To apply the Court's balancing test under such circumstances is to read the First Amendment to say "Congress shall pass no law abridging freedom of speech, press, assembly and petition unless Congress and the Supreme Court reach the joint conclusion that on balance the interest of the Government in stifling these freedoms is greater than the interest of the people in having them exercised."...

...For no number of laws against communism can have as much effect as the personal conviction which comes from having heard its arguments and

Table 5-13 *(Continued)*

rejected them, or from having once accepted its tenets and later recognized their worthlessness. . . .

Ultimately all the questions in this case really boil down to one—whether we as a people will try fearfully and futilely to preserve democracy by adopting totalitarian methods, or whether in accordance with our traditions and our Constitution we will have the confidence and courage to be free.

Hugo L. Black, dissenting, *Barenblatt v. United States*, 360 U.S. 109 (1959), at 141, 143-144, 162

Bill of Rights, criteria governing applicability to the states

The Commonwealth of Massachusetts is free to regulate the procedure of its courts in accordance with its own conception of policy and fairness unless in doing so it offends some principle of justice so rooted in the traditions and conscience of our people as to be ranked as fundamental.

Benjamin N. Cardozo, for the Court, *Snyder v. Massachusetts*, 291 U.S. 97 (1934), at 105

. . . of the very essence of a scheme of ordered liberty.

Benjamin N. Cardozo, for the Court, *Palko v. Connecticut*, 302 U.S. 319 (1937), at 325

. . . the proceedings by which this conviction was obtained do more than offend some fastidious squeamishness or private sentimentalism about combatting crime too energetically. This is conduct that shocks the conscience.

Felix Frankfurter, for the Court, *Rochin v. California*, 342 U.S. 165 (1952), at 172

Bill of Rights, purpose of

The very purpose of a Bill of rights was to withdraw certain subjects from the vicissitudes of political controversy, to place them beyond the reach of majorities and officials and to establish them as legal principles to be applied by the courts. One's right to life, liberty, and property, to free speech, a free press, freedom of worship and assembly, and other fundamental rights may not be submitted to vote; they depend on the outcome of no election.

Robert H. Jackson, for the Court, *West Virginia State Board of Education v. Barnette*, 319 U.S. 624 (1943), at 638

business affected with a public interest

Property does become clothed with a public interest when used in a manner to make it of public consequence, and affect the community at large. When, therefore, one devotes his property to a use in which the public has an interest, he, in effect, grants to the public an interest in that use, and must submit to be controlled by the public for the common good, to the extent of the interest he has thus created.

Morrison R. Waite, for the Court, *Munn v. Illinois*, 94 U.S. 113 (1877), at 126

(Table continues)

Table 5-13   *(Continued)*

---

capital punishment

These death sentences are cruel and unusual in the same way that being struck by lightening is cruel and unusual. For, of all the people convicted of . . . murders . . . many just as reprehensible, the petitioners are among the capriciously selected random handful. . . . I simply conclude that the Eighth and Fouteenth Amendments cannot . . . permit this unique penalty to be so wantonly and freakishly administered.

Potter Stewart, concurring, *Furman v. Georgia,* 408 U.S. 238 (1972), at 309-310

Sixteen years ago, this Court decreed—by a sheer act of will . . . —that the People (as in We, the People) cannot decree the death penalty, absolutely and categorically, for *any* criminal act, even (presumably) genocide; the jury must always be given the option of extending mercy. . . . Today, obscured within the fog of confusion that is our annually improvised . . . "death is different" jurisprudence, the Court strikes a further blow against the People. . . . Not only must mercy be allowed, but now only the merciful may be permitted to sit in judgment. Those who agree with the author of Exodus . . . must be banished from American juries—not because the People have so decreed, but because such jurors do not share the . . . penological preferences of this Court.

Antonin Scalia, dissenting, *Morgan v. Illinois,* 119 L. Ed. 2d 492 (1992), at 517-518

church and state, wall of separation between

Neither a state nor the Federal Government can set up a church. Neither can pass laws which aid one religion, aid all religions, or prefer one religion over another. Neither can force nor influence a person to go to or to remain away from church against his will or force him to profess a belief or disbelief in any religion. No person can be punished for entertaining or professing religious beliefs or disbeliefs, for church attendance or non-attendance. No tax in any amount, large or small, can be levied to support any religious activities or institutions, whatever they may be called, or whatever form they may adopt to teach or practice religion. Neither a state nor the Federal Government can, openly or secretly, participate in the affairs of any religious organizations or groups and vice versa. In the words of Jefferson, the clause against establishment of religion by law was intended to erect "a wall of separation between Church and State."

Hugo L. Black, for the Court, *Everson v. Board of Education,* 330 U.S. 1 (1947), at 15-16

clear and present danger doctrine

The question in every case is whether the words used are used in such circumstances and are of such a nature as to create a clear and present danger that they will bring about the substantive evils that Congress has a right to prevent. It is a question of proximity and degree. When a nation is at war many things that might be said in time of peace are such a hindrance to its effort that their utterance will not be endured so long as men fight, and that no court could regard them as protected by any constitutional right.

Table 5-13 *(Continued)*

Oliver Wendell Holmes, for the Court, *Schenck v. United States*, 249 U.S. 47 (1919), at 52

... the constitutional guarantees of free speech and free press do not permit a State to forbid or prescribe advocacy of the use of force or of law violation except where such advocacy is directed to inciting or producing imminent lawless action and is likely to incite or produce such action.
    per curiam, *Brandenburg v. Ohio*, 395 U.S. 444 (1969), at 447

commander in chief, president as

If a war be made by invasion of a foreign nation, the President is not only authorized but bound to resist force, by force. He does not initiate the war, but is bound to accept the challenge without waiting for any special legislative authority. And whether the hostile party be a foreign invader, or States organized in rebellion, it is none the less a war....
    Robert C. Grier, for the Court, *The Prize Cases*, 2 Black 635 (1863), at 668

commerce, definition of

Commerce, undoubtedly, is traffic, but it is something more; it is intercourse. It describes the commercial intercourse between nations, and parts of nations, in all its branches, and is regulated by prescribing rules for carrying on that intercourse.
    John Marshall, for the Court, *Gibbons v. Ogden*, 9 Wheat. 1 (1824), at 189-190

commercial speech

The level of discourse reaching a mailbox simply cannot be limited to that which would be suitable for a sandbox.
    Thurgood Marshall, for the Court, *Bolger v. Youngs Drug Products Corp.*, 463 U.S. 60 (1983), at 74

common law

The common law is not a brooding omnipresence in the sky, but the articulate voice of some sovereign or quasi sovereign that can be identified.
    Oliver Wendell Holmes, dissenting, *Southern Pacific Co. v. Jensen*, 244 U.S. 205 (1917), at 222

common law, federal

Except in matters governed by the Federal Constitution or by Acts of Congress, the law to be applied in any case is the law of the State. And whether the law of the State shall be declared by its Legislature in a statute or by its highest court in a decision is not a matter of federal concern. There is no federal general common law.

(Table continues)

Table 5-13 *(Continued)*

Louis D. Brandeis, for the Court, *Erie R. Co. v. Tompkins,* 304 U.S. 62 (1938), at 78

Communist Party, members of

... they are miserable merchants of unwanted ideas; their wares remain unsold. The fact that their ideas are abhorrent does not make them powerful.
William O. Douglas, dissenting, *Dennis v. United States,* 341 U.S. 494 (1951), at 589

The Constitution

There is no war between the Constitution and common sense.
Tom Clark, for the Court, *Mapp v. Ohio,* 367 U.S. 643 (1961), at 657

constitutional gloss

The Court is forever adding new stories to the temples of constitutional law, and the temples have a way of collapsing when one story too many is added.
Robert H. Jackson, concurring in the result, *Douglas v. Jeannette,* 319 U.S. 157 (1943), at 181

contraception

Since 1879, Connecticut has had on its books a law which forbids the use of contraceptives by anyone. I think this is an uncommonly silly law.
Potter Stewart, dissenting, *Griswold v. Connecticut,* 381 U.S. 479 (1965), at 527

contract, freedom of

The liberty mentioned in [the Fourteenth A]mendment ... is deemed to embrace the right of the citizen to be free in the enjoyment of all his faculties; to be free to use them in all lawful ways; to live and work where he will; to earn his livelihood by any lawful calling; to pursue any livelihood or avocation; and for that purpose to enter into all contracts which may be proper, necessary, and essential to his carrying out to a successful conclusion the purposes above mentioned.
Rufus W. Peckham, for the Court, *Allgeyer v. Louisiana,* 165 U.S. 578 (1897), at 589

It might safely be affirmed that almost all occupations more or less affect the health.... But are we all, on that account, at the mercy of legislative majorities?
... The act is ... but ... an illegal interference with the rights of individuals, both employers and employees, to make contracts regarding labor upon such terms as they may think best.... Statutes of the nature of that under review, limiting the hours in which grown and intelligent men may labor to earn their living, are mere meddlesome interferences with the rights of the individual....
Rufus W. Peckham, for the Court, *Lochner v. New York,* 198 U.S. 45 (1905), at 59, 61.

Table 5-13   *(Continued)*

What is this freedom? The Constitution does not speak of freedom of contract. It speaks of liberty and prohibits the deprivation of liberty without due process of law. In prohibiting that deprivation the Constitution does not recognize an absolute and uncontrollable liberty.... Liberty under the Constitution is thus necessarily subject to the restraints of due process, and regulation which is reasonable in relation to its subject and is adopted in the interests of the community is due process.

Charles Evans Hughes, for the Court, *West Coast Hotel Co. v. Parrish*, 300 U.S. 379 (1937), at 391

counsel, right to

The right to be heard would be, in many cases, of little avail if it did not comprehend the right to be heard by counsel. Even the intelligent and educated layman has small and sometimes no skill in the science of the law.... He requires the guiding hand of counsel at every step in the proceedings against him. Without it, though he be not guilty, he faces the danger of conviction because he does not know how to establish his innocence.

George Sutherland, for the Court, *Norris v. Alabama*, 287 U.S. 45 (1932), at 68-69

... reason and reflection require us to recognize that in our adversary system of criminal justice, any person haled into court, who is too poor to hire a lawyer, cannot be assured a fair trial unless counsel is provided for him.... That government hires lawyers to prosecute and defendants who have money hire lawyers to defend are the strongest indications of the widespread belief that lawyers in criminal courts are necessities, not luxuries. The right of one charged with a crime to counsel may not be deemed fundamental and essential to fair trials in some countries, but it is in ours.

Hugo L. Black, for the Court, *Gideon v. Wainwright*, 372 U.S. 335 (1963), at 344

debate on public issues

... debate on public issues should be uninhibited, robust, and wide-open, and that it may well include vehement, caustic, and sometimes unpleasantly sharp attacks on government and public officials.

William J. Brennan, Jr., for the Court, *New York Times Co. v. Sullivan*, 376 U.S. 254 (1964), at 270

die, right to

It cannot be disputed that the Due Process Clause protects an interest in life as well as an interest in refusing life-sustaining medical treatment.

William H. Rehnquist, for the Court, *Cruzan v. Director, Missouri Health Department*, 111 L. Ed. 2d 224 (1990), at 243

(Table continues)

Table 5-13   *(Continued)*

---

disclosure of news sources

. . . we cannot seriously entertain the notion that the First Amendment protects a newsman's agreement to conceal the criminal conduct of his source, or evidence thereof, on the theory that it is better to write about crime than to do something about it.
    Byron R. White, for the Court, *Branzburg v. Hayes,* 408 U.S. 665 (1972), at 692

dissent

Dissent is essential to an effective judiciary in a democratic society, and especially for a tribunal exercising the powers of this Court.
    Felix Frankfurter, dissenting, *Ferguson v. Moore McCormack Lines,* 352 U.S. 521 (1957), at 528

eavesdropping

The price of lawful public dissent must not be a dread of subjection to an unchecked surveillance power. Nor must the fear of unauthorized official eavesdropping deter vigorous citizen dissent and discussion of Government action in private conversation. For private dissent, no less than open public discourse, is essential to our free society.
    Lewis F. Powell, Jr., for the Court, *United States v. United States District Court,* 407 U.S. 297 (1972), at 314

emergency

While emergency does not create power, emergency may furnish the occasion for the exercise of power.
    Charles Evans Hughes, for the Court, *Home Building & Loan Assn. v. Blaisdell,* 290 U.S. 398 (1934), at 426

equal protection, violation of

In the area of economics and social welfare, a State does not violate the Equal Protection Clause merely because the classifications made by its laws are imperfect. If the classification has some "reasonable basis," it does not offend the Constitution simply because the classification "is not made with mathematical nicety or because in practice it results in some inequality."
    Potter Stewart, for the Court, *Dandridge v. Williams,* 397 U.S. 471 (1970), at 485

establishment of religion

Every analysis in this area must begin with consideration of the cumulative criteria developed by the Court over many years. Three such tests may be gleaned from our cases. First, the statute must have a secular legislative purpose; second, its principal or primary effect must be one that neither advances nor inhibits religion; finally, the statute must not foster "an excessive government entanglement with religion."

Table 5-13 *(Continued)*

Warren Burger, for the Court, *Lemon v. Kurtzman,* 403 U.S. 602 (1971), at 612-613.

exclusionary rule

. . . our holding that the exclusionary rule is an essential part of both the Fourth and the Fourteenth Amendments is not only the logical dictate of prior cases, but it also makes very good sense. . . . Presently, a federal prosecutor may make no use of evidence illegally seized, but a State's attorney across the street may, although he is operating under the enforcement prohibitions of the same Amendment. Thus, the State, by admitting evidence unlawfully seized, serves to encourage disobedience to the Federal Constitution which it is bound to uphold.

Tom C. Clark, for the Court, *Mapp v. Ohio,* 367 U.S. 643 (1961), at 657

extraordinary conditions, constitutional power over

Extraordinary conditions do not create or enlarge constitutional power.

Charles Evan Hughes, for the Court, *Schechter Poultry v. United States,* 295 U.S. 495 (1935), at 528

federalism

It is one of the happy incidents of the federal system that a single courageous State may, if its citizens choose, serve as a laboratory; and try novel social and economic experiments without risk to the rest of the country.

Louis D. Brandeis, dissenting, *New State Ice Co. v. Liebmann,* 285 U.S. 262 (1932), at 311

The [Tenth] amendment states but a truism that all is retained which has not been surrendered. There is nothing in the history of its adoption to suggest that it was more than declaratory of the relationship between the national and state governments as it had been established by the Constitution before the amendment or that its purpose was other than to allay fears that the new national government might seek to exercise powers not granted, and that the states might not be able to exercise fully their reserved powers.

Harlan Fiske Stone, for the Court, *United States v. Darby,* 312 U.S. 100 (1941), at 124

It is illuminating for purposes of reflection, if not for argument, to note that one of the greatest "fictions" of our federal system is that the Congress exercises only those powers delegated to it, while the remainder are reserved to the States or to the people.

William Rehnquist, concurring, *Hodel v. Virginia Surface Mining and Reclamation Association,* 452 U.S. 264 (1981), at 307

fighting words

There are certain well-defined and narrowly limited classes of speech, the

(Table continues)

Table 5-13   *(Continued)*

prevention and punishment of which have never been thought to raise any Constitutional problem. These include . . . "fighting" words—those which by their very utterance inflict injury or tend to incite an immediate breach of the peace.

Frank Murphy, for the Court, in *Chaplinsky v. New Hampshire*, 315 U.S. 568 (1942), at 571-572

First Amendment

If the First Amendment means anything, it means that a State has no business telling a man, sitting alone in his own house, what books he may read or what films he may watch.

Thurgood Marshall, for the Court, *Stanley v. Georgia*, 394 U.S. 557 (1969), at 565

First Amendment, principle underlying

If there is a bedrock principle underlying the First Amendment, it is that the Government may not prohibit the expression of an idea simply because society finds the idea itself offensive or disagreeable.

William J. Brennan, Jr., for the Court, *Texas v. Johnson*, 491 U.S. 397 (1989), at 414

foreign affairs, conduct of

. . . the President . . . [is] the sole organ of the Federal government in the field of international relations—a power which does not require as a basis for its exercise an act of Congress, but which, of course, like every other governmental power, must be exercised in subordination to the applicable provisions of the Constitution.

George Sutherland, for the Court, *United States v. Curtiss-Wright Export Corp.*, 299 U.S. 304 (1936), at 320

Fourteenth Amendment and Substantive Due Process

The Fourteenth Amendment does not enact Mr. Herbert Spencer's *Social Statics.*

Oliver Wendell Holmes, dissenting, *Lochner v. New York*, 198 U.S. 45 (1905) at 75

fundamental rights, freedom of speech and press as

. . . freedom of speech and of the press—which are protected by the 1st Amendment from abridgment by Congress—are among the fundamental rights and "liberties" protected by the due process clause of the 14th Amendment from impairment by the States.

Edward Terry Sanford, for the Court, *Gitlow v. New York*, 268 U.S. 652 (1925), at 666

Table 5-13   *(Continued)*

---

great cases and bad law

Great cases, like hard cases, make bad law. For great cases are called great, not by reason of the real importance in shaping the law of the future, but because of some accident of immediate overwhelming interest which appeals to the feelings and distorts the judgment. These immediate interests exercise a kind of hydraulic pressure which makes what previously was clear seem doubtful, and before which even well settled principles of law will bend.

Oliver Wendell Holmes, dissenting, *Northern Security Co. v. United States,* 193 U.S. 197 (1904), at 400-401

ideas, free trade in

Persecution for the expression of opinions seems to me perfectly logical. If you have no doubt of your premises or your power and want a certain result with all your heart you naturally express your wishes in law and sweep away all opposition. To allow opposition by speech seems to indicate that you think the speech impotent, as when a man says that he has squared the circle.... But when men have realized that time has upset many fighting faiths, they may come to believe even more than they believe the foundations of their own conduct that the ultimate good desired is better reached by free trade in ideas,— that the best test of truth is the power of the thought to get itself accepted in the competition of the market; and that truth is the only ground upon which their wishes safely can be carried out. That, at any rate, is the theory of our Constitution. It is an experiment, as all life is an experiment. Every year, if not every day, we have to wager our salvation upon some prophecy based upon imperfect knowledge. While that experiment is part of our system I think that we should be eternally vigilant against attempts to check the expression of opinions that we loathe and believe to be fraught with death, unless they so imminently threaten interference with the lawful and pressing purposes of the law that an immediate check is required to save the country.

Oliver Wendell Holmes, dissenting, *Abrams v. United States,* 250 U.S. 616 (1919), at 630

implied powers

We admit, as all must admit, that the powers of the government are limited, and that its limits are not to be transcended. But we think the sound construction of the constitution must allow to the national legislature that discretion, with respect to the means by which the powers it confers are to be carried into execution, which will enable that body to perform the high duties assigned to it, in the manner most beneficial to the people. Let the end be legitimate, let it be within the scope of the constitution, and all means which are appropriate, which are plainly adapted to that end, which are not prohibited, but consist with the letter and spirit of the constitution, are constitutional.

John Marshall, for the Court, *McCulloch v. Maryland,* 4 Wheat. 316 (1819), at 421

(Table continues)

Table 5-13   *(Continued)*

... we must never forget it is a constitution we are expounding.... a constitution intended to endure for ages to come, and, consequently, to be adapted to the various crises of human affairs.

John Marshall, for the Court, *McCulloch v. Maryland*, 4 Wheat. 316 (1819), at 407, 415

intent, legislative

Just what our forefathers did envision, or would have envisioned had they foreseen modern conditions must be divined from materials almost as enigmatic as the dreams Joseph was called upon to interpret for Pharoah. A century and half of partisan debate and scholarly specification yields no net result but only supplies more or less apt quotations from respected sources on each side of any question. They largely cancel each other.

Robert H. Jackson, concurring, *Youngstown Sheet and Tube Co. v. Sawyer*, 343 U.S. 579 (1952), at 634-635

The number of possible motivations, to begin with, is not binary, or indeed even finite. In the present case, for example, a particular legislator need not have voted for the Act either because he wanted to foster religion or because he wanted to improve education. He may have thought the bill would provide jobs for his district, or may have wanted to make amends with a faction of his party he had alienated on another vote, or he may have been a close friend of the bill's sponsor, or he may have been repaying a favor he owed the Majority Leader, or he may have hoped the Governor would appreciate his vote and make a fundraising appearance for him, or he may have been pressured to vote for a bill he disliked by a wealthy contributor or a flood of constituent mail, or he may have been seeking favorable publicity, or he may have been reluctant to hurt the feelings of a loyal staff member who worked on the bill, or he may have been mad at his wife who opposed the bill, or he may have been intoxicated and entirely unmotivated when the vote was called, or he may have accidentally voted "yes" instead of "no," or, of course, he may have had (and very likely did have) a combination of some of the above and many other motivations. To look for the sole purpose of even a single legislator is probably to look for something that does not exist.

Putting that problem aside, however, where ought we to look for the individual legislator's purpose? We cannot ... assume that every member present ... agreed with the motivation expressed in a particular legislator's pre-enactment floor or committee statement.... Can we assume ... that they all agree with the motivation expressed in the staff-prepared committee reports ... [or] post-enactment floor statements? Or post-enactment testimony from legislators, obtained expressly for the lawsuit? ... media reports on ... legislative bargaining? All these sources, of course, are eminently manipulable.

... If a state senate approves a bill by a vote of 26 to 25, and only one intended solely to advance religion, is the law unconstitutional? What if 13 of 26 had that intent? What if 3 of the 26 had the impermissible intent, but 3 of the 25 voting against the bill were motivated by religious hostility or were simply attempting to "balance" the votes of their impermissibly motivated colleagues? Or is it possible that the intent of the bill's sponsor is alone enough to invalidate it—on a theory, perhaps, that even though everyone else's intent was pure, what

Table 5-13   *(Continued)*

they produced was the fruit of a forbidden tree.
Antonin Scalia, dissenting, *Edwards v. Aguillard,* 482 U.S. 578 (1987), at 636-638

interrogation versus investigation

... interrogation under Miranda refers not only to express questioning, but also to any words or actions on the part of the police (other than those normally attendant to arrest and custody) that the police should know are reasonably likely to elicit an incriminating response from the suspect.... A practice that the police should know is reasonably likely to evoke an incriminating response from a suspect amounts to interrogation.
Potter Stewart, *Rhode Island v. Innis,* 446 U.S. 291 (1980), at 301

investigation, congressional

There is no general authority to expose the private affairs of individuals without justification in terms of the functions of the Congress.... No inquiry is an end in itself; it must be related to, and in furtherance of, a legitimate task of the Congress. Investigations conducted solely for the personal aggrandizement of the investigators or to "punish" those investigated are indefensible.
Earl Warren, for the Court, *Watkins v. United States,* 354 U.S. 178 (1957), at 187

judicial policy making

The Court is most vulnerable and comes nearest to illegitimacy when it deals with judge-made constitutional law having little or no cognizable roots in the language or design of the Constitution.
Byron R. White, for the Court, *Bowers v. Hardwick,* 478 U.S. 186 (1986), at 194

I am not so naive (nor do I think our forbears were) as to be unaware that judges in a real sense "make" law. But they make it *as judges make it,* which is to say *as though* they were "finding" it—discerning what the law is, rather than decreeing what it is today *changed to,* or what it will *tomorrow* be.
Antonin Scalia, concurring in the judgment, *James M. Beam Distilling Co. v. Georgia,* 115 L. Ed. 2d 481 (1991), at 497

... even though the Justice is not naive enough (nor does he think the Framers were naive enough) to be unaware that judges in a real sense "make" law, he suggests that judges (in an unreal sense, I suppose) should never concede that they do and must claim that they do no more than discover it, hence suggesting that there are citizens naive enough to believe them.
Byron R. White, concurring in the judgment, *James M. Beam Distilling Co. v. Georgia,* 115 L. Ed. 2d 481 (1991), at 495

(Table continues)

Table 5-13   *(Continued)*

---

judicial power

It is emphatically the province and duty of the judicial department to say what the law is.

John Marshall, for the Court, *Marbury v. Madison,* 1 Cranch 137 (1803), at 177

Judicial power, as contradistinguished from the power of the laws, has no existence. Courts are the mere instruments of the law, and can will nothing. When they are said to exercise a discretion, it is a mere legal discretion, a discretion to be exercised in discerning the course prescribed by law; and, when that is discerned, it is the duty of the court to follow it. Judicial power is never exercised for the purpose of giving effect to the will of the judge; always for the purpose of giving effect to the will of the legislature. . . .

John Marshall, for the Court, *Osborn v. Bank of the United States,* 9 Wheat. 738 (1824), at 866

. . . the only check upon our own exercise of power is our own sense of self-restraint. For the removal of unwise laws from the statute books appeal lies not to the courts but to the ballot and the processes of democratic government.

Harlan Fiske Stone, dissenting, *United States v. Butler,* 297 U.S. 1 (1936), at 79

. . . the interpretation of the Fourteenth Amendment enunciated by this Court . . . is the supreme law of the land, and Art. VI of the Constitution makes it of binding effect on the States any Thing in the Constitution or Laws of any State to the Contrary notwithstanding.

per curiam, *Cooper v. Aaron,* 358 U.S. 1 (1958), at 18

judicial restraint

. . . a Constitution is not intended to embody a particular economic theory, whether of paternalism and the organic relation of the citizen to the state or of *laissez faire.* It is made for people of fundamentally differing views, and the accident of our finding certain opinions natural and familiar, or novel, and even shocking, ought not to conclude our judgment upon the question whether statutes embodying them conflict with the Constitution of the United States.

General propositions do not decide concrete cases. The decision will depend on a judgment or intuition more subtle than any articulate major premise. But I think that the proposition just stated, if it is accepted, will carry us far toward the end. Every opinion tends to become a law. I think that the word "liberty" in the Fourteenth Amendment is perverted when it is held to prevent the natural outcome of a dominant opinion, unless it can be said that a rational and fair man necessarily would admit that the statute proposed would infringe fundamental principles as they have been understood by the traditions of our people and our law.

Oliver Wendell Holmes, dissenting, *Lochner v. New York,* 198 U.S. 45 (1905), at 75-76

One who belongs to the most vilified and persecuted minority in history is not likely to be insensible to the freedoms guaranteed by our Constitution. Were my purely personal attitude relevant I should wholeheartedly associate myself

Table 5-13   *(Continued)*

with the general libertarian views in the Court's opinion, representing as they do the thought and action of a lifetime. But as judges we are neither Jew nor Gentile, neither Catholic nor agnostic. We owe equal attachment to the Constitution and are equally bound by our judicial obligations whether we derive our citizenship for the earliest or the latest immigrants to these shores.

Felix Frankfurter, dissenting, *West Virginia v. Barnette*, 319 U.S. 624 (1943), at 646-647

The Court's authority—possessed of neither the purse nor the sword—ultimately rests on sustained public confidence in its moral sanction. Such feeling must be nourished by the Court's complete detachment, in fact and in appearance, from political entanglements and by abstention from injecting itself into the clash of political forces in political settlements.

Felix Frankfurter, dissenting, *Baker v. Carr*, 369 U.S. 186 (1962), at 267

judicial review

It is a proposition too plain to be contested, that the constitution controls any legislative act repugnant to it; or, that the legislature may alter the constitution by an ordinary act.

John Marshall, for the Court, *Marbury v. Madison*, 1 Cranch 137 (1803), at 177

To hold a governmental act to be unconstitutional is not to announce that we forbid it, but that the *Constitution* forbids it. . . .

Antonin Scalia, concurring in the result, *American Trucking Assns. v. Smith*, 110 L. Ed. 2d 148 (1990), at 174

judicial review, exercise of

When an act of Congress is appropriately challenged in the courts as not conforming to the constitutional mandate, the judicial branch of government has only one duty,—to lay the article of the Constitution which is invoked beside the statute which is challenged and to decide whether the latter squares with the former. All the Court does, or can do, is to announce its considered judgment upon the question. The only power it has, if such it may be called, is the power of judgment. The court neither approves nor condemns any legislative policy. Its delicate and difficult office is to ascertain and declare whether the legislation is in accordance with, or in contravention of, the provisions of the Constitution; and, having done that, its duty ends.

Owen J. Roberts, for the Court, *United States v. Butler*, 297 U.S. 1 (1936), at 62-63

jurisdiction

Without jurisdiction the court cannot proceed at all in any cause. Jurisdiction is power to declare the law, and when it ceases to exist, the only function remaining to the court is that of announcing the fact and dismissing the cause. And this is not less clear upon authority than upon principle.

(Table continues)

Table 5-13 *(Continued)*

Salmon P. Chase, for the Court, *Ex parte McCardle*, 7 Wall. 506 (1869), at 514

laws, faithful execution of

To contend that the obligation imposed on the President to see the laws faithfully executed implies a power to forbid their execution, is a novel construction of the Constitution, and entirely inadmissible.

Smith Thompson, for the Court, *Kendall v. United States*, 12 Pet. 524 (1838), at 613

left alone, right to be

The makers of our Constitution undertook to secure conditions favorable to the pursuit of happiness. They recognized the significance of man's spiritual nature, of his feelings and of his intellect. They knew that only a part of the pain, pleasure and satisfactions of life are to be found in material things. They sought to protect Americans in their beliefs, their thoughts, their emotions and their sensations. They conferred, as against the government, the right to be let alone—the most comprehensive of rights and the right most valued by civilized men.

Louis D. Brandeis, dissenting, *Olmstead v. United States*, 277 U.S. 438 (1928), at 478

letter of the law

It is a familiar rule that a thing may be within the letter of the statute and yet not within the statute, because not within its spirit, nor within the intention of its makers.

David J. Brewer, for the Court, *Holy Trinity Church v. United States*, 143 U.S. 457 (1892), at 459

libel

The constitutional guarantees require, we think, a federal rule that prohibits a public official from recovering damages for a defamatory falsehood relating to his conduct unless he proves that the statement was made with "actual malice"—that is, with knowledge that it was false or with reckless disregard of whether it was false or not.

William J. Brennan, Jr., for the Court, *New York Times v. Sullivan*, 376 U.S. 254 (1964), at 279-280

liberty, protection of

Experience should teach us to be most on our guard to protect liberty when the government's purposes are beneficent. Men born to freedom are naturally alert to repel invasion of their liberty by evil-minded rulers. The greatest dangers to liberty lurk in the insidious encroachment by men of zeal, well-meaning, but without understanding.

Louis D. Brandeis, dissenting, *Olmstead v. United States*, 277 U.S. 438 (1928), at 479

Table 5-13 *(Continued)*

liberty versus property

. . . the dichotomy between personal liberty and property rights is a false one. Property does not have rights. People have rights. The right to enjoy property without unlawful deprivation, no less than the right to travel, is, in truth, a personal right. In fact, a fundamental interdependence exists between the right to liberty and the personal right to property. Neither can have meaning without the other.

Potter Stewart, for the Court, *Lynch v. Household Finance Co.*, 405 U.S. 538 (1972), at 552

marriage

We deal with a right of privacy older than the Bill of Rights—older than our political parties, older than our school system. Marriage is a coming together for better or for worse, hopefully enduring, and intimate to the degree of being sacred. It is an association that promotes a way of life, not causes; a harmony in living, not political faiths; a bilateral loyalty, not commercial or social projects. Yet it is an association for as noble a purpose as any involved in our prior decisions.

William O. Douglas, for the Court, *Griswold v. Connecticut*, 381 U.S. 479 (1965), at 486

martial law

Martial law cannot arise from a threatened invasion. The necessity must be actual and present; the invasion real, such as effectually closes the courts and deposes the civil administration.

David Davis, for the Court, *Ex parte Milligan*, 4 Wall. 2 (1866), at 127

military necessity

It is said that we are dealing here with the case of imprisonment of a citizen in a concentration camp solely because of his ancestry, without evidence or inquiry concerning his loyalty and good disposition towards the United States. . . . To cast this case into outlines of racial prejudice, without reference to the real military dangers which were presented, merely confuses the issue. Korematsu was not excluded because of hostility to him or his race. He *was* excluded because we are at war with the Japanese Empire, because the properly constituted military authorities feared an invasion of our West Coast and felt constrained to take proper security measures. . . .

Hugo L. Black, for the Court, *Korematsu v. United States*, 323 U.S. 214 (1944), at 223

This exclusion of "all persons of Japanese ancestry, both alien and non-alien," from the Pacific Coast area on a plea of military necessity in the absence of martial law . . . goes over "the very brink of constitutional power" and falls into the ugly abyss of racism.

Frank Murphy, dissenting, *Korematsu v. United States*, 323 U.S. 214 (1944), at 233

(Table continues)

Table 5-13   *(Continued)*

... [This] is the case of convicting a citizen as a punishment for not submitting to imprisonment in a concentration camp, based on his ancestry, and solely because of his ancestry....

Owen J. Roberts, dissenting, *Korematsu v. United States,* 323 U.S. 214 (1944), at 226

... if any fundamental assumption underlies our system, it is that guilt is personal and not inheritable.... But here is an attempt to make an otherwise innocent act a crime merely because this prisoner is the son of parents as to whom he had no choice, and belongs to a race from which there is no way to resign....

But if we cannot confine military expedients by the Constitution, neither would I distort the Constitution to approve all that the military may deem expedient.

Robert H. Jackson, dissenting, *Korematsu v. United States,* 323 U.S. 214 (1944), at 243-245

minority groups

Groups which find themselves unable to achieve their objectives through the ballot frequently turn to the courts. Just as it was true of the opponents of New Deal legislation during the 1930s, for example, no less is it true of the Negro minority today. And, under the conditions of modern government, litigation may well be the sole practicable avenue open to a minority to petition for redress of grievances.

William J. Brennan, Jr., for the Court, *NAACP v. Button,* 371 U.S. 415 (1963), at 429-430

Miranda warnings

... we hold that when an individual is taken into custody or otherwise deprived of his freedom by the authorities in any significant way and is subject to questioning, the privilege against self-incrimination is jeopardized. Procedural safeguards must be employed to protect the privilege, and unless other fully effective means are adopted to notify the person of his right of silence and to assure that the exercise of the right will be scrupulously honored, the following measures are required. He must be warned prior to any questioning that he has the right to remain silent, that anything he says can be used against him in a court of law, that he has the right to the presence of an attorney, and that if he cannot afford an attorney one will be appointed for him prior to any questioning if he so desires. Opportunity to exercise these rights must be afforded to him throughout the interrogation. After such warnings have been given, and such opportunity afforded him, the individual may knowingly and intelligently waive these rights and agree to answer questions or make a statement. But unless and until such warnings and waiver are demonstrated by the prosecution at trial, no evidence obtained as a result of interrogation can be used against him.

Earl Warren, for the Court, *Miranda v. Arizona,* 384 U.S. 436 (1966), at 478-479

Table 5-13   *(Continued)*

miscegenation

The Fourteenth Amendment requires that the freedom of choice to marry not be restricted by invidious racial discrimination. Under our Constitution, the freedom to marry, or not to marry, a person of another race resides with the individual and cannot be infringed by the State.
Earl Warren, for the Court, *Loving v. Virginia,* 388 U.S. 1 (1967) at 12

national supremacy

Judges of equal learning and integrity, in different states, might differently interpret a statute, or a treaty of the United States, or even the constitution itself. If there were no revising authority to control these jarring and discordant judgments, and harmonize them into uniformity, the laws, the treaties, the constitution of the United States would be different in different states, and might, perhaps, never have ... the same construction, obligation, or efficacy, in any two states. The public mischiefs that would attend such a state of things would be truly deplorable ... the appellate jurisdiction must continue to be the only adequate remedy for such evils.
John Marshall, for the Court, *Martin v. Hunter's Lessee,* 1 Wheat. 304 (1816), at 348

one person, one vote

... the command of Art. I, Sec. 2, that Representatives be chosen "by the People of the several States" means that as nearly as is practicable one man's vote in a congressional election is to be worth as much as another's.
Hugo L. Black, for the Court, *Wesberry v. Sanders,* 376 U.S. 1 (1964), at 7-8

political patronage

Today the Court establishes the constitutional principle that party membership is not a permissible factor in the dispensation of government jobs, except those jobs for the performance of which party affiliation is an "appropriate requirement." ... if there is any category of jobs for whose performance party affiliation is not an appropriate requirement, it is the job of being a judge, where partisanship is not only unneeded but positively undesirable. It is, however, rare that a federal administration of one party will appoint a judge from another party. And it has always been so. See Marbury v. Madison .... Thus, the new principle that the Court today announces will be enforced by a corps of judges (the members of this Court included) who overwhelmingly owe their office to its violation. Something must be wrong here, and I suggest it is the Court.
Antonin Scalia, dissenting, *Rutan v. Republican Party of Illinois,* 111 L. Ed. 2d 52 (1990), at 78

political questions

Prominent on the surface ... is found a textually demonstrable constitutional

(Table continues)

Table 5-13   *(Continued)*

commitment of the issue to a coordinate political department; or a lack of judicially discoverable and manageable standards for resolving it; or the impossibility of deciding without an initial policy determination of a kind clearly for nonjudicial discretion; or the impossibility of a court's undertaking independent resolution without expressing lack of the respect due coordinate branches of government; or an unusual need for unquestioning adherence to a political decision already made; or the potentiality of embarrassment from multifarious pronouncements by various departments on one question.

William J. Brennan, Jr., for the Court, *Baker v. Carr*, 369 U.S. 186 (1962), at 217

political speech

... the opportunity for free political discussion to the end that government may be responsive to the will of the people and that changes may be obtained by lawful means, an opportunity essential to the security of the Republic, is a fundamental principle of our constitutional system.

Charles Evans Hughes, for the Court, *Stromberg v. California*, 283 U.S. 359 (1931), at 369

pornography

... hard-core pornography. I shall not ... attempt ... to define the kinds of material I understand to be embraced within that shorthand description; and perhaps I could never succeed in intelligibly doing so. But I know it when I see it....

Potter Stewart, concurring, *Jacobellis v. Ohio*, 378 U.S. 184 (1964), at 197

prayer

... it is no part of the business of government to compose official prayers for any group of the American people to recite as part of a religious program carried on by government.

Hugo L. Black, for the Court, *Engel v. Vitale*, 370 U.S. 421 (1962), at 425

precedent, adherence to

If there is any inconsistency or illogic in all this, it is an inconsistency and illogic of long standing that is to be remedied by the Congress and not by this Court.... there is merit in consistency even though some might claim that beneath that consistency is a layer of inconsistency.

Harry A. Blackmun, for the Court, *Flood v. Kuhn*, 407 U.S. 258 (1972), at 284

Adherence to precedent is, in the usual case, a cardinal and guiding principal of adjudication, and "[c]onsiderations of stare decisis have special force in the area of statutory interpretation, for here, unlike in the context of constitutional interpretation, the legislative power is implicated, and Congress remains free to alter what we have done."

Sandra Day O'Connor, for the Court, *California v. Federal Energy Regulatory Commission*, 109 L. Ed. 2d 474 (1990), at 486

Table 5-13   *(Continued)*

---

preferred freedoms doctrine

There may be narrower scope for operation of the presumption of constitutionality when legislation appears on its face to be within a specific prohibition of the Constitution, such as those of the first ten amendments, which are deemed equally specific when held to be embraced within the Fourteenth. . . .

It is unnecessary to consider now whether legislation which restricts those political processes which can ordinarily be expected to bring about repeal of undesirable legislation, is to be subjected to more exacting judicial scrutiny under the general prohibitions of the Fourteenth Amendment than are most other types of legislation. . . .

Nor need we enquire whether similar considerations enter into the review of statutes directed at particular religions or racial minorities: whether prejudice against discrete and insular minorities may be a special condition, which tends seriously to curtail the operations of those political processes ordinarily to be relied upon to protect minorities, and which may call for a correspondingly more searching judicial inquiry.

Harlan Fiske Stone, for the Court, *United States v. Carolene Products Co.,* 304 U.S. 144 (1938), at 152-153, note 4

preferred precedents doctrine

Considerations in favor of stare decisis are at their acme in cases involving property and contract rights, where reliance interests are involved . . . the opposite is true in cases . . . involving procedural and evidentiary rules.

William H. Rehnquist, for the Court, *Payne v. Tennessee,* 115 L. Ed. 2d 720 (1991), at 737

principle, qualification of

. . . we learned long ago that broad statements of principle, no matter how correct in the context in which they are made, are sometimes qualified by contrary decisions before the absolute limit of the stated principle is reached.

John Paul Stevens, for the Court, *Young v. American Mini Theatres, Inc.,* 427 U.S. 50 (1976), at 65

privacy

. . . specific guarantees in the Bill of Rights have penumbras, formed by emanations from those guarantees that help give them life and substance. . . . Various guarantees create zones of privacy.

William O. Douglas, for the Court, *Griswold v. Connecticut,* 381 U.S. 479 (1965), at 484

It would betray our whole plan for a tranquil and orderly society to say that a citizen, because of his personal prejudices, habits, attitudes, or beliefs, is cast outside the law's protection and cannot call for the aid of officers sworn to uphold the law and preserve the peace. The worst citizen no less than the best is

(Table continues)

Table 5-13 *(Continued)*

---

entitled to equal protection of the laws of his State and of his Nation.
　　　Hugo L. Black, dissenting, *Bell v. Maryland*, 378 U.S. 226 (1964), at 327-328

... the Fourth Amendment protects people, not places. What a person knowingly exposes to the public, even in his own home or office, is not a subject of Fourth Amendment protection.... But what he seeks to preserve as private, even if an area accessible to the public, may be constitutionally protected.
　　　Potter Stewart, for the Court, *Katz v. United States*, 389 U.S. 347 (1967), at 351-352

probable cause

In dealing with probable cause ... as the very name implies, we deal with probabilities. These are not technical; they are the factual and practical considerations of every day life on which reasonable and prudent men, not legal technicians, act.
　　　Wiley Rutledge, for the Court, *Brinegar v. United States*, 338 U.S. 160 (1949), at 175

religious people, Americans as

　　　We are a religious people whose institutions presuppose a Supreme Being.
　　　William O. Douglas, for the Court, *Zorach v. Clauson*, 343 U.S. 306 (1952), at 313

rights of students and teachers, First Amendment

　　　First Amendment rights, applied in the light of the special characteristics of the school environment, are available to teachers and students. It can hardly be argued that either students or teachers shed their constitutional rights to freedom of speech or expression at the schoolhouse gate.
　　　Abe Fortas, for the Court, *Tinker v. Des Moines Independent School District*, 393 U.S. 503 (1969), at 506

role of the Court

It is the province of a court to expound the law, not to make it.
　　　Roger B. Taney, for the Court, *Luther v. Borden*, 7 How. 1 (1849), at 41

segregation

　　　We consider the underlying fallacy of the plaintiff's argument to consist in the assumption that the enforced segregation of the two races stamps the colored race with a badge of inferiority. If this be so, it is not by reason of anything found in the act, but solely because the colored race chooses to put that construction on it.
　　　Henry Billings Brown, for the Court, *Plessy v. Ferguson*, 163 U.S. 537 (1896), at 551

Our Constitution is color blind, and neither knows nor tolerates classes among

Table 5-13   *(Continued)*

citizens. In respect of civil rights, all citizens are equal before the law. The humblest is the peer of the most powerful. The law ... takes no account of his surroundings or of his color when his civil rights ... are involved.

... the judgment this day rendered will, in time, prove to be quite as pernicious as the decision made by this tribunal in the *Dred Scott Case*. ... The destinies of the two races in this country are indissolubly linked together, and the interests of both require that the common government of all shall not permit the seeds of race hate to be planted under the sanction of law. What can more certainly arouse race hate, what more certainly create and perpetuate a feeling of distrust between these races, than state enactments which in fact proceed on the ground that colored citizens are so inferior and degraded that they cannot be allowed to sit in public coaches occupied by white citizens?

John Marshall Harlan, dissenting, *Plessy v. Ferguson*, 163 U.S. 537 (1896), at 559-560

We conclude that in the field of public education the doctrine of "separate but equal" has no place. Separate educational facilities are inherently unequal.

Earl Warren, for the Court, *Brown v. Board of Education*, 347 U.S. 483 (1954), at 495

... continued operation of segregated schools under a standard of allowing "all deliberate speed" for desegregation is no longer constitutionally permissible. ... the obligation of every school district is to terminate dual school systems at once and to operate now and hereafter only unitary schools.

per curiam, *Alexander v. Holmes County Board of Education*, 396 U.S. 19 (1969), at 20

self-incrimination

... the American system of criminal prosecution is accusatorial, not inquisitorial, and ... the Fifth Amendment privilege is its essential mainstay.

William J. Brennan, Jr., for the Court, *Malloy v. Hogan*, 378 U.S. 1 (1964), at 7

sex discrimination

Man is, or should be, woman's protector and defender. The natural and proper timidity and delicacy which belongs to the female sex evidently unfits it for many of the occupations of civil life. The constitution of the family organization, which is founded in the divine ordinance, as well as in the nature of things, indicates the domestic sphere as that which properly belongs to the domain and functions of womanhood. The harmony, not to say identity, of interests and views which belong, or should belong, to the family institution, is repugnant to the ideas of a woman adopting a distinct and independent career from that of her husband. ...

... The paramount destiny and mission of woman are to fulfil the noble and benign offices of wife and mother. This is the law of the Creator.

Joseph P. Bradley, concurring in the judgment, *Bradwell v. Illinois*, 16 Wall. 130 (1873), at 141

(Table continues)

Table 5-13   *(Continued)*

Despite the enlightened emancipation of women from the restrictions and protections of bygone years, and their entry into many parts of community life formerly considered to be reserved to men, woman is still regarded as the center of home and family life. We cannot say that it is constitutionally impermissible for a State, acting in pursuit of the general welfare, to conclude that a woman should be relieved from the civic duty of jury service unless she herself determines that such service is consistent with her own special responsibilities.
    John M. Harlan, for the Court, *Hoyt v. Florida*, 368 U.S. 57 (1961), at 61-62.

If it was ever the case that women were unqualified to sit on juries or were so situated that none of them should be required to perform jury service, that time has long since passed.
    Byron R. White, for the Court, *Taylor v. Louisiana*, 419 U.S. 522 (1975), at 537

To withstand constitutional challenge ... classifications by gender must serve important governmental objectives and must be substantially related to achievement of those objectives.
    William J. Brennan, Jr., for the Court, *Craig v. Boren*, 429 U.S. 190 (1976), at 197

slavery

    ... [Blacks] had for more than a century before been regarded as beings of an inferior order; and altogether unfit to associate with the white race, either in social or political relations; and so far inferior, that they had no rights which the white man was bound to respect; and that the negro might justly and lawfully be reduced to slavery for his benefit. He was bought and sold, and treated as an ordinary article of merchandise and traffic, whenever a profit could be made by it. This opinion was at that time fixed and universal in the civilized portion of the white race.
    Roger B. Taney, for the Court, *Scott v. Sandford*, 19 How. 393 (1857), at 407

speech

We cannot accept the view that an apparently limitless variety of conduct can be labeled "speech" whenever the person engaging in the conduct intends thereby to express an idea.
    Earl Warren, for the Court, *United States v. O'Brien*, 391 U.S. 367 (1968), at 376
standing

Have the appellants alleged such a personal stake in the outcome of the controversy as to assure that concrete adverseness which sharpens the presentation of issues upon which the court so largely depends for illumination of difficult constitutional questions? This is the gist of the question of standing.
    William J. Brennan, Jr., for the Court, *Baker v. Carr*, 369 U.S. 186 (1962), at 204

stare decisis

Ordinarily it is sound policy to adhere to prior decisions but this practice has

Table 5-13   *(Continued)*

quite properly never been a blind, inflexible rule. Courts are not omniscient. Like every other human agency, they too can profit from trial and error, from experience and reflection. As others have demonstrated, the principle commonly referred to as *stare decisis* has never been thought to extend so far as to prevent the courts from correcting their own errors. . . . Indeed, the Court has a special responsibility where questions of constitutional law are involved to review its decisions from time to time and where compelling reasons present themselves to refuse to follow erroneous precedents; otherwise its mistakes in interpreting the Constitution are extremely difficult to alleviate and needlessly so.

Hugo L. Black, dissenting, *Green v. United States*, 356 U.S. 165 (1958), at 195

sterilization

We have seen more than once that the public welfare may call upon the best citizens for their lives. It would be strange if it could not call upon those who already sap the strength of the state for these lesser sacrifices, often not felt to be such by those concerned, in order to prevent our being swamped with incompetence. It is better for all the world, if instead of waiting to execute degenerate offspring for their crime, or to let them starve for their imbecility, society can prevent those who are manifestly unfit from continuing their kind. The principle that sustains compulsory vaccination is broad enough to cover cutting the Fallopian tubes. . . . Three generations of imbeciles are enough.

Oliver Wendell Holmes, for the Court, *Buck v. Bell*, 274 U.S. 200 (1927), at 207

taxation, power of

. . . the power to tax involves the power to destroy. . . .

John Marshall, for the Court, *McCulloch v. Maryland*, 4 Wheat. 316 (1919), at 431

Tenth Amendment

Our conclusion is unaffected by the Tenth Amendment which provides: "The powers not delegated to the United States by the Constitution nor prohibited by it to the states are reserved to the states respectively or to the people." The amendment states but a truism that all is retained which has not been surrendered.

Harlan Fiske Stone, for the Court, *United States v. Darby*, 312 U.S. 100 (1941), at 123-124

thought, freedom of

. . . if there is any principle of the Constitution that more imperatively calls for attachment than any other it is the principle of free thought—not free thought for those who agree with us but freedom for the thought we hate.

Oliver Wendell Holmes, dissenting, *United States v. Schwimmer*, 279 U.S. 644 (1929), at 654-655

(Table continues)

Table 5-13 *(Continued)*

---

time of war, constitutional rights in

When peace prevails, and the authority of the government is undisputed, there is no difficulty of preserving the safeguards of liberty...; but if society is disturbed by civil commotion—if the passions of men are aroused and the restraints of law weakened, if not disregarded—these safeguards need, and should receive, the watchful care of those intrusted with the guardianship of the Constitution and laws.

David Davis, for the Court, *Ex parte Milligan*, 4 Wall. 2 (1866), at 123-124

union, nature of

The Constitution, in all its provisions, looks to an indestructible Union, composed of indestructible States.

Salmon P. Chase, for the Court, *Texas v. White*, 7 Wall. 700 (1869), at 725

Note: This table reflects the judgment of the authors.

Table 5-14 Published Biographies of the Justices

Justice (appointment number)	Biographies[a]
Baldwin, Henry (23)	Taylor, Flavia M. "The Political and Civil Career of Henry Baldwin." *Western Pennsylvania Historical Magazine* 24 (March 1941): 37-50.
Barbour, Philip P. (26)	Cynn, Paul P. "Philip Pendleton Barbour." *John P. Branch Historical Papers of Randolph-Macon College* 4 (1913): 67-77.
Black, Hugo L. (79)	Ball, Howard. *The Vision and the Dream of Justice Hugo L. Black.* University: University of Alabama Press, 1975.
	Black, Hugo L., Jr. *My Father: A Remembrance.* New York: Random House, 1975.
	Dunne, Gerald T. *Hugo Black and the Judicial Revolution.* New York: Simon and Schuster, 1977.
	Frank, John P. *Mr. Justice Black.* New York: Knopf, 1949.
	Hamilton, Virginia V. *Hugo Black: The Alabama Years.* Baton Rouge: Louisiana State University Press, 1972.
	Yarbrough, Tinsley E. *Mr. Justice Black and His Critics.* Durham, N.C.: Duke University Press, 1988.
Blackmun, Harry A. (102)	Foote, Joseph. "Mr. Justice Blackmun." *Harvard Law School Bulletin* 21 (June 1970): 18-21.
Blair, John, Jr. (5)	Drinard, J. Elliott. "John Blair." *Proceedings of the Virginia State Bar Association* 39 (1927): 436-449.
Blatchford, Samuel (49)	Hall, A. Oakey. "Justice Samuel Blatchford." *Green Bag* 5 (November 1893): 489-492.
Bradley, Joseph P. (42)	Parker, Cortlandt. *Mr. Justice Bradley of the United States Supreme Court.* Newark, N.J.: Advertiser Printing House, 1893.

(Table continues)

Table 5-14 *(Continued)*

Justice (appointment number)	Biographies[a]
Brandeis, Louis D. (69)	Freund, Paul A. *A Portrait of a Liberal Judge: Mr. Justice Brandeis, on Understanding the Supreme Court*. Boston: Little, Brown, 1957.
	Gal, Allon. *Brandeis of Boston*. Cambridge, Mass.: Harvard University Press, 1980.
	Mason, Alpheus T. *Brandeis: A Free Man's Life*. New York: Viking Press, 1946.
	Murphy, Bruce. *The Brandeis-Frankfurter Connection*. Oxford, England: Oxford University Press, 1982.
	Strum, Philippa. *Louis D. Brandeis: Justice for the People*. Cambridge, Mass.: Harvard University Press, 1984.
	Urofsky, Melvin I. *Louis D. Brandeis and the Progressive Tradition*. Boston: Little, Brown, 1981.
Brennan, William J., Jr. (94)	Hopkins, W. Wat. *Mr. Justice Brennan and Freedom of Expression*. New York: Praeger, 1991.
Brewer, David J. (52)	Eitzen, D. Stanley. *David J. Brewer, 1837-1910: A Kansan on the United States Supreme Court*. Emporia: Kansas State Teacher's College, 1964.
Brown, Henry B. (53)	Kent, Charles A. *A Memoir of Henry Billings Brown*. New York: Duffield and Company, 1915.
Burger, Warren E. (101)	Blasi, Vincent (ed.). *The Burger Court: The Counter-Revolution That Wasn't*. New Haven, Conn.: Yale University Press, 1983.
	Lamb, Charles M., and Stephen C. Halpern (eds.). *The Burger Court: Political and Judicial Profiles*. Urbana: University of Illinois Press, 1991.
	Schwartz, Bernard. *The Assent of Pragmatism: The Burger Court in Action*. Reading, Mass.: Addison-Wesley, 1990.
Burton, Harold H. (88)	Berry, Mary F. *Stability, Security and Continuity: Mr. Justice Burton and Decision-Making in the Supreme Court, 1945-1958*. Westport, Conn.: Greenwood Press, 1978.

Table 5-14 *(Continued)*

Justice (appointment number)	Biographies[a]
Butler, Pierce (73)	Brown, Francis J. *The Social and Economic Philosophy of Pierce Butler.* Washington, D.C.: Catholic University of America Press, 1945.
	Danelski, David J. *A Supreme Court Justice Is Appointed.* New York: Random House, 1964.
Byrnes, James F. (85)	Burns, Ronald. *James F. Byrnes.* New York: McGraw-Hill, 1961.
	Byrnes, James F. *All in One Lifetime.* New York: Harper, 1958 (autobiography).
Campbell, John A. (34)	Connor, Henry G. *John Archibald Campbell, Associate Justice of the United States Supreme Court, 1853-1861.* Boston: Houghton Mifflin, 1920.
	Duncan, George W. *John Archibald Campbell.* Montgomery: Alabama Historical Society, 1905.
Cardozo, Benjamin (78)	Hellman, George S. *Benjamin N. Cardozo, American Judge.* New York: McGraw-Hill, 1940.
	Levy, Berl H. *Cardozo and Frontiers of Legal Thinking.* Cleveland, Ohio: Case Western Reserve University, 1969.
	Pollard, Joseph P. *Mr. Justice Cardozo: A Liberal Mind in Action.* New York: Yorktown Press, 1935.
Catron, John (27)	Chandler, Walter. *Address on the Centenary of Associate Justice John Catron of the United States Supreme Court.* Washington, D.C.: Government Printing Office, 1937.
Chase, Salmon P. (40)	Benson, John S. *The Judicial Record of the Late Chief Justice Chase.* New York: Baker, Voorhis, and Company, 1882.
	Hart, Albert B. *Salmon Portland Chase.* Boston: Houghton Mifflin, 1899.
	Schuckers, Jacob W. *The Life and Public Services of Salmon Portland Chase.* New York: D. Appleton, 1874.

(Table continues)

Table 5-14   *(Continued)*

Justice (appointment number)	*Biographies*[a]
Chase, Samuel (10)	Elsmere, Jane S. *Justice Samuel Chase.* Muncie, Ind.: Janevar, 1980.
	Haw, James A., Francis F. Beirne, Rosamond R. Beirne, and R. Samuel Jett. *Stormy Patriot: The Life of Samuel Chase.* Baltimore: Maryland Historical Society, 1980.
Clark, Tom C. (90)	Dutton, C. B. "Mr. Justice Tom C. Clark." *Indiana Law Journal* 26 (Winter 1951): 169-184.
Clarke, John H. (70)	Warner, Hoyt L. *The Life of Mr. Justice Clarke, A Testament to the Power of Liberal Dissent in America.* Cleveland, Ohio: Case Western Reserve University, 1959.
Clifford, Nathan (35)	Clifford, Philip G. *Nathan Clifford, Democrat, 1803-1881.* New York: Putnam's, 1922.
Curtis, Benjamin R. (33)	Leach, Richard H. "Benjamin Robbins Curtis: Judicial Misfit." *New England Quarterly* 25 (December 1952): 448-462.
Cushing, William (3)	Rugg, Arthur P. "William Cushing." *Yale Law Journal* 30 (December 1920): 128-144.
Daniel, Peter V. (29)	Frank, John P. *Justice Daniel Dissenting: A Biography of Peter V. Daniel, 1784-1860.* Cambridge, Mass.: Harvard University Press, 1964.
Davis, David (38)	King, Willard L. *Lincoln's Manager, David Davis.* Cambridge, Mass.: Harvard University Press, 1960.
Day, William R. (60)	McLean, Joseph E. *William Rufus Day: Supreme Court Justice From Ohio.* Baltimore: Johns Hopkins Press, 1946.
Douglas, William O. (82)	Douglas, William O. *Go East, Young Man.* New York: Random House, 1974 (autobiography).
	Douglas, William O. *The Court Years, 1939-1975: The Autobiography of William O. Douglas.* New York: Random House, 1980 (autobiography).
	Durham, James C. *Justice William O. Douglas.* Boston: Twayne, 1981.

Table 5-14   *(Continued)*

Justice (appointment number)	*Biographies*[a]
	Simon, James F. *Independent Journey: The Life of William O. Douglas.* New York: Harper and Row, 1980.
Duvall, Gabriel (18)	Currie, David P. "The Most Insignificant Justice: A Preliminary Inquiry." *University of Chicago Law Review* 50 (Spring 1983): 466-480.
Ellsworth, Oliver (11)	Brown, William G. *The Life of Oliver Ellsworth.* New York: Macmillan, 1905.
	Lettieri, Ronald J. *Connecticut's Young Man of the Revolution, Oliver Ellsworth.* Hartford: American Revolution Bicentennial Commission of Connecticut, 1978.
Field, Stephen J. (39)	Swisher, Carl B. *Stephen J. Field: Craftsman of the Law.* Washington, D.C.: Brookings Institution, 1930.
Fortas, Abe (99)	Kalman, Laura. *Abe Fortas: A Biography.* New Haven, Conn.: Yale University Press, 1990.
	Murphy, Bruce A. *Fortas: The Rise and Ruin of a Supreme Court Justice.* New York: Morrow, 1987.
	Shogan, Robert. *A Question of Judgment: The Fortas Case and the Struggle for the Supreme Court.* Indianapolis: Bobbs-Merrill, 1972.
Frankfurter, Felix (81)	Baker, Liva. *Felix Frankfurter.* New York: Coward-McCann, 1969.
	Hirsch, Harry N. *The Enigma of Felix Frankfurter.* New York: Basic Books, 1981.
	Kurland, Philip B. *Mr. Justice Frankfurter and the Constitution.* Chicago: University of Chicago Press, 1971.
	Parrish, Michael E. *Felix Frankfurter and His Times.* New York: Free Press, 1982.
Fuller, Melville W. (51)	King, Willard L. *Melville Weston Fuller: Chief Justice of the United States, 1888-1910.* New York: Macmillan, 1950.

(Table continues)

Table 5-14   *(Continued)*

Justice (appointment number)	Biographies[a]
Goldberg, Arthur J. (98)	Goldberg, Dorothy. *A Private View of a Public Life.* New York: Charthouse, 1975.
Gray, Horace (48)	Hoar, George F. "Memoir of Horace Gray." *Massachusetts Historical Society Proceedings* 18 (January 1904): 155-187.
Grier, Robert C. (32)	Jones, Francis R. "Robert Cooper Grier." *Green Bag* 16 (April 1904): 221-224.
Harlan, John Marshall I (45)	Beth, Loren P. *John Marshall Harlan: The Last Great Whig Justice.* Lexington: University Press of Kentucky, 1992.
	Clark, Floyd B. *Constitutional Doctrines of Justice Harlan.* Baltimore: Johns Hopkins Press, 1915.
	Latham, Frank B. *The Great Dissenter: Supreme Court Justice John Marshall Harlan, 1833-1911.* New York: Cowles, 1970.
Harlan, John Marshall II (93)	Yarbrough, Tinsley E. *John Marshall Harlan: Great Dissenter of the Warren Court.* New York: Oxford University Press, 1992.
Holmes, Oliver W., Jr. (59)	Baker, Liva. *The Justice from Beacon Hill: The Life and Times of Oliver Wendell Holmes.* New York: HarperCollins, 1991.
	Bent, Silas. *Justice Oliver Wendell Holmes, A Biography.* New York: Vanguard Press, 1932.
	Biddle, Francis. *Mr. Justice Holmes.* New York: Charles Scribner's Sons, 1942.
	Bowen, Catherine D. *Yankee from Olympus: Justice Holmes and His Family.* Boston: Little, Brown, 1944.
	Howe, Mark D. *Justice Oliver Wendell Holmes,* 2 vols. Cambridge, Mass.: Harvard University Press, 1957-1963.
	Pohlman, H. L. *Justice Oliver Wendell Holmes and Utilitarian Jurisprudence.* Cambridge, Mass.: Harvard University Press, 1984.

Table 5-14 *(Continued)*

Justice (appointment number)	*Biographies*[a]
Hughes, Charles E. (63, 76)	Hendel, Samuel. *Charles Evans Hughes and the Supreme Court.* New York: King's Crown Press, 1951. Pusey, Merlo J. *Charles Evans Hughes,* 2 vols. New York: Macmillan, 1951. Pusey, Merlo J. *Mr. Chief Justice Hughes.* Chicago: University of Chicago Press, 1956. Vinson, John C. *Charles Evans Hughes.* New York: McGraw-Hill, 1961.
Hunt, Ward (43)	"Old Judge and New." *Albany Law Journal* 6 (December 14, 1872): 400-401.
Iredell, James (6)	Davis, Junius. *Alfred Moore and James Iredell: Revolutionary Patriots and Associate Justices of the Supreme Court of the United States.* Raleigh: North Carolina Society of the Sons of the Revolution, 1899. McRee, Griffith J. *Life and Correspondence of James Iredell.* New York: D. Appleton, 1857.
Jackson, Howell E. (55)	Calvani, Terry. "The Early Legal Career of Howell Jackson." *Vanderbilt Law Review* 30 (January 1977): 39-72.
Jackson, Robert H. (86)	Gerhart, Eugene C. *America's Advocate: Robert H. Jackson.* Indianapolis: Bobbs-Merrill, 1958. ———. *Supreme Court Justice Jackson: Lawyer's Judge.* New York: Q Corporation, 1961. Schubert, Glendon. *Dispassionate Justice.* New York: Bobbs-Merrill, 1969.
Jay, John (1)	Hubbard, Elbert. *John Jay, the First Chief Justice of the United States.* New York: Hartford Lunch Company, 1918. Morris, Richard B. *John Jay, the Nation, and the Court.* Boston: Boston University Press, 1967.

(Table continues)

Table 5-14   *(Continued)*

Justice (appointment number)	Biographies[a]
	Pellew, George. *John Jay.* Boston: Houghton Mifflin, 1890.
Johnson, Thomas (7)	Delaplaine, Edward S. *The Life of Thomas Johnson.* New York: F. H. Hitchock, 1927.
Johnson, William (15)	Morgan, Donald G. *Justice William Johnson, the First Dissenter.* Columbia: University of South Carolina Press, 1971.
Kennedy, Anthony (109)	Williams, Charles F. "The Opinions of Anthony Kennedy: No Time for Ideology." *American Bar Association Journal* 74 (March 1988): 56-61.
Lamar, Joseph R. (66)	Lamar, Clarinda. *The Life of Joseph Rucker Lamar, 1857-1916.* New York: Putnam's, 1926.
	Sibley, Samuel H. *Georgia's Contribution to Law: The Lamars.* New York: Newcomen Society of England, American Branch, 1948.
Lamar, Lucius Q. C. (50)	Murphy, James B. *L. Q. C. Lamar: Pragmatic Patriot.* Baton Rouge: Louisiana State University Press, 1973.
	Sibley, Samuel H. *Georgia's Contribution to Law: The Lamars.* New York: Newcomen Society of England, American Branch, 1948.
Livingston, H. Brockholst (16)	Livingston, Edwin B. *The Livingstons of Livingston Manor.* New York: Knickerbocker Press, 1910.
Lurton, Horace (62)	Tucker, David M. "Justice Horace Harmon Lurton: The Shaping of a Natural Progressive." *American Journal of Legal History* 13 (July 1969): 223-232.
Marshall, John (14)	Baker, Leonard. *John Marshall: A Life in Law.* New York: Macmillan, 1974.
	Beveridge, Albert J. *The Life of John Marshall,* 4 vols. Boston: Houghton Mifflin, 1916-1919.
	Corwin, Edward S. *John Marshall and the Constitution.* New Haven, Conn.: Yale University Press, 1919.

Table 5-14   *(Continued)*

Justice (appointment number)	*Biographies* [a]
	Crosskey, William W. *Mr. Chief Justice Marshall.* Chicago: University of Chicago Press, 1956.
	Severn, William. *John Marshall, the Man Who Made the Court Supreme.* New York: David McKay, 1969.
	Swindler, William F. *The Constitution and Chief Justice Marshall.* New York: Dodd, Mead, 1979.
Marshall, Thurgood (100)	Bland, Randall W. *Private Pressure on Public Law: The Legal Career of Justice Thurgood Marshall.* Port Washington, N.Y.: Kennikat Press, 1973.
	Davis, Michael D., and Hunter R. Clark. *Thurgood Marshall: Warrior at the Bar, Rebel on the Bench.* Secaucus, N.J.: Carol Publishing, 1992.
	Rowan, Carl T. *Dream Makers, Dream Breakers: World of Justice Thurgood Marshall.* Boston: Little, Brown, 1993.
Matthews, Stanley (47)	Jager, Ronald B. "Stanley Matthews for the Supreme Court: 'Lord Roscoe's' Downfall." *Cincinnati Historical Society Bulletin* 38 (Fall 1980): 191-208.
McKenna, Joseph (58)	McDevitt, Matthew. *Joseph McKenna, Associate Justice of the United States.* Washington, D.C.: Catholic University of America Press, 1946.
McKinley, John (28)	Hicks, Jimmie. "Associate Justice John McKinley: A Sketch." *Alabama Review* 18 (July 1965): 227-233.
McLean, John (22)	Weinsenberger, Francis P. *The Life of John McLean: A Politician on the United States Supreme Court.* Columbus: Ohio State University Press, 1937.
McReynolds, James C. (68)	Fletcher, R. V. "Mr. Justice McReynolds: An Appreciation." *Vanderbilt Law Review* 2 (December 1948): 35-46.

(Table continues)

Table 5-14 *(Continued)*

Justice (appointment number)	*Biographies*[a]
Miller, Samuel (37)	Fairman, Charles. *Mr. Justice Miller and the Supreme Court, 1862-1890.* Cambridge, Mass.: Harvard University Press, 1939.
	Gregory, Charles N. *Samuel Freeman Miller.* Iowa City: State Historical Society of Iowa, 1907.
Minton, Sherman (91)	Wallace, Henry L. "Mr. Justice Minton: Hoosier Justice on the Supreme Court." *Indiana Law Journal* 34 (Winter 1959): 145-205; 34 (Spring 1959): 377-424.
Moody, William H. (61)	Heffron, Paul T. "Profile of a Public Man." *Supreme Court Historical Society Yearbook,* 1980 (1980): 30-31, 48.
Moore, Alfred (13)	Davis, Junius. *Alfred Moore and James Iredell: Revolutionary Patriots and Associate Justices of the Supreme Court of the United States.* Raleigh: North Carolina Society of the Sons of the Revolution, 1899.
Murphy, Frank (83)	Fine, Sidney. *Frank Murphy: The Detroit Years.* Ann Arbor: University of Michigan Press, 1975.
	_____. *Frank Murphy: The New Deal Years.* Chicago: University of Chicago Press, 1979.
	_____. *Frank Murphy: The Washington Years.* Ann Arbor: University of Michigan Press, 1984.
	Howard, J. Woodford, Jr. *Mr. Justice Murphy: A Political Biography.* Princeton, N.J.: Princeton University Press, 1968.
Nelson, Samuel (30)	Leach, Richard H. "Rediscovery of Samuel Nelson." *New York History* 34 (January 1953): 64-71.
O'Connor, Sandra Day (106)	Bentley, Judith. *Justice Sandra Day O'Connor.* Englewood Cliffs, N.J.: Messner, 1983.
	Spaeth, Harold J. "Justice Sandra Day O'Connor: An Assessment." In *An Essential Safeguard,* ed. D. G. Stephenson, Jr., New York: Greenwood Press, 1991.

Table 5-14   *(Continued)*

Justice (appointment number)	*Biographies* [a]
	Woods, Harold, and Geraldine Woods. *Equal Justice: A Biography of Sandra Day O'Connor.* Minneapolis: Dillon Press, 1985.
Paterson, William (8)	O'Connor, John E. *William Paterson: Lawyer and Statesman, 1745-1806.* New Brunswick, N.J.: Rutgers University Press, 1979.
Peckham, Rufus W. (57)	Proctor, L. B. "Rufus W. Peckham." *Albany Law Journal* 55 (May 1, 1897): 286-288.
Pitney, Mahlon (67)	Belknap, Michael R. "Mr. Justice Pitney and Progressivism." *Seton Hall Law Review* 16 (1986): 381-428.
Powell, Lewis F., Jr. (103)	Kahn, Paul W. "The Court, the Community, and the Judicial Balance: The Jurisprudence of Justice Powell." *Yale Law Journal* 97 (November 1987): 1-60.
	Wilkinson, J. Harvie. *Serving Justice: A Supreme Court Clerk's View.* New York: Charterhouse, 1974.
Reed, Stanley F. (80)	O'Brien, F. William. *Justice Reed and the First Amendment: The Religion Clauses.* Washington, D.C.: Georgetown University Press, 1958.
	Prickett, Morgan D. "Stanley Forman Reed: Perspectives on a Judicial Epitaph." *Hastings Constitutional Law Quarterly* 8 (Winter 1981): 343-369.
Rehnquist, William (104, 107)	Boles, Donald E. *Mr. Justice Rehnquist, Judicial Activist: The Early Years.* Ames: Iowa State University Press, 1987.
	Davis, Derek. *Original Intent: Chief Justice Rehnquist and the Course of American Church-State Relations.* Buffalo, N.Y.: Prometheus Books, 1991.
	Davis, Sue. *Justice Rehnquist and the Constitution.* Princeton, N.J.: Princeton University Press, 1989.

(Table continues)

Table 5-14   *(Continued)*

Justice (appointment number)	*Biographies*[a]
	Savage, David G. *Turning Right: The Making of the Rehnquist Supreme Court.* New York: Wiley, 1992.
Roberts, Owen J. (77)	Leonard, Charles. *A Search for a Judicial Philosophy: Mr. Justice Roberts and the Constitutional Revolution of 1937.* Port Washington, N.Y.: Kennikat Press, 1971.
Rutledge, John (2, 9)	Barry, Richard. *Mr. Rutledge of South Carolina.* New York: Duell Sloan, and Pearce, 1942.
Rutledge, Wiley B. (87)	Harper, Fowler V. *Justice Rutledge and the Bright Constellation.* Indianapolis: Bobbs-Merrill, 1965.
	Stevens, John P. *Mr. Justice Rutledge.* Chicago: University of Chicago Press, 1956.
Sanford, Edward T. (74)	Fowler, James A. "Mr. Justice Edward Terry Sanford." *American Bar Association Journal* 17 (April 1931): 229-233.
Scalia, Antonin (108)	King, Michael P. "Justice Antonin Scalia: The First Term on the Supreme Court, 1986-1987." *Rutgers Law Journal* 20 (Fall 1988): 1-77.
Shiras, George, Jr. (54)	Shiras, George III. *Justice George Shiras, Jr., of Pittsburgh: A Chronicle of His Family, Life, and Times.* Edited by Winfield Shiras. Pittsburgh: University of Pittsburgh Press, 1953.
Souter, David H. (110)	Smith, Christopher E., and Scott P. Johnson. "Newcomer on the High Court." *South Dakota Law Review* 37 (1991): 21-43.
Stevens, John Paul (105)	Sickels, Robert J. *John Paul Stevens and the Constitution: The Search for Balance.* University Park: Pennsylvania State University Press, 1988.
Stewart, Potter (96)	Barnett, Helaine M., and Kenneth Levine. "Mr. Justice Potter Stewart." *New York University Law Review* 40 (May 1965): 526-562.
Stone, Harlan Fiske (75, 84)	Konefsky, Samuel J. *Chief Justice Stone and the Supreme Court.* New York: Macmillan, 1945.
	Mason, Alpheus T. *Harlan Fiske Stone: Pillar of the Law.* New York: Viking, 1956.

Table 5-14   *(Continued)*

Justice (appointment number)	*Biographies*[a]
Story, Joseph (19)	Dunne, Gerald T. *Justice Joseph Story and the Rise of the Supreme Court*. New York: Simon and Schuster, 1970.
	McClellan, James. *Joseph Story and the American Constitution: A Study in Political and Legal Thought*. Norman: University of Oklahoma Press, 1971.
	Newmyer, R. Kent. *Supreme Court Justice Joseph Story: Statesman of the Old Republic*. Chapel Hill: University of North Carolina Press, 1985.
Strong, William (41)	"Political Portrait of William Strong." *United States Democratic Review* 27 (September 1850): 269-275.
Sutherland, George (72)	Pascal, Joel F. *Mr. Justice Sutherland*. Chicago: University of Chicago Press, 1956.
	Pascal, Joel F. *Mr. Justice Sutherland, a Man Against the State*. Princeton, N.J.: Princeton University Press, 1951.
Swayne, Noah H. (36)	Swayne, Norman W. *The Descendants of Francis Swayne*. Philadelphia: Lippincott, 1921.
Taft, William H. (71)	Anderson, Judith I. *William Howard Taft: An Intimate History*. New York: W. W. Norton, 1981.
	Mason, Alpheus T. *William Howard Taft, Chief Justice*. New York: Simon and Schuster, 1965.
	Pringle, Henry F. *Life and Times of William Howard Taft, Chief Justice*. New York: Farrar and Rhinehart, 1939.
Taney, Roger B. (25)	Lewis, Walker. *Without Fear or Favor: A Biography of Chief Justice Roger Brooke Taney*. Boston: Houghton Mifflin, 1965.
	Schumacher, Alvin J. *Thunder on Capitol Hill: The Life of Chief Justice Roger B. Taney*. Milwaukee: Bruce Publishing Company, 1964.
	Swisher, Carl B. *Roger B. Taney*. Macmillan, 1935.

(Table continues)

Table 5-14   *(Continued)*

Justice (appointment number)	*Biographies*[a]
	_____. *Mr. Chief Justice Taney.* Chicago: University of Chicago Press, 1956.
Thomas, Clarence (111)	Gerbert, Scott D. "The Jurisprudence of Clarence Thomas." *Journal of Law and Politics* 8 (Fall 1991): 107-141.
	McCarghey, Elizabeth P. "Clarence Thomas's Record as a Judge." *Presidential Studies Quarterly* 21 (Fall 1991): 833-835.
Thompson, Smith (20)	Roper, Donald M. "Justice Smith Thompson: Politics and the New York Supreme Court in the Early Nineteenth Century." *New York Historical Society Quarterly* 51 (April 1967): 119-140.
Todd, Thomas (17)	O'Rear, Edward C. "Justice Thomas Todd." *Kentucky State Historical Society Record* 38 (February 1940): 112-119.
Trimble, Robert (21)	Goff, John S. "Mr. Justice Trimble of the United States Supreme Court." *Kentucky Historical Society Register* 58 (January 1960): 6-28.
Van Devanter, Willis (65)	Holsinger, M. Paul. "The Appointment of Supreme Court Justice Van Devanter." *American Journal of Legal History* 12 (October 1968): 324-335.
Vinson, Fred M. (89)	Frank, John P. "Fred Vinson and the Chief Justiceship." *University of Chicago Law Review* 21 (Winter 1954): 212-246.
Waite, Morrison (44)	Magrath, C. Peter. *Morrison R. Waite: The Triumph of Character.* New York: Macmillan, 1963.
	Trimble, Bruce R. *Chief Justice Waite: Defender of the Public Interest.* Princeton, N.J.: Princeton University Press, 1938.
Warren, Earl (92)	Katcher, Leo. *Earl Warren: A Political Biography.* New York: McGraw-Hill, 1967.
	Pollack, Jack H. *Earl Warren, the Judge Who Changed America.* Englewood Cliffs, N.J.: Prentice Hall, 1979.
	Schwartz, Bernard. *Super Chief.* New York: New York University Press, 1983.

Table 5-14   *(Continued)*

Justice (appointment number)	*Biographies*[a]
	White, G. Edward. *Earl Warren: A Public Life.* New York: Oxford University Press, 1982.
Washington, Bushrod (12)	Binney, Horace. *Bushrod Washington.* Philadelphia: C. Sherman and Son, 1858.
Wayne, James M. (24)	Lawrence, Alexander A. *James Moore Wayne, Southern Unionist.* Chapel Hill: University of North Carolina Press, 1943.
White, Byron R. (97)	Liebman, Lance. "Swing Man on the Supreme Court." *New York Times Magazine,* October 8, 1972, 16-17, 94-95, 98, 100.
White, Edward D. (56, 64)	Hagemann, Gerard. *The Man on the Bench: A Story of Chief Justice Edward Douglass White.* Notre Dame, Ind.: Dujarie Press, 1962.
	Highsaw, Robert B. *Edward Douglass White: Defender of the Conservative Faith.* Baton Rouge: Louisiana State University Press, 1981.
Whittaker, Charles E. (95)	Christensen, Barbara B. "Mister Justice Whittaker: The Man on the Right." *Santa Clara Law Review* 19 (1979): 1039-1062.
Wilson, James (4)	O'Donnell, May G. *James Wilson and the Natural Law Basis of Positive Law.* New York: Fordham Univeristy Press, 1937.
	Smith, Page. *James Wilson: Founding Father, 1742-1798.* Chapel Hill: Univeristy of North Carolina Press, 1956.
Woodbury, Levi (31)	Rantoul, Robert. "Mr. Justice Woodbury." *Law Reporter* 14 (November 1851): 349-361.
Woods, William B. (46)	Baynes, Thomas E. "Yankee from Georgia: A Search for Justice Woods." *Supreme Court Historical Society Yearbook,* 1978 (1978): 31-42.

[a] Wherever possible book length biographies are listed. Where full volumes are not available, articles describing the life and career of the justice are provided. The listings included here are not exhaustive.

Sources: Fenton S. Martin and Robert U. Goehlert, *The United States Supreme Court: A Bibliography* (Washington, D.C.: Congressional Quarterly, 1990); Leon Friedman and Fred L. Israel, eds, *The Justices of the United States Supreme Court: Their Lives and Major Opinions,* 5 vols. (New York: Chelsea House, 1969-1978).

6

The Justices: Voting
Behavior and Opinions

In Chapter 6 we examine the official voting behavior and opinion-writing records of the justices of the Supreme Court. This includes liberal versus conservative voting tendencies; voting interagreement among the justices; voting to overturn legislation or precedent; assignment of the majority opinion; writing the majority, concurring, and dissenting opinions; and joining one or more of the same. (The justices must also decide whether or not to hear cases appealed to them, but the vast majority of their individual votes in such cases are not officially reported.) The crucial question here is why do the justices behave as they do?

Legal professionals maintain that a justice's vote is based on some combination of the plain meaning of statutes, the intent of the framers, and precedent (also called *stare decisis*). Political scientists are more likely to look at the attitudes and values of each justice as an answer to this question. Still others argue that judicial tradition bounded by judicial restraint leads justices to defer to the wishes of Congress, the president, or the public.

The data on the voting behavior of the justices in Tables 6-1 through 6-8 are derived from the U.S. Supreme Court Judicial Database. The voting data consist of all formally decided cases on the Court's appellate docket from the 1953 through 1991 terms. In Tables 6-1 and 6-2, we look at each justice's tendency to vote in a liberal versus conservative direction, though in some issue areas (for example, criminal justice) this label fits better than in others (for example, federalism). (See the notes following the tables for further explanation.)

Table 6-1 presents the aggregate voting behavior for each justice who served between the 1953 and 1991 terms of the Court. Pre-1953 votes by those who served during the 1953 term are not included in the database or in this table. Votes are broken down by the eleven aggregate issue areas defined by the database, plus a separate civil liberties column that combines the votes from criminal procedure, civil rights, First Amendment, due process, privacy, and attorneys' cases. In the combined civil liberties cases, Justice Douglas is the most liberal of the justices, supporting that position almost 92 percent of the time. Not far behind is Justice Goldberg, who supported the liberal position nearly 90 percent of the time. A second rung of liberals consists of Justices Marshall, Fortas, Brennan, and Warren, all of whom supported the liberal position approximately 80 percent of the time. Justice Black is the remaining liberal of the group, with almost three-quarters of his votes in the liberal direction. A plurality of the justices are moderate on civil liberties issues. This group includes Frankfurter, Jackson, Burton, Clark, Minton, Harlan, Whittaker, Stewart, White, Blackmun, Powell, and Stevens. Reed, Burger, Rehnquist, O'Connor, Scalia, Kennedy, and Souter rank as conservative in civil liberties cases. In economics cases, the same tendencies hold, with some exceptions. Clark, for instance, is decidedly more liberal in economic matters than in civil liberties concerns, while Marshall approaches the moderate camp.

Because aggregate voting patterns can mask change through the judicial life cycle, we provide the annual voting behavior of each justice in Table 6-2. Data here are limited to those issues where enough cases have been decided to make annual comparisons meaningful. In addition, we have combined economics and union cases into a single economics category, as relatively few union cases are heard in any given year. While most justices demonstrate a fair amount of consistency from term to term, there are exceptions: Justice Black became markedly more moderate following the 1963 term. Justice Blackmun, who originally voted as a moderate conservative, in recent terms has voted as a moderate liberal.

Tables 6-3 through 6-5 present voting interagreement among the justices by issue area on the Warren, Burger, and Rehnquist Courts, respectively. There is little surprise here: like-minded justices tend to vote alike. Thus, Douglas voted with Goldberg over 90 percent of the time in civil rights and First Amendment cases during the Warren Court, and Brennan and Marshall were nearly inseparable on the three Courts on which they served together. Thomas has begun his career as a virtual clone of Scalia. Table 6-6 looks at interagreement among the justices in special opinions (that is, concurrences or dissents).

Data on voting behavior conclude with Tables 6-7 and 6-8, which look at cases where the Court declared legislation unconstitutional (Table 6-7) or explicitly overturned previous decisions (Table 6-8). The data are limited here because they do not tell us how justices voted in every case that the Court was asked to strike a law or overturn precedent, but only in those cases that a majority of justices in fact did so. Nevertheless, interesting results are evident. For example, Justice Frankfurter, who was reputedly opposed to the Warren Court's activism, was three times more likely to join the Court than not when it voided legislation. Rehnquist is the only justice who has consistently refused to join the Court when it strikes legislation.

After the Court reaches a decision on the merits of the case, the chief justice, or the senior associate justice in the majority if the chief justice dissents or does not participate, assigns the majority opinion to one of the members of the majority. The justices not assigned the majority opinion can either write a concurring opinion (agreeing with the decision of the majority, but not necessarily with the reasoning in its opinion), a dissenting opinion (disagreeing with both the results and the reasoning of the majority opinion), or not write at all, silently joining one or more of the opinions written by others. We detail the extent of opinion writing from the 1790 through 1991 terms of the Court in Table 6-9. A couple of points are worth noting. Extensive dissent and concurrence writing is a fairly recent phenomenon. John Marshall Harlan (I) is the only justice who did not sit on the Warren, Burger, or Rehnquist Courts who wrote more than 100 dissents. Oliver Wendell Holmes, who wrote only 72 dissenting opinions in over 5,700 cases, was known as the "Great Dissenter" not because of the quantity of his dissents, but because of their quality. No justice predating the Warren Court wrote more than 100 concurrences.

The Supreme Court database provides additional data on the opinion writing of the justices, including the number of judgments of the Court written by each justice (these are plurality rulings that occur when no majority agrees on the justification for a decision) and a division of concurring opinions into regular concurrences (joining the majority opinion, but writing separately as well) and special concurrences (explicitly disagreeing with the rationale in the majority opinion) (Table 6-10).

Table 6-11 presents the number of solo dissents authored since the 1953 term. We would expect that such dissents would come from justices at the liberal or conservative extremes of the Court's ideological spectrum. Not surprisingly, Douglas and Rehnquist have authored solo dissents on a regular basis. What cannot be explained is the solo dissent record of Justice Stevens, who is by no means an extremist. Presumably, his decision-making behavior cannot be explained by the simple liberal-conservative dichotomy. Table 6-12 lists what are in our view the most significant opinions of each justice.

Finally, in Tables 6-13 through 6-17, we examine the opinion assignment patterns of each justice who assigned an opinion between the 1953 and 1991 terms. We follow the database in assuming that the senior justice in the majority decision coalition assigned the opinion.

This assumption does not always hold, however, as sometimes justices switch votes and are not in the majority when the assignment is made. Thus, in cases where the chief justice dissents at the original conference vote but subsequently switches to the majority, we may have incorrectly listed the chief justice as having assigned the majority opinion. The same may happen when senior associate justices switch their votes.

The chief justice assigns the overwhelming number of opinions in any term. During the Warren Court, non-Warren assignments fell largely to Frankfurter, for when Warren dissented, Douglas and Black usually did too. On the Burger Court, Douglas, and then Brennan, assigned the overwhelming majority of cases when Burger dissented. On the Rehnquist Court, Brennan, until his retirement, made every assignment when the chief justice dissented. Most assigners give preference to justices who are ideologically close to them, especially in the most important cases. As an extreme example, the liberal Warren assigned but one opinion to the moderate Frankfurter in the 1959 term, while assigning ten or more opinions to five other justices. Frankfurter, though, was able to overcome this imbalance by assigning to himself the seven cases where Warren dissented and he was the senior associate in the majority.

Table 6-1 Aggregate Liberal Voting of Justices, 1953-1991 Terms

Justice	CivL	Crim	CivR	1st	DP	Priv	Atty	Un'n	Econ	FTax	Fed	JudP
Black	74.2 (925)	68.9 (399)	72.2 (277)	87.0 (192)	81.0 (42)	00.0 (3)	83.3 (12)	76.3 (135)	84.2 (467)	84.9 (126)	64.9 (111)	53.0 (362)
Reed	33.3 (108)	28.3 (53)	35.5 (31)	20.0 (15)	75.0 (8)	— (0)	100.0 (1)	81.8 (22)	52.5 (99)	75.0 (24)	52.6 (19)	55.6 (45)
Frankfurter	50.4 (369)	46.0 (174)	55.7 (88)	49.4 (79)	63.6 (22)	00.0 (1)	80.0 (5)	53.1 (64)	38.6 (241)	75.7 (70)	60.4 (53)	30.9 (152)
Douglas	91.5 (1,265)	89.3 (522)	92.7 (397)	96.8 (249)	85.9 (71)	81.8 (11)	86.7 (15)	64.9 (168)	86.3 (568)	38.6 (140)	69.0 (129)	68.7 (451)
Jackson	48.1 (27)	35.7 (14)	62.5 (8)	50.0 (4)	100.0 (1)	— (0)	— (0)	66.7 (6)	42.9 (28)	33.3 (3)	75.0 (4)	12.5 (8)
Burton	39.2 (212)	33.3 (96)	42.1 (57)	32.4 (37)	68.8 (16)	00.0 (1)	80.0 (5)	65.7 (35)	50.7 (146)	76.3 (38)	45.2 (31)	42.0 (88)
Clark	44.4 (649)	35.9 (287)	57.3 (185)	34.6 (136)	78.8 (33)	100.0 (1)	71.4 (7)	69.3 (114)	74.6 (389)	78.0 (109)	54.5 (88)	47.1 (274)
Minton	36.8 (95)	35.6 (45)	37.9 (29)	14.3 (14)	83.8 (6)	— (0)	100.0 (1)	60.0 (20)	66.3 (86)	85.7 (21)	58.8 (17)	45.9 (37)
Warren	78.5 (771)	75.1 (346)	82.8 (221)	79.9 (159)	78.8 (33)	50.0 (2)	80.0 (10)	72.0 (125)	81.9 (443)	80.0 (115)	69.1 (94)	54.8 (323)

(Table continues)

Table 6-1 (Continued)

Justice	CivL	Crim	CivR	1st	DP	Priv	Atty	Un'n	Econ	FTax	Fed	JudP
Harlan	43.7 (870)	39.4 (371)	44.8 (259)	44.1 (186)	69.2 (39)	33.3 (3)	66.7 (12)	55.4 (130)	37.7 (403)	72.1 (111)	52.9 (102)	37.3 (343)
Whittaker	43.3 (240)	43.5 (115)	46.3 (54)	37.0 (54)	60.0 (15)	00.0 (1)	100.0 (1)	42.5 (40)	32.5 (151)	57.1 (42)	66.7 (33)	43.2 (95)
Brennan	79.5 (2,417)	76.2 (944)	83.6 (769)	83.3 (408)	74.5 (192)	59.2 (49)	85.5 (55)	66.2 (234)	71.6 (867)	70.6 (180)	64.7 (238)	50.1 (733)
Stewart	51.3 (1,551)	46.1 (607)	49.9 (519)	63.9 (274)	54.8 (104)	41.4 (29)	72.2 (18)	56.9 (167)	45.0 (564)	65.9 (123)	57.8 (128)	38.8 (487)
White	42.4 (2,253)	33.2 (865)	56.1 (743)	38.3 (355)	48.3 (180)	13.2 (53)	36.8 (57)	62.7 (193)	58.3 (732)	84.8 (132)	65.6 (212)	40.9 (650)
Goldberg	88.9 (153)	80.0 (60)	98.3 (58)	89.3 (28)	80.0 (5)	100.0 (1)	100.0 (1)	65.0 (20)	65.5 (84)	78.3 (23)	55.0 (20)	55.1 (69)
Fortas	81.0 (205)	80.2 (91)	83.6 (61)	77.3 (44)	100.0 (5)	— (0)	75.0 (4)	60.0 (20)	69.3 (75)	50.0 (16)	64.7 (17)	50.6 (79)
Marshall	81.4 (1,889)	80.2 (722)	85.2 (620)	82.9 (287)	75.8 (165)	60.4 (48)	83.0 (47)	68.1 (138)	65.3 (556)	74.2 (93)	66.7 (156)	49.7 (487)
Burger	29.6 (1,430)	19.8 (515)	37.2 (500)	31.9 (213)	38.0 (129)	12.5 (40)	39.4 (33)	43.9 (107)	42.6 (423)	72.1 (68)	63.1 (111)	26.3 (354)

Blackmun	51.5 (1,791)	40.2 (672)	61.3 (582)	55.8 (269)	51.2 (168)	47.1 (51)	71.4 (49)	61.8 (131)	53.5 (546)	73.5 (83)	64.8 (159)	39.1 (453)
Powell	37.4 (1,285)	28.8 (482)	41.0 (432)	47.8 (182)	44.3 (122)	32.4 (37)	36.7 (30)	51.1 (94)	44.7 (356)	56.1 (57)	61.0 (105)	32.0 (309)
Rehnquist	20.4 (1,665)	15.3 (633)	25.6 (536)	18.7 (241)	28.0 (157)	8.2 (49)	24.5 (45)	43.7 (95)	42.2 (413)	66.3 (63)	38.7 (155)	28.5 (428)
Stevens	61.4 (1,319)	61.9 (507)	61.1 (416)	64.6 (181)	57.8 (128)	45.2 (42)	71.1 (45)	61.1 (95)	56.7 (413)	55.6 (63)	53.0 (134)	47.1 (323)
O'Connor	33.4 (886)	22.2 (352)	45.3 (258)	40.3 (129)	38.4 (86)	25.0 (24)	27.0 (37)	43.3 (60)	43.2 (266)	55.8 (43)	46.5 (99)	43.9 (228)
Scalia	29.7 (438)	25.1 (187)	36.0 (114)	32.8 (67)	29.3 (41)	30.0 (10)	26.3 (19)	36.7 (30)	45.7 (140)	70.8 (24)	58.2 (55)	32.2 (118)
Kennedy	34.7 (303)	24.1 (133)	45.3 (75)	45.8 (48)	34.8 (23)	20.0 (10)	50.0 (14)	25.0 (20)	49.1 (106)	75.0 (16)	54.3 (35)	45.9 (85)
Souter	41.7 (108)	27.1 (48)	60.6 (33)	71.4 (14)	16.7 (6)	33.3 (3)	100.0 (4)	33.3 (9)	50.0 (48)	50.0 (6)	57.1 (7)	55.9 (34)
Thomas	25.6 (43)	16.7 (18)	42.9 (14)	16.7 (6)	33.3 (3)	00.0 (1)	00.0 (1)	00.0 (1)	41.7 (24)	50.0 (2)	80.0 (5)	50.0 (16)

Note: Figures listed are the percentage of cases in which the justice took the liberal position. Figures in parentheses are the total number of cases in issue area in which the justice participated.

The issue areas are defined as follows: civil liberties (CivL); combines criminal procedure, civil rights, First Amendment, due process, privacy, and attorneys; Criminal procedure (Crim): the rights of persons accused of crime except for the due process rights of prisoners; Civil rights (CivR): non-First

Table 6-1 (Continued)

Amendment freedom cases that pertain to classifications based on race, (including native Americans), age, indigence, voting, residence, military or handicapped status, sex, or alienage; First Amendment (1st): guarantees contained therein; Due process (DP): noncriminal procedural guarantees, plus court jurisdiction over nonresident litigants and the takings clause of the Fifth Amendment; Privacy (Priv): abortion, contraception, the Freedom of Information Act and related federal statutes; Attorneys (Atty): attorneys' fees, commercial speech, admission to and removal from the bar, and disciplinary matters; Unions (Un'n): labor union activity; Economics (Econ): commercial business activity, plus litigation involving injured persons or things, employee actions vis-à-vis employers, zoning regulations, and governmental regulation of corruption other than that involving campaign spending; Federal taxation (FTax): the Internal Revenue Code and related statutes; Federalism (Fed): conflicts between the federal and state governments, excluding those between state and federal courts, and those involving the priority of federal fiscal claims; Judicial power (JudP): the exercise of the judiciary's own power and authority. The primary issue is counted in each case, except where cases contain both substantive and procedural issues, where both are counted.

The term *liberal* represents the voting direction of the justices across the various issue areas. It is most appropriate in the areas of civil liberties, criminal procedure, civil rights, First Amendment, due process, privacy, and attorneys, where it signifies pro-defendant votes in criminal procedure cases, pro-women or -minorities in civil rights cases, pro-individual against the government in First Amendment, due process, and privacy cases, and pro-attorney in attorneys' fees and bar membership cases. In takings clause cases, however, a pro-government/anti-owner vote is considered liberal. The use of the term is perhaps less appropriate in union cases, where it represents pro-union votes against both individuals and the government, and in economic cases, where it represents pro-government votes against challenges to federal regulatory authority and pro-competition, anti-business, pro-liability, pro-injured person, and pro-bankruptcy votes. In federalism and federal taxation, liberal indicates pro-national government positions; in judicial power cases, the term represents pro-judiciary positions.

Source: U.S. Supreme Court Judicial Database, with orally argued citation plus split vote as unit of analysis.

Table 6-2 Liberal Voting of the Justices, 1953-1991 Terms

Term	Civil liberties	Criminal procedure	Civil rights	First Amendment	Economics
			Black		
1953	82.1 (28)	66.7 (15)	100.0 (8)	100.0 (4)	81.1 (37)
1954	78.4 (37)	66.7 (18)	80.0 (10)	100.0 (5)	84.6 (26)
1955	83.3 (30)	66.7 (12)	100.0 (11)	100.0 (5)	87.2 (39)
1956	94.2 (52)	100.0 (18)	75.0 (12)	100.0 (15)	86.8 (38)
1957	87.3 (63)	81.3 (32)	100.0 (14)	100.0 (9)	85.3 (34)
1958	88.1 (42)	84.0 (25)	83.3 (6)	100.0 (11)	85.7 (49)
1959	91.7 (36)	87.5 (16)	100.0 (10)	100.0 (7)	89.7 (39)
1960	83.6 (67)	90.0 (30)	78.6 (14)	81.8 (22)	78.9 (38)
1961	92.1 (38)	87.5 (16)	88.9 (9)	100.0 (8)	76.3 (38)
1962	88.2 (51)	81.8 (22)	94.1 (17)	87.5 (8)	88.9 (45)
1963	87.9 (58)	90.9 (22)	85.2 (27)	88.9 (9)	82.5 (40)
1964	73.8 (42)	68.8 (16)	69.2 (13)	90.0 (10)	79.3 (29)
1965	71.7 (46)	75.0 (16)	50.0 (14)	92.3 (13)	76.9 (26)
1966	56.9 (58)	53.6 (28)	57.9 (19)	70.0 (10)	86.7 (30)

(Table continues)

Table 6-2 *(Continued)*

Term	Civil liberties	Criminal procedure	Civil rights	First Amendment	Economics
1967	60.0 (70)	47.2 (36)	62.5 (16)	78.6 (14)	73.5 (34)
1968	50.0 (62)	33.3 (27)	54.5 (22)	80.0 (10)	85.7 (21)
1969	51.6 (64)	50.0 (26)	46.2 (26)	70.0 (10)	66.7 (15)
1970	55.6 (81)	41.7 (24)	55.2 (29)	72.7 (22)	70.8 (24)
			Blackmun		
1970	34.6 (81)	12.5 (24)	51.7 (29)	31.8 (22)	47.8 (23)
1971	37.4 (91)	20.6 (34)	46.4 (28)	35.3 (17)	47.4 (38)
1972	38.9 (95)	25.7 (35)	54.5 (33)	27.8 (18)	63.6 (33)
1973	37.1 (89)	26.7 (30)	41.7 (36)	50.0 (14)	46.4 (28)
1974	46.6 (73)	45.8 (24)	48.3 (29)	55.6 (9)	64.7 (34)
1975	32.2 (90)	9.1 (33)	50.0 (28)	64.3 (14)	43.8 (32)
1976	33.3 (93)	23.3 (30)	34.3 (35)	33.3 (15)	50.0 (26)
1977	51.6 (64)	48.0 (25)	45.8 (24)	66.7 (6)	63.3 (30)
1978	45.8 (83)	37.9 (29)	52.9 (34)	37.5 (8)	46.9 (32)
1979	51.2 (84)	34.4 (32)	63.6 (22)	60.0 (10)	56.8 (37)
1980	44.8 (67)	44.0 (25)	50.0 (26)	44.4 (9)	66.7 (30)

Table 6-2   *(Continued)*

Term	Civil liberties	Criminal procedure	Civil rights	First Amendment	Economics
1981	59.3 (81)	36.8 (19)	73.5 (34)	75.0 (12)	63.6 (33)
1982	61.0 (82)	40.0 (30)	78.6 (28)	63.6 (11)	55.0 (40)
1983	43.6 (94)	20.5 (39)	65.5 (29)	75.0 (12)	48.5 (33)
1984	51.1 (88)	39.4 (33)	68.0 (25)	63.6 (11)	52.8 (36)
1985	64.9 (97)	55.8 (43)	72.4 (29)	61.5 (13)	47.4 (19)
1986	74.5 (94)	68.3 (41)	82.6 (23)	83.3 (12)	51.9 (27)
1987	65.4 (78)	53.1 (32)	76.2 (21)	76.9 (13)	54.3 (35)
1988	68.7 (83)	58.6 (29)	96.2 (26)	53.3 (15)	63.6 (22)
1989	58.6 (70)	54.3 (35)	70.0 (10)	57.1 (14)	46.2 (26)
1990	77.6 (58)	66.7 (30)	93.8 (16)	100.0 (6)	59.4 (32)
1991	73.2 (56)	57.1 (21)	83.3 (18)	87.5 (8)	67.9 (28)
			Brennan		
1956	72.7 (44)	83.3 (18)	50.0 (12)	62.5 (8)	74.4 (39)
1957	78.7 (61)	70.0 (30)	85.7 (14)	100.0 (9)	79.4 (34)
1958	79.1 (43)	73.1 (26)	66.7 (6)	100.0 (11)	75.5 (49)

(Table continues)

Table 6-2 *(Continued)*

Term	Civil liberties	Criminal procedure	Civil rights	First Amendment	Economics
1959	77.8 (36)	68.8 (16)	100.0 (10)	85.7 (7)	81.0 (42)
1960	79.1 (67)	80.0 (30)	64.3 (14)	86.4 (22)	63.2 (38)
1961	84.6 (39)	76.5 (17)	88.9 (9)	100.0 (8)	68.4 (38)
1962	84.3 (51)	77.3 (22)	94.1 (17)	87.5 (8)	82.2 (45)
1963	86.0 (57)	77.3 (22)	92.3 (26)	88.9 (9)	67.5 (40)
1964	70.5 (44)	50.0 (16)	85.7 (14)	72.7 (11)	65.5 (29)
1965	73.9 (46)	56.3 (16)	85.7 (14)	76.9 (13)	82.1 (28)
1966	78.0 (59)	75.0 (28)	84.2 (19)	81.8 (11)	73.3 (30)
1967	77.1 (70)	80.6 (36)	81.3 (16)	64.3 (14)	66.7 (33)
1968	79.4 (63)	66.7 (27)	82.6 (23)	100.0 (10)	76.2 (21)
1969	69.2 (65)	55.6 (27)	84.6 (26)	70.0 (10)	62.5 (16)
1970	75.9 (79)	70.8 (24)	82.1 (28)	68.2 (22)	68.0 (25)
1971	81.8 (88)	71.0 (31)	92.9 (28)	82.4 (17)	66.7 (39)
1972	86.3 (95)	74.3 (35)	93.9 (33)	94.4 (18)	70.0 (30)
1973	80.9 (89)	76.7 (30)	86.1 (36)	85.7 (14)	82.8 (29)
1974	80.8 (73)	83.3 (24)	86.2 (9)	66.7 (9)	73.5 (34)

Table 6-2   *(Continued)*

Term	Civil liberties	Criminal procedure	Civil rights	First Amendment	Economics
1975	84.4 (90)	78.8 (33)	85.7 (28)	100.0 (14)	63.6 (33)
1976	75.5 (94)	71.0 (31)	74.3 (35)	93.3 (15)	73.1 (26)
1977	79.3 (58)	95.0 (20)	69.6 (23)	85.7 (7)	80.6 (31)
1978	79.3 (82)	78.6 (28)	82.4 (34)	62.5 (8)	51.6 (31)
1979	82.4 (85)	78.1 (32)	86.4 (22)	100.0 (10)	80.6 (36)
1980	72.1 (68)	72.0 (25)	85.2 (27)	77.8 (9)	71.9 (32)
1981	76.5 (81)	78.9 (19)	85.3 (34)	75.0 (12)	67.6 (34)
1982	74.1 (81)	66.7 (30)	78.6 (28)	80.0 (10)	60.0 (40)
1983	74.0 (96)	75.0 (40)	82.8 (29)	84.6 (13)	57.6 (33)
1984	76.4 (89)	78.8 (33)	72.0 (25)	90.9 (11)	63.9 (36)
1985	76.5 (98)	76.7 (43)	72.4 (29)	71.4 (14)	66.7 (18)
1986	92.7 (96)	95.1 (41)	92.0 (25)	91.7 (12)	64.3 (28)
1987	82.9 (76)	83.3 (30)	81.0 (21)	100.0 (13)	69.4 (36)
1988	85.7 (84)	79.3 (29)	96.2 (26)	80.0 (15)	68.2 (22)
1989	84.3 (71)	88.6 (35)	100.0 (10)	71.4 (14)	69.2 (26)

(Table continues)

Table 6-2 *(Continued)*

Term	Civil liberties	Criminal procedure	Civil rights	First Amendment	Economics
			Burger		
1969	30.8 (65)	22.2 (27)	34.6 (26)	40.0 (10)	23.1 (13)
1970	36.3 (80)	17.4 (23)	48.3 (29)	31.8 (22)	44.0 (2425)
1971	34.1 (91)	17.6 (34)	42.9 (28)	35.3 (17)	36.8 (38)
1972	29.5 (95)	17.1 (35)	45.5 (33)	16.7 (18)	57.1 (35)
1973	30.3 (89)	20.0 (30)	38.9 (36)	28.6 (14)	37.9 (29)
1974	38.4 (73)	41.7 (24)	41.4 (29)	22.2 (9)	41.2 (34)
1975	26.7 (90)	9.1 (33)	46.4 (28)	42.9 (14)	42.4 (33)
1976	17.0 (94)	19.4 (31)	17.1 (35)	20.0 (15)	36.0 (25)
1977	36.0 (75)	48.3 (29)	25.0 (28)	50.0 (8)	51.4 (35)
1978	27.7 (83)	31.0 (29)	17.6 (34)	37.5 (8)	40.6 (32)
1979	35.3 (85)	15.6 (32)	50.0 (22)	50.0 (10)	47.2 (36)
1980	31.3 (67)	32.0 (25)	33.3 (27)	25.0 (8)	43.8 (32)
1981	23.8 (80)	0.0 (18)	26.5 (34)	50.0 (12)	35.3 (34)
1982	28.0 (82)	10.0 (30)	39.3 (28)	45.5 (11)	50.0 (40)
1983	30.9 (94)	12.8 (39)	55.2 (29)	25.0 (12)	39.4 (33)

Table 6-2   *(Continued)*

Term	Civil liberties	Criminal procedure	Civil rights	First Amendment	Economics
1984	28.1 (89)	9.1 (33)	56.0 (25)	18.2 (11)	41.7 (36)
1985	23.5 (98)	18.6 (43)	27.6 (29)	21.4 (14)	42.1 (19)
			Burton		
1953	35.7 (28)	33.3 (15)	37.5 (8)	25.0 (4)	51.3 (39)
1954	52.8 (36)	47.1 (17)	60.0 (10)	40.0 (5)	61.5 (26)
1955	43.3 (30)	33.3 (12)	45.5 (11)	40.0 (5)	56.4 (39)
1956	30.2 (53)	35.0 (20)	8.3 (12)	21.4 (14)	53.5 (43)
1957	36.5 (63)	25.0 (32)	50.0 (14)	44.4 (9)	47.1 (34)
1958	100.0 (2)	—	100.0 (2)	—	—
			Clark		
1953	44.4 (27)	26.7 (15)	62.5 (8)	66.7 (3)	60.0 (35)
1954	62.2 (37)	50.0 (18)	60.0 (10)	80.0 (5)	81.5 (27)
1955	48.3 (29)	45.5 (11)	54.4 (11)	40.0 (5)	81.1 (37)
1956	32.1 (53)	45.0 (20)	16.7 (12)	7.1 (14)	80.0 (40)
1957	30.6 (62)	25.0 (32)	21.4 (14)	11.1 (9)	66.7 (33)
1958	41.9 (43)	34.6 (26)	50.0 (6)	54.5 (11)	67.4 (46)

(Table continues)

Table 6-2 *(Continued)*

Term	Civil liberties	Criminal procedure	Civil rights	First Amendment	Economics
1959	36.1 (36)	18.8 (16)	60.0 (10)	28.6 (7)	69.0 (42)
1960	31.3 (67)	30.0 (30)	42.9 (14)	22.7 (22)	54.1 (37)
1961	43.6 (39)	35.3 (17)	66.7 (9)	25.0 (8)	71.1 (38)
1962	47.1 (51)	31.8 (22)	64.7 (17)	50.0 (8)	90.9 (44)
1963	55.2 (58)	45.5 (22)	70.4 (27)	33.3 (9)	80.0 (40)
1964	59.1 (44)	37.5 (16)	85.7 (14)	45.5 (11)	69.0 (29)
1965	58.7 (46)	37.5 (16)	78.6 (14)	53.8 (13)	75.0 (28)
1966	43.9 (57)	46.2 (26)	52.6 (19)	27.3 (11)	81.5 (27)

	Douglas				
1953	85.7 (28)	73.3 (15)	100.0 (8)	100.0 (4)	77.8 (36)
1954	78.4 (37)	72.2 (18)	80.0 (10)	100.0 (5)	88.9 (27)
1955	86.7 (30)	75.0 (12)	100.0 (11)	100.0 (5)	87.2 (39)
1956	94.3 (53)	95.0 (20)	90.9 (11)	100.0 (15)	90.7 (43)
1957	92.1 (63)	93.8 (32)	100.0 (14)	100.0 (9)	91.2 (34)
1958	93.0 (43)	92.3 (26)	83.3 (6)	100.0 (11)	93.8 (48)
1959	91.7 (36)	87.5 (16)	100.0 (10)	100.0 (7)	90.5 (42)

Table 6-2   *(Continued)*

Term	Civil liberties	Criminal procedure	Civil rights	First Amendment	Economics
1960	95.5 (67)	93.3 (30)	92.9 (14)	100.0 (22)	81.6 (38)
1961	92.3 (39)	94.1 (17)	88.9 (9)	100.0 (8)	84.2 (38)
1962	94.1 (51)	90.9 (22)	94.1 (17)	100.0 (8)	77.8 (45)
1963	98.3 (58)	100.0 (22)	100.0 (27)	88.9 (9)	68.4 (38)
1964	97.7 (44)	93.8 (16)	100.0 (14)	100.0 (11)	72.4 (29)
1965	93.5 (46)	87.5 (16)	92.9 (14)	100.0 (13)	85.7 (28)
1966	91.2 (57)	96.3 (27)	89.5 (19)	90.0 (10)	93.3 (30)
1967	91.4 (70)	91.7 (36)	81.3 (16)	100.0 (14)	66.7 (30)
1968	87.1 (62)	81.5 (27)	91.3 (23)	100.0 (9)	81.0 (21)
1969	83.1 (65)	77.8 (27)	88.5 (26)	80.0 (10)	73.3 (15)
1970	90.9 (77)	86.4 (22)	85.7 (28)	100.0 (21)	75.0 (24)
1971	94.5 (91)	88.2 (34)	96.4 (28)	100.0 (17)	68.4 (38)
1972	91.6 (95)	88.6 (35)	93.9 (33)	94.4 (18)	71.4 (35)
1973	93.3 (89)	93.3 (30)	94.4 (36)	85.7 (14)	77.8 (27)
1974	89.1 (64)	95.5 (22)	91.3 (23)	88.9 (9)	80.0 (30)

(Table continues)

Table 6-2 *(Continued)*

Term	Civil liberties	Criminal procedure	Civil rights	First Amendment	Economics
1975	—	—	—	—	100.0 (1)
			Fortas		
1965	83.7 (43)	73.3 (15)	100.0 (13)	75.0 (12)	68.2 (22)
1966	82.5 (57)	92.6 (27)	78.9 (19)	70.0 (10)	76.9 (26)
1967	80.0 (70)	80.6 (36)	75.0 (16)	78.6 (14)	57.6 (33)
1968	77.1 (35)	61.5 (13)	84.6 (13)	87.5 (8)	71.4 (14)
			Frankfurter		
1953	57.1 (28)	46.7 (15)	62.5 (8)	75.0 (4)	46.2 (39)
1954	70.3 (37)	55.6 (18)	90.9 (10)	80.0 (5)	61.5 (26)
1955	67.9 (28)	50.0 (12)	88.9 (9)	80.0 (5)	52.6 (38)
1956	51.9 (54)	65.0 (20)	25.0 (12)	53.3 (15)	33.3 (36)
1957	54.1 (61)	50.0 (32)	53.8 (13)	66.7 (9)	33.3 (33)
1958	42.5 (40)	37.5 (24)	40.0 (5)	54.5 (11)	42.2 (45)
1959	36.1 (36)	25.0 (16)	50.0 (10)	28.6 (7)	30.8 (39)
1960	34.8 (66)	36.7 (30)	42.9 (14)	23.8 (21)	41.9 (31)
1961	57.9 (19)	57.1 (7)	57.1 (7)	50.0 (2)	33.3 (18)

Table 6-2 *(Continued)*

Term	Civil liberties	Criminal procedure	Civil rights	First Amendment	Economics
			Goldberg		
1962	88.2 (51)	77.3 (22)	100.0 (17)	100.0 (8)	75.6 (40)
1963	96.6 (58)	95.5 (22)	100.0 (27)	88.9 (9)	64.9 (37)
1964	79.5 (44)	62.5 (16)	92.9 (14)	81.8 (11)	50.0 (26)
			Harlan		
1954	81.8 (11)	50.0 (4)	100.0 (4)	100.0 (1)	33.3 (3)
1955	50.0 (24)	37.5 (8)	44.4 (9)	60.0 (5)	65.6 (32)
1956	50.0 (54)	50.0 (20)	25.0 (12)	60.0 (15)	39.0 (41)
1957	42.9 (63)	43.8 (32)	35.7 (14)	44.4 (9)	32.4 (34)
1958	44.2 (43)	38.5 (26)	33.3 (6)	63.6 (11)	45.7 (46)
1959	36.1 (36)	25.0 (16)	40.0 (10)	42.9 (7)	38.1 (42)
1960	35.4 (65)	33.3 (30)	58.3 (12)	22.7 (22)	43.2 (37)
1961	51.3 (39)	52.9 (17)	55.6 (9)	37.5 (8)	36.8 (38)
1962	35.3 (41)	36.4 (22)	29.4 (17)	37.5 (8)	47.7 (44)
1963	38.6 (57)	40.9 (22)	42.3 (26)	22.2 (9)	33.3 (39)
1964	54.5 (44)	43.8 (16)	57.1 (14)	63.6 (11)	39.3 (28)

(Table continues)

Table 6-2 *(Continued)*

Term	Civil liberties	Criminal procedure	Civil rights	First Amendment	Economics
1965	37.0 (46)	18.8 (16)	35.7 (14)	53.8 (13)	37.0 (27)
1966	30.5 (59)	28.6 (28)	36.8 (19)	27.3 (11)	33.3 (30)
1967	45.7 (70)	44.4 (36)	50.0 (16)	28.6 (14)	45.5 (33)
1968	55.6 (63)	44.4 (27)	52.2 (23)	90.0 (10)	52.6 (19)
1969	46.9 (64)	37.0 (27)	52.0 (25)	60.0 (10)	37.5 (16)
1970	42.0 (81)	45.8 (24)	44.8 (29)	27.3 (22)	50.0 (24)
Jackson					
1953	48.1 (27)	35.7 (14)	62.5 (8)	50.0 (4)	47.1 (34)
Kennedy					
1987	45.7 (35)	29.4 (17)	57.1 (7)	60.0 (5)	47.4 (19)
1988	28.2 (85)	16.7 (30)	34.6 (26)	33.3 (15)	42.9 (21)
1989	24.6 (69)	14.3 (35)	25.0 (8)	35.7 (14)	46.2 (26)
1990	36.2 (58)	30.0 (30)	50.0 (16)	50.0 (6)	46.9 (32)
1991	48.2 (56)	38.1 (21)	61.1 (18)	75.0 (8)	42.9 (28)
Marshall					
1967	77.6 (49)	80.8 (26)	81.8 (11)	63.6 (11)	44.4 (9)

Table 6-2   *(Continued)*

Term	Civil liberties	Criminal procedure	Civil rights	First Amendment	Economics
1968	84.5 (58)	69.6 (23)	91.3 (23)	100.0 (9)	68.4 (18)
1969	69.5 (59)	58.3 (24)	87.0 (23)	60.0 (10)	70.0 (10)
1970	78.2 (78)	79.2 (24)	82.8 (29)	65.0 (20)	50.0 (24)
1971	85.7 (91)	85.3 (34)	78.6 (28)	94.1 (17)	53.8 (39)
1972	85.7 (91)	79.4 (34)	84.4 (32)	94.1 (17)	76.5 (34)
1973	83.9 (87)	80.0 (30)	85.7 (35)	92.9 (14)	75.9 (29)
1974	79.5 (73)	79.2 (24)	89.7 (29)	66.7 (9)	55.9 (34)
1975	83.9 (87)	75.0 (32)	88.5 (26)	100.0 (14)	54.5 (33)
1976	76.1 (92)	74.2 (31)	75.8 (33)	86.7 (15)	61.5 (26)
1977	79.7 (74)	86.2 (29)	75.0 (28)	85.7 (7)	77.1 (35)
1978	78.3 (83)	75.9 (29)	85.3 (34)	50.0 (8)	59.4 (32)
1979	86.1 (79)	86.7 (30)	86.4 (22)	100.0 (8)	70.6 (34)
1980	76.5 (68)	76.0 (25)	85.2 (27)	88.9 (9)	72.7 (30)
1981	75.9 (79)	77.8 (18)	88.2 (34)	72.7 (11)	70.6 (34)
1982	82.5 (80)	72.4 (29)	92.6 (27)	81.8 (11)	67.5 (40)

(Table continues)

Table 6-2 *(Continued)*

Term	Civil liberties	Criminal procedure	Civil rights	First Amendment	Economics
1983	75.0 (92)	76.3 (38)	82.8 (29)	76.9 (13)	56.3 (32)
1984	74.7 (87)	75.8 (33)	72.0 (25)	80.0 (10)	67.6 (34)
1985	81.4 (97)	81.4 (43)	75.0 (28)	85.7 (14)	57.9 (19)
1986	90.5 (95)	95.0 (40)	96.0 (25)	91.7 (12)	67.9 (28)
1987	83.3 (78)	87.1 (31)	81.0 (21)	100.0 (13)	75.0 (36)
1988	86.9 (84)	80.0 (30)	100.0 (26)	80.0 (15)	68.2 (22)
1989	88.6 (70)	94.3 (35)	100.0 (10)	71.4 (14)	69.2 (26)
1990	86.2 (58)	83.3 (30)	93.8 (16)	100.0 (6)	71.9 (32)
Minton					
1953	39.3 (28)	40.0 (15)	37.5 (8)	25.0 (4)	53.8 (39)
1954	36.1 (36)	29.4 (17)	40.0 (10)	20.0 (5)	74.1 (27)
1955	33.3 (30)	33.3 (12)	36.4 (11)	0.0 (5)	71.8 (39)
1956	100.0 (1)	100.0 (1)	—	—	0.0 (1)
O'Connor					
1981	34.6 (81)	10.5 (19)	41.2 (34)	58.3 (12)	53.1 (32)
1982	26.8 (82)	13.3 (30)	42.9 (28)	36.4 (11)	46.2 (39)

Table 6-2 *(Continued)*

Term	Civil liberties	Criminal procedure	Civil rights	First Amendment	Economics
1983	31.3 (96)	17.5 (40)	55.2 (29)	23.1 (13)	41.9 (31)
1984	32.6 (89)	21.2 (33)	52.0 (25)	27.3 (11)	45.7 (35)
1985	34.7 (98)	20.9 (43)	44.8 (29)	50.0 (14)	52.6 (19)
1986	30.5 (95)	22.0 (41)	33.3 (24)	50.0 (12)	46.4 (28)
1987	33.8 (77)	33.3 (30)	38.1 (21)	23.1 (13)	33.3 (36)
1988	33.3 (84)	20.0 (30)	44.0 (25)	33.3 (15)	28.6 (21)
1989	21.4 (71)	14.3 (35)	11.1 (20)	28.6 (14)	40.0 (25)
1990	39.7 (58)	26.7 (30)	62.5 (16)	50.0 (6)	43.8 (30)
1991	57.1 (56)	52.4 (21)	61.1 (18)	87.5 (8)	42.9 (28)
			Powell		
1971	34.7 (49)	17.4 (23)	60.0 (10)	33.3 (12)	33.3 (15)
1972	36.2 (94)	22.9 (35)	50.0 (32)	22.2 (18)	56.7 (30)
1973	42.0 (88)	23.3 (30)	44.4 (36)	78.6 (14)	44.0 (25)
1974	52.9 (68)	54.2 (24)	51.9 (27)	55.6 (9)	45.2 (31)
1975	35.6 (90)	18.2 (33)	50.0 (28)	50.0 (14)	48.4 (31)

(Table continues)

Table 6-2 *(Continued)*

Term	Civil liberties	Criminal procedure	Civil rights	First Amendment	Economics
1976	35.1 (94)	35.5 (31)	34.3 (35)	40.0 (15)	45.8 (24)
1977	47.3 (74)	55.2 (29)	42.9 (28)	57.1 (7)	53.1 (32)
1978	30.4 (69)	36.4 (22)	16.1 (31)	33.3 (6)	36.0 (25)
1979	42.7 (82)	37.5 (32)	40.0 (20)	44.4 (9)	51.4 (37)
1980	34.8 (66)	36.0 (25)	34.6 (26)	37.5 (8)	48.3 (29)
1981	38.3 (81)	21.1 (19)	38.2 (34)	66.7 (12)	45.5 (33)
1982	26.8 (82)	20.0 (30)	25.0 (28)	54.5 (11)	50.0 (36)
1983	34.7 (95)	17.5 (28)	50.0 (13)	53.8 (10)	28.1 (32)
1984	40.7 (59)	24.0 (25)	66.7 (15)	62.5 (8)	41.7 (24)
1985	31.6 (98)	25.6 (43)	31.0 (29)	35.7 (14)	47.4 (19)
1986	37.5 (96)	26.8 (41)	48.0 (25)	50.0 (12)	51.9 (27)
			Reed		
1953	40.0 (25)	33.3 (12)	37.5 (8)	50.0 (4)	45.9 (37)
1954	27.0 (37)	22.2 (18)	30.0 (10)	0.0 (5)	63.0 (27)
1955	26.7 (30)	33.3 (12)	27.3 (11)	0.0 (5)	66.7 (39)
1956	50.0 (16)	27.3 (11)	100.0 (2)	100.0 (1)	55.6 (18)

Table 6-2   *(Continued)*

Term	Civil liberties	Criminal procedure	Civil rights	First Amendment	Economics
			Rehnquist		
1971	25.5 (47)	10.5 (19)	40.0 (10)	33.3 (12)	33.3 (21)
1972	17.2 (93)	14.3 (35)	28.1 (32)	11.1 (18)	45.7 (35)
1973	25.0 (88)	17.2 (29)	27.8 (36)	35.7 (14)	34.5 (29)
1974	31.9 (72)	41.7 (24)	31.0 (29)	0.0 (8)	50.0 (34)
1975	18.9 (90)	9.1 (33)	35.7 (28)	28.6 (14)	36.4 (33)
1976	9.9 (81)	4.0 (25)	18.6 (32)	7.1 (14)	38.1 (21)
1977	18.7 (75)	20.7 (29)	14.3 (28)	37.5 (8)	40.0 (35)
1978	21.7 (83)	27.6 (29)	8.8 (34)	25.0 (8)	41.9 (31)
1979	10.7 (84)	0.0 (32)	13.6 (22)	0.0 (10)	38.9 (36)
1980	19.7 (66)	20.0 (25)	23.1 (26)	0.0 (8)	41.9 (31)
1981	21.0 (81)	5.3 (19)	17.6 (34)	50.0 (12)	50.0 (34)
1982	17.1 (82)	16.7 (30)	21.4 (28)	18.2 (11)	50.0 (40)
1983	24.0 (96)	7.5 (40)	44.8 (29)	15.4 (13)	41.9 (31)
1984	22.5 (89)	15.2 (33)	36.0 (25)	9.1 (11)	41.2 (34)

(Table continues)

Table 6-2 *(Continued)*

Term	Civil liberties	Criminal procedure	Civil rights	First Amendment	Economics
1985	16.5 (97)	14.0 (43)	17.9 (28)	7.1 (14)	36.8 (19)
1986	15.6 (96)	12.2 (41)	20.0 (25)	8.3 (12)	46.4 (28)
1987	29.9 (77)	25.8 (31)	33.3 (21)	25.0 (12)	37.1 (35)
1988	22.6 (84)	20.0 (30)	26.9 (26)	14.3 (14)	36.4 (22)
1989	14.3 (71)	11.4 (35)	0.0 (10)	14.3 (14)	46.2 (26)
1990	20.7 (58)	13.3 (30)	37.5 (16)	16.7 (6)	46.9 (32)
1991	32.1 (56)	23.8 (21)	50.0 (18)	37.5 (8)	50.0 (28)
			Scalia		
1986	27.7 (94)	25.0 (40)	32.0 (25)	36.4 (11)	63.0 (27)
1987	36.8 (76)	32.3 (31)	35.0 (20)	46.2 (13)	40.0 (35)
1988	33.3 (84)	30.0 (30)	38.5 (26)	33.3 (15)	40.9 (22)
1989	24.3 (70)	17.1 (35)	22.2 (9)	28.6 (14)	38.5 (26)
1990	29.3 (58)	30.0 (30)	43.8 (16)	0.0 (6)	43.8 (32)
1991	25.0 (56)	14.3 (21)	38.9 (18)	37.5 (8)	39.3 (28)
			Souter		
1990	32.1 (53)	14.8 (27)	73.3 (15)	33.3 (6)	41.4 (29)

Table 6-2   *(Continued)*

Term	Civil liberties	Criminal procedure	Civil rights	First Amendment	Economics
1991	50.9 (55)	42.9 (21)	50.0 (18)	100.0 (8)	53.6 (28)
			Stevens		
1975	54.8 (42)	33.3 (15)	87.5 (16)	50.0 (4)	66.7 (18)
1976	58.1 (93)	54.8 (31)	58.8 (34)	66.7 (15)	53.8 (26)
1977	52.7 (74)	60.7 (28)	42.9 (28)	87.5 (8)	76.5 (34)
1978	60.5 (81)	65.5 (29)	53.1 (32)	25.0 (8)	56.7 (30)
1979	60.7 (84)	56.3 (32)	52.4 (21)	100.0 (10)	61.1 (36)
1980	53.7 (67)	58.3 (24)	51.9 (27)	66.7 (9)	51.5 (33)
1981	51.3 (78)	36.8 (19)	57.6 (33)	80.0 (10)	54.5 (33)
1982	57.9 (81)	62.1 (29)	64.3 (28)	72.7 (11)	43.6 (39)
1983	57.3 (96)	55.0 (40)	72.4 (29)	38.5 (13)	57.6 (33)
1984	56.3 (87)	61.3 (31)	56.0 (25)	72.7 (11)	47.2 (36)
1985	55.7 (97)	60.5 (43)	51.7 (29)	42.9 (14)	47.4 (19)
1986	66.7 (93)	69.2 (39)	54.2 (24)	66.7 (12)	71.4 (28)
1987	62.8 (78)	71.0 (31)	57.1 (21)	53.8 (13)	62.9 (35)

(Table continues)

Table 6-2   *(Continued)*

Term	Civil liberties	Criminal procedure	Civil rights	First Amendment	Economics
1988	61.9 (84)	50.0 (30)	73.1 (26)	66.7 (15)	54.5 (22)
1989	71.4 (70)	77.1 (35)	77.8 (9)	50.0 (14)	46.2 (26)
1990	81.0 (58)	83.3 (30)	87.5 (16)	66.7 (6)	71.9 (32)
1991	80.4 (56)	76.2 (21)	77.8 (18)	100.0 (8)	53.6 (28)
			Stewart		
1958	41.0 (39)	34.6 (26)	33.3 (3)	60.0 (10)	48.8 (43)
1959	41.7 (36)	37.5 (16)	50.0 (10)	42.9 (7)	50.0 (40)
1960	53.0 (66)	58.6 (29)	50.0 (14)	45.5 (22)	48.6 (35)
1961	66.7 (39)	52.9 (17)	88.9 (9)	75.0 (8)	54.1 (37)
1962	54.9 (51)	40.9 (22)	70.6 (17)	50.0 (8)	51.1 (44)
1963	68.4 (57)	50.0 (22)	77.8 (27)	87.5 (8)	50.0 (36)
1964	55.8 (43)	43.8 (16)	64.3 (14)	60.0 (10)	53.8 (26)
1965	54.3 (46)	37.5 (16)	50.0 (14)	69.2 (13)	50.0 (28)
1966	41.4 (58)	40.7 (27)	36.8 (19)	45.5 (11)	48.3 (29)
1967	63.8 (69)	63.9 (36)	62.5 (16)	57.1 (14)	47.1 (34)
1968	54.0 (63)	37.0 (27)	47.8 (23)	100.0 (10)	42.9 (21)

Table 6-2 *(Continued)*

Term	Civil liberties	Criminal procedure	Civil rights	First Amendment	Economics
1969	41.5 (65)	29.6 (27)	50.0 (26)	50.0 (10)	40.0 (15)
1970	47.5 (80)	29.2 (24)	51.7 (29)	50.0 (22)	48.0 (25)
1971	64.8 (91)	52.9 (34)	71.4 (28)	70.6 (17)	45.9 (37)
1972	57.4 (94)	48.6 (35)	56.3 (32)	77.8 (18)	41.4 (29)
1973	52.3 (88)	40.0 (30)	54.3 (35)	78.6 (14)	36.0 (25)
1974	57.5 (73)	75.0 (24)	51.7 (29)	55.6 (9)	38.2 (34)
1975	47.8 (90)	36.4 (33)	53.6 (28)	71.4 (14)	40.6 (32)
1976	40.4 (94)	41.9 (31)	34.3 (35)	66.7 (15)	36.0 (25)
1977	54.7 (75)	62.1 (29)	39.3 (28)	75.0 (8)	61.8 (34)
1978	42.2 (83)	48.3 (29)	23.5 (34)	50.0 (8)	48.4 (31)
1979	45.9 (85)	40.6 (32)	36.4 (22)	80.0 (10)	50.0 (34)
1980	36.4 (66)	48.0 (25)	25.9 (27)	62.5 (8)	53.1 (32)
			Thomas		
1991	25.6 (43)	16.7 (18)	42.9 (14)	16.7 (6)	40.0 (25)
			Warren		
1953	38.5 (26)	21.4 (14)	62.5 (8)	50.0 (4)	66.7 (39)

(Table continues)

Table 6-2 *(Continued)*

Term	Civil liberties	Criminal procedure	Civil rights	First Amendment	Economics
1954	61.1 (36)	47.1 (17)	70.0 (10)	80.0 (5)	81.5 (27)
1955	75.9 (29)	45.5 (11)	100.0 (11)	100.0 (5)	87.2 (39)
1956	75.0 (52)	85.0 (20)	50.0 (12)	73.3 (15)	90.5 (42)
1957	83.3 (60)	75.0 (32)	92.9 (14)	100.0 (7)	82.4 (34)
1958	85.7 (42)	80.0 (25)	83.3 (6)	100.0 (11)	87.5 (48)
1959	80.0 (35)	75.0 (16)	100.0 (10)	83.3 (6)	85.7 (42)
1960	82.1 (67)	96.7 (30)	64.3 (14)	77.3 (22)	65.8 (38)
1961	92.1 (38)	94.1 (17)	87.5 (8)	100.0 (8)	78.9 (38)
1962	84.3 (51)	77.3 (22)	94.1 (17)	87.5 (8)	85.7 (42)
1963	87.9 (58)	86.4 (22)	92.6 (27)	77.8 (9)	80.0 (40)
1964	78.6 (42)	66.7 (15)	92.3 (13)	72.7 (11)	64.3 (28)
1965	77.3 (44)	66.7 (15)	84.6 (13)	76.9 (13)	78.6 (28)
1966	78.0 (59)	85.7 (28)	78.9 (19)	63.6 (11)	75.9 (29)
1967	73.9 (69)	74.3 (35)	81.3 (16)	64.3 (14)	72.7 (33)
1968	79.4 (63)	74.1 (27)	78.3 (23)	90.0 (10)	85.7 (21)

Table 6-2   *(Continued)*

Term	Civil liberties	Criminal procedure	Civil rights	First Amendment	Economics
			White		
1961	50.0 (2)	0.0 (1)	100.0 (1)	—	80.0 (8)
1962	60.8 (51)	50.0 (22)	70.6 (17)	62.5 (8)	76.2 (42)
1963	63.2 (57)	50.0 (22)	73.1 (26)	66.7 (9)	61.5 (39)
1964	60.0 (40)	43.8 (16)	69.2 (13)	62.5 (8)	67.9 (28)
1965	58.1 (43)	42.9 (14)	78.6 (14)	41.7 (12)	85.2 (27)
1966	52.6 (57)	50.0 (26)	57.9 (19)	54.5 (11)	66.7 (27)
1967	50.0 (70)	44.4 (36)	75.0 (16)	28.6 (14)	67.6 (34)
1968	61.3 (62)	50.0 (26)	56.5 (23)	90.0 (10)	66.7 (21)
1969	49.2 (65)	44.4 (27)	57.7 (26)	40.0 (10)	60.0 (15)
1970	40.0 (80)	13.0 (23)	58.6 (29)	36.4 (22)	54.2 (24)
1971	49.5 (91)	41.2 (34)	57.1 (28)	41.2 (17)	48.7 (39)
1972	31.2 (93)	26.5 (34)	56.3 (32)	5.6 (18)	57.1 (35)
1973	44.9 (89)	23.3 (30)	61.1 (36)	50.0 (14)	72.4 (29)
1974	49.3 (73)	50.0 (24)	62.1 (29)	11.1 (9)	64.7 (34)

(Table continues)

Table 6-2   *(Continued)*

Term	Civil liberties	Criminal procedure	Civil rights	First Amendment	Economics
1975	37.8 (90)	18.2 (33)	53.6 (28)	50.0 (14)	38.5 (31)
1976	35.1 (94)	32.3 (31)	45.7 (35)	20.0 (15)	46.2 (26)
1977	53.3 (75)	65.5 (29)	46.4 (28)	62.5 (8)	71.4 (35)
1978	49.4 (83)	44.8 (29)	61.8 (34)	37.5 (8)	58.1 (31)
1979	41.7 (84)	19.4 (31)	63.6 (22)	60.0 (10)	70.3 (37)
1980	44.1 (68)	40.0 (25)	55.6 (27)	44.4 (9)	56.7 (30)
1981	45.7 (81)	31.6 (19)	52.9 (34)	50.0 (12)	60.6 (33)
1982	36.6 (82)	23.3 (30)	57.1 (28)	45.5 (11)	55.0 (40)
1983	33.7 (95)	20.0 (40)	58.6 (29)	23.1 (13)	45.2 (31)
1984	30.7 (88)	18.2 (33)	52.0 (25)	9.1 (11)	51.4 (35)
1985	32.7 (98)	27.9 (43)	41.4 (29)	28.6 (14)	44.4 (18)
1986	26.3 (95)	15.0 (40)	36.0 (25)	33.3 (12)	42.9 (28)
1987	39.7 (78)	35.5 (31)	38.1 (21)	46.2 (13)	48.6 (35)
1988	31.8 (85)	20.0 (30)	38.5 (26)	26.7 (15)	45.5 (22)
1989	27.1 (70)	22.9 (35)	44.4 (9)	21.4 (14)	57.7 (26)
1990	43.1 (58)	36.7 (30)	68.8 (16)	16.7 (6)	50.0 (32)
1991	41.1 (56)	38.1 (21)	61.1 (18)	37.5 (8)	57.1 (28)

Table 6-2   *(Continued)*

Term	Civil liberties	Criminal procedure	Civil rights	First Amendment	Economics
			Whittaker		
1956	47.1 (17)	83.3 (6)	0.0 (6)	33.3 (3)	57.1 (14)
1957	47.6 (63)	40.6 (32)	57.1 (14)	44.4 (9)	32.4 (34)
1958	46.5 (43)	38.5 (26)	66.7 (6)	54.5 (11)	38.8 (49)
1959	33.3 (36)	31.3 (16)	40.0 (10)	28.6 (7)	28.6 (42)
1960	38.8 (67)	46.7 (30)	42.9 (14)	27.3 (22)	31.6 (38)
1961	57.1 (14)	60.0 (5)	75.0 (4)	50.0 (2)	28.6 (14)

Note: "—" indicates that no issue area was decided during tenure overlap. Figures listed are the percentage of cases in which the justice took the liberal position. Figures in parentheses are the total number of cases in issue area in which the justice participated. Readers should take care in interpreting the percentages since some of the figures on which they are based are quite small.

The issue areas are defined as follows: Civil liberties: combines criminal procedure, civil rights, First Amendment, due process, privacy, and attorneys; Criminal procedure: the rights of persons accused of crime except for the due process rights of prisoners; Civil rights: non-First Amendment freedom cases that pertain to classifications based on race (including native Americans), age, indigence, voting, residence, military or handicapped status, sex, or alienage; First Amendment: guarantees contained therein; Economics: labor union activity, commercial business activity, litigation involving injured persons or things, employee actions vis-à-vis employers, zoning regulations, and governmental regulation of corruption other than that involving campaign spending.

The term *liberal* represents the voting direction of justices across the various issue areas. It is most appropriate in the areas of civil liberties, criminal procedure, civil rights, First Amendment, due process, privacy, and attorneys, where it signifies pro-defendant votes in criminal procedure cases, pro-women or -minorities in civil rights cases, pro-individual against the government in First Amendment, due process, and privacy cases, and pro-attorney in attorneys' fees and bar membership cases. In takings clause cases, however, a pro-government/anti-owner vote is considered liberal. The use of the term is perhaps less appropriate in union cases, where it represents pro-union votes against both individuals and the government, and in economic cases, where it represents pro-government votes against challenges to its regulatory authority and pro-competition, anti-business, pro-liability, pro-injured person, and pro-bankruptcy votes. In federalism and federal taxation, liberal indicates pro-national government positions; in judicial power cases, the term represents pro-judiciary positions.

Source: U.S. Supreme Court Judicial Database, with orally argued citation plus split votes as unit of analysis.

Table 6-3 Voting Interagreements Among the Justices by Issue Area: The Warren Court, 1953–1968 Terms

Justice	Crim	CivR	1st	DP	Priv	Atty	Un'n	Econ	JudP	Fed	IR	FTax	Misc
							Black						
Brennan	71.0 (213)	79.7 (153)	83.5 (116)	80.0 (24)	50.0 (1)	88.9 (8)	76.5 (75)	82.7 (296)	83.8 (155)	81.5 (53)	100 (6)	76.6 (72)	100 (1)
Burton	52.2 (49)	47.4 (27)	32.4 (12)	62.5 (10)	100 (1)	80.0 (4)	77.4 (24)	57.7 (82)	75.8 (50)	42.9 (9)	66.7 (2)	76.3 (29)	50.0 (2)
Clark	51.4 (146)	63.6 (117)	41.7 (56)	69.7 (23)	0.0 (0)	85.7 (6)	82.3 (88)	83.1 (319)	81.7 (157)	65.2 (43)	100 (9)	83.3 (90)	60.0 (3)
Douglas	79.1 (276)	82.8 (183)	90.6 (144)	86.5 (32)	50.0 (1)	90.0 (9)	79.0 (94)	86.9 (378)	78.9 (173)	77.5 (62)	100 (9)	54.0 (61)	80.0 (4)
Fortas	60.4 (55)	66.7 (40)	66.7 (30)	80.0 (4)	—	100 (4)	70.0 (14)	80.8 (59)	80.5 (37)	64.2 (9)	—	62.5 (10)	—
Frankfurter	54.3 (93)	65.6 (59)	51.9 (41)	45.4 (10)	100 (1)	80.0 (4)	63.1 (36)	47.7 (121)	70.0 (77)	71.1 (27)	80.0 (4)	82.9 (58)	80.0 (4)
Goldberg	75.0 (45)	86.0 (49)	85.2 (23)	80.0 (4)	0.0 (0)	100 (1)	85.0 (17)	73.8 (62)	75.5 (34)	83.3 (15)	75.0 (3)	78.3 (18)	—
Harlan	50.7 (160)	59.6 (121)	53.9 (82)	55.8 (19)	50.0 (2)	80.0 (10)	68.5 (74)	46.3 (173)	71.8 (145)	68.5 (48)	87.5 (8)	66.6 (66)	66.7 (3)
Jackson	71.4 (10)	62.5 (5)	50.0 (2)	100 (1)	—	—	66.7 (4)	57.7 (15)	57.1 (4)	50.0 (2)	—	33.3 (1)	—

Marshall	51.0 (25)	66.6 (22)	70.0 (14)	66.7 (2)	—	100 (1)	100 (4)	66.7 (16)	95.2 (20)	75.0 (3)	—	100 (5)	—
Minton	67.3 (31)	44.8 (13)	14.3 (2)	66.7 (4)	—	100 (1)	70.0 (14)	79.5 (66)	58.8 (20)	61.5 (8)	100 (3)	100 (21)	50.0 (2)
Reed	51.9 (27)	41.9 (13)	20.0 (3)	87.5 (7)	—	100 (1)	90.5 (19)	60.0 (57)	61.0 (25)	53.3 (8)	100 (3)	87.5 (24)	75.0 (3)
Stewart	58.8 (148)	70.7 (116)	63.4 (76)	66.7 (14)	100 (2)	75.0 (3)	74.5 (64)	56.4 (162)	76.4 (120)	71.9 (41)	66.7 (4)	61.8 (47)	100 (1)
Warren	74.3 (255)	80.8 (177)	82.8 (130)	78.8 (26)	50.0 (1)	90.0 (9)	84.8 (100)	89.2 (390)	86.7 (190)	84.5 (60)	100 (8)	86.0 (98)	60.0 (3)
White	65.7 (107)	73.5 (94)	67.1 (47)	75.0 (9)	0.0 (0)	80.0 (4)	76.8 (43)	75.7 (128)	86.2 (93)	76.3 (29)	100 (4)	72.5 (29)	—
Whittaker	53.5 (61)	55.6 (30)	44.4 (24)	66.7 (10)	100 (1)	0.0 (0)	41.2 (14)	47.0 (71)	82.3 (51)	66.7 (14)	100 (2)	65.9 (27)	100 (1)
Brennan													
Black	71.0 (213)	79.7 (153)	83.5 (116)	80.0 (24)	50.0 (1)	88.9 (8)	76.5 (75)	82.7 (296)	83.8 (155)	81.5 (53)	100 (6)	76.6 (72)	100 (1)
Burton	52.1 (25)	64.3 (18)	56.3 (9)	66.7 (6)	100 (1)	75.0 (3)	85.7 (12)	61.0 (36)	87.1 (27)	60.0 (6)	—	70.6 (12)	—

(Table continues)

Table 6-3 (Continued)

Justice	Crim	CivR	1st	DP	Priv	Atty	Un'n	Econ	JudP	Fed	IR	FTax	Misc
Clark	60.0 (144)	74.2 (115)	46.6 (54)	80.8 (21)	100 (1)	83.3 (5)	82.8 (77)	91.2 (280)	87.8 (137)	84.9 (45)	100 (6)	93.1 (82)	100 (1)
Douglas	78.2 (238)	90.2 (174)	85.7 (120)	86.7 (26)	100 (2)	77.8 (7)	77.8 (81)	81.4 (289)	75.2 (149)	73.1 (49)	100 (6)	59.2 (55)	100 (1)
Fortas	86.8 (79)	93.5 (57)	80.4 (37)	100 (5)	—	75.0 (3)	94.7 (18)	84.0 (63)	93.3 (42)	85.7 (12)	—	75.0 (12)	—
Frankfurter	64.8 (81)	70.5 (43)	53.4 (31)	53.3 (8)	100 (1)	75.0 (3)	69.7 (30)	53.6 (91)	77.7 (59)	92.6 (25)	100 (2)	88.0 (44)	100 (1)
Goldberg	90.0 (54)	93.0 (53)	92.9 (26)	100 (5)	100 (1)	100 (1)	95.0 (19)	88.1 (74)	84.4 (38)	93.8 (15)	75.0 (3)	82.6 (19)	—
Harlan	62.5 (190)	58.1 (111)	52.5 (74)	66.7 (20)	100 (2)	66.7 (6)	87.7 (92)	58.1 (202)	76.3 (142)	86.4 (57)	100 (6)	78.9 (75)	100 (1)
Marshall	93.9 (46)	94.1 (32)	100 (20)	100 (3)	—	100 (1)	100 (4)	87.5 (21)	100 (22)	75.0 (3)	—	80.0 (4)	—
Reed	33.3 (3)	100 (2)	100 (1)	100 (1)	—	—	100 (1)	61.5 (8)	85.7 (6)	100 (2)	—	100 (3)	—
Stewart	72.5 (184)	71.5 (118)	71.9 (87)	95.2 (20)	0.0 (0)	50.0 (2)	81.8 (72)	69.6 (201)	81.6 (128)	92.7 (51)	66.7 (4)	79.2 (61)	100 (1)

Warren	86.0 (259)	96.3 (184)	94.2 (130)	92.6 (25)	100 (2)	88.9 (8)	94.2 (97)	92.1 (327)	91.9 (171)	89.8 (53)	100 (6)	93.7 (89)	100 (1)
White	74.2 (121)	80.5 (103)	70.8 (51)	100 (12)	100 (1)	80.0 (4)	90.9 (50)	89.4 (152)	92.5 (99)	94.4 (34)	100 (4)	90.0 (36)	—
Whittaker	66.4 (75)	64.8 (35)	46.3 (25)	73.3 (11)	100 (1)	0.0 (0)	52.5 (21)	55.0 (83)	81.3 (52)	87.0 (20)	100 (2)	73.8 (31)	100 (1)

Burton

Black	52.2 (49)	47.4 (27)	32.4 (12)	62.5 (10)	100 (1)	80.0 (4)	77.4 (24)	57.7 (82)	75.8 (50)	42.9 (9)	66.7 (2)	76.3 (29)	50.0 (2)
Brennan	52.1 (25)	64.3 (18)	56.3 (9)	66.7 (6)	100 (1)	75.0 (3)	85.7 (12)	61.0 (36)	87.1 (27)	60.0 (6)	—	70.6 (12)	—
Clark	88.4 (84)	79.0 (45)	68.6 (24)	68.8 (11)	—	60.0 (3)	85.7 (30)	71.4 (97)	86.1 (56)	91.3 (21)	66.7 (2)	84.2 (32)	75.0 (3)
Douglas	43.7 (42)	48.2 (27)	32.4 (12)	68.8 (11)	100 (1)	80.0 (4)	68.6 (24)	57.3 (82)	58.5 (38)	47.8 (11)	66.7 (2)	57.9 (22)	75.0 (3)
Frankfurter	79.2 (76)	73.2 (41)	62.2 (23)	53.3 (8)	100 (1)	60.0 (3)	71.4 (25)	72.6 (106)	85.1 (57)	73.9 (17)	66.7 (2)	76.3 (29)	75.0 (3)
Harlan	82.3 (52)	75.6 (31)	75.9 (22)	53.9 (7)	100 (1)	80.0 (4)	82.6 (19)	72.1 (62)	89.4 (42)	78.6 (11)	50.0 (2)	81.8 (18)	100 (2)

(Table continues)

Table 6-3 (Continued)

Justice	Crim	CivR	1st	DP	Priv	Atty	Un'n	Econ	JudP	Fed	IR	FTax	Misc
Jackson	71.4 (10)	75.0 (6)	50.0 (2)	100 (1)	—	—	100 (6)	85.7 (24)	57.1 (4)	100 (4)	—	33.3 (1)	—
Minton	80.0 (36)	89.6 (26)	64.3 (9)	66.7 (4)	—	100 (1)	75.0 (15)	74.1 (63)	85.3 (29)	92.3 (12)	66.7 (2)	85.7 (18)	100 (4)
Reed	84.6 (44)	80.6 (25)	66.7 (6)	75.0 (6)	—	100 (1)	95.5 (21)	80.6 (79)	87.8 (36)	86.7 (13)	66.7 (2)	83.4 (20)	75.0 (3)
Warren	62.8 (59)	64.9 (37)	48.6 (17)	50.0 (6)	100 (1)	80.0 (4)	88.6 (31)	62.8 (91)	81.3 (52)	63.6 (14)	100 (2)	73.0 (27)	100 (4)
Whittaker	86.8 (33)	86.4 (19)	100 (12)	75.0 (6)	100 (1)	100 (1)	75.0 (6)	77.5 (31)	95.4 (21)	80.0 (4)	—	55.6 (5)	—
Clark													
Black	51.4 (146)	63.6 (117)	41.7 (56)	69.7 (23)	0.0 (0)	85.7 (6)	82.3 (88)	83.1 (319)	81.7 (157)	65.2 (43)	100 (9)	83.3 (90)	60.0 (3)
Brennan	60.0 (144)	74.2 (115)	46.6 (54)	80.8 (21)	100 (1)	83.3 (5)	82.8 (77)	91.2 (280)	87.8 (137)	84.9 (45)	100 (6)	93.1 (82)	100 (1)
Burton	88.4 (84)	79.0 (45)	68.6 (24)	68.8 (11)	—	60.0 (3)	85.7 (30)	71.4 (97)	86.1 (56)	91.3 (21)	66.7 (2)	84.2 (32)	75.0 (3)
Douglas	44.1 (127)	63.6 (115)	36.0 (49)	78.8 (26)	100 (1)	71.4 (5)	72.6 (82)	79.7 (306)	70.6 (135)	72.0 (49)	100 (9)	57.0 (61)	60.0 (3)

Fortas	58.5 (24)	78.1 (25)	62.5 (15)	100 (3)	—	100 (1)	77.8 (7)	86.1 (31)	86.7 (26)	71.4 (5)	— (7)	70.0	—
Frankfurter	80.3 (139)	73.3 (66)	77.9 (60)	59.0 (13)	—	80.0 (4)	75.0 (48)	61.5 (150)	79.8 (87)	75.7 (28)	80.0 (4)	88.7 (63)	60.0 (3)
Goldberg	58.3 (35)	74.1 (43)	53.6 (15)	80.0 (4)	100 (1)	100 (1)	85.0 (17)	80.7 (67)	84.1 (37)	70.6 (12)	75.0 (3)	82.6 (19)	—
Harlan	80.8 (207)	74.1 (123)	79.8 (103)	76.7 (23)	100 (1)	85.7 (6)	76.5 (78)	57.9 (191)	79.9 (139)	81.0 (47)	87.5 (7)	78.5 (73)	100 (3)
Jackson	85.7 (12)	75.0 (6)	66.7 (2)	100 (1)	—	—	100 (6)	80.8 (21)	71.4 (5)	100 (4)	—	33.3 (1)	—
Minton	80.0 36	79.3 (23)	53.9 (7)	66.7 (4)	—	100 (1)	75.0 (15)	85.1 (68)	73.5 (25)	100 (13)	100 (3)	100 (21)	75.0 (3)
Reed	82.6 (43)	74.2 (23)	57.2 (8)	97.5 (7)	—	100 (1)	95.5 (21)	76.1 (70)	75.0 (30)	93.3 (14)	100 (3)	87.5 (21)	75.0 (3)
Stewart	80.0 (152)	81.1 (103)	71.1 (69)	88.2 (15)	0.0 (0)	50.0 (1)	82.8 (63)	69.5 (166)	83.0 (107)	90.7 (39)	66.7 (4)	76.1 (54)	100 (1)
Warren	58.8 (166)	73.1 (133)	52.6 (70)	82.8 (24)	100 (1)	85.7 (6)	88.5 (100)	90.6 (347)	87.4 (167)	77.3 (51)	100 (8)	92.6 (100)	80.0 (4)
White	81.0 (81)	83.4 (75)	73.0 (35)	87.5 (7)	100 (1)	100 (2)	83.7 (36)	86.5 (109)	90.1 (73)	81.5 (22)	100 (4)	93.9 (31)	—

(Table continues)

Table 6-3 (Continued)

Justice	Crim	CivR	1st	DP	Priv	Atty	Un'n	Econ	JudP	Fed	IR	FTax	Misc
Whittaker	84.4 (97)	77.8 (42)	88.7 (47)	73.3 (11)	—	0.0 (0)	70.0 (28)	62.8 (91)	90.3 (56)	90.0 (18)	100 (2)	64.3 (27)	100 (1)
Douglas													
Black	79.1 (276)	82.8 (183)	90.6 (144)	86.5 (32)	50.0 (1)	90.0 (9)	79.0 (94)	86.9 (378)	78.9 (173)	77.5 (62)	100 (9)	54.0 (61)	80.0 (4)
Brennan	78.2 (238)	90.2 (174)	85.7 (120)	86.7 (26)	100 (2)	77.8 (7)	77.8 (81)	81.4 (289)	75.2 (149)	73.1 (49)	100 (6)	59.2 (55)	100 (1)
Burton	43.7 (42)	48.2 (27)	32.4 (12)	68.8 (11)	100 (1)	80.0 (4)	68.6 (24)	57.3 (82)	58.5 (38)	47.8 (11)	66.7 (2)	57.9 (22)	75.0 (3)
Clark	44.1 (127)	63.6 (115)	36.0 (49)	78.8 (26)	100 (1)	71.4 (5)	72.6 (82)	79.7 (306)	70.6 (135)	72.0 (49)	100 (9)	57.0 (61)	60.0 (3)
Fortas	84.6 (77)	95.1 (58)	78.2 (36)	100 (5)	—	100 (4)	65.0 (13)	73.2 (52)	74.5 (35)	85.7 (12)	—	68.8 (11)	—
Frankfurter	54.6 (95)	61.8 (55)	49.3 (39)	45.4 (10)	100 (1)	60.0 (3)	59.4 (38)	43.6 (111)	54.5 (60)	65.0 (26)	80.0 (4)	55.7 (39)	80.0 (4)
Goldberg	85.0 (51)	96.6 (56)	92.9 (26)	80.0 (4)	100 (1)	100 (1)	73.7 (14)	74.7 (62)	72.7 (32)	72.2 (13)	75.0 (3)	50.0 (11)	—
Harlan	43.8 (140)	50.0 (102)	46.4 (71)	55.9 (19)	100 (2)	90.0 (9)	69.3 (79)	46.1 (172)	61.8 (126)	63.9 (46)	87.5 (7)	51.0 (50)	66.7 (3)

Jackson	64.2 (9)	62.5 (5)	50.0 (2)	100 (1)	—	—	16.7 (1)	60.0 (15)	42.9 (3)	75.0 (3)	—	33.3 (1)	—
Marshall	79.6 (39)	97.1 (33)	78.9 (15)	66.7 (2)	—	100 (1)	50.0 (2)	73.9 (17)	77.3 (17)	50.0 (2)	—	20.0 (1)	—
Minton	60.8 (28)	44.8 (13)	14.3 (2)	50.0 (3)	—	100 (1)	75.0 (15)	73.5 (61)	50.0 (16)	76.9 (10)	100 (3)	61.9 (13)	75.0 (3)
Reed	49.1 (26)	41.9 (13)	20.0 (3)	75.0 (6)	—	100 (1)	77.3 (17)	59.4 (57)	64.1 (25)	66.7 (10)	100 (3)	70.8 (17)	50.0 (2)
Stewart	53.2 (135)	63.9 (106)	62.5 (75)	81.0 (17)	0.0 (0)	75.0 (3)	73.9 (65)	54.4 (154)	68.1 (107)	70.2 (40)	66.7 (4)	58.7 (44)	100 (1)
Warren	81.3 (282)	90.0 (198)	81.1 (128)	84.9 (28)	100 (2)	80.0 (8)	77.4 (96)	86.7 (376)	78.0 (170)	83.5 (61)	100 (8)	54.9 (62)	80.0 (4)
White	55.2 (90)	73.6 (95)	57.7 (41)	83.3 (10)	100 (1)	80.0 (4)	67.3 (37)	76.3 (126)	76.6 (82)	73.7 (28)	100 (4)	48.8 (19)	—
Whittaker	46.1 (53)	52.9 (28)	37.0 (20)	60.0 (9)	100 (1)	100 (1)	40.0 (16)	41.3 (62)	71.9 (46)	65.2 (15)	100 (2)	68.3 (28)	100 (1)

Fortas

| Black | 60.4 (55) | 66.7 (40) | 66.7 (30) | 80.0 (4) | — | 100 (4) | 70.0 (14) | 80.8 (59) | 80.5 (37) | 64.2 (9) | — | 62.5 (10) | — |

(Table continues)

Table 6-3 (Continued)

Justice	Crim	CivR	1st	DP	Priv	Atty	Un'n	Econ	JudP	Fed	IR	FTax	Misc
Brennan	86.8 (79)	93.5 (57)	80.4 (37)	100 (5)	—	75.0 (3)	94.7 (18)	84.0 (63)	93.3 (42)	85.7 (12)	—	75.0 (12)	—
Clark	58.5 (24)	78.1 (25)	62.5 (15)	100 (3)	—	100 (1)	77.8 (7)	86.1 (31)	86.7 (26)	71.4 (5)	—	70.0 (7)	—
Douglas	84.6 (77)	95.1 (58)	78.2 (36)	100 (5)	—	100 (4)	65.0 (13)	73.2 (52)	74.5 (35)	85.7 (12)	—	68.8 (11)	—
Harlan	53.8 (49)	57.3 (35)	52.2 (24)	80.0 (4)	—	100 (4)	90.0 (18)	69.8 (51)	72.9 (35)	85.7 (12)	—	50.0 (8)	—
Marshall	88.6 (31)	100 (24)	72.2 (13)	100 (1)	—	100 (1)	100 (3)	84.2 (16)	91.7 (11)	100 (1)	—	75.0 (3)	—
Stewart	66.6 (60)	59.0 (16)	63.0 (29)	100 (5)	—	66.7 (2)	70.0 (14)	70.7 (53)	83.0 (39)	85.7 (12)	—	50.0 (8)	—
Warren	84.6 (77)	90.0 (54)	87.0 (40)	100 (5)	—	75.0 (3)	100 (19)	83.8 (62)	93.6 (44)	90.9 (10)	—	81.3 (13)	—
White	59.8 (52)	73.8 (45)	55.5 (25)	100 (5)	—	75.0 (3)	90.0 (18)	86.1 (62)	85.4 (41)	71.4 (10)	—	73.4 (11)	—
Frankfurter													
Black	54.3 (93)	65.6 (59)	51.9 (41)	45.4 (10)	100 (1)	80.0 (4)	63.1 (36)	47.7 (121)	70.0 (77)	71.1 (27)	90.0 (4)	82.9 (58)	80.0 (4)

Brennan	64.8 (81)	70.5 (43)	53.4 (31)	53.3 (8)	100 (1)	75.0 (3)	69.7 (30)	53.6 (91)	77.7 (59)	92.6 (25)	100 (2)	88.0 (44)	100 (1)
Burton	79.2 (76)	73.2 (41)	62.2 (23)	53.3 (8)	100 (1)	60.0 (3)	71.4 (25)	72.6 (106)	85.1 (57)	73.9 (17)	66.7 (2)	76.3 (29)	75.0 (3)
Clark	80.3 (139)	73.3 (66)	77.9 (60)	59.0 (13)	—	80.0 (4)	75.0 (48)	61.5 (150)	70.8 (87)	75.7 (28)	80.0 (4)	88.7 (63)	60.0 (3)
Douglas	54.6 (95)	61.8 (55)	49.3 (39)	45.4 (10)	100 (1)	60.0 (3)	59.4 (38)	43.6. (111)	54.5 (60)	65.0 (26)	80.0 (4)	55.7 (39)	80.0 (4)
Harlan	91.5 (129)	88.9 (64)	87.3 (62)	84.2 (16)	100 (1)	80.0 (4)	80.8 (42)	87.2 (170)	89.2 (82)	86.7 (26)	75.0 (3)	76.4 (42)	66.7 (3)
Jackson	78.6 (11)	75.0 (6)	25.0 (1)	100 (1)	—	—	83.3 (5)	92.8 (26)	57.1 (4)	75.0 (3)	—	66.6 (2)	—
Minton	71.7 (33)	55.2 (16)	35.7 (5)	50.0 (3)	—	100 (1)	75.0 (15)	76.7 (66)	85.3 (29)	76.9 (10)	66.7 (2)	85.7 (18)	75.0 (3)
Reed	67.9 (36)	48.4 (15)	40.0 (6)	37.5 (3)	—	100 (1)	72.7 (16)	70.7 (70)	70.7 (29)	73.3 (11)	66.7 (2)	83.4 (20)	50.0 (2)
Stewart	82.9 (63)	78.8 (26)	85.0 (34)	71.4 (5)	—	—	74.1 (20)	76.2 (77)	75.5 (34)	81.3 (13)	100 (2)	69.7 (23)	100 (1)
Warren	56.7 (97)	74.4 (67)	60.5 (46)	50.0 (9)	100 (1)	80.0 (4)	68.8 (44)	51.0 (131)	68.8 (75)	69.4 (25)	100 (4)	90.0 (63)	80.0 (4)

(Table continues)

Table 6-3 (*Continued*)

Justice	Crim	CivR	1st	DP	Priv	Atty	Un'n	Econ	JudP	Fed	IR	FTax	Misc
Whittaker	83.2 (94)	75.0 (39)	88.7 (47)	64.2 (9)	100 (1)	100 (1)	63.9 (23)	80.5 (119)	82.8 (53)	81.8 (18)	100 (2)	69.1 (29)	100 (1)
							Goldberg						
Black	75.0 (45)	86.0 (49)	85.2 (23)	80.0 (4)	0.0 (0)	100 (1)	85.0 (17)	73.8 (62)	75.5 (34)	83.3 (15)	75.0 (3)	78.3 1(8)	—
Brennan	90.0 (54)	93.0 (53)	92.9 (26)	100 (5)	100 (1)	100 (1)	95.0 (19)	88.1 (74)	84.4 (38)	93.8 (15)	75.0 (3)	82.6 (19)	—
Clark	58.3 (35)	74.1 (43)	53.6 (15)	80.0 (4)	100 (1)	100 (1)	85.0 (17)	80.7 (67)	84.1 (37)	70.6 (12)	75.0 (3)	82.6 (19)	—
Douglas	85.0 (51)	96.6 (56)	92.9 (26)	80.0 (4)	100 (1)	100 (1)	73.7 (14)	74.7 (62)	72.7 (32)	72.2 (13)	75.0 (3)	50.0 (11)	—
Harlan	56.7 (34)	43.9 (25)	39.3 (11)	60.0 (3)	100 (1)	100 (1)	85.0 (17)	63.0 (51)	86.4 (38)	83.4 (15)	75.0 (3)	82.6 (19)	—
Stewart	65.0 (39)	74.1 (43)	76.9 (20)	100 (5)	0.0 (0)	100 (1)	85.0 (17)	81.7 (67)	80.0 (36)	83.4 (15)	50.0 (2)	87.0 (20)	—
Warren	91.6 (54)	94.8 (54)	89.3 (25)	100 (5)	100 (1)	100 (1)	90.0 (18)	80.2 (65)	84.4 (38)	82.4 (14)	75.0 (3)	86.9 (20)	—
White	68.3 (41)	73.2 (41)	68.0 (17)	100 (5)	100 (1)	100 (1)	85.0 (17)	82.2 (65)	82.2 (37)	87.5 (14)	75.0 (3)	78.3 (18)	—

Harlan

Black	50.7 (160)	59.6 (121)	53.9 (82)	55.8 (19)	50.0 (2)	80.0 (10)	68.5 (74)	46.3 (173)	71.8 (145)	68.5 (48)	87.5 (8)	66.6 (66)	66.7 (3)
Brennan	62.5 (190)	58.1 (111)	52.5 (74)	66.7 (20)	100 (2)	66.7 (6)	87.7 (92)	58.1 (202)	76.3 (142)	6.4 (57)	100 (6)	78.9 (75)	100 (1)
Burton	82.3 (52)	75.6 (31)	75.9 (22)	53.9 (7)	100 (1)	80.0 (4)	82.6 (19)	72.1 (62)	89.4 (42)	78.6 (11)	50.0 (2)	81.8 (18)	100 2
Clark	80.8 (207)	74.1 (123)	79.8 (103)	76.7 (23)	100 (1)	85.7 (6)	76.5 (78)	57.9 (191)	79.9 (139)	81.0 (47)	87.5 (7)	78.5 (73)	100 (3)
Douglas	43.8 (140)	50.0 (102)	46.4 (71)	55.9 (19)	100 (2)	90.0 (9)	69.3 (79)	46.1 (172)	61.8 (126)	63.9 (46)	87.5 (7)	51.0 (50)	66.7 (3)
Fortas	53.8 (49)	57.3 (35)	52.2 (24)	80.0 (4)	—	100 (4)	90.0 (18)	69.8 (51)	72.9 (35)	85.7 (12)	—	50.0 (8)	—
Frankfurter	91.5 (129)	88.9 (64)	87.3 (62)	84.2 (16)	100 (1)	80.0 (4)	80.8 (42)	87.2 (170)	89.2 (82)	86.7 (26)	75.0 (3)	76.4 (42)	66.7 (3)
Goldberg	56.7 (34)	43.9 (25)	39.3 (11)	60.0 (3)	100 (1)	100 (1)	85.0 (17)	63.0 (51)	86.4 (38)	83.4 (15)	75.0 (3)	82.6 (19)	—
Marshall	57.1 (28)	64.7 (22)	75.0 (15)	66.7 (2)	—	100 (1)	100 (4)	72.7 (16)	81.8 (18)	75.0 (3)	—	60.0 (3)	—

(Table continues)

467

Table 6-3 (*Continued*)

Justice	Crim	CivR	1st	DP	Priv	Atty	Un'n	Econ	JudP	Fed	IR	FTax	Misc
Minton	76.9 (10)	76.9 (10)	33.3 (6)	33.3 (1)	—	100 (1)	75.0 (6)	60.7 (17)	80.0 (12)	75.0 (3)	50.0 (1)	80.0 (4)	100 (2)
Reed	73.9 (17)	73.4 (11)	42.9 (3)	60.0 (3)	—	100 (1)	60.0 (4)	59.5 (25)	76.2 (16)	83.3 (5)	50.0 (1)	75.0 (6)	100 (2)
Stewart	79.9 (203)	77.3 (126)	73.6 (89)	76.2 (16)	0.0 (0)	75.0 (3)	83.2 (74)	80.7 (225)	82.9 (131)	92.8 (52)	66.7 (4)	89.6 (69)	100 (1)
Warren	50.8 (161)	57.4 (116)	56.3 (85)	67.7 (21)	100 (1)	70.0 (7)	83.2 (94)	53.0 (197)	69.8 (141)	81.3 (52)	100 (7)	75.0 (75)	100 (3)
White	74.8 (122)	66.4 (85)	76.3 (55)	66.7 (8)	100 (1)	80.0 (4)	80.4 (45)	65.6 (107)	80.7 (88)	84.2 (32)	100 (4)	82.5 (33)	—
Whittaker	83.5 (96)	73.1 (38)	92.6 (50)	73.4 (11)	100 (1)	0.0 (0)	55.0 (22)	83.7 (123)	84.4 (54)	77.2 (17)	100 (2)	73.8 (31)	100 (1)
Jackson													
Black	71.4 (10)	62.5 (5)	50.0 (2)	100 (1)	—	—	66.7 (4)	57.7 (15)	57.1 (4)	50.0 (2)	—	33.3 (1)	—
Burton	71.4 (10)	75.0 (6)	50.0 (2)	100 (1)	—	—	100 (6)	85.7 (24)	57.1 (4)	100 (4)	—	33.3 (1)	—
Clark	85.7 (12)	75.0 (6)	66.7 (2)	100 (1)	—	—	100 (6)	80.8 (21)	71.4 (5)	100 (4)	—	33.3 (1)	—

Douglas	64.2 (9)	62.5 (5)	50.0 (2)	100 (1)	—	—	16.7 (1)	60.0 (15)	42.9 (3)	75.0 (3)	—	33.3 (1)	—
Frankfurter	78.6 (11)	75.0 (6)	25.0 (1)	100 (1)	—	—	83.3 (5)	92.8 (26)	57.1 (4)	75.0 (3)	—	66.6 (2)	—
Minton	92.9 (13)	75.0 (6)	50.0 (2)	100 (1)	—	—	66.7 (4)	75.0 (21)	71.5 (5)	100 (4)	—	33.3 (1)	—
Reed	72.7 (8)	75.0 (6)	50.0 (2)	100 (1)	—	—	100 (6)	81.5 (22)	28.6 (2)	75.0 (3)	—	33.3 (1)	—
Warren	84.6 (11)	75.0 (6)	50.0 (2)	—	—	—	100 (6)	75.0 (21)	50.0 (3)	100 (3)	—	50.0 (2)	—
Marshall													
Black	51.0 (25)	66.6 (22)	70.0 (14)	66.7 (2)	—	100 (1)	100 (4)	66.7 (16)	95.2 (20)	75.0 (3)	—	100 (5)	—
Brennan	93.9 (46)	94.1 (32)	100 (20)	100 (3)	—	100 (1)	100 (4)	87.5 (21)	100 (22)	75.0 (3)	—	80.0 (4)	—
Douglas	79.6 39	100 (34)	78.9 (15)	66.7 (2)	—	100 (1)	50.0 (2)	73.9 (17)	77.3 (17)	50.0 (2)	—	20.0 (2)	—
Fortas	(88.6) (31)	100 (24)	72.2 (13)	100 (1)	—	100 (1)	100 (3)	84.2 (16)	91.7 (11)	100 (1)	—	75.0 (3)	—

(Table continues)

Table 6-3 (Continued)

Justice	Crim	CivR	1st	DP	Priv	Atty	Un'n	Econ	JudP	Fed	IR	FTax	Misc
Stewart	71.4 (35)	64.7 (22)	95.0 (19)	100 (3)	—	—	75.0 (3)	66.6 (16)	90.9 (20)	75.0 (3)	—	50.0 (2)	—
Warren	93.9 (46)	91.2 (31)	95.0 (19)	100 (3)	—	100 (1)	100 (4)	79.2 (19)	95.5 (21)	75.0 (3)	—	80.0 (4)	—
White	68.8 (33)	67.6 (23)	75.0 (15)	100 (1)	—	100 (1)	100 (4)	83.3 (20)	90.9 (20)	75.0 (3)	—	100 (5)	—
							Minton						
Black	67.3 (31)	44.8 (13)	14.3 (2)	66.7 (4)	—	100 (1)	70.0 (14)	79.5 (66)	58.8 (20)	61.5 (8)	100 (3)	100 (21)	50.0 (2)
Burton	80.0 (36)	89.6 (26)	64.3 (9)	66.7 (4)	—	100 (1)	75.0 (15)	74.1 (63)	85.3 (29)	92.3 (12)	66.7 (2)	85.7 (18)	100 (4)
Clark	80.0 (36)	79.3 (23)	53.9 (7)	66.7 (4)	—	100 (1)	75.0 (15)	85.1 (68)	73.5 (25)	100 (13)	100 (3)	100 (21)	75.0 (3)
Douglas	60.8 (28)	44.8 (13)	14.3 (2)	50.0 (3)	—	100 (1)	75.0 (15)	73.5 (61)	50.0 (16)	76.9 (10)	100 (3)	61.9 (13)	75.0 (3)
Frankfurter	71.7 (33)	55.2 (16)	35.7 (5)	50.0 (3)	—	100 (1)	75.0 (15)	76.7 (66)	85.3 (29)	76.9 (10)	66.7 (2)	85.7 (18)	75.0 (3)
Harlan	76.9 (10)	76.9 (10)	33.3 (6)	33.3 (1)	—	100 (1)	75.0 (6)	60.7 (17)	80.0 (12)	75.0 (3)	50.0 (1)	80.0 (4)	100 (2)

Jackson	92.9 (13)	75.0 (6)	50.0 (2)	100 (1)	—	—	66.7 (4)	75.0 (21)	71.5 (5)	100 (4)	—	33.3 (1)	—
Reed	90.7 (39)	93.1 (27)	85.7 (12)	83.4 (5)	—	100 (1)	80.0 (16)	75.0 (63)	85.3 (29)	92.3 (12)	100 (3)	85.7 (18)	75.0 (3)
Warren	72.0 (36)	54.8 (17)	40.0 (6)	71.4 (5)	—	100 (1)	100 (22)	66.7 (66)	71.8 (28)	85.7 (12)	100 (2)	87.0 (20)	75.0 (3)
Reed													
Black	51.9 (27)	41.9 (13)	20.0 (3)	87.5 (7)	—	100 (1)	90.5 (19)	60.0 (57)	61.0 (25)	53.3 (8)	100 (3)	87.5 (24)	75.0 (3)
Brennan	33.3 (3)	100 (2)	100 (1)	100 (1)	—	—	100 (1)	61.5 (8)	85.7 (6)	100 (2)	—	100 (3)	—
Burton	84.6 (44)	80.6 (25)	66.7 (6)	75.0 (6)	—	100 (1)	95.5 (21)	80.6 (79)	87.8 (36)	86.7 (13)	66.7 (2)	83.4 (20)	75.0 (3)
Clark	82.6 (43)	74.2 (23)	57.2 (8)	97.5 (7)	—	100 (1)	95.5 (21)	76.1 (70)	75.0 (30)	93.3 (14)	100 (3)	87.5 (21)	75.0 (3)
Douglas	49.1 (26)	41.9 (13)	20.0 (3)	75.0 (6)	—	100 (1)	77.3 (17)	59.4 (57)	64.1 (25)	66.7 (10)	100 (3)	70.8 (17)	50.0 (2)
Frankfurter	67.9 (36)	48.4 (15)	40.0 (6)	37.5 (3)	—	100 (1)	72.7 (16)	70.7 (70)	70.7 (29)	73.3 (11)	66.7 (2)	83.4 (20)	50.0 (2)

(Table continues)

Table 6-3 *(Continued)*

Justice	Crim	CivR	1st	DP	Priv	Atty	Un'n	Econ	JudP	Fed	IR	FTax	Misc
Harlan	73.9 (17)	73.4 (11)	42.9 (3)	60.0 (3)	—	100 (1)	60.0 (4)	59.5 (25)	76.2 (16)	83.3 (5)	50.0 (1)	75.0 (6)	100 (2)
Jackson	72.7 (8)	75.0 (6)	50.0 (2)	100 (1)	—	—	100 (6)	81.5 (22)	28.6 (2)	75.0 (3)	—	33.3 (1)	—
Minton	90.7 (39)	93.1 (27)	85.7 (12)	83.4 (5)	—	100 (1)	80.0 (16)	75.0 (63)	85.3 (29)	92.3 (12)	100 (3)	85.7 (18)	75.0 (3)
Warren	72.0 (36)	54.8 (17)	40.0 (6)	71.4 (5)	—	100 (1)	100 (22)	66.7 (66)	71.8 (28)	85.7 (12)	100 (2)	87.0 (20)	75.0 (3)
						Stewart							
Black	58.8 (148)	70.7 (116)	63.4 (76)	66.7 (14)	100 (2)	75.0 (3)	74.5 (64)	56.4 (162)	76.4 (120)	71.9 (41)	66.7 (4)	61.8 (47)	100 (1)
Brennan	72.5 (184)	71.5 (118)	71.9 (87)	95.2 (20)	0.0 (0)	50.0 (2)	81.8 (72)	69.6 (201)	81.6 (128)	92.7 (51)	66.7 (4)	79.2 (61)	100 (1)
Clark	80.0 (152)	81.1 (103)	71.1 (69)	88.2 (15)	0.0 (0)	50.0 (1)	82.8 (63)	69.5 (166)	83.0 (107)	90.7 (39)	66.7 (4)	76.1 (54)	100 (1)
Douglas	53.2 (135)	63.9 (106)	62.5 (75)	81.0 (17)	0.0 (0)	75.0 (3)	73.9 (65)	54.4 (154)	68.1 (107)	70.2 (40)	66.7 (4)	58.7 (44)	100 (1)
Fortas	66.6 (60)	59.0 (16)	63.0 (29)	100 (5)	—	66.7 (2)	70.0 (14)	70.7 (53)	83.0 (39)	85.7 (12)	—	50.0 (8)	—

Frankfurter	82.9 (63)	78.8 (26)	85.0 (34)	71.4 (5)	—	—	74.1 (20)	76.2 (77)	75.5 (34)	81.3 (13)	100 (2)	69.7 (23)	100 (1)
Goldberg	65.0 (39)	74.1 (43)	76.9 (20)	100 (5)	0.0 (0)	100 (1)	85.0 (17)	81.7 (67)	80.0 (36)	83.4 (15)	50.0 (2)	87.0 (20)	—
Harlan	79.9 (203)	77.3 (126)	73.6 (89)	76.2 (16)	0.0 (0)	75.0 (3)	83.2 (74)	80.7 (225)	82.9 (131)	92.8 (52)	66.7 (4)	89.6 (69)	100 (1)
Marshall	71.4 (35)	64.7 (22)	95.0 (19)	100 (3)	—	—	75.0 (3)	66.6 (16)	90.9 (20)	75.0 (3)	—	50.0 (2)	—
Warren	61.8 155	69.9 (114)	69.2 (83)	90.5 (19)	0.0 (0)	50.0 (2)	83.9 (73)	62.4 (177)	75.9 (120)	88.0 (44)	66.7 (4)	76.6 (59)	100 (1)
White	82.1 (133)	75.2 (97)	78.6 (55)	100 (12)	0.0 (0)	50.0 (2)	78.2 (43)	71.9 (120)	83.5 (91)	89.5 (34)	50.0 (2)	79.5 (31)	—
Whittaker	76.3 (58)	87.1 (27)	85.4 (35)	85.7 (6)	—	—	56.6 (13)	76.2 (77)	83.3 (35)	100 (16)	100 (2)	90.9 (30)	100 (1)

Warren

Black	74.3 (255)	80.8 (177)	82.8 (130)	78.8 (26)	50.0 (1)	90.0 (9)	84.8 (100)	89.2 (390)	86.7 (190)	84.5 (60)	100 (8)	86.0 (98)	60.0 (3)
Brennan	86.0 (259)	96.3 (184)	94.2 (130)	92.6 (25)	100 (2)	88.9 (8)	94.2 (97)	92.1 (327)	91.9 (171)	89.8 (53)	100 (6)	93.7 (89)	100 (1)

(Table continues)

474

Table 6-3 *(Continued)*

Justice	Crim	CivR	1st	DP	Priv	Atty	Un'n	Econ	JudP	Fed	IR	FTax	Misc
Burton	62.8 (59)	64.9 (37)	48.6 (17)	50.0 (6)	100 (1)	80.0 (4)	88.6 (31)	62.8 (91)	81.3 (52)	63.6 (14)	100 (2)	73.0 (27)	100 (4)
Clark	58.8 (166)	73.1 (133)	52.6 (70)	82.8 (24)	100 (1)	85.7 (6)	88.5 (100)	90.6 (347)	87.4 (167)	77.3 (51)	100 (8)	92.6 (100)	80.0 (4)
Douglas	81.3 (282)	90.0 (198)	81.1 (128)	84.9 (28)	100 (2)	80.0 (8)	77.4 (96)	86.7 (376)	78.0 (170)	83.5 (61)	100 (8)	54.9 (62)	80.0 (4)
Fortas	84.6 (77)	90.0 (54)	87.0 (40)	100 (5)	—	75.0 (3)	100 (19)	83.8 (62)	93.6 (44)	90.9 (10)	—	81.3 (13)	—
Frankfurter	56.7 (97)	74.4 (67)	60.5 (46)	50.0 (9)	100 (1)	80.0 (4)	68.8 (44)	51.0 (131)	68.8 (75)	69.4 (25)	100 (4)	90.0 (63)	80.0 (4)
Goldberg	91.6 (54)	94.8 (54)	89.3 (25)	100 (5)	100 (1)	100 (1)	90.0 (18)	80.2 (65)	84.4 (38)	82.4 (14)	75.0 (3)	86.9 (20)	—
Harlan	50.8 (161)	57.4 (116)	56.3 (85)	67.7 (21)	100 (1)	70.0 (7)	83.2 (94)	53.0 (197)	69.8 (141)	81.3 (52)	100 (7)	75.0 (75)	100 (3)
Jackson	84.6 (11)	75.0 (6)	50.0 (2)	—	—	—	100 (6)	75.0 (21)	50.0 (3)	100 (3)	—	50.0 (2)	—
Marshall	93.9 (46)	91.2 (31)	95.0 (19)	100 (3)	—	100 (1)	100 (4)	79.2 (19)	95.5 (21)	75.0 (3)	—	80.0 (4)	—

Minton	79.1 (34)	58.6 (17)	35.7 (5)	40.0 (2)	—	—	80.0 (16)	81.4 (70)	62.5 (20)	91.7 (11)	100 (2)	100 (20)	100 (4)
Reed	72.0 (36)	54.8 (17)	40.0 (6)	71.4 (5)	—	—	100 (22)	66.7 (66)	71.8 (28)	85.7 (12)	100 (2)	87.0 (20)	75.0 (3)
Stewart	61.8 (155)	69.9 (114)	69.2 (83)	90.5 (19)	0.0 (0)	50.0 (2)	83.9 (73)	62.4 (177)	75.9 (120)	88.0 (44)	66.7 (4)	76.6 (59)	100 (1)
White	65.8 (106)	78.6 (99)	68.1 (49)	100 (12)	100 (1)	80.0 (4)	94.4 (51)	84.3 (140)	87.0 (94)	91.2 (31)	100 (4)	87.5 (35)	—
Whittaker	57.0 (65)	64.9 (35)	49.0 (25)	75.0 (12)	100 (0)	0.0 (1)	50.0 (20)	49.0 (73)	84.1 (53)	63.2 (12)	100 (2)	71.4 (30)	100 (1)
White													
Black	65.7 (107)	73.5 (94)	67.1 (47)	75.0 (9)	0.0 (0)	80.0 (4)	76.8 (43)	75.7 (128)	86.2 (93)	76.3 (29)	100 (4)	72.5 (29)	—
Brennan	74.2 (121)	80.5 (103)	70.8 (51)	100 (12)	100 (1)	80.0 (4)	90.9 (50)	89.4 (152)	92.5 (99)	94.4 (34)	100 (4)	90.0 (36)	—
Clark	81.0 (81)	83.4 (75)	73.0 (35)	87.5 (7)	100 (1)	100 (2)	83.7 (36)	86.5 (109)	90.1 (73)	81.5 (22)	100 (4)	93.9 (31)	—
Douglas	55.2 (90)	73.6 (95)	57.7 (41)	83.3 (10)	100 (1)	80.0 (4)	67.3 (37)	76.3 (126)	76.6 (82)	73.7 (28)	100 (4)	48.8 (19)	—

(Table continues)

Table 6-3 (Continued)

Justice	Crim	CivR	1st	DP	Priv	Atty	Un'n	Econ	JudP	Fed	IR	FTax	Misc
Fortas	59.8 (52)	73.8 (45)	55.5 (25)	100 (5)	—	75.0 (3)	90.0 (18)	86.1 (62)	85.4 (41)	71.4 (10)	—	73.4 (11)	—
Goldberg	68.3 (41)	73.2 (41)	68.0 (17)	100 (5)	100 (1)	100 (1)	85.0 (17)	82.2 (65)	82.2 (37)	87.5 (14)	75.0 (3)	78.3 (18)	—
Harlan	74.8 (122)	66.4 (85)	76.3 (55)	66.7 (8)	100 (1)	80.0 (4)	80.4 (45)	65.6 (107)	80.7 (88)	84.2 (32)	100 (4)	82.5 (33)	—
Marshall	68.8 (33)	67.6 (23)	75.0 (15)	100 (3)	—	100 (1)	100 (4)	83.3 (20)	90.9 (20)	75.0 (3)	—	100 (5)	—
Stewart	82.1 (133)	75.2 (97)	78.6 (55)	100 (12)	0.0 (0)	50.0 (2)	78.2 (43)	71.9 (120)	83.5 (91)	89.5 (34)	50.0 (2)	79.5 (31)	—
Warren	65.8 (106)	78.6 (99)	68.1 (49)	100 (12)	100 (1)	80.0 (4)	94.4 (51)	84.3 (140)	87.0 (94)	91.2 (31)	100 (4)	87.5 (35)	—
Whittaker													
Black	53.5 (61)	55.6 (30)	44.4 (24)	66.7 (10)	100 (1)	0.0 (0)	41.2 (14)	47.0 (71)	82.3 (51)	66.7 (14)	100 (2)	65.9 (27)	100 (1)
Brennan	66.4 (75)	64.8 (35)	46.3 (25)	73.3 (11)	100 (1)	0.0 (0)	52.5 (21)	55.0 (83)	81.3 (52)	87.0 (20)	100 (2)	73.8 (31)	100 (1)
Burton	86.8 (33)	86.4 (19)	100 (12)	75.0 (6)	100 (1)	100 (1)	75.0 (6)	77.5 (31)	95.4 (21)	80.0 (4)	—	55.6 (5)	—

Clark	84.4 (97)	77.8 (42)	88.7 (47)	73.3 (11)	—	0.0 (0)	70.0 (28)	62.8 (91)	90.3 (56)	90.0 (18)	100 (2)	64.3 (27)	100 (1)
Douglas	46.1 (53)	52.9 (28)	37.0 (20)	60.0 (9)	100 (1)	100 (1)	40.0 (16)	41.3 (62)	71.9 (46)	65.2 (15)	100 (2)	68.3 (28)	100 (1)
Frankfurter	83.2 (94)	75.0 (39)	88.7 (47)	64.2 (9)	100 (1)	100 (1)	63.9 (23)	80.5 (119)	82.8 (53)	81.8 (18)	100 (2)	69.1 (29)	100 (1)
Harlan	83.5 (96)	73.1 (38)	92.6 (50)	73.4 (11)	100 (1)	0.0 (0)	55.0 (22)	83.7 (123)	84.4 (54)	77.2 (17)	100 (2)	73.8 (31)	100 (1)
Stewart	76.3 (58)	87.1 (27)	85.4 (35)	85.7 (6)	—	—	56.6 (13)	76.2 (77)	83.3 (35)	100 (16)	100 (2)	90.9 (30)	100 (1)
Warren	57.0 (65)	64.9 (35)	49.0 (25)	75.0 (12)	100 (1)	0.0 (0)	50.0 (20)	49.0 (73)	84.1 (53)	63.2 (12)	100 (2)	71.4 (30)	100 (1)

Note: "—" indicates that no case in issue area was decided during tenure overlap. Figures listed are the percentage of cases in which the justices voted together. Figures in parentheses are the number of cases in issue area on which the pair of justices agreed during their tenures on the Warren Court. The data include all orally argued citations. Percentages should be interpreted with care since some of the figures on which they are based are quite small.

Definitions of issue areas: Criminal procedure (Crim): the rights of persons accused of crime except for the due process rights of prisoners; Civil rights (CivR): non-First Amendment freedom cases that pertain to classifications based on race (including native Americans), age, indigence, voting, residence, military or handicapped status, sex, or alienage; First Amendment (1st): guarantees contained therein; Due process (DP): noncriminal procedural guarantees, plus court jurisdiction over nonresident litigants and the takings clause of the Fifth Amendment; Privacy (Priv): abortion, contraception, the Freedom of Information Act and related federal statutes; Attorneys (Atty): attorneys' fees, commercial speech, admission to and removal from the bar, and disciplinary matters; Unions (Un'n): labor union activity; Economics (Econ): commercial business activity, plus litigation involving injured persons or things, employee actions vis-à-vis employers, zoning regulations, and governmental regulation of corruption other than that involving campaign spending; Judicial power (JudP): the exercise of the judiciary's own power and authority; Federalism (Fed): conflicts between the federal and state governments, excluding those between state and federal courts, and those involving the priority of federal fiscal claims; Interstate relations (IR): conflicts between states, such as boundary disputes, and nonproperty disputes commonly arising under the full faith and credit clause of the Constitution; Federal taxation (FTax): the Internal Revenue Code and related statutes; Miscellaneous (Misc.): legislative veto, separation of powers, and matters not included in any other issue area.

Source: U.S. Supreme Court Judicial Database, with orally argued citation plus split vote as unit of analysis.

Table 6-4 Voting Interagreements Among the Justices by Issue Area: The Burger Court, 1969-1985 Terms

Justice	Crim	CivR	1st	DP	Priv	Atty	Un'n	Econ	JudP	Fed	IR	FTax	Misc
							Black						
Blackmun	70.8 (17)	75.9 (22)	59.1 (13)	75.0 (3)	100 (1)	0.0 (0)	66.7 (6)	71.4 (10)	86.7 (13)	100 (1)	—	75.0 (3)	—
Brennan	58.0 (29)	59.3 (32)	71.9 (23)	40.0 (2)	0.0 (0)	50.0 (1)	66.7 (10)	83.4 (20)	75.8 (22)	80.0 (4)	100 (1)	63.6 (7)	—
Burger	65.3 (32)	80.0 (44)	62.6 (20)	60.0 (3)	100 (1)	50.0 (1)	60.0 (9)	59.0 (13)	78.6 (22)	80.0 (4)	100 (1)	81.8 (9)	—
Douglas	64.6 (31)	61.2 (33)	71.0 (22)	60.0 (3)	0.0 (0)	50.0 (1)	66.6 (10)	81.8 (18)	70.4 (19)	60.0 (3)	100 (1)	54.5 (6)	—
Harlan	52.0 (26)	66.7 (36)	53.1 (17)	40.0 (2)	100 (1)	0.0 (2)	80.0 (12)	60.8 (14)	79.3 (23)	100 (5)	100 (1)	81.8 (9)	—
Marshall	54.1 (26)	65.4 (34)	73.3 (22)	40.0 (2)	0.0 (0)	50.0 (1)	83.3 (10)	76.2 (16)	81.5 (22)	75.0 (3)	100 (1)	81.8 (9)	—
Stewart	56.0 (28)	74.6 (41)	65.6 (21)	40.0 (2)	0.0 (0)	0.0 (0)	53.3 (8)	43.5 (10)	82.8 (24)	60.0 (3)	100 (1)	90.9 (10)	—
White	65.3 (32)	70.9 (39)	65.7 (21)	40.0 (2)	100 (1)	0.0 (0)	64.3 (9)	73.9 (17)	75.9 (22)	80.0 (4)	100 (1)	81.8 (9)	—

	Blackmun												
Black	70.8 (17)	75.9 (22)	59.1 (13)	75.0 (3)	100 (1)	0.0 (0)	66.7 (6)	71.4 (10)	86.7 (13)	100 (1)	—	75.0 (3)	—
Brennan	54.9 (259)	70.4 (326)	61.8 (123)	66.4 (85)	87.2 (34)	78.5 (22)	78.9 (79)	73.8 (290)	81.0 (201)	86.3 (69)	81.3 (13)	79.7 (47)	66.7 (4)
Burger	82.6 (399)	78.6 (369)	76.1 (153)	86.7 (111)	66.7 (26)	63.3 (19)	73.3 (74)	80.4 (324)	85.1 (211)	91.4 (75)	87.5 (14)	81.4 (48)	50.0 (3)
Douglas	35.0 (50)	55.5 (82)	39.3 (31)	51.5 (17)	44.4 (4)	50.0 (2)	58.4 (21)	61.1 (69)	54.2 (39)	64.3 (9)	20.0 (1)	38.9 (7)	—
Harlan	66.7 (16)	93.1 (27)	77.2 (17)	75.0 (3)	100 (1)	100 (1)	77.8 (7)	76.9 (10)	93.3 (14)	100 (1)	—	75.0 (3)	—
Marshall	52.7 (252)	71.0 (327)	62.4 (121)	67.2 (84)	87.2 (34)	77.8 (21)	79.2 (80)	78.2 (312)	81.7 (201)	85.2 (63)	81.3 (13)	78.0 (46)	50.0 (3)
O'Connor	71.3 (117)	66.9 (97)	71.2 (42)	84.4 (38)	75.0 (9)	52.9 (9)	60.0 (18)	77.8 (98)	79.2 (61)	73.7 (28)	75.0 (3)	78.9 (15)	60.0 (3)
Powell	81.7 (355)	75.4 (303)	79.0 (132)	75.9 (82)	71.4 (25)	68.0 (17)	70.5 (62)	77.9 (255)	84.2 (186)	80.3 (57)	87.6 (14)	70.6 (36)	50.0 (3)
Rehnquist	77.6 (341)	65.3 (272)	65.3 (113)	80.1 (93)	58.4 (21)	51.7 (15)	69.3 (61)	75.2 (276)	82.4 (187)	60.8 (48)	87.6 (14)	72.2 (39)	33.3 (2)

(Table continues)

Table 6-4 (Continued)

Justice	Crim	CivR	1st	DP	Priv	Atty	Un'n	Econ	JudP	Fed	IR	FTax	Misc
Stevens	65.9 (209)	72.4 (215)	68.2 (75)	68.9 (60)	72.4 (21)	72.0 (18)	75.0 (48)	72.4 (194)	78.4 (123)	75.0 (48)	72.7 (8)	57.9 (22)	66.7 (4)
Stewart	74.4 (239)	79.2 (256)	68.3 (97)	74.4 (61)	63.0 (17)	91.7 (11)	64.8 (46)	73.1 (188)	81.7 (138)	61.5 (24)	75.0 (9)	59.5 (22)	0.0 (0)
White	79.4 (383)	79.5 (372)	73.6 (148)	83.5 (106)	59.0 (23)	66.6 (20)	84.1 (85)	78.5 (313)	83.9 (209)	90.2 (74)	87.6 (14)	79.7 (47)	66.7 (4)
Brennan													
Black	58.0 (29)	59.3 (32)	71.9 (23)	40.0 (2)	0.0 (0)	50.0 (1)	66.7 (10)	83.4 (20)	75.8 (22)	80.0 (4)	100 (1)	63.6 (7)	—
Blackmun	54.9 (259)	70.4 (326)	61.8 (123)	66.4 (85)	87.2 (34)	78.5 (22)	78.9 (79)	73.8 (290)	81.0 (201)	86.3 (69)	81.3 (13)	79.7 (47)	66.7 (4)
Burger	43.9 (221)	53.0 (262)	45.2 (96)	55.0 (71)	52.5 (21)	51.6 (16)	58.3 (63)	66.8 (274)	73.6 (195)	80.0 (68)	94.1 (16)	79.4 (54)	85.7 (6)
Douglas	80.2 (134)	89.6 (155)	78.7 (70)	79.4 (27)	77.7 (7)	80.0 (4)	59.5 (25)	80.5 (99)	66.3 (57)	72.2 (13)	50.0 (3)	69.2 (18)	—
Harlan	66.6 (34)	64.2 (34)	68.8 (22)	100 (5)	0.0 (0)	50.0 (1)	60.0 (9)	68.0 (17)	75.9 (22)	80.0 (4)	100 (1)	81.8 (9)	—
Marshall	92.9 (461)	94.9 (458)	92.7 (190)	89.7 (113)	94.9 (37)	100 (28)	93.3 (98)	84.4 (342)	93.5 (244)	93.6 (73)	88.2 (15)	86.8 (59)	85.7 (6)

O'Connor	41.2 (68)	64.2 (93)	55.0 (33)	62.2 (28)	75.0 (9)	33.3 (6)	63.3 (19)	72.0 (90)	81.8 (63)	75.0 (27)	75.0 (3)	68.4 (13)	80.0 (4)
Powell	51.1 (219)	56.9 (229)	56.5 (96)	62.9 (68)	63.9 (23)	56.0 (14)	64.0 (57)	69.9 (225)	72.5 (161)	77.1 (54)	81.3 (13)	83.1 (44)	85.7 (6)
Rehnquist	36.3 (158)	41.2 (172)	31.4 (55)	45.7 (53)	48.6 (18)	37.9 (11)	55.1 (49)	64.4 (234)	71.7 (165)	60.3 (47)	81.3 (13)	75.0 (42)	71.4 (5)
Stevens	71.6 (222)	75.4 (224)	71.4 (80)	67.8 (59)	70.0 (21)	80.0 (20)	73.9 (48)	72.1 (191)	74.2 (118)	74.6 (47)	72.7 (8)	69.2 (27)	85.7 (6)
Stewart	64.1 (218)	60.1 (209)	75.2 (115)	61.4 (51)	57.2 (16)	83.3 (10)	60.2 (47)	65.3 (175)	73.6 (137)	63.6 (28)	92.3 (12)	67.3 (31)	100 (2)
White	55.4 (278)	71.2 (351)	49.3 (105)	64.1 (82)	50.0 (20)	48.4 (15)	83.2 (89)	80.6 (329)	81.2 (216)	88.3 (75)	82.4 (14)	82.4 (56)	42.9 (3)
Burger													
Black	65.3 (32)	80.0 (44)	62.6 (20)	60.0 (3)	100 (1)	50.0 (1)	60.0 (9)	59.0 (13)	78.6 (22)	80.0 (4)	100 (1)	81.8 (9)	—
Blackmun	82.6 (399)	78.6 (369)	76.1 (153)	86.7 (111)	66.7 (26)	63.3 (19)	73.3 (74)	80.4 (324)	85.1 (211)	91.4 (75)	87.5 (14)	81.4 (48)	50.0 (3)
Brennan	43.9 (221)	53.0 (262)	45.2 (96)	55.0 (71)	52.5 (21)	51.6 (16)	58.3 (63)	66.8 (274)	73.6 (195)	80.0 (68)	94.1 (16)	79.4 (54)	85.7 (6)

(Table continues)

Table 6-4 (Continued)

Justice	Crim	CivR	1st	DP	Priv	Atty	Un'n	Econ	JudP	Fed	IR	FTax	Misc
Douglas	34.3 (58)	49.4 (86)	34.9 (31)	52.9 (18)	33.3 (3)	80.0 (4)	54.8 (23)	52.4 (66)	56.0 (47)	66.7 (12)	50.0 (3)	57.6 (15)	—
Harlan	78.0 (39)	87.1 (47)	78.2 (25)	80.0 (4)	100 (1)	50.0 (1)	80.0 (12)	82.6 (19)	96.5 (27)	80.0 (4)	100 (1)	81.8 (9)	—
Marshall	41.3 (210)	53.0 (259)	43.7 (90)	57.1 (72)	53.8 (21)	53.3 (16)	59.1 (62)	73.4 (304)	72.8 (190)	80.1 (64)	94.1 (16)	80.9 (55)	100 (7)
O'Connor	90.2 (148)	86.2 (125)	85.0 (51)	93.3 (42)	83.3 (10)	100 (18)	86.7 (26)	85.8 (108)	88.4 (69)	78.9 (30)	75.0 (3)	84.2 (16)	100 (5)
Powell	87.3 (384)	87.0 (354)	78.2 (133)	82.4 (89)	83.3 (30)	96.3 (26)	83.1 (74)	86.1 (285)	91.5 (204)	80.8 (59)	87.5 (14)	81.1 (43)	100 (7)
Rehnquist	90.1 (400)	86.0 (363)	85.8 (151)	93.1 (108)	91.9 (34)	87.1 (27)	86.5 (77)	85.8 (321)	92.6 (214)	61.7 (50)	87.5 (14)	78.6 (44)	85.7 (6)
Stevens	57.1 (184)	67.2 (203)	58.4 (66)	70.1 (61)	70.0 (21)	66.7 (18)	67.7 (44)	72.6 (196)	73.8 (118)	68.2 (45)	63.6 (7)	66.7 (26)	85.7 (6)
Stewart	76.7 (270)	82.2 (291)	63.6 (98)	79.5 (66)	71.4 (20)	92.8 (13)	67.9 (53)	82.3 (223)	84.3 (156)	64.5 (29)	92.3 (12)	69.5 (32)	100 (2)
White	85.0 (436)	76.1 (380)	86.0 (184)	84.4 (108)	82.5 (33)	84.9 (28)	63.6 (68)	79.8 (332)	86.8 (231)	87.5 (77)	88.2 (15)	76.5 (52)	57.1 (4)

	Douglas												
Black	64.6 (31)	61.2 (33)	71.0 (22)	60.0 (3)	0.0 (0)	50.0 (1)	66.6 (10)	81.8 (18)	70.4 (19)	60.0 (3)	100 (1)	54.5 (6)	—
Blackmun	35.0 (50)	55.5 (82)	39.3 (31)	51.5 (17)	44.4 (4)	50.0 (2)	58.4 (21)	61.1 (69)	54.2 (39)	64.3 (9)	20.0 (1)	38.9 (7)	—
Brennan	80.2 (134)	89.6 (155)	78.7 (70)	79.4 (27)	77.7 (7)	80.0 (4)	59.5 (25)	80.5 (99)	66.3 (57)	72.2 (13)	50.0 (3)	69.2 (18)	—
Burger	34.3 (58)	49.4 (86)	34.9 (31)	52.9 (18)	33.3 (3)	80.0 (4)	54.8 (23)	52.4 (66)	56.0 (47)	66.7 (12)	50.0 (3)	57.6 (15)	—
Harlan	57.1 (28)	82.3 (33)	38.7 (12)	80.0 (4)	0.0 (0)	50.0 (1)	60.0 (9)	56.5 (13)	63.0 (17)	60.0 (3)	100 (1)	72.7 (8)	—
Marshall	86.8 (145)	85.8 (145)	79.1 (68)	85.3 (29)	77.7 (7)	66.7 (2)	66.7 (26)	69.9 (86)	68.2 (58)	70.6 (12)	50.0 (3)	57.7 (15)	—
Powell	37.3 (41)	55.5 (55)	45.3 (24)	50.0 (11)	60.0 (3)	50.0 (1)	50.0 (12)	57.7 (41)	56.0 (28)	50.0 (6)	20.0 (1)	76.9 (10)	—
Rehnquist	28.6 (30)	35.3 (36)	24.5 (13)	33.4 (8)	16.7 (1)	33.3 (1)	62.5 (15)	53.9 (48)	54.7 (29)	63.7 (7)	20.0 (1)	50.0 (7)	—
Stewart	55.3 (94)	64.7 (112)	65.2 (58)	61.8 (21)	66.6 (6)	75.0 (3)	54.7 (23)	53.1 (61)	62.8 (54)	66.7 (12)	50.0 (3)	64.0 (16)	—

(Table continues)

Table 6-4 (Continued)

Justice	Crim	CivR	1st	DP	Priv	Atty	Un'n	Econ	JudP	Fed	IR	FTax	Misc
White	44.1 (74)	65.3 (113)	37.0 (33)	55.8 (19)	22.2 (2)	40.0 (2)	51.2 (21)	69.2 (88)	58.1 (50)	55.6 (10)	50.0 (3)	57.6 (15)	—
Harlan													
Black	52.0 (26)	66.7 (36)	53.1 (17)	40.0 (2)	100 (1)	0.0 (0)	80.0 (12)	60.8 (14)	79.3 (23)	100 (5)	100 (1)	81.8 (9)	—
Blackmun	66.7 (16)	93.1 (27)	77.2 (17)	75.0 (3)	100 (1)	100 (1)	77.8 (7)	76.9 (10)	93.3 (14)	100 (1)	—	75.0 (3)	—
Brennan	66.6 (34)	64.2 (34)	68.8 (22)	100 (5)	0.0 (0)	50.0 (1)	60.0 (9)	68.0 (17)	75.9 (22)	80.0 (4)	100 (1)	81.8 (9)	—
Burger	78.0 (39)	87.1 (47)	78.2 (25)	80.0 (4)	100 (1)	50.0 (1)	80.0 (12)	82.6 (19)	96.5 (27)	80.0 (4)	100 (1)	81.8 (9)	—
Douglas	57.1 (28)	82.3 (33)	38.7 (12)	80.0 (4)	0.0 (0)	50.0 (1)	60.0 (9)	56.5 (13)	63.0 (17)	60.0 (3)	100 (1)	72.7 (8)	—
Marshall	71.5 (35)	64.7 (33)	70.0 (21)	100 (5)	0.0 (0)	50.0 (1)	83.3 (10)	77.3 (17)	77.8 (21)	75.0 (3)	100 (1)	100 (11)	—
Stewart	80.4 (41)	87.1 (47)	81.2 (26)	100 (5)	100 (1)	100 (1)	60.0 (9)	83.3 (20)	89.7 (26)	60.0 (3)	100 (1)	72.7 (8)	—
White	78.0 (39)	88.9 (48)	75.1 (24)	100 (5)	100 (1)	50.0 (1)	42.9 (6)	68.0 (17)	82.8 (24)	80.0 (4)	100 (1)	100 (11)	—

	Marshall												
Black	54.1 (26)	65.4 (34)	73.3 (22)	40.0 (2)	0.0 (0)	50.0 (1)	83.3 (10)	76.2 (16)	81.5 (22)	75.0 (3)	100 (1)	81.8 (9)	—
Blackmun	52.7 (252)	71.0 (327)	62.4 (121)	67.2 (84)	87.2 (34)	77.8 (21)	79.2 (80)	78.2 (312)	81.7 (201)	85.2 (63)	81.3 (13)	78.0 (46)	50.0 (3)
Brennan	92.9 (461)	94.9 (458)	92.7 (190)	89.7 (113)	94.9 (37)	100 (28)	93.3 (98)	84.4 (342)	93.5 (244)	93.6 (73)	88.2 (15)	86.8 (59)	85.7 (6)
Burger	41.3 (210)	53.0 (259)	43.7 (90)	57.1 (72)	53.8 (21)	53.3 (16)	59.1 (62)	73.4 (304)	72.8 (190)	80.1 (64)	94.1 (16)	80.9 (55)	100 (7)
Douglas	86.8 (145)	85.8 (145)	79.1 (68)	85.3 (29)	77.7 (7)	66.7 (2)	66.7 (26)	69.9 (86)	68.2 (58)	70.6 (12)	50.0 (3)	57.7 (15)	—
Harlan	71.5 (35)	64.7 (33)	70.0 (21)	100 (5)	0.0 (0)	50.0 (1)	83.3 (10)	77.3 (17)	77.8 (21)	75.0 (3)	100 (1)	100 (11)	—
O'Connor	36.4 (59)	60.8 (87)	55.9 (33)	65.1 (28)	75.0 (9)	35.3 (6)	60.0 (18)	70.9 (88)	77.6 (59)	70.6 (24)	75.0 (3)	73.7 (14)	100 (5)
Powell	49.8 (216)	55.7 (222)	56.6 (94)	63.8 (67)	71.5 (25)	60.0 (15)	66.3 (59)	74.4 (245)	74.1 (163)	74.2 (49)	81.3 (13)	81.1 (43)	100 (7)
Rehnquist	33.6 (147)	39.1 (162)	32.2 (55)	46.9 (53)	50.0 (18)	39.3 (11)	57.3 (51)	67.9 (252)	72.3 (165)	56.8 (42)	81.3 (13)	76.8 (43)	85.7 (6)

(Table continues)

Table 6-4 (Continued)

Justice	Crim	CivR	1st	DP	Priv	Atty	Un'n	Econ	JudP	Fed	IR	FTax	Misc
Stevens	69.9 (222)	71.3 (211)	73.3 (80)	69.1 (58)	68.9 (20)	84.6 (22)	72.3 (47)	68.7 (184)	73.1 (114)	72.9 (43)	54.5 (6)	69.3 (27)	85.7 (6)
Stewart	63.4 (220)	59.7 (206)	77.0 (114)	68.3 (56)	66.7 (18)	83.3 (10)	66.7 (50)	72.9 (197)	78.2 (143)	65.9 (27)	92.3 (12)	67.4 (31)	100 (2)
White	53.2 (269)	71.5 (349)	49.7 (103)	61.6 (77)	51.3 (20)	53.3 (16)	82.8 (87)	80.9 (333)	77.9 (205)	87.5 (70)	82.4 (14)	89.7 (61)	57.1 (4)
O'Connor													
Blackmun	71.3 (117)	66.9 (97)	71.2 (42)	84.4 (38)	75.0 (9)	52.9 (9)	60.0 (18)	77.8 (98)	79.2 (61)	73.7 (28)	75.0 (3)	78.9 (15)	60.0 (3)
Brennan	41.2 (68)	64.2 (93)	55.0 (33)	62.2 (28)	75.0 (9)	33.3 (6)	63.3 (19)	72.0 (90)	81.8 (63)	75.0 (27)	75.0 (3)	68.4 (13)	80.0 (4)
Burger	90.2 (148)	86.2 (125)	85.0 (51)	93.3 (42)	83.3 (10)	100 (18)	86.7 (26)	85.8 (108)	88.4 (69)	78.9 (30)	75.0 (3)	84.2 (16)	100 (5)
Marshall	36.4 (59)	60.8 (87)	55.9 (33)	65.1 (28)	75.0 (9)	35.3 (6)	60.0 (18)	70.9 (88)	77.6 (59)	70.6 (24)	75.0 (3)	73.7 (14)	100 (5)
Powell	86.7 (136)	84.4 (113)	81.0 (47)	86.8 (33)	75.0 (9)	93.8 (15)	80.0 (24)	83.5 (91)	88.1 (67)	77.4 (24)	75.0 (3)	77.8 (14)	100 (5)
Rehnquist	93.3 (154)	79.2 (114)	80.4 (49)	91.1 (41)	91.7 (11)	100 (18)	90.0 (27)	86.3 (107)	97.5 (75)	89.5 (34)	75.0 (3)	84.2 (16)	80.0 (4)

Stevens	60.3 (99)	70.9 (102)	58.4 (35)	68.2 (30)	58.3 (7)	61.1 (11)	70.0 (21)	75.0 (93)	72.4 (55)	70.3 (26)	75.0 (3)	68.5 (13)	80.0 (4)
White	81.8 (135)	80.6 (117)	78.7 (48)	81.8 (36)	91.7 (11)	94.5 (17)	66.7 (20)	73.5 (89)	85.9 (67)	73.7 (28)	75.0 (3)	73.7 (14)	60.0 (3)
							Powell						
Blackmun	81.7 (355)	75.4 (303)	79.0 (132)	75.9 (82)	71.4 (25)	68.0 (17)	70.5 (62)	77.9 (255)	84.2 (186)	80.3 (57)	87.6 (14)	70.6 (36)	50.0 (3)
Brennan	51.1 (219)	56.9 (229)	56.5 (96)	62.9 (68)	63.9 (23)	56.0 (14)	64.0 (57)	69.9 (225)	72.5 (161)	77.1 (54)	81.3 (13)	83.1 (44)	85.7 (6)
Burger	87.3 (384)	87.0 (354)	78.2 (133)	82.4 (89)	83.3 (30)	96.3 (26)	83.1 (74)	86.1 (285)	91.5 (204)	80.8 (59)	87.5 (14)	81.1 (43)	100 (7)
Douglas	37.3 (41)	55.5 (55)	45.3 (24)	50.0 (11)	60.0 (3)	50.0 (1)	50.0 (12)	57.7 (41)	56.0 (28)	50.0 (6)	20.0 (1)	76.9 (10)	—
Marshall	49.8 (216)	55.7 (222)	56.6 (94)	63.8 (67)	71.5 (25)	60.0 (15)	66.3 (59)	74.4 (245)	74.1 (163)	74.2 (49)	81.3 (13)	81.1 (43)	100 (7)
O'Connor	86.7 (136)	84.4 (113)	81.0 (47)	86.8 (33)	75.0 (9)	93.8 (15)	80.0 (24)	83.5 (91)	88.1 (67)	77.4 (24)	75.0 (3)	77.8 (14)	100 (5)
Rehnquist	83.2 (358)	83.4 (332)	70.0 (119)	77.1 (81)	74.3 (26)	81.5 (22)	78.5 (69)	81.9 (267)	89.2 (197)	62.5 (45)	100 (16)	75.5 (40)	85.7 (6)

(Table continues)

Table 6-4 *(Continued)*

Justice	Crim	CivR	1st	DP	Priv	Atty	Un'n	Econ	JudP	Fed	IR	FTax	Misc
Stevens	63.6 (196)	68.3 (196)	61.6 (66)	62.9 (49)	76.7 (23)	72.0 (18)	71.9 (46)	72.5 (174)	74.0 (114)	82.7 (48)	54.5 (6)	67.6 (25)	85.7 (6)
Stewart	79.9 (227)	85.3 (232)	68.1 (77)	78.3 (54)	95.9 (22)	90.9 (10)	82.4 (48)	82.8 (174)	82.1 (119)	64.1 (25)	75.0 (9)	72.8 (24)	100 (2)
White	82.2 (361)	74.6 (303)	73.6 (126)	83.2 (89)	77.8 (28)	85.2 (23)	68.5 (61)	78.9 (259)	85.2 (190)	79.5 (58)	87.6 (14)	71.7 (38)	57.1 (4)
							Rehnquist						
Blackmun	77.6 (341)	65.3 (272)	65.3 (113)	80.1 (93)	58.4 (21)	51.7 (15)	69.3 (61)	75.2 (276)	82.4 (187)	60.8 (48)	87.6 (14)	72.2 (39)	33.3 (2)
Brennan	36.3 (158)	41.2 (172)	31.4 (55)	45.7 (53)	48.6 (18)	37.9 (11)	55.1 (49)	64.4 (234)	71.7 (165)	60.3 (47)	81.3 (13)	75.0 (42)	71.4 (5)
Burger	90.1 (400)	86.0 (363)	85.8 (151)	93.1 (108)	91.9 (34)	87.1 (27)	86.5 (77)	85.8 (321)	92.6 (214)	61.7 (50)	87.5 (14)	78.6 (44)	85.7 (6)
Douglas	28.6 (30)	35.3 (36)	24.5 (13)	33.4 (8)	16.7 (1)	33.3 (1)	62.5 (15)	53.9 (48)	54.7 (29)	63.7 (7)	20.0 (1)	50.0 (7)	—
Marshall	33.6 (147)	39.1 (162)	32.2 (55)	46.9 (53)	50.0 (18)	39.3 (11)	57.3 (51)	67.9 (252)	72.3 (165)	56.8 (42)	81.3 (13)	76.8 (43)	85.7 (6)
O'Connor	93.3 (154)	79.2 (114)	80.4 (49)	91.1 (41)	91.7 (11)	100 (18)	90.0 (27)	86.3 (107)	97.5 (75)	89.5 (34)	75.0 (3)	84.2 (16)	80.0 (4)

Powell	83.2 (358)	83.4 (332)	70.0 (119)	77.1 (81)	74.3 (26)	81.5 (22)	78.5 (69)	81.9 (267)	89.2 (197)	62.5 (45)	100 (16)	75.5 (40)	85.7 (6)
Stevens	54.2 (172)	63.3 (188)	51.3 (58)	64.3 (54)	66.6 (20)	55.6 (15)	62.5 (40)	69.4 (182)	74.1 (117)	69.7 (46)	54.5 (6)	77.0 (30)	71.4 (5)
Stewart	67.5 (189)	79.4 (220)	49.1 (57)	72.9 (51)	68.0 (17)	61.5 (8)	78.0 (46)	85.3 (197)	84.1 (127)	68.4 (26)	75.0 (9)	85.3 (29)	100 (2)
White	79.7 (353)	67.0 (282)	77.9 (138)	80.0 (92)	91.9 (34)	87.1 (27)	66.2 (59)	76.5 (283)	85.3 (197)	61.7 (50)	87.6 (14)	67.9 (38)	71.4 (5)

Stevens

Blackmun	65.9 (209)	72.4 (215)	68.2 (75)	68.9 (60)	72.4 (21)	72.0 (18)	75.0 (48)	72.4 (194)	78.4 (123)	75.0 (48)	72.7 (8)	57.9 (22)	66.7 (4)
Brennan	71.6 (222)	75.4 (224)	71.4 (80)	67.8 (59)	70.0 (21)	80.0 (20)	73.9 (48)	72.1 (191)	74.2 (118)	74.6 (47)	72.7 (8)	69.2 (27)	85.7 (6)
Burger	57.1 (184)	67.2 (203)	58.4 (66)	70.1 (61)	70.0 (21)	66.7 (18)	67.7 (44)	72.6 (196)	73.8 (118)	68.2 (45)	63.6 (7)	66.7 (26)	85.7 (6)
Marshall	69.9 (222)	71.3 (211)	73.3 (80)	69.1 (58)	68.9 (20)	84.6 (22)	72.3 (47)	68.7 (184)	73.1 (114)	72.9 (43)	54.5 (6)	69.3 (27)	85.7 (6)
O'Connor	60.3 (99)	70.9 (102)	58.4 (35)	68.2 (30)	58.3 (7)	61.1 (11)	70.0 (21)	75.0 (93)	72.4 (55)	70.3 (26)	75.0 (3)	68.5 (13)	80.0 (4)

(Table continues)

Table 6-4 (Continued)

Justice	Crim	CivR	1st	DP	Priv	Atty	Un'n	Econ	JudP	Fed	IR	FTax	Misc
Powell	63.6 (196)	68.3 (196)	61.6 (66)	62.9 (49)	76.7 (23)	72.0 (18)	71.9 (46)	72.5 (174)	74.0 (114)	82.7 (48)	54.5 (6)	67.6 (25)	85.7 (6)
Rehnquist	54.2 (172)	63.3 (188)	51.3 (58)	64.3 (54)	66.6 (20)	55.6 (15)	62.5 (40)	69.4 (182)	74.1 (117)	69.7 (46)	54.5 (6)	77.0 (30)	71.4 (5)
Stewart	74.9 (119)	70.9 (112)	72.3 (39)	59.6 (25)	77.8 (14)	88.9 (8)	71.5 (25)	73.7 (101)	77.5 (62)	50.0 (12)	57.1 (4)	83.4 (15)	100 (2)
White	63.0 (203)	71.5 (216)	57.9 (66)	66.3 (57)	66.6 (20)	70.4 (19)	73.9 (48)	74.1 (198)	72.3 (115)	78.8 (52)	63.6 (7)	61.6 (24)	42.9 (3)
Stewart													
Black	56.0 (28)	74.6 (41)	65.6 (21)	40.0 (2)	0.0 (0)	0.0 (0)	53.3 (8)	43.5 (10)	82.8 (24)	60.0 (3)	100 (1)	90.9 (10)	—
Blackmun	74.4 (239)	79.2 (256)	68.3 (97)	74.4 (61)	63.0 (17)	91.7 (11)	64.8 (46)	73.1 (188)	81.7 (138)	61.5 (24)	75.0 (9)	59.5 (22)	0.0 (0)
Brennan	64.1 (218)	60.1 (209)	75.2 (115)	61.4 (51)	57.2 (16)	83.3 (10)	60.2 (47)	65.3 (175)	73.6 (137)	63.6 (28)	92.3 (12)	67.3 (31)	100 (2)
Burger	76.7 (270)	82.2 (291)	63.6 (98)	79.5 (66)	71.4 (20)	92.8 (13)	67.9 (53)	82.3 (223)	84.3 (156)	64.5 (29)	92.3 (12)	69.5 (32)	100 (2)
Douglas	55.3 (94)	64.7 (112)	65.2 (58)	61.8 (21)	66.6 (6)	75.0 (3)	54.7 (23)	53.1 (61)	62.8 (54)	66.7 (12)	50.0 (3)	64.0 (16)	—

Harlan	80.4 (41)	87.1 (47)	81.2 (26)	100 (5)	0.0 (0)	100 (1)	60.0 (9)	83.3 (20)	89.7 (26)	60.0 (3)	100 (1)	72.7 (8)	—
Marshall	63.4 (220)	59.7 (206)	77.0 (114)	68.3 (56)	66.7 (18)	83.3 (10)	66.7 (50)	72.9 (197)	78.2 (143)	65.9 (27)	92.3 (12)	67.4 (31)	100 (2)
Powell	79.9 (227)	85.3 (232)	68.1 (77)	78.3 (54)	95.9 (22)	90.9 (10)	82.4 (48)	82.8 (174)	82.1 (119)	64.1 (25)	75.0 (9)	72.8 (24)	100 (2)
Rehnquist	67.5 (189)	79.4 (220)	49.1 (57)	72.9 (51)	68.0 (17)	61.5 (8)	78.0 (46)	85.3 (197)	84.1 (127)	68.4 (26)	75.0 (9)	85.3 (29)	100 (2)
Stevens	74.9 (119)	70.9 (112)	72.3 (39)	59.6 (25)	77.8 (14)	88.9 (8)	71.5 (25)	73.7 (101)	77.5 (62)	50.0 (12)	57.1 (4)	83.4 (15)	100 (2)
White	77.2 (270)	73.7 (260)	66.2 (102)	78.3 (65)	71.4 (20)	71.4 (10)	59.7 (46)	75.9 (208)	78.0 (145)	60.0 (27)	76.9 (10)	60.9 (28)	50.0 (1)
White													
Black	65.3 (32)	70.9 (39)	65.7 (21)	40.0 (2)	100 (1)	0.0 (0)	64.3 (9)	73.9 (17)	75.9 (22)	80.0 (4)	100 (1)	81.8 (9)	—
Blackmun	79.4 (383)	79.5 (372)	73.6 (148)	83.5 (106)	59.0 (23)	66.6 (20)	84.1 (85)	78.5 (313)	83.9 (209)	90.2 (74)	87.6 (14)	79.7 (47)	66.7 (4)
Brennan	55.4 (278)	71.2 (351)	49.3 (105)	64.1 (82)	50.0 (20)	48.4 (15)	83.2 (89)	80.6 (329)	81.2 (216)	88.3 (75)	82.4 (14)	82.4 (56)	42.9 (3)

(Table continues)

Table 6-4 (Continued)

Justice	Crim	CivR	1st	DP	Priv	Atty	Un'n	Econ	JudP	Fed	IR	FTax	Misc
Burger	85.0 (436)	76.1 (380)	86.0 (184)	84.4 (108)	82.5 (33)	84.9 (28)	63.6 (68)	79.8 (332)	86.8 (231)	87.5 (77)	88.2 (15)	76.5 (52)	57.1 (4)
Douglas	44.1 (74)	65.3 (113)	37.0 (33)	55.8 (19)	22.2 (2)	40.0 (2)	51.2 (21)	69.2 (88)	58.1 (50)	55.6 (10)	50.0 (3)	57.6 (15)	—
Harlan	78.0 (39)	88.9 (48)	75.1 (24)	100 (5)	100 (1)	50.0 (1)	42.9 (6)	68.0 (17)	82.8 (24)	80.0 (4)	100 (1)	100 (11)	—
Marshall	53.2 (269)	71.5 (349)	49.7 (103)	61.6 (77)	51.3 (20)	53.3 (16)	82.8 (87)	80.9 (333)	77.9 (205)	87.5 (70)	82.4 (14)	89.7 (61)	57.1 (4)
O'Connor	81.8 (135)	80.6 (117)	78.7 (48)	81.8 (36)	91.7 (11)	94.5 (17)	66.7 (20)	73.5 (89)	85.9 (67)	73.7 (28)	75.0 (3)	73.7 (14)	60.0 (3)
Powell	82.2 (361)	74.6 (303)	73.6 (126)	83.2 (89)	77.8 (28)	85.2 (23)	68.5 (61)	78.9 (259)	85.2 (190)	79.5 (58)	87.6 (14)	71.7 (38)	57.1 (4)
Rehnquist	79.7 (353)	67.0 (282)	77.9 (138)	80.0 (92)	91.9 (34)	87.1 (27)	66.2 (59)	76.5 (283)	85.3 (197)	61.7 (50)	87.6 (14)	67.9 (38)	71.4 (5)
Stevens	63.0 (203)	71.5 (216)	57.9 (66)	66.3 (57)	66.6 (20)	70.4 (19)	73.9 (48)	74.1 (198)	72.3 (115)	78.8 (52)	63.6 (7)	61.6 (24)	42.9 (3)
Stewart	77.2 (270)	73.7 (260)	66.2 (102)	78.3 (65)	71.4 (20)	71.4 (10)	59.7 (46)	75.9 (208)	78.0 (145)	60.0 (27)	76.9 (10)	60.9 (28)	50.0 (1)

Note: "—" indicates that no case in issue area was decided during tenure overlap. Figures listed are the percentage of cases in which the justices voted together. Figures in parentheses are the number of cases in issue area on which the justices agreed during their tenures on the Burger Court. The data include all orally argued citations. Readers should take care in interpreting the percentages since some of the figures on which they are based are quite small.

The issue areas are defined as follows: Criminal procedure (Crim): the rights of persons accused of crime except for the due process rights of prisoners; Civil rights (CivR): non-First Amendment freedom cases that pertain to classifications based on race (including native Americans), age, indigence, voting, residence, military or handicapped status, sex, or alienage; First Amendment (1st): guarantees contained therein; Due process (DP): noncriminal procedural guarantees, plus court jurisdiction over nonresident litigants and the takings clause of the Fifth Amendment; Privacy (Priv): abortion, contraception, the Freedom of Information Act and related federal statutes; Attorneys (Atty): attorneys' fees, commercial speech, admission to and removal from the bar, and disciplinary matters; Unions (Un'n): labor union activity; Economics (Econ): commercial business activity, plus litigation involving injured persons or things, employee actions vis-à-vis employers, zoning regulations, and governmental regulation of corruption other than that involving campaign spending; Judicial power (JudP): the exercise of the judiciary's own power and authority; Federalism (Fed): conflicts between the federal and state governments, excluding those between state and federal courts, and those involving the priority of federal fiscal claims; Interstate relations (IR): conflicts between states, such as boundary disputes, and nonproperty disputes commonly arising under the full faith and credit clause of the Constitution; Federal taxation (FTax): the Internal Revenue Code and related statutes; Miscellaneous (Misc): legislative veto, separation of powers, and matters not included in any other issue area.

Source: U.S. Supreme Court Judicial Database, with orally argued citation plus split vote as unit of analysis.

Table 6-5 Voting Intergreements Among the Justices by Issue Area: The Rehnquist Court, 1986-1990 Terms

Justice	Crim	CivR	1st	DP	Priv	Atty	Un'n	Econ	JudP	Fed	IR	FTax	Misc
							Blackmun						
Brennan	71.3 (97)	88.8 (71)	81.5 (44)	72.8 (24)	87.5 (7)	93.3 (14)	81.0 (17)	82.0 (73)	97.1 (67)	86.8 (33)	100 (6)	76.5 (13)	100 (5)
Kennedy	53.1 (60)	43.1 (25)	70.0 (28)	72.2 (13)	37.5 (3)	83.3 (10)	73.7 (14)	75.7 (59)	82.5 (47)	82.1 (23)	57.1 (4)	75.0 (9)	100 (4)
Marshall	71.4 (120)	90.7 (87)	83.3 (50)	83.4 (30)	80.0 (8)	93.8 (15)	79.3 (23)	81.4 (92)	94.2 (80)	90.2 (37)	87.5 (7)	70.0 (14)	85.7 (6)
O'Connor	50.3 (84)	50.6 (48)	55.0 (33)	63.9 (23)	70.0 (7)	52.9 (9)	75.9 (22)	70.3 (78)	91.7 (77)	74.3 (29)	87.5 (7)	80.0 (16)	85.7 (6)
Powell	58.5 (24)	56.5 (13)	50.0 (6)	78.5 (11)	100 (1)	0.0 (0)	80.0 (4)	76.2 (16)	93.3 (14)	90.9 (10)	100 (1)	75.0 (3)	100 (1)
Rehnquist	51.8 (87)	39.6 (38)	46.5 (27)	58.3 (21)	50.0 (5)	52.9 (9)	72.4 (21)	74.1 (83)	78.8 (67)	76.2 (32)	75.0 (6)	75.0 (15)	85.7 (6)
Scalia	51.8 (87)	49.5 (47)	52.5 (31)	63.9 (23)	25.0 (2)	52.9 (9)	82.7 (24)	73.0 (81)	80.5 (66)	83.4 (35)	62.5 (5)	70.0 (14)	57.1 (4)
Souter	44.4 (12)	80.0 (12)	33.3 (2)	50.0 (1)	0.0 (0)	50.0 (1)	75.0 (6)	71.4 (15)	86.7 (11)	100 (3)	100 (2)	0.0 (0)	100 (2)
Stevens	72.6 (122)	77.1 (74)	63.3 (38)	75.0 (27)	70.0 (7)	93.8 (15)	72.4 (21)	70.5 (79)	84.8 (72)	80.4 (33)	85.7 (6)	75.0 (15)	85.7 (6)

White	59.9 (100)	58.3 (56)	56.7 (34)	75.0 (27)	50.0 (5)	58.8 (10)	69.0 (20)	73.2 (82)	88.3 (75)	81.0 (34)	87.5 (7)	80.0 (16)	85.7 (6)

Brennan

Blackmun	71.3 (97)	88.8 (71)	81.5 (44)	72.8 (24)	87.5 (7)	93.3 (14)	81.0 (17)	82.0 (73)	97.1 (67)	86.8 (33)	100 (6)	76.5 (13)	100 (5)
Kennedy	35.3 (29)	38.1 (16)	52.9 (18)	60.0 (9)	57.1 (4)	80.0 (8)	45.5 (5)	74.5 (41)	81.4 (35)	79.2 (19)	60.0 (3)	80.0 (8)	100 (2)
Marshall	94.9 (129)	97.6 (80)	100 (54)	90.9 (30)	87.5 (7)	100 (14)	95.2 (20)	97.8 (89)	97.1 (67)	97.3 (36)	83.3 (5)	100 (17)	100 (5)
O'Connor	34.1 (46)	41.3 (33)	44.5 (24)	48.5 (16)	75.0 (6)	46.7 (7)	57.1 (12)	64.0 (57)	88.3 (60)	68.6 (24)	100 (6)	82.4 (14)	80.0 (4)
Powell	31.7 (13)	56.0 (14)	58.3 (7)	57.1 (8)	100 (1)	0.0 (0)	80.0 (4)	68.2 (15)	86.7 (13)	72.7 (8)	100 (1)	100 (4)	100 (1)
Rehnquist	29.4 (40)	31.7 (26)	30.8 (16)	42.4 (14)	62.5 (5)	46.7 (7)	66.7 (14)	66.7 (60)	76.8 (53)	73.7 (28)	83.3 (5)	82.4 (14)	100 (5)
Scalia	39.0 (53)	42.0 (34)	47.2 (25)	48.5 (16)	42.9 (3)	46.7 (7)	61.9 (13)	68.5 (61)	80.6 (54)	73.7 (28)	66.7 (4)	82.4 (14)	40.0 (2)
Stevens	77.2 (105)	78.3 (56)	70.4 (38)	81.8 (27)	75.0 (6)	92.9 (13)	66.7 (14)	77.8 (70)	84.1 (58)	83.8 (31)	80.0 (4)	82.4 (14)	80.0 (4)

(Table continues)

Table 6-5 *(Continued)*

Justice	Crim	CivR	1st	DP	Priv	Atty	Un'n	Econ	JudP	Fed	IR	FTax	Misc
White	35.6 (48)	47.6 (39)	46.3 (25)	63.7 (21)	62.5 (5)	53.3 (8)	61.9 (13)	72.3 (65)	84.1 (58)	81.5 (31)	83.3 (5)	76.5 (13)	100 (5)
Kennedy													
Blackmun	53.1 (60)	43.1 (25)	70.0 (28)	72.2 (13)	37.5 (3)	83.3 (10)	73.7 (14)	75.7 (59)	82.5 (47)	82.1 (23)	57.1 (4)	75.0 (9)	100 (4)
Brennan	35.3 (29)	38.1 (16)	52.9 (18)	60.0 (9)	57.1 (4)	80.0 (8)	45.5 (5)	74.5 (41)	81.4 (35)	79.2 (19)	60.0 (3)	80.0 (8)	100 (2)
Marshall	32.8 (37)	41.4 (24)	52.5 (21)	61.1 (11)	37.5 (3)	72.7 (8)	52.6 (10)	72.2 (57)	79.0 (45)	78.6 (22)	42.9 (3)	83.3 (10)	75.0 (3)
O'Connor	91.9 (103)	80.7 (46)	77.5 (31)	88.9 (16)	75.0 (6)	66.7 (8)	100 (19)	87.0 (67)	89.3 (50)	84.0 (21)	71.4 (5)	83.3 (10)	100 (4)
Rehnquist	91.2 (103)	84.5 (49)	76.9 (30)	83.3 (15)	100 (8)	75.0 (9)	89.5 (17)	88.6 (70)	84.2 (48)	89.3 (25)	85.7 (6)	100 (12)	75.0 (3)
Scalia	87.6 (99)	87.9 (51)	90.0 (36)	94.4 (17)	85.7 (6)	75.0 (9)	89.4 (17)	91.2 (72)	91.0 (51)	92.8 (26)	71.5 (5)	100 (12)	75.0 (3)
Souter	85.2 (23)	80.0 (12)	50.0 (3)	100 (2)	100 (1)	100 (2)	100 (8)	95.2 (20)	92.3 (12)	66.7 (2)	50.0 (1)	100 (2)	100 (2)
Stevens	46.9 (53)	55.1 (32)	57.5 (23)	77.8 (14)	50.0 (4)	81.8 (9)	68.4 (13)	65.8 (52)	82.5 (47)	74.1 (20)	42.9 (3)	75.0 (9)	100 (4)

White	82.3 (93)	74.1 (43)	72.5 (29)	77.8 (14)	100 (8)	91.6 (11)	84.2 (16)	84.6 (66)	86.0 (49)	82.1 (23)	42.9 (3)	75.0 (9)	75.0 (3)

Marshall

Blackmun	71.4 (120)	90.7 (87)	83.3 (50)	83.4 (30)	80.0 (8)	93.8 (15)	79.3 (23)	81.4 (92)	94.2 (80)	90.2 (37)	87.5 (7)	70.0 (14)	85.7 (6)
Brennan	94.9 (129)	97.6 (80)	100 (54)	90.9 (30)	87.5 (7)	100 (14)	95.2 (20)	97.8 (89)	97.1 (67)	97.3 (36)	83.3 (5)	100 (17)	100 (5)
Kennedy	32.8 (37)	41.4 (24)	52.5 (21)	61.1 (11)	37.5 (3)	72.7 (8)	52.6 (10)	72.2 (57)	79.0 (45)	78.6 (22)	42.9 (3)	83.3 (10)	75.0 (3)
O'Connor	32.3 (54)	45.8 (44)	45.0 (27)	58.4 (21)	70.0 (7)	50.0 (8)	55.2 (16)	61.1 (69)	85.7 (72)	65.8 (25)	75.0 (6)	80.0 (16)	71.4 (5)
Powell	31.7 (13)	52.0 (13)	58.3 (7)	78.5 (11)	100 (1)	0.0 (0)	80.0 (4)	63.6 (14)	86.7 (13)	81.8 (9)	100 (1)	100 (4)	100 (1)
Rehnquist	26.8 (45)	31.6 (31)	29.3 (17)	52.8 (19)	50.0 (5)	50.0 (8)	65.5 (19)	66.7 (76)	72.9 (62)	75.6 (31)	62.5 (5)	85.0 (17)	100 (7)
Scalia	36.3 (61)	41.2 (40)	42.4 (25)	58.3 (21)	50.0 (4)	50.0 (8)	62.0 (18)	67.3 (76)	76.8 (63)	78.0 (32)	50.0 (4)	80.0 (16)	42.9 (3)
Souter	25.9 (7)	80.0 (12)	33.3 (2)	50.0 (1)	0.0 (0)	50.0 (1)	62.5 (5)	61.9 (13)	80.0 (12)	100 (3)	100 (2)	100 (2)	50.0 (1)

(Table continues)

Table 6-5 *(Continued)*

Justice	Crim	CivR	1st	DP	Priv	Atty	Un'n	Econ	JudP	Fed	IR	FTax	Misc
Stevens	78.6 (132)	72.4 (71)	70.0 (42)	80.6 (29)	90.0 (9)	93.3 (14)	79.3 (23)	77.2 (88)	81.1 (69)	85.0 (34)	71.4 (5)	85.0 (17)	71.4 (5)
White	35.9 (60)	50.0 (49)	43.3 (26)	75.0 (27)	50.0 (5)	50.0 (8)	62.1 (18)	72.0 (82)	82.4 (70)	85.3 (35)	100 (8)	70.0 (14)	100 (7)
O'Connor													
Blackmun	50.3 (84)	50.6 (48)	55.0 (33)	63.9 (23)	70.0 (7)	52.9 (9)	75.9 (22)	70.3 (78)	91.7 (77)	74.3 (29)	87.5 (7)	80.0 (16)	85.7 (6)
Brennan	34.1 (46)	41.3 (33)	44.5 (24)	48.5 (16)	75.0 (6)	46.7 (7)	57.1 (12)	64.0 (57)	88.3 (60)	68.6 (24)	100 (6)	82.4 (14)	80.0 (4)
Kennedy	91.9 (103)	80.7 (46)	77.5 (31)	88.9 (16)	75.0 (6)	66.7 (8)	100 (19)	87.0 (67)	89.3 (50)	84.0 (21)	71.4 (5)	83.3 (10)	100 (4)
Marshall	32.8 (37)	41.4 (24)	52.5 (21)	61.1 (11)	37.5 (3)	72.7 (8)	52.6 (10)	72.2 (57)	79.0 (45)	78.6 (22)	42.9 (3)	83.3 (10)	75.0 (3)
Powell	80.5 (33)	70.8 (17)	83.3 (10)	78.5 (11)	100 (1)	100 (3)	80.0 (4)	81.8 (18)	100 (15)	72.7 (8)	100 (1)	75.0 (3)	100 (1)
Rehnquist	89.8 (150)	77.1 (74)	77.6 (45)	83.3 (30)	80.0 (8)	88.2 (15)	89.7 (26)	88.4 (99)	88.1 (74)	84.7 (33)	87.5 (7)	75.0 (15)	71.4 (5)
Scalia	86.8 (145)	80.0 (76)	76.3 (45)	88.9 (32)	62.5 (5)	88.2 (15)	86.2 (25)	85.6 (95)	85.2 (69)	82.1 (32)	75.0 (6)	80.0 (16)	71.4 (5)

Souter 96.3 (26)	93.3 (14)	83.4 (5)	100 (2)	0.0 (0)	100 (2)	100 (8)	90.5 (19)	93.3 (14)	66.7 (2)	50.0 (1)	100 (2)	100 (2)
Stevens 49.1 (82)	60.5 (58)	61.7 (37)	61.1 (22)	80.0 (8)	56.3 (9)	62.1 (18)	59.0 (66)	83.3 (70)	69.3 (27)	71.4 (5)	85.0 (17)	100 (7)
White 83.7 (139)	79.2 (76)	75.0 (45)	77.8 (28)	80.0 (8)	82.4 (14)	79.3 (23)	77.7 (87)	89.3 (75)	74.4 (29)	75.0 (6)	60.0 (12)	71.4 (5)

Powell

Blackmun 58.5 (24)	56.5 (13)	50.0 (6)	78.5 (11)	100 (1)	0.0 (0)	80.0 (4)	76.2 (16)	93.3 (14)	90.9 (10)	100 (1)	75.0 (3)	100 (1)
Brennan 31.7 (13)	56.0 (14)	58.3 (7)	57.1 (8)	100 (1)	0.0 (0)	80.0 (4)	68.2 (15)	86.7 (13)	72.7 (8)	100 (1)	100 (4)	100 (1)
Marshall 31.7 (13)	52.0 (13)	58.3 (7)	78.5 (11)	100 (1)	0.0 (0)	80.0 (4)	63.6 (14)	86.7 (13)	81.8 (9)	100 (1)	100 (4)	100 (1)
O'Connor 80.5 (33)	70.8 (17)	83.3 (10)	78.5 (11)	100 (1)	100 (3)	80.0 (4)	81.8 (18)	100 (15)	72.7 (8)	100 (1)	75.0 (3)	100 (1)
Rehnquist 85.4 (35)	72.0 (18)	58.3 (7)	78.5 (11)	100 (1)	100 (3)	80.0 (4)	86.3 (19)	100 (15)	90.9 (10)	100 (1)	75.0 (3)	100 (1)
Scalia 75.6 (31)	52.0 (13)	81.8 (9)	78.5 (11)	100 (1)	100 (3)	80.0 (4)	90.5 (19)	100 (13)	90.9 (10)	100 (1)	75.0 (3)	100 (1)

(Table continues)

Table 6-5 (Continued)

Justice	Crim	CivR	1st	DP	Priv	Atty	Un'n	Econ	JudP	Fed	IR	FTax	Misc
Stevens	51.2 (21)	60.0 (15)	66.7 (8)	50.0 (7)	100 (1)	33.3 (3)	60.0 (3)	54.5 (12)	80.0 (12)	72.7 (8)	—	50.0 (2)	100 (1)
White	82.5 (33)	80.0 (20)	83.3 (10)	78.6 (11)	100 (1)	100 (3)	40.0 (2)	86.3 (19)	86.7 (13)	72.7 (8)	100 (1)	75.0 (3)	100 (1)
Rehnquist													
Blackmun	51.8 (87)	39.6 (38)	46.5 (27)	58.3 (21)	50.0 (5)	52.9 (9)	72.4 (21)	74.1 (83)	78.8 (67)	76.2 (32)	75.0 (6)	75.0 (15)	85.7 (6)
Brennan	29.4 (40)	31.7 (26)	30.8 (16)	42.4 (14)	62.5 (5)	46.7 (7)	66.7 (14)	66.7 (60)	76.8 (53)	73.7 (28)	83.3 (5)	82.4 (14)	100 (5)
Kennedy	91.2 (103)	84.5 (49)	76.9 (30)	83.3 (15)	100 (8)	75.0 (9)	89.5 (17)	88.6 (70)	84.2 (48)	89.3 (25)	85.7 (6)	100 (12)	75.0 (3)
Marshall	26.8 (45)	31.6 (31)	29.3 (17)	52.8 (19)	50.0 (5)	50.0 (8)	65.5 (19)	66.7 (76)	72.9 (62)	75.6 (31)	62.5 (5)	85.0 (17)	100 (7)
O'Connor	89.8 (150)	77.1 (74)	77.6 (45)	83.3 (30)	80.0 (8)	88.2 (15)	89.7 (26)	88.4 (99)	88.1 (74)	84.7 (33)	87.5 (7)	75.0 (15)	71.4 (5)
Powell	85.4 (35)	72.0 (18)	58.3 (7)	78.5 (11)	100 (1)	100 (3)	80.0 (4)	86.3 (19)	100 (15)	90.9 (10)	100 (1)	75.0 (3)	100 (1)
Scalia	87.9 (146)	84.6 (82)	79.0 (45)	88.9 (32)	87.5 (7)	100 (17)	75.9 (22)	95.6 (108)	87.8 (72)	92.8 (39)	62.5 (5)	95.0 (19)	42.9 (3)

500

Souter	96.3 (26)	66.7 (10)	83.4 (5)	100 (2)	100 (1)	100 (2)	87.5 (7)	90.5 (19)	86.7 (13)	66.7 (2)	50.0 (1)	100 (2)	50.0 (1)
Stevens	45.8 (77)	53.1 (52)	55.2 (32)	55.6 (20)	60.0 (6)	56.3 (9)	72.4 (21)	59.3 (67)	80.0 (68)	75.6 (31)	57.1 (4)	70.0 (14)	71.4 (5)
White	87.4 (146)	79.6 (77)	82.7 (48)	77.8 (28)	100 (10)	82.4 (14)	89.6 (26)	79.7 (90)	85.9 (73)	85.7 (36)	62.5 (5)	85.0 (17)	100 (7)

Scalia

Blackmun	51.8 (87)	49.5 (47)	52.5 (31)	63.9 (23)	25.0 (2)	52.9 (9)	82.7 (24)	73.0 (81)	80.5 (66)	83.4 (35)	62.5 (5)	70.0 (14)	57.1 (4)
Brennan	39.0 (53)	42.0 (34)	47.2 (25)	48.5 (16)	42.9 (3)	46.7 (7)	61.9 (13)	68.5 (61)	80.6 (54)	73.7 (28)	66.7 (4)	82.4 (14)	40.0 (2)
Kennedy	87.6 (99)	87.9 (51)	90.0 (36)	94.4 (17)	85.7 (6)	75.0 (9)	89.4 (17)	91.2 (72)	91.0 (51)	92.8 (26)	71.5 (5)	100 (12)	75.0 (3)
Marshall	36.3 (61)	41.2 (40)	42.4 (25)	58.3 (21)	50.0 (4)	50.0 (8)	62.0 (18)	67.3 (76)	76.8 (63)	78.0 (32)	50.0 (4)	80.0 (16)	42.9 (3)
O'Connor	86.8 (145)	80.0 (76)	76.3 (45)	88.9 (32)	62.5 (5)	88.2 (15)	86.2 (25)	85.6 (95)	85.2 (69)	82.1 (32)	75.0 (6)	80.0 (16)	71.4 (5)
Powell	75.6 (31)	52.0 (13)	81.8 (9)	78.5 (11)	100 (1)	100 (3)	80.0 (4)	90.5 (19)	100 (13)	90.9 (10)	100 (1)	75.0 (3)	100 (1)

(Table continues)

Table 6-5 (Continued)

Justice	Crim	CivR	1st	DP	Priv	Atty	Un'n	Econ	JudP	Fed	IR	FTax	Misc
Rehnquist	87.9 (146)	84.6 (82)	79.0 (45)	88.9 (32)	87.5 (7)	100 (17)	75.9 (22)	95.6 (108)	87.8 (72)	92.8 (39)	62.5 (5)	95.0 (19)	42.9 (3)
Souter	81.5 (22)	73.3 (11)	66.7 (4)	100 (2)	100 (1)	100 (2)	87.5 (7)	95.3 (20)	78.5 (11)	100 (3)	50.0 (1)	100 (2)	100 (2)
Stevens	50.6 (85)	59.8 (58)	50.8 (30)	61.1 (22)	62.5 (5)	56.3 (9)	75.9 (22)	59.8 (67)	75.6 (62)	78.0 (32)	71.4 (5)	65.0 (13)	71.4 (5)
White	82.6 (138)	74.2 (72)	78.0 (46)	83.4 (30)	87.5 (7)	82.4 (14)	72.4 (21)	80.4 (90)	81.7 (67)	88.1 (37)	50.0 (4)	80.0 (16)	42.9 (3)
Souter													
Blackmun	44.4 (12)	80.0 (12)	33.3 (2)	50.0 (1)	0.0 (0)	50.0 (1)	75.0 (6)	71.4 (15)	86.7 (11)	100 (3)	100 (2)	0.0 (0)	100 (2)
Kennedy	85.2 (23)	80.0 (12)	50.0 (3)	100 (2)	100 (1)	100 (2)	100 (8)	95.2 (20)	92.3 (12)	66.7 (2)	50.0 (1)	100 (2)	100 (2)
Marshall	25.9 (7)	80.0 (12)	33.3 (2)	50.0 (1)	0.0 (0)	50.0 (1)	62.5 (5)	61.9 (13)	80.0 (12)	100 (3)	100 (2)	100 (2)	50.0 (1)
O'Connor	96.3 (26)	93.3 (14)	83.4 (5)	100 (2)	100 (1)	100 (2)	100 (8)	90.5 (19)	93.3 (14)	66.7 (2)	50.0 (1)	100 (2)	100 (2)
Rehnquist	96.3 (26)	66.7 (10)	83.4 (5)	100 (2)	100 (1)	100 (2)	87.5 (7)	90.5 (19)	86.7 (13)	66.7 (2)	50.0 (1)	100 (2)	50.0 (1)

							Stevens						
Scalia	81.5 (22)	73.3 (11)	66.7 (4)	100 (2)	100 (1)	100 (2)	87.5 (7)	95.3 (20)	78.5 (11)	100 (3)	50.0 (1)	100 (2)	100 (2)
Stevens	29.6 (8)	86.7 (13)	33.3 (2)	50.0 (1)	0.0 (0)	50.0 (1)	62.5 (5)	47.7 (10)	80.0 (12)	100 (3)	100 (2)	100 (2)	100 (2)
White	74.1 (20)	100 (15)	50.0 (3)	50.0 (1)	100 (1)	100 (2)	87.5 (7)	85.7 (18)	80.0 (12)	100 (3)	100 (2)	0.0 (0)	50.0 (1)
Blackmun	72.6 (122)	77.1 (74)	63.3 (38)	75.0 (27)	70.0 (7)	93.8 (15)	72.4 (21)	70.5 (79)	84.8 (72)	80.4 (33)	85.7 (6)	75.0 (15)	85.7 (6)
Brennan	77.2 (105)	78.3 (56)	70.4 (38)	81.8 (27)	75.0 (6)	92.9 (13)	66.7 (14)	77.8 (70)	84.1 (58)	83.8 (31)	80.0 (4)	82.4 (14)	80.0 (4)
Kennedy	46.9 (53)	55.1 (32)	57.5 (23)	77.8 (14)	50.0 (4)	81.8 (9)	68.4 (13)	65.8 (52)	82.5 (47)	74.1 (20)	42.9 (3)	75.0 (9)	100 (4)
Marshall	78.6 (132)	72.4 (71)	70.0 (42)	80.6 (29)	90.0 (9)	93.3 (14)	79.3 (23)	77.2 (88)	81.1 (69)	85.0 (34)	71.4 (5)	85.0 (17)	71.4 (5)
O'Connor	49.1 (82)	60.5 (58)	61.7 (37)	61.1 (22)	80.0 (8)	56.3 (9)	62.1 (18)	59.0 (66)	83.3 (70)	69.3 (27)	71.4 (5)	85.0 (17)	100 (7)
Powell	51.2 (21)	60.0 (15)	66.7 (8)	50.0 (7)	100 (1)	33.3 (3)	60.0 (3)	54.5 (12)	80.0 (12)	72.7 (8)	—	50.0 (2)	100 (1)

(Table continues)

Table 6-5 *(Continued)*

Justice	Crim	CivR	1st	DP	Priv	Atty	Un'n	Econ	JudP	Fed	IR	FTax	Misc
Rehnquist	45.8 (77)	53.1 (52)	55.2 (32)	55.6 (20)	60.0 (6)	56.3 (9)	72.4 (21)	59.3 (67)	80.0 (68)	75.6 (31)	57.1 (4)	70.0 (14)	71.4 (5)
Scalia	50.6 (85)	59.8 (58)	50.8 (30)	61.1 (22)	62.5 (5)	56.3 (9)	75.9 (22)	59.8 (67)	75.6 (62)	78.0 (32)	71.4 (5)	65.0 (13)	71.4 (5)
Souter	29.6 (8)	86.7 (13)	33.3 (2)	50.0 (1)	0.0 (0)	50.0 (1)	62.5 (5)	47.7 (10)	80.0 (12)	100 (3)	100 (2)	100 (2)	100 (2)
White	53.3 (89)	65.3 (64)	63.3 (38)	66.7 (24)	60.0 (6)	62.5 (10)	75.8 (22)	66.4 (75)	84.8 (72)	85.3 (35)	71.4 (5)	55.0 (11)	71.4 (5)
White													
Blackmun	59.9 (100)	58.3 (56)	56.7 (34)	75.0 (27)	50.0 (5)	58.8 (10)	69.0 (20)	73.2 (82)	88.3 (75)	81.0 (34)	87.5 (7)	80.0 (16)	85.7 (6)
Brennan	35.6 (48)	47.6 (39)	46.3 (25)	63.7 (21)	62.5 (5)	53.3 (8)	61.9 (13)	72.3 (65)	84.1 (58)	81.5 (31)	83.3 (5)	76.5 (13)	100 (5)
Kennedy	82.3 (93)	74.1 (43)	72.5 (29)	77.8 (14)	100 (8)	91.6 (11)	84.2 (16)	84.6 (66)	86.0 (49)	82.1 (23)	42.9 (3)	75.0 (9)	75.0 (3)
Marshall	35.9 (60)	50.0 (49)	43.3 (26)	75.0 (27)	50.0 (5)	50.0 (8)	62.1 (18)	72.0 (82)	82.4 (70)	85.3 (35)	100 (8)	70.0 (14)	100 (7)
O'Connor	83.7 (139)	79.2 (76)	75.0 (45)	77.8 (28)	80.0 (8)	82.4 (14)	79.3 (23)	77.7 (87)	89.3 (75)	74.4 (29)	75.0 (6)	60.0 (12)	71.4 (5)

Powell	82.5 (33)	80.0 (20)	83.3 (10)	78.6 (11)	100 (1)	100 (3)	40.0 (2)	86.3 (19)	86.7 (13)	72.7 (8)	100 (1)	75.0 (3)	100 (1)
Rehnquist	87.4 (146)	79.6 (77)	82.7 (48)	77.8 (28)	100 (10)	82.4 (14)	89.6 (26)	79.7 (90)	85.9 (73)	85.7 (36)	62.5 (5)	85.0 (17)	100 (7)
Scalia	82.6 (138)	74.2 (72)	78.0 (46)	83.4 (30)	87.5 (7)	82.4 (14)	72.4 (21)	80.4 (90)	81.7 (67)	88.1 (37)	50.0 (4)	80.0 (16)	42.9 (3)
Souter	74.1 (20)	100 (15)	50.0 (3)	50.0 (1)	100 (1)	100 (2)	87.5 (7)	85.7 (18)	80.0 (12)	100 (3)	100 (2)	0.0 (0)	50.0 (1)
Stevens	53.3 (89)	65.3 (64)	63.3 (38)	66.7 (24)	60.0 (6)	62.5 (10)	75.8 (22)	66.4 (75)	84.8 (72)	85.3 (35)	71.4 (5)	55.0 (11)	71.4 (5)

Note: "—" indicates no case in issue area was decided during tenure overlap. Figures listed are the percentage of cases in which the justices voted together. Figures in parentheses are the number of cases in issue area on which the justices agreed during their tenures on the Rehnquist Court, through the end of the 1990 term. The data include all orally argued citations. Readers should take care in interpreting the percentages since some of the figures on which they are based are quite small.

The issue areas are defined as follows: Criminal procedure (Crim): the rights of persons accused of crime except for the due process rights of prisoners; Civil rights (CivR): non-First Amendment freedom cases that pertain to classifications based on race (including native Americans), age, indigence, voting, residence, military or handicapped status, sex, or alienage; First Amendment (1st): guarantees contained therein; Due process (DP): noncriminal procedural guarantees, plus court jurisdiction over nonresident litigants and the takings clause of the Fifth Amendment; Privacy (Priv): abortion, contraception, the Freedom of Information Act and related federal statutes; Attorneys (Atty): attorneys' fees, commercial speech, admission to and removal from the bar, and disciplinary matters; Unions (Un'n): labor union activity; Economics (Econ): commercial business activity, plus litigation involving injured persons or

(Notes continue)

505

Table 6-5 (*Continued*)

things, employee actions vis-à-vis employers, zoning regulations, and governmental regulation of corruption other than that involving campaign spending; Judicial power (JudP): the exercise of the judiciary's own power and authority; Federalism (Fed): conflicts between the federal and state governments, excluding those between state and federal courts, and those involving the priority of federal fiscal claims; Interstate relations (IR): conflicts between states, such as boundary disputes, and nonproperty disputes commonly arising under the full faith and credit clause of the Constitution; Federal taxation (FTax): the Internal Revenue Code and related statutes; Miscellaneous (Misc): legislative veto, separation of powers, and matters not included in any other issue area.

Source: U.S. Supreme Court Judicial Database, with orally argued citation plus split vote as unit of analysis.

Table 6-6 Voting Interagreement Among the Justices in Special Opinions, 1953-1990 Terms

	Black	Blackmun	Brennan	Burger	Burton	Clark	Douglas	Fortas	Frankfurter	Goldberg	Harlan	Jackson	Kennedy	Marshall	Minton	O'Connor	Powell	Reed	Rehnquist	Scalia	Souter	Stevens	Stewart	Warren	White	Whitaker	Total
Black	—	2	21	3	2	16	166	2	3	5	17	0	—	1	1	—	—	0	—	—	—	—	19	34	11	4	307
Blackmun	1	—	101	19	—	—	3	—	—	—	2	—	3	74	—	8	30	—	22	8	1	65	14	—	49	—	400
Brennan	19	108	—	2	0	3	94	2	9	7	5	—	1	225	—	14	23	—	7	6	—	113	55	15	75	1	784
Burger	7	44	7	—	—	—	6	—	—	—	—	—	—	2	—	16	84	—	99	—	—	—	27	—	54	—	369
Burton	1	—	2	—	—	11	2	—	17	0	6	3	—	—	6	—	—	13	—	—	—	17	—	0	—	5	79
Clark	11	—	0	—	9	—	10	4	19	0	19	1	—	—	2	—	3	4	—	—	—	—	12	5	10	6	139
Douglas	141	2	90	2	0	9	—	11	9	11	46	1	—	32	3	—	—	1	2	—	—	—	31	38	17	5	416
Fortas	2	—	2	—	—	1	15	—	—	—	8	—	—	1	—	—	—	—	—	—	—	—	1	2	1	—	27
Frankfurter	5	—	7	—	11	12	6	—	—	—	58	2	—	—	1	—	—	11	—	—	—	—	4	0	—	12	121
Goldberg	4	—	4	—	—	0	7	—	—	—	7	—	—	—	—	—	—	—	—	—	—	—	7	1	—	—	25
Harlan	13	3	9	0	16	31	9	4	58	7	—	—	—	2	—	—	—	0	—	—	—	—	50	1	25	15	243
Jackson	1	—	—	—	1	0	0	—	2	—	—	—	—	—	1	—	—	0	—	—	—	—	—	0	—	—	5
Kennedy	—	0	1	—	—	—	—	—	—	—	—	—	—	0	—	10	—	—	4	18	1	2	—	—	5	—	41
Marshall	3	113	379	—	—	—	43	1	—	—	4	—	3	—	—	11	20	—	2	9	1	124	44	0	60	—	817
Minton	4	—	—	—	3	4	2	—	5	—	1	1	—	—	—	—	—	8	—	—	—	—	—	0	—	—	28

(Table continues)

Table 6-6 (Continued)

	Black	Blackmun	Brennan	Burger	Burton	Clark	Douglas	Fortas	Frankfurter	Goldberg	Harlan	Jackson	Kennedy	Marshall	Minton	O'Connor	Powell	Reed	Rehnquist	Scalia	Souter	Stevens	Stewart	Warren	White	Whitaker	Total
O'Connor	—	18	5	6	—	—	—	—	—	—	—	—	13	4	—	—	27	—	44	26	2	16	—	—	23	—	184
Powell	—	16	14	17	—	—	4	—	—	—	—	—	—	5	—	21	—	—	34	—	—	10	21	—	20	—	162
Reed	1	—	—	—	8	6	3	—	5	—	2	2	—	—	6	—	—	—	—	—	—	—	—	0	—	—	33
Rehnquist	—	33	1	42	—	—	5	—	—	—	—	—	12	5	—	53	90	—	—	29	1	36	36	—	78	—	421
Scalia	—	2	0	—	—	—	—	—	—	—	—	—	15	1	—	21	2	—	13	—	0	7	—	—	11	—	72
Souter	—	1	—	—	—	—	—	—	—	—	—	—	3	0	—	0	—	—	2	4	—	1	—	—	0	—	11
Stevens	—	35	67	4	—	—	—	—	—	—	—	—	2	55	—	16	12	—	23	5	0	—	13	—	25	—	257
Stewart	14	7	42	6	—	16	25	7	11	12	103	—	—	25	—	—	28	—	29	—	—	20	—	0	39	10	394
Warren	60	—	40	—	0	13	77	14	0	13	2	0	—	3	2	—	—	0	—	—	—	—	1	—	2	2	229
White	7	22	51	12	—	6	6	2	—	2	22	—	4	13	—	7	12	—	41	12	1	25	20	0	—	—	265
Whittaker	3	—	0	—	5	14	6	—	22	—	41	—	—	—	—	—	—	—	—	—	—	—	5	3	—	—	99
Total	297	406	843	113	55	142	489	47	160	57	332	10	56	448	22	177	331	37	322	117	7	436	360	99	505	60	[a]

Note: "Special opinions" refers to all concurring and dissenting opinions. Figures indicate agreement between justices. Jointly authored opinions count as a single opinion for each author. Rows are the number of times the justice listed on the row joined an opinion of the justice listed at the top of the column. Columns are the number of times an opinion of the justice listed at the top of the column was joined by the justice listed on the row.

[a] 5,928.

Source: U.S. Supreme Court Judicial Database, with orally argued citations as the unit of analysis.

Table 6-7 Votes in Support of and Opposition to Decisions Declaring Legislation Unconstitutional, 1953-1991 Terms

Justice	Court						Total	%	Congressional laws[a]	%
	Warren	%	Burger	%	Rehnquist	%				
Black	131-30	81.4	21-9	70.0	—	—	152-39	79.6	24-6	80.0
Blackmun	—	—	196-42	82.4	50-36	89.3	246-78	83.7	22-9	71.0
Brennan	145-0	100.0	235-14	94.4	41-1	97.6	421-15	96.6	51-3	94.4
Burger	—	—	174-80	69.0	—	—	174-80	69.0	20-8	71.4
Burton	16-10	61.5	—	—	—	—	16-10	61.5	0-3	0.0
Clark	94-31	75.2	—	—	—	—	94-31	75.2	6-8	42.9
Douglas	158-4	97.5	97-9	91.5	—	—	255-13	95.1	30-3	90.9
Fortas	46-3	93.9	—	—	—	—	46-3	93.9	11-0	100.0
Frankfurter	35-11	76.1	—	—	—	—	35-11	76.1	3-3	50.0
Goldberg	55-3	94.8	—	—	—	—	55-3	94.8	6-0	100.0
Harlan	88-66	57.1	26-4	86.7	—	—	114-70	62.0	16-14	53.3
Jackson	8-0	100.0	—	—	—	—	8-0	100.0	0-0	—
Kennedy	—	—	—	—	39-3	92.9	39-3	92.9	4-0	100.0

(Table continues)

Table 6-7 (Continued)

Justice	Court								Congressional laws[a]	%
	Warren	%	Burger	%	Rehnquist	%	Total	%		
Marshall	28-0	100.0	237-15	94.9	41-4	91.1	306-19	94.4	35-5	87.5
Minton	11-2	84.6	—	—	—	—	11-2	84.6	0-0	—
O'Connor	—	—	42-22	65.6	43-12	78.2	85-34	71.4	15	93.8
Powell	—	—	181-22	89.2	10-1	90.9	191-23	89.3	20-3	87.0
Reed	13-2	86.7	—	—	—	—	13-2	86.7	0-0	—
Rehnquist	—	—	78-129	37.7	23-31	42.6	101-160	38.7	14-14	50.0
Scalia	—	—	—	—	37-18	67.3	37-18	67.3	7-0	100.0
Souter	—	—	—	—	13-1	66.7	13-1	66.7	2-0	100.0
Stevens	—	—	115-20	85.2	47-9	83.9	162-29	84.8	14-7	66.7
Stewart	98-35	73.7	166-20	89.2	—	—	264-55	82.8	29-10	74.4
Thomas	—	—	—	—	5-4	55.6	5-4	55.6	1-0	100.0
Warren	147-12	92.5	—	—	—	—	147-12	92.5	18-6	75.0
White	91-21	81.3	196-58	77.2	40-16	71.4	327-95	77.5	30-22	57.7

	Total		Acts of Congress[a]		State and local		Total			
Whittaker	22-5	81.5	—	—	—	—	22-5	81.5	2-2	50.0
Totals	1,186-235	83.5	1,764-444	79.9	389-136	78.6	3,339-815	81.0	380-126	75.0

Note: Includes only those cases in which a majority voted to declare legislation unconstitutional. Figures to the left of the dash indicate the number of votes in favor of striking down legislation; figures to the right indicate the number of votes in favor of upholding the legislation. Percentages indicate the percent of cases in which the justice voted with the majority to declare legislation unconstitutional.

Determination of which decisions have voided acts of Congress and declared state and local legislation unconstitutional is not a clear-cut matter. The database lists only decisions in which the Court clearly indicates that it has voided a legislative enactment of some level of government. More specifically, declarations of unconstitutionality extend only to acts of Congress; state and territorial statutes, regulations, and constitutional provisions; and municipal or other local ordinances. Federal pre-emption of state or local legislation or regulations are excluded from consideration unless the opinion of the Court expressly states that the state or local enactment is unconstitutional.

[a] Excludes legislation passed by state and local power.

Source: U.S. Supreme Court Judicial Database.

Table 6-8 Votes in Support of and Opposition to Decisions Formally Altering Precedent, 1953-1991 Terms

Justice	Court Warren	%	Burger	%	Rehnquist	%	Total	%
Black	33-7	82.5	3-1	75.0	—	—	36-8	81.8
Blackmun	—	—	42-4	91.3	14-7	66.7	56-11	83.6
Brennan	38-0	100.0	31-16	66.0	9-6	60.0	78-22	78.0
Burger	—	—	41-8	83.7	—	—	41-8	83.7
Burton	2-1	66.7	—	—	—	—	2-1	66.7
Clark	13-15	46.4	—	—	—	—	13-15	46.4
Douglas	37-3	92.5	9-3	75.0	—	—	46-6	88.5
Fortas	15-1	93.8	—	—	—	—	15-1	93.8
Frankfurter	3-5	37.5	—	—	—	—	3-5	37.5
Goldberg	12-0	100.0	—	—	—	—	12-0	100.0
Harlan	16-23	41.0	3-1	75.0	—	—	19-24	44.2
Jackson	1-0	100.0	—	—	—	—	1-0	100.0
Kennedy	—	—	—	—	12-1	92.3	12-1	92.3
Marshall	9-0	100.0	33-15	68.8	9-9	50.0	51-24	68.0
Minton	1-0	100.0	—	—	—	—	1-0	100.0
O'Connor	—	—	11-2	84.6	16-5	76.2	27-7	79.4
Powell	—	—	39-4	90.7	4-1	80.0	43-5	89.6
Reed	1-0	100.0	—	—	—	—	1-0	100.0
Rehnquist	—	—	32-11	74.4	16-5	76.2	48-16	75.0
Scalia	—	—	—	—	18-3	85.7	18-3	85.7
Souter	—	—	—	—	6-0	100.0	6-0	100.0
Stevens	—	—	24-9	72.7	12-9	57.1	36-18	66.7
Stewart	24-13	64.9	33-3	91.7	—	—	57-16	78.1

Table 6-8   *(Continued)*

Justice	Warren	%	Court Burger	%	Rehnquist	%	Total	%
Thomas	—	—	—	—	2-1	66.7	2-1	66.7
Warren	37-2	94.9	—	—	—	—	37-2	94.9
White	21-11	65.6	39-8	83.0	17-4	81.0	77-23	77.0
Whittaker	3-2	60.0	—	—	—	—	3-2	60.0
Total	266-83	76.2	340-85	80.0	135-51	72.6	741-219	77.2

Note: Includes only those cases in which a majority voted to formally alter precedent. Figures to the left of the dash indicate the number of votes in favor of striking down legislation; figures to the right indicate the number of votes in favor of upholding legislation. Percentages indicate the percent of cases in which the justice voted with the majority to formally alter precedent.

Determination of whether or not the Court has formally altered precedent is not a clearcut judgment. Only those decisions in which the Court says that the decision has formally altered or "overruled" a previous decision of the Court are included. "Distinguished" precedents are not considered to have been formally altered. But those that "are disapproved," "are no longer good law," "can no longer be considered controlling," or "modify and narrow" are. Note further that the Court will occasionally assert that an earlier decision overruled a precedent even though that earlier decision contains no language to that effect. See, for example, the statement in *International Paper Co. v. Ouellette,* 479 U.S. 481 (1987), at 488, that *Illinois v. Milwaukee,* 406 U.S. 91 (1972), overruled *Ohio v. Wyandotte Chemicals Corp.,* 401 U.S. 493 (1971). Consequently, the list of overrulings for a given period of time need not remain constant because language in cases decided subsequent to that period may indicate that an earlier case overruled decisions even where not explicitly stated.

Source: U.S. Supreme Court Judicial Database.

Table 6-9   Opinions of the Court, Dissenting Opinions, and Concurring Opinions, 1790-1991 Terms

Justice	Instances of participation in opinions[a] (N)	Opinions of the Court (N)	Dissenting opinions (N)	Concurring opinions (N)
Baldwin	609	39	11	7
Barbour	210	17	2	1
Black	3,754	481	310	88
Blackmun	3,043	287	231	243
Blair	29	0	0	0
Blatchford	3,496	427	2	0
Bradley	5,343	389	60	17
Brandeis	3,874	455	65	10
Brennan	4,427	428	456	258
Brewer	4,405	533	57	8
Brown	3,408	453	44	10
Burger	2,394	247	118	119
Burton	1,259	96	50	15
Butler	2,811	325	35	6
Byrnes	147	16	0	0
Campbell	696	92	18	5
Cardozo	2,134	129	23	2
Catron	1,730	157	26	12
Salmon Chase	1,226	134	8	2
Samuel Chase	188	1	1	1
Clark	1,717	214	98	24
Clarke	1,200	128	22	2
Clifford	3,428	395	60	8
Curtis	427	48	8	3
Cushing	217	4	0	3
Daniel	1,253	87	47	9
Davis	2,250	192	10	2
Day	4,160	430	22	2
Douglas	4,157	524	486	154
Duvall	958	16	1	1
Ellsworth	35	9	0	0
Field	7,455	544	84	19
Fortas	379	38	33	24
Frankfurter	2,681	247	251	132
Fuller	4,687	750	32	1
Goldberg	345	36	23	28
Gray	5,366	450	11	4
Grier	1,903	194	12	2
Harlan I	7,927	737	119	17
Harlan II	1,826	165	311	204
Holmes	5,767	873	72	14
Hughes	3,155	395	17	2
Hunt	1,902	141	5	4
Iredell	55	0	1	1

Table 6-9   *(Continued)*

Justice	Instances of participation in opinions[a] (N)	Opinions of the Court (N)	Dissenting opinions (N)	Concurring opinions (N)
H. Jackson	762	46	4	0
R. Jackson	1,441	150	107	47
Jay	25	1	0	0
T. Johnson	10	0	0	0
W. Johnson	1,057	109	30	11
Kennedy	554	58	29	39
J. Lamar	1,485	112	2	0
L.Q.C. Lamar	1,304	101	2	1
Livingston	513	38	7	3
Lurton	1,211	96	2	0
J. Marshall	1,111	508	6	0
T. Marshall	3,187	317	328	105
Matthews	2,668	233	5	2
McKenna	5,580	646	30	4
McKinley	793	19	3	1
McLean	1,855	245	33	5
McReynolds	4,789	488	65	7
Miller	5,839	608	67	6
Minton	603	66	35	7
Moody	700	62	4	0
Moore	25	0	0	0
Murphy	1,336	132	66	18
Nelson	2,408	290	22	6
O'Connor	1,523	169	98	107
Paterson	112	1	1	0
Peckham	2,695	312	8	2
Pitney	2,455	249	19	5
Powell	2,126	242	152	186
Reed	2,215	228	79	21
Rehnquist	2,859	314	259	183
Roberts	2,237	296	67	2
J. Rutledge	5	0	0	0
W. Rutledge	873	65	59	34
Sanford	1,457	129	3	1
Scalia	782	74	67	108
Shiras	2,381	251	15	0
Souter	212	20	5	8
Stevens	2,279	232	372	239
Stewart	2,863	304	225	173
Stone	3,392	456	93	37
Story	1,340	270	13	1
Strong	2,126	238	19	2

(Table continues)

Table 6-9   *(Continued)*

Justice	Instances of participation in opinions[a] (N)	Opinions of the Court (N)	Dissenting opinions (N)	Concurring opinions (N)
Sutherland	2,535	288	23	2
Swayne	2,874	335	9	3
Taft	1,680	255	2	1
Taney	1,708	260	14	7
Thomas	92	7	6	6
Thompson	834	87	10	2
Todd	608	12	0	1
Trimble	127	16	0	0
Van Devanter	5,220	360	4	1
Vinson	654	76	12	0
Waite	3,863	872	23	2
Warren	1,754	165	56	21
Washington	851	69	1	0
Wayne	2,040	144	5	6
B. White	3,976	442	298	234
E. White	5,807	680	49	11
Whittaker	561	42	52	18
Wilson	48	2	1	0
Woodbury	406	42	9	2
Woods	2,144	164	1	0

Note: Given that we used two data sources to assemble this table, readers should be aware that differences probably exist in the way those collecting the data defined opinions of the Court, dissenting opinions, and concurring opinions. We only report their results and make no attempt to impose consistency on the data.

[a] Figures for justices seated prior to 1953 are approximations based on the number of majority opinions decided during their tenures.

Sources: For justices seated before the 1953 term: Albert P. Blaustein and Roy M Mersky, *The First One Hundred Justices* (Hamden, Conn.: Shoe String Press, 1978), 142-146; for justices seated during and after the 1953 term: U.S. Supreme Court Judicial Database, with orally argued citation as the unit of analysis.

Table 6-10 Opinion Writing, 1953–1991 Terms

Justice[a]	Instances of participation in opinions	Opinions of the Court	Judgments of the Court[b]	Dissents	Concurrences Regular[c]	Concurrences Special[d]	Dissents (jurisdictional)[e]	Nonconcurring member of the majority[f]
Black	1,994	194 (9.7)	6 (0.3)	238 (11.9)	52 (2.6)	70 (3.5)	0 —	1,434 (71.9)
Blackmun	3,043	287 (9.4)	10 (0.3)	231 (7.6)	102 (3.4)	141 (4.6)	3 (0.1)	2,269 (74.6)
Brennan	4,427	428 (9.7)	24 (0.5)	456 (10.3)	113 (2.6)	145 (3.3)	0 —	3,261 (73.7)
Burger	2,394	247 (10.3)	11 (0.5)	118 (4.9)	76 (3.1)	43 (1.8)	1 (0.0)	1,898 (79.3)
Burton	522	36 (6.9)	0 —	35 (6.7)	3 (0.6)	6 (1.1)	0 —	442 (84.7)
Clark	1,530	171 (11.2)	1 (0.1)	103 (6.7)	11 (0.7)	21 (1.4)	1 (0.1)	1,222 (79.9)
Douglas	2,588	258 (10.1)	2 (0.1)	481 (18.8)	96 (3.8)	90 (3.5)	7 (0.3)	1,654 (63.9)
Fortas	379	38 (10.0)	2 (0.5)	33 (8.7)	11 (2.9)	13 (3.4)	1 (0.3)	281 (74.1)
Frankfurter	918	78 (8.5)	6 (0.7)	104 (11.3)	25 (2.7)	40 (4.4)	20 (2.2)	645 (70.3)
Goldberg	345	36 (10.4)	0 —	23 (6.7)	14 (4.6)	14 (4.6)	1 (0.3)	257 (74.5)

(Table continues)

Table 6-10 (Continued)

Justice[a]	Instances of participation in opinions	Opinions of the Court	Judgments of the Court[b]	Dissents	Concurrences Regular[c]	Concurrences Special[d]	Dissents (jurisdictional)[e]	Nonconcurring member of the majority[f]
Harlan	1,826	165 (9.0)	6 (0.3)	311 (17.0)	81 (4.4)	123 (6.7)	2 (0.1)	1,138 (62.3)
Jackson	75	5 (6.7)	2 (2.7)	7 (9.3)	2 (2.7)	0 (—)	0 (—)	59 (78.7)
Kennedy	554	58 (10.6)	1 (0.2)	29 (5.8)	21 (3.8)	18 (2.5)	0 (—)	427 (77.1)
Marshall	3,187	317 (9.9)	5 (0.2)	328 (10.3)	42 (1.3)	63 (2.0)	2 (0.1)	2,430 (76.3)
Minton	277	22 (7.9)	0 (—)	17 (6.1)	0 (—)	2 (0.7)	1 (0.4)	235 (84.8)
O'Connor	1,523	169 (11.1)	5 (0.3)	98 (6.4)	57 (3.7)	50 (3.3)	0 (—)	1,144 (75.1)
Powell	2,126	242 (11.4)	12 (0.6)	152 (7.1)	109 (5.1)	77 (3.6)	0 (—)	1,534 (72.2)
Reed	316	27 (8.5)	0 (—)	27 (8.5)	3 (0.9)	3 (0.9)	0 (—)	256 (81.0)
Rehnquist	2,859	314 (11.0)	14 (0.5)	259 (9.1)	36 (1.3)	47 (1.6)	2 (0.1)	2,187 (76.5)
Scalia	782	74 (9.5)	3 (0.4)	67 (8.6)	31 (4.0)	77 (9.8)	0 (—)	530 (67.8)

Souter	212	20 (9.4)	2 (0.9)	5 (2.4)	3 (1.4)	5 (2.4)	1 (0.5)	176 (83.0)
Stevens	2,279	232 (10.2)	13 (0.6)	372 (16.3)	99 (4.3)	140 (6.1)	7 (0.1)	1,416 (62.1)
Stewart	2,863	304 (10.6)	10 (0.3)	225 (7.9)	72 (2.5)	101 (3.5)	4 (0.1)	2,147 (75.0)
Thomas	92	7 (7.6)	1 (1.1)	6 (6.5)	2 (2.2)	4 (4.3)	0 —	72 (78.3)
Warren	1,754	165 (9.4)	5 (0.3)	56 (3.2)	10 (0.6)	11 (0.6)	1 (0.1)	1,506 (85.9)
White	3,976	442 (11.1)	19 (0.5)	298 (7.5)	97 (2.4)	137 (3.4)	2 (0.1)	2,981 (75.0)
Whittaker	561	42 (7.5)	0 —	52 (9.3)	6 (1.1)	12 (2.1)	0 —	449 (80.0)

Note: Figures in parentheses are percentage of listed activity relative to overall participation. Data include all orally argued case citations.

[a] For those justices seated prior to 1953, data are not completely descriptive of their careers.
[b] Plurality rulings that occur when no majority agrees on the justification for a decision.
[c] Joined majority opinion but wrote separately as well.
[d] Explicitly disagreed with rationale in majority opinion.
[e] Include dissent (in the form of an opinion) from a dismissal or denial of certiorari, dissent from summary affirmation of an appeal, or dissent from the Court's assertion of jurisdiction.
[f] Wrote no opinion.

Source: U.S. Supreme Court Judicial Database.

Table 6-11   Number of Solo Dissents, 1953-1991 Terms

Justice[a]	Solo dissents	Solo dissents as % of participations in solo dissent cases[b]
Black	50	13.8
Blackmun	20	5.4
Brennan	22	3.3
Burger	14	4.3
Burton	2	2.9
Clark	21	8.3
Douglas	208	45.2
Fortas	2	1.8
Frankfurter	12	9.8
Goldberg	0	—
Harlan	79	22.5
Jackson	0	—
Kennedy	1	2.2
Marshall	33	8.1
Minton	0	—
O'Connor	7	4.8
Powell	11	4.2
Reed	6	19.4
Rehnquist	68	21.5
Scalia	11	18.3
Souter	0	—
Stevens	80	32.8
Stewart	28	5.6
Thomas	1	11.1
Warren	4	1.2
White	35	6.0
Whittaker	13	17.1
Total	728	

Note: Jurisdictional dissents and dissents from denials of certiorari are excluded. Unit of analysis is docket number of orally argued cases.

[a] For those justices seated prior to 1953, data are not completely descriptive of their careers.
[b] Indicates percentage of cases in which justice was the solo dissenter in cases containing solo dissents.

Source: U. S. Supreme Court Judicial Database.

Table 6-12 Significant Opinions

Justice (appointment number)	Case	Opinion [a]	Subject matter
Baldwin, Henry (23)	Groves v. Slaughter (1841)	C	Slave trade
Barbour, Philip P. (26)	City of New York v. Miln (1837)	M	Foreign commerce
Black, Hugo L. (79)	Korematsu v. United States (1944)	M	Presidential war powers
	Everson v. Board of Education (1947)	M	Religious establishment
	Youngstown Sheet and Tube v. Sawyer (1952)	M	Presidential war powers
	Engle v. Vitale (1962)	M	Religious establishment, school prayer
	Gideon v. Wainwright (1963)	M	Right to counsel
	Wesberry v. Sanders (1964)	M	Reapportionment
Blackmun, Harry A. (102)	Roe v. Wade (1973)	M	Abortion
	Bates v. State Bar of Arizona (1977)	M	Commercial expression
	Garcia v. San Antonio Metropolitan Transit Authority (1985)	M	Federalism
	Mistretta v. United States (1989)	M	Judicial-legislative powers
Blair, John, Jr. (5)	Chisholm v. Georgia (1793)	S	Federal court jurisdiction
Blatchford, Samuel (49)	Chicago, Milwaukee and St. Paul Railroad v. Minnesota (1890)	M	Substantive due process
	Budd v. New York (1892)	M	Commerce, due process
	Counselman v. Hitchcock (1892)	M	Self-incrimination
Bradley, Joseph P. (42)	Ex parte Siebold (1880)	M	Voting rights
	The Civil Rights Cases (1883)	M	Civil rights
	Boyd v. United States (1886)	M	Search and seizure

(Table continues)

Table 6-12 (Continued)

Justice (appointment number)	Case	Opinion[a]	Subject matter
Brandeis, Louis D. (69)	Truax v. Corrigan (1921)	D	Labor, due process, equal protection
	Olmstead v. United States (1928)	D	Wiretapping, privacy
	O'Gorman and Young v. Hartford Fire Insurance Co. (1931)	M	State insurance regulations
Brennan, William J., Jr. (94)	Roth v. United States (1957)	M	Obscenity
	Baker v. Carr (1962)	M	Reapportionment
	New York Times v. Sullivan (1964)	M	Libel
	Craig v. Boren (1976)	M	Sex discrimination
	Texas v. Johnson (1989)	M	Freedom of expression
Brewer, David J. (52)	In re Debs (1895)	M	Commerce, labor
	Muller v. Oregon (1908)	M	Commerce, due process, state police powers
Brown, Henry B. (53)	Pollock v. Farmers' Loan and Trust (1895)	D	Federal income tax
	Plessy v. Ferguson (1896)	M	Racial discrimination
	Holden v. Hardy (1898)	M	Contracts, due process
Burger, Warren E. (101)	Swann v. Charlotte-Mecklenburg Board of Education (1971)	M	School desegregation
	Lemon v. Kurtzman (1971)	M	Religious establishment
	Miller v. California (1973)	M	Obscenity
	United States v. Nixon (1974)	M	Executive privilege
	INS v. Chadha (1983)	M	Legislative veto
Burton, Harold H. (88)	Henderson v. United States (1950)	M	Racial discrimination
	Joint Anti-Fascist Refugee Committee v. McGrath (1951)	M	Subversive activities
Butler, Pierce (73)	Powell v. Alabama (1932)	D	Right to counsel
	Morehead v. New York ex rel.Tipaldo (1936)	M	Substantive due process
	Breedlove v. Suttles (1937)	M	Poll taxes

Byrnes, James F. (85)	Edwards v. California (1941)	M	Right to interstate travel
Campbell, John A. (34)	Dodge v. Woolsey (1856)	D	Contracts, state taxation
	Scott v. Sandford (1857)	C	Slavery
Cardozo, Benjamin (78)	Nixon v. Condon (1932)	M	Racial discrimination, voting rights
	Steward Machine Co. v. Davis (1937)	M	Federal taxing and spending powers
	Palko v. Connecticut (1937)	M	Application of the Bill of Rights to the states
Catron, John (27)	The License Cases (1847)	C	State taxation powers
	Scott v. Sandford (1857)	C	Slavery
Chase, Salmon P. (40)	Mississippi v. Johnson (1867)	M	Presidential immunity
	Ex parte McCardle (1869)	M	Appellate jurisdiction
	Hepburn v. Griswold (1870)	M	Legal tender
Chase, Samuel (10)	Ware v. Hylton (1796)	S	Treaty powers
	Calder v. Bull (1798)	S	Ex post facto laws
Clark, Tom C. (90)	Watkins v. United States (1957)	D	Legislative investigations
	Mapp v. Ohio (1961)	M	Exclusionary rule
	Heart of Atlanta Motel v. United States (1964)	M	Racial discrimination
Clarke, John H. (70)	Abrams v. United States (1919)	M	Freedom of expression
	American Column and Lumber Co. v. United States (1921)	M	Antitrust
Clifford, Nathan (35)	Knox v. Lee (1871)	D	Legal tender

(Table continues)

Table 6-12 *(Continued)*

Justice (appointment number)	Case	Opinion[a]	Subject matter
Curtis, Benjamin R. (33)	*Cooley v. Board of Wardens* (1852)	M	Foreign commerce
	Scott v. Sandford (1857)	D	Slavery
Cushing, William (3)	*Chisholm v. Georgia* (1793)	S	Federal court jurisdiction
	Ware v. Hylton (1796)	S	Treaty powers
Daniel, Peter V. (29)	*West River Bridge v. Dix* (1848)	M	Contract clause
	Scott v. Sandford (1857)	C	Slavery
Davis, David (38)	*Ex parte Milligan* (1866)	M	Presidential war powers
Day, William R. (60)	*Weeks v. United States* (1914)	M	Search and seizure
	Hammer v. Dagenhart (1918)	M	Child labor
	United States v. United States Steel Corp. (1920)	D	Antitrust
Douglas, William O. (82)	*Murdock v. Pennsylvania* (1943)	M	Free exercise of religion
	Terminiello v. Chicago (1949)	M	Freedom of speech
	Griswold v. Connecticut (1965)	M	Privacy
	Harper v. Virginia State Board of Elections (1966)	M	Poll taxes
	Adderley v. Florida (1966)	D	Freedom of expression
Duvall, Gabriel (18)	*LeGrand v. Darnall* (1829)	M	Slavery
Ellsworth, Oliver (11)	*Wiscart v. Dauchy* (1796)	S	Appellate jurisdiction
Field, Stephen J. (39)	*Cumming v. Missouri* (1867)	M	Loyalty oaths
	Paul v. Virginia (1869)	M	Commerce, insurance
	Munn v. Illinois (1877)	D	Commerce, due process

Fortas, Abe (99)	*In re Gault* (1967)	Juvenile rights	M
	Tinker v. Des Moines (1969)	Freedom of expression	M
Frankfurter, Felix (81)	*Minersville School District v. Gobitis* (1940)	Free exercise of religion	M
	Colegrove v. Green (1946)	Reapportionment	M
	Wolf v. Colorado (1949)	Search and seizure	M
	Mallory v. United States (1957)	Criminal due process	M
Fuller, Melville W. (51)	*United States v. E.C. Knight* (1895)	Commerce	M
	Pollock v. Farmers' Loan and Trust (1895)	Federal income tax	M
	Champion v. Ames (1903)	Federal police powers	D
	Loewe v. Lawler (1908)	Labor	M
Goldberg, Arthur J. (98)	*Escobedo v. Illinois* (1964)	Self-incrimination, counsel	M
	Griswold v. Connecticut (1965)	Privacy	C
Gray, Horace (48)	*Julliard v. Greenman* (1884)	Legal tender	M
	United States v. Wong Kim Ark (1898)	Citizenship	M
Grier, Robert C. (32)	*The Prize Cases* (1863)	Presidential war powers	M
Harlan, John Marshall I (45)	*Pollock v. Farmers' Loan and Trust* (1895)	Federal income tax	D
	Plessy v. Ferguson (1896)	Racial discrimination	D
	Champion v. Ames (1903)	Federal police powers	M
	Northern Securities v. United States (1904)	Commerce	M
Harlan, John Marshall II (93)	*NAACP v. Alabama* (1958)	Freedom of association	M
	Barenblatt v. United States (1959)	Legislative investigations	M
	Scales v. United States (1961)	Subversive activities	M

(Table continues)

Table 6-12 (Continued)

Justice (appointment number)	Case	Opinion[a]	Subject matter
	Reynolds v. Sims (1964)	D	Reapportionment
	Miranda v. Arizona (1966)	D	Self-incrimination
Holmes, Oliver W., Jr. (59)	Swift and Co. v. United States (1905)	M	Commerce
	Schenck v. United States (1919)	M	Freedom of expression
	Abrams v. United States (1919)	D	Freedom of expression
	Missouri v. Holland (1920)	M	Treaty powers
	Moore v. Dempsey (1923)	M	Fair trials
	Buck v. Bell (1927)	M	Compulsory sterilization
Hughes, Charles E. (63, 76)	Shreveport Rate Case (1914)	M	Commerce
	Near v. Minnesota (1931)	M	Freedom of the press
	Home Building and Loan Association v. Blaisdell (1934)	M	Contracts
	Schechter Poultry Corp. v. United States (1935)	M	Commerce
	West Coast Hotel v. Parrish (1937)	M	Substantive due process
	N.L.R.B. v. Jones & Laughlin Steel Corp. (1937)	M	Commerce
Hunt, Ward (43)	United States v. Reese (1876)	D	Voting rights
Iredell, James (6)	Chisholm v. Georgia (1793)	D	Federal court jurisdiction
	Calder v. Bull (1798)	S	Ex post facto laws
Jackson, Howell E. (55)	Pollock v. Farmers' Loan and Trust (1895)	D	Federal income tax
Jackson, Robert H. (86)	West Virginia State Board of Education v. Barnette (1943)	M	Free exercise of religion
	Korematsu v. United States (1944)	D	Presidential war powers
	Fay v. New York (1947)	M	Juries
	Youngstown Sheet and Tube Co. v. Sawyer (1952)	C	Presidential war powers

Justice	Case		Topic
Jay, John (1)	Chisholm v. Georgia (1793)	S	Federal court jurisdiction
	Glass v. The Sloop Betsy (1794)	S	Admiralty
Johnson, Thomas (7)	None		
Johnson, William (15)	Martin v. Hunter's Lessee (1816)	C	Judicial power
	Anderson v. Dunn (1821)	M	Congressional power
	Gibbons v. Ogden (1824)	C	Commerce clause
Kennedy, Anthony (109)	Skinner v. Railway Labor Executives Association (1989)	M	Drug testing
	Masson v. New Yorker Magazine (1991)	M	Libel
	Freeman v. Pitts (1992)	M	School desegregation
	Lee v. Weisman (1992)	M	Religious establishment
Lamar, Joseph R. (66)	Gompers v. Buck's Stove and Range Co. (1911)	M	Contempt, labor
Lamar, Lucius Q. C. (50)	Kidd v. Pearson (1888)	M	Commerce
	In re Neagle (1890)	D	Presidential power
	McCall v. California (1890)	M	Commerce, state taxation
Livingston, H. Brockholst (16)	Riggs v. Lindsay (1813)	M	Business law
	The Euphrates (1814)	M	Prize case
Lurton, Horace (62)	Coyle v. Smith (1911)	M	Statehood powers
	Henry v. A. B. Dick Co. (1912)	M	Patents
Marshall, John (14)	Marbury v. Madison (1803)	M	Judicial review
	Fletcher v. Peck (1810)	M	Contract clause
	McCulloch v. Maryland (1819)	M	Federalism

(Table continues)

Table 6-12 *(Continued)*

Justice (appointment number)	Case	Opinion[a]	Subject matter
Marshall, Thurgood (100)	*Dartmouth College v. Woodward* (1819)	M	Contract clause
	Gibbons v. Ogden (1824)	M	Commerce clause
	Benton v. Maryland (1969)	M	Double jeopardy
	Furman v. Georgia (1972)	C	Capital punishment
	San Antonio Independent School District v. Rodriguez (1973)	D	Economic discrimination
Matthews, Stanley (47)	*Hurtado v. California* (1884)	M	Application of the Bill of Rights to the states
	Yick Wo v. Hopkins (1886)	M	Equal protection
McKenna, Joseph (58)	*Weems v. United States* (1910)	M	Cruel and unusual punishment
	Hipolite Egg Co. v. United States (1911)	M	Commerce
	United States v. United States Steel Corp. (1920)	M	Antitrust
McKinley, John (28)	*Bank of Augusta v. Earle* (1839)	D	Corporations
	Pollard's Lessee v. Hagen (1845)	M	Land claims
McLean, John (22)	*Wheaton v. Peters* (1834)	M	Copyright
	Cooley v. Board of Wardens (1852)	D	Foreign commerce
	Scott v. Sandford (1857)	D	Slavery
McReynolds, James C. (68)	*Myer v. Nebraska* (1923)	M	Freedom of speech
	Pierce v. Society of Sisters (1925)	M	Free exercise of religion
	The Gold Clause Cases (1935)	D	Gold standard
	N.L.R.B. v. Jones & Laughlin Steel Corp. (1937)	D	Commerce

Justice	Case		Topic
Miller, Samuel (37)	Slaughterhouse Cases (1873)	M	Privileges and immunities, due process of law
	Kilbourn v. Thompson (1881)	M	Congressional power
	Ex parte Yarbrough (1884)	M	Voting rights
Minton, Sherman (91)	United States v. Rabinowitz (1950)	M	Search and seizure
	Adler v. Board of Education (1952)	M	Subversive activities
Moody, William H. (61)	First Employers' Liability Case (1908)	D	Commerce
	Twining v. New Jersey (1908)	M	Application of the Bill of Rights to the states
Moore, Alfred (13)	None		
Murphy, Frank (83)	Thornhill v. Alabama (1940)	M	Freedom of expression
	Chaplinsky v. New Hampshire (1942)	M	Freedom of speech
	Wolf v. Colorado (1949)	D	Search and seizure
Nelson, Samuel (30)	Scott v. Sandford (1857)	C	Slavery
O'Connor, Sandra Day (106)	Garcia v. San Antonio Metropolitan Transit Authority (1985)	D	Federalism
	Tison v. Arizona (1987)	M	Capital punishment
	City of Richmond v. J.A. Croson Co. (1989)	M	Affirmative action
Paterson, William (8)	Talbot v. Jansen (1795)	S	Prize case
	Hylton v. United States (1796)	S	Taxation
Peckham, Rufus W. (57)	Allgeyer v. Louisiana (1897)	M	Substantive due process
	Maxwell v. Dow (1900)	M	Application of the Bill of Rights to the states
	Lochner v. New York (1905)	M	Substantive due process

(Table continues)

Table 6-12 *(Continued)*

Justice (appointment number)	Case	Opinion[a]	Subject matter
Pitney, Mahlon (67)	*Frank v. Mangum* (1915)	M	Fair trials
	Duplex Printing Press Co. v. Deering (1921)	M	Antitrust
Powell, Lewis F., Jr. (103)	*San Antonio Independent School District v. Rodriguez* (1973)	M	Economic discrimination
	Regents of the University of California v. Bakke (1978)	M	Affirmative action
	McCleskey v. Kemp (1987)	M	Capital punishment
Reed, Stanley F. (80)	*McNabb v. United States* (1943)	D	Self-incrimination
	Smith v. Allwright (1944)	M	Elections and voting
	Louisiana ex rel. Francis v. Resweber (1947)	M	Capital punishment
Rehnquist, William (104, 107)	*National League of Cities v. Usery* (1976)	M	Federalism
	Rostker v. Goldberg (1981)	M	Military draft, sex discrimination
	Dames & Moore v. Regan (1981)	M	Presidential power
	Mueller v. Allen (1983)	M	Religious establishment
	Morrison v. Olson (1988)	M	Separation of powers
Roberts, Owen J. (77)	*Nebbia v. New York* (1934)	M	Substantive due process
	Grovey v. Townsend (1935)	M	Elections and voting
	United States v. Butler (1936)	M	Federal commerce, taxing and spending powers
	Cantwell v. Connecticut (1940)	M	Free exercise of religion
Rutledge, John (2, 9)	None		
Rutledge, Wiley B. (87)	*Thomas v. Collins* (1945)	M	Speech, labor
	In re Yamashita (1946)	D	War tribunals

Justice	Case		Topic
Sanford, Edward T. (74)	Gitlow v. New York (1925)	M	Freedom of speech, press
	Whitney v. California (1927)	M	Freedom of association
Scalia, Antonin (108)	Johnson v. Transportation Agency of Santa Clara County (1987)	D	Affirmative action
	Nollan v. California Coastal Commission (1987)	M	Takings clause
	R.A.V. v. City of St. Paul (1992)	M	Freedom of expression
Shiras, George, Jr. (54)	Brass v. North Dakota (1894)	M	Commerce, due process
	Wong Wing v. United States (1896)	M	Alien discrimination
Souter, David H. (110)	Yates v. Evatt (1991)	M	Juries
	Sochor v. Florida (1992)	M	Capital punishment
Stevens, John Paul (105)	Payton v. New York (1980)	M	Search and seizure
	NAACP v. Claiborne Hardware Co. (1982)	M	Freedom of expression
	Wallace v. Jaffree (1985)	M	Religious establishment, school prayer
Stewart, Potter (96)	Katz v. United States (1967)	M	Search and seizure, privacy
	Jones v. Alfred H. Mayer (1968)	M	Civil rights
	Gregg v. Georgia (1976)	M	Capital punishment
	Gannett Co. v. DePasquale (1979)	M	Freedom of the press
Stone, Harlan Fiske (75, 84)	United States v. Butler (1936)	D	Federal commerce, taxing and spending powers
	Minersville School District v. Gobitis (1940)	D	Free exercise of religion
	United States v. Darby Lumber Company (1941)	M	Child labor
	United States v. Classic (1941)	M	Elections and voting

(Table continues)

Table 6-12 (Continued)

Justice (appointment number)	Case	Opinion[a]	Subject matter
Story, Joseph (19)	Martin v. Hunter's Lessee (1816)	M	Judicial power
	Martin v. Mott (1827)	M	Presidential power
	Charles River Bridge v. Warren Bridge (1837)	D	Contract clause
Strong, William (41)	Knox v. Lee (1871)	M	Legal tender
	Strauder v. West Virginia (1880)	M	Racial discrimination, juries
Sutherland, George (72)	Adkins v. Children's Hospital (1923)	M	Substantive due process
	Powell v. Alabama (1932)	M	Right to counsel
	Carter v. Carter Coal Co. (1936)	M	Commerce
	United States v. Curtiss-Wright Export Corp. (1936)	M	Presidential power
Swayne, Noah H. (36)	Slaughterhouse Cases (1873)	D	Privileges and immunities, due process of law
	Springer v. United States (1881)	M	Federal income tax
Taft, William H. (71)	Bailey v. Drexel Furniture Co. (1922)	M	Child labor
	United States v. Lanza (1922)	M	Double jeopardy
	Adkins v. Children's Hospital (1923)	D	Substantive due process
	Myers v. United States (1926)	M	Presidential power
	Olmstead v. United States (1928)	M	Wiretapping, privacy
Taney, Roger B. (25)	Charles River Bridge v. Warren Bridge (1837)	M	Contract clause
	Luther v. Borden (1849)	M	Guarantee clause
	Scott v. Sandford (1857)	M	Slavery

Thomas, Clarence (111)	*Hudson v. McMillan* (1992)	D	Cruel and unusual punishment
Thompson, Smith (20)	*Mason v. Haile* (1827)	M	Contract clause
	Cherokee Nation v. Georgia (1831)	D	Native Americans
	Kendall v. United States (1838)	M	Federal court jurisdiction
Todd, Thomas (17)	*Preston v. Browder* (1816)	M	Land
	Riggs v. Tayloe (1824)	M	Evidence
Trimble, Robert (21)	*Ogden v. Saunders* (1827)	C	Contracts, bankruptcy
	The Antelope (1827)	M	Slave trade
Van Devanter, Willis (65)	*Dillon v. Gloss* (1921)	M	Constitutional amendment ratification
	McGrain v. Daugherty (1927)	M	Investigation powers of Congress
Vinson, Fred M. (89)	*Shelley v. Kraemer* (1948)	M	Racial discrimination
	Sweatt v. Painter (1950)	M	Racial discrimination
	Feiner v. New York (1951)	M	Freedom of speech
Waite, Morrison (44)	*United States v. Reese* (1876)	M	Voting rights
	Munn v. Illinois (1877)	M	Commerce, due process
	Stone v. Mississippi (1880)	M	Contracts, police powers
Warren, Earl (92)	*Brown v. Board of Education* (1954)	M	Racial discrimination
	Reynolds v. Sims (1964)	M	Reapportionment
	South Carolina v. Katzenbach (1966)	M	Voting rights
	Miranda v. Arizona (1966)	M	Self-incrimination
	Powell v. McCormack (1969)	M	Congressional membership

(Table continues)

Table 6-12 (Continued)

Justice (appointment number)	Case	Opinion [a]	Subject matter
Washington, Bushrod (12)	Dartmouth College v. Woodward (1819)	C	Contract clause
	Ogden v. Saunders (1827)	M	Contracts, bankruptcy
Wayne, James M. (24)	Dobbins v. Erie County (1842)	M	State taxation
	Louisville Railroad Co. v. Letson (1844)	M	Corporations
	Cooley v. Board of Wardens (1852)	D	Foreign commerce
White, Byron R. (97)	Branzburg v. Hayes (1972)	M	Freedom of the press
	Washington v. Davis (1976)	M	Racial discrimination
	United States v. Leon (1984)	M	Exclusionary rule
	Bowers v. Hardwick (1986)	M	Privacy, homosexuality
White, Edward D. (56, 64)	McCray v. United States (1904)	M	Federal regulatory taxes
	Standard Oil Co. v. United States (1911)	M	Antitrust
	Selective Draft Law Cases (1918)	M	Military draft
Whittaker, Charles E. (95)	Staub v. City of Baxley (1958)	M	Freedom of expression
Wilson, James (4)	Chisholm v. Georgia (1793)	S	Federal court jurisdiction
Woodbury, Levi (31)	Jones v. Van Zandt (1847)	M	Slavery
	Planters' Bank v. Sharp (1848)	M	Contracts, banking
Woods, William B. (46)	United States v. Harris (1883)	M	Civil rights
	Presser v. Illinois (1886)	M	Right to bear arms

Note: Opinions listed here have been selected by the authors because they were written in significant cases or are particularly representative of a justice's judicial philosophy.

[a] M=majority opinion; C=concurring opinion; D=dissenting opinion; S=seriatim opinion.

Table 6-13 Assignment and Authorship of Majority Opinion, 1953-1960 Terms

Term/ assigner[a]	Black	Reed	Frankfurter	Douglas	Jackson	Burton	Clark	Minton	Warren	Harlan	Whittaker	Brennan	Stewart	Total
1953														
Warren	9	4	6	6	4	6	7	4	9	—	—	—	—	55
Black	0	1	0	0	1	0	0	2	0	—	—	—	—	4
Reed	0	2	2	0	2	0	0	0	0	—	—	—	—	6
Total	9	7	8	6	7	6	7	6	9	—	—	—	—	65
1954														
Warren	9	4	8	11	—	6	14	6	12	1	—	—	—	71
Black	0	2	1	0	—	0	0	1	0	0	—	—	—	4
Reed	0	0	2	0	—	0	0	0	0	1	—	—	—	3
Total	9	6	11	11	—	6	14	7	12	2	—	—	—	78
1955														
Warren	9	4	9	10	—	6	7	8	8	8	—	—	—	69
Black	0	0	0	0	—	0	0	1	0	0	—	—	—	1
Reed	0	5	0	0	—	2	4	0	0	1	—	—	—	12
Total	9	9	9	10	—	8	11	9	8	9	—	—	—	82
1956														
Warren	10	2	7	13	—	7	11	—	12	9	3	—	—	85
Black	1	0	0	0	—	1	0	—	0	1	0	—	—	3
Reed	0	3	0	0	—	1	1	—	0	1	0	—	—	6
Frankfurter	0	0	4	0	—	0	2	—	0	0	0	—	—	6
Total	11	5	11	13	—	9	14	—	12	11	3	—	—	100

(Table continues)

535

Table 6-13 (Continued)

Term/assigner[a]	Author													Total
	Black	Reed	Frankfurter	Douglas	Jackson	Burton	Clark	Minton	Warren	Harlan	Whittaker	Brennan	Stewart	
1957														
Warren	11	—	4	12	—	4	8	—	11	7	8	10	—	75
Black	1	—	0	1	—	0	0	—	0	0	0	2	—	4
Frankfurter	0	—	6	0	—	3	7	—	0	8	0	1	—	25
Total	12	—	10	13	—	7	15	—	11	15	8	13	—	104
1958														
Warren	10	—	5	12	—	—	8	—	10	4	9	9	7	74
Black	0	—	1	0	—	—	0	—	0	3	0	1	0	6
Frankfurter	0	—	5	0	—	—	3	—	0	5	0	3	3	19
Total	10	—	11	12	—	—	11	—	10	12	9	13	10	99
1959														
Warren	10	—	1	10	—	—	12	—	11	5	6	12	9	76
Black	1	—	0	1	—	—	0	—	0	1	0	0	0	3
Frankfurter	0	—	7	0	—	—	4	—	0	3	1	0	2	17
Douglas	0	—	0	0	—	—	0	—	0	1	0	0	0	1
Total	11	—	8	11	—	—	16	—	11	10	7	12	11	97
1960														
Warren	13	—	7	13	—	—	11	—	11	7	10	11	7	90
Black	1	—	0	0	—	—	0	—	0	0	1	0	0	2
Frankfurter	0	—	5	0	—	—	2	—	0	4	1	1	5	18
Total	14	—	12	13	—	—	13	—	11	11	12	12	12	110

[a] Assumes senior justice in the majority decision coalition assigned the opinion. The reader should be aware, however, that sometimes justices switch votes after the original conference. Thus, where the chief justice dissents initially, but switches to the majority after the original conference, he is possibly listed incorrectly as having assigned the majority opinion. The same holds when senior associate justices switch their votes.

Source: U.S. Supreme Court Judicial Database, with citation as unit of analysis.

Table 6-14 Assignment and Authorship of Majority Opinion, 1961-1968 Terms

Term/assigner[a]	Author													
	Black	Frankfurter	Douglas	Clark	Warren	Harlan	Whittaker	Brennan	Stewart	White	Goldberg	Fortas	Marshall	Total
1961														
Warren	11	3	11	7	10	8	1	9	10	3	—	—	—	73
Black	1	0	0	1	0	0	0	0	0	0	—	—	—	2
Frankfurter	0	1	0	2	0	0	1	1	1	0	—	—	—	6
Clark	0	0	0	1	0	2	0	0	1	0	—	—	—	4
Total	12	4	11	11	10	10	2	10	12	3	—	—	—	85
1962														
Warren	10	—	10	10	12	9	—	12	12	13	12	—	—	100
Black	1	—	1	2	0	1	—	0	0	0	0	—	—	5
Douglas	0	—	2	0	0	1	—	1	0	0	0	—	—	4
Clark	0	—	0	0	0	1	—	0	0	0	0	—	—	1
Total	11	—	13	12	12	12	—	13	12	13	12	—	—	110
1963														
Warren	12	—	12	11	11	10	—	12	12	10	14	—	—	104
Black	0	—	0	1	0	0	—	1	1	0	0	—	—	3
Douglas	0	—	0	0	0	0	—	0	0	1	0	—	—	1
Clark	0	—	0	1	0	0	—	0	0	1	0	—	—	2
Harlan	0	—	0	0	0	1	—	0	0	0	0	—	—	1
Total	12	—	12	13	11	11	—	13	13	12	14	—	—	111
1964														
Warren	10	—	9	12	10	8	—	10	7	7	9	—	—	82
Black	0	—	1	0	0	1	—	0	1	2	1	—	—	6
Douglas	0	—	0	0	0	0	—	0	1	1	0	—	—	2
Harlan	0	—	0	0	0	1	—	0	0	0	0	—	—	1
Total	10	—	10	12	10	10	—	10	9	10	10	—	—	91

(Table continues)

Table 6-14 *(Continued)*

Term/assigner[a]	Black	Frankfurter	Douglas	Clark	Warren	Harlan	Whittaker	Brennan	Stewart	White	Goldberg	Fortas	Marshall	*Total*
1965														
Warren	9	—	12	10	9	7	—	11	10	11	—	10	—	89
Black	2	—	0	0	0	0	—	1	1	0	—	0	—	4
Clark	0	—	0	1	0	1	—	1	1	0	—	0	—	4
Total	11	—	12	11	9	8	—	13	12	11	—	10	—	97
1966														
Warren	7	—	12	12	11	6	—	9	7	10	—	11	—	85
Black	4	—	0	0	0	3	—	2	4	0	—	0	—	15
Total	11	—	12	12	11	9	—	11	11	10	—	11	—	100
1967														
Warren	12	—	12	—	11	9	—	12	14	11	—	11	9	101
Black	1	—	1	—	0	4	—	0	0	1	—	0	0	7
Douglas	0	—	0	—	0	0	—	1	0	0	—	0	0	1
Harlan	0	—	0	—	0	0	—	0	0	0	—	0	1	1
Total	13	—	13	—	11	13	—	13	14	12	—	11	10	110
1968														
Warren	10	—	11	—	12	8	—	9	10	10	—	8	12	90
Black	1	—	1	—	0	0	—	0	0	0	—	0	0	2
Douglas	0	—	0	—	0	1	—	2	0	0	—	0	0	3
Harlan	0	—	0	—	0	1	—	1	1	0	—	0	1	4
Total	11	—	12	—	12	10	—	12	11	10	—	8	13	99

Author

[a] Assumes senior justice in the majority decision coalition assigned the opinion. The reader should be aware, however, that sometimes justices switch votes after the original conference. Thus, where the chief justice dissents initially, but switches to the majority after the original conference, he is possibly listed incorrectly as having assigned the majority opinion. The same holds when senior associate justices switch their votes.

Source: U.S. Supreme Court Judicial Database, with citation as unit of analysis.

Table 6-15 Assignment and Authorship of Majority Opinion, 1969-1977 Terms

Term/ assigner[a]	Author												Total
	Black	Douglas	Harlan	Brennan	Stewart	White	Marshall	Burger	Blackmun	Powell	Rehnquist	Stevens	
1969													
Burger	6	8	6	4	10	9	7	11	—	—	—	—	61
Black	4	3	1	3	1	4	2	0	—	—	—	—	18
Douglas	0	2	2	3	1	0	1	0	—	—	—	—	9
Total	10	13	9	10	12	13	10	11	—	—	—	—	88
1970													
Burger	11	11	6	10	13	12	9	13	10	—	—	—	95
Black	3	1	2	0	1	1	0	0	0	—	—	—	8
Douglas	0	2	2	1	2	0	0	0	0	—	—	—	7
Total	14	14	10	11	16	13	9	13	10	—	—	—	110
1971													
Burger	—	10	—	11	12	15	11	12	12	12	11	—	106
Douglas	—	3	—	7	6	2	4	0	0	0	0	—	22
Brennan	—	0	—	0	0	1	0	0	0	0	0	—	1
Total	—	13	—	18	18	18	15	12	12	12	11	—	129
1972													
Burger	—	13	—	9	12	15	12	19	14	13	15	—	122
Douglas	—	3	—	4	2	2	0	0	0	3	0	—	14
Brennan	—	0	—	0	2	0	0	0	0	1	1	—	4
Total	—	16	—	13	16	17	12	19	14	17	16	—	140
1973													
Burger	—	13	—	12	14	16	11	14	14	14	16	—	124
Douglas	—	1	—	3	2	3	2	0	1	1	1	—	14

(Table continues)

Table 6-15 *(Continued)*

Term/assigner[a]	Author												Total
	Black	Douglas	Harlan	Brennan	Stewart	White	Marshall	Burger	Blackmun	Powell	Rehnquist	Stevens	
Brennan	—	0	—	0	2	0	0	0	0	1	1	—	4
Stewart	—	0	—	0	0	0	0	0	0	1	0	—	1
Total	—	14	—	15	18	19	13	14	15	17	18	—	143
1974													
Burger	—	6	—	12	10	13	10	14	11	16	15	—	107
Douglas	—	0	—	3	5	3	0	0	2	1	0	—	14
Brennan	—	0	—	0	1	0	1	0	0	0	0	—	2
Total	—	6	—	15	16	16	11	14	13	17	15	—	123
1975													
Burger	—	—	—	13	14	13	16	17	14	16	16	6	125
Brennan	—	—	—	3	2	2	1	0	2	0	0	3	13
Total	—	—	—	16	16	15	17	17	16	16	16	9	138
1976													
Burger	—	—	—	6	10	13	11	15	11	12	15	12	105
Brennan	—	—	—	7	3	2	1	0	3	3	0	1	20
Stewart	—	—	—	0	1	0	0	0	0	0	0	0	1
Total	—	—	—	13	14	15	12	15	14	15	15	13	126
1977													
Burger	—	—	—	7	9	10	15	16	10	13	12	11	103
Brennan	—	—	—	7	6	3	0	0	2	2	0	2	22
Stewart	—	—	—	0	0	0	0	0	0	0	2	1	3
White	—	—	—	0	0	1	0	0	0	0	0	0	1
Total	—	—	—	14	15	14	15	16	12	15	14	14	129

a Assumes senior justice in the majority opinion coalition assigned the opinion. The reader should be aware, however, that sometimes justices switch votes after the original conference. Thus, where the chief justice dissents initially, but switches to the majority after the original conference, he is possibly listed incorrectly as having assigned the majority opinion. The same holds when senior associate justices switch their votes.

Source: U.S. Supreme Court Judicial Database, with citation as unit of analysis.

Table 6-16 Assignment and Authorship of Majority Opinion, 1978-1985 Terms

Term/assigner[a]	Author										Total
	Brennan	Stewart	White	Marshall	Burger	Blackmun	Powell	Rehnquist	Stevens	O'Connor	
1978											
Burger	6	13	15	12	17	9	10	16	13	—	111
Brennan	7	1	1	1	0	4	2	0	2	—	18
Stewart	0	1	0	0	0	0	0	0	0	—	1
Total	13	15	16	13	17	13	12	16	15	—	130
1979											
Burger	9	12	13	12	15	13	15	15	11	—	115
Brennan	5	3	2	1	0	1	1	0	3	—	16
Stewart	0	0	0	1	0	0	0	0	0	—	1
Total	14	15	15	14	15	14	16	15	14	—	132
1980											
Burger	5	14	11	12	13	11	13	15	10	—	104
Brennan	8	0	3	1	0	1	2	0	1	—	16
Stewart	0	2	0	0	0	0	0	0	0	—	2
White	0	0	1	0	0	0	0	0	0	—	1
Total	13	16	15	13	13	12	15	15	11	—	123
1981											
Burger	3	—	16	9	16	9	14	16	12	11	106
Brennan	12	—	3	5	0	5	2	1	3	1	32
White	0	—	0	0	0	0	0	0	0	1	1
Blackmun	0	—	0	0	0	1	0	0	0	0	1
Marshall	0	—	0	1	0	0	0	0	0	0	1
Total	15	—	19	15	16	15	16	17	15	13	141

(*Table continues*)

Table 6-16 (Continued)

Term/assigner[a]	Author										
	Brennan	Stewart	White	Marshall	Burger	Blackmun	Powell	Rehnquist	Stevens	O'Connor	Total
1982											
Burger	7	—	18	16	17	14	16	20	15	16	139
Brennan	8	—	1	0	0	1	2	0	0	0	12
Total	15	—	19	16	17	15	18	20	15	16	151
1983											
Burger	9	—	17	15	18	14	17	19	16	17	142
Brennan	5	—	1	0	0	2	1	0	0	0	9
Total	14	—	18	15	18	16	18	19	16	17	151
1984											
Burger	6	—	15	12	17	13	12	16	15	16	122
Brennan	7	—	3	1	0	3	1	1	1	0	17
Total	13	—	18	13	17	16	13	17	16	16	139
1985											
Burger	6	—	17	12	14	10	16	18	15	16	124
Brennan	7	—	1	3	0	4	2	0	2	1	20
White	0	—	1	0	0	0	0	1	0	0	2
Total	13	—	19	15	14	14	18	19	17	17	146

[a] Assumes senior justice in the majority decision coalition assigned the opinion. The reader should be aware, however, that sometimes justices switch votes after the original conference. Thus, where the chief justice dissents initially, but switches to the majority after the original conference, he is possibly listed incorrectly as having assigned the opinion. The same holds when senior associate justices switch their votes.

Source: U.S. Supreme Court Judicial Database, with citation as unit of analysis.

Table 6-17 Assignment and Authorship of Majority Opinion, 1986-1991 Terms

Term/assigner[a]	Author												
	Brennan	White	Marshall	Blackmun	Powell	Rehnquist	Stevens	O'Connor	Scalia	Kennedy	Souter	Thomas	Total
1986													
Rehnquist	4	15	10	7	18	17	12	18	10	—	—	—	111
Brennan	12	2	6	6	2	0	4	0	2	—	—	—	34
Total	16	17	16	13	20	17	16	18	12	—	—	—	145
1987													
Rehnquist	10	19	13	11	—	15	14	14	14	4	—	—	114
Brennan	6	1	2	4	—	0	5	2	2	3	—	—	25
Total	16	20	15	15	—	15	19	16	16	7	—	—	139
1988													
Rehnquist	8	17	12	12	—	15	14	12	11	13	—	—	114
Brennan	8	0	2	2	—	0	2	1	1	2	—	—	18
Total	16	17	14	14	—	15	16	13	12	15	—	—	132
1989													
Rehnquist	5	14	12	11	—	15	10	14	14	12	—	—	107
Brennan	8	3	2	2	—	0	3	3	0	1	—	—	22
Total	13	17	14	13	—	15	13	17	14	13	—	—	129
1990													
Rehnquist	—	10	11	10	—	14	9	15	11	9	7	—	96
White	—	4	0	0	—	0	3	0	0	3	1	—	11
Marshall	—	0	1	1	—	0	1	1	0	1	0	—	5
Blackmun	—	0	0	0	—	0	1	0	0	0	0	—	1
Total	—	14	12	11	—	14	14	16	11	13	8	—	113

(Table continues)

Table 6-17 (Continued)

Term/assigner[a]	Author												Total
	Brennan	White	Marshall	Blackmun	Powell	Rehnquist	Stevens	O'Connor	Scalia	Kennedy	Souter	Thomas	
1991													
Rehnquist	—	11	—	9	—	11	9	13	10	7	10	8	88
White	—	4	—	0	—	0	3	1	2	2	2	0	14
Blackmun	—	0	—	1	—	0	0	0	0	2	1	0	4
Total	—	15	—	10	—	11	12	14	12	11	13	8	106

[a] Assumes senior justice in the majority decision coalition assigned the opinion. The reader should be aware, however, that sometimes justices switch votes. Thus, where the chief justice dissents initially, but switches to the majority after the original conference, he is possibly listed incorrectly as having assigned the majority opinion. The same holds when senior associate justices switch their votes.

Source: U.S. Supreme Court Judicial Database, with citation as unit of analysis.

7
The Supreme Court and the Political Environment

In the preceding chapters we present data on the internal processes and behavior of the Supreme Court and its members. Here, we consider the relationship between the Court and the political environment within which it functions. Congress, the executive branch, state governments, and interest groups all interact with the judiciary, each in a distinctive fashion that is oftentimes bounded by tradition or even constitutional mandate. Consider Congress, which is the focus of Tables 7-1 through 7-7. At least five points of interaction exist between Congress and the Court. First, Congress can propose amendments that are designed to overturn Court decisions[1] or change the Court's jurisdiction, composition, benefits, and so forth. Table 7-1 lists amendments proposed by Congress and ratified by the states in response to Supreme Court decisions. Note that this has occurred only five times in the more than two hundred years of government operation, and despite the fact that "the number of [proposed] constitutional amendments designed to overcome a ruling of the Supreme Court would fill a congressman's wastebasket."[2]

Another aspect of the Court-congressional dynamic is both more direct and increasingly employed. As shown in Table 7-2, members of Congress are filing amicus curiae ("friend of the Court") briefs in Court cases with growing regularity. Almost 75 percent of all amicus curiae filings have occurred since 1980. In addition, participation in amicus curiae activity has taken on a pluralistic gloss. In more cases than ever members of Congress are filing on both sides of the issue under consideration. The briefs submitted in *Webster v. Reproductive Health Services* (1989),[3] which involved state-imposed restrictions on abortion, provide a good example: 9 senators and 44 representatives filed on behalf of the pro-life side, while 25 senators and 115 representatives filed in support of the pro-choice position.

A third point of interaction between Congress and the Court is congressionally enacted legislation, which itself often becomes the subject of litigation. In Chapter 2, we provide information on congressional acts overturned by the Court (see Table 2-13). Table 7-3 lists those laws most litigated during the Warren, Burger, and Rehnquist Court eras. Table 7-4 provides parallel data on highly litigated constitutional provisions. Some issues remain perennial subjects of Court litigation. For example, the Internal Revenue Code and the National Labor Relations Act appear in high numbers in all three eras. Others, though, change with the times. Title VII of the Civil Rights Act of 1964, enacted five years prior to the end of the Warren Court era, does not appear until the Burger years, where it trailed the Social Security Act, the National Labor Relations Act, and the Internal Revenue Code. By the Rehnquist Court years, however, only the Federal Rules of Civil Procedure and the Internal Revenue and Bankruptcy Codes surpassed it in frequency.

A fourth point of interaction occurs between the Court and the judiciary committees of Congress. Among other things, these committees make budgetary recommendations for the federal judiciary and consider bills of interest to the Court. The Senate Judiciary Committee has the additional function of holding confirmation hearings on nominees to the federal bench, including the Supreme Court. In Chapter 4, we provide information on the outcomes of the confirmation process as it pertains to Supreme Court justices (Table 4-12). Tables 7-5 and 7-6 list the names of those who have served as chairs of the judiciary committees of the Senate and House, respectively.

Finally, Congress can impeach federal judges, including Supreme Court justices. Article I of the Constitution specifies that the House "shall have the sole Power of Impeachment" and that the Senate "shall have the sole Power to try all Impeachments." Members of Congress have threatened to initiate proceedings against at least three justices (see Table 5-7), but, as is evident in Table 7-7, the House has voted articles of impeachment against only one, Samuel Chase; the Senate has never convicted a member of the Court. This has not been true of lower court judges, seven of whom have been convicted of impeachable charges. Interestingly, three of those seven convictions were handed down in the 1980s.

The executive branch is a second participant in judicial affairs. Most notably, presidents are responsible for nominating Supreme Court justices. This is a subject we consider in some detail in Chapter 4 (see Tables 4-10 and 4-11). Another less obvious though no less important activity is the role of the executive branch as a participant in Court cases. The office of the U.S. solicitor general, located within the Department of Justice (see Figures 7-1 and 7-2), is responsible for representing the U.S. government, including many (but not all) of its agencies, before the Court. In Tables 7-8 and 7-9 we provide the names of those who have served as attorney general and solicitor general, respectively. More interesting still may be the data contained in Tables 7-10 through 7-16, where we present varied data on the relative success of the U.S. government and its agencies from 1953-1992. The reader will draw his or her own conclusion about the government's record, but one thing is certain: regardless of the particular ideology or partisanship of the administration in office, or even the legal issue under review, solicitors general carry great weight with the justices. Why is the U.S. government, as represented by the solicitor general, such a successful courtroom player? Those who have studied the issue offer a variety of reasons. Most significantly, the solicitor general will bring before the Court only those cases he or she deems important. This helps explain the solicitor general's high rate of success in getting the Court to hear his or her cases. The solicitor general's legal expertise and the embodiment of the interests of the nation are additional explanations.[4]

The United States is not the only governmental entity to litigate before the Supreme Court. The states and the officials and offices under their authority often appear as parties and amici curiae. Taken collectively, the data in Tables 7-17 through 7-19 suggest that the states are significantly less successful than the U.S. government. Between 1953 and 1991, their average success rate was about 20 percent lower than that of the solicitor general. Yet definitive conclusions cannot be drawn simply by comparing percentages. While it is true that the federal government has a better aggregated rate of success than the states, these statistics can be deceiving. For one thing, we must take into account the states' comparative success within the distinct Court eras. As political scientists Sheehan, Mishler, and Songer note, "state governments fared better against the federal government during the early Burger years but much worse during the Rehnquist years."[5] However, it may not be simply a matter of parties determining their own fates. Research by Sheehan and his colleagues indicates that the ideology of the Court affects its disposition of all kinds of cases, including those brought by states. Those readers who are interested in comparing the relative success of the various governmental entities before the Court should use the tables contained in this chapter in conjunction with data presented in Chapters 3 and 6 in order to obtain a fair assessment.

That governmental units such as legislatures, executives, states, and so forth play some role in Court litigation is not surprising. After all, the doctrines of checks and balances and federalism suggest that "dialogues" will inevitably occur between and among the branches and components of our government.[6] What may be surprising is that points of interaction also exist between the Court and extra-institutional entities, in particular, interest groups. Attorneys representing a range of organized interests commonly lobby the Court. During the 1987 term alone, over a thousand organized interests participated in about 80 percent of the cases decided with an opinion.

While it is certainly true that interest groups wish to influence the Court as ardently as they do Congress and the executive, judicial lobbying is nevertheless a significantly different enterprise from that which occurs in congressional or executive corridors. The "rules of the legal game" simply prohibit groups from directly approaching judges and justices in the same manner as they would members of Congress or the executive. Instead, interest group organizations have had to develop a uniquely "judicial" approach to lobbying the Court: they sponsor cases (that is, interest groups provide legal representation to parties to suits),[7] they intervene in litigation (that is, interest groups "voluntarily interpose" in suits),[8] and they file or cosign amicus curiae briefs.[9]

Tables 7-20 through 7-22 provide information on interest group involvement as amici curiae. We limit our look into the world of organizational litigation to the amicus curiae strategy for many reasons, not the least of which is that attorneys filing as amici curiae generally list their organizational affiliation on the cover of their briefs, while those sponsoring cases often do not. Accordingly, it is relatively easy to discern whether a group participated as an amicus and far more difficult to determine if it sponsored a case.[10] The data in Table 7-20 indicate that group participation as amicus curiae has increased considerably over the past six decades: between 1928 and 1940, organized interests filed amicus curiae briefs in only 181 cases; in 1988 alone, that figure was 136. Table 7-21 shows the wide array of groups that participate as amicus curiae. Commercial and governmental interests dominated pressure group activity during the 1987 term, but many other types of groups filed briefs as well. Finally, Table 7-22 indicates that the justices occasionally cite amicus curiae briefs in their opinions. While these data do not prove that justices are swayed by amici arguments, they do show that some members of the Court consider them in developing their opinions.

Notes

1. There are four routes by which to amend the Constitution: (1) Proposal passed by two-thirds vote of both houses of Congress and ratified by approval of three-fourths of the state legislatures, (2) proposal passed by two-thirds vote of both houses of Congress and ratified by approval of three-fourths of the state conventions, (3) proposal passed by national convention established by Congress upon request of two-thirds of the states and ratified by approval of three-fourths of the state legislatures, and (4) proposal passed by national convention established by Congress upon

request of two-thirds of the states and ratified by approval of three-fourths of the state conventions.

2. Joseph T. Keenan, *The Constitution of the United States* (Chicago: Dorsey, 1988), 43.

3. 492 U.S. 490.

4. For a recent review of this literature, see Jeffrey A. Segal, "Courts, Executives, and Legislatures," in John B. Gates and Charles A. Johnson, eds., *The American Courts* (Washington, D.C.: CQ Press, 1991).

5. Reginald S. Sheehan, William Mishler, and Donald R. Songer, "Ideology, Status, and Differential Success of Direct Parties before the Supreme Court," *American Political Science Review* 86 (1992), 466.

6. For more on this point, see Louis Fisher, *Constitutional Dialogues* (Princeton, N.J.: Princeton University Press, 1988).

7. *Brown v. Board of Education*, 347 U.S. 483 (1954), sponsored by the NAACP Legal Defense and Educational Fund, provides a classic example. For other examples, see Jack Greenberg, *Judicial Process and Social Change* (St. Paul, Minn.: West, 1977); Clement E. Vose, *Caucasians Only* (Berkeley: University of California Press, 1959); and Karen O'Connor, *Women's Organizations' Use of the Court* (Lexington, Mass.: Lexington Books, 1980).

8. *Harris v. McRae*, 448 U.S. 297 (1980), which involved the constitutionality of a federal act (the Hyde Amendment) limiting the use of Medicaid funds for abortions, provides an example. In that case, a pro-life organization (Americans United for Life Legal Defense Fund) represented intervenor Henry Hyde (R-Ill.), who did not believe that the Carter administration would ably defend the amendment. For more on intervention, see Emma Coleman Jones's articles, "Litigation Without Representation: The Need for Intervention in Affirmative Action Litigation," *Harvard Civil Rights-Civil Liberties* 14 (1979), 31, and "Problems and Prospects of Participation in Affirmative Action Litigation: A Role for Intervenors," *University of California, Davis, Law Review* 13 (1980), 221.

9. For more information on the role of amici curiae and their history in the Supreme Court, see Samuel Krislov, "The *Amicus Curiae* Brief: From Friendship to Advocacy," *Yale Law Journal* 72 (1963), 694, and Gregory A. Caldeira and John R. Wright, "The Discuss List: Agenda Building in the Supreme Court," *Law and Society Review* 24 (1990), 807.

10. We want to stress that researchers interested in amicus curiae participation should not rely on the *U.S. Reports* as they do not provide complete information. Rather, researchers should consult the briefs filed in cases. Consider *Coker v. Georgia*, 433 U.S. 583 (1977), in which the American Civil Liberties Union (ACLU) filed an amicus curiae brief. It appears in the *U.S. Reports* in the following form: "*Ruth Bader Ginsburg, Melvin L. Wulf, Marjorie Mazen Smith,* and *Nancy Stearns* filed a brief for the American Civil Liberties Union et al. as *amici curiae* urging reversal." The *U.S. Reports* identifies this as an "et al." brief. This means that "others" signed on to it. The brief within the microfiche record of *Coker* names these "others" specifically: "Brief *amici curiae* of the American Civil Liberties Union, the Center for Constitutional Rights, the National Organization for Women Legal Defense and Education Fund, the Women's Law Project, the Center for Women Policy Studies, the Women's Legal Defense Fund, and Equal Rights Advocates, Inc." The ACLU may have been the lead interest, but six other groups (the "et al." in the *U.S. Reports)* signed the brief.

Table 7-1 Amendments to the U.S. Constitution Overturning Supreme Court Decisions

Amendment	Date ratified	Supreme Court decision overturned
Eleventh	February 7, 1795	Chisholm v. Georgia (1793)
Thirteenth	December 6, 1865	Scott v. Sandford (1857)
Fourteenth	July 9, 1868	Scott v. Sandford (1857)
Sixteenth	February 3, 1913	Pollock v. Farmer's Loan and Trust Co. (1895)
Twenty-sixth	July 1, 1971	Oregon v. Mitchell (1970)

Table 7-2   Cases in Which Members of Congress Filed Amicus Curiae Briefs, 1900-1990

Pacific States Telegraph and Telephone Co. v. Oregon, 223 U.S. 118 (1912)
Myers v. United States, 272 U.S. 52 (1926)
National Life Insurance Co. v. United States, 277 U.S. 508 (1928)
The Pocket Veto Case, 279 U.S. 655 (1929)
Edwards v. United States, 286 U.S. 482 (1932)
Jurney v. MacCracken, 294 U.S. 125 (1935)
Wright v. United States, 302 U.S. 583 (1938)
United States v. Bekins, 304 U.S. 27 (1938)
Edwards v. California, 314 U.S. 160 (1941)
Shapiro v. United States, 335 U.S. 1 (1948)
Henderson v. United States, 339 U.S. 816 (1950)
United States v. Louisiana, 363 U.S. 1 (1960)
United States v. Florida, 363 U.S. 121 (1960)
New York Times v. United States, 403 U.S. 713 (1971)
Williamson v. United States, 405 U.S. 1026 (1972)
United States v. United States District Court, 407 U.S. 297 (1972)
Laird v. Tatum, 408 U.S. 1 (1972)
Regional Rail Reorganization Act Cases, 419 U.S. 102 (1974)
Ripon Society v. National Republican Party, 424 U.S. 933 (1976)
Hutchinson v. Proxmire, 443 U.S. 111 (1979)
Harris v. McRae, 448 U.S. 297 (1980)
McCarty v. McCarty, 453 U.S. 210 (1981)
Lehman v. Nakshian, 453 U.S. 156 (1981)
Rostker v. Goldberg, 453 U.S. 57 (1981)
Federal Election Commission v. Democratic Senatorial Campaign Committee, 454 U.S. 27 (1981)
Weinberger v. Rossi, 456 U.S. 25 (1982)
North Haven Board of Education v. Bell, 456 U.S. 512 (1982)
Nixon v. Fitzgerald, 457 U.S. 731 (1982)
Harlow v. Fitzgerald, 457 U.S. 800 (1982)
Crawford v. Board of Education of City of Los Angeles, 458 U.S. 527 (1982)
Bob Jones University v. United States, 461 U.S. 574 (1983)
United States v. Ptasynski, 462 U.S. 74 (1983)
Bush v. Lucas, 462 U.S. 367 (1983)
Immigration and Naturalization Service v. Chadha, 462 U.S. 919 (1983)
Grove City College v. Bell, 465 U.S. 555 (1984)
Consolidated Rail Corp. v. Darrone, 465 U.S. 624 (1984)
Heckler v. Mathews, 465 U.S. 728 (1984)
Monsanto v. Spray-Rite Service Corp., 465 U.S. 752 (1984)
Federal Communications Commission v. League of Women Voters, 468 U.S. 364 (1984)
Wallace v. Jaffree, 472 U.S. 38 (1985)
Jean v. Nelson, 472 U.S. 846 (1985)
Atascadero State Hospital v. Scanlon, 473 U.S. 234 (1985)
Bender v. Williamsport Area School District, 475 U.S. 534 (1986)
Diamond v. Charles, 476 U.S. 54 (1986)
Wygant v. Jackson Board of Education, 476 U.S. 267 (1986)

(Table continues)

Table 7-2 *(Continued)*

Bowen v. American Hospital Association, 476 U.S. 610 (1986)
Thornburgh v. American College of Obstetricians and Gynecologists, 476 U.S. 747 (1986)
Meritor Savings Bank v. Vinson, 477 U.S. 57 (1986)
Riverside v. Rivera, 477 U.S. 561 (1986)
Japan Whaling Association v. American Cetacean Society, 478 U.S. 221 (1986)
Tashjian v. Republican Party of Connecticut, 479 U.S. 208 (1986)
California Federal Savings and Loan v. Guerra, 479 U.S. 272 (1987)
School Board of Nassau County v. Arline, 480 U.S. 273 (1987)
Meese v. Keene, 481 U.S. 465 (1987)
Edwards v. Aguillard, 482 U.S. 578 (1987)
South Dakota v. Dole, 483 U.S. 203 (1987)
Honig v. Doe, 484 U.S. 305 (1988)
United States v. Providence Journal Co., 485 U.S. 305 (1988)
Huffman v. Western Nuclear, 486 U.S. 663 (1988)
Pierce v. Underwood, 487 U.S. 552 (1988)
Bowen v. Kendrick, 487 U.S. 589 (1988)
Morrison v. Olson, 487 U.S. 654 (1988)
Communications Workers v. Beck, 487 U.S. 735 (1988)
United States v. Mistretta, 488 U.S. 361 (1989)
Board of Estimate of the City of New York v. Morris, 489 U.S. 688 (1989)
U.S. Department of Justice v. Reporters Committee for Freedom of Press, 489 U.S. 749 (1989)
American Foreign Service Association v. Garfinkel, 490 U.S. 153 (1989)
Patterson v. McLean Credit Union, 491 U.S. 164 (1989)
Sable Communications v. Federal Communications Commission, 492 U.S. 115 (1989)
Webster v. Reproductive Health Services, 492 U.S. 490 (1989)
Dole v. United Steelworkers, 494 U.S. 26 (1990)
Adams Fruit Co. v. Ramsford Barrett, 494 U.S. 638 (1990)
United States v. Eichman, 496 U.S. 310 (1990)
Eli Lilly v. Medtronic, 496 U.S. 661 (1990)
Minnesota v. Hodgson, 497 U.S. 490 (1989)
Lujan v. National Wildlife Federation, 497 U.S. 871 (1990)
Metro Broadcasting v. Federal Communications Commission, 110 S.Ct. 2997 (1990)

Note: Amicus curiae (or "friend of the court") is a person (or group), not a party to a case, who submits views in the form of written briefs and/or oral arguments on how the case should be decided.

Source: Cases obtained by authors through LEXIS.

Table 7-3 Most Litigated Laws, Warren Through Rehnquist Courts

Court (terms)	Law	Number of cases
Warren (1953–1968)	Internal Revenue Code	122
	National Labor Relations Act, as amended	116
	Interstate Commerce Act, as amended	103
	Natural Gas and Natural Gas Policy Acts	62
	Immigration and Naturalization, Immigration, and Nationality Acts, as amended	53
	Sherman Anti-Trust Act	49
	Criminal Procedure, Federal Rules of	46
	Clayton Act	40
	Federal Rules of Civil Procedure, including Appellate Procedure	40
	Labor-Management Relations Act	32
	Federal Employers' Liability Act	25
	Railway Labor Act	25
	Bankruptcy Code, Bankruptcy Act, and Bankruptcy Reform Act of 1978	23
	Supreme Court Jurisdiction: State Courts, Appeal, Certiorari (28 USC 1257)	21
	Selective Service, Military Selective Service, and Universal Military Service and Training Acts	19
Burger (1969–1985)	Social Security Act (Aid to Families with Dependent Children, Medicaid, Medicare, Social Security Disability Benefits Reform Act, and Supplemental Security Income)	92
	National Labor Relations Act, as amended	91
	Internal Revenue Code	77
	Civil Rights Act of 1964, Title VII	67
	Civil Rights Act, section 1983	48
	Federal Rules of Civil Procedure, including Appellate Procedure	46
	Securities Act of 1933, Securities and Exchange Act, and Williams Act	38
	Sherman Anti-Trust Act	35

(Table continues)

Table 7-3 *(Continued)*

Court *(terms)*	Law	Number of cases
	Habeas Corpus (28 USC 2241-2255)	30
	Clayton Act	26
	Natural Gas and Natural Gas Policy Acts	25
	Interstate Commerce Act, as amended	24
	Omnibus Crime Control and Safe Streets, National Firearms, Organized Crime Control, and Gun Control Acts (excluding RICO)	24
	Communications Act of 1934	21
	Freedom of Information, Sunshine, and Privacy Acts	21
	Longshoremen and Harbor Workers' Compensation Act	21
	Voting Rights Act of 1965, plus amendments	21
Rehnquist (1986-1991)	Federal Rules of Civil Procedure, including Appellate Procedure	33
	Internal Revenue Code	28
	Bankruptcy Code, Bankruptcy Act, and Bankruptcy Reform Act of 1978	21
	Civil Rights Act of 1964, Title VII	19
	Civil Rights Act, section 1983	18
	Employee Retirement Income Security Act, as amended	15
	Social Security Act (Aid to Families with Dependent Children, Medicaid, Medicare, Social Security Disability Benefits Reform Act, and Supplemental Security Income)	13
	Federal Rules of Evidence	10
	National Labor Relations Act, as amended	10
	Securities Act of 1933, Securities and Exchange Act, and Williams Act	9
	Administrative Procedure and Administrative Orders Review Acts	9
	Federal Rules of Criminal Procedure	9

Source: U.S. Supreme Court Judicial Database.

Table 7-4 Most Litigated Constitutional Provisions, Warren Through Rehnquist Courts

Court (terms)	Constitutional provision	Number of cases
Warren (1953–1968)	Fourteenth Amendment, equal protection clause	127
	Fourteenth Amendment, due process clause	125
	First Amendment, freedom of speech, press, and assembly clauses	74
	Fourth Amendment[a]	62
	Fifth Amendment, self-incrimination clause[a]	54
	Article I, section 8, interstate commerce clause	37
	Sixth Amendment, right to counsel[a]	36
	Article VI, supremacy clause	36
	Fifth Amendment, due process clause	31
	First Amendment, freedom of association[a]	24
	Sixth Amendment, confrontation, cross examination, and compulsory process clauses[a]	21
	Fifth Amendment, double jeopardy clause[a]	20
	Fifth Amendment, takings clause[a]	20
	Article IV, section 1, full faith and credit	12
	Sixth Amendment, trial by jury clause[a]	12
Burger (1969–1985)	Fourteenth Amendment, due process clause	214
	Fourteenth Amendment, equal protection clause	185
	First Amendment, freedom of speech, press, and assembly clauses[a]	168
	Fourth Amendment[a]	112
	Article III, section 2, case or controversy requirement	88
	Article I, section 8, interstate commerce clause	71
	Fifth Amendment, due process clause	62
	Fifth Amendment, double jeopardy clause[a]	50
	Fifth Amendment, equal protection component	50

(Table continues)

Table 7-4 (Continued)

Court (terms)	Constitutional provision	Number of cases
	Fifth Amendment, self-incrimination clause[a]	47
	Fifth Amendment, takings clause[a]	42
	First Amendment, establishment of religion clause[a]	41
	Sixth Amendment, right to counsel[a]	40
	Eighth Amendment, cruel and unusual punishment clause[a]	35
	First Amendment, freedom of association[a]	24
	Article VI, supremacy clause	23
Rehnquist (1986-1991)	First Amendment, freedom of speech, press, and assembly clauses	61
	Fourteenth Amendment, due process clause	56
	Article III, section 2, case or controversy requirement	34
	Fourth Amendment[a]	30
	Eighth Amendment, cruel and unusual punishment clause[a]	30
	Fourteenth Amendment, equal protection clause	27
	Article I, section 8, interstate commerce clause	27
	Fifth Amendment, due process clause	18
	First Amendment, establishment of religion clause[a]	17
	Fifth Amendment, takings clause[a]	17
	First Amendment, freedom of association[a]	14
	Sixth Amendment, confrontation, cross examination, and compulsory process clauses[a]	13
	Sixth Amendment, right to counsel[a]	13
	Fifth Amendment, equal protection component	11
	Article VI, supremacy clause	11

[a] Where a state or local government allegedly abridged a provision of the Bill of Rights that has been made binding on the states because it has been incorporated into the due process clause of the Fourteenth Amendment, identification is to the specific provision rather than the due process clause.

Source: U.S. Supreme Court Judicial Database.

Table 7-5 Chairs of the Senate Committee on the Judiciary

Name	Years of service	State	Party [a]
Dudley Chase	1815-1817	Vermont	Jacksonian Democrat
John J. Crittenden	1817-1818	Kentucky	Unionist
James Burrill, Jr.	1818-1819	Rhode Island	[b]
William Smith	1819-1823	South Carolina	Democrat
Martin Van Buren	1823-1828	New York	Democrat
John M. Berrien	1828-1829	Georgia	Democrat
John Rowan	1829-1831	New York	Democrat
William L. Marcy	1831-1832	New York	Jacksonian Democrat
William Wilkins	1832-1833	Pennsylvania	Democrat
John M. Clayton	1833-1836	Delaware	National Republican
Felix Grundy	1836-1838	Tennessee	War Democrat
Garret D. Wall	1838-1841	New Jersey	Democrat
John M. Berrien	1841-1844	Georgia	Whig
Chester Ashley	1844-1847	Arkansas	Democrat
Andrew P. Butler	1847-1857	South Carolina	States Rights Democrat
James A. Bayard	1857-1860	Delaware	Democrat
Lyman Trumbull	1860-1872	Illinois	Republican
George F. Edmunds	1872-1879	Vermont	Republican
Allen G. Thurman	1879-1881	Ohio	Democrat
George F. Edmunds	1881-1891	Vermont	Republican
George F. Hoar	1891-1893	Massachusetts	Republican
James L. Pugh	1893-1895	Alabama	Democrat
George F. Hoar	1895-1904	Massachusetts	Republican
Orville H. Platt	1904-1905	Connecticut	Republican
Clarence D. Clark	1905-1913	Wyoming	Republican
Charles A. Culberson	1913-1919	Texas	Democrat
Knute Nelson	1919-1923	Minnesota	Republican
Frank B. Brandegee	1923-1925	Connecticut	Republican
Albert B. Cummins	1925-1926	Iowa	Republican
William E. Borah	1926-1927	Idaho	Republican
George W. Norris	1927-1933	Nebraska	Republican
Henry F. Ashurst	1933-1941	Arizona	Democrat
Frederick Van Nuys	1941-1945	Indiana	Democrat
Pat McCarran	1945-1947	Nevada	Democrat
Alexander Wiley	1947-1949	Wisconsin	Republican
Pat McCarran	1949-1953	Nevada	Democrat
William Langer	1953-1955	North Dakota	Republican
Harley M. Kilgore	1955-1957	West Virginia	Democrat
James O. Eastland	1957-1979	Mississippi	Democrat
Edward M. Kennedy	1979-1981	Massachusetts	Democrat
Strom Thurmond	1981-1987	South Carolina	Republican
Joseph Biden	1987-	Delaware	Democrat

[a] During the nineteenth century, members of Congress commonly changed political parties. Listed here is party with which member was affiliated at time of service as chair.
[b] No party affiliation.

Source: U.S. Senate, *History of the Committee on the Judiciary United States Senate 1816-1967,* Sen. Doc. No. 78, 90th Cong., 2d sess. (Washington, D.C.: Government Printing Office, 1968), 131-133; *CQ's Guide to Congress* (Washington, D.C.: Congressional Quarterly, 1982).

Table 7-6   Chairs of the House Committee on the Judiciary

Name	Years of service	State	Party [a]
Charles Jared Ingersoll	1813-1815	Pennsylvania	Democrat
Hugh Nelson	1815-1819	Virginia	Democrat
John Sergeant	1819-1822	Pennsylvania	Federalist
Hugh Nelson	1822-1823	Virginia	Democrat
Daniel Webster	1823-1827	Massachusetts	Federalist
Philip Pendelton Barbour	1827-1829	Virginia	Democrat
James Buchanan	1829-1831	Pennsylvania	Democrat
Warren Ransom Davis	1831-1832	South Carolina	States' Rights Democrat
John Bell	1832-1834	Tennessee	Whig
Thomas Flournoy Foster	1834-1835	Georgia	Democrat
Samuel Beardsley	1835-1836	New York	Democrat
Francis Thomas	1836-1839	Maryland	Democrat
John Sergeant	1839-1841	Pennsylvania	Federalist
Daniel Dewey Barnard	1841-1843	New York	Whig
William Wilkins	1843-1844	Pennsylvania	Democrat
Romulus Mitchell Saunders	1844-1845	North Carolina	Democrat
George Oscar Rathbun	1845-1847	New York	Democrat
Joseph Reed Ingersoll	1847-1849	Pennsylvania	Whig
James Thompson	1849-1851	Pennsylvania	Democrat
James Xavier McLanahan	1851-1853	Pennsylvania	Democrat
Frederick Perry Stanton	1853-1855	Tennessee	Democrat
George Abel Simmons	1855-1857	New York	Whig
George Smith Houston	1857-1859	Alabama	Democrat
John Hickman	1859-1861	Pennsylvania	Douglas Democrat
John Hickman	1861-1863	Pennsylvania	Republican
James Falcolner Wilson	1863-1869	Iowa	Republican
John Armour Bingham	1869-1873	Ohio	Republican
Ben Franklin Butler	1873-1875	Massachusetts	Republican
James Proctor Knott	1875-1881	Kentucky	Democrat
Thomas Bracket Reed	1881-1883	Maine	Republican
John Randolph Tucker	1883-1887	Virginia	Democrat
David Browning Culberson	1887-1889	Texas	Democrat
Ezra Booth Taylor	1889-1891	Ohio	Republican
David Browning Culberson	1891-1895	Texas	Democrat
David Bremner Henderson	1895-1899	Iowa	Republican
George Washington Ray	1899-1903	New York	Republican
John James Jenkins	1903-1909	Wisconsin	Republican
Richard Wayne Parker	1909-1911	New Jersey	Republican
Henry De Lamar Clayton	1911-1915	Alabama	Democrat
Edwin Yates Webb	1915-1919	North Carolina	Democrat
Andrew John Volstead	1919-1923	Minnesota	Republican
George Scott Graham	1923-1931	Pennsylvania	Republican
Hatton William Sumners	1931-1946	Texas	Democrat
Earl Cory Michener	1947-1948	Michigan	Republican
Emanuel Cellar	1949-1952	New York	Democrat

Table 7-6   *(Continued)*

Name	Years of service	State	Party [a]
Chauncey W. Reed	1953-1954	Illinois	Republican
Emanuel Cellar	1955-1972	New York	Democrat
Peter W. Rodino, Jr.	1973-1988	New Jersey	Democrat
Jack Brooks	1989-	Texas	Democrat

[a] During the nineteenth century, members of Congress commonly changed political parties. Listed here is party with which member was affiliated at time of service as chair.

Source: U.S. House, *History of the Committee on the Judiciary of the House of Representatives,* Committee Print, Serial no. 15, 97th Cong., 2d sess. (Washington, D.C.: Government Printing Office, 1982), 144-145; *CQ's Guide to Congress* (Washington, D.C.: Congressional Quarterly, 1982).

Table 7-7 Impeachment of Federal Judges and Justices

Name (Court)	House	Senate
John Pickering (District Court, N.H.)	Voted (45-8) four articles of impeachment, most of which involved his judicial conduct (e.g., his handling of a lawsuit; being drunk and committing blasphemy on the bench), in December 1803.	Convicted (19-7) on all charges in March 1804.
Samuel Chase (Supreme Court)	Voted (72-32) eight articles of impeachment, six of which involved his actions "while presiding on circuit at treason and sedition trials," in March 1804. The other two centered on "addresses delivered to grand juries."	Acquitted (varying votes) on all charges in March 1805.
James H. Peck (District Court, Fla.)	Voted (123-49) one article charging him with "wrongfully convicting an attorney of contempt" in April 1830.	Acquitted (22-21) in January 1831.
Wes H. Humphreys (District Court, Tenn.)	Voted (voice vote) seven articles, all centering on the fact that he "ceased holding court and acted as a judge for the Confederacy," in May 1862.	Convicted (38-0) on six of seven charges in June 1862.
Charles Swayne (District Court, Fla.)	Voted (voice vote) twelve articles, charged with "padding expense accounts, using railroad property in receivership, and misusing contempt of power," in December 1904.	Acquitted (varying votes) on all charges in February 1905.
Robert W. Archibald (Commerce Court)	Voted (223-1) thirteen articles, many of which involved allegations of influence peddling, in July 1912.	Convicted (voice vote) on five charges in January 1913.
George W. English (District Court, Ill.)	Voted (306-2) five articles, charged with "partiality, tyranny, and oppression" (e.g., accepting gifts) in November 1926.	Resigned in December 1926; proceedings dismissed (70-9) in December.

Harold Louderback (District Court, Calif.)	Voted (183-142) five articles, including "registering to vote at a fictitious residence" and "appointing incompetent receivers and allowing them excessive fees," in February 1933.	Acquitted (varying votes) on all charges in May 1933.
Halstead L. Ritter (District Court, Fla.)	Voted (181-146) seven articles, including income tax evasion and continuing to practice law while a judge, in March 1936. The last article charged that he brought "his court into scandal and disrepute."	Convicted (56-28) on the last count only in April 1936.
Harry E. Claibourne (District Court, Nev.)	Voted (406-0) four articles, stemming from his conviction of income tax evasion, in July 1986.	Convicted (varying votes) on three of the four counts in October 1986.
Alcee L. Hastings (District Court, Fla.)	Voted (413-3) seventeen articles, centering on a bribery charge for which he was acquitted in February 1983, in August 1988.	Convicted on eight of the seventeen counts in October 1989.
Walter L. Nixon (District Court, Miss.)	Voted (417-0) three articles, stemming from his 1986 conviction for perjury, in May 1989.	Convicted on two of the three counts in November 1989.

Sources: U.S. Department of Justice, *The Law of Impeachment* (Washington, D.C.: Government Printing Office, February 22, 1974), Appendix 1; Henry J. Abraham, *The Judicial Process*, 5th ed. (New York: Oxford University Press, 1986), 46-48; Congressional Quarterly, *1989 Almanac* (Washington, D.C.: Congressional Quarterly, 1990), 231, 234. For further information on the articles of impeachment voted by the House of Representatives (prior to 1973), see U.S. House, Committee on the Judiciary, *Impeachment—Selected Materials*, 93d Cong., 1st sess. (Washington, D.C.: Government Printing Office, 1973), 125-203.

Table 7-8 Attorneys General of the United States

Name	Term	Appointing president
Edmund Jennings Randolph	September 26, 1789-January 2, 1794	Washington
William Bradford	January 27, 1794-August 23, 1795	Washington
Charles Lee	December 10, 1795-February 18, 1801	Washington/J. Adams
Levi Lincoln	March 5, 1801- March 3, 1805	Jefferson
John Breckenridge	August 7, 1805-December 14, 1806	Jefferson
Caesar Augustus Rodney	January 20, 1807-December 11, 1811	Jefferson/Madison
William Pinkney	December 11, 1811-February 10, 1814	Madison
Richard Rush	February 10, 1814-November 13, 1817	Madison
William Wirt	November 13, 1817-March 3, 1829	Monroe/J.Q. Adams
John MacPherson Berrien	March 9, 1829-July 20, 1831	Jackson
Roger Brooke Taney	July 20, 1831-September 24, 1833	Jackson
Benjamin Franklin Butler	July 5, 1833-September 1, 1838	Jackson/Van Buren
Felix Grundy	July 5, 1838-December 1, 1839[a]	Van Buren
Henry Dilworth Gilpin	January 11, 1840-March 4, 1841	Van Buren
John Jordan Crittenden	March 3, 1841-September 13, 1841	W. Harrison//Tyler
Hugh Swinton Legare	September 13, 1841-June 20, 1843	Tyler
John Nelson	July 1, 1843-March 3, 1845	Tyler
John Young Mason	March 6, 1845-September 9, 1846	Polk
Nathan Clifford	September 17, 1846-March 17, 1848	Polk
Isaac Toucey	June 21, 1848-March 3, 1849	Polk
Reverdy Johnson	March 8, 1849-July 20, 1850	Taylor
John Jordan Crittenden	July 22, 1850-March 3, 1853	Fillmore
Caleb Cushing	March 7, 1853-March 3, 1857	Pierce
Jeremiah Sullivan Black	March 6, 1857-December 17, 1860	Buchanan
Edwin McMasters Stanton	December 20, 1860-March 3, 1861	Buchanan
Edward Bates	March 5, 1861-September 1864	Lincoln
James Speed	December 2, 1864-July 17, 1866	Lincoln/A. Johnson
Henry Stanbery	July 23, 1866-March 12, 1868	A. Johnson
William Maxwell Evarts	July 15, 1868-March 3, 1869	A. Johnson

Ebenezer Rockwood Hoar	March 5, 1869-June 23, 1870	Grant
Amos Tappan Akerman	June 23, 1870-January 10, 1872	Grant
George Henry Williams	December 14, 1871-May 15, 1875 [b]	Grant
Edwards Pierrepont	April 26, 1875-May 22, 1876 [c]	Grant
Alphonso Taft	May 22, 1876-March 11, 1877	Grant
Charles Devens	March 12, 1877-March 6, 1881	Hayes
(Isaac) Wayne MacVeagh	March 5, 1881-September 24, 1881 [d]	Garfield
Benjamin Harris Brewster	December 19, 1881- March 5, 1885 [e]	Arthur
Augustus Hill Garland	March 6, 1885-March 5, 1889	Cleveland
William Henry Harrison Miller	March 5, 1889-March 6, 1893	B. Harrison
Richard Oliney	March 6, 1893-June 7, 1895	Cleveland
Judson Harmon	June 8, 1895-March 5, 1897	Cleveland
Joseph McKenna	March 5, 1897-January 25, 1898	McKinley
John William Griggs	June 25, 1898-March 29, 1901	McKinley
Philander Chase Knox	April 5, 1901-June 30, 1904	McKinley
William Henry Moody	July 1, 1904-December 17, 1906	T. Roosevelt
Charles Joseph Bonaparte	December 17, 1906-March 4, 1909	T. Roosevelt
George Woodward Wickersham	March 5, 1909-March 5, 1913	Taft
James Clark McReynolds	March 5, 1913-August 29, 1914	Wilson
Thomas Watt Gregory	August 20, 1914-March 4, 1919	Wilson
Alexander Mitchell Palmer	March 5, 1919-March 5, 1921	Wilson
Harry Micajah Daugherty	March 4, 1921-March 28, 1924	Harding
Harlan Fiske Stone	April 7, 1924-February 3, 1925	Coolidge
John T. Sargent	March 17, 1925-March 5, 1929	Coolidge
William DeWitt Mitchell	March 5, 1929-March 3, 1933	Hoover
Homer Stille Cummings	March 4, 1933-January 2, 1939	F. Roosevelt
Frank Murphy	January 2, 1939-January 18, 1940	F. Roosevelt
Robert Houghwout Jackson	January 18, 1940-July 10, 1941	F. Roosevelt
Francis Biddle	September 15, 1941-June 30, 1945	F. Roosevelt
Tom Campbell Clark	June 15, 1945-August 24, 1949 [f]	Truman
James Howard McGrath	August 24, 1949-April 7, 1952	Truman
James Patrick McGranery	May 27, 1952-January 20, 1953	Truman

(Table continues)

Table 7-8 (Continued)

Name	Term	Appointing president
Herbert Brownell, Jr.	January 21, 1953-November 8, 1957	Eisenhower
William Pierce Rogers	November 8, 1957-January 20, 1961	Eisenhower
Robert Francis Kennedy	January 21, 1961-September 3, 1964	Kennedy
Nicholas deBelleville Katzenbach	February 11, 1965-October 2, 1966 [g]	L. Johnson
Ramsey Clark	February 3, 1967-January 20, 1969	L. Johnson
John Newton Mitchell	January 21, 1969-March 1, 1972	Nixon
Richard Gordon Kleindienst	June 12, 1972-May 24, 1973 [h]	Nixon
Elliot Lee Richardson	May 25, 1973-October 20, 1973	Nixon
William Bart Saxbe	January 4, 1974-February 3, 1975	Nixon
Edward Hirsch Levi	February 6, 1975-January 20, 1977	Ford
Griffin Boyette Bell	January 26, 1977-August 16, 1979	Carter
Benjamin R. Civiletti	August 16, 1979-January 19, 1981	Carter
William French Smith	January 23, 1981-February 24, 1985	Reagan
Edwin Meese, III	February 25, 1985-August 12, 1988	Reagan
Richard L. Thornburgh	August 12, 1988-August 9, 1991	Reagan/Bush
William P. Barr	November 25, 1991-January 20, 1993	Bush
Janet Reno	March 12, 1993-	Clinton

[a] Appointed July 5, 1838, to take effect September 1, 1838.
[b] Appointed December 14, 1871, to take effect January 10, 1872.
[c] Appointed April 26, 1875, to take effect May 15, 1875.
[d] Resigned September 22, 1881, but served to October 23, 1881.
[e] Did not take the oath of office until January 2, 1882.
[f] Entered on duty July 1, 1945.
[g] Served as acting attorney general from September 4, 1964, until appointed.
[h] Served as acting attorney general from March 2, 1972, until appointed.

Source: U.S. Department of Justice, *Register of the U.S. Department of Justice and the Federal Courts*, 55th ed. (Washington, D.C.: Government Printing Office, 1990), 151.

Figure 7-1 Organizational Chart of the Department of Justice

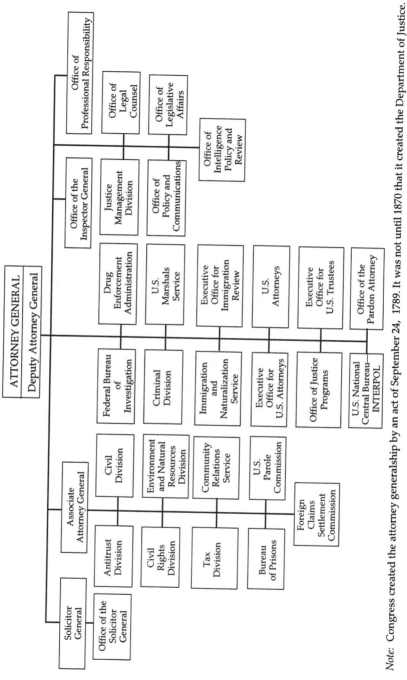

Note: Congress created the attorney generalship by an act of September 24, 1789. It was not until 1870 that it created the Department of Justice.

Source: U.S. Department of Justice, *Legal Activities 1992-1993* (Washington, D.C.: Office of Attorney Personnel Management, 1992).

Table 7-9 Solicitors General of the United States

Name	Term	Appointing president
Benjamin H. Bristow	October 11, 1870-November 15, 1872	Grant
Samuel F. Phillips	November 15, 1872-May 3, 1885	Grant
John Goode	May 1, 1885-August 5, 1886	Cleveland
George A. Jenks	July 30, 1886-May 29, 1889	Cleveland
Orlow W. Chapman	May 29, 1889-January 19, 1890	B. Harrison
William Howard Taft	February 4, 1890-March 20, 1892	B. Harrison
Charles H. Aldrich	March 21, 1892-May 28, 1893	B. Harrison
Lawrence Maxwell, Jr.	April 6, 1893-January 30, 1895	Cleveland
Holmes Conrad	February 6, 1895-July 8, 1897	Cleveland
John K. Richards	July 1, 1897-March 6, 1903	McKinley
Henry M. Hoyt	February 25, 1903-March 31, 1909 [a]	T. Roosevelt
Lloyd Wheaton Bowers	April 1, 1909-September 9, 1910	Taft
Frederick W. Lehman	December 12, 1910-July 15, 1912	Taft
William Marshall Bullitt	July 16, 1912-March 11, 1913	Taft
John William Davis	August 30, 1913-November 26, 1918	Wilson
Alexander C. King	November 27, 1918-May 23, 1920	Wilson
William L. Frierson	June 11, 1920-June 30, 1921	Wilson
James M. Beck	June 30, 1921-June 7, 1925	Harding
William D. Mitchell	June 4, 1925-April 5, 1929 [b]	Coolidge
Charles Evans Hughes, Jr.	May 27, 1929-March 16, 1930	Hoover
Thomas D. Thacher	March 22, 1930-May 4, 1933 [c]	Hoover
James Crawford Biggs	May 4, 1933-March 24, 1935	F. Roosevelt
Stanley Reed	March 23, 1935-January 30, 1938 [d]	F. Roosevelt
Robert H. Jackson	March 5, 1938-January 17, 1940	F. Roosevelt
Francis Biddle	January 22, 1940-September 4, 1941	F. Roosevelt
Charles Fahy	November 15, 1941-September 27, 1945	F. Roosevelt
J. Howard McGrath	October 4, 1945-October 7, 1946 [e]	Truman
Philip B. Perlman	July 30, 1947-August 15, 1952 [f]	Truman

Walter J. Cummings, Jr.	December 2, 1952-March 1, 1953	Truman
Simon E. Sobeloff	February 10, 1954-July 19, 1956[g]	Eisenhower
J. Lee Rankin	August 4, 1956-January 23, 1961	Eisenhower
Archibald Cox	January 24, 1961-July 31, 1965	Kennedy
Thurgood Marshall	August 11, 1965-August 30, 1967	L. Johnson
Erwin N. Griswold	October 12, 1967-June 25, 1973	L. Johnson
Robert H. Bork	June 19, 1973-January 20, 1977	Nixon
Wade Hampton McCree, Jr.	March 28, 1977-August 5, 1981	Carter
Rex E. Lee	August 6, 1981-May 31, 1985	Reagan
Charles Fried	October 25, 1985-January 20, 1989	Reagan
Kenneth Starr	May 27, 1989-January 20, 1993	Bush
Drew S. Days III	June 7, 1993-	Clinton

[a] Took the oath of office and entered on duty March 16, 1909.
[b] Took the oath of office and entered on duty June 8, 1925.
[c] Took the oath of office and entered on duty April 17, 1930.
[d] Took the oath of office and entered on duty March 25, 1935.
[e] Took the oath of office and entered on duty October 8, 1945.
[f] Took the oath of office and entered on duty July 31, 1947.
[g] Took the oath of office and entered on duty February 25, 1954.

Source: U.S. Department of Justice, Register of the U.S. Department of Justice and the Federal Courts, 54th ed. (Washington, D.C.: Government Printing Office, 1988), 143.

Figure 7-2 Organizational Chart of the Office of the U.S. Solicitor General

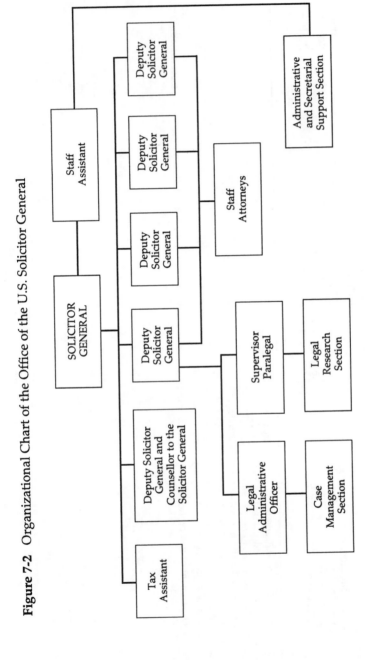

Note: Congress created the solicitor generalship on June 22, 1870.

Table 7-10   Success Rate of the United States as a Party to a Case Before the Supreme Court, 1953-1991 Terms

Term	Total number of cases[a]	% won
1953	26	61.5
1954	34	61.8
1955	41	46.3
1956	59	44.1
1957	48	58.3
1958	35	62.9
1959	56	62.5
1960	51	68.6
1961	36	44.4
1962	36	61.1
1963	37	56.8
1964	24	79.2
1965	39	56.4
1966	30	60.0
1967	40	65.0
1968	31	61.3
1969	26	65.4
1970	40	70.0
1971	23	43.5
1972	40	72.5
1973	31	71.0
1974	38	68.4
1975	33	84.8
1976	30	50.0
1977	33	57.6
1978	20	65.0
1979	38	65.8
1980	16	66.8
1981	18	72.2
1982	25	52.0
1983	30	83.3
1984	25	76.0
1985	25	88.0
1986	26	61.5
1987	24	66.7
1988	15	80.0
1989	23	56.5
1990	14	64.3
1991	21	57.1
Total	1,237	63.0

[a] Includes those cases where the *U.S. Reports* names the United States a party to the case, and criminal and habeas corpus cases where the *U.S. Reports* lists as the party the name of the official or office of the person who prosecutes or has custody of the accused or convicted person. If the United States is not the first named party in multiple party litigation, the case is not included.

Source: U.S. Supreme Court Judicial Database, with orally argued docket as unit of analysis.

Table 7-11   Success Rate of the United States as a Party to a Case Before the Supreme Court by Issue Area, 1953-1990 Terms

Term	Total number of cases[a]	% won
Criminal procedure	465	62.8
Civil rights	100	60.0
First Amendment	90	41.1
Due process	34	79.4
Privacy	3	100.0
Attorneys	4	50.0
Unions	9	88.9
Economic activity	255	63.9
Judicial power	79	64.6
Federalism	37	64.9
Federal taxation	131	70.2
Miscellaneous	9	77.8
Total	1,216	63.0

Note: The issue areas are defined as follows: Criminal procedure: the rights of persons accused of crime except for the due process rights of prisoners; Civil rights: non-First Amendment freedom cases that pertain to classifications based on race (including native Americans), age, indigence, voting, residence, military or handicapped status, sex, or alienage; First Amendment: guarantees contained therein; Due process: noncriminal procedural guarantees, plus court jurisdiction over nonresident litigants and the takings clause of the Fifth Amendment; Privacy: abortion, contraception, the Freedom of Information Act and related federal statutes; Attorneys: attorneys' fees, commercial speech, admission to and removal from the bar, and disciplinary matters; Unions: labor union activity; Economic activity: commercial business activity, plus litigation involving injured persons or things, employee actions vis-à-vis employers, zoning regulations, and governmental regulation of corruption other than that involving campaign spending; Judicial power: the exercise of the judiciary's own power and authority; Federalism: conflicts between the federal and state governments, excluding those between state and federal courts, and those involving the priority of federal fiscal claims; Federal taxation: the Internal Revenue Code and related statutes; Miscellaneous: Legislative veto, separation of powers, and matters not included in any other issue area.

[a] Includes those cases where the *U.S. Reports* names the United States a party to the case, and criminal and habeas corpus cases where the *U.S. Reports* lists as the party the name of the official or office of the person who prosecutes or has custody of the accused or convicted person. If the United States is not the first named party in multiple party litigation, the case is not included.

Source: U.S. Supreme Court Judicial Database, with orally argued docket as unit of analysis.

Table 7-12   Success Rate of the Solicitor General as an Amicus Curiae in Cases Before the Supreme Court by President, 1952-1990 Terms

President	Total number of cases [a]	% won
Eisenhower	42	83.3
Kennedy	48	87.5
Johnson	41	82.9
Nixon	79	70.9
Ford	38	71.1
Carter	86	65.1
Reagan [b]	123	67.5
Bush [c]	99	75.8

[a] Includes all cases where solicitor general filed an amicus curiae brief and the Court decided the case with an opinion on the merits.
[b] Includes 1980-1982 and 1986-1987 terms.
[c] Includes 1988-1990 terms.

Source: 1952-1982: Jeffrey A. Segal, "Courts, Executives, and Legislatures," in John B. Gates and Charles A. Johnson, eds., *The American Courts: A Critical Assessment* (Washington, D.C.: CQ Press, 1991), 379; updated by the authors.

Table 7-13   Success Rate of the Solicitor General as an Amicus Curiae in Cases Before the Supreme Court by Issue Area, 1952-1982 Terms

Issue	Total number of cases[a]	% won
Criminal procedure	36	80.6
Civil rights	141	73.0
First Amendment	1	74.5
Economic activity	66	77.3
Judicial power	33	72.7
Federalism	26	73.1

Note: Issue areas are defined as follows: Criminal procedure: the rights of persons accused of crime except for the due process rights of prisoners; Civil rights: non-First Amendment freedom cases that pertain to classifications based on race (including native American), age, indigence, voting, residence, military or handicapped status, sex, or alienage; First Amendment: guarantees contained therein; Economic activity: commercial business activity, plus litigation involving injured persons or things, employee actions vis-à-vis employers, zoning regulations, and governmental regulation of corruption other than that involving campaign spending; Judicial power: the exercise of the judiciary's own power and authority; Federalism: conflicts between the federal and state governments, excluding those between state and federal courts, and those involving the priority of federal fiscal claims.

[a] Includes all cases where solicitor general filed amicus curiae brief and the Court decided the case with an opinion on the merits.

Source: Jeffrey A. Segal, "Amicus Curiae Briefs by the Solicitor General during the Warren and Burger Courts," *Western Political Quarterly* 41 (1988): 139.

Table 7-14 Success Rate of Federal Agencies as a Party to a Case Before the Supreme Court, 1953-1990 Terms

Term	Total number of cases[a]	% won
1953	28	50.0
1954	18	77.8
1955	29	55.2
1956	28	78.6
1957	39	41.0
1958	25	80.0
1959	29	69.0
1960	21	52.4
1961	18	61.1
1962	22	68.2
1963	16	68.8
1964	29	72.4
1965	19	68.4
1966	30	63.3
1967	34	82.4
1968	14	78.6
1969	24	45.8
1970	18	44.4
1971	26	73.1
1972	25	80.0
1973	32	65.6
1974	24	75.0
1975	38	57.9
1976	25	84.0
1977	27	77.8
1978	25	64.0
1979	24	70.8
1980	33	78.8
1981	24	83.3
1982	44	72.7
1983	41	80.5
1984	34	82.4
1985	28	57.1
1986	21	71.4
1987	37	59.5
1988	24	62.5
1989	24	70.8
1990	16	37.5
Total	1,013	67.7

Note: See Table 7-16 for list of federal agencies included.

[a] Includes cases where the *U.S. Reports* lists name of federal agency or the head of the agency as a party to a case.

Source: U.S. Supreme Court Judicial Database, with orally argued docket as unit of analysis.

Table 7-15 Success Rate of Federal Agencies as a Party to a Case Before the Supreme Court by Issue Area, 1953-1990 Terms

Issue	Total number of cases[a]	% won
Criminal procedure	19	63.2
Civil rights	173	60.7
First Amendment	71	57.7
Due process	27	81.5
Privacy	30	83.3
Attorneys	9	55.6
Unions	175	68.0
Economic activity	250	75.6
Judicial power	131	59.5
Federalism	24	58.3
Federal taxation	96	74.0
Miscellaneous	8	62.5
Total	1,013	67.7

Note: Issue areas are defined as follows: Criminal procedure: the rights of persons accused of crime except for the due process rights of prisoners; Civil rights: non-First Amendment freedom cases that pertain to classifications based on race (including native Americans), age, indigence, voting, residence, military or handicapped status, sex, or alienage; First Amendment: guarantees contained therein; Due process: noncriminal procedural guarantees, plus court jurisdiction over nonresident litigants and the takings clause of the Fifth Amendment; Privacy: abortion, contraception, the Freedom of Information Act and related federal statutes; Attorneys: attorneys' fees, commercial speech, admission to and removal from the bar, and disciplinary matters; Unions: labor union activity; Economic activity: commercial business activity, plus litigation involving injured persons or things, employee actions vis-à-vis employers, zoning regulations, and governmental regulation of corruption other than that involving campaign spending; Judicial power: the exercise of the judiciary's own power and authority; Federalism: conflicts between the federal and state governments, excluding those between state and federal courts, and those involving the priority of federal fiscal claims; Federal taxation: the Internal Revenue Code and related statutes; Miscellaneous: legislative veto, separation of powers, and matters not included in any other issue area.

[a] Includes cases where the *U.S. Reports* lists name of federal agency or the head of the agency as a party to a case.

Source: U.S. Supreme Court Judicial Database, with orally argued docket as unit of analysis.

Table 7-16   Success Rates of Federal Agencies as a Party to a Case Before the Supreme Court by Agency, 1953-1990 Terms

Agency [a]	Total number of cases [b]	% won
Atomic Energy Commission	1	0.0
Air Force	4	50.0
Department of Agriculture	20	55.0
Army	5	20.0
Civil Aeronautics Board	5	40.0
Central Intelligence Agency	3	66.7
Commodity Futures Trading Commission	2	100.0
Department of Commerce	2	100.0
Comptroller of Currency	6	33.3
Comptroller General	3	33.3
Consumer Product Safety Commission	2	50.0
Civil Rights Commission	2	100.0
Civil Service Commission	6	33.3
Customs Service	1	100.0
Department of Defense	31	83.9
Department of Education	6	83.3
Department of Energy	2	50.0
Department of Health and Human Services	39	69.2
Department of Health, Education and Welfare	30	86.7
Department of Housing and Urban Development	4	50.0
Department of Interior	36	75.0
Department of Justice	37	51.4
Department of Labor	53	71.7
Department of State	16	18.8
Department of Transportation	5	80.0
Department of Treasury	18	66.7
Employees' Compensation Commission	4	100.0
Environmental Protection Agency	27	81.5
Equal Employment Opportunity Commission	14	78.6
Federal Aviation Administration	1	100.0
Federal Bureau of Investigation	1	100.0
Federal Communications Commission	18	60.0
Food and Drug Administration	3	100.0
Federal Deposit Insurance Corporation	3	100.0
Federal Elections Commission	8	50.0
Federal Energy Administration	1	100.0
Federal Energy Regulatory Commission	9	100.0
Federal Housing Administration	1	100.0
Federal Labor Relations Authority	4	0.0
Federal Maritime Board	1	0.0
Federal Maritime Commission	5	40.0
Federal Power Commission	59	76.3
Federal Reserve Board	7	71.4
Federal Savings and Loan Insurance Corporation	2	50.0

(Table continues)

Table 7-16   *(Continued)*

Agency[a]	Total number of cases[b]	% won
Federal Trade Commission	37	86.5
General Services Administration	3	100.0
Interstate Commerce Commission	46	67.4
Immigration and Naturalization Service	57	57.9
Internal Revenue Service	106	70.8
Information Security Oversight Office	1	0.0
Navy	2	100.0
National Labor Relations Board	158	69.6
National Mediation Board	2	100.0
National Railway Adjustment Board	1	100.0
Nuclear Regulatory Commission	4	100.0
Office of Personnel Management	4	50.0
Occupational Safety and Health Administration	1	0.0
Occupational Safety and Health Review Commission	3	66.7
Office of Workers' Compensation Programs	6	0.0
Patent Office	1	100.0
Pension Benefit Guaranty Corporation	1	100.0
Public Health Service	1	0.0
Railroad Retirement Board	1	100.0
Renegotiation Board	2	100.0
Selective Service System	5	60.0
Small Business Administration	1	100.0
Subversive Activities Control Board	5	20.0
Tennessee Valley Authority	2	50.0
United States Parole Commission	12	41.7
United States Postal Service	6	33.3
Veterans' Administration	5	60.0
Wage Stabilization Board	1	0.0

[a] Note that agencies occasionally change names or otherwise alter their structure. They may also cease to exist.
[b] Includes cases where the *U.S. Reports* lists federal agency or the head of the agency as a party to a case.

Source: U.S. Supreme Court Judicial Database, with orally argued docket as unit of analysis.

Table 7-17   Success Rate of States as a Party to a Case Before the
Supreme Court, 1953-1990 Terms

Term	Total number of cases[a]	% won
1953	17	35.3
1954	7	14.3
1955	10	60.0
1956	13	23.1
1957	21	66.7
1958	18	55.6
1959	15	33.3
1960	33	51.5
1961	20	35.0
1962	29	27.6
1963	23	21.7
1964	27	14.8
1965	19	26.3
1966	34	38.2
1967	30	26.7
1968	31	35.5
1969	41	43.9
1970	57	54.4
1971	64	42.2
1972	62	59.7
1973	37	48.6
1974	43	46.5
1975	44	59.1
1976	62	45.2
1977	48	52.1
1978	46	60.9
1979	35	37.1
1980	36	61.1
1981	46	34.8
1982	55	58.2
1983	45	48.9
1984	37	56.8
1985	52	65.4
1986	48	54.2
1987	31	45.2
1988	33	63.6
1989	38	68.4
1990	31	58.1
Total	1,338	48.3

[a] Includes those cases where the *U.S. Reports* names a state a party to a case, and criminal and habeas corpus cases where the *U.S. Reports* list as the party the name of the official or office of the person who prosecutes or has custody of the accused or convicted person. If a state is not the first named party in multiple party litigation, the case is not included.

Source: U.S. Supreme Court Judicial Database, with orally argued docket as unit of analysis.

Table 7-18   Success Rate of States as a Party to a Case Before the
Supreme Court by Issue Area, 1953-1990 Terms

Issue	Total number of cases[a]	% won
Criminal procedure	544	53.1
Civil rights	252	36.9
First Amendment	119	37.0
Due process	52	57.7
Privacy	21	47.6
Attorneys	10	50.0
Unions	3	33.3
Economic activity	122	48.4
Judicial power	133	63.9
Federalism	79	35.4
Federal taxation	2	50.0
Miscellaneous	1	100.0
Total	1,338	48.3

Note: The issue areas are defined as follows: Criminal procedure: the rights of persons accused of crime except for the due process rights of prisoners; Civil rights: non-First Amendment freedom cases that pertain to classifications based on race (including native Americans), age, indigence, voting, residence, military or handicapped status, sex, or alienage; First Amendment: guarantees contained therein; Due process: noncriminal procedural guarantees, plus court jurisdiction over nonresident litigants and the takings clause of the Fifth Amendment; Privacy: abortion, contraception, the Freedom of Information Act and related federal statutes; Attorneys: attorneys' fees, commercial speech, admission to and removal from the bar, and disciplinary matters; Unions: labor union activity; Economic activity: commercial business activity, plus litigation involving injured persons or things, employee actions vis-à-vis employers, zoning regulations, and governmental regulation of corruption other than that involving campaign spending; Judicial power: the exercise of the judiciary's own power and authority; Federalism: conflicts between the federal and state governments, excluding those between state and federal courts, and those involving the priority of federal fiscal claims; Federal taxation: the Internal Revenue Code and related statutes; Miscellaneous: legislative veto, separation of powers, and matters not included in any other issue area.

[a] Includes those cases where the *U.S. Reports* name a state a party to a case, and criminal and habeas corpus cases where the *U.S. Reports* list as the party the name of the official or office of the person who prosecutes or has custody of the accused or convicted person. If a state is not the first named party in multiple party litigation, the case is not included.

Source: U.S. Supreme Court Judicial Database, with orally argued docket as unit of analysis.

Table 7-19   Success Rates of States as a Party to a Case Before the Supreme Court by State, 1953-1990 Terms

State	Total number of cases[a]	% won
Alabama	38	28.9
Alaska	11	54.5
Arizona	43	46.5
Arkansas	17	29.4
California	139	57.6
Colorado	8	50.0
Connecticut	23	34.8
Delaware	5	60.0
Florida	69	55.1
Georgia	47	36.2
Hawaii	6	16.7
Idaho	8	25.0
Illinois	73	53.4
Indiana	16	50.0
Iowa	20	44.4
Kansas	3	33.3
Kentucky	25	48.0
Louisiana	53	32.7
Maine	8	37.5
Maryland	45	62.2
Massachusetts	38	68.4
Michigan	25	64.0
Minnesota	14	50.0
Mississippi	27	33.3
Missouri	20	30.0
Montana	9	55.6
Nebraska	9	55.6
Nevada	6	50.0
New Hampshire	8	0.0
New Jersey	26	50.0
New Mexico	15	33.3
New York	109	56.0
North Carolina	30	33.3
North Dakota	4	50.0
Ohio	54	44.4
Oklahoma	16	31.3
Oregon	19	68.4
Pennsylvania	52	44.2
Rhode Island	7	42.9
South Carolina	16	43.8
South Dakota	9	44.4
Tennessee	23	60.9
Texas	68	41.1
Utah	5	80.0
Vermont	5	20.0

(Table continues)

Table 7-19   *(Continued)*

State	Total number of cases[a]	% won
Virginia	32	37.5
Washington	27	51.9
West Virginia	8	75.0
Wisconsin	16	43.8
Wyoming	3	33.3

[a] Includes those cases where the *U.S. Reports* name a state a party to a case, and criminal and habeas corpus cases where the *U.S. Reports* list as the party the name of the official or office of the person who prosecutes or has custody of the accused or convicted person. If a state is not the first named party in multiple party litigation, the case is not included.

Source: U.S. Supreme Court Judicial Database, with orally argued docket as unit of analysis.

Table 7-20 Frequency of Amicus Curiae Participation in Non-commercial Supreme Court Litigation, Selected Years

Years	Cases with amicus curiae briefs		Total number of cases [a]
	%	N	
1928-1940	1.6	3	181
1941-1952	18.2	67	368
1953-1966	23.8	149	626
1970-1980	53.5	449	841
1988 [b]	80.1	109	136

[a] Includes all noncommercial litigation, comprising elections, free speech, free press, indigents, military, race discrimination, freedom of information, sex discrimination, unions, criminal procedures, state/federal employees, church-state, and conscientious objectors.
[b] Represents the 1987 term.

Source: Lee Epstein, "Courts and Interest Groups," in *The American Courts: A Critical Assessment*, ed. John B. Gates and Charles A. Johnson (Washington, D.C.: CQ Press, 1991), 351. For more information, see Karen O'Connor and Lee Epstein, "Amicus Curiae Participation in U.S. Supreme Court Litigation: An Appraisal of Hakman's 'Folklore'," *Law and Society Review* 16 (1981-1982): 318-319.

Table 7-21 Amicus Curiae Participants in Supreme Court Litigation, 1987 Term

Amicus curiae participant	Number of cases [a]	Percentage of total cases decided on their merits
Commercial interests	111	24.3
Government	111	24.3
Legal	59	12.9
Civil liberties	49	10.7
Religion	22	4.8
Public affairs	20	4.4
Women	17	3.7
Health	17	3.7
Education	15	3.3
Labor	15	3.3
Consumer	7	1.5
Other groups	13	2.9
Total	456	

[a] Includes only the interest that filed the brief, not co-signers.

Source: Lee Epstein, "Courts and Interest Groups," in *The American Courts: A Critical Assessment*, ed. John B. Gates and Charles A. Johnson (Washington, D.C.: CQ Press, 1991), 356.

Table 7-22 Justices' Citations to Amicus Curiae Briefs, 1953-1991

Justice [a]	Number of citations to amici curiae	Number of citations to amici curiae divided by total opinions written [b]
Black	297	.53
Blackmun	531	.69
Brennan	755	.65
Burger	337	.68
Burton	17	.21
Clark	109	.36
Douglas	416	.45
Fortas	43	.44
Frankfurter	74	.29
Goldberg	87	.39
Harlan	252	.37
Jackson	10	.63
Kennedy	82	.65
Marshall	505	.71
Minton	8	.20
O'Connor	292	.77
Powell	458	.77
Reed	20	.33
Rehnquist	453	.53
Scalia	157	.62
Souter	10	.29
Stevens	607	.71
Stewart	363	.51
Thomas	7	.35
Warren	99	.40
White	660	.66
Whittaker	28	.25

[a] For justices joining the Court prior to 1953, data are not completely descriptive of careers.
[b] Includes opinions of the court, judgments, and dissenting and concurring (regular and special) opinions.

Sources: LEXIS; U.S. Supreme Court Judicial Database.

8

The Supreme Court and Public Opinion

The relationship between the Supreme Court and public opinion brings together questions of vital interest to Court-watchers. First, is the Supreme Court influenced by public opinion? Second, does the Supreme Court have the capability to influence public opinion through its rulings? This second question can be expanded to include issues of public support for the Court and the extent to which the Court is able to influence the public's opinion about itself.

High-profile decisions by and large reflect public opinion.[1] Whether the Court is actually *influenced* by public opinion is harder to gauge. There is little reason to think so. The justices, unlike state court judges, are immune from majoritarian pressures. The public neither elects nor removes them from office. Moreover, the justices are not supposed to represent majoritarian concerns. Justice Robert H. Jackson stated this convincingly in *West Virginia Board of Education v. Barnette* (1943):

> The very purpose of a Bill of Rights was to withdraw certain subjects from the vicissitudes of political controversy, to place them beyond the reach of majorities and officials and to establish them as legal principles to be applied by the courts. One's right to life, liberty, and property, to free speech, a free press, freedom of worship and assembly, and other fundamental rights may not be submitted to vote; they depend on the outcome of no elections.[2]

With the exceptions of the Court's interpretation of the cruel and unusual punishments clause, the due process clause, and its definition of obscenity, the Court has stood by Jackson's exhortation. In the three excepted areas, however, justification for the Court's results, as laid out in the majority opinion, if not the result itself, often rests on public opinion.

The question as to whether the Court influences public opinion and legitimates public policy was first asked by Robert Dahl in 1957.[3]

Dahl, in the course of arguing that the Court had not historically filled its normative role as the protector of minority rights, claimed that its power could nevertheless be justified by its ability to legitimate the decisions of other branches of government. The overwhelming majority of research on this subject, however, has found the Court to be without power to influence public opinion.[4]

In this chapter we present a series of polls on public opinion concerning matters with which the Court has dealt. The four basic sources used to compile this data are The General Social Survey, The Harris Survey, The Gallup Poll, and the *New York Times* surveys. Some care must be taken in interpreting survey results, as small differences in question wording can lead to substantial differences in aggregate responses. For instance, a majority of Americans support a woman's right to terminate her pregnancy, while at the same time a majority of Americans also believe that the killing of the unborn should be prohibited. Moreover, special care should be taken in interpreting Harris surveys, whose questions tend to lean in the Democratic/liberal direction. For example, The Harris Survey's questions on affirmative action contain the tag "provided there are no strict quotas." Jane Mansbridge's award-winning *Why We Lost the ERA* [5] documents Harris's change to a more favorable question wording about the proposed amendment in the days before the Illinois legislature was scheduled to vote, in an effort to claim increased support for women's rights.

We begin with political tolerance (Tables 8-1 through 8-5). Americans are notably inconsistent in response to questions about political tolerance. On the one hand, there is almost universal support of statements such as "The right of everyone to freedom of speech, no matter what his or her views, must be upheld." On the other hand, when questions are phrased in the context of particular groups, for example, communists, homosexuals, or atheists, libertarianism drops markedly. Thus, only a bare majority of Americans believe that atheists, communists, or militarists should be allowed to teach at colleges or universities. With the exception of racists' rights, however, a trend toward respect for the rights of all groups is evident.

We next turn from the rights of association to the rights of the accused. Table 8-6 demonstrates strong support for capital punishment, dating as far back as 1936. And despite twelve years of Reagan-Bush appointments to the federal bench, about 80 percent of the survey respondents believe that courts are too lenient with criminals (see Table 8-7). Presumably, such responses are based on the actions of state courts, where the overwhelming majority of criminal cases are tried. Nevertheless, the public's support for the "peace forces" in society does not extend to the use of wiretapping (see Table 8-8).

We next consider the "American dilemma": the question of race

(Tables 8-9 through 8-13). *Brown v. Board of Education,* [6] the school desegregation case, mustered support by a majority of Americans (54 percent) in 1954, and that support grew throughout the decade. Laws against intermarriage are supported today by only the most insistent racists (16.9 percent), as is the "right" of whites to live in segregated housing (17.2 percent). On the other hand, racial busing remains anathema to most Americans. Support for racial preference in hiring garners a less than majority approval rate, while support for affirmative action appears high, though, as noted in Table 8-13, it drops markedly when the question wording is changed.

Women's rights and abortion are the subjects of Tables 8-14 through 8-19. The percentage of Americans who believe that a woman's job is to take care of the home (18.6 percent) is at about the same level as the percentage of people who are opposed to racial intermarriage. On abortion, the results are far more complex. The most interesting results are in Table 8-18, which shows that only a minority of Americans support abortion on demand (40.8 percent) or advocate a total ban on abortion (see, for example, the "chance of defect" column). Thus, the middle ground recently taken by the Court in *Planned Parenthood v. Casey* [7] may be closest to the public's opinion on this issue. Support for *Roe v. Wade* [8] appears high, though only 20 percent of Americans support abortions in the second trimester of pregnancy (see the note to Table 8-19). More so than many other issues, the answers received on matters of abortion depend on the exact manner in which the question is asked.

Other social issues are presented in Tables 8-20 through 8-23. We note briefly the American public's opposition to homosexuality and pornography, and support for school prayer and the right to die. Only the school prayer responses differ from the most relevant Court decisions.

We present the public's perception of the Court itself in Tables 8-24 through 8-30. While only a minority of Americans have a great deal of confidence in the Court, we should note that confidence in Congress is certainly no higher. As is evident in Table 8-29, one plausible explanation as to why the Supreme Court is unable to influence public opinion is that most Americans are largely unaware of its activities. Less than ten percent of Americans can name the chief justice of the United States (William Rehnquist) or the most well known associate justice (Sandra Day O'Connor). Only 6 out of 1,005 persons were able to name John Paul Stevens as an associate justice. Yet 54 percent of survey respondents were able to name correctly the judge on the television program "The People's Court" (Table 8-30). Such data provide a stunning picture of the American public's general ignorance of the Court and its day-to-day activity.

Notes

1. Thomas Marshall, *Public Opinion and the Supreme Court* (New York: Unwin/Hyman, 1989).
2. 319 U.S. 624, at 638.
3. Robert Dahl, "Decision-Making in a Democracy: The Supreme Court as National Policy-Maker," *Journal of Public Law* 6 (1957): 279-296.
4. See Gregory A. Caldeira, "Courts and Public Opinion," in *The American Courts: A Critical Assessment*, ed. John B. Gates and Charles A. Johnson (Washington, D.C.: CQ Press, 1991), and Charles H. Franklin and Liane C. Kosaki, "The Republican Schoolmaster: The Supreme Court, Public Opinion, and Abortion," *American Political Science Review* 83 (1989): 751-772.
5. Jane Mansbridge, *Why We Lost the ERA* (Chicago: University of Chicago Press, 1986).
6. 347 U.S. 483 (1974).
7. 120 L. Ed. 2d 674 (1992).
8. 410 U.S. 113 (1973).

Table 8-1   Respondents Allowing Atheists to Perform Specified Activity (percent)

Year	Community	Library	College
1972	65.0	60.4	39.9
1973	65.3	60.8	40.6
1974	61.7	59.8	41.7
1976	64.0	59.5	41.3
1977	62.2	58.4	38.7
1980	66.1	61.9	45.3
1982	61.3	57.6	43.3
1984	68.0	63.6	45.7
1985	64.6	60.4	45.3
1987	67.9	64.1	45.6
1988	69.7	63.7	45.2
1989	71.6	67.1	51.0
1990	72.3	66.4	50.2
1991	71.8	69.1	51.9

Note: Questions: (Community) "Suppose someone who is against all churches and religion wanted to make a speech in your community. Should he be allowed to speak or not?" (Library) "If some people in your community suggested that a book he wrote against churches and religion should be taken out of the library, would you favor removing this book or not?" (College) "Should such a person be allowed to teach in a college or university, or not?"

Source: General Social Survey, National Opinion Research Center, University of Chicago, various years.

Table 8-2 Respondents Allowing Racists to Perform Specified Activity (percent)

Year	Community	Library	College
1976	60.6	59.5	40.4
1977	58.4	60.8	40.7
1980	61.4	63.7	42.9
1982	56.2	56.3	39.8
1984	57.3	62.9	40.6
1985	55.3	60.0	42.0
1987	59.0	61.3	41.3
1988	61.0	61.7	41.4
1989	61.7	64.8	45.7
1990	62.5	64.0	44.6
1991	62.1	65.5	41.9

Note: Questions: (Community) "Suppose someone who believes blacks are genetically inferior wanted to make a speech in your community. Should he be allowed to speak or not?" (Library) "If someone in your community suggested that a book he wrote that said blacks are inferior should be taken out of the library, would you favor removing it?" (College) "Should such a person be allowed to teach in a college or university, or not?"

Source: General Social Survey, National Opinion Research Center, University of Chicago, various years.

Table 8-3 Respondents Allowing Homosexuals to Perform Specified Activity (percent)

Year	Community	Library	College
1973	60.7	53.5	47.3
1974	62.3	54.8	50.1
1976	61.8	55.4	52.0
1977	61.7	55.2	49.2
1980	65.9	58.1	54.6
1982	63.5	54.0	53.9
1984	67.9	59.3	58.7
1985	66.6	55.3	57.8
1987	67.1	56.5	56.1
1988	69.7	60.3	56.5
1989	76.1	63.8	63.3
1990	73.5	63.9	62.3
1991	75.7	68.3	63.2

Note: Questions: (Community) "Suppose someone who admits he is a homosexual wanted to make a speech in your community, should he be allowed to speak or not?" (Library) "If some people in your community suggested that a book he wrote in favor of homosexuality should be taken out of the library, would you favor removing this book, or not?" (College) "Should such a person be allowed to teach in a college or university, or not?"

Source: General Social Survey, National Opinion Research Center, University of Chicago, various years.

Table 8-4   Respondents Allowing Communists to Perform Specified
Activity (percent)

Year	Community	Library	College
1972	51.8	52.8	32.1
1973	59.7	58.2	38.9
1974	57.7	58.4	41.6
1976	54.5	55.9	41.4
1977	55.3	55.0	38.6
1980	55.1	57.2	40.5
1982	53.9	53.8	42.6
1984	59.1	59.3	45.6
1985	56.8	57.0	44.1
1987	58.6	59.3	46.0
1988	60.2	59.3	47.5
1989	64.1	61.3	50.2
1990	64.2	63.7	51.4
1991	67.1	67.2	53.6

Note: Questions: (Community) "Suppose someone who admits he is a communist wanted to make a speech in your community. Should he be allowed to speak, or not?" (Library) "Suppose he wrote a book that is in your public library. Somebody in the community suggests that the book should be removed from the public library. Would you favor removing it, or not?" (College) "Suppose he is teaching in a college. Should he be fired or not?"

Source: General Social Survey, National Opinion Research Center, University of Chicago, various years.

Table 8-5 Respondents Allowing Militarists to Perform Specified Activity (percent)

Year	Community	Library	College
1976	54.2	55.9	36.9
1977	50.5	54.4	33.9
1980	56.8	58.0	39.3
1982	51.6	52.5	36.5
1984	56.8	59.0	41.0
1985	54.4	56.2	39.6
1987	54.6	56.1	38.1
1988	55.6	56.4	37.1
1989	59.1	59.1	40.2
1990	56.8	60.1	43.0
1991	61.9	66.6	42.7

Note: Questions: (Community) "Suppose someone who advocates doing away with elections and letting the military run the country wanted to make a speech in your community. Should he be allowed to speak or not?" (Library) "Suppose he wrote a book advocating doing away with elections and letting the military run the country. Somebody in your community suggests the book be removed from the public library. Would you favor removing it, or not?" (College) "Should such a person be allowed to teach in a college or university, or not?"

Source: General Social Survey, National Opinion Research Center, University of Chicago, various years.

Table 8-6 Respondents Favoring Capital Punishment, Various Polls (percent)

Year	General Social Survey	Harris	Gallup	New York Times
1936	—	—	61	—
1937	—	—	65	—
1953	—	—	68	—
1960	—	—	51	—
1965	—	38	45	—
1966	—	—	42	—
1969	—	48	51	—
1970	—	47	—	—
1971	—	—	49	—
1972	52.8	—	57	—
1973	59.7	59	—	—
1974	62.9	—	64	—
1975	59.8	—	—	—
1976	65.4	67	65	—
1977	66.8	—	—	—
1978	66.3	—	62	—
1980	66.9	—	—	—
1981	—	—	66	—
1982	67.9	—	—	—
1983	73.1	68	—	—
1984	69.9	—	—	—
1985	75.2	—	—	—
1986	71.2	—	—	—
1987	64.1	—	—	—
1988	70.6	—	—	77
1989	73.7	—	—	71
1990	74.2	—	—	72
1991	71.1	—	76	—

Note: "—" indicates survey not conducted in that year. Question: "Do you believe in capital punishment for persons convicted of murder or are you opposed to it?" The Harris Survey asked: "Do you believe in capital punishment or are you opposed to it?"

Sources: General Social Survey, National Opinion Research Center, University of Chicago, various years; The Harris Survey, February 10, 1983, 2; *The Gallup Poll* (1985), 36 and (1991), 43; *New York Times* press release.

Table 8-7 Respondents Believing Courts Are Too Lenient

Year	Percentage	Year	Percentage
1972	66.1	1983	85.2
1973	72.6	1984	80.9
1974	77.0	1985	83.7
1975	78.8	1986	85.2
1976	80.7	1987	77.9
1977	82.9	1988	81.3
1978	84.7	1989	83.6
1980	83.0	1990	82.4
1982	82.3	1991	79.2

Note: Question: "In general, do you think the courts in this area deal too harshly or not harshly enough with criminals?"

Source: General Social Survey, National Opinion Research Center, University of Chicago, various years.

Table 8-8 Respondents Approving of Wiretapping

Year	General Social Survey	Gallup
1949	—	22
1969	—	46
1974	16.5	—
1975	16.2	—
1977	18.4	—
1978	19.0	—
1982	16.7	—
1983	18.5	—
1985	22.8	—
1986	22.2	—
1988	20.2	—
1989	26.1	—
1990	21.9	—
1991	24.1	—

Note: "—" indicates survey not conducted in that year. Question: (General Social Survey) "Everything considered, would you say that, in general, you approve or disapprove of wiretapping?" (The Gallup Poll) "Do you think it is right, or not, to get evidence for use in a court trial by means of wiretapping?"

Sources: General Social Survey, National Opinion Research Center, University of Chicago, various years; *The Gallup Poll* 2 (1935-1971), 844.

Table 8-9   Respondents Approving of *Brown v. Board of Education*

Date	Percentage
May 1954	54
April 1955	56
November 1955	59
December 1956	63
April 1957	62
July 1957	58
September 1957	59
May 1959	57
May 1961	62

Source: The Gallup Poll (1981), 26.

Table 8-10   Respondents Disapproving of Racial Intermarriage and Approving of Segregated Housing (percent)

Year	Favor laws against racial intermarriage	Believe whites have right to segregated housing
1970	35.0	—
1971	—	—
1972	31.9	31.2
1973	32.4	—
1974	33.7	—
1975	37.6	—
1976	31.6	35.0
1977	27.7	36.3
1978	—	—
1979	—	—
1980	29.1	30.1
1981	—	—
1982	24.9	23.7
1983	—	—
1984	23.5	24.6
1985	25.2	24.4
1986	—	—
1987	20.3	20.1
1988	21.8	21.5
1989	20.1	20.7
1990	18.6	21.6
1991	16.9	17.2

Note: "—" indicates survey not conducted in that year. Questions asked of nonblacks only through 1977. Questions: (General Social Survey) "Do you think there should be laws against marriage between (Negroes/blacks) and whites?" (The Gallup Poll) "Some states have laws making it a crime for a white person and a Negro to marry. Do you approve or disapprove of such laws?"

Source: 1970: *The Gallup Poll* 3 (1935-1971), 2263; 1971-1991: General Social Survey, National Opinion Research Center, University of Chicago, various years.

Table 8-11 Respondents Approving of Busing, Various Polls (percent)

Year	General Social Survey	Harris	Gallup
1970	—	—	11
1971	—	17	18
1972	19.4	17	—
1973	—	—	—
1974	20.1	—	35[a]
1975	17.2	20	—
1976	15.7	14	—
1977	16.2	—	—
1978	20.0	—	—
1979	—	—	—
1980	—	—	22
1981	—	—	—
1982	25.8	—	—
1983	22.8	—	—
1984	—	—	—
1985	21.9	—	—
1986	29.3	41	—
1987	—	—	—
1988	32.4	—	—
1989	27.6	—	—
1990	32.9	—	—
1991	34.2	—	—

Note: "—" indicates survey not conducted in that year. Questions: (General Social Survey, The Harris Survey) "In general, do you favor or oppose the busing of black and white school children from one school district to another?" (The Gallup Poll) "Do you favor or oppose busing children to achieve a better racial balance?"

[a] Percentage of respondents giving a positive response out of those giving a positive or negative response.

Sources: General Social Survey, National Opinion Research Center, University of Chicago, various years; The Harris Survey, January 5, 1987, 3; *The Gallup Poll* 3 (1935-1971), 2243, 2323 and (1981), 21.

Table 8-12   Respondents Favoring Racial
Preferences in Hiring or Promotion
Where There Has Been Past
Discrimination

Date	Percentage
May 1985	42
April 1987	50
July 1987	40
September 1987	37
May 1990	33
December 1990	32
January 1992	49
February 1992	39

Note: Question: "Do you believe that where there has been job discrimination against blacks in the past, preference in hiring or promotion should be given to blacks today?"

Source: New York Times press release.

Table 8-13   Respondents Favoring Affirmative
Action

Date	Percentage
January 1982	72
July 1982	69
September 1983	61
July 1984	65
September 1985	75
July 1987	69
June 1991	75
September 1991 [a]	70

Note: Question: "Do you favor or oppose federal laws requiring affirmative action programs for women and minorities provided there are no rigid quotas?"

[a] When "affirmative action" is replaced by "racial preferences," support drops to 46 percent.

Source: The Harris Poll, July 14, 1991, 3, and September 15, 1991, 2.

Table 8-14   Respondents Believing a Woman's Job Is to Take Care of the Home

Year	Percentage
1974	34.3
1975	34.6
1977	37.2
1978	30.9
1982	27.5
1983	22.3
1985	25.7
1986	23.4
1988	20.3
1989	19.1
1990	17.1
1991	18.6

Note: Question: "Women should take care of running their homes and leave running the country to men (agree/ disagree)?"

Source: General Social Survey, National Opinion Research Center, University of Chicago, various years.

Table 8-15   Respondents Favoring the Proposed Equal Rights Amendment

Date	Percentage[a]
April 1982	53
July 1982	59
May 1983	62
July 1985	61

Note: Question: "Do you strongly favor, somewhat favor, somewhat oppose, or strongly oppose the Equal Rights Amendment?"

[a] Includes "strongly favor" and "somewhat favor" responses.

Source: The Harris Survey, August 9, 1982, 3, May 14, 1984, 2, and August 19, 1985, 3.

Table 8-16   Respondents Believing Abortion Should Be Legal, Selected Polls (percent)

Date	New York Times	Gallup
April 1975	—	21
December 1977	—	22
February 1979	—	22
July 1980	—	25
May 1981	—	23
May 1983	—	23
September 1988	—	24
September 1989	40	—
November 1989	41	—
January 1990	39	—
April 1990	—	31
August 1990	41	—
June 1991	37	—
August 1991	41	—
September 1991	42	33
January 1992	40	—
March 1992	44	—

Note: "—" indicates survey not conducted in that year. Questions: *(New York Times)* "Which of these comes closest to your views? 1) Abortion should be generally available to all who want it, or 2) Abortion should be available but under stricter limits than it is now, or 3) Abortion should not be permitted." (The Gallup Poll) "Do you think abortion should be legal under any circumstances, legal only under some circumstances, or illegal under all circumstances?" The percentages represent those who selected "1" in the *New York Times* poll and "under any circumstances" in the Gallup.

Sources: New York Times press release; *The Gallup Poll* (1978), 29, 509, (1988), 206, (April 1990), 3, and (September 1991), 52.

Table 8-17 Respondents Believing Information on Birth Control
Should Be Legally Available, Selected Polls (percent)

Year	General Social Survey	Gallup
1936	—	70
1959	—	72
1964	—	81
1974	91.2	—
1975	89.3	—
1977	90.8	—
1982	89.5	—
1983	90.1	—

Note: "—" indicates survey not conducted in that year. Questions: (General Social Survey) "Do you think birth control information should be available to anyone who wants it, or not?" (The Gallup Poll) 1936, "Should the distribution of information on birth control be made legal?" After 1936, "Do you think birth control information should be available to anyone who wants it, or not?"

Sources: General Social Survey, National Opinion Research Center, University of Chicago, various years; *The Gallup Poll* 1 (1935-1971) and (1935-1971), 1654.

Table 8-18 Respondents Supporting Legal Abortion Under Special Circumstances (percent)

Year	Chance of defect	Wants no more children	Health endangered	Can't afford	Rape	Not married	Any reason
1965	54.0	—	77.0	18.0	—	—	—
1972	74.3	37.6	83.0	45.6	74.1	40.5	—
1973	82.2	46.1	90.6	51.7	80.6	47.3	—
1974	82.6	44.6	90.4	52.3	82.7	47.9	—
1975	80.3	43.8	88.2	50.5	79.9	45.8	—
1976	81.6	44.6	88.7	50.8	80.4	48.2	—
1977	83.1	44.4	88.0	51.6	80.5	47.5	36.5
1978	80.1	39.0	88.3	45.4	80.4	39.6	32.2
1979	—	—	—	—	—	—	—
1980	80.3	45.2	87.7	49.6	80.2	46.3	39.4
1981	—	—	—	—	—	—	—
1982	78.4	43.4	87.5	46.7	79.8	43.2	36.5
1983	74.7	37.0	85.3	41.2	77.9	36.8	34.3
1984	77.4	41.1	87.0	44.4	76.7	42.6	37.2
1985	76.1	39.1	86.8	42.4	78.0	39.9	35.7
1986	—	—	—	—	—	—	—
1987	74.8	39.3	84.4	42.8	75.6	38.5	37.3
1988	76.2	38.8	85.6	40.4	76.7	37.6	34.6
1989	78.3	42.7	87.5	45.8	79.9	43.3	38.6
1990	78.0	43.2	88.8	45.3	80.7	43.1	41.5
1991	79.4	42.7	88.0	46.1	82.3	42.9	40.8

Note: "—" indicates survey not conducted in that year. Questions: "Please tell me whether or not you think it should be possible for a pregnant woman to obtain a *legal* abortion if A) there is a strong chance of serious defect in the baby, B) She is married and does not want any more children, C) the woman's own health is seriously endangered by the pregnancy, D) the family has a very low income and can't afford any more children, E) She became pregnant as the result of rape, F) She is not married and does not want to marry the man, or G) the woman wants it for any reason?"

Sources: The Gallup Poll 3 (1935-1971), 1985; General Social Survey, National Opinion Research Center, University of Chicago, various years.

Table 8-19   Respondents Supporting *Roe v. Wade,* Selected Polls (percent)

Date	Harris	Gallup
February 1974	52	—
November 1974	—	47
April 1975	54	—
March 1976	54	—
August 1976	59	—
October 1976	60	—
July 1977	53	—
July 1978	—	—
February 1979	60	—
February 1980	—	—
May 1981	56	45
May 1982	—	—
June 1983	—	50
June 1984	—	—
September 1985	50	—
January 1986	—	49
January 1987	—	—
December 1988	—	57
January 1989	56	—
July 1989	61	58
August 1989	59	—
October 1989	58	—
October 1990	—	—
June 1991	—	52
July 1991	—	56
September 1991	—	57

Note: "—" indicates survey not conducted in that year. Questions: (The Harris Survey) "In 1973, the U.S. Supreme Court decided that state laws which made it a crime to have an abortion up to three months of pregnancy were unconstitutional, and that the decision of whether or not to have an abortion should be left to the woman and her doctor to decide. In general, do you favor or oppose the U.S. Supreme Court decision making abortion up to three months of pregnancy legal?" (The Gallup Poll) "In 1973, the Supreme Court ruled that states cannot place restrictions on a woman's right to an abortion during the first three months of pregnancy. Would you like to see this ruling overturned or not?" The wording of these questions is inaccurate. The decision in fact legalized abortion in the first six months of pregnancy. In 1975, Harris found only 20 percent approval for legalized abortions between the third and sixth months of pregnancy.

Sources: The Harris Survey, August 18, 1977, 2, March 7, 1979, 2, January 29, 1989, 2, and November 26, 1989, 2; *The Gallup Poll* (1981), 113, (1983), 139, (1986), 49, (1989), 20, (July 1991), 21, and (September 1992), 52.

Table 8-20   Respondents Believing Homosexual
Behavior Is Wrong

Year	Percentage[a]
1973	76.3
1974	71.8
1976	72.5
1977	73.7
1980	75.5
1982	76.2
1984	75.1
1985	76.7
1987	79.2
1988	78.2
1989	74.2
1990	77.1
1991	74.2

Note: Question: "Do you believe that sexual relations between two adults of the same sex is always wrong, almost always wrong, wrong only sometimes, or not wrong at all?"

[a] Includes "always" and "almost always" responses.

Source: General Social Survey, National Opinion Research Center, University of Chicago, various years.

Table 8-21   Respondents Believing Pornography
Leads to a Breakdown in Morals

Year	Percentage
1973	52.8
1975	51.3
1976	54.6
1978	56.8
1980	60.0
1983	58.3
1984	61.3
1986	61.9
1987	59.0
1988	61.8
1989	62.1
1990	60.8
1991	59.6

Note: Question: "Sexual materials lead to a breakdown in morals (yes/no)?"

Source: General Social Survey, National Opinion Research Center, University of Chicago, various years.

Table 8-22   Respondents Approving of Supreme Court Decisions
Preventing Organized Prayer or Bible Readings in Schools,
Selected Polls (percent)

Year	General Social Survey	Gallup
1963	—	24
1974	30.7	—
1975	35.3	—
1977	33.4	—
1982	34.1	—
1983	39.5	—
1985	43.0	—
1986	37.0	—
1988	37.2	—
1989	40.9	—
1990	40.0	—
1991	38.3	—

Note: "—" indicates survey not conducted in that year. Question: "The U.S. Supreme Court has ruled that no state or local government may require the reading of the Lord's Prayer or Bible verses in public schools. What are your views on this?"

Sources: General Social Survey, National Opinion Research Center, University of Chicago; *The Gallup Poll* 3 (1935-1971), 1837.

Table 8-23 Respondents Supporting an Individual's Right to Die, Various Polls (percent)

Year	General Social Survey	Gallup	Harris
1936	—	—	—
1947	—	37	—
1973	—	53	—
1977	59.3	—	66
1978	57.7	—	—
1981	—	—	73
1982	55.2	—	—
1983	62.9	—	—
1985	63.6	—	80
1986	65.6	—	—
1988	65.6	—	—
1989	65.3	—	—
1990	68.4	—	—
1991	70.2	65	—

Note: "—" indicates survey not conducted in that year. Questions: (General Social Survey, The Gallup Poll) "Do you believe that doctors should be allowed by law to end an incurable patient's life if the patient and his family request it?" (The Harris Survey) "Do you believe families should be allowed to tell doctors to end life support for comatose terminally ill patients?"

Sources: General Social Survey, National Opinion Research Center, University of Chicago, various years; *The Gallup Poll* 1 (1935-1971), 656 and (January 1991), 51; The Harris Survey, March 4, 1985, 3.

Table 8-24 Respondents Believing the Supreme Court Is Too Liberal or Too Conservative (percent)

Year	Too liberal	Too conservative	About right	Unsure
1973	35	26	17	22
1986	34	38	10	17
1987	38	38	8	18
1991	30	42	9	19

Note: Question: "In general, do you think the U.S. Supreme Court is too liberal or too conservative?"

Source: *New York Times* press release.

Table 8-25 Respondents Having a Great Deal of Confidence in the Supreme Court, Various Polls (percent)

Year	General Social Survey	Harris	Gallup
1963	—	—	43
1966	—	50	—
1967	—	—	45
1968	—	—	36
1969	—	—	33
1971	—	23	—
1972	—	28	—
1973	31.3	33	37
1974	33.2	40	—
1975	30.7	28	49
1976	35.2	22	—
1977	35.5	29	—
1978	38.0	29	—
1979	—	28	45
1980	24.6	28	47
1981	—	29	—
1982	29.2	25	—
1983	27.1	33	42
1984	32.9	35	—
1985	—	28	55
1986	29.5	32	53
1987	34.2	30	52
1988	34.5	32	56
1989	34.4	15	—
1990	35.0	32	—
1991	36.7	23	—
1991	—	30	—

Note: "—" indicates survey not conducted that year. Questions: (General Social Survey, The Harris Poll) "As far as people running the U.S. Supreme Court are concerned, would you say you have a great deal of confidence, only some confidence, or hardly any confidence?" (The Gallup Poll) 1963-1973, "In general, what kind of rating would you give the Supreme Court?" After 1975, "Would you tell me how much confidence you have in the Supreme Court: a great deal, quite a lot, some, or very little?"

Sources: General Social Survey, National Opinion Research Center, University of Chicago, various years; The Harris Poll, March 22, 1992, 2; *The Gallup Poll* 3 (1935-1971), 1836, 2147, 2200, 1 (1972-1977), 140, 528, (1980), 245, (1983), 174, (1986), 275, and (1987), 141.

Table 8-26   Public Reaction to Franklin D. Roosevelt's Plan to Enlarge the Supreme Court

Interview dates (1937)	Favor plan	Oppose plan	Don't know
February 10-15	38.4%	44.8%	17%
February 17-22	44.1	45.9	10
February 24-March 1	42.3	45.1	12
March 3- March 8	41.9	49.1	9
March 12-March 17	45.9	44.1	10
March 17-March 22	45.4	43.6	11
March 24-March 29	44.2	40.8	15
April 1-April 6	43.7	42.1	14
April 7-April 12	44.1	45.9	10
April 14-April 19	40.9	46.1	13
April 21-April 26	39.9	45.1	15
April 28-May 1	38.7	47.3	14
May 5-May 10	36.5	46.5	17
May 12-May 17	37.4	45.7	17
May 19-May 24	30.7	44.3	25
May 26-May 31	30.8	46.2	23
June 3-June 8	34.9	48.2	17
June 9-June 14	37.4	49.6	13

Note: On February 5, 1937, President Franklin D. Roosevelt announced a plan to reorganize the federal court system. Among his proposals was the creation of one new seat on the Supreme Court for every justice who had attained the age of 70 but remained in active service. At the time of his proposal, six sitting justices were over 70.

Questions: February 10-April 12, "Are you in favor of President Roosevelt's proposal regarding the Supreme Court?" April 14-June 14, "Should Congress pass the President's Supreme Court plan?"

Source: American Institute of Public Opinion (Gallup), 1937 Studies: #68-86.

Table 8-27 Members of State, District, and Territorial Bars Favoring Franklin D. Roosevelt's Plan to Enlarge the Supreme Court (1937)

State	Percentage	Total number of respondents
Alabama	27.0	596
Arizona	23.4	274
Arkansas	35.1	501
California	21.1	4,585
Colorado	15.2	794
Connecticut	16.6	757
Delaware	18.3	115
District of Columbia	19.2	1,298
Florida	31.1	1,007
Georgia	31.1	809
Idaho	20.3	256
Illinois	18.3	6,457
Indiana	17.2	1,861
Iowa	11.5	1,430
Kansas	13.7	931
Kentucky	22.9	955
Louisiana	22.6	702
Maine	10.9	384
Maryland	18.1	1,084
Massachusetts	12.0	2,515
Michigan	18.1	2,281
Minnesota	16.5	1,606
Mississippi	41.2	461
Missouri	19.3	2,529
Montana	21.1	322
Nebraska	15.0	1,130
Nevada	23.1	134
New Hampshire	10.5	191
New Jersey	26.3	2,149
New Mexico	15.5	148
New York	22.9	10,788
North Carolina	32.1	842
North Dakota	17.3	294
Ohio	16.9	4,375
Oklahoma	27.2	1,465
Oregon	14.4	785
Pennsylvania	19.1	3,932
Rhode Island	10.6	322
South Carolina	31.2	343
South Dakota	14.5	413
Tennessee	26.5	861
Texas	25.7	2,736
Utah	14.1	327
Vermont	7.6	184
Virginia	23.4	1,085
Washington	16.3	1,261

Table 8-27   *(Continued)*

State	Percentage	Total number of respondents
West Virginia	16.5	672
Wisconsin	21.6	1,391
Wyoming	15.4	130
Territorial	26.3	19
Total	20.3	70,487

Note: On February 5, 1937, President Franklin D. Roosevelt announced a plan to reorganize the Federal court system. Among his proposals was the creation of one new seat on the Supreme Court for every justice who had attained the age of 70 but remained in active service. At the time of his proposal, six sitting justices were over 70.

Source: U.S. Senate, Committee on the Judiciary, *Hearings on a Bill to Reorganize the Judicial Branch of Government, April 5 to 15, 1937,* 76th Cong., 1st sess. 1937 (Supplement to hearing of April 15, 1937).

Table 8-28   Respondents Supporting or Opposing Nominees for the Supreme Court

Nominee	Date of survey	Favor	Oppose	Not sure
Black	September 1937[a]	56	44	0
Carswell	April 1970[b]	32	34	34
O'Connor	July 1981[a]	86	8	6
O'Connor	July 1981[b]	79	14	7
Rehnquist	August 1986[b, c]	30	58	12
Bork	August 1987[a]	31	25	44
Bork	September 1987[d]	14	13	73
Bork	September 1987[d]	21	27	52
Bork	October 1987[b, c]	29	57	14
Thomas	July 1991[a]	52	17	31
Thomas	July 1991[b]	59	27	14
Thomas	August 1991[a]	56	23	21
Thomas	August 1991[b]	59	32	9
Thomas	September 1991[a]	54	25	21
Thomas	September 1991[b]	53	39	8
Thomas	October 9, 1991[d]	24	11	65
Thomas	October 9-13, 1991[b, c]	58	38	4
Thomas	October 10-13, 1991[a, c]	53	30	17
Thomas	October 13, 1991[d]	45	20	35
Thomas	October 14, 1991[d]	57	19	24
Thomas	October 14, 1991[a, c]	58	30	12

[a] The Gallup Poll
[b] The Harris Survey
[c] Respondents were informed of charges against nominee prior to being asked question.
[d] *New York Times* Poll

Sources: The Harris Survey Yearbook of Public Opinion (1971), 21; The Harris Survey, July 20, 1981, 3, August 3, 1986, 3, September 28, 1987, 2, and October 15, 1991, 4; *The Gallup Poll* 1 (1935-1971), 71, (1987), 221, (July 1991), 18, (August 1991), 53, (September 1991), 45, and (October 1991), 26; *New York Times* press release.

Table 8-29   Respondents Able to Name 1989
Supreme Court Justices

Justice	Percentage
O'Connor	23
Rehnquist	9
Kennedy	7
Scalia	6
Marshall	5
Blackmun	4
Brennan	3
White	3
Stevens	1

Note: 71 percent of respondents could not name any justice;
only two of the 1,005 respondents correctly named all nine.

Source: Washington Post National Weekly Edition, June 26-July 2,
1989, p. 37.

Table 8-30   Respondents Able to Name the Judge
of the Television Show "The People's
Court"

Justice	Percentage
Wapner	54
Other	1
Don't know	42

Source: Washington Post National Weekly Edition, June 26-July 2,
1989, p. 37.

9

The Impact of the Supreme Court

Once the U.S. Supreme Court hands down a decision, does that ruling have any legal, political, or social impact? Answers provided by scholars range from the definite "no" to the absolute "yes." Most analysts, however, are circumspect, suggesting that the impact of a Court decision depends on the way various "populations" (for example, judges, lawyers, politicians, citizens) respond to it.[1]

Addressing the question of the Court's impact is beyond the scope of this book.[2] What we do provide, however, are data pertaining to specific Supreme Court rulings in the areas of abortion, capital punishment, school desegregation, voting rights, campaign contributions, and reapportionment. This information will help analysts and students understand better the Court and will provide a base from which to conduct further scholarly endeavors. We wish to make clear from the outset, though, that we do not assume causal links between specific Court cases and the data presented. Simply because we present data on voter registration rates, for example, does not necessarily mean that the Court's rulings have had any impact on those figures. This said, we may now consider the tables appearing in this chapter and the Court cases associated with them.

Tables 9-1 and 9-2 present data on legal abortions carried out in the United States, providing information on the number of abortions and on the characteristics of women who have had the procedure. The Supreme Court's involvement in the issue of abortion began in earnest with *Roe v. Wade* (1973).[3] In this landmark decision, the Court found that the right to privacy encompasses the decision whether or not to bear a child, and it set out a "trimester" scheme, which legalized the abortion procedure prior to viability. As evident in Table 9-1, in absolute terms the number of legal abortions skyrocketed from 18,000 in 1968 to 1,590,000 in 1988. Percentagewise, though, the biggest growth period occurred just prior to the *Roe* decision. This has led some scholars to conclude that the Court's 1973 decision did not have much impact on exercise of the abortion right. Others argue that these numbers would have remained flat had the Court not acted. In either case, it will be interesting to see how recent events affect a woman's right to choose, in particular the Court's alteration of *Roe* in *Planned Parenthood of Southeastern Pennsylvania v. Casey* (1992),[4] in which the Court articulated an undue burden standard applying to laws regulating abortions performed during all gestational periods.

Table 9-3 presents data on another highly charged issue: capital punishment. Prior to the 1970s, the Supreme Court had never issued an explicit ruling on the constitutionality of capital punishment.[5] Accordingly, states were free to impose sentences of death. The data displayed in Table 9-3 indicate that, at least through the 1950s, many states did in fact use execution as a form of criminal punishment. By the 1960s and 1970s, however, the pace of executions had slowed considerably. Although a number of reasons exist for this slowdown, two in particular are important. The first is that in the mid 1960s a civil rights litigating group, the NAACP Legal Defense and Educational Fund, developed a legal strategy to stop all executions in the United States. Now referred to as "moratorium," this strategy proved quite effective. In 1968, for the first time in U.S. history, no legalized executions occurred.[6] The second explanation derives from a Supreme Court case, *Furman v. Georgia* (1972),[7] in which five of the justices held that the procedures used by the states to impose capital punishment violated the Constitution.[8]

Largely as a result of the moratorium strategy and *Furman*, no executions took place in the United States between 1968 and 1976. This is not to say that states had eradicated capital punishment or that judges and juries were not imposing sentences of death. In fact, immediately after the *Furman* decision, many states rewrote their laws to conform to the Court's ruling. In *Gregg v. Georgia* (1976),[9] the Court held that these new laws were constitutional so long as they met certain procedural standards and did not impose mandatory death sentences. Accordingly, states are once again free to invoke the death penalty and, in fact, if they continue at their current pace, over nine hundred individuals will be executed during the 1990s.

Tables 9-4, 9-5, and 9-6 present data pertaining to yet another controversial issue: school desegregation. Beginning in the late 1930s, the Supreme Court chipped away at the "separate but equal" doctrine it had articulated in *Plessy v. Ferguson* (1896).[10] But it was not until 1954, in the landmark case of *Brown v. Board of Education*,[11] that it fully overturned *Plessy*. A year later, the Court ordered that school desegregation take place "with all deliberate speed" and gave federal district courts the requisite oversight responsibilities. In *Swann v. Charlotte-*

Mecklenburg County Board of Education (1971),[12] the justices reaffirmed the broad powers of district courts in enforcing *Brown*, allowing them to use "a wide arsenal of student placement strategies, including rearrangement of attendance zones and the politically unpopular imposition of forced busing." [13]

Three trends visible in the tables are particularly worth noting. The first is simply that change has occurred. In the 1950s, schools in the South were almost completely segregated (see Table 9-4); thirty years later, 43 percent of the black student population attended schools with fewer than half minority students and 65 percent of the white student population attended schools that were less than 90 percent white (see Table 9-6). The second trend is that, while change has occurred, it has been slow to arrive. As important as *Brown v. Board of Education* was, it (and its progeny of the 1960s) did not lead to overnight desegregation of public schools. As the data reveal, it was not until the late 1960s and into the 1970s that the promise of *Brown* seemed at least somewhat fulfilled. Finally, and relatedly, many school systems today remain segregated, though not unconstitutionally so. To be sure, the data support a trend toward desegregation (particularly in the South), yet they also reveal that a large proportion of the white student population continues to attend schools that are over 90 percent white.

The remaining tables present data on voting and the electoral process. Table 9-7 contains information on white versus minority voter registration rates in eleven southern states. The Court's long involvement in the area of race discrimination in the electoral process stems from the attempts of southern states to circumvent the Fifteenth Amendment by keeping blacks out of the voting booth. As Chief Justice Earl Warren wrote in *South Carolina v. Katzenbach* (1966),

> beginning in 1890, the States of Alabama, Georgia, Louisiana, Mississippi, North Carolina, South Carolina, and Virginia enacted tests still in use which were specifically designed to prevent Negroes from voting. Typically they made the ability to read and write a registration qualification and also required completion of a registration form. These laws were based on the fact that as of 1890 in each of the named States, more than two-thirds of the adult Negroes were illiterate while less than one-quarter of the adult whites were unable to read or write. At the same time, alternate tests were prescribed in all of the named States to assure that white illiterates would not be deprived of the franchise. These included grandfather clauses, property qualifications, "good character" tests, and the requirement that registrants "understand" or "interpret" certain matter.[14]

Despite the efforts of the Supreme Court, Congress, and the Justice Department to remove these and other barriers, the South continued to stymie black voting. Table 9-7 shows that as late as 1960 registration rates for nonwhites hovered around 29 percent compared with 61 percent for whites. "Figures such as these convinced Congress ... that a more aggressive policy was required. The result was the Voting Rights Act of 1965, the most comprehensive statute ever enacted by Congress to enforce the guarantees of the Fifteenth Amendment."[15] Led by South Carolina, five southern states immediately challenged the Act as exceeding the constitutional power of the federal government. In *South Carolina v. Katzenbach* (1965),[16] however, the Supreme Court upheld the Act, writing that "[h]opefully, millions of non-white Americans will now be able to participate for the first time on an equal basis in the government under which they live." Based on the data presented in Table 9-7, at the very least, minority and white registration in the South are now roughly comparable.

Tables 9-8 and 9-9 contain information on another dimension of electoral activity, that involving political action committees (PACs). PACs are nonpolitical party committees set up in accordance with federal law to collect money and disburse it to preferred candidates. As the tables reveal, there were only about 700 PACs prior to 1976, and they spent relatively little: about $53 million compared with $358 million in 1990. What happened? What explains the astounding growth of PACs? Part of the answer lies with a 1976 Supreme Court decision, *Buckley v. Valeo*.[17] There the Court reviewed several 1974 amendments to the Federal Election Campaign Act of 1971 designed to reform political campaigns. The resulting decision was mixed: the justices struck down provisions mandating ceilings on independent political expenditures but upheld limits on direct campaign contributions. PACs were a natural, albeit perhaps unintended, outgrowth of this ruling.[18] To circumvent the individual spending limits, individuals and organizations created these PACs. Some were established by existing interest groups (connected PACs); others (nonconnected PACs) were formed solely to acquire and then give money to candidates and campaigns. In any case, they are now a major, institutionalized force operating in the electoral process.

Finally, Table 9-10 provides data on a third dimension of voting: reapportionment. Prior to 1963, states were free to devise (or "apportion") legislative districts as they saw fit. Some states, however, never bothered to reapportion, even after massive population shifts that saw large numbers emigrate from rural areas into the cities. In *Colegrove v. Green* (1946),[19] the Supreme Court dismissed a challenge to Illinois' congressional districts (which the legislature had failed to reapportion since 1901), ruling that the case presented a political rather than legal question. In the early 1960s, the justices had a change of heart. In a series of cases beginning with *Baker v. Carr* (1962),[20] the Court mandated that states reapportion their districts on the basis of the one person, one vote principle. The results of those rulings are depicted in Table 9-10.

Notes

1. See, for example, Charles A. Johnson and Bradley C. Canon, *Judicial Policies: Implementation and Impact*. (Washington, D.C.: CQ Press, 1984).
2. See Selected Readings list at the end of the book for some leading works on the Court's impact. Also, given the limited focus of this book, we do not provide data on lower federal and state court responses to Supreme Court rulings (that is, the "legal" impact of decisions). For readers interested in this literature, we highly recommend the following articles: Charles A. Johnson, "Lower Court Reactions to Supreme Court Decisions: A Quantitative Examination," *American Journal of Political Science* 23 (1979): 792-804; Charles A. Johnson, "Law, Politics, and Judicial Decision Making: Lower Federal Court Uses of Supreme Court Decisions," *Law and Society Review* 21 (1987): 325-340; Bradley C. Canon, "Organizational Contumacy in the Transmission of Legal Policies: The *Mapp, Escobedo, Miranda, and Gault* Cases," *Villanova Law Review* 20 (1974): 50-79; Donald Songer, "Alternative Approaches to the Study of Judicial Impact: *Miranda* in Five State Courts," *American Politics Quarterly* 16 (1988): 425-444.
3. 410 U.S. 113. Prior to 1973, the Court decided several cases involving reproductive issues, with *Griswold v. Connecticut*, 381 U.S. 479 (1965) among the most significant. It also decided at least one abortion-related case prior to *Roe, United States v. Vuitch*, 402 U.S. 62 (1971).
4. 120 L. Ed. 2d 674.
5. Of course, it had decided cases in which defendants had been sentenced to death, but the primary issue in those cases was not the constitutionality of capital punishment. In addition, prior to 1972 the Court decided cases examining procedures surrounding the imposition of death sentences.
6. For more information on moratorium, see Lee Epstein and Joseph Kobylka, *The Supreme Court and Legal Change* (Chapel Hill: University of North Carolina Press, 1992), and Michael Meltsner, *Cruel and Unusual* (New York: Random House, 1973).
7. 408 U.S. 238.
8. The Court issued a per curiam opinion. Each justice wrote separately.
9. 428 U.S. 153.
10. 163 U.S. 537.
11. 347 U.S. 483.
12. 402 U.S. 1.
13. Lee Epstein and Thomas G. Walker, *Constitutional Law for a Changing America—Rights, Liberties, and Justice* (Washington, D.C.: CQ Press, 1992), 549.
14. 383 U.S. 301, at 310-311.
15. Epstein and Walker, *Constitutional Law for a Changing America*, 593-594.
16. 383 U.S. 301.
17. 424 U.S. 1.
18. A 1975 Federal Election Commission (FEC) ruling also paved the way for the creation of corporate PACs. More specifically, in 1975 the Sun Oil Company sought the FEC's permission to use its funds to create a PAC, which would solicit contributions from employees and stockholders. The FEC granted the company's request, with the proviso that contributions be truly voluntary.
19. 328 U.S. 459.
20. 369 U.S. 186.

Table 9-1 Legal Abortions, 1966-1989

Year	Number	Change from previous year	Percent change from previous year
1966	8,000		
1967	9,000	+1,000	+13
1968	18,000	+9,000	+100
1969	22,700	+4,700	+26
1970	193,500	+170,800	+752
1971	485,800	+292,300	+151
1972	586,800	+101,000	+21
1973	744,600	+157,800	+27
1974	898,600	+154,000	+21
1975	1,034,200	+135,600	+15
1976	1,179,300	+145,100	+14
1977	1,316,700	+137,400	+12
1978	1,409,600	+92,900	+7
1979	1,497,700	+88,100	+6
1980	1,553,900	+56,200	+4
1981	1,577,300	+23,400	+2
1982	1,573,900	−3,400	−0.2
1983	1,575,000	+1,100	−0.07
1984	1,577,200	+2,200	+0.1
1985	1,588,600	+11,400	+0.7
1986	1,574,000	−14,600	−0.92
1987	1,559,100	−14,900	−0.95
1988	1,590,800	+31,700	+2
1989	1,396,658 (incomplete)		

Sources: 1966-1973: Gerald N. Rosenberg, *The Hollow Hope* (Chicago: University of Chicago Press, 1991), 180; 1973-1988: Harold W. Stanley and Richard G. Niemi, *Vital Statistics on American Politics*, 3d ed. (Washington, D.C.: CQ Press, 1992), 34; 1989: Planned Parenthood Federation.

Table 9-2 Legal Abortions by Selected Characteristics, Selected Years

Characteristic	Number (1,000)				Abortion ratio[a]			
	1973	1980	1985	1987	1973	1980	1985	1987
Age								
Under 15	12	15	17	16	476	607	624	607
15-19	232	445	399	391	280	451	462	456
20-24	241	549	548	516	181	310	328	322
25-29	130	304	336	333	128	213	219	214
30-34	73	153	181	189	165	213	203	198
35-39	41	67	87	92	246	317	280	268
40 and over	17	21	21	22	334	461	409	376
Race								
White	549	1,094	1,076	1,017	178	274	265	252
Nonwhite	196	460	513	542	252	392	397	393
Marital status								
Married	216	320	281	275	74	98	88	87
Unmarried	528	1,234	1,307	1,284	564	649	605	570
Number of prior live births								
None	411	900	872	821	242	365	358	341
1	115	305	349	360	108	208	219	222
2	104	216	240	248	190	283	288	285
3	61	83	85	88	228	288	281	276
4 or more	55	51	43	43	196	251	230	224
Number of prior induced abortions								
None	NA	1,043	944	901	NA	NA	NA	NA
1	NA	373	416	416	NA	NA	NA	NA
2 or more	NA	138	228	242	NA	NA	NA	NA
Weeks of gestation								
Less than 9	284	800	818	792[b]	NA	NA	NA	NA
9-10	222	417	429	417[b]	NA	NA	NA	NA
11-12	131	202	199	194[b]	NA	NA	NA	NA
13 or more	108	136	142	156[b]	NA	NA	NA	NA

Note: "NA" indicates not available.

[a] Number of abortions per 1,000 abortions and live births. Live births are those which occurred from July of the year shown through June 30 of the following year.

[b] Figures not exactly comparable to those for earlier years because of a change in the method of calculation.

Source: U.S. Bureau of the Census, *Statistical Abstract of the United States: 1991*, 111th ed. (Washington, D.C.: Government Printing Office, 1991), 71.

Table 9-3 The Death Penalty: Numbers Executed (1930-1992) and Death Row Populations

State or authority	Number executed							Death row population[b]
	1930s	1940s	1950s	1960s	1970s	1980s	1990-1992[a]	
Alabama	60	50	20	5	0	7	2	113
Alaska	0	0	0[c]	—	—	—	—	—
Arizona	17	9	8	4	0	0	1	102
Arkansas	53	8	18	9	0	0	4	33
California	108	80	74	30	0	0	1	331
Colorado	25	13	3	6	0	0	0	3
Connecticut	5	10	5	1	0	0	0	4
Delaware	8	4	0[d]	0[d]	0	0	1	6
District of Columbia	20	NA	4	0	0[e]	—	—	—
Florida	44	65	49	12	1	20	6	319
Georgia	137	130	85	14	0	14	0	110
Hawaii	0	0	0[f]	—	—	—	—	—
Idaho	0	NA	3	0	0	0	0	23
Illinois	61	18	9	2	0	0	1	146
Indiana	31	7	2	1	0	2	0	55
Iowa	8	7	1	2[g]	—	—	—	—
Kansas	0[h]	5	5	5	0[i]	—	—	—
Kentucky	52	34	16	1	0	0	0	26
Louisiana	58	47	27	1	0	18	1	39
Maine	—	—	—	—	—	—	—	—
Maryland	16	45	6	1	0	0	0	15
Massachusetts	18	9	0	0[k]	0	0[j]	—	—
Michigan	0	0	0	0	—	—	—	—
Minnesota	—	—	—	—	—	—	—	—
Mississippi	48	60	36	10	0	4	0	53
Missouri	36	15	7	4	0	1	5	82
Montana	5	1	0	0	0	0	0	8

619

Nebraska	0	2	2	0	0	0	0	12
Nevada	8	0	9	2	1	3	1	61
New Hampshire	1	0	0	0	0	0	0	0
New Jersey	40	NA	17	3	0	0	0	7
New Mexico	2	NA	3	1	0[m]	0	0	1
New York	153	114	52	10[l]	0	—	—	—
North Carolina	131	12	19	1	0	3	1	110
North Dakota	—	—	—	—	—	—	—	—
Ohio	82	1	32	7	0	0	0	118
Oklahoma	34	NA	7	6	0	0	3	120
Oregon	2	12	4	1[n]	0[o]	0	0	15
Pennsylvania	82	6	31	3	0	0	0	143
Rhode Island	—	—	—	—	—	—	—	—
South Carolina	67	61	26	8	0	2	1	45
South Dakota	0[p]	1	0	0	0	0	0	0
Tennessee	47	37	8	1	0	0	0	104
Texas	120	NA	74	29	0	33	14	356
Utah	2	NA	6	1	1	2	1	12
Vermont	1	1	2	0[q]	—	—	—	—
Virginia	28	35	23	6	0	8	6	51
Washington	23	NA	6	2	0	0	0	9
West Virginia	20	11	9	[r]	—	—	—	—
Wisconsin	—	—	—	—	—	—	—	—
Wyoming	4	2	0	1	0	0	1	0
U.S. government	10	13	9	1	0	0	0	1
U.S. military[s]	NA	NA	NA	NA	NA	NA	0	5
Total[t]	1,667	925	717	191	3	117	50	2,638[u]

Note: "—" indicates death penalty abolished prior to 1930. "NA" indicates data not available.

(Notes continue)

Table 9-3 (Continued)

a Through October 1992.

b As of summer 1992.

c Death penalty abolished in 1957.

d Death penalty abolished in 1958 but restored in 1961.

e Death penalty abolished in 1972.

f Death penalty abolished in 1957.

g Death penalty abolished in 1872, restored in 1876, and abolished again in 1965.

h Death penalty restored in 1935 after having been abolished in 1907.

i Death penalty abolished in 1972.

j Death penalty declared unconstitutional in 1980.

k Death penalty abolished in 1846 but retained for treason until 1963.

l Death penalty abolished in 1966 but retained for some civil offenses.

m Death penalty restored in 1974, then declared unconstitutional in 1977.

n Death penalty abolished in 1964.

o Death penalty restored in 1970s.

p Death penalty restored in 1939 after having been abolished in 1915.

q Death penalty abolished in 1965.

r Death penalty abolished in 1965 but retained for some civil offenses.

s Since 1930, 160 executions have been carried out under military authority. Breakdown by decade is not available.

t The national total counts multiple death-sentence inmates once. However, they are included in the state total for each state where they are sentenced to death.

u Number of inmates; some are multiply-sentenced and are listed in each state.

Sources: 1930-1991: Harold W. Stanley and Richard G. Niemi, *Vital Statistics on American Politics*, 3d ed. (Washington, D.C.: CQ Press, 1992), 30-32, and Franklin E. Zimring and Gordon Hawkins, *Capital Punishment and the American Agenda* (New York: Cambridge University Press, 1986), 31, 43. 1992: NAACP Legal Defense and Educational Fund.

Table 9-4 Black Children in Elementary and Secondary Schools with White Children: Southern and Border States, 1954-1973

Year	Southern states[a]		Border states[b]	
	Percentage[c]	Number	Percentage[c]	Number
1954-1955	0.001	23	NA	NA
1955-1956	0.12	2,782	NA	NA
1956-1957	0.14	3,514	39.6	106,878
1957-1958	0.15	3,829	41.4	127,677
1958-1959	0.13	3,456	44.4	142,352
1959-1960	0.16	4,216	45.4	191,114
1960-1961	0.16	4,308	49.0	212,895
1961-1962	0.24	6,725	52.5	240,226
1962-1963	0.45	12,868	51.8	251,797
1963-1964	1.20	34,105	54.8	281,731
1964-1965	2.30	66,135	58.3	313,919
1965-1966	6.10	184,308	68.9	384,992
1966-1967	16.90	489,900	71.4	456,258
1968-1969	32.00	942,600	74.7	475,000
1970-1971	85.90	2,707,000	76.8	512,000
1972-1973	91.30	2,886,300	77.3	524,800

Note: "NA" indicates not available.

[a] Includes Alabama, Arkansas, Florida, Georgia, Louisiana, Mississippi, North Carolina, South Carolina, Tennessee, Texas, and Virginia.

[b] Includes Delaware, the District of Columbia, Kentucky, Maryland, Missouri, Oklahoma, and West Virginia.

[c] Percentage of black students out of all black schoolchildren attending school with white students.

Source: Gerald N. Rosenberg, *The Hollow Hope* (Chicago: University of Chicago Press, 1991), 50.

Table 9-5   Black Children in Elementary and Secondary Schools with White Children by Southern or Border State, 1960 and 1970

	1960-61		1970-71	
Region/state	Percentage[a]	Number	Percentage[a]	Number
South				
Alabama	0.000	0	80.0	216,000
Arkansas	0.100	113	91.4	97,000
Florida	0.010	28	90.1	299,500
Georgia	0.000	0	83.1	303,700
Louisiana	0.0004	1	75.9	258,800
Mississippi	0.000	0	89.1	242,600
North Carolina	0.030	82	93.1	327,700
South Carolina	0.000	0	92.9	242,600
Tennessee	0.250	376	74.1	140,500
Texas	1.200	3,500	85.9	346,100
Virginia	0.100	208	89.6	232,500
Border				
Delaware	45.0	6,738	100.0	27,000
District of Columbia	84.1	81,392	66.4	91,400
Kentucky	47.7	20,000 (est.)	96.6	64,000
Maryland	33.6	45,943	74.2	163,500
Missouri	41.7	35,000 (est.)	69.7	100,900
Oklahoma	24.0	9,822	89.3	47,000
West Virginia	66.6	14,000 (est.)	98.9	18,800

[a] Percentage of black students out of all black schoolchildren attending school with white students.

Source: Gerald N. Rosenberg, *The Hollow Hope* (Chicago: University of Chicago Press, 1991), 345-347.

Table 9-6   School Desegregation by Region, 1968-1986

Region/year	Percentage of black student population in school with more than half minority students	Percentage of hispanic student population in school with more than half minority students	Percentage of white student population in school 90-100 percent white
South [a]			
1968	80.9	69.6	70.6
1972	55.3	69.9	38.0
1976	54.9	70.9	34.6
1980	57.1	76.0	35.0
1984	56.9	75.4	—
1986	58.0	75.2	—
Border [b]			
1968	71.6	—	80.0
1972	67.2	—	75.9
1976	60.1	—	64.8
1980	59.2	—	64.1
1984	62.5	—	—
1986	59.3	29.9	—
Northeast [c]			
1968	66.8	74.8	83.0
1972	69.9	74.4	82.9
1976	72.5	74.9	81.4
1980	79.9	76.3	80.2
1984	73.1	77.5	—
1986	72.8	78.2	—
Midwest [d]			
1968	77.3	31.8	89.4
1972	75.3	34.4	87.5
1976	70.3	39.3	84.7
1980	69.5	46.6	81.2
1984	70.7	53.9	—
1986	69.8	54.3	—
West [e]			
1968	72.2	42.4	63.0
1972	68.1	44.7	56.0
1976	67.4	52.7	49.9
1980	66.8	63.5	43.3
1984	66.9	68.4	—
1986	68.2	69.9	—

(Table continues)

Table 9-6   *(Continued)*

Region/year	Percentage of black student population in school with more than half minority students	Percentage of hispanic student population in school with more than half minority students	Percentage of white student population in school 90-100 percent white
Total [f]			
1968	76.6	54.8	78.4
1972	63.6	56.6	68.9
1976	62.4	60.8	64.9
1980	62.9	68.1	61.2
1984	63.5	70.6	—
1986	63.3	71.5	—

Note: "—" indicates data not available.

[a] Includes Alabama, Arkansas, Florida, Georgia, Louisiana, Mississippi, North Carolina, South Carolina, Tennessee, Texas, and Virginia.

[b] Includes Delaware, District of Columbia, Kentucky, Maryland, Missouri, Oklahoma, and West Virginia.

[c] Includes Connecticut, Maine, Massachusetts, New Hampshire, New Jersey, New York, Pennsylvania, Rhode Island, and Vermont.

[d] Includes Illinois, Indiana, Iowa, Kansas, Michigan, Minnesota, Nebraska, North Dakota, Ohio, South Dakota, and Wisconsin.

[e] Includes Arizona, California, Colorado, Idaho, Montana, Nevada, New Mexico, Oregon, Utah, Washington, and Wyoming.

[f] Excludes Alaska and Hawaii.

Source: Harold W. Stanley and Richard G. Niemi, *Vital Statistics on American Politics,* 3d ed. (Washington, D.C.: CQ Press, 1992), 389-390.

Table 9-7   Voter Registration Rates in Eleven Southern States by Race, Selected Years

Year/state	Whites		Nonwhites	
	Number registered	Percentage of white voting age population	Number registered	Percentage of nonwhite voting age population
1960				
Alabama	860,000	63.6	66,000	13.7
Arkansas	518,000	60.9	73,000	38.0
Florida	1,819,000	69.3	183,000	39.4
Georgia	1,020,000	56.8	180,000	29.3
Louisiana	993,000	76.9	159,000	31.1
Mississippi	478,000	63.9	22,000	5.2
North Carolina	1,861,000	92.1	210,000	39.1
South Carolina	481,000	57.1	58,000	13.7
Tennessee	1,300,000	73.0	185,000	59.1
Texas	2,079,000	42.5	227,000	35.5
Virginia	867,000	46.1	100,000	23.1
Total	12,276,000	61.1	1,463,000	29.1
1970				
Alabama	1,311,000	85.0	315,000	66.0
Arkansas	728,000	74.1	153,000	82.3
Florida	2,495,000	65.5	302,000	55.3
Georgia	1,615,000	71.7	395,000	57.2
Louisiana	1,143,000	77.0	319,000	57.4
Mississippi	690,000	82.1	286,000	71.0
North Carolina	1,640,000	68.1	305,000	51.3
South Carolina	668,000	62.3	221,000	56.1
Tennessee	1,600,000	78.5	242,000	71.6
Texas	3,599,000	62.0	550,000	72.6
Virginia	1,496,000	64.5	269,000	57.0
Total	16,985,000	69.2	3,357,000	62.0
1980				
Alabama	1,700,000	81.4	350,000	55.8
Arkansas	1,056,000	76.9	130,000	57.2
Florida	4,331,000	67.7	489,000	58.3
Georgia	1,800,000	63.0	450,000	48.6
Louisiana	1,550,000	74.8	465,000	60.7
Mississippi	1,152,000	98.9	330,000	62.3
North Carolina	2,314,000	70.1	440,000	51.3
South Carolina	916,000	58.5	320,000	53.7
Tennessee	2,200,000	78.5	300,000	64.0
Texas	6,020,000	75.1	620,000	56.0
Virginia	1,942,000	62.2	360,000	53.2
Total	24,981,000	71.9	4,254,000	55.8

(Table continues)

Table 9-7 *(Continued)*

Year/state	Whites		Nonwhites	
	Number registered	Percentage of white voting age population	Number registered	Percentage of nonwhite voting age population
1986[a]				
Alabama	1,807,000	77.5	509,000	68.9
Arkansas	1,030,000	67.2	157,000	57.9
Florida	4,677,000	66.9	576,000	58.2
Georgia	1,990,000	62.3	576,000	52.8
Louisiana	1,580,000	67.8	551,000	60.6
Mississippi	1,193,000	91.6	450,000	70.8
North Carolina	2,468,000	67.4	585,000	58.4
South Carolina	932,000	53.4	371,000	52.5
Tennessee	2,186,000	70.0	358,000	65.3
Texas	7,068,000	79.0	875,000	68.0
Virginia	2,097,000	60.3	442,000	56.2
Total	27,028,000	69.9	5,450,000	60.8

[a] As of August 1986.

Source: U.S. Bureau of the Census, *Statistical Abstract of the United States* (Washington, D.C.: Government Printing Office, 1980, 1989, 1990). Original data source is Voter Educational Project, Atlanta, Georgia.

Table 9-8 Political Action Committees (PACs), 1974-1992

Date	Connected PACs[a]					Nonconnected PACs[b]	Total
	Corporate	Labor	Trade/health/membership	Cooperative	Corporation without stock		
December 1974	89	201	318[c]	c	c	c	608
November 1975	139	226	357[c]	c	c	c	722
December 1976	433	224	489[c]	c	c	c	1,146
December 1977	550	234	438	8	20	110	1,360
December 1978	785	217	453	12	24	162	1,653
December 1979	950	240	514	12	32	247	1,995
December 1980	1,206	297	576	42	56	374	2,551
December 1981	1,329	318	614	41	68	531	2,901
December 1982	1,469	380	649	47	103	723	3,371
December 1983	1,538	378	643	51	122	793	3,525
December 1984	1,682	394	698	52	130	1,053	4,009
December 1985	1,710	388	695	54	142	1,003	3,992
December 1986	1,744	384	745	56	151	1,077	4,157
December 1987	1,775	364	865	59	145	957	4,165
December 1988	1,816	354	786	59	138	1,115	4,268
December 1989	1,796	349	777	59	137	1,060	4,178
December 1990	1,795	346	774	59	136	1,062	4,172
December 1991	1,738	338	742	57	136	1,083	4,094
July 1992	1,731	344	759	56	144	1,091	4,125

[a] Operate in association with sponsoring organization that often covers operating and fund-raising costs.
[b] Operates independently.
[c] Trade/membership/health category includes all PACs except corporate and labor.

Sources: 1974-1990: Harold W. Stanley and Richard G. Niemi, *Vital Statistics on American Politics*, 3d ed. (Washington, D.C.: CQ Press, 1992), 175; 1991-1992: Federal Election Commission.

Table 9-9   Receipts, Expenditures, and Contributions of PACs, 1975-1992

Election cycle	Receipts (millions)	Expenditures (millions)	Contributions to congressional candidates (millions)	Percentage contributed to congressional candidates
1975-1976	$54.0	$52.9	$22.6	42
1977-1978	80.0	77.4	34.1	43
1979-1980	137.7	131.2	55.2	40
1981-1982	199.5	190.2	83.6	42
1983-1984	288.7	266.8	105.3	36
1985-1986	353.4	340.0	132.7	38
1987-1988	384.6	364.2	151.2	39
1989-1990	372.4	358.1	149.8	40
1991-1992 [a]	283.7	247.7	111.4	45

Note: Figures are in current dollars.

[a] Through June 30, 1992.

Sources: 1974-1990: Harold W. Stanley and Richard G. Niemi, *Vital Statistics on American Politics,* 3d ed. (Washington, D.C.: CQ Press, 1992), 178; 1991-1992: Federal Election Commission.

Table 9-10 Legislative Reapportionment Deviations from Equality in Size of Congressional Districts, 1960s and 1980s (percent)

State	1960s [a] Positive	Negative	1980s total [b]
Alabama	21.4	17.2	2.45
Alaska	AL	AL	AL
Arizona	52.9	54.3	0.08
Arkansas	28.8	25.4	0.73
California	424.4	27.0	0.08 [c]
Colorado	49.1	55.4	0.002
Connecticut	63.2	24.5	0.46
Delaware	AL	AL	AL
Florida	60.3	42.5	0.13
Georgia	108.9	31.0	NA
Hawaii	AL	AL	<0.01
Idaho	22.9	22.9	0.04
Illinois	31.6	33.6	0.03
Indiana	64.6	31.4	2.96
Iowa	12.3	10.4	0.05
Kansas	23.9	14.3	0.34
Kentucky	40.8	19.2	1.39
Louisiana	31.6	35.2	0.42 [d]
Maine	4.3	4.3	0.001
Maryland	86.3	37.3	0.35
Massachusetts	11.6	12.3	1.09
Michigan	85.3	71.4	<0.01
Minnesota	13.2	12.0	0.01
Mississsippi	39.9	32.3	NA
Missouri	17.3	12.4	0.18
Montana	18.7	18.7	AL
Nebraska	12.8	14.0	0.23
Nevada	AL	AL	0.60
New Hampshire	9.3	9.3	0.24
New Jersey	44.8	36.9	0.69 [c]
New Mexico	AL	AL	0.87 [d]
New York	15.1	14.4	1.64
North Carolina	18.7	36.9	1.76 [d]
North Dakota	5.4	5.4	AL
Ohio	79.5	41.6	0.68
Oklahoma	42.5	41.3	0.58
Oregon	18.2	40.0	0.15
Pennsylvania	31.9	27.7	0.24
Rhode Island	7.0	7.0	0.02
South Carolina	33.9	31.4	0.28 [c]
South Dakota	46.3	46.3	AL
Tennessee	58.2	43.6	2.40
Texas	118.5	48.5	0.28
Utah	28.6	28.6	0.43

(Table continues)

Table 9-10   *(Continued)*

State	1960s [a]		1980s total [b]
	Positive	Negative	
Vermont	AL	AL	AL
Virginia	36.0	21.1	1.81
Washington	25.2	16.0	0.06
West Virginia	13.4	18.6	0.50
Wisconsin	40.1	34.2	0.14
Wyoming	AL	AL	AL

Note: "AL" indcates at-large district (only one congressional representative); "NA" indicates not available.

[a] Maximum percentage deviation (positive and negative) from the average district population. Data from 1962.
[b] Total deviations from the average (the sum of the largest deviations from above and below the average). Data as of April 1983.
[c] New plan needed.
[d] Subject to court review.

Source: Harold W. Stanley and Richard G. Niemi, *Vital Statistics on American Politics*, 3d ed. (Washington, D.C.: CQ Press, 1992), 40-42.

10

The Supreme Court in the Judicial System

When the Constitutional Convention met in Philadelphia in 1787, the delegates faced difficult decisions with respect to the judiciary. Committed to a separation of powers philosophy, the Convention realized the need for a judiciary to provide a check and balance to the legislative and executive branches. But what kind of judicial system should be created?

The Framers had three alternatives. First, they could allow the already existing state courts to handle legal disputes growing out of federal law. This alternative had the drawback of commingling federal and state functions, as well as failing to complete the necessary structures for a sound separation of powers system. Second, they could abolish the state courts and replace them with a new set of federal courts. This was politically unacceptable. Not only would such a move violate principles of federalism but also it would enrage sitting state court judges who wielded significant political power in their states. Opposition from these judges would jeopardize the ratification process. Finally, the delegates could create a federal court system that would coexist with the state court system. This was politically and philosophically acceptable, but because there was not yet a body of federal law and no federal legal disputes to decide, it was impossible to know precisely what kind of a judicial system would be needed.

The Convention selected the third alternative, but because of the uncertainty surrounding the question of a properly constructed judiciary, the Framers' description of the judicial branch in Article III is very sketchy. The Constitution creates a single Supreme Court, but mentions no other judicial bodies. Instead, it confers upon Congress the authority to create inferior courts as the legislature deems necessary. The Framers' decision to allow the state courts to continue in operation while permitting Congress to develop a federal judiciary resulted in contemporary America's well-developed system of courts that function below the United States Supreme Court (see Figure 10-1). In Chapter 10 we provide data regarding the state judiciaries and the lower federal courts.

The first set of tables (10-1 through 10-17) examines the federal judiciary. Today's lower federal courts fall into three categories. The courts of appeals occupy the rung of the judicial ladder immediately below the Supreme Court. The business of the courts of appeals is to review the decisions of the federal trial courts and various federal administrative agencies when disappointed litigants appeal. Each of the twelve regular courts of appeals has jurisdiction over a particular geographical area known as a circuit (see Figure 10-2). Appeals are normally heard by panels of three appellate judges. The decisions of the courts of appeals are reviewable only by the Supreme Court. The legal interpretations of the courts of appeals, if not reversed by the Supreme Court, are binding on all lower federal and state courts within the particular circuit. As the nation grew westward and the reach of federal law expanded, the size and workload of the courts of appeals increased. Tables 10-1 through 10-9 illustrate the growth of the courts of appeals, from the initial three-circuit court system of 1789 to the present system of twelve. Table 10-1 shows the development of the circuit court system, while Tables 10-2 and 10-3 chart the increase in number of court of appeals judgeships and how they are distributed by circuit, respectively. Next we examine the caseload of the courts of appeals by the growth in cases filed and terminated (Table 10-4) and by general subject categories (Tables 10-5 and 10-6). We also provide information on appellate court appointments (Tables 10-7 and 10-8) and on the important matter of how the Supreme Court has treated appeals from the various circuit courts (Table 10-9).

The district courts constitute the second level of federal tribunals. The United States today is divided into 94 judicial districts (see Figure 10-2). Eighty-nine of these operate within the various states, with each state having between one and four districts, depending upon caseload demands. Additional districts exist for the District of Columbia, Puerto Rico, and three federal territories (Guam, Northern Mariana Islands, and the Virgin Islands). Each of these judicial districts has a district court. The federal district courts function as the primary trial court of general jurisdiction for the federal system. Most federal court cases begin at this level. Tables 10-10 through 10-14 provide data on the district courts. Table 10-10 shows the growth of district court judgeships over time, while Table 10-11 illustrates how they are distributed among the various judicial districts. Table 10-12 examines the growth in civil and criminal cases in the district courts over time. A review of presidential appointments to district judgeships appears in Table 10-13. Finally, in Table 10-14, we examine how the decisions of the district courts have been reviewed when appealed to the United States Supreme Court.

The final group of federal courts are those possessing limited jurisdiction. Such courts normally hear cases on specific subject matter, and fall into one of two categories. The first we call Article I, or legislative, courts (Table 10-15). These tribunals have been created by Congress to help the legislature carry out its responsibilities as outlined in Article I of the Constitution. Examples are the United States Tax Court, the United States Court of Military Appeals, and the United States Court of Federal Claims. Because these courts have been created under Article I, the judges sitting on them do not enjoy the same constitutional benefits as judges serving on courts that are part of the regular judiciary. For example, Article I judges do not enjoy life tenure, instead serving designated terms. The second category of special courts contains those tribunals we call Article III, or constitutional, courts (Table 10-16). These courts have been created by Congress under Article III of the Constitution to create courts inferior to the Supreme Court. Judges on these bodies do enjoy life tenure and the other Article III provisions designed to ensure judicial independence. Examples are the United States Court of International Trade and the Court of Appeals for the Federal Circuit. Table 10-17 reveals how decisions appealed from these specialized courts have fared when reviewed by the United States Supreme Court.

The Supreme Court interacts with state judiciaries as well as with the lower federal courts. Consequently, the final set of tables in this chapter examines the state judiciaries. Over the past two centuries, state judiciaries have flourished. This growth has run contrary to the fears of many state advocates at the time of the Constitutional Convention who predicted that if the federal judiciary grew in size and power, the state courts would decline or even disappear. Tables 10-18 and 10-19 summarize the organization and structure of the various state judiciaries, including the number of judges, how they are selected, and the terms they serve. Tables 10-20 and 10-21 provide data on the mandatory and discretionary caseloads of the state appellate courts, and Table 10-22 illustrates the manner in which state appellate judges write and report their opinions. In Tables 10-23 and 10-24, we report the criminal and civil caseloads of the state trial courts. Table 10-25 explains where the major opinions from the various state courts can be found in the West Regional Reporter system, an ongoing compendium of published court opinions that can be found in any law library. Finally, Table 10-26 reviews the United States Supreme Court's record on decisions appealed to the justices from the various state courts.

Figure 10-1 The American Court System

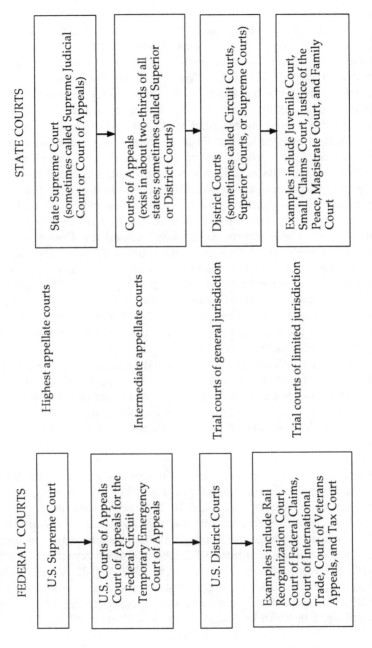

Source: Lee Epstein and Thomas G. Walker, *Constitutional Law for a Changing America* (Washington, D.C.: CQ Press, 1992), 662.

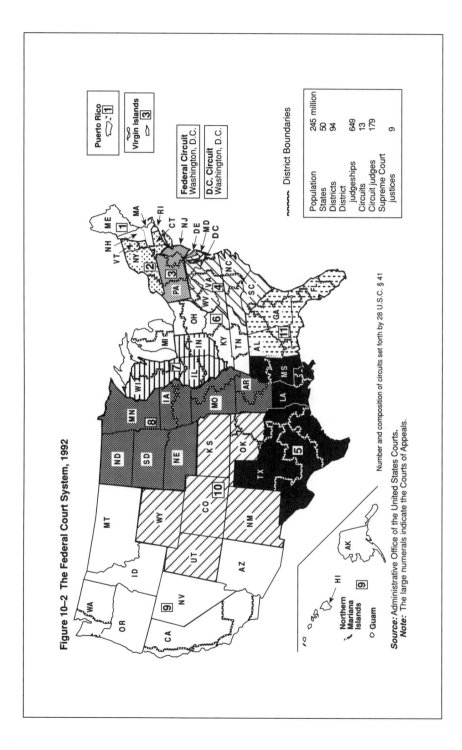

Figure 10–2 The Federal Court System, 1992

Population	245 million
States	50
Districts	94
District judgeships	649
Circuits	13
Circuit judges	179
Supreme Court justices	9

▬▬▬ District Boundaries

Puerto Rico [1]

Virgin Islands [3]

Federal Circuit
Washington, D.C.

D.C. Circuit
Washington, D.C.

Number and composition of circuits set forth by 28 U.S.C. § 41

Northern Mariana Islands [9]

○ Guam

Source: Administrative Office of the United States Courts.
Note: The large numerals indicate the Courts of Appeals.

Table 10-1 The Development of the Federal Courts of Appeals

Year of congressional action	Circuit/states in circuit													
	First	Second	Third	Fourth	Fifth	Sixth	Seventh	Eighth	Ninth	California	District of Columbia	Tenth	Eleventh	Federal
1802	NH, MA, RI	CT, NY, VT	NJ, PA	MD, DE	VA, NC	SC, GA					[a]			
1807							TN, KY, OH							
1837	NH, MA, RI, ME						IL, IN, OH	MO, KY, TN	AL, LA[b], MS, AR					
1842				MD, DE, VA	AL, LA	SC, NC, GA	MI, IN, IL, OH		MS, AR					
1855										CA				
1862				MD, DE, VA, NC, SC, WV	FL, GA, AL, MS	TX, LA, AR, TN, KY	IN, OH	WI, IL, MI	MN, IA, MO, KS					

Year									Abolished	Abolished
1863									[a]	CA, OR
1866	PA, NJ, DE	MD, VA, NC, SC, WV	FL, GA, AL, MS, LA, TX	TN, KY, OH, MI	WI, IN, IL	KS, MO, IA, MN, AR[c]	CA, NV, OR		[a]	Abolished
1891		MD, VA, NC, SC, WV				KS, MO, IA, MN, AR, ND, SD, NE, CO, WY	CA, NV, OR, WA, ID, MT			
1893									[a]	
1929	PR, ME, NH, MA, RI					ND, SD, NE, MN, IA, MO, AR	CA, NV, OR, WA, ID, MT, HI, AZ		[a]	NM, CO, OK, KS, WY, UT

(Table continues)

Table 10-1 *(Continued)*

	Circuit/states in circuit													
Year of congressional action	First	Second	Third	Fourth	Fifth	Sixth	Seventh	Eighth	Ninth	California	District of Columbia	Tenth	Eleventh	Federal
1948			PA, NJ, DE, VI		FL, GA, AL, MS, LA, TX, CZ				CA, NV, OR, WA, ID, MT, HI, AZ, AK		Formally specified circuit			
1980					TX, MS, LA									
1982														Created[d]
Present									CA, NV, OR, WA, ID, MT, HI, AZ,				FL, GA, AL	

AK,
GU,
MP

Note: The Judiciary Act of 1789 created three circuits, the Eastern, Middle, and Southern. By an act of February 13, 1801, Congress provided for the establishment of six circuit courts, "comprising the Thirteen original states, the States of Kentucky, Tennessee, and Vermont, and the districts of Maine and Ohio." Congress repealed the 1801 Act, but an act passed in 1802 retained some elements of its predecessor, including the enlarged number of circuits.

Three other important laws relating to the development of the courts of appeals were passed in 1802, 1869, and 1891. In 1802, Congress provided "that circuits shall consist of a Supreme Court Justice residing within the district and the district judge of the district. This act thereby dispenses with specifically designated circuit judges." In 1869, a circuit court judge was appointed for each of the "then existing nine judicial circuits." Not until 1891, however, did Congress create separate federal intermediate appellate courts.

[a] The Judiciary Act of 1801 created separate circuit court judgeships and a federal intermediate court for the District of Columbia. In 1802, Congress repealed that part of the law establishing circuit judgeships, but not that which created the D.C. Court. In 1863, it replaced the D.C. intermediate court with the Supreme Court for the District of Columbia and, finally, in 1893, it replaced the D.C. Supreme Court with the Court of Appeals for the District of Columbia.

[b] Except for the Western District of Louisiana.

[c] Except for the Western District of Arkansas.

[d] Created out of the Court of Claims and Court of Customs and Patent Appeals.

Source: Russell R. Wheeler and Cynthia Harrison, *Creating the Federal Judicial System* (Washington, D.C.: Federal Judicial Center, 1989). For more information on the development of the circuit courts of appeals, see U.S. Senate, Committee on the Judiciary, *Legislative History of the United States Circuit Courts of Appeals and the Judges Who Served during the Period 1801 through March 1958*, 85th Cong., 2d sess. (Washington, D.C.: Government Printing Office, 1958), 3. For more information on the evolution of the District of Columbia District Court, see John R. Schmidhauser, *Judges and Justices* (Boston: Little, Brown, 1979), 45–47.

Table 10-2   The Growth in Court of Appeals
Judgeships, 1895-1990

Year	Judgeships
1895	20 [a]
1900	25 [a]
1905	28 [a]
1910	30 [a]
1915	32
1920	34
1925	42
1930	45
1935	47
1940	57
1945	59
1950	65
1955	68
1960	68
1965	78
1970	97
1975	97
1980	132
1985	156
1990	168

Note: Figures from 1895-1935 are the numbers of actual sitting judges in regular service; figures from 1940-1990 are the number of judgeships authorized by Congress.

[a] Includes judges of circuit courts remaining in office after 1891 creation of the federal courts of appeals.

Sources: 1895-1935: Richard A. Posner, *Federal Courts: Crisis and Reform* (Cambridge, Mass.: Harvard University Press, 1985), appendix B; 1940-1990: Administrative Office of the United States Courts and the United States Code.

Table 10-3 Authorized Judgeships, U.S. Courts of Appeals, 1992

Circuits (states)	Authorized judgeships
District of Columbia	12
First (Maine, Massachusetts, New Hampshire, Puerto Rico)	6
Second (Connecticut, New York, Vermont)	13
Third (Delaware, New Jersey, Pennsylvania,Virgin Islands)	14
Fourth (Maryland, North Carolina, South Carolina,Virginia, West Virginia)	15
Fifth (Louisiana, Mississippi, Texas)	17
Sixth (Kentucky, Michigan, Ohio, Tennessee)	16
Seventh (Illinois, Indiana, Wisconsin)	11
Eighth (Arkansas, Iowa, Minnesota, Missouri, Nebraska, North Dakota, South Dakota)	11
Ninth (Alaska, Arizona, California, Guam, Hawaii, Idaho, Montana, Nevada, Northern Mariana Islands, Oregon, Washington)	28
Tenth (Colorado, Kansas, New Mexico, Oklahoma, Utah, Wyoming)	12
Eleventh (Alabama, Florida, Georgia)	12
The Federal Circuit	12
Total	179

Source: United States Code.

Table 10-4   Caseload of the U.S. Courts of Appeals, 1915-1936

Fiscal year	Cases filed	Cases terminated	Cases pending at end of fiscal year
1915	1,452	NA	NA
1916	1,518	NA	NA
1917	1,447	NA	NA
1918	1,320	1,477	793
1919	1,324	1,338	785
1920	1,308	1,242	843
1921	1,471	1,352	944
1922	1,601	1,588	978
1923	1,704	1,731	950
1924	2,131	1,898	1,084
1925	2,156	2,162	1,179
1926	2,278	2,208	1,145
1927	2,525	2,601	1,340
1928	2,610	2,493	1,455
1929	2,926	2,826	1,555
1930	2,874	2,898	1,531
1931	2,893	2,992	1,432
1932	3,305	3,198	1,539
1933	3,105	3,177	1,467
1934	3,406	3,261	1,612
1935	3,514	3,452	1,674
1936	3,521	3,526	1,669

Note: "NA" indicates not available. Data for 1915-1928 include the nine existing circuits and the District of Columbia; data for 1928-1936 include the ten existing circuits and the District of Columbia.

Sources: 1915-1926 (cases filed), 1927-1936 U.S. Senate, *Hearings before a Subcommittee of the Committee on the Judiciary,* 75th Cong., 1st sess., February 24, 1937 (Washington, D.C.: Government Printing Office, 1937). 1918-1926 (cases terminated and cases pending): U.S. House, *Hearing before the Committee on the Judiciary,* 70th Cong., 1st sess., February 3 and March 2, 1928 (Washington, D.C.: Government Printing Office, 1928).

Table 10-5 Caseload of the U.S. Courts of Appeals, 1942-1989

Year	Cases commenced					Cases terminated					Cases disposed of[a]				Median months[b]
	Crim.	U.S. civil	Priv. civil	Admin. appeals	Total	Crim.	U.S. civil	Priv. civil	Admin. appeals	Total	Affirmed/ granted	Reversed/ denied	Other	Total	
1942	339	510	—	835	3,228	287	486	—	830	2,999	—	573	—	2,292	7.7
1943	363	581	950	826	3,093	319	529	1,089	841	3,197	1,563	600	63	2,226	6.5
1944	437	621	954	717	3,072	395	599	967	738	3,039	1,568	547	33	2,148	6.5
1945	486	651	758	511	2,730	469	633	836	566	2,848	1,413	556	23	1,992	7.0
1946	400	690	894	418	2,627	418	640	829	503	2,621	1,299	477	29	1,805	6.8
1947	370	770	861	499	2,615	383	780	853	412	2,654	1,317	509	61	1,887	6.9
1948	359	677	1,118	381	2,758	356	702	925	359	2,577	1,269	483	69	1,821	6.3
1949	309	791	1,171	491	2,989	318	655	1,132	418	2,753	1,421	544	80	2,045	7.1
1950	308	708	1,114	485	2,830	342	783	1,184	541	3,064	1,700	528	127	2,355	7.1
1951	298	677	1,172	566	2,982	291	688	1,119	481	2,829	1,438	572	126	2,136	6.7
1952	391	724	1,133	610	3,079	362	687	1,141	598	3,048	1,629	588	91	2,308	7.3
1953	454	815	1,106	639	3,226	398	700	1,124	621	3,043	1,710	641	85	2,436	7.0
1954	550	875	1,124	659	3,481	460	809	986	689	3,192	1,632	668	127	2,427	7.1
1955	677	811	1,363	576	3,695	670	893	1,289	523	3,654	1,907	777	125	2,809	7.3
1956	557	872	1,361	609	3,588	573	865	1,445	626	3,734	2,082	743	148	2,973	7.4
1957	535	895	1,464	618	3,701	544	905	1,388	666	3,687	1,949	621	139	2,709	7.1
1958	599	836	1,447	625	3,694	596	878	1,482	567	3,704	2,013	689	129	2,831	7.0
1959	616	802	1,501	606	3,754	633	831	1,473	601	3,753	1,935	648	122	2,705	6.7
1960	623	788	1,534	737	3,899	580	750	1,517	660	3,713	1,924	656	101	2,681	6.8
1961	616	903	1,617	846	4,204	628	881	1,482	825	4,049	2,023	692	94	2,806	6.8
1962	773	1,066	1,692	1,024	4,823	622	936	1,508	855	4,167	2,101	680	114	2,895	7.1
1963	965	1,054	2,030	1,141	5,437	862	1,049	1,894	962	5,011	2,261	791	120	3,172	7.3
1964	1,043	1,309	2,299	983	6,023	917	1,183	2,159	1,105	5,700	2,660	765	127	3,552	7.4
1965	1,223	1,387	2,677	1,106	6,766	1,014	1,229	2,183	1,004	5,771	2,635	773	138	3,546	8.0
1966	1,458	1,338	2,809	1,254	7,183	1,214	1,309	2,552	1,141	6,571	3,026	866	195	4,087	8.3
1967	1,665	1,372	3,101	1,385	7,903	1,524	1,378	2,968	1,257	7,527	3,340	954	174	4,468	8.8
1968	2,098	1,500	3,569	1,545	9,116	1,754	1,356	3,268	1,512	8,264	3,449	1,009	160	4,668	7.8

(Table continues)

Table 10-5 (Continued)

Year	Cases commenced					Cases terminated					Cases disposed of[a]				
	Crim.	U.S. civil	Priv. civil	Admin. appeals	Total	Crim.	U.S. civil	Priv. civil	Admin. appeals	Total	Affirmed/ granted	Reversed/ denied	Other	Total	Median months[b]
1969	2,508	1,823	4,197	1,345	10,248	2,022	1,559	3,679	1,394	9,014	3,838	1,072	211	5,121	8.3
1970	2,660	2,167	4,834	1,522	11,662	2,581	1,912	4,367	1,407	10,699	4,626	1,280	233	6,139	8.2
1971	3,197	2,367	5,234	1,383	12,788	3,047	2,258	5,065	1,503	12,368	5,765	1,377	464	7,606	7.6
1972	3,980	2,604	5,795	1,509	14,535	3,799	2,512	5,399	1,448	13,828	6,207	1,664	666	8,537	6.6
1973	4,453	2,704	6,172	1,616	15,629	4,210	2,722	6,030	1,493	15,112	7,163	1,693	762	9,618	6.4
1974	4,067	3,267	6,157	2,205	16,436	4,299	2,791	5,847	1,734	15,422	6,429	1,579	443	8,451	6.8
1975	4,187	2,981	6,511	2,290	16,658	4,005	3,094	6,252	1,909	16,000	6,763	1,632	682	9,077	7.4
1976	4,650	3,327	7,077	2,515	18,408	4,238	2,853	6,248	2,359	16,426	6,995	1,680	676	9,351	7.1
1977	4,738	3,622	7,358	2,564	19,119	4,554	3,198	6,680	2,510	17,784	7,826	1,715	1,859	11,400	7.1
1978	4,487	3,928	7,324	2,382	18,918	4,461	3,437	6,813	2,256	17,714	6,717	1,536	597	8,850	8.0
1979	4,102	3,983	8,922	2,922	20,219	4,320	3,857	7,175	2,602	18,928	7,125	1,548	688	9,361	8.1
1980	4,405	4,654	10,200	2,950	23,200	3,993	4,346	8,942	2,643	20,887	8,017	1,845	745	10,607	8.9
1981	4,377	4,940	12,074	3,800	26,362	4,192	5,021	11,327	3,303	25,066	9,004	2,246	918	12,168	9.3
1982	4,767	5,517	13,267	3,118	27,946	4,552	5,508	13,115	3,549	27,984	9,560	2,138	1,022	12,720	8.9
1983	4,790	5,820	14,429	3,069	29,630	4,777	5,585	13,710	3,260	28,660	10,174	2,173	870	13,217	8.6
1984	4,881	6,259	15,466	3,045	31,490	4,876	6,074	15,309	3,212	31,185	10,961	2,382	984	14,327	8.3
1985	4,989	6,744	16,827	3,179	33,360	4,892	6,363	15,743	2,760	31,387	12,286	2,770	1,313	16,369	10.3
1986	5,134	6,415	17,876	3,187	34,292	5,134	6,535	17,276	3,235	33,774	13,398	3,249	1,552	18,199	10.3
1987	5,260	6,292	19,246	2,723	35,176	5,039	6,227	18,338	3,237	34,444	13,681	2,924	1,897	18,502	10.3
1988	6,012	6,210	20,464	3,043	37,524	5,284	6,386	19,798	2,625	35,888	14,953	2,664	1,561	19,178	10.1
1989	8,020	6,349	20,626	2,965	39,734	6,297	6,127	20,313	2,914	37,372	15,240	2,617	1,465	19,322	10.3

Note: Crim. = Criminal; Priv. civil = Private civil; Admin. appeals = Administrative appeals. "—" indicates data not available.

[a] Includes cases terminated on the merits after hearing or submission. 1975-1989 data not comparable to prior years due to changes in criteria. 1942-1985, figure is from filing of complete record to final disposition; 1985-1989, figure is from filing of notice of appeal to final disposition.

[b] 1942-1970, figure is from filing of complete record to final disposition.

Sources: 1942-1970: *Historical Statistics of the United States, Colonial Times to 1970* (Washington, D.C.: Government Printing Office, 1975); 1971-1989: *Statistical Abstract of the United States* (Washington, D.C.: Government Printing Office, successive years).

Table 10-6 Caseload of the U.S. Courts of Appeals, 1990-1992

Action	1990	1991	1992
Cases commenced	40,898	42,033	46,032
Criminal	9,493	9,949	10,956
U.S. prisoner petitions	2,263	2,390	2,569
Other U.S. civil	4,363	4,273	4,544
Private prisoner petitions	7,676	8,188	9,202
Other private civil	12,812	12,610	13,660
Bankruptcy	1,087	1,247	1,444
Administrative appeals	2,578	2,764	3,052
Original proceedings	524	612	605
Cases terminated	38,520	41,414	42,933
Criminal	7,509	9,198	9,830
U.S. prisoner petitions	2,049	2,316	2,441
Other U.S. civil	4,330	4,263	4,356
Private prisoner petitions	7,499	8,115	8,330
Other private civil	12,870	12,583	13,298
Bankruptcy	1,040	1,201	1,280
Administrative appeals	2,582	3,148	2,801
Original proceedings	641	590	597
Cases disposed of[a]	21,006	22,707	23,162
Affirmed or enforced	16,629	17,988	18,463
Dismissed	1,186	1,370	1,196
Reversed	2,565	2,503	2,681
Remanded	404	595	473
Other	222	251	349
Median months[b]	10.1	10.2	10.5

[a] Includes cases terminated on the merits after hearing or submission.
[b] Figures are from filing of notice of appeal to final disposition.

Source: Administrative Office of the United States Courts, Statistics Division, Analysis and Reports Branch.

Table 10-7   Presidential Appointments to the Circuit Courts and Courts of Appeal by Political Party

		Appointees			
President	Party affiliation	Member of same party	Member of other party or independent	Unknown party affiliation	Total
J. Adams	Federalist	7	0	7	14
Jefferson	Democrat-Republican	0	0	3	3
Grant	Republican	3	3	4	10
Hayes	Republican	2	1	1	4
Arthur	Republican	4	0	1	5
Cleveland	Democrat	6	1	5	12
B. Harrison	Republican	8	2	2	12
McKinley	Republican	3	2	0	5
T. Roosevelt	Republican	14	3	3	20
Taft	Republican	11	2	0	13
Wilson	Democrat	19	1	0	20
Harding	Republican	6	0	0	6
Coolidge	Republican	15	2	0	17
Hoover	Republican	12	4	0	16
F. Roosevelt	Democrat	45	3	0	48
Truman	Democrat	23	3	0	26
Eisenhower	Republican	42	3	0	45
Kennedy	Democrat	20	1	0	21
L. Johnson	Democrat	38	2	0	40
Nixon	Republican	42	3	0	45
Ford	Republican	11	1	0	12
Carter	Democrat	46	10	0	56
Reagan	Republican	76	2	0	78
Bush	Republican	33	4	0	37
Total		486	53	26	565

Sources: Adams to Truman: U.S. Senate, Committee on the Judiciary, *Legislative History of the United States Circuit Courts of Appeals and the Judges Who Served during the Period 1801 through March 1958*, 85th Cong., 2d sess. (Washington, D.C.: Government Printing Office, 1958), 4; Eisenhower and Kennedy: Sheldon Goldman, "Characteristics of Eisenhower and Kennedy Appointees to the Lower Federal Courts," *Western Political Quarterly* 18 (1965): 760; Johnson to Bush: Sheldon Goldman, "The Bush Imprint on the Judiciary: Carrying on a Tradition," *Judicature* 74 (1991): 302-303; Sheldon Goldman, "Bush's Judicial Legacy: The Final Imprint," *Judicature* 76 (1993): 293.

Table 10-8 Party Identification of Appellate Court Judges by Historic Era

Party	1789-1828	1829-1861	1862-1888	1889-1919	1920-1932	1933-1976	Carter	Reagan/Bush
Democratic			4 (12)	34 (43)	9 (19.1)	134 (55.1)	46 (82.1)	
Republican			25 (74)	41 (52.6)	38 (80.9)	100 (42.0)	4 (7.1)	109 (96.5)
Federalist	23 (76.7)							
Jeffersonian	7 (23.3)							
Jacksonian Democrat		3 (100)						
Whig								
Free Soil								
No affiliation			4 (12)	3 (3.8)		5 (21.5)		1 (0.9)
Know-Nothing			1 (2)					
Liberal						1 (0.4)		
Independent						1 (0.4)	6 (10.7)	3 (2.7)

Note: Figures are number of judges; figures in parentheses are percentage of total judges on bench.

Sources: 1789-1976: John R. Schmidhauser, *Judges and Justices* (Boston: Little, Brown, 1979), 87; Carter and Reagan/Bush: Sheldon Goldman, "The Bush Imprint on the Judiciary: Carrying on a Tradition," *Judicature* 74 (1991): 302-303; Sheldon Goldman, "Bush's Judicial Legacy: The Final Imprint," *Judicature* 76 (1993): 293.

Table 10-9   U.S. Circuit Court Decisions Affirmed by the Supreme
Court, 1953-1991

	Circuit					
Term	First	Second	Third	Fourth	Fifth	Sixth
1953	2 (100.0)	4 (50.0)	2 (100.0)	2 (100.0)	5 (31.3)	2 (66.7)
1954	2 (66.7)	7 (46.7)	4 (57.1)	1 (50.0)	5 (38.5)	3 (42.9)
1955	—	8 (57.1)	6 (75.0)	0 (0.0)	4 (36.4)	1 (33.3)
1956	2 (66.7)	6 (42.9)	2 (28.6)	2 (66.7)	2 (20.0)	2 (33.3)
1957	1 (33.3)	5 (41.7)	4 (66.7)	0 (0.0)	3 (25.0)	5 (45.5)
1958	0 (0.0)	8 (66.7)	8 (61.5)	6 (85.7)	3 (25.0)	1 (50.0)
1959	0 (0.0)	8 (72.2)	4 (50.0)	1 (25.0)	7 (38.9)	3 (37.5)
1960	4 (50.0)	3 (76.5)	0 (0.0)	1 (25.0)	3 (50.0)	4 (57.1)
1961	0 (0.0)	4 (36.4)	0 (0.0)	1 (33.3)	3 (30.0)	1 (33.3)
1962	2 (40.0)	7 (46.7)	0 (0.0)	0 (0.0)	1 (11.1)	1 (16.7)
1963	1 (33.3)	4 (28.6)	1 (33.3)	0 (0.0)	0 (0.0)	0 (0.0)
1964	0 (0.0)	7 (58.3)	3 (60.0)	0 (0.0)	2 (18.2)	3 (50.0)
1965	0 (0.0)	4 (33.3)	1 (100.0)	2 (66.7)	6 (35.3)	1 (14.3)
1966	3 (100.0)	6 (50.0)	0 (0.0)	0 (0.0)	6 (50.0)	5 (71.4)
1967	2 (50.0)	8 (50.0)	2 (18.2)	2 (66.7)	1 (20.0)	2 (22.2)
1968	1 (33.3)	1 (25.0)	0 (0.0)	1 (33.3)	3 (33.3)	1 (16.7)
1969	—	3 (30.0)	2 (100.0)	0 (0.0)	3 (25.0)	3 (37.5)
1970	1 (50.0)	3 (60.0)	1 (33.3)	2 (50.0)	5 (31.3)	3 (42.9)
1971	1 (25.0)	8 (57.1)	1 (100.0)	1 (16.7)	5 (29.4)	6 (85.7)
1972	1 (50.0)	6 (60.0)	1 (25.0)	7 (77.8)	3 (42.9)	2 (25.0)
1973	1 (33.3)	4 (28.6)	1 (12.5)	4 (50.0)	6 (66.7)	5 (27.8)
1974	1 (100.0)	7 (50.0)	6 (54.5)	0 (0.0)	3 (30.0)	1 (16.7)
1975	0 (0.0)	6 (54.5)	2 (28.6)	6 (66.7)	4 (22.2)	3 (30.0)
1976	2 (100.0)	3 (30.0)	3 (50.0)	5 (41.7)	7 (36.8)	3 (27.3)
1977	4 (80.0)	4 (25.0)	2 (50.0)	3 (50.0)	7 (43.8)	2 (20.0)
1978	—	3 (25.0)	4 (50.0)	2 (40.0)	4 (28.6)	2 (28.6)
1979	0 (0.0)	9 (64.3)	2 (20.0)	3 (75.0)	13 (65.0)	2 (33.3)
1980	0 (0.0)	4 (44.4)	3 (17.6)	0 (0.0)	9 (56.3)	4 (57.1)
1981	3 (50.0)	3 (65.0)	3 (18.8)	3 (33.3)	7 (35.0)	3 (50.0)
1982	2 (33.3)	5 (35.7)	2 (40.0)	6 (60.0)	6 (30.0)	3 (50.0)
1983	2 (28.6)	4 (36.4)	8 (53.3)	5 (55.6)	3 (37.5)	4 (44.4)
1984	4 (66.7)	8 (53.3)	3 (30.0)	3 (37.5)	1 (25.0)	9 (50.0)
1985	1 (25.0)	6 (86.7)	9 (69.2)	5 (35.7)	3 (42.9)	7 (43.8)
1986	3 (75.0)	2 (11.1)	9 (64.3)	1 (16.7)	7 (53.8)	2 (25.0)
1987	5 (83.3)	3 (75.0)	3 (42.9)	5 (45.5)	9 (69.2)	7 (70.0)
1988	1 (100.0)	10 (55.6)	6 (54.5)	6 (60.0)	6 (60.0)	1 (16.7)
1989	2 (100.0)	3 (27.3)	9 (75.0)	4 (40.0)	2 (20.0)	0 (0.0)
1990	0 (0.0)	7 (87.5)	5 (83.3)	3 (30.0)	8 (42.1)	2 (40.0)
1991	2 (33.3)	3 (27.3)	4 (57.1)	2 (40.0)	7 (50.0)	1 (14.3)
Total	56 (44.8)	204 (47.9)	126 (43.8)	95 (41.3)	182 (36.8)	110 (37.5)

Table 10-9   *(Continued)*

			Circuit			
Term	Seventh	Eighth	Ninth	Tenth	Eleventh	District of Columbia
1953	—	2 (66.7)	8 (80.0)	0 (0.0)		9 (69.2)
1954	0 (0.0)	0 (0.0)	1 (20.0)	3 (75.0)		1 (11.1)
1955	2 (50.0)	3 (100.0)	5 (50.0)	1 (25.0)		0 (0.0)
1956	5 (45.5)	4 (80.0)	4 (25.0)	0 (0.0)		3 (33.3)
1957	5 (55.6)	2 (66.7)	6 (66.7)	5 (71.4)		4 (23.5)
1958	2 (40.0)	5 (62.5)	1 (11.1)	1 (33.3)		4 (22.2)
1959	4 (36.4)	0 (0.0)	4 (36.4)	3 (75.0)		4 (44.4)
1960	6 (40.0)	2 (100.0)	3 (37.5)	0 (0.0)		4 (33.3)
1961	2 (33.3)	—	1 (16.7)	1 (50.0)		3 (15.8)
1962	2 (40.0)	1 (100.0)	2 (22.2)	0 (0.0)		6 (75.0)
1963	4 (50.0)	0 (0.0)	2 (25.0)	0 (0.0)		2 (50.0)
1964	3 (50.0)	2 (66.7)	3 (60.0)	1 (33.3)		2 (16.7)
1965	2 (25.0)	1 (25.0)	1 (16.7)	1 (50.0)		2 (33.3)
1966	1 (12.5)	0 (0.0)	2 (25.0)	3 (50.0)		2 (28.6)
1967	0 (0.0)	0 (0.0)	2 (15.4)	9 (50.0)		1 (9.1)
1968	1 (16.7)	1 (16.7)	1 (14.3)	2 (33.3)		1 (25.0)
1969	0 (0.0)	1 (20.0)	3 (37.5)	1 (20.0)		2 (33.3)
1970	4 (44.4)	—	6 (42.9)	1 (33.3)		2 (50.0)
1971	3 (37.5)	1 (14.3)	6 (54.5)	1 (20.0)		1 (16.7)
1972	2 (25.0)	1 (20.0)	4 (23.5)	0 (0.0)		4 (26.7)
1973	2 (18.2)	1 (50.0)	9 (56.3)	1 (33.3)		6 (35.3)
1974	3 (60.0)	0 (0.0)	4 (36.4)	0 (0.0)		4 (22.2)
1975	3 (50.0)	2 (50.0)	9 (33.3)	0 (0.0)		7 (41.2)
1976	4 (40.0)	4 (33.3)	5 (55.6)	1 (33.3)		1 (16.7)
1977	1 (8.3)	2 (28.6)	1 (6.3)	1 (50.0)		3 (18.8)
1978	8 (57.1)	3 (23.1)	3 (27.3)	0 (0.0)		0 (0.0)
1979	4 (66.7)	1 (33.3)	1 (8.3)	4 (66.7)		3 (25.0)
1980	1 (20.0)	1 (16.7)	7 (36.8)	0 (0.0)		5 (31.3)
1981	4 (38.4)	5 (62.5)	7 (70.0)	4 (80.0)		0 (0.0)
1982	4 (44.4)	4 (36.4)	10 (34.5)	2 (66.7)		5 (18.5)
1983	6 (85.7)	4 (33.3)	2 (6.1)	1 (16.7)	2 (33.3)	0 (0.0)
1984	5 (45.5)	2 (33.3)	7 (25.0)	3 (50.0)	7 (70.0)	1 (14.3)
1985	4 (66.7)	1 (16.7)	8 (44.4)	1 (50.0)	2 (33.3)	3 (23.1)
1986	2 (33.3)	3 (42.9)	12 (57.1)	0 (0.0)	4 (33.3)	1 (14.3)
1987	1 (20.0)	4 (40.0)	10 (55.6)	5 (55.6)	3 (60.0)	9 (64.3)
1988	4 (44.4)	4 (40.0)	9 (42.9)	0 (0.0)	5 (50.0)	4 (50.0)
1989	3 (50.0)	6 (66.7)	8 (50.0)	1 (25.0)	5 (83.3)	4 (50.0)
1990	2 (25.0)	1 (33.3)	3 (23.1)	0 (0.0)	2 (40.0)	2 (28.6)
1991	2 (40.0)	1 (33.3)	5 (35.7)	2 (28.6)	3 (30.0)	0 (0.0)
Total	111 (37.5)	75 (37.3)	185 (34.8)	59 (35.1)	33 (47.1)	115 (27.4)

Note: "—" indicates no cases decided. Figures are total number of cases affirmed. Figures in parentheses are percentage of cases affirmed. All orally argued docket numbers, excluding cases arising under the Court's original jurisdiction, are included. Because the formal dispositions the Court makes do not necessarily correspond to who wins the case, the focus here is on the prevailing party. If the petitioning party prevails in whole or in part, the case is counted as a reversal; otherwise as an affirmation.

Source: U.S. Supreme Court Judicial Database.

Table 10-10   The Growth in District Court Judgeships, 1790-1990

Year	Judgeships	Year	Judgeships
1790	13	1895	65
1795	15	1900	65
1800	16	1905	74
1805	19	1910	88
1810	19	1915	93
1815	22	1920	99
1820	27	1925	128
1825	28	1930	146
1830	28	1935	134
1835	28	1940	190
1840	31	1945	193
1845	33	1950	215
1850	39	1955	244
1855	39	1960	245
1860	45	1965	307
1865	49	1970	401
1870	50	1975	400
1875	53	1980	516
1880	54	1985	575
1885	56	1990	576
1890	58		

Note: Figures from 1790-1880 and 1940-1990 are the number of judgeships authorized by Congress; figures from 1885-1935 are the numbers of actual sitting judges in regular service.

Sources: 1790-1935: Richard A. Posner, *Federal Courts: Crisis and Reform* (Cambridge, Mass.: Harvard University Press, 1985), appendix B. 1940-1990: Administrative Office of the United States Courts and the United States Code.

Table 10-11 Authorized Judgeships, U.S. District Courts, 1992

Districts	Authorized judgeships
Alabama	
Northern	7
Middle	3
Southern	3
Alaska	3
Arizona	8
Arkansas	
Eastern	5
Western	3
California	
Northern	14
Eastern	6
Central	27
Southern	8
Colorado	7
Connecticut	8
Delaware	4
District of Columbia	15
Florida	
Northern	4
Middle	11
Southern	16
Georgia	
Northern	11
Middle	4
Southern	3
Hawaii	3
Idaho	2
Illinois	
Northern	22
Central	3
Southern	3
Indiana	
Northern	5
Southern	5
Iowa	
Northern	2
Southern	3
Kansas	5
Kentucky	
Eastern	4
Western	4
Eastern and Western	1[a]
Louisiana	
Eastern	13
Middle	2
Western	7

(Table continues)

Table 10-11   *(Continued)*

Districts	Authorized judgeships
Maine	3
Maryland	10
Massachusetts	13
Michigan	
Eastern	15
Western	4
Minnesota	7
Mississippi	
Northern	3
Southern	6
Missouri	
Eastern	6
Western	5
Eastern and Western	2[a]
Montana	3
Nebraska	3
Nevada	4
New Hampshire	3
New Jersey	17
New Mexico	5
New York	
Northern	4
Southern	28
Eastern	15
Western	4
North Carolina	
Eastern	4
Middle	4
Western	3
North Dakota	2
Ohio	
Northern	11
Southern	8
Oklahoma	
Northern	3
Eastern	1
Western	6
Northern, Eastern, and Western	1[a]
Oregon	6
Pennsylvania	
Eastern	22
Middle	6
Western	10
Puerto Rico	7
Rhode Island	3
South Carolina	9
South Dakota	3

Table 10-11 *(Continued)*

Districts	Authorized judgeships
Tennessee	
Eastern	5
Middle	4
Western	5
Texas	
Northern	12
Southern	18
Eastern	7
Western	10
Utah	5
Vermont	2
Virginia	
Eastern	9
Western	4
Washington	
Eastern	4
Western	7
West Virginia	
Northern	3
Southern	5
Wisconsin	
Eastern	4
Western	2
Wyoming	3
Total	632

[a] Congressionally created authorized judgeship designated to serve two or more districts.
Source: United States Code.

Table 10-12 Criminal and Civil Cases in the U.S. District Courts, 1871-1992

	Criminal cases		Civil cases	
Year	Cases commenced[a]	Cases disposed of	Cases commenced[a]	Cases terminated
1871	NA	8,187	NA	NA
1872	NA	8,092	NA	NA
1873	NA	6,713	NA	8,851
1874	NA	6,018	NA	10,845
1875	NA	6,045	NA	11,801
1876	NA	7,095	NA	10,883
1877	NA	8,013	NA	10,098
1878	NA	10,644	NA	12,451
1879	NA	13,717	NA	11,005
1880	NA	9,269	NA	11,026
1881	NA	11,488	NA	10,086
1882	NA	7,494	NA	9,395
1883	NA	7,792	NA	9,904
1884	NA	12,542	NA	10,256
1885	NA	11,977	NA	10,588
1886	NA	14,479	NA	11,464
1887	NA	12,905	NA	11,066
1888	NA	14,599	NA	10,249
1889	NA	14,588	NA	10,283
1890	NA	16,016	NA	10,228
1891	NA	18,327	NA	11,172
1892	NA	18,725	NA	13,263
1893	NA	21,935	NA	12,018
1894	NA	21,744	NA	13,500
1895	NA	25,724	NA	12,672
1896	NA	26,271	NA	12,347
1897	NA	18,134	NA	12,246
1898	NA	16,814	NA	13,758
1899	NA	17,341	NA	10,908
1900	NA	17,033	NA	12,061
1901	NA	16,837	NA	13,264
1902	NA	16,149	NA	12,766
1903	NA	16,034	NA	12,219
1904	18,488	17,453	14,888	13,052
1905	18,900	18,168	16,002	14,126
1906	17,435	16,337	15,986	15,550
1907	18,332	16,006	18,434	14,517
1908	13,345	12,942	14,905	11,611
1909	14,505	13,959	13,127	11,882
1910	14,864	15,371	13,788	12,909
1911	15,057	14,702	14,001	12,525
1912	15,953	16,158	14,993	14,875
1913	16,753	16,757	14,935	17,994
1914	18,399	18,128	16,288	18,115

Table 10-12 *(Continued)*

Year	Criminal cases		Civil cases	
	Cases commenced [a]	Cases disposed of	Cases commenced [a]	Cases terminated
1915	19,868	19,120	15,268	18,812
1916	20,243	20,432	17,352	29,898
1917	19,628	17,671	17,551	22,926
1918	35,096	30,949	16,756	30,962
1919	47,433	35,734	18,800	28,337
1920	55,587	34,230	22,109	18,883
1921	54,487	47,399	32,175	23,187
1922	60,722	53,165	31,745	26,166
1923	71,077	68,152	30,716	29,256
1924	70,168	73,488	34,301	31,443
1925	76,136	92,711	38,035	37,504
1926	68,582	76,536	38,721	38,723
1927	64,164	67,279	40,856	42,507
1928	83,37	88,366	44,445	41,230
1929	86,348	85,328	45,287	44,390
1930	87,305	82,609	48,325	48,465
1931	NA	NA	49,332	49,385
1932	NA	NA	60,515	55,636
1933	NA	NA	NA	NA
1934	NA	NA	NA	NA
1935	35,500	NA	36,000	NA
1936	36,000	NA	39,500	NA
1937	35,464	NA	32,771	NA
1938	34,178	NA	33,477	NA
1939	34,803	NA	33,733	NA
1940	33,401	NA	34,734	NA
1941	31,823	NA	38,477	38,561
1942	33,294	NA	38,140	38,352
1943	36,588	NA	36,789	36,044
1944	39,621	NA	38,499	37,086
1945	39,429	41,653	60,965	52,300
1946	33,203	36,482	67,835	61,000
1947	33,652	36,635	58,956	54,515
1948	32,097	34,242	46,725	48,791
1949	34,432	36,264	53,421	48,396
1950	36,383	37,675	54,622	53,259
1951	38,670	41,066	51,600	52,119
1952	37,950	38,622	58,428	53,150
1953	37,291	37,762	64,001	57,490
1954	41,808	42,989	59,461	57,903
1955	35,310	38,990	59,375	58,974
1956	28,739	31,811	62,394	67,700
1957	28,120	29,725	62,380	63,568

(Table continues)

Table 10-12 *(Continued)*

	Criminal cases		Civil cases	
Year	Cases commenced[a]	Cases disposed of	Cases commenced[a]	Cases terminated
1958	28,897	30,469	67,115	61,285
1959	28,729	30,729	57,800	62,172
1960	28,137	30,512	59,284	61,829
1961	28,460	32,671	58,293	55,416
1962	37,665	33,110	61,836	57,996
1963	39,920	34,845	63,630	62,379
1964	30,268	33,381	66,930	63,954
1965	33,334	33,718	67,678	65,478
1966	31,494	31,975	70,906	66,184
1967	32,207	31,535	70,961	70,172
1968	32,571	31,843	71,449	68,873
1969	35,413	32,796	77,193	73,354
1970	39,959	36,356	87,321	80,435
1971	41,290	44,615	93,396	85,638
1972	47,043	49,516	96,173	94,256
1973	38,449	46,724	98,560	97,402
1974	36,105	48,014	103,530	96,701
1975	41,100	49,200	117,300	103,800
1976	39,100	51,600	130,600	115,500
1977	39,800	53,200	138,600	123,200
1978	34,600	45,900	138,600	123,200
1979	31,500	41,200	154,700	140,000
1980	28,000	36,600	168,800	155,000
1981	30,400	38,100	180,600	172,900
1982	31,600	40,500	206,200	185,500
1983	34,900	43,300	241,800	213,600
1984	35,900	44,500	261,500	241,800
1985	38,500	47,400	273,700	268,600
1986	40,400	50,000	254,800	265,800
1987	42,200	54,200	239,000	237,500
1988	43,500	52,800	239,600	238,100
1989	44,900	54,600	233,500	234,600
1990	48,094	44,295	217,879	213,922
1991	45,733	42,787	207,690	211,713
1992	48,342	43,493	226,895	239,633

Note: "NA" indicates not available.
[a] Excludes transfers from one court to another.

Sources: 1871-1930: American Law Institute, *A Study of the Business of the Federal Courts* (Philadelphia: American Law Institute, 1934); 1935-1936: approximations from Chart 2, 1942 Annual Report of the Administrative Office; 1936-1940: 1940 Annual Report of the Administrative Office; 1941-1970: U.S. Bureau of the Census, *Historical Statistics of the United States, Colonial Times to 1970* (Washington, D.C.: Government Printing Office, 1975); 1971-1989: U.S. Bureau of the Census, *Statistical Abstract of the United States* (Washington, D.C.: Government Printing Office), successive editions; 1990-1992: Administrative Office of the United States Courts, Statistics Division, Analysis and Reports Branch.

Table 10-13 Presidential Appointments to the U.S. District Courts by Political Party, Cleveland to Bush

President	Party affiliation	Appointees			
		Member of same party	Member of other party or independent	Unknown party affiliation	Total
Cleveland	Democrat	30	0	0	30
B. Harrison	Republican	18	1	0	19
McKinley	Republican	19	0	0	19
T. Roosevelt	Republican	55	0	0	55
Taft	Republican	26	6	0	32
Wilson	Democrat	54	1	0	55
Harding	Republican	37	1	0	38
Coolidge	Republican	49	2	0	51
Hoover	Republican	30	3	0	33
F. Roosevelt	Democrat	151	10	0	161
Truman	Democrat	105	10	0	115
Eisenhower	Republican	116	9	0	125
Kennedy	Democrat	93	10	0	103
L. Johnson	Democrat	115	7	0	122
Nixon	Republican	166	13	0	179
Ford	Republican	41	11	0	52
Carter	Democrat	187	15	0	202
Reagan	Republican	270	20	0	290
Bush	Republican	131	17	0	148
Total		1,693	136	0	1,829

Sources: Cleveland to Truman: Estimated from Stephen T. Early, Jr., *Constitutional Courts of the United States* (Totowa, N.J.: Littlefield, Adams, 1977), 88; Eisenhower and Kennedy: Sheldon Goldman, "Characteristics of Eisenhower and Kennedy Appointees to the Lower Federal Courts," *Western Political Quarterly* 18 (1965): 760; Johnson to Bush: Sheldon Goldman, "The Bush Imprint on the Judiciary: Carrying on a Tradition," *Judicature* 74 (1991): 302-303; Sheldon Goldman, "Bush's Judicial Legacy: The Final Imprint," *Judicature* 76 (1993): 287.

Table 10-14 U.S. District Court Decisions Affirmed by the Warren, Burger, and Rehnquist Courts, 1953-1990 Terms

District court	Warren (1953-1968)		Burger (1969-1985)		Rehnquist (1986-1990)		Total	
	N	Percentage	N	Percentage	N	Percentage	N	Percentage
Alabama, MD	3	42.9	0	0.0	—	—	3	30.0
Alabama, ND	0	0.0	2	40.0	—	—	2	28.9
Alaska, D	0	0.0	0	0.0	—	—	0	0.0
Arizona, D	—	—	4	80.0	—	—	4	80.0
Arkansas, MD	—	—	1	33.3	—	—	1	33.3
Arkansas, WD	3	37.5	0	0.0	—	—	3	23.1
California, CD	—	—	7	33.3	2	66.7	9	37.5
California, ED	—	—	1	50.0	0	0.0	1	33.3
California, ND	4	40.0	6	30.0	—	—	10	33.3
California, SD	3	30.0	0	0.0	—	—	3	23.1
Colorado, D	5	62.5	2	66.7	—	—	7	63.3
Connecticut, D	3	33.3	1	11.9	—	—	4	22.2
Delaware, D	3	75.0	—	—	—	—	3	75.0
District of Columbia, D	12	44.0	19	48.7	4	40.0	35	47.3
Florida, MD	2	40.0	0	0.0	—	—	2	20.0
Florida, ND	0	0.0	0	0.0	—	—	0	0.0
Florida, SD	0	0.0	0	0.0	—	—	0	0.0
Georgia, MD	0	0.0	1	50.0	—	—	1	25.0
Georgia, ND	1	9.1	5	83.3	1	100.0	7	38.9
Georgia, SD	3	100.0	0	0.0	0	0.0	3	75.0
Hawaii, D	0	0.0	—	—	0	0.0	1	100.0
Idaho, D	—	—	1	100.0	—	—	11	40.7
Illinois, ND	8	36.4	3	60.0	—	—	1	20.0
Illinois, SD	1	25.0	0	0.0	—	—	1	25.0
Indiana, ND	1	100.0	0	0.0	0	0.0	0	0.0
Indiana, SD	0	0.0	0	0.0	—	—		

Iowa, ND	0	0.0	1	100.0	—	—	1	50.0
Iowa, SD	1	100.0	0	0.0	—	—	1	33.3
Kansas, D	0	0.0	1	33.3	—	—	1	16.7
Kentucky, ED	0	0.0	1	50.0	—	—	1	33.3
Kentucky, WD	0	0.0	—	—	—	—	0	0.0
Louisiana, ED	4	44.4	1	33.3	0	0.0	5	41.7
Louisiana, MD	—	—	—	—	—	—	0	0.0
Louisiana, WD	0	0.0	—	—	—	—	0	0.0
Maine, D	—	—	—	—	—	—	—	—
Maryland, D	1	33.3	3	37.5	—	—	4	36.4
Massachusetts, D	4	36.4	5	35.7	—	—	9	36.0
Michigan, ED	2	50.0	1	50.0	—	—	3	50.0
Michigan, WD	1	100.0	—	—	—	—	1	100.0
Minnesota, D	3	100.0	3	37.5	—	—	6	54.5
Mississippi, ND	—	—	0	0.0	—	—	0	0.0
Mississippi, SD	1	14.3	0	0.0	—	—	1	6.3
Missouri, ED	1	20.0	0	0.0	—	—	1	12.5
Missouri, WD	4	66.7	0	0.0	1	50.0	5	55.6
Montana, D	—	—	3	75.0	—	—	3	75.0
Nebraska, D	1	33.3	1	50.0	—	—	2	40.0
Nevada, D	—	—	0	0.0	—	—	0	0.0
New Hampshire, D	—	—	1	100.0	—	—	1	100.0
New Jersey, D	0	0.0	2	50.0	—	—	2	25.8
New Mexico, D	—	—	0	0.0	—	—	0	0.0
New York, ED	1	16.7	3	42.9	—	—	4	30.8
New York, ND	0	0.0	2	100.0	—	—	2	66.7
New York, SD	20	44.4	16	34.8	1	100.0	37	40.2
New York, WD	0	0.0	2	33.3	—	—	2	25.0
North Carolina, ED	—	—	2	66.7	—	—	2	66.7
North Carolina, MD	0	0.0	—	—	—	—	0	0.0

(Table continues)

Table 10-14 (Continued)

District court	Warren (1953-1968) N	Percentage	Burger (1969-1985) N	Percentage	Rehnquist (1986-1990) N	Percentage	Total N	Percentage
North Carolina, WD	—	—	2	50.0	0	0.0	2	33.3
North Dakota, D	—	—	0	0.0	—	—	0	0.0
Ohio, ND	0	0.0	0	0.0	—	—	0	0.0
Ohio, SD	2	40.0	3	75.0	0	0.0	5	55.6
Oklahoma, ND	—	—	—	—	—	—	0	0.0
Oklahoma, WD	1	25.0	2	33.3	—	—	3	30.0
Oregon, D	—	—	0	0.0	—	—	0	0.0
Pennsylvania, ED	4	50.0	7	38.9	—	—	11	42.3
Pennsylvania, MD	2	50.0	0	0.0	—	—	2	33.3
Pennsylvania, WD	0	0.0	0	0.0	—	—	0	0.0
Puerto Rico, D	—	—	1	50.0	—	—	1	50.0
Rhode Island, D	4	80.0	2	50.0	—	—	6	66.7
South Carolina, D	1	33.3	—	—	—	—	1	33.3
South Carolina, ED	0	0.0	1	20.0	—	—	0	0.0
South Dakota, D	0	0.0	0	0.0	—	—	1	16.7
Tennessee, MD	1	25.0	—	—	—	—	1	20.0
Tennessee, WD	0	0.0	1	33.3	—	—	0	0.0
Texas, ED	—	—	1	33.3	—	—	1	33.3
Texas, ND	0	0.0	4	57.1	—	—	4	44.4
Texas, SD	4	44.4	0	0.0	—	—	4	28.6
Texas, WD	2	66.7	2	18.2	—	—	4	28.6
Utah, D	1	9.1	1	100.0	0	0.0	2	14.3
Vermont, D	0	0.0	3	100.0	1	100.0	4	57.1
Virginia, ED	1	12.5	2	25.0	1	33.3	4	21.1
Virginia, WD	—	—	1	50.0	—	—	1	50.0
Washington, ED	—	—	0	0.0	—	—	0	0.0

Washington, WD	3	60.0	1	25.0	1	100.0	5	50.0
West Virginia, SD	1	50.0	0	0.0	—	—	1	25.0
Wisconsin, ED	2	50.0	2	33.3	—	—	4	40.0
Wisconsin, WD	—	—	0	0.0	—	—	0	0.0
Wyoming, D	—	—	1	33.3	—	—	1	33.3
Total	125	34.8	137	34.1	12	40.0	274	34.6

Note: "—" indicates no cases decided. *N*s are the number of cases affirmed; percentages are the number of cases affirmed expressed as a percentage of the total number of cases. D=single-district state. ED=eastern district. MD=middle district. ND=northern district. SD=southern district. WD=western district. All orally argued docket numbers, excluding cases arising under the Court's original jurisdiction, are included. Because the formal dispositions the Court makes do not necessarily correspond to who wins the case, the focus here is on the prevailing party. If the petitioning party prevails in whole or in part, the case is counted as a reversal; otherwise as an affirmation.

Only district court decisions directly reviewed by the Supreme Court are included. Because the disposition made of district court decisions after intervention by the courts of appeals is problematic at best, they are excluded from consideration.

Source: U.S. Supreme Court Judicial Database.

Table 10-15   Article I Special Jurisdiction Courts

Court	Characteristics
Bankruptcy Courts	*Status:* After years of controversy over the question of Article I versus Article III status for bankruptcy judges, Congress reorganized the federal bankruptcy courts in 1984. The result is a hybrid creation. Bankruptcy courts are established as a unit within the federal district court, yet the bankruptcy judges are Article I officers.
	Jurisdiction: The bankruptcy courts, operating within the federal district court system, have jurisdiction over personal and corporate bankruptcy filings.
	Judges: Congress has authorized a number of bankruptcy judge positions for each judicial district based on the district's caseload demands. The judges are chosen by the judges of the court of appeals for the respective circuit. In those districts with more than one bankruptcy judge, the district court designates a chief judge of the bankruptcy court. Bankruptcy judges serve for terms of 14 years. They may be removed from office by the Judicial Council of the circuit, but only for reasons of incompetence, misconduct, neglect of duty, or physical or mental disability.
	Location: One in each federal judicial district.
	Appeals: Go to the federal district court. Legislation also authorizes the establishment of an appeals panel of bankruptcy judges within the districts. After a bankruptcy judge's decisions are reviewed by the district court or the appeals panel, further appeal may be made to the appropriate court of appeals.
Territorial Courts	*Status:* From time to time Congress has created courts to deal with legal disputes arising in territories administered by the United States. Three such courts currently exist: Guam, Virgin Islands, and the Northern Mariana Islands. While the courts in these territories function in much the same manner as the United States district courts, their judges do not have Article III status.
	Jurisdiction: Jurisdiction over disputes involving federal and local law arising within their geographical jurisdiction.

Table 10-15   *(Continued)*

Court	Characteristics
	Judges: Guam and the Northern Mariana Islands courts have one judge each; the court for the Virgin Islands has two judges. Judges are appointed by the president and confirmed by the Senate, and serve for 10-year terms.
	Location: Located in their respective territories.
	Appeals: Appeals from the decisions of the territorial courts of Guam and the Northern Mariana Islands go to the Court of Appeals for the Ninth Circuit. Appeals from the decisions of the territorial court for the Virgin Islands go to the Court of Appeals for the Third Circuit.
United States Court of Federal Claims	*Status:* Created by Congress in 1982 as a successor to the Court of Claims, which operated from 1855-1982.
	Jurisdiction: Trial court having authority to hear suits involving monetary claims against the United States government.
	Judges: Staffed by 16 judges who are nominated by the president and confirmed by the Senate. Members of the court serve for terms of 15 years. The chief judge must be under 70 years of age when chosen and may serve until reaching the age of 70 or until the president designates another judge to be chief. Judges may be removed from office by the United States Court of Appeals for the Federal Circuit, but only for reasons of incompetency, misconduct, neglect of duty, engaging in the practice of law, or physical or mental disability.
	Location: Washington, D.C., but cases may be heard nationwide.
	Appeals: Decisions may be appealed to the United States Court of Appeals for the Federal Circuit.
United States Court of Military Appeals	*Status:* Created by Congress in 1950.
	Jurisdiction: An appellate tribunal to review the decisions of military courts martial.

(Table continues)

Table 10-15   *(Continued)*

Court	Characteristics
	Judges: Staffed by five judges, who are nominated by the president and confirmed by the Senate. Judges must be civilians at the time of their appointment and persons who have served 20 or more years in the military are not eligible. No more than three judges may be of the same political party. They serve terms of 15 years. The chief judge is designated by the president. Judges may be removed by the president only for neglect of duty, malfeasance in office, or mental or physical disability.
	Location: Washington, D.C.
	Appeals: Decisions are reviewable only on certiorari to the United States Supreme Court.
United States Court of Veterans Appeals	*Status:* Created by Congress in 1988.
	Jurisdiction: Exclusive appellate jurisdiction over decisions of the Board of Veterans Appeals, a unit of the Veterans Administration.
	Judges: Staffed by one chief judge and two to six associate judges. The judges are appointed by the president, confirmed by the Senate, and serve 15-year terms. No more than the smallest possible majority of the judges may be of the same political party. Judges may be removed by the president only on grounds of misconduct, neglect of duty, or engaging in the practice of law.
	Location: Washington, D.C., but cases may be heard nationwide.
	Appeals: Decisions may be appealed to the Court of Appeals for the Federal Circuit.
United States Tax Court	*Status:* Originally created by Congress in 1924 as an administrative agency in the executive branch. It was known as the United States Board of Tax Appeals until 1942, when it received its current name. In 1969, Congress moved it out of the executive branch and made it an Article I tribunal.
	Jurisdiction: A trial court that handles suits filed by taxpayers who are dissatisfied with the decisions of the appeals division of the Internal Revenue Service.

Table 10-15 *(Continued)*

Court	Characteristics
	Judges: Staffed by 19 judges, who are appointed by the president, confirmed by the Senate, and serve a term of 15 years. The chief judge is elected by the members of the court for a two-year term. The court is empowered to appoint special trial judges who assist the court with its work and serve at the pleasure of the court. Judges must be under the age of 65 when appointed and can be removed by the president only for inefficiency, neglect of duty, or malfeasance. *Location:* Headquartered in Washington, D.C., but judges hear cases throughout the United States at locations convenient to taxpayers. *Appeals:* Taken to the United States court of appeals for the appropriate circuit.

Note: Article I courts, also known as legislative courts, are those created by Congress to assist the legislature in carrying out congressional functions described in Article I of the Constitution. Because they are created under Article I of the Constitution, these courts do not enjoy the same status ascribed to federal courts. Article I judges, for example, do not serve during good behavior and are not protected against salary reduction.

Sources: United States Code; *The United States Government Manual 1991/92* (Washington, D.C.: Office of the Federal Register of the National Archives and Records Administration, 1992); Kenneth R. Redden, *Federal Special Court Litigation* (Charlottesville, Va.: The Michie Company, 1982).

Table 10-16 Article III Special Jurisdiction Courts

Court	Characteristics
Court of Appeals for the Federal Circuit	*Status:* Created by Congress in 1982. It is the result of a merger of the appellate jurisdictions of the United States Court of Claims and the United States Court of Customs and Patent Appeals. It enjoys the same status as the regional courts of appeals.
	Jurisdiction: Jurisdiction over patent, trademark, and copyright disputes, and certain administrative law issues. It hears cases appealed from district courts, the United States Claims Court, the United States Court of International Trade, the United States Court of Veterans Appeals, and designated administrative agencies.
	Judges: Staffed by twelve judges who serve on the Court of Appeals for the Federal Circuit. They are appointed by the president and confirmed by the Senate. The chief judge is the member of the court with the greatest seniority who is under the age of 65. The chief judge serves for a term of seven years.
	Location: Washington, D.C.
	Appeals: Reviewable under writ of certiorari to the United States Supreme Court.
Foreign Intelligence Surveillance Court	*Status:* Established by Congress in 1978.
	Jurisdiction: Jurisdiction over executive branch requests for warrants to engage in domestic electronic surveillance for the purposes of gathering foreign intelligence.
	Judges: Staffed by seven district court judges from seven different circuits designated by the chief justice of the United States. Judges may serve no more than seven years. All hearings, procedures, and decisions are classified. Staffed on a monthly rotational basis with the judge on duty authorized to act individually. Service is part time and is in addition to judges' regular judicial duties.
	Location: Washington, D.C.

Table 10-16   *(Continued)*

Court	Characteristics
	Appeals: The chief justice is authorized to appoint three federal judges to serve as a review panel for cases in which the government wishes to appeal a warrant denial. Decisions of this appeal panel may be reviewed upon government petition for a writ of certiorari to the Supreme Court.
Judicial Panel on Multidistrict Litigation	*Status:* Created by Congress in 1968 in an effort to streamline the judicial process with respect to lawsuits filed in separate districts that involve common factual questions.
	Jurisdiction: Empowered to transfer temporarily to a single district civil cases pending in different districts that involve common questions of fact. This action allows pretrial and discovery procedures to be conducted at a single location to improve the efficiency of the system.
	Judges: Staffed by seven judges, who are designated by the chief justice of the United States from among district and court of appeals judges. The chief justice from time to time changes the members of the panel. Two or more of the judges may not be from the same circuit. The chief judge of the panel is also appointed by the chief justice. Duty on the panel is part time and is in addition to the other responsibilities the members of the panel may have.
	Location: Headquartered in Washington, D.C., but the panel holds hearings in each of the circuits on a rotating basis.
	Appeals: Panel decisions not to transfer a case are not reviewable. Other actions may be appealed to the appropriate court of appeals.
The Special Court (Created by the Regional Rail Reorganization Act of 1973)	*Status:* Created by Congress in 1973 to handle matters related to the reorganization of financially bankrupt railroads in the Northeast and Midwest.
	Jurisdiction: Jurisdiction over the transfer of assets from insolvent to solvent railroads in the designated regions.

(Table continues)

Table 10-16   *(Continued)*

Court	Characteristics
	Judges: Staffed by five judges, who are appointed from the ranks of district court and court of appeals judges to the Special Court by the Judicial Panel on Multidistrict Litigation. Service on the Special Court is part time and is in addition to the regular duties of its members.
	Location: Washington, D.C.
	Appeals: Decisions of the Special Court are reviewable under certiorari to the United States Supreme Court.
United States Court of International Trade	*Status:* Created by Congress in 1980. It traces its roots to 1890 as the Board of United States General Appraisers, which became the United States Customs Court in 1926. In 1956, the Customs Court became an Article III tribunal. The 1980 legislation reorganized the Customs Court into its present form as the Court of International Trade.
	Jurisdiction: Jurisdiction over civil cases arising from federal trade and import laws. This includes such matters as customs, duties, and trade regulations.
	Judges: Nine judges serve on the Court of International Trade. They are appointed by the president and confirmed by the Senate. Not more than five of the judges may be of the same political party. The chief judge is designated by the president. The chief judge must be less than 70 years of age when selected and serves in that capacity until reaching the age of 70 or until the president designates a replacement.
	Location: Headquartered in New York City, but may hear cases in other cities as well.
	Appeals: Taken to the Court of Appeals for the Federal Circuit.

Note: Article III courts, also known as constitutional courts, are those created by Congress under its authority in Article III of the Constitution to establish lower federal courts. These courts are part of the judicial branch and judges serving on them enjoy all of the protections specified in Article III (terms of good behavior, no reduction in salary, removeable only by impeachment, etc.).

Sources: United States Code; *The United States Government Manual 1991/92* (Washington, D.C.: Office of the Federal Register of the National Archives and Records Administration, 1992); Kenneth R. Redden, *Federal Special Court Litigation* (Charlottesville, Va.: The Michie Company, 1982).

Table 10-17 Specialized Court Decisions Affirmed by the Warren, Burger, and Rehnquist Courts

Specialized court	Warren (1953-1969)		Burger (1969-1986)		Rehnquist (1986-1991)		Total	
	N	Percentage	N	Percentage	N	Percentage	N	Percentage
Customs and Patent Appeals	0	0.0	4	57.1	—	—	4	50.0
Court of Claims[a]	11	29.7	8	40.0	—	—	19	33.3
Federal Circuit	—	—	1	14.3	6	46.2	7	35.0
Temporary Emergency Court of Appeals	—	—	1	100.0	—	—	1	100.0
Military Appeals	—	—	—	—	1	100.0	1	100.0
Total	11	28.9	14	40.0	7	50.0	32	36.8

Note: "—" indicates no cases decided. *N*s are the number of docket numbers, excluding cases arising under the Court's original jurisdiction, are included. Because the formal dispositions the Court makes do not necessarily correspond to who wins the case, the focus here is on the prevailing party. If the petitioning party prevails in whole or in part, the case is counted as a reversal; otherwise, as an affirmation.

[a] This court is now called the Court of Federal Claims.

Source: U.S. Supreme Court Judicial Database.

Table 10-18 State Court Systems: Organization and Selection of Judges

State	Name of court of last resort	Number of justices	Length of term (years)[a]	Selection process	Intermediate court
Alabama	Supreme Court	9	6	Partisan ballot	Yes
Alaska	Supreme Court	5	10	Merit	Yes
Arizona	Supreme Court	5	6	Merit	Yes
Arkansas	Supreme Court	7	8	Partisan ballot	Yes
California	Supreme Court	7	12	Gubernatorial[b]	Yes
Colorado	Supreme Court	7	10	Merit	Yes
Connecticut	Supreme Court	7	8	Modified merit[c]	Yes
Delaware	Supreme Court	5	12	Gubernatorial	No
Florida	Supreme Court	7	6	Merit	Yes
Georgia	Supreme Court	7	6	Nonpartisan ballot	Yes
Hawaii	Supreme Court	5	10	Modified merit[d]	Yes
Idaho	Supreme Court	5	6	Nonpartisan ballot	Yes
Illinois	Supreme Court	7	10	Partisan election[b]	Yes
Indiana	Supreme Court	5	10	Merit	Yes
Iowa	Supreme Court	9	8	Merit	Yes
Kansas	Supreme Court	7	6	Merit	Yes
Kentucky	Supreme Court	7	8	Nonpartisan ballot	Yes
Louisiana	Supreme Court	7	10	Nonpartisan ballot	Yes
Maine	Supreme Judicial Court	7	7	Gubernatorial	Yes
Maryland	Court of Appeals	7	10	Merit[e]	Yes
Massachusetts	Supreme Judicial Court	7	to age 70	Gubernatorial	Yes
Michigan	Supreme Court	7	8	Nonpartisan ballot	Yes
Minnesota	Supreme Court	7	6	Nonpartisan ballot	Yes
Mississippi	Supreme Court	9	8	Partisan ballot	No
Missouri	Supreme Court	7	12	Merit	Yes
Montana	Supreme Court	7	8	Nonpartisan ballot	No
Nebraska	Supreme Court	7	6	Merit	No
Nevada	Supreme Court	5	7	Nonpartisan ballot	No
New Hampshire	Supreme Court	5	to age 70	Gubernatorial	No

State	Court			Selection	
New Jersey	Supreme Court	7	7	Gubernatorial	Yes
New Mexico	Supreme Court	8	5	Modified merit [f]	Yes
New York	Court of Appeals	14	7	Gubernatorial	Yes
North Carolina	Supreme Court	8	7	Partisan ballot	Yes
North Dakota	Supreme Court	10	5	Nonpartisan ballot	Yes
Ohio	Supreme Court	6	7	Nonpartisan ballot [g]	Yes
Oklahoma	Supreme Court	6	9	Merit	Yes
	Criminal Court of Appeals	6	3	Merit	
Oregon	Supreme Court	6	7	Nonpartisan ballot	Yes
Pennsylvania	Supreme Court	10	7	Partisan ballot [h]	Yes
Rhode Island	Supreme Court	life	5	Legislative	No
South Carolina	Supreme Court	10	5	Legislative	Yes
South Dakota	Supreme Court	8	5	Merit	No
Tennessee	Supreme Court	8	9	Partisan ballot	Yes
	Criminal Court of Appeals	6	9	Partisan ballot	
Texas	Supreme Court	6	9	Partisan ballot	Yes
Utah	Supreme Court	10	5	Merit	Yes
Vermont	Supreme Court	6	5	Modified merit [i]	No
Virginia	Supreme Court	12	7	Legislative	Yes
Washington	Supreme Court	6	9	Nonpartisan ballot	Yes
West Virginia	Supreme Court	12	5	Partisan ballot	No
Wisconsin	Supreme Court	12	7	Nonpartisan ballot	Yes
Wyoming	Supreme Court	8	5	Merit	No

[a] Term is for retention period. Initial term may be shorter.
[b] Judges run unopposed in retention elections.
[c] Judicial Review Council recommends reappointment.
[d] Reappointment by the Judicial Selection Commission.
[e] Advice and consent of Senate required.
[f] Judges can be opposed in first retention election.
[g] Nominees selected in partisan primaries.
[h] Retention by nonpartisan ballot.
[i] Selected with advice and consent of Senate; retained unless removed by state legislature.

Source: The Book of States 1990-91 (Lexington, Ky.: Council of State Governments, 1990), 207-212.

Table 10-19 Authorized Judgeships and Support Personnel in State Appellate Courts, 1990

State	Authorized justices/judges		Lawyer support personnel	
	Court of last resort	Intermediate appellate court	Court of last resort	Intermediate appellate court
Alabama	9	3 [a] 5 [a]	18	6 [a] 10 [a]
Alaska	5	3	11	8
Arizona	5	21	16	48
Arkansas	7	6	15	16
California	7	88	50	206
Colorado	7	16	14	26
Connecticut	7	9	14	14
Delaware	5	NA	5	NA
District of Columbia	9	NA	27	NA
Florida	7	57	15	102
Georgia	7	9	17	28
Hawaii	5	3	14	6
Idaho	5	3	11	6
Illinois	7	50	24	88
Indiana	5	13	13	10
Iowa	9	6	16	6
Kansas	7	10	7	18
Kentucky	7	14	11	22
Louisiana	7	48	27	103
Maine	7	NA	9	NA
Maryland	7	13	14	29
Massachusetts	7	14	20	31
Michigan	7	24	15	84
Minnesota	7	15	10	36

State			
Mississippi	9	NA	NA
Missouri	7	32	135
Montana	7	NA	NA
Nebraska	7	NA	NA
Nevada	5	NA	NA
New Hampshire	5	NA	NA
New Jersey	7	28	60
New Mexico	5	7	20
New York	7	47[b]	25[b]
		15[b]	171[b]
North Carolina	7	12	28
North Dakota	5	3	0
Ohio	7	59	Varies
Oklahoma	9	5[c]	6[c]
		12[c]	12[c]
Oregon	7	10	18
Pennsylvania	7	15[d]	NA
		9[d]	57[d]
Rhode Island	5	NA	NA
South Carolina	5	6	11
South Dakota	5	NA	NA
Tennessee	5	9[e]	9[e]
		12[e]	12[e]
Texas	9	9[f]	42[f]
		80[f]	217[f]
Utah	5	7	9
Vermont	5	NA	NA
Virginia	7	10	12
Washington	9	17	32

(Table continues)

Table 10-19 (Continued)

State	Authorized justices/judges		Lawyer support personnel	
	Court of last resort	Intermediate appellate court	Court of last resort	Intermediate appellate court
West Virginia	5	NA	20	NA
Wisconsin	7	13	10	25
Wyoming	5	NA	20	NA

Note: "NA" indicates not applicable.

a Alabama has multiple appellate courts. Figures on top are for Court of Civil Appeals; figures on bottom are for Court of Criminal Appeals.
b New York has multiple appellate courts. Figures on top are for Appellate Division; figures on bottom are for Appellate Terms.
c Oklahoma has multiple appellate courts. Figures on top are for Court of Appeals; figures on bottom are for Court of Criminal Appeals.
d Pennsylvania has multiple appellate courts. Figures on top are for Commonwealth Court; figures on bottom are for Superior Court.
e Tennessee has multiple appellate courts. Figures on top are for Court of Appeals; figures on bottom are for Court of Criminal Appeals.
f Texas has multiple appellate courts. Figures on top are for Court of Criminal Appeals; figures on bottom are for Courts of Appeals.

Source: Court Statistics Project, State Court Caseload Statistics: Annual Report 1990 (Williamsburg, Va.: National Center for State Courts in Cooperation with the Conference of State Court Administrators, 1992), 102-106.

Table 10-20 Mandatory Caseloads in State Appellate Courts, 1984-1990

	1984		1985		1986		1987		1988		1989		1990	
State court	Filings (N)	Dispo-sitions (N)	Filings (N)	Dispo-sitions (N)	Filings (N)	Dispo-sitions (N)	Filings (N)	Dispo-sitions (N)	Filings (N)	Dispo-sitions (N)	Filings (N)	Dispo-sitions (N)	Filings (N)	Dispo-sitions (N)
	States with one court of last resort and one intermediate appellate court													
Alaska														
Supreme Court	320	347	334	287	318	355	368	291	363	394	342	298	342	349
Court of Appeals	467	449	446	406	505	589	469	429	435	403	404	431	429	387
Arizona														
Supreme Court	105 [a]	111 [a]	81 [a]	87 [a]	118 [a]	70 [a]	116 [a]	86 [a]	112 [a]	79 [a]	159 [a]	133 [a]	92	162
Court of Appeals	2,753	2,598	2,843	2,953	3,352	3,445	3,451	3,372	3,902	3,240	3,858	3,478	4,491	3,659
Arkansas														
Supreme Court	479 [b]	448 [b]	439 [b]	451 [b]	411 [b]	404 [b]	459 [b]	416 [b]	400 [b]	457 [b]	443 [b]	421 [b]	482	448
Court of Appeals	855	827	846	895	951	840	949	983	899	827	1,079	978	1,096	1,016
California														
Supreme Court	222 [c]	NA	284 [c]	NA	236 [c]	NA	315 [c]	73	319 [c]	101	380 [c]	46	522	20
Courts of Appeal	10,118	NA	10,252	NA	10,035	NA	9,985	10,669	10,954	10,577	11,542	13,886	13,012	14,584
Colorado														
Supreme Court	256	NA	200	NA	205	NA	214	NA	197	NA	205	NA	228	NA
Court of Appeals	1,580	1,411	1,626	1,396	1,862	1,590	1,930	1,602	1,964	2,028	2,012	2,193	2,269	2,105
Connecticut														
Supreme Court	NA	NA	NA	NA	NA	NA	58	NA	86	NA	274	296	281	285
Appellate Court	1,362 [d]	568 [d]	934 [d]	877 [d]	953 [d]	1,055 [d]	945	893	995	1,026	985	1,135	1,107	1,107
Florida														
Supreme Court	587	530	597	639	629	644	581	548	510	534	642	580	617	595
District Courts of Appeal	11,770	11,941	12,262	12,540	13,502	12,847	13,861	13,591	14,195	13,599	13,924	14,073	14,386	14,503

(Table continues)

Table 10-20 (Continued)

State court	1984 Filings (N)	1984 Dispositions (N)	1985 Filings (N)	1985 Dispositions (N)	1986 Filings (N)	1986 Dispositions (N)	1987 Filings (N)	1987 Dispositions (N)	1988 Filings (N)	1988 Dispositions (N)	1989 Filings (N)	1989 Dispositions (N)	1990 Filings (N)	1990 Dispositions (N)
Georgia														
Supreme Court	633[e]	NA	692[e]	NA	616[e]	NA	640[e]	NA	639[e]	NA	674	NA	690	502
Court of Appeals	2,070[f]	2,090[f]	1,946[f]	NA	2,666[f]	NA	2,071[f]	1,961	2,306[f]	1,986	2,361[f]	1,918	2,384	1,535
Hawaii														
Supreme Court	471[d]	454[d]	496[d]	516[d]	604[d]	691[d]	616[d]	579[d]	715[d]	609[d]	650[d]	749[d]	489	565
Intermediate Court of Appeals	101	125	132	105	132	132	134	142	120	129	140	138	138	120
Idaho														
Supreme Court	349[g]	352[g]	348[g]	333[g]	288[g]	359[g]	289[g]	295[g]	382[g]	332[g]	366[g]	347[g]	349	369
Court of Appeals	146	175	149	282	174	174	181	174	227	162	221	231	215	204
Illinois														
Supreme Court	118	120	167	152	218	207	176	152	275	292	153	191	199	185[h]
Appellate Court	7,134[h]	6,891[h]	7,611[h]	6,961[h]	7,550[h]	7,007[h]	7,954[h]	7,451[h]	8,119[h]	7,648[h]	8,139[h]	7,722[h]	8,191[h]	7,951[h]
Indiana														
Supreme Court	NA	357	NA	359	NA	470	409	384	NA	380	336	418	199	259
Court of Appeals	1,150[h]	1,137[h]	1,037[h]	1,062[h]	1,073[h]	1,116[h]	1,149[h]	1,130[h]	1,222[h]	1,137[h]	1,516	1,334	1,966	1,657
Iowa														
Supreme Court	NA	846[i]	NA	868[i]	1,528	933[i]	877[i]	944[i]	801[i]	899[i]	1,303	970[i]	1,211	947[i]
Court of Appeals	569	532	730	637	552	589	618	578	728	669	678	799	743	662
Kansas														
Supreme Court	169	343	177	344	189	331	214	333	347	459	179	290	165	267
Court of Appeals	1,041[d]	1,045[d]	1,087[d]	989[d]	1,131[d]	1,106[d]	1,127[d]	1,143[d]	1,176[d]	1,174[d]	1,154[d]	1,218[d]	1,201[d]	1,152[d]
Kentucky														
Supreme Court	221	280	282	259	251	253	261	271	258	302	304	305	281	278
Court of Appeals	2,725	2,696	3,156	2,757	2,769	2,661	2,691	2,304	2,665	2,243	2,712	2,438	2,569	2,463

	1	2	3	4	5	6	7	8	9	10	11	12	13	14
Louisiana														
Supreme Court	147[j]	NA	NA	79[j]	112	71	135	123	124	134	108	105	82	95
Courts of Appeal	3,870[k]	NA	NA	3,578[k]	3,695	3,944	3,846	3,380	3,967	3,429	3,562	3,646	3,835	3,517
Maryland														
Court of Appeals	220[l]	230[l]	218[l]	232[l]	238[l]	188[l]	233[l]	222[l]	242[l]	183[l]	205[l]	221[l]	261	244
Court of Special Appeals	1,777	1,877	1,642	1,807	1,644	1,552	1,714	1,777	1,754	1,762	1,841	1,811	2,006	1,808
Massachusetts														
Supreme Judicial Court	141	NA	129	NA	86	NA	72	NA	96	NA	75	NA	86	NA
Appeals Court	1,375[h]	NA	1,301[h]	NA	1,352[h]	NA	1,434[h]	NA	1,394[h]	NA	1,451[h]	NA	1,568	1,171
Michigan														
Supreme Court	5	NA	3	NA	4	NA	5	NA	4	NA	4	NA	2	NA
Court of Appeals	4,796	NA	5,187	NA	NA	NA	8,186[g]	7,502[g]	8,559[g]	8,497[g]	10,951[g]	8,983[g]	12,340[g]	10,503[g]
Minnesota														
Supreme Court	NA	NA	NA	NA	175	157	241	204	271	250	248	242	282	260
Court of Appeals	NA	NA	NA	NA	1,767	1,848	1,924	1,916	2,065	1,949	1,772	1,872	2,157	2,042
Missouri														
Supreme Court	161[l]	158[l]	187[l]	170[l]	164[l]	115[l]	93[l]	133[l]	63	60	227	227	247	267
Court of Appeals	2,852	3,159	3,166	3,177	3,147	3,206	3,055	3,259	3,315	3,145	3,659	3,331	3,565	3,568
New Jersey														
Supreme Court	368	408	227	251	236	237	349	381	357	349	413	383	387	401
Appellate Division of Superior Court	6,224[h]	6,262[h]	6,037[h]	6,056[h]	6,106[h]	6,611[h]	6,277[h]	6,400[h]	6,458[h]	6,494[h]	6,492[h]	6,531[h]	7,007	6,284
New Mexico														
Supreme Court	322	NA	303	NA	325	NA	320	NA	296	NA	368	365	297	313
Court of Appeals	572	NA	662	NA	671	NA	604	853	648	690	777	741	797	763
North Carolina														
Supreme Court	230	219	222	183	249	245	182	192	147	213	109	95	116	102
Court of Appeals	1,314[e,m]	1,412[e,m]	1,375[e,m]	1,464[e,m]	1,381[e,m]	1,626[e,m]	1,265[e,m]	1,310[e,m]	1,351[e,m]	1,272[e,m]	1,378	1,188[e,m]	1,378	1,366

(Table continues)

Table 10-20 (Continued)

State court	1984 Filings (N)	1984 Dispositions (N)	1985 Filings (N)	1985 Dispositions (N)	1986 Filings (N)	1986 Dispositions (N)	1987 Filings (N)	1987 Dispositions (N)	1988 Filings (N)	1988 Dispositions (N)	1989 Filings (N)	1989 Dispositions (N)	1990 Filings (N)	1990 Dispositions (N)
North Dakota														
Supreme Court	370	331	338	335	377	357	382	357	367	405	397	381	429	439
Court of Appeals	[n]	[n]	[n]	[n]	[n]	[n]	[n]	[n]	9	13	0	0	13	7
Ohio														
Supreme Court	338	320	442	383	491	414	422	380	500	462	535	457	682	531
Court of Appeals	9,383	9,124	9,522	9,491	9,683	9,296	9,983	9,393	10,005	9,668	10,771	9,871	10,721	10,928
Oregon														
Supreme Court	205	390[h]	180	296[h]	145	262[h]	176	313[h]	192	322[h]	217	301[h]	194	271[h]
Court of Appeals	3,828	3,759	3,981	3,784	4,146	4,014	4,305	4,232	3,739	3,985	3,795	3,601	4,584	3,725
South Carolina														
Supreme Court	479	NA	451	NA	519	NA	511	596	624	385	463	537	602	537
Court of Appeals	404	441	391	398	351	374	440	368	307	367	448	377	370	367
Utah														
Supreme Court	640	NA	628	NA	623	NA	474	521	443	617	498	642	566	556
Court of Appeals	NA	NA	NA	NA	NA	NA	560[o]	NA	721	NA	764	785	629	691
Virginia														
Supreme Court	NA	NA	NA	NA	NA	NA	NA	NA	NA	NA	NA	NA	13	13
Court of Appeals	[n]	[n]	538	216	419	476	422	NA	455	NA	443	NA	464	NA
Washington														
Supreme Court	228[d]	176[d]	194[d]	184[d]	162[d]	209[d]	135[d]	148[d]	123[d]	154[d]	101[d]	127[d]	148[d]	139[d]
Court of Appeals	2,866	2,724	3,270	2,994	3,535	3,238	3,238	3,870	3,157	3,289	3,222	2,902	3,653	3,086
Wisconsin														
Supreme Court	98	NA	91	NA	NA	NA	NA	NA	NA	NA	NA	NA	NA	NA
Court of Appeals	2,239	2,223	2,358	2,501	2,053	2,178	2,185	2,206	2,147	2,368	2,355	2,414	2,853	2,612

States with no intermediate appellate court

Court														
Delaware Supreme Court	331[g]	354[g]	406[g]	373[g]	417[g]	415[g]	397[g]	419[g]	473[g]	407[g]	517[g]	480[g]	483[g]	553[g]
District of Columbia Court of Appeals	1,810[1]	1,510[1]	1,770[1]	1,568[1]	1,556	1,568	1,500	1,595	1,624	1,602	1,515	1,598	1,650	1,798
Maine Supreme Judicial Court	61	494	NA	506	59	521	631[p]	495	528[p]	507[p]	540	452	622[p]	475[p]
Mississippi Supreme Court	838	637	815	853	1,010	912	891	831	919	793	773	840	961	944
Montana Supreme Court	NA	NA	NA	NA	566	355	546	NA	597	NA	627	618[g]	633	624
Nebraska Supreme Court	1,002[g]	NA	997[g]	NA	1,014[g]	NA	1,196[g]	964[g]	1,103[g]	1,094[g]	1,497[g]	1,277[g]	1,207[g]	1,022[g]
Nevada Supreme Court	799	788	777	867	853	854	856	1013	991	922	997	1,047	1,089	1,057
New Hampshire Supreme Court	NA	NA	NA	NA	NA	NA	NA	NA	NA	NA	NA	NA	NA	NA
Rhode Island Supreme Court	409	447	403	393	389	478	323	402	410	403	455	396	465	476
South Dakota Supreme Court	344[q]	NA	358[q]	NA	363[q]	NA	422[q]	NA	428[q]	463[q]	387[q]	484[q]	403[q]	434[q]
Vermont Supreme Court	623[r]	532	575	506	550	535	538	527	620	593	619	624	590	685
West Virginia Supreme Court of Appeals	NA	NA	NA	NA	NA	NA	NA	NA	NA	NA	NA	NA	NA	NA
Wyoming Supreme Court	331	250	306	347	342	327	320	302	357	334	321	363	314	287

(Table continues)

Table 10-20 (Continued)

States with multiple appellate courts at any level

State court	1984 Filings (N)	1984 Dispositions (N)	1985 Filings (N)	1985 Dispositions (N)	1986 Filings (N)	1986 Dispositions (N)	1987 Filings (N)	1987 Dispositions (N)	1988 Filings (N)	1988 Dispositions (N)	1989 Filings (N)	1989 Dispositions (N)	1990 Filings (N)	1990 Dispositions (N)
Alabama														
Supreme Court	745	NA	798	797	827	940	998	1,017	829	994	908	620	998	569
Court of Civil Appeals	532	536	548	516	530	548	584	518	529	576	556	528	651	641
Court of Criminal Appeals	1,400	1,480	1,520	1,424	1,537	1,745	1,695	1,819	1,784	1,774	2,132	1,927	2,042	1,904
New York														
Court of Appeals	NA	391	NA	401	680	350	409	369	324	369	330	295	302	287
Appellate Division	NA	NA	135	135	NA	NA	9,205[h]	13,392[h]	10,740[h]	13,225[h]	11,338[h]	14,534[h]	10,577[h]	2,540[h]
Appellate Terms	NA	NA	NA	NA	NA	NA	2,208	2,133	2,192	21,214	2,461	2,034	2,245	2,179
Oklahoma														
Supreme Court	789	229[s]	1,128	149[s]	788	174[s]	1,105	813	809	852	862	NA	1,033	NA
Court of Appeals	788	801	635	693	971	856	931	728	1,362	1,215	1,373	1,337	1,323	1,038
Court of Criminal Appeals	502	645	NA	404	NA	536	980[h]	626	1,046[h]	693	1,192[h]	773	1,445[h]	774
Pennsylvania														
Supreme Court	268	NA	142	NA	92	NA	80	NA	121	NA	94	NA	225	NA
Commonwealth Court	4,012	NA	3,554	NA	3,737[t]	NA	3,030[t]	4,053[t]	3,164[t]	4,392[t]	3,115[t]	3,973[t]	3,491	3,519[t]
Superior Court	5,793[h]	5,908[h]	5,878[h]	8,355[h]	5,989[h]	7,410[h]	6,137[h]	6,253[h]	6,439[h]	6,416[h]	6,040[h]	6,218[h]	6,291	6,079
Tennessee														
Supreme Court	216	NA	139	NA	146	NA	170	NA	161	NA	161	NA	107	NA
Court of Appeals	951	1,010	999	1,010	1,173	1,330	1,003	1,033	889	1,015	889	1,015	980	924

Court of Criminal Appeals Texas	868[h]	851[h]	850[h]	891[h]	885	946[h]	811[h]	747[h]	994	794[h]	994	794[h]	1,002	843[h]
Supreme Court	0	0	1	1	2	2	3	3	3	3	3	1	3	3
Court of Criminal Appeals														
Appeals	1,959	2,237	1,998	2,085	2,221	2,027	2,450	2,448	3,578	3,546	3,504	3,806	2,281	2,487
Courts of Appeals	7,386	8,274	7,954	7,981	7,832	8,161	7,857	7,824	8,250	7,984	8,813	8,414	8,062	8,134

Note: "NA" indicates data not available.

[a] Does not include mandatory judge disciplinary cases.
[b] Includes a few discretionary petitions but not mandatory attorney disciplinary cases and certified questions from the federal courts.
[c] Does not include judge disciplinary cases.
[d] Includes a few discretionary petitions that were granted review.
[e] Includes a few discretionary petitions that were granted review and refiled as appeals.
[f] Includes all discretionary petitions that were granted review and refiled as appeals.
[g] Includes discretionary petitions that were granted review.
[h] Includes all discretionary petitions that were granted review.
[i] Includes some discretionary petitions that were dismissed by the court.
[j] Includes a few discretionary appeals.
[k] Includes refiled discretionary petitions that were granted review.
[l] Includes discretionary petitions that were granted review and refiled as appeals.
[m] Includes some cases where relief, not review, was granted.
[n] Court did not exist during that year.
[o] Represents an 11-month reporting period.
[p] Includes discretionary opinions but not mandatory and advisory opinion cases.
[q] Includes discretionary advisory opinion.
[r] Includes discretionary petitions that were granted review and decided.
[s] Does not include mandatory appeals of final judgments, mandatory disciplinary cases, and mandatory interlocutory decisions.
[t] Does not include transfer from the Superior Court and Court of Common Pleas.

Source: Court Statistics Project, *State Court Caseload Statistics: Annual Report 1990* (Williamsburg, Va.: National Center for State Courts in Cooperation with the Conference of State Court Administrators, 1992), 150-158.

Table 10-21 Discretionary Caseloads in State Appellate Courts, 1984-1990

State court	1984 Filings (N)	1984 Dispositions (N)	1985 Filings (N)	1985 Dispositions (N)	1986 Filings (N)	1986 Dispositions (N)	1987 Filings (N)	1987 Dispositions (N)	1988 Filings (N)	1988 Dispositions (N)	1989 Filings (N)	1989 Dispositions (N)	1990 Filings (N)	1990 Dispositions (N)
				States with one court of last resort and one intermediate appellate court										
Alaska														
Supreme Court	221	220	194	197	313	290	219	231	244	255	251	243	231	235
Court of Appeals	63	77	64	54	83	99	54	54	62	66	62	56	61	64
Arizona														
Supreme Court	1,016[a]	1,048	1,161[a]	1,078[a]	1,156[a]	1,156	995[a]	1,054	1,018[a]	905	1,004[a]	995	1,044[a]	1,006
Court of Appeals	50	59	40	45	49	48	51	45	60	63	52	53	83	56
Arkansas														
Supreme Court	NA	NA	NA	NA	NA	NA	NA	NA	NA	NA	NA	NA	NA	NA
Court of Appeals	NJ	NJ	NJ	NJ	NJ	NJ	NJ	NJ	NJ	NJ	NJ	NJ	NJ	NJ
California														
Supreme Court	3,991	NA	4,346	NA	4,808	NA	4,558	4,004	4,351	4,052	4,214	4,442	4,662	4,442
Courts of Appeal	5,838	NA	5,938	NA	6,234	NA	6,732	6,776	7,005	7,334	6,966	7,070	7,236	7,438
Colorado														
Supreme Court	813	NA	767	NA	783	NA	756	1,063	825	1,001[b]	993	1,215[b]	1,072	1,261
Appellate Court	NJ	NJ	NJ	NJ	NJ	NJ	NJ	NJ	NJ	NJ	NJ	NJ	NJ	NJ
Florida														
Supreme Court	1,056	1,060	1,175	1,123	1,097	1,260	1,270	1,223	1,316	1,426	1,111	965	1,303	NA
District Courts of Appeal	1,970	1,669	1,975	1,683	2,294	1,751	2,282	1,887	2,285	1,839	2,259	1,893	2,457	NA
Georgia														
Supreme Court	941	NA	975	NA	980	NA	1,006	1,524[c]	998	1,616[c]	1,101	1,885[c]	1,079	1,559[c]
Court of Appeals	623	629	641	NA	647	NA	733	701	717	683	809	706	794	794

Hawaii														
Supreme Court	32	35	41	39	43	45	57	58	45	42	42	45	43	43
Intermediate Court of Appeals	NJ	NJ	NJ	NJ	NJ	NJ	NJ	NJ	NJ	NJ	NJ	NJ	NJ	NJ
Idaho														
Supreme Court	60	55	92	99	77	71	82	76	76	84	91	88	77	86
Court of Appeals	NJ	NJ	NJ	NJ	NJ	NJ	NJ	NJ	NJ	NJ	NJ	NJ	NJ	NJ
Illinois														
Supreme Court	1,675	1,715	1,579	1,673	1,637	1,622	1,673	1,633	1,558	1,482	1,558	1,484	1,582	1,498
Appellate Court	NA	NA	NA	NA	NA	NA	NA	NA	NA	NA	NA	NA	NA	NA
Indiana														
Supreme Court	NA	356	NA	325	NA	355	404	437	NA	494	565	599	690	629
Court of Appeals	NA	NA	NA	NA	NA	NA	NA	NA	NA	NA	81	76	112	116
Iowa														
Supreme Court	NA	479 d	NA	497 d	352	520 d	327	317 d	371	291 d	NA	303 d	NA	311
Court of Appeals	NJ	NJ	NJ	NJ	NJ	NJ	NJ	NJ	NJ	NJ	NJ	NJ	NJ	NJ
Kansas														
Supreme Court	NA	NA	NA	NA	NA	NA	NA	NA	NA	NA	526	NA	461	NA
Court of Appeals	NA	NA	NA	NA	NA	NA	NA	NA	NA	NA	NA	NA	NA	NA
Kentucky														
Supreme Court	986	793	813	1,044	847	898	693 e	706 e	686 e	678	748 e	640 e	753 e	718
Court of Appeals	79	73	96	87	94	107	90	71	92	77	89	89	59	76
Louisiana														
Supreme Court	2,126 f	NA	2,313 f	NA	2,455	2,230	2,673	2,660	2,657	2,404	2,776	2,633	2,684	2,870
Courts of Appeal	1,842	NA	2,538	NA	3,016	2,935	3,541	3,460	3,877	3,802	4,189	4,138	3,980	3,945
Maryland														
Court of Appeals	761	785	713	678	607	700	655	562	682	776	598	543	626	608
Court of Special Appeals	308	308	192	192	240	185	294	294	220	220	230	230	204	204

(Table continues)

Table 10-21 (Continued)

State court	1984 Filings (N)	1984 Dispositions (N)	1985 Filings (N)	1985 Dispositions (N)	1986 Filings (N)	1986 Dispositions (N)	1987 Filings (N)	1987 Dispositions (N)	1988 Filings (N)	1988 Dispositions (N)	1989 Filings (N)	1989 Dispositions (N)	1990 Filings (N)	1990 Dispositions (N)
Massachusetts														
Supreme Judicial Court	1,246	NA	1,336	NA	1,473	NA	336	NA	563	NA	592	NA	444	NA
Appeals Court	NA	NA	NA	NA	NA	NA	NA	NA	886	NA	959	NA	916	916
Michigan														
Supreme Court	2,347	2,495[g]	2,069	2,314[g]	2,042	2,397[g]	2,082	2,168[g]	2,662	2,254[g]	2,805	2,453[g]	2,507	2,755
Court of Appeals	NA	NA	2,249	NA	NA	NA	NA	NA	NA	NA	NA	NA	NA	NA
Missouri														
Supreme Court	846	812[h]	981	980[h]	989	953[h]	1,033	997[h]	1,056	1,064	857	871	809	823
Court of Appeals	NJ	NJ	NJ	NJ	NJ	NJ	NJ	NJ	NJ	NJ	NJ	NJ	NJ	NJ
New Jersey														
Supreme Court	1,142	1,075[i]	1,053[i]	1,025[i]	1,382[i]	1,378[i]	1,382[i]	1,411[i]	1,354[i]	1,398[i]	1,482[i]	1,472[i]	1,217[i]	1,200[i]
Appellate Division of Superior Court	NA	NA	NA	NA	NA	NA	NA	NA	NA	NA	NA	NA	NA	NA
New Mexico														
Supreme Court	174	NA	155	NA	202	NA	350	NA	295	NA	366	344	414	402
Court of Appeals	57	NA	68	NA	52	NA	57	NA	64	NA	44	NA	46	NA
North Carolina														
Supreme Court	541	465	620	665	735	748	676	637	636	727	447	397	626	601
Court of Appeals	471	423	484	462	546	560	483	483	446	446	385	385	451	431
North Dakota														
Supreme Court	NA	NA	NA	NA	NA	NA	NA	NA	6	5	0	0	NA	NA
Court of Appeals	j	j	j	j	j	j	j	j	NA	NA	NA	NA	NA	NA

Jurisdiction / Court														
Ohio														
Supreme Court	1,704	1,293	1,644	1,428	1,733	1,532	1,846	1,598	1,770	1,621	1,686	1,372	1,872	1,413
Court of Appeals	NJ	NJ	NJ	NJ	NJ	NJ	NJ	NJ	NJ	NJ	NJ	NJ	NJ	NJ
Oregon														
Supreme Court	870	NA	903	873	990	1,013	1,086	1,042	857	871	709	733	791	707
Court of Appeals	NJ	NA	NJ	NA	NJ	NA	NJ	NA	NJ	NA	NJ	NA	NJ	NA
South Carolina														
Supreme Court	NA	NA	NA	NA	24[k]	NA	32[k]	NA	26[k]	NA	43[k]	NA	61	NA
Court of Appeals	NJ	NJ	NJ	NJ	NJ	NJ	NJ	NJ	NJ	NJ	NJ	NJ	NJ	NJ
Utah														
Supreme Court	NA	NA	42	NA	51	NA	30	NA	61	NA	36	NA	48	NA
Court of Appeals	NA	NA	NA	NA	NA	NA	10	NA	20	NA	NA	NA	NA	NA
Virginia														
Supreme Court	1,915	1,919	1,043	1,321	1,193	1,095	1,441	1,169	1,439	1,655	1,573	1,800	1,740	1,610
Court of Appeals	j	j	1,103	637	1,113	881	1,201	1,743	1,291	1,454	1,523	1,777	1,570	2,140
Washington														
Supreme Court	881[l]	905[l]	906[l]	907[l]	897[l]	786[l]	1,151[l]	1,093[l]	947[m]	1,060[m]	821[m]	829[m]	891[m]	883[m]
Court of Appeals	263	270	320	283	371	317	346	388	372	388	318	305	351	354
Wisconsin														
Supreme Court	718	721[n]	761	699	836	765	869	725	915	866	896	802	842	728
Court of Appeals	245	209	228	228	241	241	221	188	228	162	191	148	NA	NA
States with no intermediate appellate court														
Delaware														
Supreme Court	5[°]	5	3[°]	2	3[°]	3	4[°]	4	4[°]	3	6[°]	5	1[°]	5
District of Columbia														
Court of Appeals	85	NA	81	77	76	72	96	87	61	65	49	49	45	45

(Table continues)

Table 10-21 (*Continued*)

State court	1984 Filings (N)	1984 Dispositions (N)	1985 Filings (N)	1985 Dispositions (N)	1986 Filings (N)	1986 Dispositions (N)	1987 Filings (N)	1987 Dispositions (N)	1988 Filings (N)	1988 Dispositions (N)	1989 Filings (N)	1989 Dispositions (N)	1990 Filings (N)	1990 Dispositions (N)
Maine Supreme Judicial Court	NA	52	NA	68	NA	67	NA	40	NA	NA	NA	NA	NA	NA
Mississippi Supreme Court	2	1	4	4	3	3	2	2	0	0	43	32	64	59
Montana Supreme Court	NA	NA	NA	NA	36	19	25	NA	31	NA	6	NA	NA	NA
Nebraska Supreme Court	NA	NA	NA	NA	NA	NA	NA	NA	NA	NA	NA	NA	NA	NA
New Hampshire Supreme Court	603[P]	550[P]	574[P]	602	534[P]	415[P]	516[P]	451[P]	504	543	567	532	627	567
Rhode Island Supreme Court	202	218	288	219	168	199	219	241	189	178	179	169	177	197
South Dakota Supreme Court	27[q]	NA	17[q]	NA	32[q]	NA	27[q]	NA	35[q]	NA	39[q]	NA	49	NA
Vermont Supreme Court	25	26	19	20	24	21	31	26	32	32	34	35	32	36
West Virginia Supreme Court of Appeals	1,282	1,124	1,372	1,268	1,585	1,396	2,037	1,909	1,621	1,775	1,644	1,735	1,623	1,586
Wyoming Supreme Court	NA	NA	NA	NA	NA	NA	NA	NA	NA	NA	NA	NA	NA	NA

States with multiple appellate courts at any level

Court													
Alabama													
Supreme Court	712	NA	606	588	763	582	713	654	765	603	806	1,104	867	1,248
Court of Civil Appeals	NJ	NJ	NJ	NJ	NJ	NJ	NJ	NJ	NJ	NJ	NJ	NJ	NJ	NJ
Court of Criminal Appeals	NJ	NJ	NJ	NJ	NJ	NJ	NJ	NJ	NJ	NJ	NJ	NJ	NJ	NJ
New York													
Court of Appeals	NA	3,477	NA	3,505	NA	3,349	NA	3,478	4,280	3,392	4,411	3,621	4,499	3,808
Appellate Division	NA	NA	NA	NA	NA	NA	NA	NA	NA	NA	NA	NA	NA	NA
Appellate Terms	NA	NA	NA	NA	NA	NA	NA	NA	NA	NA	NA	NA	NA	NA
Oklahoma													
Supreme Court	388	NA	295	NA	340	NA	293	237	295	231	443	446	446	NA
Court of Appeals	NJ	NJ	NJ	NJ	NJ	NJ	NJ	NJ	NJ	NJ	NJ	NJ	NJ	NJ
Court of Criminal Appeals	284	256	NA	267	NA	264	NA	283	NA	291	NA	312	NA	412
Pennsylvania													
Supreme Court	1,537	NA	2,579	NA	2,242	NA	1,936	NA	2,207	NA	2,227	NA	3,645	NA
Commonwealth Court	82	NA	81	NA	NA	NA	115	NA	45	NA	29	NA	36	NA
Superior Court	NA	NA	NA	NA	NA	NA	NA	NA	NA	NA	NA	NA	NA	NA
Tennessee													
Supreme Court	842	NA	772	NA	765	NA	758	1,087	758	1,087	820	1,057	731	772
Court of Appeals	57	NA	82	NA	74	NA	77	77	77	77	103	97	109	74
Court of Criminal Appeals	NA	NA	NA	NA	NA	NA	NA	NA	NA	NA	67	35	NA	NA
Texas													
Supreme Court	1,130	1,034	1,169	1,187	1,228	1,166	1,176	1,261	1,243	1,168	1,126	1,096	1,206	1,166

(Table continues)

Table 10-21 (Continued)

State court	1984 Filings (N)	1984 Dispositions (N)	1985 Filings (N)	1985 Dispositions (N)	1986 Filings (N)	1986 Dispositions (N)	1987 Filings (N)	1987 Dispositions (N)	1988 Filings (N)	1988 Dispositions (N)	1989 Filings (N)	1989 Dispositions (N)	1990 Filings (N)	1990 Dispositions (N)
Court of Criminal Appeals	1,281	1,081	1,360	1,046	1,360	1,100	1,339	1,672	1,416	1,437	1,792	2,107	1,380	1,352
Courts of Appeals	NJ	NJ	NJ	NJ	NJ	NJ	NJ	NJ	NJ	NJ	NJ	NJ	NJ	NJ

Note: "NA" indicates data not available; "NJ" indicates court does not have jurisdiction.

[a] Includes mandatory judge disciplinary cases.
[b] Includes mandatory jurisdiction cases.
[c] Represents some double counting as figure includes mandatory appeals and discretionary appeals that were granted and refiled as appeals.
[d] Does not include some discretionary original proceedings.
[e] Does not include some discretionary petitions.
[f] Does not include some discretionary petitions, which are reported with mandatory jurisdiction caseload.
[g] Includes a few mandatory jurisdiction cases.
[h] Does not include a few original proceedings.
[i] Does not include discretionary interlocutory decision cases.
[j] Court did not exist during year.
[k] Does not include discretionary petitions that were denied or otherwise dismissed/withdrawn or settled.
[l] Includes mandatory certified questions from federal courts but not some discretionary petitions.
[m] Does not include some discretionary cases that are reported with mandatory jurisdiction cases.
[n] Includes all disposed mandatory jurisdiction cases.
[o] Does not include some discretionary interlocutory decision cases, which are reported with mandatory jurisdiction cases.
[p] Includes discretionary judge disciplinary cases.
[q] Does not include advisory opinions that are reported with mandatory jurisdiction cases.

Source: Court Statistics Project, *State Court Caseload Statistics: Annual Report 1990* (Williamsburg, Va.: National Center for State Courts in Cooperation with the Conference of State Court Administrators, 1992), 160-167.

Table 10-22 Opinions Reported by State Appellate Courts, 1990

| State/court | Opinion count | | Composition of opinion count | | | Total dispositions by signed opinion |
	Per case	Per written document	Signed	Per curiam	Memo	
	States with one court of last resort and one intermediate appellate court					
Alaska						
Supreme Court	Yes	No	Yes	No	No	180
Court of Appeals	Yes	No	Yes	No	No	119
Arizona						
Supreme Court	Yes	No	Yes	Yes	No	116
Court of Appeals	Yes	No	Yes	Yes	Some	288
Arkansas						
Supreme Court	Yes	No	Yes	Yes	Yes	373
Court of Appeals	Yes	No	Yes	Yes	No	623
California						
Supreme Court	Yes	No	Yes	Yes	Some	100
Courts of Appeal	Yes	No	Yes	Yes	Some	10,416
Colorado						
Supreme Court	Yes	No	Yes	Yes	No	237
Appellate Court	Yes	No	Yes	No	Some	384
Connecticut						
Supreme Court	Yes	No	Yes	Yes	Some	246
Appellate Court	Yes	No	Yes	Yes	Some	413

(Table continues)

Table 10-22 (Continued)

State/court	Opinion count		Composition of opinion count			Total dispositions by signed opinion
	Per case	Per written document	Signed	Per curiam	Memo	
Florida						
Supreme Court	Yes	No	Yes	Yes	No	199
District Courts of Appeal	Yes	No	Yes	Yes	No	4,492
Georgia						
Supreme Court	Yes	No	Yes	Yes	No	310
Court of Appeals	Yes	No	Yes	No	No	1,922
Hawaii						
Supreme Court	Yes	No	Yes	Yes	Some	318
Intermediate Court of Appeals	Yes	No	Yes	Yes	Yes	118
Idaho						
Supreme Court	No	Yes	Yes	Yes	Yes	NA
Court of Appeals	No	Yes	Yes	Yes	No	NA
Illinois						
Supreme Court	Yes	No	Yes	Yes	No	NA
Appellate Court	Yes	No	Yes	Yes	Some	2,082
Indiana						
Supreme Court	Yes	No	Yes	Yes	No	219
Court of Appeals	Yes	Yes	Yes	Yes	Yes	1,685
Iowa						
Supreme Court	No	Yes	Yes	No	No	249
Court of Appeals	Yes	No	Yes	No	No	551

Kansas						
Supreme Court	Yes	No	Yes	Yes	Some	200
Court of Appeals	Yes	No	Yes	Yes	Some	886
Kentucky						
Supreme Court	Yes	No	Yes	Yes	Some	NA
Court of Appeals	Yes	No	Yes	Yes	Some	NA
Louisiana						
Supreme Court	No	Yes	Yes	Yes	Some	135
Courts of Appeal	No	Yes	Yes	Yes	Yes	3,195
Maryland						
Court of Appeals	Yes	No	Yes	No	No	142
Court of Special Appeals	Yes	No	Yes	No	No	205
Massachusetts						
Supreme Judicial Court	No	Yes	Yes	No	No	236
Appeals Court	No	Yes	Yes	Yes	Yes	163
Michigan						
Supreme Court	Yes	No	Yes	Yes	No	71
Court of Appeals	Yes	No	Yes	Yes	Some	4,729
Minnesota						
Supreme Court	Yes	No	Yes	No	No	157
Court of Appeals	Yes	No	Yes	No	No	437
Missouri						
Supreme Court	Yes	No	Yes	Yes	Some	130
Court of Appeals	Yes	No	Yes	Yes	Some	1,884
New Jersey						
Supreme Court	No	Yes	Yes	No	No	87
Appellate Division of Superior Court	Yes	No	Yes	Yes	Yes	3,397

(Table continues)

Table 10-22 (Continued)

State/court	Opinion count		Composition of opinion count			Total dispositions by signed opinion
	Per case	Per written document	Signed	Per curiam	Memo	
New Mexico						
Supreme Court	Yes	No	Yes	No	Some	166
Court of Appeals	No	Yes	Yes	No	No	164
North Carolina						
Supreme Court	Yes	No	Yes	No	Some	93
Court of Appeals	Yes	No	Yes	No	Yes	1,221
North Dakota						
Supreme Court	Yes	No	Yes	Yes	No	281
Court of Appeals	Yes	No	No	No	No	NA
Ohio						
Supreme Court	Yes	No	Yes	No	Yes	NA
Court of Appeals	Yes	No	Yes	No	Yes	7,127
Oregon						
Supreme Court	Yes	No	Yes	Yes	No	91
Court of Appeals	Yes	No	Yes	No	No	499
South Carolina						
Supreme Court	Yes	No	Yes	Yes	No	178
Court of Appeals	Yes	No	Yes	Yes	No	339
Utah						
Supreme Court	Yes	No	Yes	Yes	No	111
Court of Appeals	Yes	No	Yes	Yes	No	244
Virginia						
Supreme Court	Yes	No	Yes	Yes	No	164
Court of Appeals	Yes	No	Yes	Yes	No	564

Washington						
Supreme Court	Yes	No	Yes	Yes	Some	119
Court of Appeals	Yes	No	Yes	Yes	Some	1,358
Wisconsin						
Supreme Court	Yes	No	Yes	Yes	No	101
Court of Appeals	Yes	No	Yes	No	No	1,265
States with no intermediate appellate court						
Delaware						
Supreme Court	Yes	No	Yes	No	No	77
District of Columbia						
Court of Appeals	Yes	No	Yes	Yes	No	369
Maine						
Supreme Judicial Court	No	Yes	Yes	No	No	259
Mississippi						
Supreme Court	Yes	No	Yes	No	Yes	375
Montana						
Supreme Court	Yes	No	Yes	No	No	387
Nebraska						
Supreme Court	Yes	No	Yes	Yes	Yes	322
Nevada						
Supreme Court	No	Yes	Yes	Yes	No	155
New Hampshire						
Supreme Court	Yes	No	Yes	Yes	No	139
Rhode Island						
Supreme Court	Yes	No	Yes	No	No	163
South Dakota						
Supreme Court	Yes	No	Yes	Yes	No	159

(Table continues)

Table 10-22 (Continued)

State/court	Opinion count		Composition of opinion count			Total dispositions by signed opinion
	Per case	Per written document	Signed	Per curiam	Memo	
Vermont						
Supreme Court	Yes	No	Yes	No	No	211
West Virginia						
Supreme Court of Appeals	Yes	No	Yes	Yes	Some	278
Wyoming						
Supreme Court	Yes	No	Yes	Yes	Some	161
States with multiple appellate courts at any level						
Alabama						
Supreme Court	Yes	No	Yes	Yes	Some	703
Court of Civil Appeals	Yes	No	Yes	Yes	Yes	404
Court of Criminal Appeals	Yes	No	Yes	No	Some	418
New York						
Court of Appeals	No	Yes	Yes	No	No	120
Appellate Division	No	Yes	Yes	Yes	Some	NA
Appellate Terms	No	Yes	Yes	Yes	Some	NA
Oklahoma						
Supreme Court	Yes	No	Yes	Yes	No	313
Court of Appeals	Yes	No	Yes	Yes	No	NA
Court of Criminal Appeals	Yes	No	Yes	Yes	Yes	1,038

Pennsylvania						
Supreme Court	Yes	No	Yes	No	No	209
Commonwealth Court	Yes	No	Yes	Yes	Yes	4,193
Superior Court	No	Yes	Yes	Yes	Yes	1,556
Tennessee						
Supreme Court	Yes	No	Yes	Yes	Some	157
Court of Appeals	Yes	No	Yes	Yes	Some	789
Court of Criminal Appeals	Yes	No	Yes	Yes	Some	748
Texas						
Supreme Court	No	Yes	Yes	No	No	66
Court of Criminal Appeals	Yes	No	Yes	No	No	170
Courts of Appeals	Yes	No	Yes	No	No	4,839

Note: "NA" indicates data not available; "Yes" indicates court follows this method when counting opinions; "No" indicates court does not follow this method when counting opinion.

Source: Court Statistics Project, *State Court Caseload Statistics: Annual Report 1990* (Williamsburg, Va.: National Center for State Courts in Cooperation with the Conference of State Court Administrators, 1992), 102-106.

Table 10-23 Criminal Filings in General and Limited Jurisdiction State Courts, 1990

State	Criminal filings in general jurisdiction courts	Criminal filings in limited jurisdiction courts	Total criminal filings	Population ranking
Alabama	43,945	265,410	309,355	22
Alaska	2,718	27,209	29,927	51
Arizona	29,073	283,055	312,128	24
California	154,482	1,028,634	1,183,116	1
Colorado	21,054	81,153	102,207	26
Connecticut	176,301	a	176,301	28
Delaware	6,833	99,289	106,122	47
District of Columbia	40,310	b	40,310	49
Florida	193,740	439,131	632,871	4
Hawaii	7,917	39,030	46,947	42
Idaho	67,520	b	67,520	43
Illinois	447,565	b	447,565	6
Indiana	112,555	131,480	244,035	14
Iowa	60,942	b	60,942	31
Kansas	40,376	12,415	52,791	33
Kentucky	15,111	168,401	183,512	23
Lousiana	155,490	148,376	303,866	21
Maryland	60,229	213,306	273,535	19
Massachusetts	391,658	b	391,658	13
Michigan	45,616	287,771	333,387	8
Minnesota	178,504	b	178,504	20
Missouri	139,971	a	139,971	15
Nebraska	6,524	81,562	88,086	37
New Hampshire	12,756	42,351	55,107	41
New Jersey	61,098	404,847	465,945	9
New Mexico	11,502	63,439	74,941	38
New York	79,322	481,397	560,719	2
North Carolina	108,784	544,588	653,372	10
North Dakota	1,775	18,248	20,023	48
Ohio	55,949	507,441	563,390	7
Oklahoma	75,352	a	75,352	29
Oregon	28,523	117,811	146,334	30
Pennsylvania	139,699	573,273	712,972	5
Puerto Rico	35,539	47,069	82,608	27
Rhode Island	6,671	46,728	53,399	44
South Carolina	101,461	252,668	354,129	25
South Dakota	36,128	b	36,128	46
Texas	168,269	1,622,159	1,790,428	3
Utah	4,608	91,952	96,560	36
Vermont	22,087	a	22,087	50
Virginia	97,266	476,372	573,638	12
Washington	28,047	231,218	259,265	18
West Virginia	6,820	128,287	135,107	35
Wisconsin	89,648	NA	89,648	16
Wyoming	1,503	14,374	15,877	52

(Notes follow)

Table 10-23   *(Continued)*

Note: "NA" indicates not available. Some states are not included here because they were not listed in source.

[a] Court does not have criminal jurisdiction.

[b] No court of limited jurisdiction.

Source: Court Statistics Project, *State Court Caseload Statistics: Annual Report 1990* (Williamsburg, Va.: National Center for State Courts in Cooperation with the Conference of State Court Administrators, 1992), 27.

Table 10-24   Civil Filings in General and Limited Jurisdiction State Courts, 1990

State	Civil filings in general jurisdiction courts	Civil filings in limited jurisdiction courts	Total civil filings	Population ranking
Alabama	94,189	169,364	263,553	22
Alaska	13,861	19,408	33,269	51
Arizona	111,080	138,499	249,579	24
California	685,816	1,135,866	1,821,682	1
Colorado	99,429	114,830	214,259	26
Connecticut	173,337	57,467	230,804	28
Delware	9,255	60,779	70,034	47
District of Columbia	141,053	a	141,053	49
Florida	557,913	354,358	912,271	4
Hawaii	28,179	24,510	52,689	42
Idaho	62,075	a	62,075	43
Illinois	695,416	a	695,416	6
Indiana	294,730	146,310	441,040	14
Iowa	184,692	a	184,692	31
Kansas	160,398	b	160,398	33
Kentucky	67,914	148,803	216,717	23
Louisiana	185,872	66,208	252,080	21
Maine	6,893	66,462	73,355	39
Maryland	128,893	738,202	867,095	19
Massachusetts	560,420	a	560,420	13
Michigan	207,022	519,315	726,337	8
Minnesota	215,792	a	215,792	20
Missouri	264,923	b	264,923	15
Nebraska	51,504	57,557	109,061	37
New Hampshire	33,709	75,221	108,930	41
New Jersey	844,051	6,324	850,375	9
New York	219,605	1,091,762	1,311,367	2
North Carolina	115,005	501,625	616,630	10
North Dakota	18,131	16,269	34,400	48
Ohio	398,357	416,975	815,332	7
Oklahoma	205,833	NA	205,833	29
Oregon	93,972	89,127	183,099	30
Pennsylvania	302,739	384,429	687,168	5
Puerto Rico	70,961	57,970	128,931	27
South Carolina	55,151	248,567	303,718	25
South Dakota	40,573	a	40,573	46
Texas	454,991	425,419	880,410	3
Utah	29,947	105,901	135,848	36
Vermont	35,375	4,496	39,871	50
Virginia	113,927	1,184,078	1,298,005	12
Washington	147,111	111,760	258,871	18
West Virginia	43,658	51,363	95,021	35
Wisconsin	341,909	b	341,909	16
Wyoming	10,744	22,887	33,631	52

(Notes follow)

Table 10-24 *(Continued)*

Note: "NA" indicates not available. Some states are not included here because they were not listed in source.

[a] No court of limited jurisdiction.
[b] Court does not have civil jurisdiction.

Source: Court Statistics Project, *State Court Caseload Statistics: Annual Report 1990* (Williamsburg, Va.: National Center for State Courts in Cooperation with the Conference of State Court Administrators, 1992), 11.

Table 10-25 West's Regional Reporters of State Court Decisions, 1992

Atlantic Reporter (A. 2d)
Connecticut, Delaware, District of Columbia, Maine, Maryland, New Hampshire, New Jersey, Pennsylvania, Rhode Island, Vermont

North Eastern Reporter (N.E. 2d)
Illinois, Indiana, Massachusetts, New York, Ohio

North Western Reporter (N.W. 2d)
Iowa, Michigan, Minnesota, Nebraska, North Dakota, South Dakota, Wisconsin

Pacific Reporter (P. 2d)
Alaska, Arizona, California, Colorado, Hawaii, Idaho, Kansas, Montana, Nevada, New Mexico, Oklahoma, Oregon, Utah, Washington, Wyoming

South Eastern Reporter (S.E. 2d)
Georgia, North Carolina, South Carolina, Virginia, West Virginia

Southern Reporter (So. 2d)
Alabama, Florida, Louisiana, Mississippi

South Western Reporter (S.W. 2d)
Arkansas, Kentucky, Missouri, Tennessee, Texas

Note: West's regional reporters contain opinions of particular state courts.

Table 10-26 State and Territorial Court Decisions Affirmed by the Warren, Burger, and Rehnquist Courts

State	Warren (1953-1969 Terms)		Burger (1969-1986 Terms)		Rehnquist (1986-1990 Terms)		Total	
	N	Percentage	N	Percentage	N	Percentage	N	Percentage
Alabama	5	17.2	5	26.3	1	25.0	11	21.2
Alaska	1	33.3	0	0.0	—	—	1	16.7
Arizona	1	12.5	5	35.7	6	66.7	12	38.7
Arkansas	0	0.0	2	66.7	3	42.9	5	25.0
California	30	52.6	24	40.7	14	50.0	68	47.2
Colorado	0	0.0	5	83.3	0	0.0	5	41.7
Connecticut	3	37.5	4	66.7	0	0.0	7	46.7
Delaware	4	57.1	2	40.0	0	0.0	6	46.2
District of Columbia	—	—	4	50.0	—	—	4	50.0
Florida	14	45.2	15	46.9	4	30.8	33	43.4
Georgia	3	17.6	11	37.9	1	33.3	15	30.0
Hawaii	—	—	0	0.0	—	—	0	0.0
Idaho	0	0.0	0	0.0	1	33.3	1	12.5
Illinois	7	35.0	10	31.3	9	50.0	26	37.1
Indiana	3	75.0	3	42.9	1	50.0	7	53.8
Iowa	4	40.0	2	66.7	1	33.3	7	43.8
Kansas	1	12.5	1	50.0	2	66.7	4	30.8
Kentucky	1	14.3	5	35.7	2	40.0	8	30.8
Louisiana	9	32.1	5	26.3	1	50.0	15	30.6
Maine	—	—	2	50.0	1	100.0	3	60.0
Maryland	4	25.0	10	71.4	0	0.0	14	37.8
Massachusetts	2	40.0	8	47.1	0	0.0	10	41.7
Michigan	6	54.5	5	35.7	4	44.4	15	44.1
Minnesota	1	50.0	3	33.3	1	33.3	5	38.5
Mississippi	1	25.0	2	20.0	3	37.5	6	27.3
Missouri	3	30.0	0	0.0	4	80.0	7	31.8
Montana	—	—	1	50.0	1	100.0	2	66.7
Nebraska	2	50.0	1	25.0	0	0.0	3	33.3
Nevada	0	0.0	—	—	1	25.0	1	20.0
New Hampshire	1	25.0	1	14.3	—	—	2	20.0
New Jersey	4	50.0	5	35.7	2	66.7	11	44.0
New Mexico	2	66.7	2	22.2	1	100.0	5	38.5
New York	27	50.0	14	35.0	3	42.9	44	43.6
North Carolina	2	16.7	5	50.0	2	66.7	9	36.0
North Dakota	1	100.0	0	0.0	1	50.0	2	33.3
Ohio	10	33.3	6	25.0	4	50.0	20	32.3
Oklahoma	2	33.3	1	14.3	1	33.3	4	25.0
Oregon	0	0.0	4	36.4	0	0.0	4	21.1
Pennsylvania	3	30.0	5	41.7	3	33.3	11	35.5
Puerto Rico	—	—	2	66.7	—	—	2	66.7
Rhode Island	0	0.0	1	50.0	—	—	1	33.3

(Table continues)

Table 10-26   *(Continued)*

State	Warren (1953-1969 Terms)		Burger (1969-1986 Terms)		Rehnquist (1986-1990 Terms)		Total	
	N	Percentage	*N*	Percentage	*N*	Percentage	*N*	Percentage
South Carolina	1	10.0	3	50.0	1	20.0	5	23.8
South Dakota	—	—	1	20.0	1	100.0	2	33.3
Tennessee	2	28.6	2	28.6	2	66.7	6	35.3
Texas	8	19.5	3	14.3	2	28.6	13	18.8
Utah	1	25.0	1	50.0	—	—	2	33.3
Vermont	—	—	2	66.7	1	100.0	3	75.0
Virginia	4	25.0	1	14.3	1	33.3	6	23.1
Washington	6	30.0	3	20.0	0	0.0	9	23.1
West Virginia	3	60.0	2	50.0	0	0.0	5	38.5
Wisconsin	4	57.1	2	22.2	3	50.0	9	40.9
Wyoming	—	—	1	100.0	1	100.0	2	100.0
Total	186	33.9	202	35.4	90	40.9	478	35.7

Note: "—" indicates no cases decided. *N*s are the number of cases affirmed; percentages are the number of cases affirmed expressed as a percentage of the total number of cases. All orally argued docket numbers, excluding cases arising under the Court's original jurisdiction, are included. Because the formal dispositions the Court makes do not necessarily correspond to who wins the case, the focus here is on the prevailing party. If the petitioning party prevails in whole or in part, the case is counted as a reversal; otherwise as an affirmation.

Source: U.S. Supreme Court Judicial Database.

Constitution of the United States

We the People of the United States, in Order to form a more perfect Union, establish Justice, insure domestic Tranquility, provide for the common defence, promote the general Welfare, and secure the Blessings of Liberty to ourselves and our Posterity, do ordain and establish this Constitution for the United States of America.

Article I

Section 1. All legislative Powers herein granted shall be vested in a Congress of the United States, which shall consist of a Senate and House of Representatives.

Section 2. The House of Representatives shall be composed of Members chosen every second Year by the People of the several States, and the Electors in each State shall have the Qualifications requisite for Electors of the most numerous Branch of the State Legislature.

No Person shall be a Representative who shall not have attained to the age of twenty five Years, and been seven Years a Citizen of the United States, and who shall not, when elected, be an Inhabitant of that State in which he shall be chosen.

[Representatives and direct Taxes shall be apportioned among the several States which may be included within this Union, according to their respective Numbers, which shall be determined by adding to the whole Number of free Persons, including those bound to Service for a Term of Years, and excluding Indians not taxed, three fifths of all other Persons.][1] The actual Enumeration shall be made within three Years after the first Meeting of the Congress of the United States, and within every subsequent Term of ten Years, in such Manner as they shall by Law direct. The Number of Representatives shall not exceed one for

every thirty Thousand, but each State shall have at Least one Represen-
tative; and until such enumeration shall be made, the State of New
Hampshire shall be entitled to chuse three, Massachusetts eight, Rhode-
Island and Providence Plantations one, Connecticut five, New-York six,
New Jersey four, Pennsylvania eight, Delaware one, Maryland six, Vir-
ginia ten, North Carolina five, South Carolina five, and Georgia three.

When vacancies happen in the Representation from any State, the
Executive Authority thereof shall issue Writs of Election to fill such
Vacancies.

The House of Representatives shall chuse their Speaker and other
Officers; and shall have the sole Power of Impeachment.

Section 3.   The Senate of the United States shall be composed of
two Senators from each State, [chosen by the Legislature thereof,][2] for
six Years; and each Senator shall have one Vote.

Immediately after they shall be assembled in Consequence of the
first Election, they shall be divided as equally as may be into three
Classes. The Seats of the Senators of the first Class shall be vacated at
the Expiration of the second Year, of the second Class at the Expiration
of the fourth Year, and of the third Class at the Expiration of the sixth
Year, so that one third may be chosen every second Year; [and if
Vacancies happen by Resignation, or otherwise, during the Recess of
the Legislature of any State, the Executive thereof may make temporary
Appointments until the next Meeting of the Legislature, which shall
then fill such Vacancies.][3]

No Person shall be a Senator who shall not have attained to the
Age of thirty Years, and been nine Years a Citizen of the United States,
and who shall not, when elected, be an Inhabitant of that State for
which he shall be chosen.

The Vice President of the United States shall be President of the
Senate, but shall have no Vote, unless they be equally divided.

The Senate shall chuse their other Officers, and also a President
pro tempore, in the Absence of the Vice President, or when he shall
exercise the Office of President of the United States.

The Senate shall have the sole Power to try all Impeachments.
When sitting for that Purpose, they shall be on Oath or Affirmation.
When the President of the United States is tried, the Chief Justice shall
preside: And no Person shall be convicted without the Concurrence of
two thirds of the Members present.

Judgment in Cases of Impeachment shall not extend further than
to removal from Office, and disqualification to hold and enjoy any
Office of honor, Trust or Profit under the United States: but the Party
convicted shall nevertheless be liable and subject to Indictment, Trial,
Judgment and Punishment, according to Law.

Section 4.   The Times, Places and Manner of holding Elections for Senators and Representatives, shall be prescribed in each State by the Legislature thereof; but the Congress may at any time by Law make or alter such Regulations, except as to the Places of chusing Senators.

The Congress shall assemble at least once in every Year, and such Meeting shall [be on the first Monday in December],[4] unless they shall by Law appoint a different Day.

Section 5.   Each House shall be the Judge of the Elections, Returns and Qualifications of its own Members, and a Majority of each shall constitute a Quorum to do Business; but a smaller Number may adjourn from day to day, and may be authorized to compel the Attendance of absent Members, in such Manner, and under such Penalties as each House may provide.

Each House may determine the Rules of its Proceedings, punish its Members for disorderly Behaviour, and, with the Concurrence of two thirds, expel a Member.

Each House shall keep a Journal of its Proceedings, and from time to time publish the same, excepting such Parts as may in their Judgment require Secrecy; and the Yeas and Nays of the Members of either House on any question shall, at the Desire of one fifth of those Present, be entered on the Journal.

Neither House, during the Session of Congress, shall, without the Consent of the other, adjourn for more than three days, nor to any other Place than that in which the two Houses shall be sitting.

Section 6.   The Senators and Representatives shall receive a Compensation for their Services, to be ascertained by Law, and paid out of the Treasury of the United States. They shall in all Cases, except Treason, Felony and Breach of the Peace, be privileged from Arrest during their Attendance at the Session of their respective Houses, and in going to and returning from the same; and for any Speech or Debate in either House, they shall not be questioned in any other Place.

No Senator or Representative shall, during the Time for which he was elected, be appointed to any civil Office under the Authority of the United States, which shall have been created, or the Emoluments whereof shall have been encreased during such time; and no Person holding any Office under the United States, shall be a Member of either House during his Continuance in Office.

Section 7.   All Bills for raising Revenue shall originate in the House of Representatives; but the Senate may propose or concur with Amendments as on other Bills.

Every Bill which shall have passed the House of Representatives and the Senate, shall, before it become a Law, be presented to the President of the United States; If he approve he shall sign it, but if not he shall return it, with his Objections to that House in which it shall have originated, who shall enter the Objections at large on their Journal, and proceed to reconsider it. If after such Reconsideration two thirds of that House shall agree to pass the Bill, it shall be sent, together with the Objections, to the other House, by which it shall likewise be reconsidered, and if approved by two thirds of that House, it shall become a Law. But in all such Cases the Votes of both Houses shall be determined by yeas and Nays, and the Names of the Persons voting for and against the Bill shall be entered on the Journal of each House respectively. If any Bill shall not be returned by the President within ten Days (Sundays excepted) after it shall have been presented to him, the Same shall be a Law, in like Manner as if he had signed it, unless the Congress by their Adjournment prevent its Return, in which Case it shall not be a Law.

Every Order, Resolution, or Vote to which the Concurrence of the Senate and House of Representatives may be necessary (except on a question of Adjournment) shall be presented to the President of the United States; and before the Same shall take Effect, shall be approved by him, or being disapproved by him, shall be repassed by two thirds of the Senate and House of Representatives, according to the Rules and Limitations prescribed in the Case of a Bill.

Section 8.   The Congress shall have Power To lay and collect Taxes, Duties, Imposts and Excises, to pay the Debts and provide for the common Defence and general Welfare of the United States; but all Duties, Imposts and Excises shall be uniform throughout the United States;

To borrow Money on the credit of the United States;

To regulate Commerce with foreign Nations, and among the several States, and with the Indian Tribes;

To establish an uniform Rule of Naturalization, and uniform Laws on the subject of Bankruptcies throughout the United States;

To coin Money, regulate the Value thereof, and of foreign Coin, and fix the Standard of Weights and Measures;

To provide for the Punishment of counterfeiting the Securities and current Coin of the United States;

To establish Post Offices and post Roads;

To promote the Progress of Science and useful Arts, by securing for limited Times to Authors and Inventors the exclusive Right to their respective Writings and Discoveries;

To constitute Tribunals inferior to the supreme Court;

To define and punish Piracies and Felonies committed on the high

Seas, and Offences against the Law of Nations;

To declare War, grant Letters of Marque and Reprisal, and make Rules concerning Captures on Land and Water;

To raise and support Armies, but no Appropriation of Money to that Use shall be for a longer Term than two Years;

To provide and maintain a Navy;

To make Rules for the Government and Regulation of the land and naval Forces;

To provide for calling forth the Militia to execute the Laws of the Union, suppress Insurrections and repel Invasions;

To provide for organizing, arming, and disciplining, the Militia, and for governing such Part of them as may be employed in the Service of the United States, reserving to the States respectively, the Appointment of the Officers, and the Authority of training the Militia according to the discipline prescribed by Congress;

To exercise exclusive Legislation in all Cases whatsoever, over such District (not exceeding ten Miles square) as may, by Cession of particular States, and the Acceptance of Congress, become the Seat of the Government of the United States, and to exercise like Authority over all Places purchased by the Consent of the Legislature of the State in which the Same shall be, for the Erection of Forts, Magazines, Arsenals, dock-Yards, and other needful Buildings; —And

To make all Laws which shall be necessary and proper for carrying into Execution the foregoing Powers, and all other Powers vested by this Constitution in the Government of the United States, or in any Department or Officer thereof.

Section 9.   The Migration or Importation of such Persons as any of the States now existing shall think proper to admit, shall not be prohibited by the Congress prior to the Year one thousand eight hundred and eight, but a Tax or duty may be imposed on such Importation, not exceeding ten dollars for each Person.

The Privilege of the Writ of Habeas Corpus shall not be suspended, unless when in Cases of Rebellion or Invasion the public Safety may require it.

No Bill of Attainder or ex post facto Law shall be passed.

No Capitation, or other direct, Tax shall be laid, unless in Proportion to the Census or Enumeration herein before directed to be taken.[5]

No Tax or Duty shall be laid on Articles exported from any State.

No Preference shall be given by any Regulation of Commerce or Revenue to the Ports of one State over those of another; nor shall Vessels bound to, or from, one State, be obliged to enter, clear, or pay Duties in another.

No Money shall be drawn from the Treasury, but in Consequence of Appropriations made by Law; and a regular Statement and Account of the Receipts and Expenditures of all public Money shall be published from time to time.

No Title of Nobility shall be granted by the United States: And no Person holding any Office of Profit or Trust under them, shall, without the Consent of the Congress, accept of any present, Emolument, Office, or Title, of any kind whatever, from any King, Prince, or foreign State.

Section 10. No State shall enter into any Treaty, Alliance, or Confederation; grant Letters of Marque and Reprisal; coin Money; emit Bills of Credit; make any Thing but gold and silver Coin a Tender in Payment of Debts; pass any Bill of Attainder, ex post facto Law, or Law impairing the Obligation of Contracts, or grant any Title of Nobility.

No State shall, without the Consent of the Congress, lay any Imposts or Duties on Imports or Exports, except what may be absolutely necessary for executing it's inspection Laws: and the net Produce of all Duties and Imposts, laid by any State on Imports or Exports, shall be for the Use of the Treasury of the United States; and all such Laws shall be subject to the Revision and Controul of the Congress.

No State shall, without the Consent of Congress, lay any Duty of Tonnage, keep Troops, or Ships of War in time of Peace, enter into any Agreement or Compact with another State, or with a foreign Power, or engage in War, unless actually invaded, or in such imminent Danger as will not admit of delay.

Article II

Section 1. The executive Power shall be vested in a President of the United States of America. He shall hold his Office during the Term of four Years, and, together with the Vice President, chosen for the same Term, be elected, as follows:

Each State shall appoint, in such Manner as the Legislature thereof may direct, a Number of Electors, equal to the whole Number of Senators and Representatives to which the State may be entitled in the Congress: but no Senator or Representative, or Person holding an Office of Trust or Profit under the United States, shall be appointed an Elector.

[The Electors shall meet in their respective States, and vote by Ballot for two Persons, of whom one at least shall not be an Inhabitant of the same State with themselves. And they shall make a List of all the Persons voted for, and of the Number of Votes for each; which List they shall sign and certify, and transmit sealed to the Seat of the Government of the United States, directed to the President of the

Senate. The President of the Senate shall, in the Presence of the Senate and House of Representatives, open all the Certificates, and the Votes shall then be counted. The Person having the greatest Number of Votes shall be the President, if such Number be a Majority of the whole Number of Electors appointed; and if there be more than one who have such Majority, and have an equal Number of Votes, then the House of Representatives shall immediately chuse by Ballot one of them for President; and if no Person have a Majority, then from the five highest on the list the said House shall in like Manner chuse the President. But in chusing the President, the Votes shall be taken by States, the Representation from each State having one Vote; a quorum for this Purpose shall consist of a Member or Members from two thirds of the States, and a Majority of all the States shall be necessary to a Choice. In every Case, after the Choice of the President, the Person having the greatest Number of Votes of the Electors shall be the Vice President. But if there should remain two or more who have equal Votes, the Senate shall chuse from them by Ballot the Vice President.][6]

The Congress may determine the Time of chusing the Electors, and the Day on which they shall give their Votes; which Day shall be the same throughout the United States.

No Person except a natural born Citizen, or a Citizen of the United States, at the time of the Adoption of this Constitution, shall be eligible to the Office of President; neither shall any Person be eligible to that Office who shall not have attained to the Age of thirty five Years, and been fourteen Years a Resident within the United States.

In Case of the Removal of the President from Office, or of his Death, Resignation, or Inability to discharge the Powers and Duties of the said Office,[7] the Same shall devolve on the Vice President, and the Congress may by Law provide for the Case of Removal, Death, Resignation or Inability, both of the President and Vice President, declaring what Officer shall then act as President, and such Officer shall act accordingly, until the Disability be removed, or a President shall be elected.

The President shall, at stated Times, receive for his Services, a Compensation, which shall neither be encreased nor diminished during the Period for which he shall have been elected, and he shall not receive within that Period any other Emolument from the United States, or any of them.

Before he enter on the Execution of his Office, he shall take the following Oath or Affirmation:—"I do solemnly swear (or affirm) that I will faithfully execute the Office of President of the United States, and will to the best of my Ability, preserve, protect and defend the Constitution of the United States."

Section 2.   The President shall be Commander in Chief of the Army and Navy of the United States, and of the Militia of the several States, when called into the actual Service of the United States; he may require the Opinion, in writing, of the principal Officer in each of the executive Departments, upon any Subject relating to the Duties of their respective Offices, and he shall have Power to grant Reprieves and Pardons for Offences against the United States, except in Cases of Impeachment.

He shall have Power, by and with the Advice and Consent of the Senate, to make Treaties, provided two thirds of the Senators present concur; and he shall nominate, and by and with the Advice and Consent of the Senate, shall appoint Ambassadors, other public Ministers and Consuls, Judges of the supreme Court, and all other Officers of the United States, whose Appointments are not herein otherwise provided for, and which shall be established by Law: but the Congress may by Law vest the Appointment of such inferior Officers, as they think proper, in the President alone, in the Courts of Law, or in the Heads of Departments.

The President shall have Power to fill up all Vacancies that may happen during the Recess of the Senate, by granting Commissions which shall expire at the End of their next Session.

Section 3.   He shall from time to time give to the Congress Information of the State of the Union, and recommend to their Consideration such Measures as he shall judge necessary and expedient; he may, on extraordinary Occasions, convene both Houses, or either of them, and in Case of Disagreement between them, with Respect to the Time of Adjournment, he may adjourn them to such Time as he shall think proper; he shall receive Ambassadors and other public Ministers; he shall take Care that the Laws be faithfully executed, and shall Commission all the Officers of the United States.

Section 4.   The President, Vice President and all civil Officers of the United States, shall be removed from Office on Impeachment for, and Conviction of, Treason, Bribery, or other high Crimes and Misdemeanors.

Article III

Section 1.   The judicial Power of the United States, shall be vested in one supreme Court, and in such inferior Courts as the Congress may from time to time ordain and establish. The Judges, both of the supreme and inferior Courts, shall hold their Offices during good Behaviour, and shall, at stated Times, receive for their Services, a Compensation, which shall not be diminished during their Continuance in Office.

Section 2.   The judicial Power shall extend to all Cases, in Law and Equity, arising under this Constitution, the Laws of the United States, and Treaties made, or which shall be made, under their Authority; — to all Cases affecting Ambassadors, other public Ministers and Consuls; — to all Cases of admiralty and maritime Jurisdiction; — to Controversies to which the United States shall be a Party; — to Controversies between two or more States; — between a State and Citizens of another State;[8] — between Citizens of different States; — between Citizens of the same State claiming Lands under Grants of different States, and between a State, or the Citizens thereof, and foreign States, Citizens or Subjects.[8]

In all Cases affecting Ambassadors, other public Ministers and Consuls, and those in which a State shall be Party, the supreme Court shall have original Jurisdiction. In all the other Cases before mentioned, the supreme Court shall have appellate Jurisdiction, both as to Law and Fact, with such Exceptions, and under such Regulations as the Congress shall make.

The Trial of all Crimes, except in Cases of Impeachment, shall be by Jury; and such Trial shall be held in the State where the said Crimes shall have been committed; but when not committed within any State, the Trial shall be at such Place or Places as the Congress may by Law have directed.

Section 3.   Treason against the United States, shall consist only in levying War against them, or in adhering to their Enemies, giving them Aid and Comfort. No Person shall be convicted of Treason unless on the Testimony of two Witnesses to the same overt Act, or on Confession in open Court.

The Congress shall have Power to declare the Punishment of Treason, but no Attainder of Treason shall work Corruption of Blood, or Forfeiture except during the Life of the Person attainted.

Article IV

Section 1.   Full Faith and Credit shall be given in each State to the public Acts, Records, and judicial Proceedings of every other State. And the Congress may by general Laws prescribe the Manner in which such Acts, Records and Proceedings shall be proved, and the Effect thereof.

Section 2.   The Citizens of each State shall be entitled to all Privileges and Immunities of Citizens in the several States.

A Person charged in any State with Treason, Felony, or other Crime, who shall flee from Justice, and be found in another State, shall on Demand of the executive Authority of the State from which he fled, be delivered up, to be removed to the State having Jurisdiction of the Crime.

[No Person held to Service or Labour in one State, under the Laws thereof, escaping into another, shall, in Consequence of any Law or Regulation therein, be discharged from such Service or Labour, but shall be delivered up on Claim of the Party to whom such Service or Labour may be due.][9]

Section 3.   New States may be admitted by the Congress into this Union; but no new State shall be formed or erected within the Jurisdiction of any other State; nor any State be formed by the Junction of two or more States, or Parts of States, without the Consent of the Legislatures of the States concerned as well as of the Congress.

The Congress shall have Power to dispose of and make all needful Rules and Regulations respecting the Territory or other Property belonging to the United States; and nothing in this Constitution shall be so construed as to Prejudice any Claims of the United States, or of any particular State.

Section 4.   The United States shall guarantee to every State in this Union a Republican Form of Government, and shall protect each of them against Invasion; and on Application of the Legislature, or of the Executive (when the Legislature cannot be convened) against domestic Violence.

Article V

The Congress, whenever two thirds of both Houses shall deem it necessary, shall propose Amendments to this Constitution, or, on the Application of the Legislatures of two thirds of the several States, shall call a Convention for proposing Amendments, which, in either Case, shall be valid to all Intents and Purposes, as Part of this Constitution, when ratified by the Legislatures of three fourths of the several States, or by Conventions in three fourths thereof, as the one or the other Mode of Ratification may be proposed by the Congress; Provided [that no Amendment which may be made prior to the Year One thousand eight hundred and eight shall in any Manner affect the first and fourth Clauses in the Ninth Section of the first Article; and][10] that no State, without its Consent, shall be deprived of its equal Suffrage in the Senate.

Article VI

All Debts contracted and Engagements entered into, before the Adoption of this Constitution, shall be as valid against the United States under this Constitution, as under the Confederation.

This Constitution, and the Laws of the United States which shall be made in Pursuance thereof; and all Treaties made, or which shall be made, under the Authority of the United States, shall be the supreme Law of the Land; and the Judges in every State shall be bound thereby, any Thing in the Constitution or Laws of any State to the Contrary notwithstanding.

The Senators and Representatives before mentioned, and the Members of the several State Legislatures, and all executive and judicial Officers, both of the United States and of the several States, shall be bound by Oath or Affirmation, to support this Constitution; but no religious Test shall ever be required as a Qualification to any Office or public Trust under the United States.

Article VII

The Ratification of the Conventions of nine States, shall be sufficient for the Establishment of this Constitution between the States so ratifying the Same.

Done in Convention by the Unanimous Consent of the States present the Seventeenth Day of September in the Year of our Lord one thousand seven hundred and Eighty seven and of the Independence of the United States of America the Twelfth. IN WITNESS whereof We have hereunto subscribed our Names,

George Washington,
President and
deputy from Virginia.

New Hampshire:	John Langdon, Nicholas Gilman.
Massachusetts:	Nathaniel Gorham, Rufus King.
Connecticut:	William Samuel Johnson, Roger Sherman.

New York:	Alexander Hamilton.
New Jersey:	William Livingston, David Brearley, William Paterson, Jonathan Dayton.
Pennsylvania:	Benjamin Franklin, Thomas Mifflin, Robert Morris, George Clymer, Thomas FitzSimons, Jared Ingersoll, James Wilson, Gouverneur Morris.
Delaware:	George Read, Gunning Bedford Jr., John Dickinson, Richard Bassett, Jacob Broom.
Maryland:	James McHenry, Daniel of St. Thomas Jenifer, Daniel Carroll.
Virginia:	John Blair, James Madison Jr.
North Carolina:	William Blount, Richard Dobbs Spaight, Hugh Williamson.
South Carolina:	John Rutledge, Charles Cotesworth Pinckney, Charles Pinckney, Pierce Butler.
Georgia:	William Few, Abraham Baldwin.

[The language of the original Constitution, not including the Amendments, was adopted by a convention of the states on September 17, 1787, and was subsequently ratified by the states on the following dates: Delaware, December 7, 1787; Pennsylvania, December 12, 1787; New Jersey, December 18, 1787; Georgia, January 2, 1788; Connecticut, January 9, 1788; Massachusetts, February 6, 1788; Maryland, April 28, 1788; South Carolina, May 23, 1788; New Hampshire, June 21, 1788.

Ratification was completed on June 21, 1788.

The Constitution subsequently was ratified by Virginia, June 25, 1788; New York, July 26, 1788; North Carolina, November 21, 1789; Rhode Island, May 29, 1790; and Vermont, January 10, 1791.]

Amendments

Amendment I

(First ten amendments ratified December 15, 1791.)

Congress shall make no law respecting an establishment of religion, or prohibiting the free exercise thereof; or abridging the freedom of speech, or of the press; or the right of the people peaceably to assemble, and to petition the Government for a redress of grievances.

Amendment II

A well regulated Militia, being necessary to the security of a free State, the right of the people to keep and bear Arms, shall not be infringed.

Amendment III

No Soldier shall, in time of peace be quartered in any house, without the consent of the Owner, nor in time of war, but in a manner to be prescribed by law.

Amendment IV

The right of the people to be secure in their persons, houses, papers, and effects, against unreasonable searches and seizures, shall not be violated, and no Warrants shall issue, but upon probable cause, supported by Oath or affirmation, and particularly describing the place to be searched, and the persons or things to be seized.

Amendment V

No person shall be held to answer for a capital, or otherwise infamous crime, unless on a presentment or indictment of a Grand Jury, except in cases arising in the land or naval forces, or in the Militia, when in actual service in time of War or public danger; nor shall any person be subject for the same offence to be twice put in jeopardy of life or limb; nor shall be compelled in any criminal case to be a witness against himself, nor be deprived of life, liberty, or property, without due process of law; nor shall private property be taken for public use, without just compensation.

Amendment VI

In all criminal prosecutions, the accused shall enjoy the right to a speedy and public trial, by an impartial jury of the State and district wherein the crime shall have been committed, which district shall have been previously ascertained by law, and to be informed of the nature and cause of the accusation; to be confronted with the witnesses against him; to have compulsory process for obtaining witnesses in his favor, and to have the Assistance of Counsel for his defence.

Amendment VII

In Suits at common law, where the value in controversy shall exceed twenty dollars, the right of trial by jury shall be preserved, and no fact tried by a jury, shall be otherwise re-examined in any Court of the United States, than according to the rules of the common law.

Amendment VIII

Excessive bail shall not be required, nor excessive fines imposed, nor cruel and unusual punishments inflicted.

Amendment IX

The enumeration in the Constitution, of certain rights, shall not be construed to deny or disparage others retained by the people.

Amendment X

The powers not delegated to the United States by the Constitution, nor prohibited by it to the States, are reserved to the States respectively, or to the people.

Amendment XI *(Ratified February 7, 1795)*

The Judicial power of the United States shall not be construed to extend to any suit in law or equity, commenced or prosecuted against one of the United States by Citizens of another State, or by Citizens or Subjects of any Foreign State.

Amendment XII *(Ratified June 15, 1804)*

The Electors shall meet in their respective states and vote by ballot for President and Vice-President, one of whom, at least, shall not be an inhabitant of the same state with themselves; they shall name in their ballots the person voted for as President, and in distinct ballots the person voted for as Vice-President, and they shall make distinct lists of all persons voted for as President, and of all persons voted for as Vice-President, and of the number of votes for each, which lists they shall sign and certify, and transmit sealed to the seat of the government of the United States, directed to the President of the Senate; — The President of the Senate shall, in the presence of the Senate and House of Representatives, open all the certificates and the votes shall then be counted; — The person having the greatest number of votes for President, shall be the President, if such number be a majority of the whole number of Electors appointed; and if no person have such majority, then from the persons having the highest numbers not exceeding three on the list of those voted for as President, the House of Representatives shall choose immediately, by ballot, the President. But in choosing the President, the votes shall be taken by states, the representation from each state having one vote; a quorum for this purpose shall consist of a member or members from two-thirds of the states, and a majority of all the states shall be necessary to a choice. [And if the House of Representatives shall not choose a President whenever the right of choice shall devolve upon them, before the fourth day of March next following, then the Vice-President shall act as President, as in the case of the death or other constitutional disability of the President. —][11] The person having the greatest number of votes as Vice-President, shall be the Vice-President, if such number be a majority of the whole number of Electors appointed, and if no person have a majority, then from the two highest numbers on the list, the Senate shall choose the Vice-President; a quorum for the purpose shall consist of two-thirds of the whole number of Senators, and a majority of the whole number shall be necessary to a choice. But no person constitutionally ineligible to the office of President shall be eligible to that of Vice-President of the United States.

Amendment XIII *(Ratified December 6, 1865)*

Section 1.   Neither slavery nor involuntary servitude, except as a punishment for crime whereof the party shall have been duly convicted, shall exist within the United States, or any place subject to their jurisdiction.

Section 2. Congress shall have power to enforce this article by appropriate legislation.

Amendment XIV *(Ratified July 9, 1868)*

Section 1. All persons born or naturalized in the United States, and subject to the jurisdiction thereof, are citizens of the United States and of the State wherein they reside. No State shall make or enforce any law which shall abridge the privileges or immunities of citizens of the United States; nor shall any State deprive any person of life, liberty, or property, without due process of law; nor deny to any person within its jurisdiction the equal protection of the laws.

Section 2. Representatives shall be apportioned among the several States according to their respective numbers, counting the whole number of persons in each State, excluding Indians not taxed. But when the right to vote at any election for the choice of electors for President and Vice President of the United States, Representatives in Congress, the Executive and Judicial officers of a State, or the members of the Legislature thereof, is denied to any of the male inhabitants of such State, being twenty-one years of age,[12] and citizens of the United States, or in any way abridged, except for participation in rebellion, or other crime, the basis of representation therein shall be reduced in the proportion which the number of such male citizens shall bear to the whole number of male citizens twenty-one years of age in such State.

Section 3. No person shall be a Senator or Representative in Congress, or elector of President and Vice President, or hold any office, civil or military, under the United States, or under any State, who, having previously taken an oath, as a member of Congress, or as an officer of the United States, or as a member of any State legislature, or as an executive or judicial officer of any State, to support the Constitution of the United States, shall have engaged in insurrection or rebellion against the same, or given aid or comfort to the enemies thereof. But Congress may by a vote of two-thirds of each House, remove such disability.

Section 4. The validity of the public debt of the United States, authorized by law, including debts incurred for payment of pensions and bounties for services in suppressing insurrection or rebellion, shall not be questioned. But neither the United States nor any State shall assume or pay any debt or obligation incurred in aid of insurrection or rebellion against the United States, or any claim for the loss or emancipation of any slave; but all such debts, obligations and claims shall be held illegal and void.

Section 5.   The Congress shall have power to enforce, by appropriate legislation, the provisions of this article.

Amendment XV *(Ratified February 3, 1870)*

Section 1.   The right of citizens of the United States to vote shall not be denied or abridged by the United States or by any State on account of race, color, or previous condition of servitude.

Section 2.   The Congress shall have power to enforce this article by appropriate legislation.

Amendment XVI *(Ratified February 3, 1913)*

The Congress shall have power to lay and collect taxes on incomes, from whatever source derived, without apportionment among the several States, and without regard to any census or enumeration.

Amendment XVII *(Ratified April 8, 1913)*

The Senate of the United States shall be composed of two Senators from each State, elected by the people thereof, for six years; and each Senator shall have one vote. The electors in each State shall have the qualifications requisite for electors of the most numerous branch of the State legislatures.

When vacancies happen in the representation of any State in the Senate, the executive authority of such State shall issue writs of election to fill such vacancies: *Provided,* That the legislature of any State may empower the executive thereof to make temporary appointments until the people fill the vacancies by election as the legislature may direct.

This amendment shall not be so construed as to affect the election or term of any Senator chosen before it becomes valid as part of the Constitution.

Amendment XVIII *(Ratified January 16, 1919)*

Section 1.   After one year from the ratification of this article the manufacture, sale, or transportation of intoxicating liquors within, the importation thereof into, or the exportation thereof from the United

States and all territory subject to the jurisdiction thereof for beverage purposes is hereby prohibited.

Section 2. The Congress and the several States shall have concurrent power to enforce this article by appropriate legislation.

Section 3. This article shall be inoperative unless it shall have been ratified as an amendment to the Constitution by the legislatures of the several States, as provided in the Constitution, within seven years from the date of the submission hereof to the States by the Congress.][13]

Amendment XIX *(Ratified August 18, 1920)*

The right of citizens of the United States to vote shall not be denied or abridged by the United States or by any State on account of sex.

Congress shall have power to enforce this article by appropriate legislation.

Amendment XX *(Ratified January 23, 1933)*

Section 1. The terms of the President and Vice President shall end at noon on the 20th day of January, and the terms of Senators and Representatives at noon on the 3d day of January, of the years in which such terms would have ended if this article had not been ratified; and the terms of their successors shall then begin.

Section 2. The Congress shall assemble at least once in every year, and such meeting shall begin at noon on the 3d day of January, unless they shall by law appoint a different day.

Section 3.[14] If, at the time fixed for the beginning of the term of the President, the President elect shall have died, the Vice President elect shall become President. If a President shall not have been chosen before the time fixed for the beginning of his term, or if the President elect shall have failed to qualify, then the Vice President elect shall act as President until a President shall have qualified; and the Congress may by law provide for the case wherein neither a President elect nor a Vice President elect shall have qualified, declaring who shall then act as President, or the manner in which one who is to act shall be selected, and such person shall act accordingly until a President or Vice President shall have qualified.

Section 4.   The Congress may by law provide for the case of the death of any of the persons from whom the House of Representatives may choose a President whenever the right of choice shall have devolved upon them, and for the case of the death of any of the persons from whom the Senate may choose a Vice President whenever the right of choice shall have devolved upon them.

Section 5.   Sections 1 and 2 shall take effect on the 15th day of October following the ratification of this article.

Section 6.   This article shall be inoperative unless it shall have been ratified as an amendment to the Constitution by the legislatures of three-fourths of the several States within seven years from the date of its submission.

Amendment XXI *(Ratified December 5, 1933)*

Section 1.   The eighteenth article of amendment to the Constitution of the United States is hereby repealed.

Section 2.   The transportation or importation into any State, Territory, or possession of the United States for delivery or use therein of intoxicating liquors, in violation of the laws thereof, is hereby prohibited.

Section 3.   This article shall be inoperative unless it shall have been ratified as an amendment to the Constitution by conventions in the several States, as provided in the Constitution, within seven years from the date of the submission hereof to the States by the Congress.

Amendment XXII *(Ratified February 27, 1951)*

Section 1.   No person shall be elected to the office of the President more than twice, and no person who has held the office of President, or acted as President, for more than two years of a term to which some other person was elected President shall be elected to the office of the President more than once. But this Article shall not apply to any person holding the office of President when this Article was proposed by the Congress, and shall not prevent any person who may be holding the office of President, or acting as President, during the term within which this Article become operative from holding the office of President or acting as President during the remainder of such term.

Section 2. This article shall be inoperative unless it shall have been ratified as an amendment to the Constitution by the legislatures of three-fourths of the several States within seven years from the date of its submission to the States by the Congress.

Amendment XXIII *(Ratified March 29, 1961)*

Section 1. The District constituting the seat of Government of the United States shall appoint in such manner as the Congress may direct:

A number of electors of President and Vice President equal to the whole number of Senators and Representatives in Congress to which the District would be entitled if it were a State, but in no event more than the least populous State; they shall be in addition to those appointed by the States, but they shall be considered, for the purposes of the election of President and Vice President, to be electors appointed by a State; and they shall meet in the District and perform such duties as provided by the twelfth article of amendment.

Section 2. The Congress shall have power to enforce this article by appropriate legislation.

Amendment XXIV *(Ratified January 23, 1964)*

Section 1. The right of citizens of the United States to vote in any primary or other election for President or Vice President, for electors for President or Vice President, or for Senator or Representative in Congress, shall not be denied or abridged by the United States or any State by reason of failure to pay any poll tax or other tax.

Section 2. The Congress shall have power to enforce this article by appropriate legislation.

Amendment XXV *(Ratified February 10, 1967)*

Section 1. In case of the removal of the President from office or of his death or resignation, the Vice President shall become President.

Section 2. Whenever there is a vacancy in the office of the Vice President, the President shall nominate a Vice President who shall take office upon confirmation by a majority vote of both Houses of Congress.

Section 3. Whenever the President transmits to the President pro tempore of the Senate and the Speaker of the House of Representatives his written declaration that he is unable to discharge the powers and duties of his office, and until he transmits to them a written declaration to the contrary, such powers and duties shall be discharged by the Vice President as Acting President.

Section 4.   Whenever the Vice President and a majority of either the principal officers of the executive departments or of such other body as Congress may by law provide, transmit to the President pro tempore of the Senate and the Speaker of the House of Representatives their written declaration that the President is unable to discharge the powers and duties of his office, the Vice President shall immediately assume the powers and duties of the office as Acting President.

Thereafter, when the President transmits to the President pro tempore of the Senate and the Speaker of the House of Representatives his written declaration that no inability exists, he shall resume the powers and duties of his office unless the Vice President and a majority of either the principal officers of the executive department or of such other body as Congress may by law provide, transmit within four days to the President pro tempore of the Senate and the Speaker of the House of Representatives their written declaration that the President is unable to discharge the powers and duties of his office. Thereupon Congress shall decide the issue, assembling within forty-eight hours for that purpose if not in session. If the Congress, within twenty-one days after receipt of the latter written declaration, or, if Congress is not in session, within twenty-one days after Congress is required to assemble, determines by two-thirds vote of both Houses that the President is unable to discharge the powers and duties of his office, the Vice President shall continue to discharge the same as Acting President; otherwise, the President shall resume the powers and duties of his office.

Amendment XXVI *(Ratified July 1, 1971)*

Section 1.   The right of citizens of the United States, who are eighteen years of age or older, to vote shall not be denied or abridged by the United States or by any State on account of age.

Section 2.   The Congress shall have power to enforce this article by appropriate legislation.

Amendment XXVII *(Ratified May 7, 1992)*

No law varying the compensation for the services of the Senators and

Representatives shall take effect, until an election of Representatives shall have intervened.

Notes

1. The part in brackets was changed by section 2 of the Fourteenth Amendment.
2. The part in brackets was changed by the first paragraph of the Seventeenth Amendment.
3. The part in brackets was changed by the second paragraph of the Seventeenth Amendment.
4. The part in brackets was changed by section 2 of the Twentieth Amendment.
5. The Sixteenth Amendment gave Congress the power to tax incomes.
6. The material in brackets has been superseded by the Twelfth Amendment.
7. This provision has been affected by the Twenty-fifth Amendment.
8. These clauses were affected by the Eleventh Amendment.
9. This paragraph has been superseded by the Thirteenth Amendment.
10. Obsolete.
11. The part in brackets has been superseded by section 3 of the Twentieth Amendment.
12. See the Nineteenth and Twenty-sixth Amendments.
13. This Amendment was repealed by section 1 of the Twenty-first Amendment.
14. See the Twenty-fifth Amendment.

Source: U.S. Congress, House, Committee on the Judiciary, *The Constitution of the United States of America, as Amended,* 100th Cong., 1st sess., 1987, H Doc 100-94.

Selected Readings

Introduction

Abraham, Henry J. *The Judiciary: The Supreme Court in the Governmental Process.* 8th ed. Dubuque, Iowa: Brown, 1991.

Baum, Lawrence. *The Supreme Court.* 4th ed. Washington, D.C.: CQ Press, 1992.

Brigham, John. *The Cult of the Court.* Philadelphia: Temple University Press, 1987.

Elliott, Stephen P., ed. *A Reference Guide to the United States Supreme Court.* New York: Facts on File, 1986.

Frank, John P. *Marble Palace: The Supreme Court in American Life.* New York: Knopf, 1958.

Krislov, Samuel. *The Supreme Court in the Political Process.* New York: Macmillan, 1965.

McCloskey, Robert G. *The American Supreme Court.* Chicago: University of Chicago Press, 1960.

_____. *The Modern Supreme Court.* Cambridge: Harvard University Press, 1972.

Martin, Fenton, and Robert U. Goehlert. *The U.S. Supreme Court: A Bibliography.* Washington, D.C.: CQ Press, 1990.

O'Brien, David M. *Storm Center.* 2d ed. New York: W. W. Norton, 1990.

Rohde, David W., and Harold J. Spaeth. *Supreme Court Decision Making.* San Francisco: Freeman, 1976.

Schmidhauser, John R. *The Supreme Court: Its Politics, Personality and Procedures.* New York: Holt, Rinehart, and Winston, 1960.

Segal, Jeffrey A., and Harold J. Spaeth. *The Supreme Court and the Attitudinal Model.* New York: Cambridge University Press, 1993.

Shnayerson, Robert. *The Illustrated History of the Supreme Court of the United States.* New York: Abrams, 1986.

Spaeth, Harold J. *Supreme Court Policy Making.* San Francisco: Freeman, 1974.

Walker, Thomas G., and Lee Epstein. *The Supreme Court: An Introduction.* New York: St. Martin's Press, 1992.

Wasby, Stephen L. *The Supreme Court in the Federal Judicial System.* 3d ed. Chicago: Nelson-Hall, 1988.

Witt, Elder. *Congressional Quarterly's Guide to the U.S. Supreme Court.* 2d ed. Washington, D.C.: Congressional Quarterly, 1990.

Chapter One   The Supreme Court: An Institutional Perspective

Dunne, Gerald T. "Proprietors, Sometimes Predators: Early Court Reporters." *Supreme Court Historical Society Yearbook* (1976): 61-72.

Epstein, Lee, and Thomas G. Walker. *Constitutional Law for a Changing America: Institutional Powers and Constraints.* Washington, D.C.: CQ Press, 1992.

Frank, John P. *Marble Palace: The Supreme Court in American Life.* New York: Knopf, 1958.

Goebel, Julius, Jr. *Antecedents and Beginnings to 1801: The History of the Supreme Court of the United States.* New York: Macmillan, 1971.

Hall, Kermit L. *The Magic Mirror: Law in American History.* New York: Oxford University Press, 1989.

Joyce, Craig. "The Rise of the Supreme Court Reporter: An Institutional Perspective on Marshall Court Ascendancy." *Michigan Law Review* 83 (1985): 1291-1391.

Kelly, Alfred H., Winfred A. Harbison, and Herman Belz. *The American Constitution: Its Origins and Development.* New York: W. W. Norton, 1991.

Rehnquist, William H. *The Supreme Court: How It Was, How It Is.* New York: Morrow, 1987.

Richard, Williams L. "Supreme Court of the United States: The Staff that Keeps on Operating." *Smithsonian* 7 (1977): 39-49.

Urofsky, Melvin I. *A March of Liberty: A Constitutional History of the United States.* New York: Knopf, 1988.

Warren, Charles. *The Supreme Court in United States History.* Boston: Little, Brown, 1926.

Chapter Two   The Supreme Court's
Review Process, Caseload, and Cases

Review Process

Brenner, Saul. "The New Certiorari Game." *Journal of Politics* 41 (1979): 649-655.

Caldeira, Gregory A., and John R. Wright. "Organized Interests and Agenda Setting in the U.S. Supreme Court." *American Political Science Review* 82 (1988): 1109-1127.

New York University Supreme Court Project. "Summaries of Cases Granted Certiorari During the 1982 Term." *New York University Law Review* 59 (1984): 823-1003, 1403-1929.

Pacelle, Richard L., Jr. *The Transformation of the Supreme Court's Agenda.* Boulder, Colo.: Westview, 1991.

Palmer, Jan. "An Econometric Analysis of the U.S. Supreme Court's Certiorari Decisions." *Public Choice* 39 (1982): 387-398.

Perry, H. W., Jr. "Agenda Setting and Case Selection." In *The American Courts: A Critical Assessment*, edited by John B. Gates and Charles A. Johnson. Washington, D.C.: CQ Press, 1991.

_____. *Deciding to Decide: Agenda Setting in the United States Supreme Court.* Cambridge: Harvard University Press, 1991.

Provine, Doris Marie. *Case Selection in the United States Supreme Court.* Chicago: University of Chicago Press, 1980.

Tanenhaus, Joseph, Marvin Schick, Matthew Muraskin, and Daniel Rosen. "The Supreme Court's Certiorari Jurisdiction: Cue Theory." In *Judicial Decision Making*, edited by Glendon Schubert. New York: Free Press, 1963.

Caseload

Bickel, Alexander M. *The Caseload of the Supreme Court, and What, If Anything, to Do about It.* Washington, D.C.: American Enterprise Institute for Public Policy Research, 1973.

Casper, Gerhard, and Richard Posner. *The Workload of the Supreme Court.* Chicago: American Bar Foundation, 1974.

Federal Judicial Center. *Case Load of the Supreme Court: A Report of the Study Group.* Washington, D.C.: Administrative Office of the U.S. Courts, 1972.

Frankfurter, Felix, and James M. Landis. *The Business of the Supreme Court: A Study in the Federal Judicial System.* New York: Macmillan, 1928.

McLauchlan, William P. "Courts and Caseloads." In *The American Courts: A Critical Assessment*, edited by John B. Gates and Charles A. Johnson. Washington, D.C.: CQ Press, 1991.

_____. *Federal Court Caseloads.* New York: Praeger, 1984.

Cases

Adamany, David. "Legitimacy, Realigning Elections and the Supreme Court." *Wisconsin Law Review* (1973): 790-846.

_____. "The Supreme Court." In *The American Courts: A Critical Assessment,* edited by John B. Gates and Charles A. Johnson. Washington, D.C.: CQ Press, 1991.

Bickel, Alexander. *The Least Dangerous Branch of Government.* Indianapolis: Bobbs-Merrill, 1962.

Casper, Jonathan D. "The Supreme Court and National Policy Making." *American Political Science Review* 70 (1976): 50-63.

Choper, Jesse H. *Judicial Review and the National Political Process.* Chicago: University of Chicago Press, 1980.

Cortner, Richard C. *The Supreme Court and the Second Bill of Rights.* Madison: University of Wisconsin Press, 1981.

Dahl, Robert A. "Decision-Making in a Democracy: The Supreme Court as a National Policy-Maker." *Journal of Public Law* 6 (1957): 279-295.

_____. *Pluralist Democracy in the United States.* Chicago: Rand McNally, 1967.

Ely, John Hart. *Democracy and Distrust.* Cambridge: Harvard University Press, 1980.

Epstein, Lee, and Joseph F. Kobylka. *The Supreme Court and Legal Change.* Chapel Hill: University of North Carolina Press, 1992.

Funston, Richard. *A Vital National Seminar: The Supreme Court in American Political Life.* Palo Alto, Calif.: Mayfield, 1978.

Gates, John B. *The Supreme Court and Partisan Realignment.* Boulder, Colo.: Westview, 1991.

Halpern, Stephen, and Charles Lamb, eds. *Supreme Court Activism and Restraint.* Lexington, Mass.: Lexington Books, 1982.

Lasser, William. *The Limits of Judicial Power.* Chapel Hill: University of North Carolina Press, 1988.

Chapter Three   The Supreme Court's
Opinion, Decision, and Outcome Trends

Epstein, Lee, Thomas G. Walker, and William J. Dixon. "The Supreme Court and Criminal Justice Disputes: A Neo-Institutional Perspective." *American Journal of Political Science* 33 (1989): 825.

George, Tracey E., and Lee Epstein. "On the Nature of Supreme Court Decision Making." *American Political Science Review* 86 (1992): 323.

Halpern, Stephen C., and Kenneth N. Vines. "Institutional Disunity, the Judges' Bill and the Role of the Supreme Court." *Western Political Quarterly* 30 (1977): 471.

Peterson, Steven. "Dissent in American Courts." *Journal of Politics* 43 (1981): 412.

Segal, Jeffrey A. "Predicting Supreme Court Cases Probabilistically: The Search and Seizure Cases, 1962-1981." *American Political Science Review* 78 (1984): 891.

Stephens, Richard. "The Function of Concurring and Dissenting Opinions in Courts of Last Resort." *University of Florida Law Review* 5 (1952): 394.

Walker, Thomas G., Lee Epstein, and William J. Dixon. "On the Mysterious Demise of Consensual Norms in the United States Supreme Court." *Journal of Politics* 50 (1988): 361.

Zobell, Karl M. "Division of Opinion in the Supreme Court: A History of Judicial Disintegration." *Cornell Law Quarterly* 44 (1959): 186.

Chapter Four   The Justices: Backgrounds, Nominations, and Confirmations

Abraham, Henry J. *Justices and Presidents*. New York: Oxford University Press, 1992.

Bork, Robert H. *The Tempting of America*. New York: Simon and Schuster, 1990.

Chase, Harold W. *Federal Judges: The Appointing Process*. Minneapolis: University of Minnesota Press, 1972.

Danelski, David J. *A Supreme Court Justice is Appointed*. New York: Random House, 1964.

Goldman, Sheldon. "Federal Judicial Recruitment." In *The American Courts: A Critical Assessment*, edited by John B. Gates and Charles A. Johnson. Washington, D.C.: CQ Press, 1991.

Harris, Richard. *Decision*. New York: Dutton, 1970.

Pritchett, C. Herman. *The Roosevelt Court*. New York: Macmillan, 1948.

Schmidhauser, John R. *Judges and Justices*. Boston: Little, Brown, 1979.

Simon, James F. *In His Own Image*. New York: McKay, 1973.

Chapter Five   The Justices: Post-Confirmation Activities and Departures from the Court

Atkinson, David N. "Bowing to the Inevitable: Supreme Court Deaths and Resignations, 1789-1864." *Arizona State Law Journal* (1982): 615-640.

_____. "Retirement and Death on the United States Supreme Court: From Van Devanter to Douglas." *University of Missouri at Kansas City Law Review* 45 (1976): 1-27.

Bell, Peter A. "Extrajudicial Activity of Supreme Court Justices." *Stanford Law Review* 22 (1970): 587-617.

Christensen, George A. "Here Lies the Supreme Court: Gravesites of the Justices." *Supreme Court Historical Society Yearbook* (1983): 17-30.

Fairman, Charles. "Retirement of Federal Judges." *Harvard Law Review* 51 (1938): 397-430.

Frank, John P. "Conflict of Interest and U.S. Supreme Court Justices." *American Journal of Comparative Law* 18 (1970): 744-761.

McKay, Robert B. "The Judiciary and Non-Judicial Activities." *Law and Contemporary Problems* 35 (1970): 9-36.

Pusey, Merlo J. "Disability on the Court." *Supreme Court Historical Society Yearbook* (1979): 63.

Wheeler, Russell. "Extrajudicial Activities of Early Supreme Court Justices." *Supreme Court Review* (1973): 123-158.

Chapter Six   The Justices: Voting Behavior and Opinions

Baum, Lawrence. *The Supreme Court.* 4th ed. Washington, D.C.: CQ Press, 1992.

Carter, Lief H. *Reason in Law.* 3d ed. Glenview, Ill.: Scott, Foresman, 1988.

Gibson, James L. "Decision Making in Appellate Courts." In *The American Courts: A Critical Assessment,* edited by John B. Gates and Charles A. Johnson. Washington, D.C.: CQ Press, 1991.

Murphy, Walter F. *Elements of Judicial Strategy.* Chicago: University of Chicago Press, 1964.

O'Brien, David. *Storm Center.* New York: W. W. Norton, 1986.

Pritchett, C. Herman. *The Roosevelt Court.* New York: Macmillan, 1948.

Rohde, David W., and Harold J. Spaeth. *Supreme Court Decision Making.* San Francisco: Freeman, 1976.

Schubert, Glendon A. *Quantitative Analysis of Judicial Behavior.* Glencoe, Ill.: Free Press, 1959.

Segal, Jeffrey A., and Harold J. Spaeth. *The Supreme Court and the Attitudinal Model.* New York: Cambridge University Press, 1993.

Chapter Seven   The Supreme Court and the Political Environment

The Legislature and the Supreme Court

Berger, Raoul. *Congress v. The Supreme Court.* Cambridge: Harvard University Press, 1969.

Fisher, Louis. *Constitutional Dialogues.* Princeton, N.J.: Princeton University Press, 1988.

Handberg, Roger, and Harold F. Hill, Jr. "Court Curbing, Court Reversals, and Judicial Review: The Supreme Court versus Congress. *Law and Society Review* 14 (1980): 309-322.

Murphy, Walter F. *Congress and the Court.* Chicago: University of Chicago Press, 1962.

Pritchett, C. Herman. *Congress versus the Supreme Court.* Minneapolis: University of Minnesota Press, 1961.

Schmidhauser, John R., and Larry L. Berg. *The Supreme Court and Congress.* New York: Free Press, 1972.

Segal, Jeffrey A. "Courts, Executives, and Legislatures." In *The American Courts: A Critical Assessment*, edited by John B. Gates and Charles A. Johnson. Washington, D.C.: CQ Press, 1991.

Warren, Charles. *Congress, the Constitution, and the Supreme Court.* Boston: Little, Brown, 1925.

The Executive and the Supreme Court

Abraham, Henry J. *Justices and Presidents.* New York: Oxford University Press, 1992.

Caplan, Lincoln. *The Tenth Justice.* New York: Knopf, 1987.

"Government Litigation in the Supreme Court: The Roles of the Solicitor General." *Yale Law Journal* 78 (1969): 1442-1481.

O'Connor, Karen. "The Amicus Curiae Role of the U.S. Solicitor General in Supreme Court Litigation." *Judicature* 66 (1983): 256-264.

Puro, Steven. "The United States as Amicus Curiae." In *Courts, Law and Judicial Processes*, edited by S. Sidney Ulmer. New York: Free Press, 1971.

Scigliano, Robert. *The Supreme Court and the Presidency.* New York: Free Press, 1971.

Segal, Jeffrey A. "Amicus Curiae Briefs by the Solicitor General during the Warren and Burger Courts." *Western Political Quarterly* 41 (1988): 135-144.

_____. "Supreme Court Support for the Solicitor General: The Effect of Presidential Appointments." *Western Political Quarterly* 43 (1990): 137-152.

Segal, Jeffrey A., and Cheryl D. Reedy. "The Supreme Court and Sex Discrimination: The Role of the Solicitor General." *Western Political Quarterly* 41 (1988): 553-568.

Ulmer, S. Sidney. "Governmental Litigants, Underdogs, and Civil Liberties in the Supreme Court: 1903-1968 Terms." *Journal of Politics* 47 (1985): 899-909.

The States and the Supreme Court

Baker, Stewart A., and James R. Asperger. "Towards a Center for State and Local Legal Advocacy." *Catholic University Law Review* 31 (1982): 367-373.

Epstein, Lee, and Karen O'Connor. "States and the U.S. Supreme Court: An Examination of Litigation Outcomes." *Social Science Quarterly* 69 (1988): 660-674.

Howard, A. E. Dick. "The States and the Supreme Court." *Catholic University Law Review* 31 (1982): 375-438.

Morris, Thomas R. "States before the U.S. Supreme Court: State Attorneys General as Amicus Curiae." *Judicature* 70 (1987): 298-305.

Schmidhauser, John R. *The Supreme Court as Final Arbiter in Federal-State Relations, 1789-1957*. Chapel Hill: University of North Carolina Press, 1958.

Sheehan, Reginald S., William Mishler, and Donald R. Songer. "Ideology, Status, and Differential Success of Direct Parties before the Supreme Court." *American Political Science Review* 86 (1992): 464-471.

Spaeth, Harold J. "Burger Court Review of State Court Civil Liberties Decisions." *Judicature* 68 (1985): 285-291.

Sprague, John D. *Voting Patterns of the U.S. Supreme Court: Cases in Federalism, 1889-1959*. Indianapolis: Bobbs-Merrill, 1968.

Interest Groups and the Supreme Court

Barker, Lucius. "Third Parties in Litigation: A Systematic View of the Judicial Function." *Journal of Politics* 29 (1967): 41-69.

Behuniak-Long, Susan. "Friendly Fire: Amici Curiae and *Webster v. Reproductive Health Services*." *Judicature* 74 (1991): 261-270.

Caldeira, Gregory A., and John R. Wright. "Amici before the Supreme Court." *Journal of Politics* 52 (1990): 782-806.

——. "Interest Groups and Agenda-Setting in the Supreme Court of the United States." *American Political Science Review* 82 (1988): 1109-1127.

Cortner, Richard C. "Strategies and Tactics of Litigants in Constitutional Cases." *Journal of Public Law* 17 (1968): 287-307.

Epstein, Lee. *Conservatives in Court*. Knoxville: University of Tennessee

Press, 1985.

―――. "Courts and Interest Groups." In *The American Courts: A Critical Assessment*, edited by John B. Gates and Charles A. Johnson. Washington, D.C.: CQ Press, 1991.

Kluger, Richard. *Simple Justice*. New York: Knopf, 1976.

Kobylka, Joseph F. *The Politics of Obscenity*. Westport, Conn.: Greenwood Press, 1990.

Krislov, Samuel. "The Amicus Curiae Brief: From Friendship to Advocacy." *Yale Law Journal* 72 (1963): 694-721.

Lawrence, Susan E. *The Poor in Court*. Princeton, N.J.: Princeton University Press, 1990.

O'Connor, Karen. *Women's Organizations' Use of the Court*. Lexington, Mass.: Lexington Books, 1980.

Pfeffer, Leo. "Amici in Church-State Litigation." *Law and Contemporary Problems* 44 (1981): 83-110.

Scheppele, Kim, and Jack L. Walker, Jr. "The Litigation Strategies of Interest Groups." In *Mobilizing Interest Groups in America*, edited by Jack L. Walker, Jr. Ann Arbor: University of Michigan Press, 1991.

Sorauf, Frank J. *The Wall of Separation: Constitutional Politics of Church and State*. Princeton, N.J.: Princeton University Press, 1976.

Vose, Clement E. *Caucasians Only*. Berkeley and Los Angeles: University of California Press, 1959.

―――. "Litigation as a Form of Pressure Group Activity." *Annals of the American Academy of Political and Social Science* 319 (1958): 20-31.

Wasby, Stephen L. "The Multi-Faceted Elephant: Litigator Perspectives on Planned Litigation for Social Change." *Capital University Law Review* 15 (1986): 143-189.

Chapter Eight   The Supreme Court and Public Opinion

Adamany, David W., and Joel B. Grossman. "Support for the Supreme Court as a National Policymaker." *Law and Policy Quarterly* 5 (1983): 405-437.

Caldeira, Gregory A. "Courts and Public Opinion." In *The American Courts: A Critical Assessment*, edited by John B. Gates and Charles A. Johnson. Washington, D.C.: CQ Press, 1991.

Franklin, Charles H., and Liane C. Kosaki. "The Republican Schoolmaster: The Supreme Court, Public Opinion, and Abortion." *American Political Science Review* 83 (1989): 751-772.

Marshall, Thomas. *Public Opinion and the Supreme Court*. New York: Longman, 1989.

Muir, William K., Jr. *Law and Attitude Change*. Chicago: University of Chicago Press, 1967.

Rosenberg, Gerald N. *The Hollow Hope.* Chicago: University of Chicago Press, 1991. (Chapters 4 and 8.)

Tanenhaus, Joseph, and Walter Murphy. "Patterns of Public Support for the Supreme Court: A Panel Study." *Journal of Politics* 43 (1981): 24-39.

Chapter Nine   The Impact of the Supreme Court

Becker, Theodore L., ed. *The Impact of Supreme Court Decisions.* New York: Oxford University Press, 1969.

Becker, Theodore L., and Malcolm Feeley, eds. *The Impact of Supreme Court Decisions.* New York: Oxford University Press, 1973.

Bond, Jon, and Charles A. Johnson. "Implementing a Permissive Policy: Hospital Abortion Services after *Roe v. Wade.*" *American Journal of Political Science* 26 (1982): 1-24.

Bullock, Charles S., III, and Charles M. Lamb, eds. *Implementation of Civil Rights Policy.* Monterey, Calif.: Brooks-Cole, 1984.

Canon, Bradley C. "Courts and Policy: Compliance, Implementation, and Impact." In *The American Courts: A Critical Assessment,* edited by John B. Gates and Charles A. Johnson. Washington, D.C.: CQ Press, 1991.

Dolbeare, Kenneth M., and Phillip E. Hammond. *The School Prayer Decisions.* Chicago: University of Chicago Press, 1971.

Dometrius, Nelson C., and Lee Sigelman. "Modeling the Impact of Supreme Court Decisions: *Wygant v. Board.*" *Journal of Politics* 50 (1988): 131-149.

Hansen, Susan B. "State Implementation of Supreme Court Decisions: Abortion Rates Since *Roe v. Wade.*" *Journal of Politics* 42 (1980): 372-395.

Hanson, Roger, and Robert Crew. "The Policy Impact of Reapportionment." *Law and Society Review* 8 (1973): 69-94.

Johnson, Charles A., and Bradley C. Canon. *Judicial Policies: Implementation and Impact.* Washington, D.C.: CQ Press, 1984.

McCubbins, Matthew, and Thomas Schwartz. "Congress, the Courts, and Public Policy: Consequences of the One Man, One Vote Rule." *American Journal of Political Science* 32 (1988): 388-415.

Peltason, Jack. *Fifty-Eight Lonely Men.* New York: Harcourt, Brace and World, 1961.

Rosenberg, Gerald N. *The Hollow Hope.* Chicago: University of Chicago Press, 1991.

Sorauf, Frank J. "*Zorach v. Clauson:* The Impact of a Supreme Court Decision." *American Political Science Review* 53 (1959): 777-791.

Vines, Kenneth. "Federal District Court Judges and Race Relations Cases in the South." *Journal of Politics* 26 (1964): 337-357.

Wasby, Stephen L. *The Impact of the United States Supreme Court.* Homewood, Ill.: Dorsey Press, 1970.

Chapter Ten   The Supreme Court in the Judicial System

Carp, Robert A., and C. K. Rowland. *Policymaking and Politics in the Federal District Courts.* Knoxville: University of Tennessee Press, 1983.
Court Statistics Project. *State Court Caseload Statistics: Annual Report 1990.* Williamsburg, Va.: National Center for State Courts in Cooperation with the Conference of State Court Administrators, 1992.
Early, Stephen T., Jr. *Constitutional Courts of the United States.* Totowa, N.J.: Littlefield, Adams, 1977.
Henderson, Dwight F. *Courts for a New Nation.* Washington, D.C.: Public Affairs Press, 1971.
Howard, J. Woodford, Jr. *Courts of Appeals in the Federal Judicial System.* Princeton, N.J.: Princeton University Press, 1981.
Jacob, Herbert. *Urban Justice.* Englewood Cliffs, N.J.: Prentice Hall, 1973.
Klonoski, James R., and Robert I. Mendelsohn, eds. *The Politics of Local Justice.* Boston: Little, Brown, 1970.
Posner, Richard A. *Federal Courts: Crisis and Reform.* Cambridge: Harvard University Press, 1985.
Redden, Kenneth R. *Federal Special Court Litigation.* Charlottesville, Va.: The Michie Company, 1982.
Richardson, Richard J., and Kenneth N. Vines. *The Politics of Federal Courts.* Boston: Little, Brown, 1970.
Stumpf, Harry P., and John H. Culver. *The Politics of State Courts.* New York: Longman, 1992.
Tarr, G. Alan, and Mary C. A. Porter. *State Supreme Courts in State and Nation.* New Haven, Conn.: Yale University Press, 1988.
Watson, Richard A., and Rondal G. Downing. *The Politics of Bench and Bar.* New York: Wiley, 1969.

Index

Issue area. *See* Cases, policy areas.
  See also Voting interagreement

Jackson, Robert H., 424, 583
Johnson, Charles A., 549, 586, 615
Johnson, Thomas, 297
Jones, Emma Coleman, 549
Judgments of the Court, 146, 164, 425
Judicial Conference, United States, 3
Judicial review, 48
Judiciary Act of 1801, 297
Judiciary Act of 1925, 46
Judiciary Committee, 546
  chairs of, 557, 558-559
Jurisdiction, 29-30
Justices, 175-179. *See also* Opinions;
  Voting behavior
  academic position, 229-239
  as author, 370-381
  biographies of, 407-421
  birth and childhood, 180-192
  children, 222-228
  circuit assignments, 314-320
  classic statements of, 382-406
  death, 343-353
  departure from Court, 327-335
  education, 207-221
  extra-judicial activities, 321-325
  family background, 193-206
  impeachment, 326
  judicial experience, 256-264
  legal training, 207-221
  length of service, 300-302
  marriage, 222-228
  military experience, 240-241
  opinion writing, 514-519
  personal papers, 354-369
  political experience, 242-255
  post-Court activities, 338-342
  private practice, 229-239
  reputation of, 336-337
  significant opinions, 521-534

Keenan, Joseph T., 549
Kennedy, Anthony M., 424
Keogh v. Orient Fire Insurance Co., 10
Kobylka, Joseph, 615
Kosaki, Liane C., 586
Krislov, Samuel, 549

Legislation, 26-28
  most litigated, 553-554

Liberal voting
  aggregate by justice, 427-430
  aggregate by justice by term, 431-455
Lobbying, 547-548

McReynolds, James, 172
Mansbridge, Jane, 584, 586
Marbury v. Madison, 48
Marshall, John, 9, 48
Marshall, Thomas, 586
Marshall, Thurgood, 172, 424
Meltsner, Michael, 615
Mersky, Roy M., 3
Minton, Sherman, 424
Mishler, William, 547, 549
Moody, William, 172
Morse v. Anderson, 49
Murphy, Frank, 172

National Labor Relations Act, 546
National Opinion Research Center, 2
Natural courts, 303-313
Nelson, Samuel, 173
New York Times surveys, 584
Nominees, 265-273
  appointment anomalies, 292-295
  confirmation factors, 291
  federal district judgeships, 632
  nominated by, 274-283
  public opinion and, 608
  Senate action on, 284-290

O'Connor, Karen, 549
O'Connor, Sandra Day, 172, 424, 585
Opinions. *See also* Judgments of the
  Court; Voting behavior
  assignment of, 425-426, 535-543
  authors of, 535-543
  concurring, 4, 154-158, 425, 514-516
  dissenting, 149-153, 425, 514-516
  majority, 4, 535-543
  participation in, 514-516
  per curiam, 4-5, 72-73
  signed, 46-47, 72-73, 514-516
  writing of, 517-519

Palko v. Connecticut, 7
Palmer, Jan, 7